"An important work for Egyptologists all
as a major contribution to the history of E
context."—Dan Deac, *Journal of Ancient H*

"Professor Donald Malcolm Reid is one of the most prolific scholars in the
field of modern Egyptian history. This work fills in a major lacuna, the role
of Egyptians in archaeology and the museum world during the first half of
the 20th century."—Jere Bacharach, University of Washington

"Reid leaves no stone unturned, revealing stories of intrigue, cooperation,
and contestation, setting them assiduously into the context of Egyptian
political history. The history of archeology becomes, in his masterful telling,
one of multiple pasts and manifold identities."— Beth Baron, CUNY

"A very important contribution to the development of, and changes in, the
perception of our national culture as viewed by the West and how this vision
affected Egyptians and Egyptian archeology . . . promises to be as important
in its field as *Whose Pharaohs?* has been."—Fayza Haikal, The American
University in Cairo

"*Contesting Antiquity in Egypt* would be of interest to scholars across
humanistic disciplines. It will act as a valuable reference to those studying
symbols of national ideology as well as ones scavenging for minute biblio-
graphical information on a great many twentieth-century Egyptian cultural
movers."—*Arab Studies Quarterly*

"A valuable piece of scholarship: not only in terms of the history of archaeology and museums in Egypt, but also concerning how we think about the
making of the past in formerly colonized countries."—William Carruthers,
Public Archaeology

"Highly recommended. . . . Of particular importance is Reid's emphasis on
Egyptian scholars who pioneered the study of the above fields and the role
they played in wresting control of Egyptology from earlier French, British,
German, and US colonial dominance. Of equal interest is the constant tension
and rivalry between French and British archaeologists for control of Egyptology and their role in subordinating indigenous scholarship. Intrigues to con-

trol the news related to the discovery of Tutankhamen, controversies regarding the division of archaeological remains, and personal hostilities between famed archaeologists all make for an interesting read."—*Choice*

"Reid, who always has a good eye for an anecdote, shows how impossible it is to separate culture from the imperial machinations and rivalries of the time.... The really important thing about Reid's new book is that he brings the often neglected contributions of Egyptian scholars into this narrative."—Raphael Cormack, *Apollo*

"A fascinating history of historians."—*AramcoWorld*

Contesting Antiquity in Egypt

Archaeologies, Museums
& the Struggle for Identities
from World War I
to Nasser

Donald Malcolm Reid

The American University in Cairo Press
Cairo New York

This paperback edition published in 2019 by
The American University in Cairo Press
113 Sharia Kasr el Aini, Cairo, Egypt
200 Park Ave., Suite 1700 New York, NY 10166
www.aucpress.com

Dar el Kutub No. 1953/19
ISBN 978 977 416 938 0

Dar el Kutub Cataloging-in-Publication Data

Reid, Donald Malcolm
        Contesting Antiquity in Egypt: Archaeologies, Museums, and the Struggle for Identities
from World War I to Nasser / Donald Malcolm Reid.—Cairo: The American University in
Cairo Press, 2019
        p. cm.
        ISBN 978 977 416 938 0
        1. Egyptology—History
        2. Excavations—(Archaeology)—Egypt
        932

1 2 3 4 5   23 22 21 20 19

Designed by Adam el-Sehemy
Printed in The United States of America

For my Grandchildren: Juliette, Malcolm, and Ben

and

For the Grandchildren of Egypt

Contents

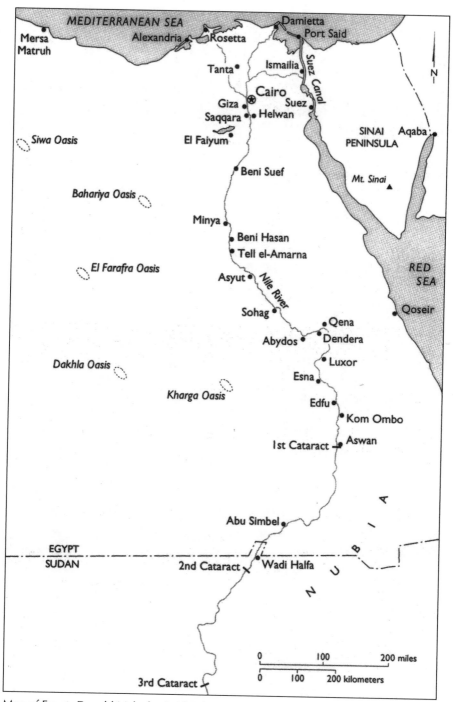

Map of Egypt. *Donald Malcolm Reid, Whose Pharaohs? (Berkeley: University of California Press, 2002, and Cairo: AUC Press, 2003), xvii. Adapted with permission of the University of California Press.*

Figures

Tables

Abbreviations

ASAE	*Annales du service des antiquités de l'Égypte*
BIÉ	*Bulletin de l'institut de l'Égypte*
BSAC	*Bulletin de la société d'archéologie copte*
BSAA	*Bulletin de la société archéologique d'Alexandrie*
BComité	*Bulletin de la comité de conservation des monuments de l'art arabe*
BSOAS	*Bulletin of the School of Oriental and African Studies*, University of London
CNRS	Centre national de la recherche scientifique (Paris)
CUA	Cairo University Archives
DAI	Deutsches Archäologisches Institut—Abteilung Kairo, German Archaeological Institute—Cairo Department. Unless specified otherwise, DAI refers to the Cairo Department, not the parent organization in Germany.
DOG	Deutsche Orient Gesellschaft (German Oriental Society)
DWQ	Dar al-Wathaiq al-Qawmiya (Egyptian National Archives)
EEF	The Egypt Exploration Fund. In 1919 it became the Egypt Exploration Society (EES).
EG	*The Egyptian Gazette*
EES	The Egypt Exploration Society (Egypt Exploration Fund until 1919)
FO	Foreign Office records in United Kingdom National Archives
GEM	Grand Egyptian Museum, Cairo
ICIC	International Committee on Intellectual Cooperation

IIIC	International Institute of Intellectual Cooperation
IGS	International Geographic Society
ICO	International Congress of Orientalists
IFAO	Institut français d'archéologie orientale du Caire
JEA	*Journal of Egyptian Archaeology*
MAÉ	Ministère des affaires étrangeres, France
MFA	Museum of Fine Arts, Boston
MMA	Metropolitan Museum of Art, New York ("the Met")
NMEC	National Museum of Egyptian Civilization, Cairo
NYT	*The New York Times*
OI	Oriental Institute, University of Chicago
OIA	Oriental Institute Archives, University of Chicago
TCA	Thomas Cook Archives, Peterborough, UK
UKNA	United Kingdom National Archives. "UKNA" omitted before "FO" (Foreign Office) references in notes.
USNA	United States National Archives
WWWE4	Morris L. Bierbrier, ed., *Who Was Who in Egyptology*, 4th ed. (London: The Egypt Exploration Society, 2012)
WWWE3	refers to the third edition, edited by Morris L. Bierbrier, (1995).
WWWE2	refers to the second edition, edited by Eric Uphill, (1972).
WWWE1	refers to the first edition, edited by Warren R. Dawson, (1951).
£E	Egyptian pounds

Note on Transliteration, Translation, and Dates

For transliteration, I have generally followed the system preferred by the AUC Press, which is close to that of the *International Journal of Middle East Studies*. Familiar English spellings are preferred for such proper names as Cairo, Luxor, Nasser, and Naguib Mahfouz. "Fuad" and "Faruq" are used instead of these kings' own spellings Fouad and Farouk. Diacritical marks and the symbols for *'ayn* (') and *hamza* (') have been omitted in most cases. I have tried to follow the preferences of living Egyptians who have indicated to me the English spellings they use for their names. Alternative spellings are sometimes provided in parentheses at first mention.

Translations of quotations into English are my own unless otherwise indicated.

CE and BCE (and occasionally AD and BC) dates have been preferred to Islamic AH (*anno Hegirae*) dates.

Acknowledgments

R esearch for this book was made possible by grants from the National Endowment for the Humanities (through the American Research Center in Egypt), the Binational Fulbright Commission, the Fulbright-Hays Faculty Research Abroad program, and Georgia State University. During three academic years in Egypt (1987–88, 1998–99, and 2005), I was variously sponsored by Dr. Gaballah Ali Gaballah, secretary-general of the Supreme Council of Antiquities; Dr. Hassanein Rabie, vice president of Cairo University; Dr. Raouf Abbas Hamed, vice dean of the Faculty of Arts at Cairo University; Dr. Mukhtar El Kasibani of the Faculty of Archaeology, Cairo University; and the American Research Center in Egypt. At Georgia State University, Dean Ahmed Abdelal and successive history department chairs Hugh Hudson, Diane Willen, and Timothy Crimmins enthusiastically supported my research. At the University of Washington, Scott Noegel, chair of the Department of Near Eastern Languages and Civilization, provided hospitality and assistance, and I owe a special debt of gratitude to Jere Bacharach.

Professors Farhat J. Ziadeh and L. Carl Brown stand out as lifelong mentors. Over forty years of friendship with the late William L. Cleveland and with F. Robert Hunter have left their mark on all my work. Other friends and colleagues who have greatly assisted me include the late Ahmed Abdalla, Jeffrey Abt, Beth Baron, Edmund Burke III, Bruce Craig, Éric Gady, Israel Gershoni, Arthur Goldschmidt Jr., James Jankowski, Alaa El-Habashi, Fayza Haikal, Kenneth Perkins, Michael J. Reimer, John Rodenbeck, Paula Sanders, Jason Thompson, Mai Trad, the late George Scanlon, Dr. Samir Simaika, Donald Whitcomb, and Caroline Williams. Dr. Abd al-Munim Ibrahim al-Dusuqi Jumayi (Abdel Moneim Gameiy) and the late Mr. Makram Naguib long provided me with hospitality and assistance in Egypt.

My wife Barbara Reid made the best of companions on the long journey, reading and critiquing every step of the way. My daughter Jamila Reid was most helpful with technical assistance.

At the American University in Cairo Press, I am most grateful to Neil Hewison, Nadia Naqib, Nadine El-Hadi, the rest of the ever-helpful staff, and two insightful anonymous readers.

Responsibility for the ideas presented is, of course, my own.

Introduction

Four museums founded in Egypt in the half century between 1858 and 1908 each represented a vital segment of the country's past and an emerging field of scholarly specialization: the Museum of Egyptian Antiquities, the Graeco–Roman Museum, the Museum of Arab Art, and the Coptic Museum (see figs. 1–4).[1]

During this same half century, Western imperialism peaked worldwide and Europeans fastened imperial control over Egypt. It was no coincidence that both the founding directors and their immediate successors at three of the four museums were Europeans, the Coptic Museum being the only exception. This was colonial museology, and it grew up in tandem with colonial archaeology.

As European nation-states came of age in the nineteenth century, museums and archaeology played critical roles in constructing each nation's ideas of its distinctive heritage and identity. Throughout the century, European empires old and new also enlisted archaeology and museums in the service of defining, legitimating, and projecting imperial claims. Meanwhile, museums, universities, and learned societies—building on Enlightenment ideals of rationally and empirically based universal knowledge, or 'science'—were constructing modern academic disciplines. Dedication to universal knowledge was potentially at odds with allegiance to particular nations and empires, but many scholars found ways to rationalize commitment to science, nationalism, and imperialism all at once. For example, Auguste Mariette and Gaston Maspero, who dominated Egypt's pre-1914 Antiquities Service and Egyptian Museum, simultaneously labored on behalf of Egyptological 'science,' French nationalism, and French imperialism.

Where did this leave modern Egyptians? Like Europeans, they had their own traditions, both scholarly and folk, surrounding Egypt's

1

pre-Islamic and pre-Christian antiquities. This inheritance ranged from fascination with pharaonic antiquities to revulsion at their paganism. Throughout the long nineteenth century stretching from 1798 to 1914, Egyptians struggled to come to grips with both the shock of European conquest and colonization and the challenge presented by Europe's emerging new forms of knowledge. Political and economic colonization provoked resistance and a long struggle for independence. Meanwhile, Napoleon Bonaparte's military expedition to Egypt in 1798 had unearthed the Rosetta Stone, and in 1822 Jean-François Champollion's decipherment of its hieroglyphic text laid the foundation for modern Egyptology. Cultural colonization—as in Egypt's antiquities museums—elicited a dual response. One was a struggle to educate Egyptian Egyptologists who could compete as equals with Western specialists and hope eventually to replace them. In the other struggle, Egyptians impressed with pharaonic achievements tried to persuade their countrymen that museums and archaeology could make inspiring contributions to the causes of national revival and independence. The present author's *Whose Pharaohs? Archaeology, Museums, and Egyptian National Identity from Napoleon to World War I* treats these themes over the long century from 1798 to 1914.[2]

Contesting Antiquity in Egypt picks up the story in 1914 and carries it forward to the 1952 revolution. By 1914, colonial control—locked in

1 The Egyptian Museum (Museum of Egyptian Antiquities), Cairo. *Photo: D. Reid.*

2 The Greco–Roman Museum, Alexandria. *Photo: D. Reid.*

by British military occupation in 1882—was coming under increasing challenge. Repression under martial law during World War I fueled the national uprising of 1919. In reaction, the British tried to protect their strategic interests by unilaterally declaring Egypt independent, but with major restrictions. The ensuing 'semicolonial' era lasted until the 1952 revolution of Nasser's Free Officers. These three semicolonial decades of partial and fitful imperial retreat and intermittent nationalist advance proved immensely frustrating to Europeans and Egyptians alike.

During this semicolonial era, Egyptians had won enough autonomy to establish university programs in archaeology and challenge slowly receding colonial control over their academic and cultural institutions. The Egyptianization of archaeological and museum posts proceeded only unevenly, however, and the colonizers clung to some key posts into the 1950s. This study highlights the still often neglected careers of several generations of Egyptians in the archaeologies represented by the four museums. It examines their views in relation to both the international

3 The Museum of Arab Art, Cairo (since 1952, Museum of Islamic Art). *Photo: D. Reid.*

4 The Coptic Museum, Cairo. *Photo: D. Reid.*

scholarly communities to which they belonged and their roles in critical internal debates among Egyptians over heritage and identity.

Egyptian archaeological and museological development were part of a global process in which states and peoples struggled to transform themselves into modern nation-states and empires. In the first half of the twentieth century, imperial nations—Britain, France, Germany, Russia, Italy, the United States, and Japan—were caught up in a global contest for political, economic, and cultural influence. In colonized lands such as Egypt and India, museums and archaeology became significant arenas in the struggle for independence. In independent but semiperipheral countries such as Greece, Mexico, and post–World War I Turkey and Iran, efforts to harness the study and display of the past to nationalist agendas variously reflected features of archaeology characteristic of both colonizing and colonized countries.

Each of the antiquities museums inherited by semicolonial Egypt from the prewar colonial era evolved with its own idiosyncratic timing, motivation, and mission. Together, however, the four institutions had by 1914 cobbled together a four-museum paradigm for parceling out Egypt's antiquities, archaeology, and premodern history. The Egyptian Museum and Egyptology emphasized the pharaonic era, the Greco–Roman Museum and classical studies centered on the Ptolemaic and Roman–Byzantine age, the Coptic Museum and Coptic studies stressed Christian aspects of both the Roman–Byzantine and Islamic eras, and the Museum of Arab Art and Islamic studies treated the Islamic age. In this book, "archaeology" and "archaeologist" are sometimes used in a loose sense for the four fields and their practitioners.

In 1992, an Egyptian intellectual attending a conference in France identified himself as coming "from Arab-Afro-Asian Egypt with its four civilizations, Pharaonic, Graeco-Roman, Coptic, and Islamic."[3] Clearly, the four-museum paradigm had taken hold. There are other possible chronological and thematic ways of dividing up Egypt's long past, but the four-museum paradigm has not lost its power and offers a convenient way of organizing this study.[4]

The Egyptian Museum—with its pharaonic concentration—was first on the scene and remains by far the largest, most famous, and most visited museum in Egypt.[5] Founded in Cairo in 1858 along with the Egyptian Antiquities Service, it opened to the public in 1863. The Museum of Arab Art came next, opening in 1884. It was a creation of the Committee for the Conservation of Monuments of Arab Art (the Comité), which had been established three years earlier.[6] The Greco–Roman Museum was founded third, in 1892. Appropriately, it was not located in Cairo but in Alexandria.

The seaport city named for its founder, Alexander the Great, had served as Egypt's capital throughout its millennium of Greek and Roman rule.

Great Britain's military occupation in 1882 gave it the strongest hand during the colonial age, but citizens of other European powers also joined in, giving imperialism on the Nile a European transnational flavor. This was reflected formally in such institutions as the Mixed Courts and Caisse de la dette publique and informally in the mix of Europeans holding posts in the Antiquities Service, the Comité, and Egyptian state schools. Although the parceling out was never formally negotiated, the European founding directors of three museums and the Khedival Library (now the National Library, Dar al-Kutub al-Misriya) turned them into spheres of influence for four different countries. From Mariette through Maspero and beyond, French directors made the Antiquities Service and Egyptian Museum primarily a French archaeological protectorate. The Khedival Library became the domain of German Orientalist directors—five in a row from 1873 to 1914. Three successive Italians directed the Greco–Roman Museum from its inception to 1952, except for a break forced by World War II. Austro–Hungarian influence made itself felt at the Comité and Museum of Arab Art. Although Julius Franz, architect in chief of the Comité and founding curator of the Museum of Arab Art, was German born, he had studied architecture in Vienna, as had his hand-picked Hungarian successor, Max Herz. The British lacked a comparable specific enclave of cultural influence but had the satisfaction of running the whole country.

The Coptic Museum, founded in 1908, was unique in having an Egyptian founding director—Murqus (Marcus) Simaika—and in not falling into the cultural orbit of any particular European power. It benefited from a specific Egyptian constituency—Coptic Christians. Nevertheless, it too was a product of the colonial age and owed much to European inspiration.

Each of the four museums was eventually enshrined in a landmark building reflecting both architectural fashions and the parameters of the collections within. The Egyptian Museum (1902), designed by French architect Marcel Dourgnon (1858–1911)[7], was Beaux Arts neoclassical in style, with a pharaonic flourish or two (see fig. 1). The edifice exuded European imperial dominance. The inscriptions on its façade were in Latin and celebrated famous pharaohs and the European founding fathers of Egyptology (see figs. 5 and 6).[8]

The Greco–Roman Museum had the façade of a Doric temple, with ΜΟΥΣΕΙΟΝ ("MUSEUM") in Greek over its entrance (see fig. 2). The Museum of Arab Art was in Islamic revival style, more specifically neo-Mamluk (see fig. 3). The building's upper floor, which had a separate entrance, housed the Khedival Library. At first glance, the architectural

5 Imperial Latin. Dedicatory inscription, Egyptian Museum, Cairo. *Photo: D. Reid.*

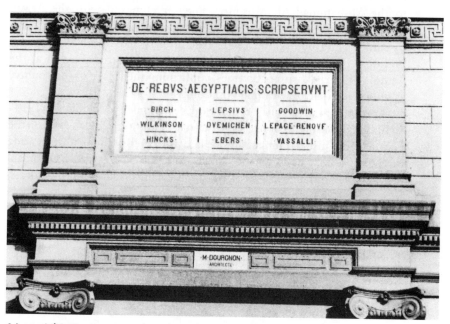

6 Imperial Latin. European founders of Egyptology, Egyptian Museum, Cairo.
Photo: D. Reid.

message of the Coptic Museum was less clear; its façade was inspired by the Fatimid Mosque of al-Aqmar (see fig. 4). On closer inspection, crosses on the façade, Coptic inscriptions, and the bust of Murqus Simaika before the entry proclaimed its Coptic Christian character.

How might the disjointed Egyptian past suggested by these four museums be knitted into a larger whole? A set of postage stamps issued in January 1914—when consul general Lord Kitchener was in the saddle and British power still strong—offered a colonial answer: Egypt was "an antique land" now under benevolent British protection (see fig. 7).

Hitherto, Pyramid-and-Sphinx designs—a choice largely reflecting European perceptions of the land—had monopolized regular Egyptian postage stamps since 1867 (see fig. 7, row 1). Kitchener's set of 1914 retained the pharaonic emphasis—six out of ten scenes—but tacked on a postpharaonic coda connecting to the British imperial present (see fig. 7, rows 2 & 3). Of the set's four nonpharaonic scenes, a 'colonial picturesque' Nile felucca with palm trees evoked timeless rusticity. Two stamps featured nineteenth-century monuments of the reigning dynasty's founder, Muhammad Ali: Ras al-Tin Palace and his landmark mosque atop the Cairo Citadel. Only one stamp recognized Cairo's great medieval Islamic monuments, and this only incidentally as foreground to the Muhammad Ali Mosque.[9] The set climaxed with the Aswan Dam, a suggestion perhaps that this British colonial wonder rivaled the Pyramids. The one-pound (£E1) banknote issued by the British-run National Bank of Egypt in 1914 (not shown) featured a pylon at the Temple of Karnak with palm trees, confirming the image of the country as quintessentially one of pharaonic ruins.[10]

Archaeological as much as political developments delimit the 1914–1952 timeframe of this book. The Ottoman Empire entered the war on the German and Austro–Hungarian side late in 1914. Britain finally cast aside the pretense that its Egyptian 'veiled protectorate' was really Ottoman, deposed the last khedive (Abbas II), and formally declared a protectorate. In archaeology, both Antiquities director general Maspero and his subordinate Ahmad Kamal, the only Egyptian Egyptologist yet to have won a sliver of international recognition, retired that same year—1914. The war halted German and Austro–Hungarian excavations, and French, British, and American digging slowed to a crawl. The last German director of the Khedival Library, Dr. A. Schaade, and Max Herz, the Hungarian curator of the Museum of Arab Art and chief architect of the Comité, were expelled as enemy aliens, opening two small bright spots for nationalists during those dark days of British martial law. With no European successors in sight, Herz's assistant Ali Bahgat moved up to become director of

7 A colonial vision of Egypt's heritage: Lord Kitchener's postage stamps of 1914. Top row: Pyramid-and-Sphinx designs monopolized regular Egyptian postage stamps from 1879 to 1914. Second and third rows: set issued in January 1914 under Lord Kitchener. Fourth row: statue of Ramesses II, added to the 1914 set in 1915.

the Museum of Arab Art, and liberal nationalist Ahmad Lutfi al-Sayyid became the first Egyptian to direct the National Library.

The 1922–1952 semicolonial era has also been called Egypt's age of parliamentary monarchy and (the last phase of) its 'Liberal Age.'[11] The period is sometimes classified as 'postcolonial' or 'neocolonial,' but the preference here is to save these terms for the 1950s and after, when formal political independence had been fully achieved. The Free Officers overthrew King Faruq in July 1952, and the Suez War of 1956 set the seal on full Egyptian independence. In archaeology, 1952 makes a good terminal date. King Faruq's overthrow ended the Egyptian career of his protégé Étienne Drioton and ninety-four years of French direction of the Antiquities Service. Within a year or so of the revolution, Egyptians occupied all of the country's key archaeological posts. This came at a price, however. Egypt lost four formidable European scholars—Drioton in Egyptology, K.A.C. Creswell in Islamic architecture, Gaston Wiet in Islamic art, and Achille Adriani in Greco–Roman art and archaeology.[12]

Contesting Antiquity in Egypt continues on the path of *Whose Pharaohs?* in emphasizing five thematic strands. First, it knits together the more familiar history of Western archaeologists with that of their relatively neglected Egyptian counterparts. Even after Michel Foucault, Edward Said, and several decades of postmodernism, positivist assumptions about Western progressive, objective, 'scientific' knowledge still underlie much writing about Egyptian archaeology. Nineteenth-century pioneers (Champollion, Richard Lepsius, and Mariette), turn-of-the-century successors (Gaston Maspero, Flinders Petrie, and Adolf Erman), and early twentieth-century heroes (Howard Carter, Ludwig Borchardt, James Henry Breasted, and George Reisner) still dominate the stage. Egyptians flicker in the shadows as trusty foremen, loyal servants, laborers, tomb robbers, antiquities dealers, obstructionist officials, and benighted nationalists.

Continuing to write Egyptians into the history of archaeology in their own country, this book highlights three Egyptian founding fathers— Ahmad Kamal (1849–1923, Egyptology), Ali Bahgat (1848–1924, Islamic archaeology), and Murqus Simaika (1864–1944, Coptic archaeology). Although Kamal and Bahgat were fifteen or sixteen years older than Simaika, the three shared something of a common generational consciousness. All three attended reformed schools where they learned European languages, thereby opening the door to their archaeological careers. All completed formal schooling before the British conquest of 1882 and lived most of their professional lives during the ensuing forty years of intense colonial occupation. Unlike Kamal and Bahgat, Simaika was not a professional scholar or a field archaeologist. He was an amateur—a lover of Coptic antiquity whose position as a notable facilitated his campaign to preserve Coptic monuments, create a Coptic Museum, and foster scholarship by organizing church and monastery libraries. Kamal died in 1923, followed by Bahgat in 1924. The younger Simaika lived well into the semicolonial era, dying in 1944. After the three pioneers, this book takes up the careers of succeeding generations in each discipline.

The emphasis on Egyptians and developments *in* Egypt means that *Contesting Antiquity* makes no attempt at a comprehensive history of Egyptology, Greco–Roman studies, Islamic art and archaeology, or Coptology. Egyptologists like Adolf Erman and Alan Gardiner, who worked mainly back home in their studies, universities, or museum halls, figure only on the margins. In contrast, Egyptologists Maspero, Petrie, Carter, Borchardt, and Reisner, along with Islamic specialists Gaston Wiet and K.A.C. Creswell, loom large because of their long, influential careers in

Egypt. On the popular level, Western 'Egyptomania' comes in mainly as needed for background, while in-country Egyptian 'pharaonism' is closely examined.

The second theme is to bring the histories of Egyptology, Greco–Roman studies, Coptology, and Islamic art and archaeology together in a single work. The plural "archaeologies" in the book's title is intended to emphasize that Egypt has archaeologies other than the pharaonic. Specialists in each of the four disciplines are usually leery of venturing beyond their own circumscribed field. Differences in Egypt's languages, writing systems, and religions across the ages make specialization essential, but disciplinary boundaries and periodizations can become blinders.

Juxtaposing the four museums and their respective archaeologies points up the inherited biases in the vocabulary with which we have to work. Logically, "Egyptology," "the Egyptian Museum," and the *Journal of Egyptian Archaeology* should all concentrate on the study of Egypt at any period. In fact, however, all center on ancient Egypt—primarily pharaonic, but with Greco–Roman and (because of the continuity of the language) Coptic studies often tacked on.[13] This standard definition of Egyptology implicitly slights Islamic and modern Egypt. Did "Egypt cease to be Egypt when it ceased to be ancient"?[14] The pharaonic Egyptian Museum dwarfed the other three antiquities museums, and Egyptology and its popular analogues ('Egyptomania' in the West, 'pharaonism' in Egypt) outshone Islamic, Coptic, and Greco–Roman archaeologies in Egypt in both Western and Egyptian eyes. Standard antiquities tours overwhelmingly stress the pharaonic to the near exclusion of the other three archaeologies. Although pointing out such issues, this book itself admittedly reflects the weight of the tradition by devoting over twice as many pages to the pharaonic as to the other three archaeologies combined. Islam of course looms far larger than pharaonic Egypt in the consciousness of most Egyptians, but this mostly found expression in arenas other than the Comité, the Museum of Arab Art, and Islamic archaeology.

The third thematic strand centers on the tension between politics and the ideal of objective, universal science. Both Westerners and Egyptians felt the competing pulls of trying to be good citizens of two imagined communities—one political and particularist (whether Western imperialist or Egyptian nationalist), and the other internationalist and scientific. British, French, German, Italian, and American archaeologists all showed varying degrees of imperialist tendencies in their Egyptian activities. Some tried to close Western ranks under the pious mantle of progressive science, dismissing Egyptians as mere chauvinists. "For the native," remarked Frantz Fanon, "objectivity is always directed against him."[15] In the West, archaeologists reacting against the nationalistic excesses of World War II reasserted positivist claims to be objective, value-free scientists. Even the latest edition of the indispensible *Who Was Who in Egyptology* only lightly alludes to the political, social, and ideological matrices in which its subjects lived and worked.[16] Mariette and Maspero are rightly celebrated as great Egyptologists, but they were also influential actors in both the French and the European transnational imperialism of their day.

A fourth theme is the integration of the history of archaeology, museums, and heritage into the mainstream history of Egypt. Historians of modern Egypt usually leave the history of archaeology to archaeologists or to popular writers. Egyptologists and other archaeologists have unique insights into the internal histories of their disciplines, but externalist studies by historians and social scientists may do better at setting disciplinary histories more fully into the political, social, and cultural contexts of the day.

Finally, the fifth thematic strand examines both scholarly and popular interest in the Egyptian past, treating the two as a continuum rather than as polar opposites. On the scholarly side, *Contesting Antiquity* emphasizes institution building, individual careers, and increasing specialization and professionalization. Scholarly histories of Egyptology and other archaeological disciplines often sidestep popular enthusiasms—which can be embarrassing, comical, and fantastic—about the object of their study. A burgeoning literature on 'Egyptomania' now takes seriously pharaonic themes in Western painting, architecture, photography, clothing styles, fiction, travel literature, novels, popular songs, classical music, world's fairs, guidebooks, postcards, and movies. After London's Great (or Crystal Palace) Exhibition of 1851, a world's fair without an Egyptian exhibit hardly seemed worthy of the name.

Because this study emphasizes Egyptians and developments *within* Egypt, 'pharaonism' receives more attention than Western 'Egyptomania.' 'Pharaonism' is used here for modern Egyptians' popular interest in, and often identification with, ancient Egypt. The Arabic equivalent— *al-fir'awniya*—was probably coined in the 1920s and is usually associated with Egyptian territorial nationalism. Pharaonism assumes an enduring cultural and sometimes biological heritage from ancient Egypt, which becomes a source of inspiration for revival and independence. In varying degrees, pharaonism shows up in politics, journalism, literature, folklore, architecture, painting, sculpture, and music.[17]

The term has one significant drawback. For Muslims, 'pharaoh' calls up the idolatrous pharaoh of the Quran (and the Bible) who persecuted Moses and the Israelite believers in the one true God. In modern times, denouncing an autocratic ruler or political opponent as 'pharaoh' is strong abuse, and few Egyptians choose to call themselves 'pharaonists.' Although it is often assumed that pharaonism is an opposite of Islamism, mild pharaonism need not be incompatible with Islamic or Arab national- ist allegiances. Many Egyptian Muslims and Copts treasure ancient Egypt along with their other heritages. How else could Egypt's wildly popular national football team be called 'the Pharaohs'? 'Pharaonism' is used in this book for convenience, and in a neutral sense.

'Pharaonism' is a less suitable term for contexts outside Egypt. For popular Western enthusiasm for ancient Egypt, the playful 'Egyptoma- nia' often serves. There is no clear line where scholarly Egyptology leaves off and Egyptomania begins. Promoters of world's fairs enlisted Egyp- tologists Mariette and Heinrich Brugsch and Comité architect Max Herz to guarantee the authenticity of pharaonic and Islamic Egyptian displays. Western painters and photographers of Egypt ranged from casual tourists to archaeological specialists. Georg Ebers wrote Egyptological mono- graphs with one hand and pharaonic novels with the other. Mariette the Egyptologist ran the Antiquities Service and Egyptian Museum, while Mariette the Egyptomaniac dreamed up the fantasy that became Verdi's *Aida*. Mariette insisted on meticulous authenticity for the opera's sets and costumes. But what did authenticity mean in a modern European musical extravaganza that no ancient Egyptian would have understood?

In the realm of theory, three books and the discussions they stimu- lated echo through the long-range background to this book—Edward Said's *Orientalism*, Benedict Anderson's *Imagined Communities*, and Bruce Trigger's *A History of Archaeological Thought*.[18] Said accused Orientalists of complicity in imposing Western imperialism on the Islamic world. Ander- son asserted that nations are not primordial, enduring entities but modern mental imaginings enabled by the rise of print capitalism. Calling attention to the political dimensions of archaeology, Trigger helped inspire a flurry of works probing the links between archaeology, nations, and empires. All three books caught the rising tide of the 'new cultural history.'

Historians of Egypt and the Middle East are often torn between acclaiming Said's insights and exasperation at *Orientalism*'s sweep- ing indictments. Timothy Mitchell built on Said's insights, while Jason Thompson, Mercedes Volait, and John MacKenzie found his blanket condemnations of Orientalists at odds with the individuals they studied closely.[19] Israel Gershoni, James Jankowski, and Ziad Fahmy are among those who creatively adapted Bendict Anderson's thesis to Egypt.[20]

Since Trigger's survey, numerous works have probed the ideologi- cal links between archaeology, nations, and empires.[21] For the Middle East, Wendy Shaw has studied Ottoman archaeology and museums, and

Magnus Bernhardsson has done the same for Iraq.[22] Donald Reid and Elliott Colla have examined Egyptian archaeology from both Western and Egyptian sources and perspectives, Jill Kamil has written a biography of Egyptologist Labib Habachi, and Éric Gady has detailed the politics of French Egyptology.[23] The tangled politics of Israeli and Palestinian archaeology have also come under scrutiny.[24]

The plural "identities" in the subtitle of this work is intended to signal that the imperialist/nationalist dichotomy does not come close to conveying the complexity of the disciplines, ideologies, actors, motivations, and social forces involved. Western imperialism versus Egyptian nationalism is a necessary framework, but it is neither simple nor sufficient. Some archaeologists, whether Western or Egyptian, were more political than others, and personal rivalries between compatriots often trumped national solidarity. Beginnings have been made, or should be, at writing histories of Egyptian archaeology from below or from the viewpoints of such "fragments of the nation"[25] as women, Copts, Upper Egyptians, tourist guides, antiquities dealers, boat crews, hotel workers, Islamists, and archaeological workers from the villages of Quft, Nazlat al-Samman (by the Giza Pyramids), and Qurna (across the river from Luxor).[26]

Despite the continuing urgency of "rescuing history from the nation,"[27] however, much remains to be done in the history of Egyptian archaeology in "rescuing the nation from the empire." Without underestimating either nationalist excesses or postcolonial disappointments in Egypt, the injustices of the colonial age still need a fuller reckoning. The intention is neither to belittle Western nor to exaggerate Egyptian achievements in archaeology but to point up inequalities of power, challenge assumptions that "never the twain shall meet," and work for disciplinary histories that no longer read like Western monologues into imagined Egyptian silence.

This book draws on published and archival sources in Arabic and Western languages, supplemented by interviews with over fifty Egyptian archaeologists over the course of three decades. It uses unpublished documents from Egypt (the National Archives—Dar al-Wathaiq al-Qawmiya, the archives of the Ministry of Finance—Dar al-Mahfuzat, and the archives of Cairo University), France (the archives of the Ministère des affaires ètrangères), the UK (the National Archives), and the US (National Archives, Oriental Institute of the University of Chicago, the Museum of Fine Arts—Boston, University of Pennsylvania's University Museum). The author's most remarkable find was the previously unexploited memoirs of Murqus Simaika, the founder of the Coptic Museum.

Contesting Antiquity in Egypt is divided into three parts. Part one briefly reviews approaches to ancient Egypt over the long century from

Napoleon in 1798 to 1914 and then concentrates on Egyptology and pharaonism from World War I through the 1920s, with the discovery of Tutankhamun's tomb as the touchstone. Part two sets aside the pharaonic theme to explore less familiar aspects of Egypt's heritage—the history of tourism (with its intimate ties to archaeology), and the histories of the Greco–Roman, Coptic, and Arab/Islamic museums and their associated archaeologies down to 1952. Pioneers in these postpharaonic archaeologies all shaped their fields with the dominant Egyptological paradigm in mind. Returning to 1930, part three picks up the histories of Egyptology and pharaonism and carries them down to Nasser's revolution.

In part one, chapter 1 briefly surveys Egyptological developments from 1798 to 1914 before closely examining the effects of World War I and the 1919 national uprising on archaeology and popular pharaonism among Egyptians. Chapter 2 takes up Howard Carter's discovery of the tomb of Tutankhamun in 1922 and its impact on archaeology, Egyptian and imperial politics, and popular Egyptian consciousness. Chapter 3 discusses British, French, German, and American Egyptology as practiced in Egypt through the remainder of the 1920s. Covering the same chronological ground, Chapter 4 examines the establishment of the Egyptology program at the Egyptian (now Cairo) University and the training there, and in some cases in Europe, of two generations of Egyptian Egyptologists. It concludes with a survey of popular pharaonism to 1930.

Putting the pharaonic heritage temporarily on hold, each of the chapters of part two follows another theme all the way from 1914 to 1952. Chapter 5 focuses on Western tourism to Egypt with attention to guidebooks, hotels, and guides as well as to Hassan Fathy's failed attempt to move Qurna villagers away from the Tombs of the Nobles and down to his utopian New Qurna in the agricultural plain. Chapter 6 looks at Islamic art and archaeology, highlighting the careers of Ali Bahgat, French Orientalist Gaston Wiet at the Museum of Arab Art, and British historian of Islamic architecture K.A.C. Creswell, who introduced Islamic archaeology to Cairo University. The Comité de conservation des monuments de l'art arabe also looms large in this chapter.

Chapter 7, on Copts and Coptic archaeology, emphasizes the careers of two notables of different generations: Murqus Simaika, founder of the Coptic Museum in 1908, and Mirrit Boutros Ghali, founder of the Société d'archéologie copte in 1934. Its treatment also includes two issues entangled in the delicate relations between Copts and Muslims—the nationalization of the Coptic Museum in 1931 and the special affinity of many Copts for pharaonic Egypt. Chapter 8 turns to Egypt's Greco–Roman heritage, emphasizing the centrality of classics to European imperial discourse and the attempts of a few Egyptians to develop expertise in the field and appropriate it for their own purposes. The Greco–Roman Museum in Alexandria, which Italians directed for half a century, looms large here. The development of university-level classical studies in Cairo and Alexandria rounds out the story.

Returning to pharaonic themes in part three, chapter 9 follows the careers of second-generation Egyptologists Selim Hassan and Sami Gabra through the 1930s. It discusses Hermann Junker's displacement of Ludwig Borchardt, a Jew, at the head of German archaeology in Egypt and the effects on the two Egyptologists of the Nazis' rise to power back home. Chapter 9 also highlights Selim Hassan's challenge to French and British control of the Antiquities Service and how his defeat forced him out of public life until the 1952 revolution.

Chapter 10 follows Egyptian debates over pharaonism in relation to Islam and Arabism in the 1930s and 1940s. Diverse views on Saad Zaghlul's neo-pharaonic tomb and Mukhtar's monumental statues of Zaghlul come in here. So do the pharaonist proclivities of writer-politicians Muhammad Husayn Haykal and Ahmad Husayn (of Young Egypt) and of writers Salama Musa, Tawfiq al-Hakim, and Naguib Mahfouz.

Chapter 11, on the dozen years leading up to the 1952 revolution, charts the retreat of Europeans in the Antiquities Service and the Egyptianization of university Egyptology. Under the guidance of Director General of Antiquities Étienne Drioton, King Faruq personally dabbled in 'royal archaeology.' In the year before the revolution, separate crises with France and Britain severely damaged their archaeological interests in Egypt. Drioton's abrupt departure along with his patron King Faruq nearly completed the Egyptianization of the country's archaeological institutions. Old-new aspirations and inequities of power metamorphosed and reemerged—in archaeology as in politics—as Egypt entered its postcolonial age. Nasser and the Free Officers opened a new chapter in Egyptian archaeology. In that chapter, the Aswan High Dam would loom large—in national and Cold War politics; socioeconomic development; salvage archaeology coordinated through the United Nations Educational, Scientific, and Cultural Organization (UNESCO); and in the tragic displacement of the Nubian people.

Part One

Egyptology and Pharaonism to 1930

1

Egyptology and Pharaonism in Egypt before Tutankhamun

S ailing home to France for the last time in July 1914, retiring director
general of the Egyptian Antiquities Service Gaston Maspero could
look back with satisfaction on 116 years since Napoleon's conquest
of Egypt, ninety-two since Jean-François Champollion's decipherment of
hieroglyphs, fifty-six since Auguste Mariette's founding of the Egyptian
Antiquities Service,[1] and thirty-three since first taking up his own post in
Cairo. The French could perhaps be pardoned their sometime boast that
Egyptology was a French science.[2]

This chapter begins with a brief review of the development of Western
Egyptology over the long nineteenth century from 1798 to 1914. In addition to the French, scholars and archaeologists from Britain, Germany,
Italy, and other European countries all participated in constructing the
discipline. Around the turn of the twentieth century, Americans joined
in. National and personal rivalries often subverted ideals of scientific
objectivity and international collaboration, and Egyptology remained
resolutely Eurocentric. The rather conventional sketch of the history of
nineteenth-century Egyptology in the next few pages sets the stage for a
central theme of the book: bringing in modern Egyptians—both those
who struggled to establish Egyptology as a scholarly specialty and those
who promoted ancient Egypt among the wider public. The career of
Ahmad Kamal Pasha epitomizes the struggle to develop Egyptian Egyptology, and Ahmad Lutfi al-Sayyid stands out among the intellectuals who
campaigned to popularize it in modern Egypt in the decade leading up
to World War I. The chapter then turns to the critical years of World
War I—a trying time for British and French colonizers, Egyptians, and
all archaeologists alike. The hopes and disappointments of the Egyptian
uprising of 1919 ('revolution' in nationalist terminology) come next. The

chapter concludes with an overview of the substantial evidence of phara-onism among the public on the eve of Tutankhamun's bursting on the scene in November 1922.

French and British Egyptology from Champollion and Thomas Young to Maspero and Petrie

Until Champollion's breakthrough toward decipherment of hieroglyphs in 1822, what Europeans knew about ancient Egypt was gleaned from the Bible; classical works by writers such as Herodotus and Manetho; and travel accounts by medieval and later European travelers—includ-ing crusaders, pilgrims, and merchants. From the Renaissance through the European Enlightenment, comparing classical accounts with on-the-ground observations in Egypt emerged as a new method of research. Humanist rediscovery of the classical texts of Horapollo's *Hieroglyphica* and the *Corpus Hermeticum* also fed mystical fantasies of pharaonic Egypt as the fount of occult wisdom. Such traditions passed underground from human-ists to Rosicrucians and Freemasons and on to New Age circles today.

In 1798, Napoleon's expedition to Egypt opened up a new era. Brit-ish, Ottoman, Mamluk, and popular Egyptian resistance quickly turned the expedition into a military disaster, but the accompanying French savants managed to salvage a scholarly triumph—the encyclopedic *Description de l'Égypte*. French soldiers digging fortifications also chanced upon the Rosetta Stone, which bore inscriptions in three scripts—hiero-glyphs, demotic, and Greek. Seizing the stone as spoils of war, the British ensconced it in the British Museum, but their scholars, led by polymath physician Thomas Young, made little progress in deciphering its hiero-glyphic text. A Frenchman won the honor instead: in 1822 Jean-François Champollion (1790–1832) announced his breakthrough toward decipher-ing hieroglyphs. By the time of his death ten years later at only forty-two, Champollion had published a grammar of ancient Egyptian, founded the Egyptian Department at the Louvre, led an archaeological expedition to Egypt, urged Egyptian governor Muhammad Ali to preserve antiquities, and inaugurated academic Egyptology through the chair created for him at the Collège de France.

Picking up on Champollion's legacy after a lull, Auguste Mariette (1821–1881) discovered the Serapeum—the tomb of the Apis sacred bulls—at Saqqara in 1850. Four years later, the accession of Muhammad Ali's son Said Pasha opened the door to Ferdinand de Lesseps's proj-ect to dig the Suez Canal. With French influence in Egypt riding high throughout Napoleon III's reign (1851–1870), Said appointed Mariette director of antiquities in 1858 (see fig. 8). Mariette obtained a monopoly on excavation and filled the museum he opened at Bulaq in 1863 (the Egyptian Museum) with pharaonic antiquities. He achieved at least partial success in stemming the frenzied outflow of antiquities to Western museums and private collections.

In 1880, Gaston Maspero arrived in Cairo to found what soon became the Institut français d'archéologie oriental du Caire (IFAO). This put him on the spot to keep the directorship of the Antiquities Service in French hands when Mariette died in January 1881. Khedive Ismail's (r. 1863–79) bankruptcy and deposition at the hands of European creditors had opened the way for Col. Ahmad Urabi's revolt against European encroachment, Khedive Tawfiq (r. 1879–92), and Egypt's Turkish-speaking Ottoman elite.[3] In 1882, the British bombarded Alexandria, defeated Urabi, and occupied the country. During his two terms directing the Egyptian Antiquities Service (1881–86, 1899–1914), Maspero's adroit diplomacy managed to keep it in French hands despite the British occupation. In 1899, Maspero negotiated an informal archaeological entente which prefigured the famous Anglo–French Entente of 1904. He welcomed British officials into the Antiquities Service, and in the 1904 Entente agreement, Britain formally recognized France's claim to direct the Egyptian Antiquities Service.

8 Auguste Mariette's sarcophagus and statue, garden of the Egyptian Museum, Cairo. *Photo: D. Reid.*

Two months before Maspero sailed from Egypt for the last time in June 1914, his British contemporary Flinders Petrie (1853–1942) wound up his usual winter excavations and headed home to England. Petrie spiritedly continued the British–French rivalry over Egypt and Egyptology, which went back to Admiral Nelson's sinking of Napoleon's fleet at the Battle of the Nile, Champollion's trumping Thomas Young in the decipherment of the Rosetta Stone, and British consul Henry Salt's (1780–1827) contest with French consul Bernardino Drovetti (1776–1852) in collecting pharaonic antiquities for European museums. Britain was far behind France (as well as Germany) in establishing Egyptology as a university specialty and a profession. With only scant and sporadic state support, British Egyptology long remained the domain of private patronage and amateurs. Tomb copyist Gardiner Wilkinson (1797–1875) and his Orientalist friend Edward W. Lane (author of *Manners and Customs of the Modern Egyptians*) were neither university nor museum based.[4] As an official at the British Museum for nearly fifty years, Samuel Birch (1813–1885) came closer to being a professional Egyptologist. He was also a sinologist, however, and never ventured out to see Egypt for himself. Birch's successor, E.A.W. Budge (1857–1934), kept the British Museum active in Egyptology through the Maspero–Petrie era.

Petrie was thus not atypical in arriving in British Egyptology by a nonacademic road. This contrasted with his contemporary Maspero, who also first set foot in Egypt in 1880. Maspero came up through the elite schools of Paris and excelled as an academic, administrator, and museum curator. Petrie, on the other hand, was a self-taught field archaeologist with almost no formal schooling. He worked out meticulous techniques of excavation and record keeping, paid close attention to everyday objects, and published his results promptly. He refined stratigraphic excavation and established relative chronologies, especially with pottery, through seriation. Never lingering at any site for long, he dug all over Egypt and in Palestine, sometimes for the Egypt Exploration Fund (EEF) but more often for his own Egyptian Research Account and British School of Archaeology in Egypt (BSAE). Archaeologists today are less impressed with some of Petrie's other successive enthusiasms: believing in secret wisdom encoded in the architecture of the Great Pyramid, attempting to prove the literal historical accuracy of the Bible, and seeing races and racial conquests as the critical determinants of the history of civilizations.[5]

Alongside and sometimes overlapping with Petrie, the EEF (since 1919 the Egypt Exploration Society, EES) was another key force in British Egyptology in the 1880–1914 era.[6] Novelist Amelia Edwards (1831–1892) and British Museum numismatist and Orientalist Reginald

Stuart Poole took the lead in organizing the privately funded EEF in 1882. Britain's conquest of Egypt in the very year of the EEF's founding formalized an imperial antiquities regime privileging Westerners. David Gange has emphasized the centrality of religion in shaping nineteenth-century British interest in ancient Egypt. Until after midcentury, apocalyptic sermons, literature, and paintings depicted it as a monstrous pagan land cursed by God for persecuting Moses and the chosen people. In the 1870s and 1880s, the emphasis shifted as Biblical literalists embraced archaeology as a scientific ally they hoped would discredit higher criticism of the Bible and skepticism of scriptural truths.[7] The EEF's early public appeals highlighted its search for the lost Biblical cities in the Nile Delta associated with Moses and the Exodus. The EEF soon broadened its horizons, and in 1892 a bequest in Amelia Edwards's will first propelled Egyptology into a British university. She endowed a chair of Egyptology at University College London. As she had wished, Petrie became its first occupant.

The pharaonic emphasis of the January 1914 set of Egyptian postage stamps discussed in the introduction was in tune with Consul General Lord Kitchener's archaeological interests. A collector of antiquities himself, he proposed to erect a fallen colossus of Ramesses II from Memphis in front of the Cairo train station. A stamp of Ramesses II issued in 1915 probably reflects this unrealized colonial project (fig. 7, row 4).[8] Ironically, Egyptian nationalists—the regime of Nasser's Free Officers—would accomplish the project forty years later (fig. 78.).[9] The switch from French to English as the European language on Kitchener's stamp set of January 1914 anticipated Britain's declaration of a formal protectorate over Egypt late that same year. In the meantime, World War I had broken out, and Kitchener had been called home to become secretary of state for war.

The Coming of the Germans

As early as the 1840s with Richard Lepsius, Germans began to challenge the French for leadership in Egyptology. [10] Germany's and Italy's late unifications—by West European standards—meant that their Egyptological activity was dispersed well beyond their eventual national capitals of Berlin and Rome. Late unification and the weakness of their universities may have encouraged some Italians to pursue the field under foreign auspices. Italian-born Bernardino Drovetti (1776–1852) collected antiquities while serving as French consul at Cairo, Giovanni Battista Belzoni (1778–1823) collected for British consul Henry Salt and exhibited in London, and Giuseppe Passalacqua (1797–1865) became the first director of Berlin's Egyptian Museum.

Richard Lepsius (1810–84) and Heinrich Brugsch (1827–94) put German archaeology on the map in Egypt itself. Just missing the chance to study hieroglyphs with the master, Lepsius arrived in Paris to study the year after Champollion's death. King of Prussia Friedrich Wilhelm IV personally funded Lepsius's archaeological expedition to Egypt from 1842 to 1845. Lepsius returned to a Berlin University chair created especially for him and later added the directorship of Berlin's Egyptian Museum. He published his expedition's results in twelve volumes—*Denkmäler aus Ägypten und Aethiopien* (1849–59). Although Heinrich Brugsch earned his doctorate at Berlin, he emerged as a younger rival rather than as a student of Lepsius. Arriving in Egypt in 1853 on a Prussian state scientific mission, Brugsch assisted Mariette in working on the Saqqara Serapeum. In 1864, he returned to Egypt as Prussian consul and from 1869 to 1874 directed Egypt's ephemeral School of Egyptology in Cairo. Based at the University of Göttingen from 1867, he contributed to all phases of Egyptian philology.

After forcing Chancellor Bismarck into retirement in 1890, Kaiser Wilhelm II worked to expand German influence in the central Ottoman Empire. Egypt, already in British hands, received less German imperial attention. The projected Berlin-to-Baghdad railroad potentially rivaled the Suez Canal as a link to India and the Far East. In 1898, the kaiser visited Constantinople (Istanbul), Damascus, and Jerusalem. German excavations in Greece and western Anatolia, driven by the reverence for Greece and Rome in German high culture, concentrated on classical sites. Biblical associations also came into play with German excavations in Mesopotamia and Egypt. The kaiser encouraged the founding of the German Oriental Society (Deutsche Orient Gesellschaft, DOG) in the same year he visited the Near East. The DOG grew out of a nongovernmental Orient-Committee formed in 1887 to sponsor excavation in Mesopotamia. Textile millionaire James Simon (1851–1932), a German Jewish patron of Berlin museums and charities, provided much of the funding for DOG excavations in both Mesopotamia and Egypt.[11]

Lepsius's and Brugsch's work in Egypt had been only episodic; Ludwig Borchardt (1863–1938) labored to establish a more permanent German archaeological base there. Borchardt earned both a Technische Hochschule degree in architecture and an Egyptology doctorate under Lepsius's successor, Adolf Erman (1854–1937), at Berlin. Erman's priority in backing Borchardt's activities in Egypt beginning in 1895 was to obtain copies of texts to support his ambitious project of a Berlin dictionary of Egyptian.[12] Funded by the Prussian Academy of Sciences, Erman's dictionary challenged older French leadership in Egyptian philology. Borchardt's excavations and research on ancient Egyptian architecture sometimes caused friction with his philologically focused mentor and others in Erman's circle back in Germany. After helping consolidate the temples of Philae before their flooding by the Aswan Dam, Borchardt directed an international commission to catalogue the collections of the Cairo Museum. In 1899, Erman arranged for Borchardt's appointment as scientific attaché at the German consulate.[13] With funds from James Simon through the DOG and his own resources, Borchardt excavated Fifth Dynasty solar temples and pyramids at Abu Gurob and Abusir. In 1907 Erman arranged for the founding of the Imperial German Institute for Egyptian Archaeology (Kaiserlich Deutsche Institut für Ägyptische Altertumskunde), with Borchardt as director.[14] Despite its impressive-sounding name, the sparsely staffed and meagerly funded Institute was not in the same league as IFAO. The Institute's headquarters were in Borchardt's privately owned villa in Zamalek (Cairo) and an adjoining villa acquired in 1908, and the "German House" he built for research at al-Qurna (Thebes) was privately funded and on land donated by Khedive Abbas II[15] (see fig. 9).

9 The first "German House" at al-Qurna. Designed by Ludwig Borchardt, 1905; destroyed by the British in 1915. *Courtesy of the Swiss Institute of Architectural and Archaeological Research on Ancient Egypt in Cairo.*

For the last three seasons before the war, Borchardt dug at Akhetaten, modern Tell al-Amarna. Akhenaten had moved his capital there from Thebes—a sharp break with the old gods in favor of the sole sun god, Aten. Borchardt's pioneering settlement archaeology contrasted with the usual emphasis on excavating tombs and temples. He left field supervision largely to his assistant, Hermann Ranke, but was on hand in December 1912 when the bust of Queen Nefertiti turned up in the workshop of the sculptor Thutmose. Chapter 3 takes up the uproar that followed the bust's public display in Berlin in 1923 and its publication.

America Stakes a Claim

Although the United States had no professional Egyptologists until the 1890s, amateur American interest in ancient Egypt was long standing and diverse. Tracing esoteric wisdom back to the pharaohs, Freemasons among the founding fathers put a pyramid capped by an "All-Seeing Eye" on the Great Seal of the United States in 1782; Americans still encounter it daily on the dollar bill. Bible-centered Americans saw Egypt as a land of plenty, oppression and plagues, divine deliverance, and refuge for the Holy Family. Classically minded elites associated the land of the Nile with Herodotus, Alexander, Cleopatra, Anthony, and Caesar. In the 1870s, American industrialists and financiers joined older elites uneasy about popular democracy in funding art museums in Boston, New York, and Philadelphia as a means of public education. William Vanderbilt funded the transport of one of "Cleopatra's Needles" from Alexandria to New York's Central Park, where the obelisk went up behind the Metropolitan Museum in 1881. The long-delayed completion of the Washington Monument four years later gave the District of Columbia the world's tallest obelisk.[16]

In 1896, Edwin Blashfield finished his painting *Evolution of Civilization* in the collar of the Library of Congress's dome. The figures representing Egypt and America sit side by side; civilization is shown as beginning in Egypt with "Written Records" and progressing around the dome to culminate in contemporary America, whose contribution is "Science" (see fig. 10).[17]

In the 1890s, American museums out to build up Egyptian collections subscribed to Britain's EEF, but aspiring Egyptologists headed to Germany for doctoral studies. Returning with German PhDs in many fields, Americans built research universities by grafting seminars and laboratories onto homegrown undergraduate colleges. Egyptologists George Reisner, James Breasted, and Albert Lythgoe were all born between 1865 and 1868, studied in Germany in the 1890s, established university or museum bases back home, led their first Egyptian expeditions between 1899 and 1906, and died between 1934 and 1942.[18]

10 Civilization from Egyptian dawn to American climax. Section of Edwin Blashfield's *Evolution of Civilization*, collar of the dome, Thomas Jefferson Building, Library of Congress, Washington DC, 1896. *Photo: Carol Highsmith, Library of Congress, public domain.*

Reisner studied Semitic languages at Harvard and went to Berlin intending to pursue Assyriology but ended up studying Egyptology under Adolf Erman. Erman arranged for Reisner to join Borchardt's international catalogue commission at Cairo. In 1899, Reisner led a University of California expedition financed by Phoebe A. Hearst, the widow of mining magnate George Hearst and mother of press baron William Randolph Hearst. Digging at half a dozen sites, Reisner worked out meticulous excavation techniques. After a plunge in gold mining profits forced Hearst to cut off support in 1905, Reisner returned to Harvard to teach Semitic archaeology. Harvard and the Boston Museum of Fine Arts (MFA) agreed to cosponsor him on an Egyptian expedition. In 1910, joint appointments as assistant professor of Egyptology at Harvard and curator of the Egyptian Department at the MFA regularized the arrangement which kept him in the field almost uninterruptedly until his death in Cairo in 1942.[19]

After trying pharmacy and the ministry, Reisner's fellow mid-Westerner James Henry Breasted also came to Egyptology through Hebrew and Semitic languages.[20] Standard Oil baron John D. Rockefeller recruited William Rainey Harper, Breasted's Hebrew professor at Yale, to found the University of Chicago. Harper dispatched Breasted to Berlin for a PhD in Egyptian philology under Erman, and Breasted returned to spend his entire career at Chicago. In contrast to Reisner, a field archaeologist, Breasted excelled in philology and history. He eschewed the glamor of excavation and emphasized the urgency of copying and publishing fast-perishing inscriptions. From 1905 to 1907, a Rockefeller grant funded Breasted's epigraphic expedition to record the historical inscriptions of Nubia.[21]

In 1906, the Metropolitan Museum of Art (MMA) and Brooklyn Museum joined Reisner and Breasted with field expeditions to Egypt, and in 1907 the University of Pennsylvania's Museum of Archaeology and Anthropology (University Museum) also jumped in. Financial tycoon J.P. Morgan came to dominate the MMA's board in 1905 and decided the museum needed its own Egyptian department and expedition. Alfred Lythgoe, like Reisner a product of Harvard and Germany, became Morgan's man. Lythgoe had studied at Bonn, learned field archaeology under Reisner, and in 1902 became founding curator of the Boston MFA's Egyptian department. Transferring to the Met in 1906, he founded his second museum Egyptian department and led the Met's expedition to the Middle Kingdom pyramid site at Lisht.[22]

A German rite of passage was no longer indispensable. The MMA's Herbert Winlock had been fascinated as a boy with mummies in the Smithsonian, where his astronomer father was assistant secretary.[23] At Harvard in 1905, Lythgoe invited Winlock to join the Harvard–Boston Giza expedition; Winlock "accepted with a shout loud enough for the echoes of it still to fill my soul."[24] He followed Lythgoe to the MMA in 1906, excelled at field archaeology, headed the Met's expedition at Deir al-Bahari, and eventually directed the MMA.

Europeans often envied the resources American millionaires poured into Egyptology. The sixth American expedition in the field in 1907— the peak of prewar American field Egyptology—was financed by Rhode Island mining magnate Theodore Davis (1837–1915). Like Britain's Lord Carnarvon, Davis had the private wealth to dig as a hobby and made spectacular discoveries in the Valley of the Kings (1903–12). Unusually for his day, Davis relinquished most of his finds to the Cairo Museum, which named a room in his honor.[25]

Maspero toyed with hiring one of Reisner's apprentices for the Antiquities Service until he discovered that the Harvard–Boston expedition paid them more in six months than his own inspectors made in a year.[26] The MMA in turn outbid Reisner and the MFA, luring Lythgoe and Briton Arthur Mace away with higher salaries.[27] In 1912, the MMA erected its landmark domed expedition house near Hatshepsut's Deir al-Bahari

11 Americans living in style: Dig house of the Metropolitan Museum of Art, al-Qurna, built 1912. *Photo: D. Reid.*

temple at Thebes (see fig. 11). J.P. Morgan thought MMA excavators should live in style, but his personal generosity came up short:

> It was called Morgan House until someone realized that the great financier had merely advanced the money as a loan and then paid himself back out of museum funds; after that it was known as Metropolitan House.[28]

Ahmad Kamal Pasha, Pioneer of Egyptian Egyptology and Pharaonism

Against this background of the prevailing Eurocentric narrative of nineteenth-century Egyptology, attention may now be turned to the countervailing themes of the emergence among modern Egyptians of both specialist Egyptology and a wider pharaonism among the general public. The same fateful summer of 1914 when Maspero left Egypt for good, Petrie for six years, and Borchardt for nine, the retirement of their colleague Ahmad Kamal from the Antiquities Service passed almost unnoticed.[29] Kamal devoted his life to a two-pronged struggle during the colonial age: to prove himself as a professional Egyptologist and to persuade his countrymen of the importance of their pharaonic heritage as a source of inspiration for modern revival and the struggle for independence (see fig. 12).

Five years younger than Maspero and two older than Petrie, Kamal was born in Cairo in 1851 to a Muslim father of Cretan origin who had probably entered state service under Muhammad Ali. In Cairo's elite Primary School (*Mubtadiyan*) and Preparatory School (*Tajhiziya*), Kamal learned the French that would enable him to enter the School of Egyptology when Khedive Ismail's minister of education, Ali Mubarak, opened it in 1869 and appointed German Egyptologist Heinrich Brugsch as its director. Mariette could not conceive of Egyptians as possible professional

12 Ahmad Kamal and the
coffin of Queen Ahmose
Nefertari from the Deir
al-Bahari cache of royal
mummies. *Photo: É. Brugsch,
in Edward Wilson, "Finding
Pharaoh," as reproduced in
John Romer,* Valley of the
Kings *(New York, 1994),
139.* As Contesting Antiquity
was on press, an argument
was made that this photo
depicts not Ahmad Kamal but
his colleague at the Bulaq
Museum Emile Brugsch. See
Dylan Bickerstaffe, "Emile
Brugsch & the Royal Mum-
mies at Bulaq," *KMT* 26, No.
1 (Spring 2015): 18–26.

colleagues and worried about German influence encroaching on his own antiquities domain. He refused to hire the school's graduates, and in 1874 the School of Egyptology closed. Unable to enter the field for which he had prepared, Ahmad Kamal had to fall back on teaching German in the schools and translating for state offices.

While a student, Kamal may have met the elderly Rifaa Rafi al-Tahtawi (1801–1873), who had shown an early interest in ancient Egypt, and would likely have encountered al-Tahtawi's school textbooks. After a religious education at al-Azhar, al-Tahtawi studied in Paris for five years (1826–31) while serving as chaplain to a student educational mission of Muhammad Ali's. Under the tutelage of Edmé-François Jomard, an engineer veteran of Napoleon's Egyptian expedition, and Sylvestre de Sacy, the dean of French Orientalism, al-Tahtawi read widely in French. Champollion person-ally reported to Muhammad Ali on al-Tahtawi's progress in his studies.[30]

Al-Tahtawi is mainly remembered for his book describing life in Paris, for heading a bureau that translated French works for use in Egyptian schools, and for editing official publications. In 1835 Muhammad Ali also put al-Tahtawi in charge of collecting antiquities in a precursor of the Egyptian Museum. In 1868, al-Tahtawi drew on both Arabic and French sources for a pioneering Arabic history of ancient Egypt up to the Islamic conquest.

Okasha El Daly's *Egyptology: the Missing Millennium: Ancient Egypt in Medieval Arabic Writings* showed that medieval Muslims were not necessarily hostile to ancient Egypt, as often assumed because of the blasphemous Quranic (and Biblical) pharaoh who persecuted Moses and the Israelites. Sufis and other Muslims admired the monuments and legendary wisdom of pharaonic Egypt.[31] In both Coptic and Muslim folklore, echoes of ancient Egyptian beliefs lived on.[32]

Shortly before Mariette died in January 1881, Prime Minister Riyad Pasha secured, probably at the urging of minister of education Ali Mubarak, Ahmad Kamal's appointment as secretary translator at the Bulaq Museum. More open-minded than Mariette, Maspero supported the small school of Egyptology Kamal directed at the museum from 1881 to 1886 and hired several of its graduates. Unfortunately the school was sacrificed in order to fund the hires.

Maspero's successor, Eugène Grébaut (1846–1915, in office 1886–92),[33] advertised an opening that ruled out Egyptians: it required knowledge of hieroglyphs, hieratic, demotic, Coptic, Greek, and Latin. Grébaut's student Georges Daressy won the post. Nevertheless, Grébaut did bring Kamal into the Antiquities Service cadre as assistant curator, if only as a maneuver to keep Britons out. When Kamal heard a rumor that H. Brugsch's younger brother Émile Brugsch was leaving his more senior assistant curatorship and that foreigners coveted the post, he petitioned Prime Minister Mustafa Fahmi:

The sole indigenous Egyptologist and former student of Brugsch Pasha ...I have been waiting during twenty-two years of government service to be promoted and rewarded for my sincere and beneficial services to the country.... Being assistant curator and in view of my seniority, merit, and Egyptian law, I respectfully take the liberty of confidentially asking you to help me obtain this post despite all foreign demands.[34]

Kamal appended an Arabic note to his petition in French, pointing out that although a French assistant curator (Daressy) had similar knowledge and education, he himself also knew Arabic and had twenty-one years of service to the Frenchman's six. Kamal's appeal on patriotic grounds to hire an Egyptian went unheeded. In any event, É. Brugsch stayed on until January 1914. The Institut égyptien elected Daressy to membership a decade before electing Kamal. Grébaut's successor, Jacques de Morgan (1857–1924, in office 1892–97),[35] reportedly wanted to dismiss Kamal and refused to speak to him for a whole year. Upon returning as Antiquities director in 1899, Maspero entrusted Kamal with archaeological and publication responsibilities but did not promote him. In 1913, Daressy was promoted over Kamal's head to secretary general of the Service, and in January 1914 James Quibell passed Kamal by to become museum curator. Both Europeans were over a dozen years Kamal's junior.

Kamal followed a two-track publication strategy, writing in French for Western colleagues and in Arabic for the Egyptian public. His French works included two volumes of the Egyptian Museum's *Catalogue générale* and items in the *Annales du service des antiquités de l'Égypte* (*ASAE*), often reporting on his salvage work at plundered sites. His Arabic publications—invisible to European colleagues—included a grammar of ancient Egyptian, which highlighted its affinities with Arabic, and Arabic translations of guidebooks to the Egyptian and Greco–Roman museums. He wrote for the monthly *al-Muqtataf* and in 1886 did a twelve-part series on archaeology for *al-Ahram*.[36] Sometime between 1906 and 1908, Kamal gave a series of lectures on ancient Egypt at the Higher Schools Club, and in 1908–1909 he taught a course at the private Egyptian University. Only Lord Cromer's retirement in 1907 had made the university itself possible; he had blocked it out of the not unrealistic fear that it might become a center of discontent with British rule. Maspero sat on the Egyptian University's board and would have had to recommend his subordinate Kamal to teach the course.

Kamal's lectures impressed Taha Hussein, the blind student from al-Azhar who would become a controversial professor, writer, and public intellectual after World War I. Hussein emphasized the breadth of the European-inspired university's curriculum compared to what he had experienced at al-Azhar and what a cousin had encountered at Dar al-Ulum, a teacher's college that combined traditional Arabic–Islamic and European-style subjects:

> I had not forgotten a day when I was arguing with my cousin, then a student at *Dar al-Ulum*, and he, the *Dar al-Ulumi*, had said to me, the Azharite: "What do you know about knowledge, anyway? You're just an ignoramus, versed in mere grammar and fiqh. You've never had a single lesson in the history of the Pharaohs. Have you ever heard the names of Rameses and Akhenaton?"[37]

But now, here I was in a university class-room listening to Professor Ahmad Kamal . . . talking about ancient Egyptian civilization. . . . Here he was making his point by reference to words from ancient Egyptian which he related to Arabic, Hebrew, and Syriac, as the evidence required.

No sooner had I accosted my cousin than I drew myself up in proud scorn of him and that *Dar al-Ulum* about which he had been preening himself. "Do you learn Semitic languages at *Dar al-Ulum*?" I querried. My cousin replied in the negative. Whereupon I proudly explained hieroglyphics to him and how the ancient Egyptians wrote, also alluding to Hebrew and Syriac.

Kamal's published university lectures only reached the Fifteenth Dynasty; for some reason, he did not continue the course the following year. An Italian and three successive Egyptians followed him in teaching History of the Ancient East. In the early 1920s, Taha Hussein taught the course as mainly Greek and Roman history, with special attention to Ptolemaic and Roman Egypt.[38]

Meanwhile, in 1910 Kamal set up an Egyptology section in the Higher Teachers College. A second cohort of students entered in 1912. Maspero did not hire Selim Hassan or any other graduates, however, and in 1913 or 1914 the program closed. Ahmad Kamal's son Hassan Kamal went on to Oxford intending to study Egyptology but came home with a British medical degree instead. Kamal's students Selim Hassan, Mahmoud Hamza, and Shafiq Ghurbal had to fall back on teaching secondary school. A decade passed before Selim Hassan and Hamza found a way back to Egyptology. Ghurbal went on to become a noted modern historian. With no program for training in place, it looked as though another generation of potential Egyptologists might be lost. Partly due to Kamal's efforts, however, pharaonism was stirring among a wider public.[39]

Pharaonism on the Eve of World War I

The proliferation of Western expeditions, swelling tourism, and Ahmad Kamal's proselytizing all quickened Egyptians' interest in the pharaohs. In the realm of politics, three events in 1907 spurred the creation of the Watani, Umma, and several minor political parties: the execution of peasants who clashed with British soldiers hunting pigeons at Dinshaway, Cromer's retirement after a quarter of a century, and an economic depression. Mustafa Kamil (1874–1908) of the Watani Party and Ahmad Lutfi al-Sayyid (1872–1963) of the Umma Party were both nationalist lawyers in their mid thirties who included pride in pharaonic Egypt in their political and cultural visions. Lutfi al-Sayyid in particular, as general secretary of Umma and editor of its daily *al-Jarida*, emphasized pharaonism as a vital component of Egyptian national identity.

The landed notables of the Umma Party included later national hero Saad Zaghlul, who had married into the Turco-Circassian aristocracy. (He married the daughter of Mustafa Fahmi, the prime minister whom Cromer valued for his docility.) Having prospered under British rule, Umma Party landlords did not push for immediate independence. Instead they advocated top-down leadership by notables and gradual educational, social, and constitutional reform.

Lutfi al-Sayyid's grandfather and father had both been *umda*s (mayors) of their Delta village in Daqhaliya province. He attended the village Quran school, made the critical transfer to the state primary school in Mansura, and continued on to the elite Khedival Secondary School in Cairo. At the Cairo School of Law in the 1890s, Lutfi al-Sayyid's contemporaries included three future prime ministers (Ismail Sidqi, Abd al-Khaliq Tharwat, and Muhammad Tawfiq Nasim). As editor of the Ummah Party's *al-Jarida* from 1907 to 1914, Lutfi al-Sayyid preached loyalty to a unique Egyptian nation rooted in the territory of the Nile valley and in the pharaonic past. The political/religious loyalty many Egyptians felt for the sultan-caliph in Istanbul left him unmoved. In 1910, Muslim–Coptic tension came to a head when a follower of the Watani Party assassinated Egypt's first Coptic prime minister, Boutros Ghali.

Lutfi al-Sayyid insisted that a common ancient Egyptian heritage bound Muslims and Copts together and that successive conquerors, including the Arabs, had long since become Egyptianized.[40] He pressed for more pharaonic emphasis in the schools: "For the truth of the matter is that we do not know as much about the stature of our fatherland and its glory as the tourists do!"[41]

> I don't ask that each Egyptian show proof of capacity of observation of a Champollion, encyclopedic knowledge of Egyptian antiquities of a Maspero or the archaeological competence of a [Ahmad] Kamal Bey. What we need are regular lectures and permanent teaching, at the Egyptian University or in other scientific establishments, of a sort that the sons of Egypt can have access to familiarity with their past, not in a scientific and precise manner, but in the manner in which the European tourists who visit our country know our history and that of our ancestors.[42]

Al-Sayyid even praised ancient Egyptian travelers and merchants for spying out foreign lands as a prelude to imperial expansion, just as nineteenth-century French and British travelers had done.[43]

The charismatic Mustafa Kamil died at thirty-three, a year after founding the Watani Party in 1907. He was the son of an ethnic Egyptian army officer at a time when Turco-Circassians still monopolized the upper ranks. After primary and secondary school, Cairo-born Kamil obtained a law degree from the University of Toulouse. Although Kamil's successor as party leader, Muhammad Farid (1868–1919), was of upper-class Turkish extraction, most of the party's activists came from the growing ranks of the *effendiya*—a middle stratum of officials, professionals, and students from state schools who characteristically wore European-style coat, trousers, and tie, along with a tarboosh (fez). They tended toward conservatism on religious and social issues, such as the emancipation of women, and looked to the Ottoman sultan-caliph for support even while demanding immediate and complete Egyptian independence from Britain.[44] Among Watanists, Ottoman and Pan-Islamic loyalties coexisted with territorial Egyptian nationalism, including strands of pharaonism. Mustafa Kamil hailed Egyptian Muslims and Copts as "one family" descended from the ancient Egyptians, denied that Egyptians were primarily of external Arab descent, and praised Egypt as the first cradle from which civilization had spread.[45] Choosing the quintessentially pharaonic Sphinx as their emblem, Watanists founded several Sphinx student societies in Europe. In March 1914, London's Sphinx Society hosted a tea party at the Savoy Hotel for Muhammad Farid, whom the British had exiled in 1912. In July 1914, on the eve of the Great War, the Sphinx Society of Geneva welcomed Farid in a ceremony replete with a sphinx flag and sphinx badges.[46]

Also in 1914, a bronze statue of Mustafa Kamil that Watanists had commissioned from French sculptor Leopold Savine reached Cairo (see fig. 13). The head of a sphinx supports the orating Kamil, and a *fellaha* (peasant woman) on a plaque on the statue's pedestal heeds his call. Joining the sphinx and *fellaha* as national symbols anticipated Mahmoud Mukhtar's famous postwar sculpture *The Revival of Egypt*. The erection of Kamil's statue in a public square in Kitchener's Cairo was out of the question, so it was relegated to the courtyard of the private Mustafa Kamil School until 1940. Then Prime Minister Ali Mahir, challenging the popularity of the late Zaghlul and the Wafd, erected it in the renamed square that still bears Kamil's name.[47]

A third political voice until his deposition in 1914, Khedive Abbas Hilmi II, also made use of pharaonist appeals. Inheriting the throne in 1892 at seventeen, Abbas clashed with Lord Cromer and encouraged Lutfi al-Sayyid and Mustafa Kamil in anti-British activities. Al-Sayyid soon went his own way, but Abbas and Kamil collaborated until falling out in 1904. In 1898, the cover of an educational magazine showed

13 Mustafa Kamil
draws strength from
the Sphinx. By Leopold
Savine, sculptor, 1910;
erected in Mustafa
Kamil Square, Cairo,
1940. *Photo: D. Reid.*

Abbas presiding over an Egyptian renaissance inspired by the Sphinx and Pyramids.[48] Abbas's court poet Ahmad Shawqi (1868–1932) was of Turkish, Circassian, Kurdish, Arab, and Greek descent, but lack of Egyptian blood was no barrier to his pharaonism—"a romance that riveted his attention most of his life."[49] Shawqi studied law in France. The Arabic poem he recited in 1894 at the International Conference of Orientalists in Geneva included a long section extolling the pharaohs. Around the turn of the century, Shawqi wrote three historical romances set in pharaonic times.[50]

Nor did being Syrian Christian immigrants inhibit Salim and Bishara Taqla from naming the daily they founded in 1875 *al-Ahram* (The Pyramids). Even if rarely on a conscious level, the name of this famous newspaper still provides Egyptians a daily reminder of their pharaonic heritage.

14 Pyramids, palms, and a Nile village on the cover of magazine *Fatat al-Nil* (Young Woman of the Nile), 1913. *Dust jacket of Beth Baron,* The Women's Awakening in Egypt.

Pharaonism also cropped up in a range of social and ideological contexts in the women's press. Labiba Hashim (c. 1880–1947), who founded *Fatat al-sharq* (Young Woman of the East) in 1906, was a Syrian Christian who promoted Muslim–Christian unity. In 1914, her magazine hailed Queen Ahmose Nefertari, founding mother of the New Kingdom, as the first Egyptian woman actually to rule despite there being a male heir.[51] Malaka Saad, the Coptic founder of *al-Jins al-latif* (The Gentle Sex), published an exemplary biography of Queen Hatshepsut in 1913 praising the intelligence and political skill she shared with her father, Thutmose I.[52] More noteworthy was Sarah al-Mihiya's choice of the Pyramids—along with the sun, crescent moon, palm trees, and a village by the Nile—for the cover of *Fatat al-Nil* (Young Woman of the Nile) in 1913 (see fig. 14). Al-Mihiya, a pious Muslim steeped in Islamic learning, deplored unveiling and public mingling of the sexes. Yet her devotion to Islam and conservative social views in no way conflicted with her embrace of Egyptian specificity with the Nile name of her magazine title and the Pyramids on its cover.[53]

Wartime Distortions: Egyptian and European Travail, American Opportunity

After the Ottoman Empire plunged into World War I on the German side on October 29, 1914, Britain severed Egypt's nominal tie to Istanbul and proclaimed a protectorate and martial law. Khedive Abbas II was deposed in favor of his pliable uncle Husayn Kamil, who was proclaimed sultan as a slap at his Ottoman former suzerain. Over one hundred thousand Egyptian laborers were conscripted for the war effort, draft animals were requisitioned, and restrictions severely reduced the area allowed for the lucrative cotton crop. Demand from British imperial forces in Egypt raised the price of wheat and other commodities, and inflation hit the public hard.

Maspero left Cairo for the last time on July 7, 1914. Two weeks later, he was elected perpetual secretary of the Academy of Inscriptions in Paris. On August 4 the Germans invaded Belgium and France. Maspero's son Jean, a Byzantine papyrologist, died fighting in the Argonne in 1915, and in June 1916 Gaston Maspero died suddenly as he was about to address the Academy.[54]

The war dealt a savage blow to the Europe-centered international scholarly networks so carefully built up over the nineteenth century. In October 1914, German professors and artists declared in the "Manifesto of the Ninety-Three" "to the civilized world" that war had been forced on Germany and its peace-loving Kaiser. Alleged German atrocities in Belgium were lies; Germans had fired only in self defense and

> our troops with aching hearts, were obliged to fire a part of the town [Louvain] as a punishment. . . . Have faith in us! Believe that we shall carry on this war to the end as a civilized nation, to whom the legacy of a Goethe, a Beethoven, and a Kant, is just as sacred as its own hearths and homes.[55]

Classical history professor Édouard Meyer threw his prestige behind the Manifesto and—unlike some—never recanted.[56]

Like Maspero, Adolf Erman, the dean of German Egyptology, lost a son in the war. Erman, Friedrich von Bissing, and Georg Steindorff sent condolences to the Masperos via their Swiss colleague Edouard Naville, but Louise Maspero could not bring herself to reply until after the war. Already in 1912, Pierre Lacau had singled Ludwig Borchardt out as "the enemy."[57] Even Naville and Reisner—both Berlin trained—and the Russian Golenischeff called the Germans "Boches"—a slur comparable to calling Germans "Huns"—when writing to French friends.[58]

In Cairo, the German Archaeological Institute was sequestered and Germany was stripped of the cultural enclave five German Orientalist successive directors had built up at the National Library since 1873.[59] The United States tended German interests in Cairo, with Reisner advising on archaeological matters, until entering the war itself in 1917; then Sweden took over.[60] IFAO director George Foucart asked the British to award to France Germany's Tell al-Amarna concession, the German House at Qurna, and the German and Austro–Hungarian concessions at Giza. Instead, the British demolished the German House at Thebes—a "center of illicit antiquities trade and otherwise undesireable."[61]

Five out of nine Frenchmen in the Antiquities Service were mobilized,[62] and IFAO was similarly decimated. Pierre Lacau, aged forty, followed

Maspero as director general of the Service on October 7, 1914, but his absence on the French front left fifty-year-old Georges Daressy to mind the store. Like Maspero and Erman, Daressy lost a son in the war.[63] Even as the British and French fought side by side in Flanders, the French feared the official British protectorate in Egypt would destroy Maspero's delicate archaeological entente.[64] In September 1915 Lacau conceded that—like military service—defending France's predominance in the Antiquities Service was also a patriotic duty, and came to Egypt. He returned to the army in 1916, however, and only being wounded and catching pleurisy in 1917 persuaded him to take up his Cairo post for good.

French fears for their archaeological position in Egypt were not imaginary. Hearing that Georges Legrain, director of works at Karnak, had died, Lord Carnarvon suggested that in the absence of a French successor, a Briton should occupy the post. In 1917, EEF president General Francis Grenfell urged taking the Antiquities Service away from the French. Egyptologists Alan Gardiner, Percy Newberry, and Eric Peet backed him up. Rev. Archibald Sayce, an Assyriologist interested in Egyptology, suggested allowing the French to keep the museum, conservation, and exhibiting but installing a British inspector general of archaeology in the Egyptian police who would direct inspectors, guards, excavations, and publications.[65]

World War I interrupted the excavations of both Petrie and the EEF after some thirty years in the field that nearly coincided with the British occupation itself. The EEF and Petrie's British School of Archaeology in Egypt (BSAE), launched in 1905, competed for much the same pool of British and American supporters. Learning that the EEF was about to launch its *Journal of Egyptian Archaeology*, Petrie beat it into print by one month in December 1913 with his magazine, *Ancient Egypt*.[66] In 1915, *Ancient Egypt* mourned the loss at Gallipoli of former BSAE excavator James Alfred Dixon[67] and solicited donations for the Officers' Families Fund. Hilda Petrie's argument for continuing wartime meetings of her husband's Egyptian Research Students' Association suggests a mostly female membership: "Knitting can be pursued by all the members except the lecturer, so the meetings need not mean waste of time."[68] In 1917, Petrie finally suspended *Ancient Egypt*: "To continue any journal which does not help the war is treachery to our own cause. Paper, printing, and postal work are all needed to be reduced."[69] That same year, however, Howard Carter felt sufficiently free from wartime duties to resume digging for Lord Carnarvon in the Valley of the Kings.

Italian excavations in Egypt came to a halt with the war. From an average of about twenty-two Western expeditions a year from half a dozen countries in the decade leading up to the war,[70] the number plunged nearly to zero. The Metropolitan's Herbert Winlock stayed at his desk in New York until joining the Coastal Artillery. Arthur Mace's British army service interrupted the MMA's work at Lisht. In the winter of 1915, Reisner's Harvard–Boston team was the only one working in Egypt and the Sudan, compared to fourteen to sixteen previously. Hundreds of villagers from Quft—where Petrie had begun recruiting laborers in the 1890s—were out of work; only Reisner's expedition offered respite for a few families.[71] Early in 1917, *Ancient Egypt* reported:

> There is, naturally, no British party out excavating, nor, indeed, is there from any European country; the Antiquities Department itself, like all other Government Departments, is denuded of all available men.
>
> Meanwhile, the United States continue to excavate.[72]

Not entering the war until 1917 and spared fighting on their own soil, only Americans were available to take up a little of the slack. Reisner's Harvard–Boston MFA expedition dug at Giza into 1916 and in Nubia throughout the war. Writing from Harvard Camp, Giza, in 1919, Reisner noted that he had not been home since 1912 and pleaded not to be recalled.[73] For the Metropolitan, Ambrose Lansing's work on Amenhotep III's palace complex at Malqata near Medinat Habu kept on the payroll some Egyptians who would be needed for postwar work. Lansing resumed the Met's work at Lisht from 1916 to 1918.[74] With Palestine in enemy Ottoman hands, Clarence Fisher moved the University of Pennsylvania's University Museum expedition back to Egypt in 1915, digging at Dendera and Memphis until 1919. Petrie lashed out at Lacau for turning the concession at Memphis over to Fisher but later conceded that Fisher had assumed that Petrie had relinquished the site.[75]

With Ahmad Kamal retired and no process in place for training successors, Egyptians in archaeology had no way to benefit from the wartime travails of their British and French colonial masters. In 1916, Kamal read a paper at the Institut égyptien that drew a sharp rebuke from his former colleague Daressy. At the peak of his career, Daressy was directing the Service in Lacau's absence and writing much of the *Annales du service des antiquités de l'Égypte* himself. Kamal derived the Greek word for Egypt—*Aiguptos*—from the name of the Upper Egyptian town of Coptos, not from the name of Ptah's shrine in Memphis, "Ha Ka Ptah," as proposed by H. Brugsch. Kamal's patriotism inclined him to seek an Egyptian root for *Misr*, the Arabic name for Egypt, rather than to see it as originated by Semitic neighbors.[76] Daressy berated Kamal for "assertions which cannot be accepted by Egyptologists. . . . The author sins gravely from a philological and historical point of view," giving hieroglyphic signs different Arabic letter equivalents and switching their order as needed.[77] He accused Kamal of ignoring historical context and exaggerating the Semitic influence on Egyptian. Kamal retorted that Egyptian dialects had differed on the phonetic values of some signs and that he had followed philological rules on metathesis. He defended his derivation of many Arabic words from Egyptian and even declared: "Egyptian is the mother language of Arabic and therefore of Hebrew."[78]

Daressy had the stronger case, but his attempt almost to read his retired colleague out of the profession followed years of personal friction in the colonial context of the Cairo Museum. Kamal had published over thirty items (many of them short notices) in the *ASAE*, which Daressy now edited. After this quarrel, the *ASAE* carried nothing further by Kamal. Kamal's nationalism did color his scholarship, but few Western Egyptologists were without sin in this regard.

Petrie was contemptuous of Ahmad Kamal's excavation reports in *ASAE*:

> There is no trace of the archaeological necessity of recording groups, there is nothing said but what could be seen by looking at the plunder in a museum. At Deir Rifeh work was carried on similarly, devoid of all archaeological value. . . . Happily it had been excavated, with a record and publication of the groups of objects, by the British School [Petrie's organization] (*Gizeh and Rifeh*), and so there was less left for the senseless plundering carried on under the Museum supervision.[79]

Petrie was equally caustic on Daressy's work, as reported in the *ASAE*:

> This stele, though brought to Cairo, was yet so fissured that it has fallen to pieces and is lost. It does not seem to be known that no matter how fragmentary a stone may be, or how rotten wood has become, flooding with melted paraffin wax will always consolidate it enough for preservation.[80]

In 1917, High Commissioner Wingate decided that Egypt was sufficiently under control to plan for a state university, which Cromer had always feared. Lacau chaired the archaeological committee of the resulting University Commission. IFAO director George Foucart, Islamic archaeologist Ali Bahgat, Ahmad Kamal, and another Egyptian also sat on the committee. Archaeology not being a priority of Wingate's, there was no British member. The committee proposed chairs of Egyptology and Islamic archaeology, with ethnography (Foucart's enthusiasm) and Coptic archaeology as future possibilities. Instruction would be in English and French, supplemented—despite the war—by German. Arabic would be used only for lectures to the public.[81] In any event, the 1919 revolution intervened, and the university commission's report was published and shelved.

Pharaonism from the 1919 Revolution to the Discovery of Tutankhamun's Tomb

> Pardon us oh Wingate! But our country has had enough!
> You took our camels, donkeys, barley, and wheat aplenty,
> Now leave us alone! . . .
> Laborers and soldiers were forced to travel, leaving their land
> They headed to Mount Lebanon and to the battlefields and the trenches! . . .
> We are the sons of the Pharaohs, which no one can dispute.
> When necessary we can fight with clubs, sticks and even head butts.
> Long live Egypt! Long live Egypt! Best of all nations; mother of the brave;
> And this has been for all times.[82]

According to British intelligence, "little boys in the street and the ladies in the harem" chanted these verses in the national rising against the British in March 1919. Twenty years later, an Egyptian writer emphasized the pharaonic, not Arab or Muslim, inspiration of 1919:

> When Egypt rose up, songs and ballads began to speak of the "children of the Pharaohs" or of "Egypt, Mother of the Pyramids." . . . Then the names of Ramses and Thutmose were on every tongue. But had Egyptians at that time asserted that they were "the children of the Arabs," or substituted for Ramses and Thutmose the names of Khalid ibn al Walid or 'Amr ibn al-'As, or sung of the relics and ruins of Arabia, then there would have been no revolution to achieve independence.[83]

Popular pride in ancient Egypt as an inspiration for national revival and independence had indeed taken firm root before the discovery of Tutankhamun's tomb in November 1922.

The 1919 revolution gave birth to the Wafd Party, which originated in the delegation *(wafd)* of Saad Zaghlul and two colleagues to High Commissioner Wingate in November 1918. They sought permission to travel to Europe to make the case for independence. Woodrow Wilson's call for self-determination had aroused their hopes. Zaghlul, Lutfi al-Sayyid, and many other early Wafdists came from the prewar Umma Party. The British attempt to crush the Wafd by deporting Zaghlul and three comrades to Malta touched off the countrywide uprising that Egyptians call the 1919 revolution.[84] It cut across generational, gender, confessional, and class lines. Zaghlul was sixty; future novelist Naguib Mahfouz, who saw the British shoot down demonstrators near the Mosque of Sayyidna Husayn, was seven.[85] Veiled upperclass women joined the demonstrations, and Muslim and Coptic religious leaders stressed interfaith unity. A poster shows Saad Zaghlul about to free Egypt (a woman in imagined pharaonic garb) from shackles held by the British lion. The caption translates: "Have patience, Egypt, for patience is the key to final release from suffering." (see fig. 15)

The British replaced Wingate with General Allenby, the conqueror of Palestine and Syria, but the military strongman quickly pivoted to diplomacy. Zaghlul and his comrades were allowed to proceed to Paris,

15 Saad Zaghlul calls for patience while he frees Egypt, a 'pharaonically' dressed woman, from the British lion. Poster, ca.1919–1920. *Cover of Byron Canon,* Politics of Law and the Courts in Nineteenth-Century Egypt *(Salt Lake City: University of Utah Press, 1988).*

Table A. Iconic Pharaonist Works and Pharaonists of the Generation of 1919

Saad Zaghlul's Tomb	Mustafa Fahmi (1886–1972)	Architect
	Salama Musa (1887–1958)	Literary journalist
Nahdat Misr (The Revival of Egypt)	Muhammad Nagi (1888–1956)	Painter
	Muh. Husayn Haykal (1888–1956)	Literary journalist; politician
Nahdat Misr (The Revival of Egypt)	Mahmoud Mukhtar (1891–1934)	Sculptor
Awdat al-Ruh (Return of the Spirit)	Tawfiq al-Hakim (1898–1987)	Writer

but to their dismay, the United States recognized Britain's Egyptian protectorate just as they arrived. Most Egyptians boycotted Lord Milner's later fact-finding mission to Egypt, and in 1921, independence negotiations with Zaghlul and Prime Minister Adli Yakan broke down.

The cultural and political leaders who reached maturity around this critical time became known as "the generation of 1919"; cultural leaders among them were in their early thirties and are sometimes called "the generation of 1889," roughly the median year of their births.[86] Table A lists several of this generation's iconic pharaonist works and their creators.

Egyptian territorial nationalism of the 1920s usually included a pharaonist component. Western fascination with ancient Egypt (in its popular form, "Egyptomania") stimulated pharaonism among Egyptians, but this was not simply a cultural import. Pharaonism drew, for example, on anti-Bedouin prejudices of the settled fellahin and townspeople. In colloquial Egyptian Arabic, "Arab" refers to the nomadic Bedouin of presumed Arabian origin.

Mahmoud Mukhtar's sculpture *Nahdat Misr* (The Revival of Egypt) and Muhammad Nagi's mural-scale painting of the same name were already on their way to becoming national monuments before the discovery of Tutankhamun's tomb (see figs. 16 and 17).

Inspired by the 1919 rising, both works blended ancient and modern symbols in affirmation of an awakened national spirit believed to have

16 *Nahdat Misr* (The Revival of Egypt or The Procession of Isis), by Muhammad Nagi; placed in the parliament building, Cairo, 1924. *Hamed Said, ed.,* Contemporary Art in Egypt *(Cairo: Ministry of Culture and National Guidance in cooperation with the Publishing House "Jugoslavija," 1964). Printed in Zagreb., Black and white illustration number 120.*

endured since the pharaohs. In Nagi's painting, the goddess Isis rides through the Nile countryside with peasant men, women, and children in train. In Mukhtar's sculpture, a sphinx stretches to stand up as a peasant woman lifts her veil. Both *Revival*s romanticized the fellahin and chose a woman to represent Egypt. Both artists had studied in capitals of European art—Nagi in Florence and Mukhtar in Paris—and both masterpieces won recognition in Paris before being seized upon back home as embodiments of the revolutionary spirit of 1919 and enshrined as national monuments.[87]

Muhammad Nagi (1888–1956) and Mahmoud Mukhtar (1891–1934) were born three years apart into families that respectively represented two main strata of the landed elite—the Turco-Circassian aristocracy and indigenous village *umdas*. Nagi grew up in Alexandria, Mukhtar in Cairo.

Nagi's Turkish grandfather had been governor of the Sudan and the Red Sea provinces, and the artist's father had directed customs in Alexandria. Nagi cherished bucolic memories of peasant life on the family's Abu Hummus estate in the Delta near Mansura. The Swiss School in Alexandria immersed Nagi in urban Egyptian and European culture. Italian Futurist and symbolist poet Giuseppe Ungaretti, later a Mussolini supporter, was a classmate. After earning a law degree at the University of Lyon (1910), Nagi pursued his own muse for four years at Florence's Academy of Fine Arts.

Mahmoud Mukhtar was an *umda*'s son from a Delta village near al-Mahalla al-Kubra. His mother, resented by an older co-wife, took him home to her village before moving to Cairo in 1902. Mukhtar entered the School of Fine Arts when Prince Yusuf Kamal opened it in 1908. Guillaume Laplagne, the director and teacher of sculpture, became his first mentor. In 1911, Prince Kamal sent Mukhtar on to the École des Beaux Arts in Paris, where he lived for most of the next nine years. Like al-Tahtawi before him, Mukhtar awakened to ancient Egypt while studying in Europe. His Beaux-Arts comrades hailed him as "Ramses II" and paraded him naked through the streets while offering him sacrifices of food and drink. In 1912, Mukhtar's *Aida* statue (also on a pharaonic theme) became the first sculpture by an Arab to be internationally exhibited.[88]

Nagi experienced pharaonic art on site and firsthand by copying tomb paintings at Thebes while on a visit home to Egypt in 1911. He also imbibed French impressionism at its source, moving to Giverny for

17 *Nahdat Misr* (The Revival of Egypt), by Mahmoud Mukhtar; unveiled in 1928 before the Cairo Railway Station, and moved in 1954 to Giza to stand at the square leading to Cairo University. *Photo: D. Reid.*

a time to associate with Claude Monet. The 1919 revolution inspired him to begin painting *Revival of Egypt* in his Cairo studio. After it won a prize in Paris in 1922, it was chosen to decorate the Cairo parliament building, inaugurated in March 1924 along with the first parliament under the 1923 constitution.

A white marble version of Mukhtar's *Revival of Egypt* won a gold medal at the Salon des Artistes in the Grand Palais, Paris, in 1920. Future president of the Egyptian Senate Wisa Wasif viewed it there. Amin al-Rafii, editor of the Wafdist *al-Akhbar*, launched a campaign for a monumental version for Cairo and raised £E6,500 in six months.[89] Returning home in 1920 for the first time in six years, Mukhtar received a hero's welcome. He rejected bronze in favor of Aswan pink granite—which was appropriately pharaonic—for the monumental version. In 1921, Adli Yakan's cabinet decided to place it in Railroad Station Square. In the spring of 1922—with Tutankhamun still five months away—on-site work officially began. Political squabbles hampered Mukhtar at every turn, and not until 1928 did King Fuad finally unveil the monument.

Postwar pharaonism was by no means confined to the generation of 1919. Ahmad Shawqi (1868–1932), who turned fifty in 1919, returned from Spanish exile still writing on Arabic–Islamic and pharaonic themes alike. Ninety-four of 153 verses of a poem of his on the Nile published in 1921 were pharaonic themed. Shawqi had once visited the Pyramids every week; now he could see them from the balcony of his home.[90] That same year, Shawqi's younger critics Abbas Mahmud al-Aqqad and Ibrahim Abd al-Qadir al-Mazini published a two-volume collection of modernist poems, *al-Diwan*. These writers of the generation of 1919 rejected Shawqi's neoclassical formality but like him included pharaonist poems in their repertoire.[91]

In tune with Benedict Anderson's theory of print capitalism fostering "imagined communities" of modern nations, nonofficial Arabic periodicals first began publication in the 1860s under Khedive Ismail. As Ziad Fahmy noted, however:

> most Egyptians did not read . . . the intellectual writings of Taha Husayn, Lutfi al-Sayyid, or Salama Musa, or even the nationalistic novels of Muhammad Husayn Haykal, Naguib Mahfuz, and Tawfiq al-Hakim.[92]

Adult literacy was only 4.8 percent in the 1897 census (9.1 percent for males and 0.7 percent for females); even more than doubling that by 1927 to 11.8 percent (19.6 percent males, 3.9 percent females)[93] left the vast majority illiterate. Reading aloud in coffee houses and at home greatly enlarged the audience. Colloquial Arabic in the satirical press, cartoons, vaudeville, popular songs, and—between the wars—records, films, and radio (Fahmy's "media capitalism") brought many more in on "imagining the nation."

Nagi's and Mukhtar's representations of Egypt as a woman coincided with women's demonstrations in 1919 and a growing female presence in literature, the press, and on stage. In 1923, upperclass women led by Hoda Shaarawi began unveiling and founded the Egyptian Feminist Union (EFU). [94] Not surprisingly, Egyptian women often included a pharaonist component in their self-expression.

On a popular level, singer-actress Munira al-Mahdiya's (1884–1965) December 1919 melodrama *In Just a Couple of Days* depicted the national struggle. Sayyid Darwish (1892–1923) supplied the music. She turned thirty-five in 1919, and he twenty-seven. From a poor peasant family near Zaqaziq, al-Mahdiya lost her father early and dropped out of a French convent primary school to sing for a living. Darwish grew up poor and fatherless in Alexandria, working as a Quran reciter and manual laborer. He recited poetry and played the oud, worked for a theatrical troupe, and became a composer. [95] Al-Mahdiya played herself, representing Egypt, in *In Just a Couple of Days*. A public prosecutor (representing Saad Zaghlul) pursued the villain Marco, an agent of British and foreign interests. She sang before the Great Pyramid:

> Sleep oh Khufu, and rest in safety
> We confronted (the enemy) and we saw suffering and pain though no more
> Who can ever forget this experience?
> Oh glorious one, builder of the pyramid
> Christians and Muslims, all volunteer to be in your service
> Their unity is an enduring one, and tomorrow we will be the most civilized Nation. [96]

Yaqub Sannu had pioneered pharaonic cartoons in his 1870s journal *Abu Naddara al-Zarqa*, showing Egypt as a pharaonic queen threatened by European imperialism and as a sphinx being flogged by Britain. In cartoons, which used colloquial Arabic and became more popular after 1919, Egypt is often a 'pharaonic' woman, with a cobra headdress, bare or sandaled feet, and bracelets. [97] A 1919 cartoon on boycotting the Milner Mission has "Syria" dancing with a French officer and "Fiume" with an Italian, but pharaonic "Egypt" spurns her British suitor. [98] In a 1920 cartoon, a pharaonic woman invites Prime Minister Clemenceau—a Roman with a bloody sword and a shield labeled "peace conference"—to take note of a pharaonic temple labeled "Egypt." [99] In a 1921 cartoon, a pharaonic female "Egypt" reaches for the fruit of "complete independence," which the Wafd—a man in a tarboosh—is plucking for her from "the tree of freedom."[100]

In the early decades of the press, thick face veils, which seemed at odds with modernity and awakening, hampered cartoonists' use of upperclass women to personify Egypt. Once face veils were lightened, and after 1923 discarded, upperclass women often personified the nation.[101] In a 1920 cartoon, "Mother Egypt" sits on a sphinx, nursing businessman Talaat Harb's new baby, Bank Misr (see fig. 18). She wears the light, white face veil (yashmak) of the upper classes and fashionable high heels. The caption reads: "the Egyptian Nation, the beloved, splendid Egyptian Nation sitting on its oldest and most famous manifestation—the Sphinx." Older brothers—foreign banks—look on with "jealousy and rage, but they cheer each other on by saying: 'Will the baby live? Will the baby live?' We say: 'Yes the baby will live if he continues to nurse from the breast of his mother.'"[102]

Proliferating advertisements in the press also exploited pharaonic themes. A 1922 ad features a fair-skinned 'Cleopatra-type' gazing dreamily as two dark men stir a tureen. The caption says:

In the days of the ancient Egyptians, olive oil and palm olive oil were among the most important and greatest necessities and beauty aids. Palm-olive soap is manufactured today from olive oil and palm oil.[103]

18 "Mother Egypt," sitting on a sphinx, nurses Bank Misr (Bank of Egypt), 1920. Older brothers—the foreign banks—look on with "jealousy and rage, but they cheer each other on by saying 'Will the baby live? Will the baby live?' We say: 'Yes, the baby will live if he continues to nurse from the breast of his mother.'" Al-Lataif al-Musawwara, *Aug. 2, 1920, as shown in Pollard, Nurturing the Nation, 191.*

But Europeanized elites had no monopoly on pharaonism. Labiba Ahmad's Islamic-oriented *al-Nahda al-nisaiya* (Women's Revival) featured Mukhtar's iconic *Revival of Egypt* on its cover from 1921. Although the editor herself wore a face veil until the mid-1920s, she did not hesitate to choose Mukhtar's sphinx and peasant woman lifting her veil to symbolize the magazine.[104]

On October 4, 1922—exactly one month before Howard Carter's crew hit on the entrance to the tomb of Tutankhamun—the leading daily *al-Ahram* featured a front-page article by awestruck budding Egyptologist Selim Hassan on the Egyptian collection in the Louvre.[105] This was the fourth in a series of articles on Egyptian collections Hassan had visited that summer, the other museums being in Vienna, Berlin, and Hildesheim (Germany). Hassan both questioned the means through which these rich collections had been acquired and challenged his countrymen: "How can foreigners be more interested in the heritage of our country and in promoting the study of the language of our ancestors than we are?"[106]

Independence and pharaonism were in the air. It was time for Tutankhamun.

2

Nationalizing Tutankhamun

In 1922, archaeology and politics in Egypt converged more closely than ever before or since. In February Britain declared Egypt independent (albeit with severe restrictions), and in November Howard Carter, working for Lord Carnarvon, uncovered Tutankhamun's tomb. Weary Britons, beset by postwar economic troubles, political instability, and fears of imperial decline, welcomed the discovery as a wonderful relief. Hurrying home after opening the tomb, Carnarvon reported directly to King George V and Queen Mary at Buckingham Palace. To Egyptians, Tutankhamun's treasures offered—at a critical moment—a ringing affirmation of past glory and a spur to modern revival. Perhaps to their surprise, their newly declared independence proved to have teeth enough to enable Egypt, after sharp dispute, to keep the entire find as the glory of the Cairo Museum.

Fifty years later in 1972, both Egypt and its former colonial master renewed their claims on the legacy of Tutankhamun with postage stamps celebrating the fiftieth anniversary of the discovery (see fig. 19).[1]

Yet the dazzling Tutankhamun exhibition the British Museum put on with relics on loan from Cairo reflected a high degree of international collaboration. "Britain's moment in the Middle East," as Elizabeth Monroe called the 1914 to 1971 period,[2] came close to bracketing the two peaks of the British–Egyptian encounter over Tutankhamun. The first peak, in the early 1920s, featured clashes over ownership of the find, management of publicity, visiting arrangements, and supervision of the archaeological work (see table B). The second peak, the London exhibition of 1972, sealed the passing of Britain's empire in the Middle East; British troops had finally relinquished their Persian Gulf bases only the year before. Neither Britons nor Egyptians had forgotten their quarrel over Tutankhamun, but the exhibition held out the hope of better relations in the emerging postcolonial age.

19 Tutankhamun fifty years on: A British stamp (top) and Egyptian stamps, 1972, on the occasion of the British Museum exhibition and the fiftieth anniversary of the discovery.

This chapter charts the rhythm of the first stage of the long cycle of British and Egyptian interest in Tutankhamun, which had high points in the 1920s and again in the early 1970s.[3] The two peaks and intervening four-decade trough were closely bound up with the overarching issue of imperial domination and Egyptian independence. From an imperial perspective, the find in 1922 was already a moment too late. Had the discovery come ten years earlier—as in the case of the bust of Nefertiti still in Berlin—Tutankhamun's treasures might be scattered among the British Museum, Carnarvon's castle Highclere, the Metropolitan Museum of Art, and the Cairo's Egyptian Museum.

Tutankhamun provided inspiration for both the takeoff of Egyptian professional Egyptology and for a wave of pharaonism—Egyptian popular pride in their pharaonic heritage. By the early 1930s, however, with hopes for full independence thwarted and a Frenchman still directing the Antiquities Service, Tutankhamun was fading into the background of both British and Egyptian consciousness. Only decolonization in the 1950s—full political independence and control of its own Antiquities Service—made it possible for Egypt to consider lending abroad the stunning exhibits which so revived popular and scholarly interest in the pharaoh. Table B tallies keyword listings for Tutankhamun in *The Times*, suggesting clearly the long-term rhythm of remembering and forgetting the pharaoh over fifty years.

Table B. Remembering and Forgetting Tutankhamun: Keyword listings for Tutankhamen (and variant spellings) in The Times by month.

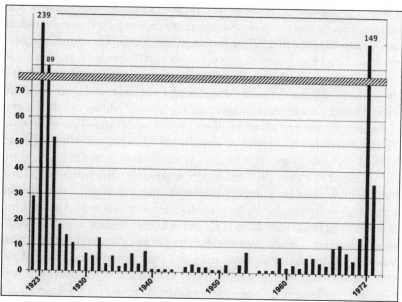

Business and advertising listings excluded. *The Times Digital Archive.*

From 'Independence' to the Return of the Wafd, 1922–1936

Between 1922 and 1936, the Tutankhamun story unfolded alongside the struggle for independence in an evolving Egyptian parliamentary monarchy in which the British were never far in the background. In the wake of the 1919 uprising, High Commissioner Allenby quickly recognized that the protectorate could no longer be sustained. An investigatory commission led by Lord Milner and ensuing talks with Saad Zaghlul and Prime Minister Adli Yakan failed to find middle ground between demands for full independence and Britain's defense of its imperial interests. Allenby persuaded the Foreign Office to break the impasse by unilaterally declaring Egypt independent on February 28, 1922. France seized the moment to become the first country to recognize Egyptian independence.[4] Britain reserved freedom of action, however, in imperial communications, defense of Egypt against foreign attack or interference, the protection of foreign and minority interests, and Sudanese affairs. Although a commission was appointed to draft a constitution, tellingly, 'independent' Egypt was not independent enough to join the League of Nations. Egypt was allowed to reconstitute its Ministry of Foreign Affairs, which the British had disbanded in 1914, but diplomatic missions to and from Cairo ranked only as legations, not embassies, with only ministers plenipotentiary, not ambassadors, at their heads. Britain's representative in Cairo remained a high commissioner, as under the protectorate.[5] An arrangement was negotiated whereby the many European officials in Egyptian government service had to retire by 1927 or forfeit an indemnity. Thereafter, the government hired Europeans only on periodically renewable contracts.

In addition to the British, three forces competed in high politics through the semicolonial era: the palace under King Fuad and then Faruq; the Wafd Party of Saad Zaghlul and his successor, Mustafa al-Nahhas; and the Liberal Constitutionalists and other small elitist parties. Mustafa Kamil's Watani Party survived but had dwindled to a shadow of its prewar self. King Fuad worked tirelessly to establish himself as an absolute monarch.[6] The Wafd had emerged from the 1919 revolution as the only party with a mass base, but notables irked by Zaghlul's leadership seceded in 1922 to form the Liberal Constitutionalist Party, and other schisms followed. Ahmad Lutfi al-Sayyid and most other Liberal Constitutionalist leaders were large landowners and intellectuals from the defunct Umma Party and lacked a mass following. With the Wafd boycotting the commission that produced the 1923 constitution, royalists and Liberal Constitutionalists provided for a bicameral parliament and reserved considerable power for the king.

The Wafd's resounding victory in the January 1924 election transformed it into a staunch defender of the constitution it had originally opposed. Prime Minister Zaghlul brought a judicious mix of political veterans and new Wafdist politicians into his cabinet. Negotiations for a treaty with Ramsay MacDonald's Labour cabinet broke down over the future of the Sudan. The November 1924 assassination in Cairo of Sir Lee Stack, sirdar of the Egyptian army and governor general of the Sudan, led Allenby to demand an indemnity of £E500,000 and evacuation of all Egyptian troops from the Sudan. Zaghlul resigned, but London recalled Allenby for perceived weakness. From 1916 to 1946, six British proconsuls in Egypt in a row were called home under a cloud. The first four, including Allenby, never held diplomatic posts again.[7]

It was King Fuad's turn. He detested Zaghlul as a dangerous rival and worked tirelessly to undercut the Wafd and the 1923 constitution. Prime Minister Ahmad Ziwar's palace governments, however, could not prevent the Wafd from winning parliamentary elections in 1925 and 1926. In 1926–27, with Britain vetoing Zaghlul's return as prime minister, Liberal Constitutionalists Adli Yakan and then Abd al-Khaliq Tharwat headed coalition cabinets with the Wafd. In 1928 Oxford-educated Muhammad Mahmud, betraying both principles in the name of his Liberal

Constitutionalist Party, formed a pro-palace cabinet and suspended the constitution. Mustafa al-Nahhas, who headed the Wafd after Zaghlul's death in 1927, led a Wafdist cabinet for a few months in 1930. With the Depression deepening, however, another palace coup spearheaded by Ismail Sidqi replaced the 1923 constitution with an authoritarian one. By 1934, this last bid of Fuad's for palace rule was faltering in the face of rising protests. In the spring of 1936, the Wafd swept back into power under the restored 1923 constitution as the king lay dying.

On the economic front, British investment in Egypt peaked just before World War I, and trade between the two countries just after it. In 1919, 46 percent of Egypt's imports came from Great Britain and 53 percent of Egyptian exports (mainly cotton) went to it. Thereafter, Egypt's fitful path toward full independence loosely paralleled the erosion of its economic ties to Britain. Immediately after World War I, Britain supplied 70 percent of Egypt's imported textiles, but by 1922 cheaper Japanese, Italian, and Indian imports had slashed this to 21 percent. By 1938, British investment in Egypt had fallen to less than a fourth of the pre-1914 figure. In 1939, Egypt received 28 percent of its imports from Britain and sent 36 percent of its exports to it.[8]

Under Cromer, growth in the overwhelmingly agricultural economy, with the Aswan Dam as the central symbol, had been impressive. This slowed by 1914, however, and population increase began to outstrip growth in agricultural production. The influx of imperial troops during World War I drove up cotton prices, but after the war, plunges in world cotton prices periodically hurt big landowners and peasants alike. Short of a radical redistribution of wealth, industrialization seemed a way out. Talaat Harb pitched Bank Misr in 1920 as a patriotic alternative to foreign banks and built up a range of Misr Group industries. The Federation of Egyptian Industries, formed in 1922, lobbied for tariffs on imported manufactures and against labor unions. Profits, however, trumped patriotic purity. In 1937, Misr Group partnered with a British firm to form Egypt's largest textile factory, Misr Fine Spinning and Weaving and Beida Dyers, at al-Mahalla al-Kubra. Muhammad Ahmad Abboud, a Glasgow-educated engineer with a Scottish wife who built up a rival business group, never had any compunctions about collaboration with European-owned businesses.

Colonial Absence: Where Were the Egyptian Egyptologists?

Egyptian Egyptology, like large-scale Egyptian-owned industry, scarcely existed at the end of World War I but began to make headway in the wake of the 1919 revolution and the partial independence of 1922. Exactly a century after Champollion's decipherment, the dual sensations of greater independence and the discovery of Tutankhamun's tomb accelerated the growth of both specialist Egyptian Egyptology and of pharaonism among the Egyptian public.

Like Petrie, Howard Carter (1874–1939) had little formal education. Hired at age seventeen as an EEF artist copyist, he joined the Antiquities Service when Maspero opened it to Britons. He resigned several years later after a fracas with French tourists. Maspero nevertheless recommended him as a field archaeologist to hobbyist Lord Carnarvon, which set the pair on the path that would lead to Tutankhamun. George Herbert (1866–1923), the fifth Earl of Carnarvon, was born at Highclere Castle and studied at Eton and Trinity College, Cambridge. After an automobile accident damaged his health, he began wintering in Egypt. Three years after he began digging at Thebes in 1906, he hired Howard Carter to conduct his excavations. By 1917, Carter's war work had let up sufficiently for him to start digging in the Valley of the Kings, where Lord Carnarvon had obtained his concession after Theodore Davis stopped excavating there in 1912. Carnarvon was on the verge of giving up on the Valley when on November 4, 1922, Carter's crew hit on the first step of the tomb of Tutankhamun. The Metropolitan Museum of Art's expedition, working over the mountain ridge at Deir al-Bahari, quickly seconded specialists to assist in recording and clearing, conserving the tomb's objects, and shipping them to the Cairo Museum.

Carter paid warm tribute to his Egyptian headmen and crew,[9] who loyally carried out the subaltern tasks according to the colonial and class order of the day. Otherwise, Egyptians flicker in the background of standard accounts of the discovery as dignitaries and antiquities officials or stand in the way as obstructive nationalists. Carter cannot be personally faulted for having no Egyptian Egyptologists on his staff. Ahmad Kamal, the only one with a modicum of Western recognition, was seventy-one, had been retired for eight years, and was not primarily a field archaeologist. Few Western archaeologists of the day could imagine Egyptians as fellow 'scientists' or professionals.

In 1919, the Milner Mission reported that the Antiquities Service had seven Europeans in top posts, nine Egyptian inspectors, and a number of Egyptian guards. A few months later, the Milner report was amended to say that French direction of the Service must continue.[10] Only nine months before the February 1922 declaration of independence started the clock ticking on the retirement of hundreds of Europeans from state service, Adli Yakan's cabinet docilely created two new curatorships at the Egyptian Museum explicitly for Europeans—one French and one

British. The justification was that the posts required "special scientific training," "which the Egyptian inspectors now in the Service do not possess."[11] Pierre Lacau's assistant Georges Daressy was blunt: "not a single one [Egyptian] [was] capable of conducting a large-scale excavation in a scientific manner." Daressy did add as an afterthought: "meanwhile the Antiquities Service is studying a project for preparing young Egyptians for scientific posts of the Museum."[12]

The experience of Dr. Saleh Bey Hamdi, the exception to the absence of Egyptian professional specialists on Carter's team, only confirmed colonial exclusion. Hamdi was director of Alexandria sanitary services and former head of the Cairo School of Medicine. He was invited to join Dr. Douglas Derry, professor of anatomy at the Cairo School of Medicine, in dissecting the king's mummy. In *The Tomb of Tut.Ankh.Amen*, Carter thanked both Derry and Hamdi. However, neither the title page of the volume nor the appended report on the anatomical work included Hamdi's name alongside Derry's. Derry buried his sole mention of his collaborator on the sixth page of the report. Harry Burton's photograph of the dissection poses Derry and Carter as the active investigators (see figure 20). With director general Lacau at his side, Carter peers intently through a magnifying glass as Derry makes the first incision. Although Hamdi is in the foreground, he seems a mere bystander, caught awkwardly looking at the camera rather than the task at hand. [13]

Colonial hierarchies continued to haunt Ahmad Kamal in retirement. Two months before the discovery of Tutankhamun's tomb, a conference in Champollion's native Grenoble celebrated the centennial of his decipherment. Twenty-five Frenchmen gave papers, including Pierre Lacau, Kamal's old rival Daressy, and twenty-two-year-old Étienne Drioton, future director general of Egyptian Antiquities. Two speakers each from Belgium, Italy, Switzerland, and Denmark, and one each from the United States, Russia, and the Netherlands set an international tone.[14]

Germans and Egyptians were notably absent from the podium. Not only did Germany have a powerful tradition of Egyptology; a German had written the standard biography of Champollion—in German.[15] The wounds of World War I were still too raw, however, for Germans to have been invited. More significant for our purpose was the absence of Egyptian speakers. Ahmad Kamal came all the way from Cairo to attend, but the subaltern could not speak.[16] By Kamal's side, his former student Selim Hassan—now assistant curator in training at the Egyptian Museum—had had to pay his own way.[17]

Around this time, Kamal petitioned the Ministry of Education to publish the twenty-two volume dictionary of ancient Egyptian he had

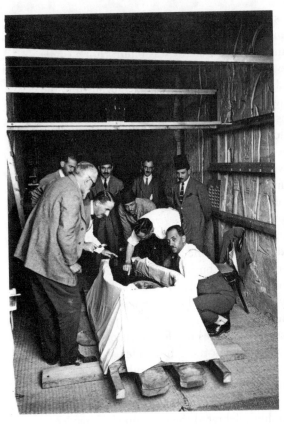

20 Overlooking Saleh Bey
Hamdi: The dissection of the
mummy of Tutankhamun.
Derry makes the initial incision
while Carter (with magnifying
class) and Antiquities Director Lacau (left) peer intently.
Hamdi seems a bystander:
Although in the foreground, he
is caught awkwardly looking at
the camera instead of the task
at hand. *Photo: Harry Burton,
courtesy of Griffith Institute,
Oxford University.*

long been compiling. It gave Arabic, French, and Coptic equivalents
for Egyptian words. The volume for the Arabic letter *sin* alone ran to
1,072 manuscript pages. Kamal asserted that as a native speaker of Arabic,
he could see Egyptian's affinity to Arabic and other Semitic languages,
which had eluded most Westerners. As a sample, a three-man committee evaluated Kamal's volume for the letter *qaf* for the government press.
American George Reisner recommended publication, and Briton Cecil
Firth seems to have agreed, but Lacau's opposition, which included criticism of Kamal's French, sank the project.[18] Kamal died soon after. Not
until 2002 did the Supreme Council of Antiquities undertake the publication of a facsimile edition.[19] The work's chance of influencing Egyptian
philology had long since passed.[20] Even had it come out simultaneously
with the great Berlin dictionary (1926–31), its being in Arabic would have
put it beyond the reach of most Western Egyptologists.

In the last year of his life, Ahmad Kamal and two of his former students came forward to explain the significance of Tutankhamun's tomb

in the Arabic press.[21] One of these students was Ahmad Kamal's own son Hassan (Ahmad) Kamal (1896–1974), who had gone on to Oxford in 1912 to study Egyptology but came home with a University of London medical degree instead. Hassan Kamal eventually became first deputy minister of health and a bey, but he especially enjoyed writing on Egyptological topics in Arabic for his countrymen.[22] Hassan Kamal contrasted his father's solitary lexicographical toil with the team compiling Adolf Erman's Egyptian dictionary in Berlin.[23] Chief inspector of antiquities for Upper Egypt Reginald Engelbach at first rebuffed the attempt of Selim Hassan—another former student of Ahmad Kamal's—to see Tutankhamun's tomb, but Carter intervened in Hassan's favor.[24]

Upon Ahmad Kamal's death in 1923, obituaries appeared in *The Journal of Egyptian Archaeology, Bulletin de l'institut d'Égypte*, and the Arabic press. He had published more items in the *Annales du service des antiquités de l'Égypte* than all his Egyptian contemporaries combined, but the journal ignored his passing. The first edition of *Who Was Who in Egyptology* (1951) omitted him.[25] The second edition of *Who Was Who in Egyptology* in 1972 included him, as did subsequent editions. Only decolonization finally cleared the way for Kamal's rehabilitation. Gamal Mukhtar published an appreciation in Arabic in 1963. In 1981 the *ASAE* finally made amends,[26] and Kamal's and other Egyptians' busts were added to those of Europeans enshrined behind Mariette's monument in the garden of the Egyptian Museum (see fig. 83).

Ahmad Kamal's hard road contrasted with the successful career of his more famous contemporary Osman Hamdi Bey (1842–1910) in Istanbul. Hamdi directed Istanbul's Imperial Museum and the Ottoman antiquities service from 1881 until his death in 1910. Ottoman independence, though precarious, accounts for much of the difference. The cosmopolitan son of a former grand vizier, Hamdi studied law and Orientalist painting in Paris, founded Istanbul's Academy of Fine Arts, and excavated in Sidon and elsewhere.[27] He succeeded a German as director of the Imperial Museum in Istanbul in 1881—the same year that Maspero followed Mariette in Egypt. Hamdi wrestled with museological and archaeological issues through the height of the European imperial age. Colonized Egypt trailed by seventy years in having one of its own nationals take over direction of its antiquities and archaeology. Kamal signed an article shortly before he died "Neglected Archaeologist."[28]

Private remarks by three American Egyptologists shortly before the Tutankhamun discovery drive home the Orientalist, imperialist, and racial prejudices of the day. James Henry Breasted wrote home at the beginning of November, 1919:

We reached Alexandria Thursday morning. . . . There had been rioting the day before. . . . The country people have had enough and are ready to settle down under British authority; but the little tarbushed effendis in Cairo and Alexandria are still making trouble. . . . There is trouble in the air, and the outbreak in Cairo is likely to come at any minute. You need not have the slightest anxiety. The trouble will be confined to certain quarters, just as was the negro rioting in Chicago. The authorities are quite ready and indeed are hoping that the lid may blow off very violently in order to show the agitators the strong hand at once and without mercy. The country is full of British troops.[29]

Breasted's great rival George Reisner is rightly remembered for his fatherly concern for his workers, unusual training of Egyptians for photography and recording excavations, and care not to antagonize Egyptian nationalists. Yet after a mob attack on Europeans in Alexandria in 1921, he wrote:

The old anti-Christian fanaticism is still in existence, and the native brutality of a half-civilized people is still alive in the hearts of the Egyptians. . . .
     The people of Egypt are, in spite of all their vanity and pretensions, still a half-savage race. They have been held in check by force since the days of Mohammed Ali (or more correctly Menes). . . . The people stand in intellectual and religious opposition to all that is called European,—blind, ignorant, and uncomprehending opposition. The lust of blood and plunder is part of the constitution of every man and woman. Over 90 per cent of the inhabitants can neither read nor write.[30]

In 1915, Clarence Fisher, who had worked under Reisner for eight years, began digging at Memphis for the University of Pennsylvania's University Museum. Mahmud Ahmed Said el Mayyit, a former Qufti headman (rais) of Reisner's, managed the crew until Fisher dismissed him on charges of dishonesty. Mahmud's brother Said Ahmed, however, was Reisner's current rais at Giza, and Reisner took Mahmud back into his crew. Fisher protested:

Dr. Reisner's present attitude is an acknowledgement that he regards the word of a native black man as more to be relied on than the word of two white men such as Mr. Sanborn and myself, the representatives of a sister University.[31]

To Reisner, Fisher wrote:

It is usually accepted that the word of a white man is better than that of a native, but I am sorry to say that several times during the past two years you have thought it best to think otherwise.

If you intend to support Mahmud el Mayyit—continue him in your service . . . it is intended as an insult not only to us personally but to the University of Pennsylvania. It certainly will destroy any other white man's authority over these people.[32]

It was not only working class Egyptians who came up short in Western eyes. In 1920, Herbert Winlock of the Metropolitan Museum was asked if he would take "an educated, high-class Egyptian on the excavation work." "Certainly not," he replied, for while they would not steal, "and many of them are delightful, cultivated people," after having been "a dominated race for thousands of years," they had developed "an intellectual facility to twist facts,"

that *facility* of mind, which enables an Egyptian, or any Oriental for that matter, however cultivated, to see the thing as he *wants* to see it. For instance with such a man with me, when some relic was discovered, supposing that I was in need of more evidence to prove something, say that Rameses III. ruled before Ramesses II., he would do everything he could to prove it—in order to please me.

To clinch his case, Winlock ridiculed the maneuvering of Saad Zaghlul and his rivals in negotiating with Britain. However, James Quibell of the Antiquities Service protested—was it because he was a Scot?—"That is going a bit too strong. I do not blame the Egyptians for wanting to govern themselves." [33]

Rhythms of Memory and Forgetting

The Tutankhamun discovery spun threads of British and Egyptian individual, family, and institutional memories lasting as long as fifty years down to the London exhibition of 1972.[34] I.E.S. Edwards, the British Museum Egyptologist who organized the show, had thrilled to the discovery as a boy.[35] Lady Evelyn Herbert (later Beauchamp) entered the tomb with her father, Lord Carnarvon, and Howard Carter in 1922 and attended the Museum's celebratory dinner fifty years later. 'Tutmania' was part of a rich tradition of Western Egyptomania in fields as diverse as architecture, literature, painting, women's fashion, music, and mummy movies. The death of Lord Carnarvon from an infected mosquito bite just months after the discovery fueled "curse of the pharaoh" stories, which still flourish.[36] British deeds and memories in connection with Tutankhamun have been studied from many angles; Egyptian views are still far less charted. Egyptian memories clustered in such institutions—*lieux de mémoire* in themselves—as the Egyptian Museum, the Antiquities Service, the Valley of the Kings, the village of Qurna, the town of Luxor, and its Winter Palace Hotel.

Fever-pitch attention to Tutankhamun—in the metropole, its rebellious Egyptian province, and beyond—could not be sustained indefinitely. Early news of the discovery tracked the rhythm of Egyptian winter archaeological and tourist 'seasons,' interspersed with long summer lulls. "The best time for a tour in Egypt," pronounced Baedeker, "is between November 1st and May 1st."[37] Then tourists departed, and well-to-do European and Egyptian residents fled the summer heat for Europe or the sea breezes of Alexandria. Western archaeologists headed home to mount exhibits, write, lecture, and prepare their next season's campaign.

News of "King Tut" pouring out of the Valley of the Kings during the winter of 1922–23 was stretched into May by Lord Carnarvon's untimely death in April and finally trailed off in June. The second winter season, 1923–24, brought a frenzy of coverage, which was highlighted by the

Table C. Seasonal Rhythms of Archaeology and Tourism in Egypt: Keyword listings for Tutankhamen (and variant spellings) in The Times by month.

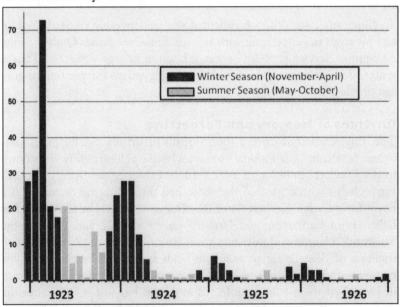

Business and advertising listings and racehorses named Tutankhamen excluded. *The Times Digital Archive.*

opening of the sarcophagus, Carter's strike, the Antiquities Service's seizure of the tomb, and Carter's suit against the Egyptian government (see table C).[38] The catalog of the Library of Congress shows the initial flush of books on Tutankhamun, with nine published in 1923 and three more in 1924. Carter's third season was delayed by politics, as will be seen. It opened late (in January 1925) and attracted little coverage as he conserved objects already brought out of the tomb. Journalistic interest flared up again in the fourth winter (1925–26), with the opening of the nesting coffins and unwrapping of the mummy. The next six seasons attracted only minimal publicity. Carter's dispatch of the gilded shrines to Cairo in 1932 wound up his fieldwork, and in 1933 he published the third and final volume of his popular account.

Thereafter, news of Tutankhamun fell off sharply for almost thirty years. The Anglo–Egyptian Treaty of 1936 ultimately failed to resolve the basic conflict between the two nations. Carter's intended six-volume specialized report never got off the ground. Tutankhamun remained the star attraction in the Valley of the Kings and Cairo Museum, but until the 1960s these were directly available only to Egyptians and the limited numbers of foreign tourists who made it to Egypt despite the Depression, World War II, and their unstable aftermath. Only the postcolonial age under Nasser would clear the way for Egypt to lend Tutankhamun objects for exhibition abroad in the 1960s. The accompanying increase in tourism and publications on the "boy king" recharged the memory of Tutankhamun in Britain, Egypt, and beyond.

Who Owns the News?

Three disputes over Tutankhamun during the first two seasons left their marks on British and Egyptian collective memories. Would Lord Carnarvon's sale of exclusive press rights to *The Times* of London stand? Would the Antiquities Service award the foreign excavators their customary share, or would Egypt's as yet untested independence enable it to keep the entire hoard as a unique national treasure? Finally, how would the French-directed Antiquities Service exercise its right to supervise the work, including visits to the tomb?

In a revealing act of imperial privilege, Lord Carnarvon ignored the press of the country in which he was digging and invited only London *Times* correspondent Arthur Merton to the opening.[39] Merton scooped the world on November 30, 1922, with news of the discovery. Six weeks later, Carnarvon sold exclusive publication rights to *The Times* for £5000 and 75 percent of future royalties on sales to other papers. Other Western papers and the Egyptian press came together, for once, in opposing the monopoly. Britain's *Daily Express* and *Daily Mail*, Reuters news agency, and *The New York Times* rushed special correspondents to Luxor to challenge what Egyptologist-turned-journalist Arthur Weigall dubbed "Tutankhamen and Co. Ltd."[40]

In the second season, Carter tried to finesse the problem by naming Merton to his staff and having him follow up his exclusive evening dispatches to *The Times* with free releases to the Egyptian press the next morning. But under pressure from critics of the monopoly, Lacau and his superior, the minister of public works, tried to deny Merton privileged access to the tomb.[41] The British-run *Egyptian Gazette* joined its metropolitan colleagues in the attack:

> Certain British officials in the Egyptian Government service who sympathise strongly with Lord Carnarvon, hope to avert the Egyptian Government's assumption of powers and privileges now enjoyed for discoveries, but they are sadly handicapped by Lord Carnarvon's arrangement with certain people in London to capitalize the news of this great find.[42]

In the Arabic press, the Watani Party's *al-Liwa* protested:

> But Lord Carnarvon has succeeded in seizing the Valley of the Kings where the precious treasures—Tutankhamen, and his sacred and valuable relics have been discovered. . . . Wealth lies in making propaganda about these contents. People all over the world desire to read the exact description of the finds, from both the technical and historic points of view, and every word that is written on the subject is being paid for by all the readers in the world. How many millions of pounds or even piastres will enter the pockets of Lord Carnarvon? Do not forget the prices of photographs and cinema films and all propaganda materials.[43]

Al-Ahram charged that *The Times* "has been attempting to force us to take our news regarding Egyptian treasures from a non-Egyptian newspaper" and that allowing free access to all foreign correspondents would have

> published in all parts of the world the characteristics of Egyptian civilisation and the glorious antiquities of that civilisation. . . . Had these antiquities been discovered in another country the Government of that country would have invited foreign journalists, at the expense of the state to see the finds and publish all possible details about them, for it is obvious that this would serve as propaganda to attract the attention of the world to the nation possessed of such relics denoting its advanced state of civilisation in the past. We all know that the Powers sympathised, and still sympathise, with the Hellenic State . . . owing to their recognition of the favours conferred by the civilisation of Athens on the civilisation of the world.[44]

Ownership of the Find

Upon founding the Antiquities Service in 1858, Auguste Mariette obtained a monopoly on excavation and tried to retain everything of value for the museum he opened in Bulaq, Cairo, in 1863. His successor, Maspero, however, faced the different challenge of maintaining French control of the Service despite British occupation of the country. He welcomed in foreign excavators and usually let them take home half their finds. Maspero's leniency and the Cairo Museum's selling of 'duplicates' enabled British and American excavators, who were not government funded, to impress their donors at home with museum prizes. Since the French Ministry of Education funded IFAO, its excavators were under less pressure to impress private donors with a flow of museum showpieces.[45] This legal outflow of antiquities from colonized Egypt contrasted with Italy, where few foreigners were allowed even to dig, and Greece, where foreign excavators had to renounce any claim to their finds.

Georges Daressy, standing in during Pierre Lacau's absence, had signed Carnarvon's concession for the Valley of the Kings on April 18, 1915. Renewed annually thereafter, the contract stipulated that Egypt would retain the mummies, coffins, and sarcophagi of kings, princes, and high priests, as well as all the contents of any tomb found intact. If a tomb had been "already searched," the Service would retain objects of "capital importance" and divide the rest so that the "Permittee's share will sufficiently recompense him for the pain and labour of the undertaking."[46]

Less than three weeks before the Tutankhamun discovery, Pierre Lacau announced his intention to replace the customary fifty-fifty division; instead, the Antiquities Service would claim everything found, and any awards to foreign expeditions would be gifts given at its discretion.[47] Lacau also announced that in the future, excavation concessions should only be awarded to institutions, not individuals (such as Lord Carnarvon and Theodore Davis). Robert Mond had been excavating and conserving tombs at Sheikh Abdel Qurna on his own for fifteen years; now he was obliged to affiliate with a scientific body in order to continue. The EES readily agreed to sponsor his work.[48] Chapter 3 takes up the furious British and American reactions to Lacau's proposed changes, which did not apply to Carnarvon's existing, annually renewed, concession.

Carter initially pronounced Tutankhamun's tomb intact, but he soon discovered that it had twice sustained minor looting shortly after burial. The superficial looting might have worked in Carnarvon's favor, since his concession stipulated that everything found in an intact tomb went to the Antiquities Service. In any case, Carnarvon felt certain of a rich share. He assured the Metropolitan's Albert Lythgoe that in return for his museum's assistance, "I'm going to give you a part of the things which I receive." "Of course, I shall have to give something to the British Museum, but I intend to see that the Metropolitan is *well taken care of*."⁴⁹

The disposition of the find was still unsettled when Carnarvon died in Cairo in early April 1923. Lacau authorized Carter to continue the Valley of the Kings concession on behalf of Lady Carnarvon. In a letter to Carter on January 10, 1924, however, Lacau "implicitly stated that the tomb and its contents were the property of Egypt."⁵⁰

Ahmad Shawqi, the great Arabic neoclassical poet, warned that Carter might make off with Egypt's patrimony:

> Our forefathers, and their greatest [Tutankhamun], are an inheritance that
>   We should be careful not to let pass into the hands of others.
>   We should refuse to allow our patrimony to be mistreated, or for
> thieves to steal it away. . . .
>   Aren't those who kidnapped the living Caliph [Wahid al-Din] capable
> of stealing off
>   With dead kings?

Shawqi urged the mummy-king to avenge himself on Carter as he had on Carnarvon: "I said to you, 'Strike his hand and cut it off! And send his way the nuisance of mosquitoes.'"⁵¹

Shawqi and his fellow neoclassical poet Khalil Mutran (1872–1949), who also wrote on Tutankhamun, showing that neither the young nor indigenous Egyptians had a monopoly on pharaonic themes. Shawqi, like King Fuad, turned fifty in 1919. Mutran, four years younger, was born in 1868 like Lutfi al-Sayyid. Neither Shawqi's mixed Turkish, Circassian, Kurdish, and Greek blood nor Mutran's Lebanese Christian roots prevented them from embracing pharaonism. Baalbek-born Khalil Mutran settled in Egypt in 1892, where his fellow Greek Catholic immigrants from Lebanon had already seized on the ultimate pharaonic symbol—*al-Ahram* (The Pyramids)—as the name for their famous newspaper. Mutran is mainly remembered for Lebanese and Arab nationalist themes, but in addition to Tutankhamun he also composed poems on Ramesses and the Pyramids.⁵² Shawqi, who is especially remembered for his pride in the Islamic and Arabic heritage, considered "Tutankhamun" his finest poem.⁵³

Supervision of the Work, Carter's Strike, and the Seizure of the Tomb

Carnarvon's concession stipulated the Antiquities Service's "right not only to supervise the work, but also to alter the manner of the execution if they so deem proper for the success of the undertaking."[54] After decades of colonial indulgence toward Western excavators, Egyptians pressed for the vigorous application of these stipulations.

Fikri Abaza complained in *al-Ahram*:

There in that old valley which is filled with hidden marvels and secrets—the Valley of the Kings, an absolute despotic government has arisen on the ruins of the ancient Pharaohic [sic], and of the modern Egyptian Government. That Government is the Government of Lord Carnarvon and Mr. Carter Limited. Does anybody dare to dispute it within the boundaries of that Valley? It is exploring there without any control on its work.

The Carnarvon Government permits and explains, and prevents and grants, it invites the Ministers of Egypt, out of courtesy and generosity, to see the Kings of Egypt, as it invites the officials of the Ministry of Public Works and the Antiquities Department to see its finds. This Government, gentlemen, deals in skulls and bones—the skulls and bones of our forefathers, may Allah be merciful to them and to us. (The words in Arabic are only said about the dead). Lord Carnarvon is exploiting the mortal remains of our ancient fathers before our eyes, and he fails to give the grandchildren any information about their forefathers. What era do we live in and to which Government do we submit?[55]

My young king, are they going to transport you to the museum and set you next to the Qasr al-Nil barracks to add insult to injury? So that, my free king, you might look out over your occupied country? So that you might see your enslaved people? So that you might learn that those who robbed your grave now dig another for your nation?[56]

In February and March 1923, *al-Ahram* ran articles entitled "Tutankhamun Speaks," "Tutankhamun Addresses Egypt's Interests," and "Tutankhamun Holds the Ministry Accountable." Egypt's film industry was launched that same year with *In the Country of Tut-Ankh-Amun*.[57] *Ramsis*, a short-lived magazine with a Coptic editor, published "Yaqzat Firawn" (A Pharaoh Awakes), a story in which an Egyptian god awakens Tutankhamun as archaeologists are about to break into his tomb and urges him to flee. The mummy-king, however, is resigned to the fact that the days of pharaonic power are over. He decides instead to put on his finest garments and jewelry to impress his discoverers. Elliott Colla points out that although in Western fiction, mummies are usually the object of horror or disruptive desire, in Egyptian fiction they often represent benevolent ancestors and patriarchs seeking restitution for Egypt.[58]

Tourists, journalists, officials, and archaeologists clamoring for a glimpse of the tomb slowed Carter's hot, tedious work to a crawl. Under pressure from Egyptian public opinion and the government, Lacau intervened in matters related to Carter's schedule and the flow of visitors to the tomb. In January 1924, two British and two American Egyptologists associated with Carter sent a rebuke to Lacau:

> Unless the unnecessary difficulties now obstructing the work in the Tomb of Tutankhamen are moderated . . . you, as Director General of Antiquities are failing completely to carry out the obligations of your high office to protect the scientific procedure of this all-important task. It is hardly necessary for us to call attention to the unfortunate effect of such failure of your administration upon the public and the great scientific world now so eagerly following the progress of the task.[59]

On February 13, 1924, Carter's feud with the Egyptian government boiled over. The previous day, in the presence of dignitaries, he had raised the stone lid of the sarcophagus. Now he planned to show the tomb first to the world press, then to the wives of his coworkers. The Ministry of Public Works, however, forbade the special viewing for the wives. Carter locked the tomb in a fury and posted a notice in Luxor in the Winter Palace Hotel:

> Owing to impossible restrictions and discourtesies on the part of the Public Works Department and its Antiquities Service, all my collaborators in protest have refused to work any further upon the scientific investigations of the discovery of the tomb of Tut.ankh.amen. . . . The tomb will be closed, and no further work can be carried out.[60]

Carter badly underestimated Saad Zaghlul's new Wafdist government, which was fresh from victory in the first parliamentary elections under the 1923 constitution. Arabic newspapers and magazines across a wide political spectrum attacked Carter. *Al-Mahrusa* urged the cabinet to stand fast "so that Mr. Carter may know that we have a real government." *Al-Balagh* said the government "must put an end to the ambitions which the weakness of preceding Ministries allowed Mr. Carter to nourish" and cancel the concession:

> Egypt has suffered enough from this foreigner, who, under the nose of the Egyptian public and of a high official of the Government, closes the tomb of Pharaoh as though it were the tomb of his own father.[61]

Even *al-Muqattam*, long a champion of the British occupation, reflected:

We hope that this incident will open the eyes of both the Government and the nation to the fact that it is time for Egyptians to study their own antiquities and practice the task of excavation and dealing with antiquities. It is not worthy of a great State to be monopolized by foreigners, while the inhabitants of this country stand by as onlookers in regret at not having the means to do otherwise.[62]

In the Arabic press, only Muhammad Husayn Haykal's Liberal Constitutionalist *al-Siyasa*, which harried the Wafd at every turn, defended Carter. Wafdist papers had earlier criticized Haykal for translating part of Carter and Mace's *Tomb of Tut.Ankh.Amen*.[63] On the cancelled visit of the wives, *al-Siyasa* wrote:

The incident makes us laugh. . . . Why did the Minister of Public Works refuse Mr. Carter's demand to permit the wives of his collaborators to visit the Tomb several days before others? Is it not natural for the wives of excavators to see the antiquities discovered before others? Is it not natural for the wives of Ministers to hear important news of the Ministry before they become known to the public? And even if it is not natural would it not be an act of courage to agree to the ladies' visit? What patriotic interests and national dignity required the refusal of the request? To tell the truth, the Minister of Public Works was too strict where strictness was not required.[64]

Al-Nizam, however, wrote:

This excavator, not content with the desire of laying his hand on antique curiosities and having a free hand in dealing with the dead, wanted to exercise influence over the Egyptian Ministers, the former Ministries having encouraged him to do so by their mildness. He imagined himself a kind of King of Wady al-Muluk. Mr. Carter was accustomed to open the doors of the Tomb of Tutankhamen whenever he liked and for any one he cared to admit, thanks to the courtesy and mildness of Abdul Hamid Pasha Suleiman, but when the Zaghloul Ministry was formed he found himself before an entirely different Minister . . . .[65]

Murqus (Marcos) Hanna, the "entirely different Minister," canceled the concession and banished Carter from the tomb. He dispatched Lacau to saw off the locks, take possession, and secure the sarcophagus lid, which Carter had left dangling precariously. The uproar increased when an uncatalogued head of Tutankhamun emerging from a lotus blossom was found packed in a Fortnum and Mason's wine crate in Carter's work space in the tomb of Ramesses XI.

Going beyond his usual appeal to 'science,' Carter accused the Egyptians of having insulted ladies, complaining in a telegram to Prime Minister Zaghlul of

> a great insult I have received from officials Antiquities Service, preventing me to-day taking members of families of my collaborators to visit Tut.ankh.amen's Tomb. Feel sure Your Excellency would disapprove of this ungentlemanly action which is also illegal and unjustifiable.[66]

Zaghlul, however, shot back:

> The science which you rightly invoke cannot allow that, for a private viewing which you would like to take place, you and your colleagues should abandon the investigations which are of a superior interest not only to Egypt but to the whole world.[67]

Murqus Hanna made it look as though inviting foreign wives had slighted Egyptian ladies of higher rank: "not even the wives of Cabinet Ministers could be admitted to the tomb until after the days set aside for the *scientific* study of the sarcophagus."[68]

Carter stormed off to the Mixed Courts, which had tried cases involving foreign interests since 1876. He sued to be made "sequestrator" of the tomb, free of interference from the Antiquities Service, and for a favorable ruling on division of the find. Unfortunately, he chose as his lawyer F.M. Maxwell, who had earlier sought the death penalty for Hanna, the very minister of public works Carter was now suing. Now, Maxwell neglected to bring proof that he represented Lady Carnarvon to the opening hearing. *Al-Nizam* wrote of "Carter the Mad":

> Carter's insanity has been conspicuous in the action he has taken against the Government; he sent Mr. Maxwell, the well known Military court lawyer, to plead for him on behalf of the Carnarvons without giving him any legal warrant to do so. Mr. Howard Carter may have imagined that the mere sending of Mr. Maxwell to the Mixed Court by his order, and without legal authorization, was enough to make the Court obey. . . . Why should he not imagine that if he considers himself the Dictator of

the Valley of the Kings, and even of Egypt herself. . . . Why should he not imagine this while he believes that he is a descendant of the Pharaohs and the heir of Tutankhamen.[69]

Maxwell's declaration that the government had entered the tomb "like a bandit" sank any chance of an out-of-court settlement. The Mixed Court of Appeals ruled the dispute an internal administrative matter and threw out the case.

Meanwhile, a week before the March 1924 opening of the first parliament under the 1923 constitution, the Wafd staged a national celebration at the tomb. *Al-Hilal* linked the occasion to the new parliamentary era and noted with pride that in a ceremony in Paris, the Egyptian delegate had been officially received alongside representatives of the great powers.[70] Special trains whisked Hanna, members of parliament, and diplomats to Luxor. High Commissioner Lord Allenby's attendance signaled that Carter was on his own, and Prime Minister Ramsey MacDonald telegrammed: "Urge Carter on highest authority to stop legal proceedings. Make amicable arrangement with Egyptian authorities."[71]

Ahmad Shawqi wrote of Tutankhamun:

He traveled forty centuries, considering them until he came home, and found there. . . .
  England, and its army, and its lord, brandishing its Indian sword, protecting its India.[72]

But liberation from the British was now at hand:

Pharaoh, the time of self-rule is in effect, and the dynasty of arrogant lords has passed.
  Now the foreign tyrants in every land must relinquish their rule over their subjects.[73]

The foreign tyrants compared to the British were the Hyksos, whom Tutankhamun's Eighteenth Dynasty forebears had driven back into Syria–Palestine (not the Hittites as Elliott Colla has it).

Shawqi's "Tutankhamun and the Parliament" divided its praise of the new constitutional monarchy between Zaghlul's Wafdist cabinet and King Fuad:

She [Young Egypt] spread out her roses along the road, and received her heart [King Fuad] and her Wafd delegation . . .

Tutankhamen has established Egypt's representative body, fortified its convocation, and he conferred the promise [of self-government] to this happy generation.

Tutankhamen has returned his authority to our sons![74]

Britain's *Outlook* deplored the "continued insults of these hysterical children who are playing at self-government," and *The Egyptian Gazette* later denounced "the tawdry triumph, with its fireworks and fantasias, of a government seeking in the burial ground of kings the *panem et circenses* wherewith to flatter the mob."[75] Charles Breasted, the son of American Egyptologist James Henry Breasted, deplored "the intoxicating effect of sudden freedom and independence upon an ignorant, decadent, mongrel people, totally unfit for self rule."[76]

The British press was by no means as solidly behind Carter as *al-Balagh* charged.[77] The *Westminster Gazette* opined:

Scientific research is very difficult to adapt to the purposes of popular entertainment. If Mr. Howard Carter had been content to set quietly to work, to recover what he could, and study it carefully and methodically, and to make his report when the work was completed, or his interim reports at various stages, he would probably have remained undisturbed. – But to make the whole affair a 'stunt' by creating a monopoly in news with regard to it and then publishing pictures and descriptions from day to day, was a direct invitation to the world to become excited, and if the tomb has become a place of pilgrimage for the tourist, discussion and controversy have arisen, and the Egyptian Government has begun to wonder whether they or the concessionaires really own the Valley, the adoption of methods new to Egyptology must be held largely to blame.[78]

An editorial in the British-run *Egyptian Gazette* was surprisingly open to Egyptian views:

Mr. Carter would appear to have failed to realize the significance of the changes that have been taking place in the political situation here during the past two years. . . . We do not know exactly to what degree of efficiency the organization of the Egyptian Department of Antiquities has been brought, but it is no doubt fully equal to the task of carrying on Mr. Carter's work. . . .

When the immediate danger to the tomb has been removed, the Government will not, of course, have need for hurry in carrying out whatever plans it may have in view. It would need an 'archeological mission' to Europe to equip some young Egyptians to engage on the uncompleted task of Mr. Carter. A few years more or less counts for nothing beside the centuries of Tutankhamen's undisturbed respose. But it would count for a good deal if these relics of 'the ancient glories of Egypt' were finally disposed of at the hands of the new Egypt that is so conscious of its rights.[79]

Sometimes the Arabic press turned inward with advice to fellow Egyptians:

The antiquities of the Valley of the Kings, which form a material fortune, must be a moral fortune for us, and we ought to know how to use it in the service of our national movement. . . . The Ministry of Education should fix certain days every month for visits by the students of our schools to the relics of their forefathers either where they have been discovered or in museums, so that they may read in them and learn how to make a good history of their own.[80]

In "The Spirit of Tutankhamen stirs the whole world," the newspaper *Misr* wondered:

Are we really roused as others have been roused by the discovery of the tomb of that great king and the contents thereof? Has this increased our sense of the greatness of our country, and made us zealous for its glorious history and wonderful antiquities, as foreigners are? . . . Countrymen! The discoveries of your country—recent and old—show that your Egypt was the educator of nations, the creator of laws and social regimes, the creator of science, and philosophy, the inventor of fine arts and marvelous hand industries. . . .

Countrymen, unity has a wonderful power, and the ancient history of Egypt is full of proofs of the unity and fraternity of the Egyptians, who worked sincerely for the welfare of the country, and reaped the glorious results of their co-operation. You have seen with your own eyes the fruits of unity which materialized four years ago in Egypt when the nation stood solidly to work for the interests of the country with determination. You have seen also how the energy slackened and how our opponents profited at our expense when the ranks of the nation were divided into parties and groups and they began to fight each other. . . . Before the epoch of King Tutankhamen Egypt was occupied by the Hyksos, but when the Egyptians of that time worked together for the welfare of their country with true sincerity and unity they succeeded in saving the country from the hands of those foreigners. Thus they attained to great prosperity and power, especially at the time of King Akhenaton, who purified Egypt from Hyksos, and his successor King Tutankhamen.[81]

If *Misr*'s history was muddled—Egypt was in turmoil under Akhenaten and Tutankhamun, and the Hyksos had been driven out nearly two centuries earlier—the moral was clear.

Tutankhamun's Eighteenth Dynasty forebears had followed up the expulsion of the Hyksos by conquering an empire stretching from Syria into the Sudan. Now Tutankhamun demanded of Prime Minister Abd al-Khaliq Tharwat how many kingdoms *he* had conquered and mocked him for extolling Britain's proclamation of hemmed-in Egyptian independence: "When was Egypt other than independent? Who lost its independence?"[82]

Westerners' fascination with Tutankhamun as a symbol of Egypt—along with the Pyramids, Sphinx, Nefertiti, and Cleopatra—helped define him as a national icon for Egyptians as well. This was not unlike the Eiffel Tower and Gallic cock for France. "Pierre Nora was right: 'Because foreigners take the Eiffel Tower to be the very image of France, the country has strongly internalized the world's regard.'"[83] "First proposed, if not imposed, by foreigners, the cock nevertheless became an authentic symbol for France, a symbol as rich in content as if it had been chosen by the French themselves."[84]

Tut Goes to Wembley: The British Empire Exhibition

While the stalemate over the tomb festered in 1924, King George V and Queen Mary opened the British Empire Exhibition at Wembley, northwest of central London, for a two-season run. It featured a replica of the tomb. Tutankhamun's situation at Wembley was rather like Egypt's relationship to the Empire—too important to be left out but included in an anomalous and confusing way. "When you come to think of it," mocked *Punch*, "what *is* the imperial status of Egypt? Is it autonomous under a Khedive, or is it a British Protectorate under Howard Carter, or what?"[85] The Tutankhamun relics at Wembley were only replicas. Were Egypt's British-declared independence, the borrowed clauses of its Belgian-inspired constitution, and its new parliament real? Replicas? Fakes? No one quite knew.

Promoted as "The British Empire in Microcosm," Wembley advertised "a comprehensive survey of the wealth and resources of the British Commonwealth of Nations."[86] Omitting Tut would have disappointed a public saturated with news of this British discovery. With the tomb closed and Carter locked out, "it seems as though the model of the tomb in the British Empire Exhibition grounds at Wembley must do duty for the real one as a place of pilgrimage for visitors."[87] But having touted Egypt's independence, Britain could hardly display the pharaoh's wares alongside those of India, Canada, and Malaya.

So 'Tut-ankh-amen's Tomb' at Wembley ended up among the 'joy jaunts' of the Amusement Park: the "Giant Switchback, 'Caterpillar,' Water Chute, 'Jack and Jill,' and 'Derby Racer.'"[88] One wonders if Egyptian visitors were amused. Carter was not, but for a different reason. He sued on the grounds that the replicas William Aumonier and twelve skilled craftsmen had fashioned under the supervision of Egyptologist Arthur Weigall had illegally relied on photographs taken by the Carnarvon expedition. The defendants were able to prove, however, that they had drawn instead on photos and sketches by Weigall and his friends.[89]

Punch reported that Aumonier's Tottenham Court Road studio was on Tutankhamen Court Road and concocted a mock pedigree, rather in the spirit of Rome's legendary descent from Aeneas of Troy or Britain's Trojan ancestor Brutus:

> TUT-ANKH-AMEN was not really buried at Luxor at all but only a nameless man in his stead, and the young king wandered off and found a boat and went down the Nile, and when he came to the sea there was a ship with grave Phoenician traders on the decks, and he went aboard and hid in the bales, and so came to Cornwall, and from the West Country right up to London along the traders way. . . . Thus TUT-ANKH-AMEN was the earliest of all the gipsies to come into this land, and taught men the art of working in metal and the making of furniture, having a little booth first of all not very far from Goodge Street Station [i.e., Aumonier's studio].[90]

French and American Threads of Memory

Discovering, remembering, and forgetting Tutankhamun was not, of course, an exclusively Egyptian and British affair. French and American supporting actors participated in the drama of discovery. France and the United States shared in the relative neglect of Tutankhamun for decades after the first sensational early years. Then their landmark exhibitions in the 1960s helped revive his memory and pave the way for the British Musum exhibition of 1972. Antiquities director Pierre Lacau was heir to a tradition of Franco–British Egyptological rivalry threading back through Maspero, Mariette, and Champollion to Britain's seizure of the Rosetta Stone in 1801 and enshrinement of it in the British Museum. Lacau was forced to take Egyptian nationalism more seriously than had his predecessors. British and American accounts often dismiss him as an intrusive bureaucrat who harassed Carter and caved in to unreasonable Egyptian demands. Éric Gady has countered with a sympathetic reading of Lacau's handling of the discovery.[91] Place names in Cairo still honor the memory of Champollion, Mariette, and Maspero, but not Lacau. Lacau's vigorous defense of Egypt's rights in the Tutankhamun affair was overshadowed in nationalist eyes by his rearguard struggle to retain French control of the Antiquities Service.

Lacau's assistant Gustave Lefebvre installed the original Tutankhamun display in the Egyptian Museum in the mid-1920s. On a popular level, Paris's *Exposition internationale des arts décoratifs et industriels modernes* of 1925, which gave 'art deco' its name, fostered French versions of 'Tutmania.' Bernard Bruyère, who followed Carter's work from his own excavation across the mountain ridge at the tomb workers' village of Deir al-Medina, lived to savor the Tutankhamun exhibition in Paris in 1967.

Coming of age at the turn of the century, American Egyptology was closely intertwined with its British counterpart at a time when American political and economic activities in Egypt were still too marginal to worry the British. Carter had dug for American millionaire Theodore Davis before going to work for Carnarvon. Carter and Carnarvon both helped the Metropolitan Museum purchase antiquities, and Met staff quickly came to their aid on Tutankhamun's tomb. Two of the staffers the Metropolitan seconded to Carter—photographer Harry Burton and Arthur Mace—were themselves British.[92] Carter chose the United States and Canada for his lecture tour in the spring of 1924 while locked out of the tomb. *The New York Times* once even mistakenly called Carter American.[93] President Calvin Coolidge invited him to the White House twice.

James Henry Breasted, who had recently established the Oriental Institute of the University of Chicago, assisted Carter with the inscribed seals of the tomb and tried in vain to mediate Carter's dispute with the Egyptian government.[94] As will be seen in chapter 3, Breasted's proposal in 1926 of a new Rockefeller-funded Cairo museum to be under Western tutelage for at least thirty years misread Egypt's postwar politics as badly as had Carter.

Transnational alignments and intranational rivalries undercut attempts at national solidarity on Tutankhamun. Georges Foucart, director of IFAO, intrigued against his compatriot, Antiquities director Lacau. Lacau's British subordinates James Quibell and Reginald Engelbach supported their French chief.

Flinders Petrie and Francis Griffith refused to join fellow Britons Alan Gardiner and Percy Newberry in denouncing Lacau over Tutankhamun. Hopes for British–American solidarity (imagined as "Anglo-Saxon") were also ruined by Breasted's cold relationship with his compatriot George Reisner. Reisner was contemptuous of Carter's qualifications as an archaeologist,[95] and significantly it was Yale, not Reisner's Harvard, that awarded Carter an honorary doctorate. Among Egyptians, Muhammad Husayn Haykal's Liberal Constitutionalist *al-Siyasa*, as already noted, stood alone in breaking nationalist ranks to support Carter.

Climax and Tapering Off

Carter's popular book only alludes to the political upheavals of the era and the dispute that nearly aborted his work. He saved the details—and his rage—for his privately printed booklet of June 1924, *Tut.Ankh.Amen: The Politics of Discovery.* Even Carter's close associates were shocked at his publishing Egyptian government correspondence concerning the tomb. They prevailed upon him to suppress the publication, but the damage was done.[96]

Late in 1924, the assassination in Cairo of Sir Lee Stack, commander (sirdar) of the Egyptian army and governor general of the Sudan, handed Allenby and King Fuad the opportunity to replace Zaghlul and the Wafd with a palace government under Ahmad Ziwar. Hoping that progress on Tutankhamun might ease other British–Egyptian tensions, Allenby pressed Ziwar and Carter to settle.[97] Carter and Lady Carnarvon agreed to renounce *The Times*'s news monopoly and all claims to objects from the tomb. In return, Egypt promised Lady Carnarvon a gift of duplicates. In January 1925, ten months after the strike and lockout, Carter was quietly allowed to resume work in the tomb. Prime Minister Ziwar called on him there in February.[98] As King Fuad worked tirelessly to build a royal autocracy in the enlarged political space conceded to Egypt by the British, he wrapped himself in the mantle of pharaonic glory evoked by the treasures of the pharaoh. He visited the tomb with Antiquities director Lacau and laid claim to Tutankhamun's legacy by superimposing his own photo on a corner of a picture of a statue of the young pharaoh (see fig. 21). The caption on the latter photo reads, "his majesty our lord King Fuad the First, the best omen for the future of the independent kingdom of the Valley of the Nile."[99] (Chapter 4 further explores this theme.)

Between 1923 and 1932, the Tutankhamun collection gradually went on display as the prime attraction of Cairo's Egyptian Museum. This monument was itself, as already noted, a colonial *lieu de mémoire* in Ismailiya Square (now Midan al-Tahrir, Liberation Square).[100] Next door, on the Nile, the forbidding Qasr al-Nil barracks housed Britain's occupying troops. Just north along the Nile, the Anglican Cathedral of All Saints was added in the 1930s—"as heavy and purposeful as a power station."[101] Several blocks to the south stood the Residency, which Cromer had built. The villas of Garden City, Zamalek, and Heliopolis housed the well-to-do, both Western and Egyptian. Heading eastward from the museum, one came to the British Turf Club—"which would not have looked out of place in St. James's Street"—and the famous Shepheard's Hotel. To the west, across the Qasr al-Nil Bridge, lay the Gezira Sporting Club. Of these imperial *lieux de mémoire*, the Egyptian Museum, British Embassy,

21 King Fuad lays claim to Tutankhamun. a: Fuad and Antiquities Director General Pierre Lacau (left center) emerge from the tomb. b: Fuad claims Tutankhamun by juxtaposing his own portrait on that of a statue of the pharaoh. *Zaki Fahmi,* Safwat al-asr fi tarikh, *105, 112.*

and Gezira Club would survive Nasser's revolution; the Qasr al-Nil barracks, Cathedral, Turf Club, and old Shepheard's would not.

As Tutankhamun's funerary mask and coffins went on display in 1926, it was said that

> all Cairo is flocking to pay its five piastres a head at the turnstile, to secure entrance to the halls where archaeological treasures have stood for many years past, a focus of interest to *savants* and tourists, but, by the majority of Cairenes, sadly neglected. . . .
>
> Schoolmasters and school mistresses are planning organized mass visits of their pupils, hardened residents who have remained indifferent to all the stir hitherto made about Tutankhamen and his buried treasures are being roused from their lethargy to pay their first visit in thirty years to the Museum, and on all sides there are signs of an awakening curiosity regarding the life and times of the Boy Pharaoh. . . .
>
> There is much speculation among the crowds on the possible value of the coffin, should the Egyptian Government ever take the unthinkable decision to sell it. Here fancy ranges unchecked by knowledge from a hundred thousand sterling to ten millions.[102]

Thomas Cook & Son had just managed to bring out a postwar edition of *Cook's Handbook for Egypt and the Sudan* in 1921 when the discovery of Tutankhamun's tomb abruptly made it obsolete. Not until 1925 did Cook plug the gaping hole with a temporary patch—a twenty-eight-page supplement on recent archaeological finds bound into the 1921 edition.[103] When the firm finally produced a new edition in 1929, it had to compete with a new edition of Baedeker's classic Egyptian guide. Of the many tombs in the Valley of the Kings, Baedeker awarded only those of Seti I and Ramesses III more space than Tutankhamun's cramped and hurriedly decorated burial place. Although only half of the Tutankhamun collection had gone on display by 1929, the relics from his short, obscure reign filled five of the twenty-three pages Baedeker gave to the whole museum covering over three thousand years of history.[104]

The rhythms of Tutankhamun coverage in *al-Ahram* resembled those in Western media—intense attention in the first two seasons, renewed interest in 1926, sparse notices into the early 1930s, and then near silence.[105] The magazines *al-Hilal* and *al-Muqtataf* provided frequent coverage during the first two seasons, and *al-Hilal* was inspired to frame the symbolic namesake crescent moon on its cover page with pharaonic columns[106] (see fig. 34). One of the few books on Tutankhamun in Arabic between the wars was the account of a visit to the tomb by students from Cairo's Khedival Secondary School in March 1926.[107]

After the unwrapping of the mummy and dispatch of the coffins to Cairo in February 1926, *The Times* index lists only three Tutankhamun items for the rest of the year. Table C shows the fall in keyword mentions in *The Times* thereafter. Carter's six remaining seasons in the tomb were only minimally reported. Four of the six *Times* articles of 1930 dealt with financial reimbursement to the Carnarvon estate and Egypt's decision, stiffened by the Wafd's brief return to power, not to give away any duplicates from the tomb. After Carter ended his fieldwork in 1932 and published the third and last volume of *The Tomb of Tut.Ankh.Amen* the following year, the pharaoh nearly vanished from the news for almost thirty years.

The glare of Tutankhamun publicity in the 1920s cast other archaeological news in Egypt into the shade. Chapter 3 takes up the wide range of other Western archaeological activities in Egypt during the decade, and chapter 4 turns to the simultaneous takeoffs in the 1920s of both professional Egyptian Egyptology and of pharaonism among the Egyptian public.

3
Western Egyptology in Egypt in the Wake of Tutankhamun, 1922–1930

Tutankhamun aside, the uncharted currents of the emerging semi-colonial age forced continual renegotiation among Pierre Lacau of the Antiquities Service, Western archaeological expeditions, and a series of unstable Egyptian governments ranging from palace dictatorships to nationalist governments led by the Wafd. Despite the political uncertainties of the decade, and occasional flare-ups of the old Franco-British Egyptological rivalry, Egyptian archaeology flourished in the 1920s. A feud between Lacau and IFAO director George Foucart undercut French hopes for national solidarity in Egyptological matters. Dismayed by the weakening of British control in Egypt, Flinders Petrie left to excavate in "Egypt over the Border"—the new British mandate in Palestine. The Egypt Exploration Society (EES, the former EEF) took over the former German concession at Tell al-Amarna, and Bernard Bruyère led the IFAO expedition at another former German concession, the tomb workers' village at Deir al-Medina.

The uproar in 1923 over the prewar circumstances in which Borchardt had exported the bust of Nefertiti to Berlin largely blocked renewed German excavations until 1929. Hermann Junker, however, was able to resume his prewar work at Giza under Austrian auspices. American Egyptology had manged to keep its toe in the door throughout the war and now surged back with George Reisner's Harvard–Boston expedition at Giza and Herbert Winlock's Metropolitan Museum of Art excavations at Deir al-Bahari. James Henry Breasted's new Oriental Institute (OI) at the University of Chicago soon sprawled throughout the Middle East. Its Egyptian activities centered on the long-term project of the epigraphic recording of the temple of Ramesses III at Medinat Habu. Breasted overreached, however, in proposing a new Rockefeller-funded museum in Cairo; it foundered on the shoals of Egyptian nationalism.

Franco-British Rivalry in the Era of Pierre Lacau

In 1919 Alan Gardiner and director of the British Museum Sir Frederick Kenyon represented the EES on an Archaeological Joint Committee which assessed archaeological prospects in the Near East for the British Academy. Lord Carnarvon wanted archaeology to follow the flag; he pressed Foreign Secretary Arthur Balfour to trade France a free archaeological hand in Syria and Armenia for a British one in Egypt.[1] Gardiner lobbied for a British archaeological institute in Cairo which could counter IFAO's on-the-spot advantage. Sir John Evans agreed, writing in *The Times* that without state support, the EES and Petrie's BSAE could not compete adequately with the French, Germans, and Americans. Petrie, however, declared a British institute pointless unless an expanded Egyptian Antiquities Service undertook to hire its British graduates at decent salaries.[2] Nothing came of it. Proposals for a British institute in Cairo cropped up again at intervals of a generation, after World War II in 1946, and again in 1970–74.[3]

In December 1922, a month after the Tutankhamun discovery, Petrie organized a meeting at University College London to create a British–American front to roll back Lacau's plan to abolish the customary fifty-fifty divisions of finds. Albert Lythgoe of the Metropolitan and Petrie drafted a protest, signed by Alan Gardiner and others, and sent it to Egypt's council of ministers, High Commissioner Allenby, and Lacau. Lythgoe and Breasted rallied the support of American minister to Egypt Morton Howell and the State Department. Egypt responded in April 1923 with the concession that it would postpone Lacau's changes until after the 1923–24 season.[4]

Lacau's British and American detractors accused him of caving in to unreasonable Egyptian demands. They missed the Frenchman's conviction that he was defending the interests of 'science' and ignored their own inability to rally united fronts among their own countrymen. As already noted, Britons James Quibell and Cecil Firth backed their Antiquities Service chief Lacau, and among Americans, Reisner supported Lacau against Lythgoe and Breasted. Neither IFAO's George Foucart nor the Louvre's Georges Bénédite believed that Lacau, an employee of the Egyptian government, was acting in the best interests of French archaeology.

Lacau insisted that once the British and Americans accepted the *principle* of Egypt's right to everything excavated from its soil, he would *in practice* award reasonable shares to foreign expeditions to take home. His opponents dismissed such personal assurances and until 1926 kept trying to roll back his proposed changes. In 1925, Lythgoe dramatized his protest by refusing to send Metropolitan expeditions to Lisht and

Deir al-Bahari. Reisner, however, dashed hopes for American solidarity and warned American minister Morton Howell that diplomatic pressure would backfire. As for the British, Alan Gardiner and the EES lobbied High Commissioner Allenby, his successor Lord Lloyd, the Foreign Office, and even the British prime minister. As with Tutankhamun, however, the British government had too much at stake in Egypt to invest much political capital in disputing archaeological spoils.

In April 1926, however, even France came together with the United States and Britain in delivering simultaneous diplomatic notes pressing for favorable clarification on divisions of finds. The Wafd's election victory the following month, however, boded ill for their cause. Howell hastened to obtain assurances from Ziwar's outgoing cabinet that divisions of finds would continue, though with some restrictions. The incoming Liberal Constitutionalist–Wafdist coalition (headed by Adli Yakan since the British vetoed Zaghlul's return as prime minister) let Ziwar's statement stand.[5]

The headstrong Petrie would have none of it. He had refrained from going out to Egypt for three winter seasons between 1922 and 1926, and during the fourth (1923–24) he recorded rock-cut tombs at Qau rather than excavate, thus avoiding the question of a division of finds. Guy Brunton, Caton-Thompson, and A.J. Arkell did lead expeditions for Petrie's BSAE during these years but at prehistoric sites unlikely to yield striking museum pieces. Even so, the divisions were disappointing. Petrie's magazine *Ancient Egypt* complained: "Further work on great clearances for new discoveries is checked by the illegal claims of the Department of Antiquities."[6] In June 1926 Petrie called it quits, announcing that he was leaving to dig in "Egypt over the Border"—Palestine—where he assumed British mandatory authorities had more control.[7]

Reluctantly conceding that guaranteed fifty-fifty divisions were a thing of the past, the EES and the Met hoped for the best from Lacau's divisions. From 1921 to 1936, the EES dug at Akhenaten's short-lived capital at Tell al-Amarna. Petrie had made a sondage there (1891–92), and Norman de Garis Davis had copied private tombs for the EEF's Archaeological Survey (1901–1907). Ludwig Borchardt's expedition took over the site in 1907 and dug there several seasons until forced out by the war. Borchardt hoped to resume there once the conflict was over, so the award of the concession to the EEF in 1920 provoked an acrimonious exchange of letters between Adolf Erman and his former pupil Alan Gardiner.[8] The EES's interwar work at Amarna suffered from turnovers of directors and scant publication.[9] When the EES complained about meager shares in the divisions, High Commissioner Lloyd agreed to speak to Lacau but declined to go over his head to Egypt's prime minister.[10]

Lacau's defense of Egypt's interests won him little appreciation from Egyptian nationalists, for whom his very presence perpetuated colonial archaeology. His own tenure was far from assured. In 1923, the clock began ticking on a four-year transition, during which Europeans could retire from Egyptian state service and receive an indemnity. The French consul general warned of the blow to French interests should Lacau leave. IFAO no longer had a credible successor in the wings; the vacancy might go to an American or a Belgian—such as, Jean Capart.[11] The French Ministry of Foreign Affairs (MAE) implored Lacau to remain "at the head of this service so important for science and for French influence." He agreed to soldier on until full implementation of the retirement law in April 1927. Should the burden prove too heavy, however, and if Egypt vetoed a French successor, he would at least insist that the Service retain a minimum of two Frenchmen and two Britons and that it exclude Germans.[12]

When the April 1927 deadline arrived, Lacau decided to gamble, staying on as a contract worker subject to periodic renewal. Only a year into his first three-year contract, however, he complained that thirty years in Egypt had worn him down. Friction with High Commissioner Lord Lloyd, a Gallophobe, and Prime Minister Muhammad Mahmud, who was "de formation anglais," were taking their toll. King Fuad, however, persuaded Lacau to stay by granting him longer leaves. When Wafdists in the 1930 parliament criticized his six-month summer leaves in France, a face-saving compromise cut his leave to three months but tacked on a month and a half for special reasons.[13]

French Archaeology and the Feud between Pierre Lacau and George Foucart

Pierre Lacau's falling out with IFAO director George Foucart (1865–1943) is a salutary reminder that archaeological factions rarely split cleanly along national lines. In 1915, Foucart stepped into the IFAO directorship, which Lacau had vacated for the Antiquities Service. Both Foucart and Lacau were determined to prove their devotion to France, yet in the dozen years their respective directorships in Cairo overlapped, they drifted apart.

George Foucart was the son of Hellenist Paul Foucart, former director of the École française at Athens, professor at the Collège de France, and member of the Académie des inscriptions et belles-lettres. In 1894, George's father helped him obtain an Egyptian Antiquities Service inspectorship under Jacques de Morgan. Forced out on charges of being too friendly to the British, George Foucart taught at the universities of Bordeaux and Aix-en-Provence until 1915, when he leapt at a chance to vindicate himself by returning to Cairo as director of IFAO.[14]

France emerged from World War I victorious but shaken and insecure. In July 1918, four months before the armistice, the Quai d'Orsay organized the *Service des oeuvres françaises à l'étranger* to combat the anticipated resurgence of German cultural influence abroad and the continuing "Anglo-Saxon" challenge.[15] With finances strained, Foucart welcomed *Service des oeuvres* grants to IFAO to supplement ministry of public instruction funding.[16] Feeling isolated after the Franco–Belgian occupation of the German Ruhr in 1923 and the financial crisis of 1924, France turned to rely more on the League of Nations. In 1922 France had been instrumental in founding the International Committee on Intellectual Cooperation (ICIC)—"the forgotten UNESCO"—under the Organization of Intellectual Cooperation of the League of Nations. In 1926, France founded and funded the International Institute of Intellectual Cooperation (IIIC) as the executive of ICIC and provided it offices in Paris in the Palais Royale.[17]

Philosopher Henri Bergson initially chaired the ICIC, whose members included Marie Curie and Albert Einstein, the latter an acceptable German because of his pacifism. Except for the French, ICIC members acted more as independent intellectuals than as national representatives. Britain and the United States, often suspicious of state-sponsored culture, tended to dismiss ICIC as a tool of French propaganda and contributed nothing to its budget. Italy was the only major power other than France to help fund it. British classicist Gilbert Murray and American astronomer George Hale—a close friend of Breasted's[18]—were active in ICIC, and the Rockefeller Foundation helped fund it. ICIC's limitations reflected those of the League itself—lack of official US support, the late entry of Germany (1926) and the USSR (1934), and the secessions of Germany (1933) and Italy (1937).

Returning to Egypt in 1915, Foucart vowed that this time no one would be able to question his patriotism. It was he, rather than Lacau, who followed Maspero on the board of the private Egyptian University. In 1918 Foucart accepted the presidency of Egypt's Geographical Society (EGS); Lacau contented himself with the vice presidency.[19] Sultan Fuad (as already noted, king from 1922) revived the Geographical Society as an instrument of royal propaganda. The EGS published histories and collections of documents glorifying Fuad as an enlightened patron and worthy son of Khedive Ismail, grandson of Ibrahim Pasha, and great-grandson of Muhammad Ali.

IFAO's most notable post–World War I excavation was Bernard Bruyère's excavation at Deir al-Medina of the village and cemetery of New Kingdom royal tomb workers at Thebes. The Deir al-Medina concession was in a sense spoils of war, the Germans having held it until 1914. Except for an interval during World War II, Bruyère dug there from 1921 to 1951.[20]

Émile Chassinat (IFAO director, 1898–1912) had established IFAO's famous scholarly press in 1899. Chassinat had inherited M. Rochemonteix's project of publishing the vast temple of Horus at Edfu. Rochemonteix had died in 1891 at forty-two, just before the publication of the first volume. Chassinat's acrimonious ouster as IFAO director in 1912 (for failing to train French Egyptologists and his alleged role in selling papyri to American tycoon J.P. Morgan) left the Edfu project in limbo. After taking over IFAO in 1915, Foucart shared an interest with Lacau in enabling Chassinat to get the Edfu project back on track. The second Edfu volume came out in 1924. The project of the Epigraphic Survey of the University of Chicago's Oriental Institute to publish Ramesses III's Medinat Habu temple spurred the French to finish Edfu. National honor was at stake, pleaded Foucart, and Edfu volumes three through fourteen followed from 1928 to 1934. In any event, the OI did not finish its eight volumes on Ramesses III's Medinat Habu temple until 1970.[21]

Foucart and Lacau fell out. Calling on Prime Minister Ziwar in December 1924 to negotiate the resumption of work on Tutankhamun's tomb, Howard Carter was surprised to find Foucart on hand and eager to blame Lacau for the clash over the tomb.[22] Foucart also believed that Lacau's proposed restrictions on exporting antiquities betrayed French interests and would hamper acquisitions by the Louvre. The French minister to Egypt also wanted to join the Americans in demanding that foreign expeditions be guaranteed half of their finds.[23]

It was Foucart's failure as a courtier with King Fuad that finally did him in. Hosting the first postwar congress of the International Geographic Society in Cairo in 1925 should have been a triumph for Foucart as president of Egypt's Royal Geographic Society. A striking set of commemorative postage stamps celebrated the event. The ibis-headed scribal god of wisdom, Thoth (Djehouty), rendered Fuad's name in hieroglyphs in a royal cartouche (see fig. 22).[24] Foucart somehow angered the king, who denied him a postcongress decoration and deposed him as president of the Royal Geographic Society. The Gallophilic king even allowed a Briton to succeed Foucart. Clearly, IFAO would remain out of royal favor as long as Foucart headed it. In 1927, Pierre Jouguet succeeded Foucart as director of IFAO, and the organization returned to Fuad's good graces. Unable to regain favor with either the king or IFAO, Foucart stayed on sadly in Cairo, worked as a tour guide for Messageries maritimes, and died in Zamalek in 1943.[25]

Punishing the Germans for the War and Nefertiti

One thing on which Foucart and Lacau saw eye to eye was their reluctance to see Germans return to Egyptian archaeology after the war.[26] Toward the end of the war, Foucart exhorted some thirty IFAO-associated researchers to publish as a means of enhancing French scientific prestige vis-à-vis the Germans and Austrians. He and his successor as IFAO director, Pierre Jouguet, both favored awarding some fellowships to foreigners to enhance French prestige at German expense.

With Americans swelling Allied ranks on the western front in September 1918, Foucart proposed allocating them two IFAO fellowships. Later, IFAO gave fellowships to K.A.C. Creswell of Britain and Eugenio Griffini of Italy. Foucart was close to Belgian sugar magnate Henry Naus Bey (Sucreries d' Égypte) and Belgian Egyptologist Jean Capart; Capart's protégé Marcelle Werbrouck obtained an IFAO fellowship. In keeping with France's postwar search for allies among the new states on Germany's eastern flank, IFAO awarded Jaroslav Černý, a Czech, a fellowship, and made Kazimierz Michalowski of the University of Warsaw coexcavator with IFAO at Deir al-Medina. From neutral nations, Ernst Andersson (pseudonym of Ernst Akmar), a Swede, and Swiss Arabic epigrapher Max van Berchem also held IFAO fellowships.[27]

In 1920 the Swedish consul general looking after the German Institute in Zamalek forwarded to British authorities a petition that it be desequestered.[28] Ludwig Borchardt claimed that the institute's premises were his private property, not that of the German government. Lacau and his British subordinate Cecil Firth, both war veterans, opposed letting Borchardt return, especially if he were again to combine diplomatic status with direction of the German Institute.[29] Firth offered to live in the sequestered residence if the Swedish consul moved out.[30] In the summer of 1921, the British were on the brink of selling Borchardt's two Zamalek villas and archaeological library. Reisner, who had studied in Berlin and worked with Borchardt on the Egyptian Museum's catalogue commission, objected. He conceded that Borchardt's "manners made him many enemies in Egypt," but emphasized that "they did not lessen his services to Egyptology."[31] Twelve Swiss scholars also signed a petition on Borchardt's behalf.[32]

Meanwhile, in 1920, over two years before the dispute over the bust of Nefertiti exploded, the award of a concession to Britain's EES to excavate at Tell al-Amarna roiled relations between German Egyptologists on one side and the French and British on the other. Borchardt had excavated there until 1914 and hoped to resume after the war. Learning of EES plans through a newspaper article, Adolf Erman wrote Alan Gardiner, his erstwhile student who had collaborated for years on the Berlin Egyptian dictionary project, denouncing EES intentions as "robbery." He hoped Gardiner would champion the Germans' moral right to the site, but Gardiner replied:

> Do you really imagine that the French Director of the Service of Antiquities, who has seen one sixth of his country overrun and devastated by the German armies would willingly countenance the resumption of German excavations in Egypt, so long as he could possibly prevent it? And do you think it likely that the British who stood shoulder to shoulder with the French in defending Egypt against Turkish and German invaders, would be disposed in this matter to adopt the German point of view in preference to the French?[33]

Erman wrote back emphasizing Germany's suffering under the "hunger blockade" imposed by the Allies. However, he and Gardiner then moved to patch up relations on the basis of old friendship and scholarly collaboration. Thomas Gertzen notes that not only postwar nationalistic bitterness contributed to the quarrel; it also reflected the increasing independence of "the Anglo-Saxon branch of Berlin School Egyptology." Since 1914, Britain had had its own specialized *Journal of Egyptian Antiquities*, and Gardiner was beginning to write his own grammar of Egyptian.[34]

Germany and Egypt restored consular relations in 1921, and after Egypt was declared independent in 1922, the German consulate was upgraded to a legation.[35] In May 1923, High Commissioner Allenby informed Whitehall that excluding Germans, Austrians, and Bulgarians could no longer be justified and requested that Borchardt be readmitted.[36] Borchardt reached Cairo at the end of October 1923 and reopened the Institute in 1924. The French consul general worried lest Germany try to reclaim the Deir al-Medina concession, where Bruyère was now digging for IFAO.[37] No one was more surprised than Borchardt when Lacau not only received him correctly in November 1923 but even allowed him several small surveys and excavations despite the general ban on excavations by German institutions involved in the Nefertiti affair.

Young French Antiquities Service inspector Gustave Lefebvre had made the still-disputed on-site division of the finds at Tell al-Amarna back in January 1913. The bust of the queen was already packed and perhaps in dim light, and Lefebvre may have been misled by a cropped photo. Lefebvre had already agreed that plaster objects could go to Berlin. Borchardt's inventory listed merely a "plaster bust of a princess of the royal family"; it was actually limestone with a layer of plaster. In Berlin, the Kaiser viewed the bust privately in 1913 in the home of DOG treasurer James Simon, whose financing of the dig made him owner of the German share. In 1920 Simon presented the bust to Berlin's Egyptian Museum.[38]

For a decade after shipping the bust home in 1913, Borchardt feared lest its display and publication stir up trouble in Egypt for German archaeologists. Erman's successor as director of Berlin's Egyptian Museum, Heinrich Schäfer, had no such qualms and put the bust on display early in 1923. The reaction was swift; already on February 22, 1923, the EES, which had taken over the German concession at Tell al-Amarna, alluded to the bust in a fundraising appeal in *The Times*:

> Those of your readers who are impressed by the magnitude of the splendour of the discovery at Thebes [the tomb of Tutankhamun] and by the beauty of the German finds at Amarna, are asked to help in discovering similar treasures, if it be possible, for our national and local museums in Britain and America.[39]

In Cairo, Lacau grilled his assistant, Gustave Lefebvre, who denied any clear memory of having seen the bust when making the division of finds with Borchardt in 1913. Conceding from the beginning that Lefebvre had made a mistake in allowing the export of the bust, Lacau made his case for its return to Egypt on moral rather than legal grounds. Demanding its return, Egypt refused to authorize excavations by Borchardt, the German Archaeological Institute, the DOG, or the Berlin Museum until 1929. (The above-mentioned small operations which Lacau allowed Borchardt were a surprising minor exception). In a tally of expeditions in the field for the 1926–27 season, Foucart did not mention Germany: there were six from the United States, five each from Great Britain and France, two from the Antiquities Service, and one each from Austria and the Archaeological Society of Alexandria.[40] Borchardt obtained private funds to rebuild the German House at Qurna, but for the most part he had no choice but to concentrate on preparing for publication works based on his prewar fieldwork.

In Egyptology and other fields, it took about a decade to paper over the rift the war had torn in scholarly internationalism. A month after the Treaty of Versailles in June 1919, the Allies excluded Germans from the International Research Council (IRC) founded in Brussels. The French and the Belgians were particularly intransigent.

German and Austrian representation at the Eleventh International Geographical Congress, which Egypt's Royal Geographical Society hosted for the International Geographical Union in 1925, became controversial. Egypt's initial invitations in June 1922 had included

Germans and Austrians. The secretary of Britain's Royal Geographic Society was outraged that "our enemies" might attend: "It would be impossible to associate peacefully with a people who behaved as the Germans did. . .. we have nothing to do with pigs."[41] Joining the International Research Council that summer obliged Egypt to observe the Council's boycott. Germans and Austrians were excluded from subsequent invitations to the Cairo congress and did not attend.

That same year, however, the tide began to turn against the boycott.[42] The Locarno Conference of October 1925 and ensuing treaties cleared the way for Germany to join the League of Nations in 1926. In 1925, 47 percent of international scholarly meetings excluded Germans; by 1929 the figure had fallen to 15 percent.[43] At the League of Nations' International Committee on Intellectual Cooperation (ICIC), Briton Gilbert Murray urged the French to engage with liberals from the Weimar Republic. The International Research Council repealed its German exclusion policy in 1926 and in 1931 further distanced itself from its exclusionist past by changing its name to the International Council of Scientific Unions (ICSU). Germans participated in the International Congress of Orientalists convened at Oxford in 1928, the first since the war.[44]

Albert Einstein obtained a seat on the ICIC as early as 1922. As a pacifist and a Jew, he was atypical of Germany's professorial elite. In "the spirit of Locarno," German scholars joined in ICIC activities after 1925, but the IRC boycott had so angered Germans that they counterboycotted it even after it had relented and changed its name to ICSU.[45] Tragically, the ending of Allied scholarly boycotts barely preceded the new confrontations after Hitler's rise to power in 1933.

Like his Berlin-educated compatriot Reisner, Breasted reached out to German colleagues soon after the war. Financial chaos in Germany prevented the publication of Erman's Berlin dictionary of Egyptian until Breasted persuaded John D. Rockefeller Jr. to come to the rescue. In his memoirs, Erman gave an ironic nod to this "enemy" funding. Until the war ruptured ties and "sent our best youths to die," he wrote, the project had had two contributors each from the United States, Britain, and Denmark, and one each from France, Ireland, and Sweden.[46] In 1926, Adolf Erman and Kurt Sethe protested the exclusion of Germans from the international board of the proposed new Rockefeller Cairo museum in 1926. Breasted replied that French and British opinion had left him no choice.[47] In any case, Egyptian nationalist opposition sank the project in April 1926. By the time Breasted was toying with reviving the proposal the following year, he thought Franco–German rapprochement had perhaps progressed enough to add Germans to the board.

As late as April 1929, British war veteran Cecil Firth refused to represent the Egyptian Antiquities Service at the Berlin centennial of the German Archaeological Institute of Rome: "I don't like Germans." Henri Gauthier and assistant curator Mahmud Hamza represented Egypt instead. Both presented papers. None of the foreign societies congratulating Berlin on this occasion were French.[48]

In May 1929 King Fuad made a state visit to Germany with the intention of normalizing Egyptian–German relations. The German art world held its breath for fear of losing the bust of Nefertiti.[49] A German cartoon entitled "You wish!" showed the portly monarch beckoning to the bust of Nefertiti in the Berlin Museum. King Fuad: "Come back to Egypt with me, beautiful Nefertiti, and I'll make you my favorite wife in the harem!" Nefertiti: "Out of the question, my little Fuad, I'm better off in Berlin in a glass case than in Cairo as make-believe queen by England's grace and favor!" (see fig. 22)[50]

In fact, Fuad never raised the issue with his Berlin hosts. Once his visit had been successfully accomplished, Egypt proposed that Berlin return Nefertiti in exchange for two statues from the Cairo museum. Heinrich Schäfer, director of Berlin's Egyptian Museum, and the bust's original owner, James Simon, were amenable, and in October Pierre Lacau visited Berlin and obtained the consent of the Prussian minister of culture. By May 1930, Lacau and Schäfer had agreed that in exchange for the return of the bust of Nefertiti, Berlin would receive an Old Kingdom statue of the priest Ranefer and a New Kingdom statue of Amenhotep son of Hapu. Borchardt, however, also went to Berlin, "where this 'prussian,'—if he had not been a Jew, he would have certainly been a militant nazi— still had influential friends."[51] He lobbied against the deal, and there was a storm in the press. Germany and Egypt both changed governments in the spring of 1930, and the Germans backed away from the deal. When Chancellor Hitler's Nazi ministers revived the idea of returning the bust in 1933–34, he angrily vetoed the overture: "What the German people have, they keep."[52] Hitler dreamed of a new Egyptian Museum starring Nefertiti alone under a central dome; this would be part of a new museum complex when he transformed Berlin into Germania, capital of Europe or the world.[53]

The Nefertiti dispute remains unresolved to this day, but Borchardt's retirement in 1928 and the succession in 1929 of Hermann Junker as head of a reorganized German Archaeological Institute—Cairo Department (DAI) ended the ban on German excavations in Egypt. The commemorative volumes for the seventy-fifth and 100th anniversaries (1982 and 2007) of the Institute assume the continuity of the similarly

22 Nefertiti stays in Berlin. a: On a visit to Berlin in 1929, King Fuad implores Nefertiti: "Come back to Egypt with me, beautiful Nefertiti, and I'll make you my favorite wife in the harem!" Nefertiti: "Out of the question, my little Fuad, I'm better off in Berlin in a glass case than in Cairo as make-believe queen by England's grace and favor!" *Cartoon in* Kladderadatsch, *undated clipping in Swiss Institute for Egyptian Architecture and Archaeology, Cairo.* b: "The Queen Neferet-Iti will remain a prisoner. Thus decides Hitler, who, declaring he has fallen in love, obstinately refuses to return her to Egypt." La bourse égyptienne, March 31, 1934. a and b *Trümpler, ed.,* Das Grosse Spiel, *303, 305. Courtesy of the Swiss Institute of Architectural and Archaeological Research on Ancient Egypt in Cairo.*

named institutes but skate over Borchardt's unhappy retirement. Susanne Voss has explored Borchardt's disagreements with Georg Steindorff, Heinrich Schäfer, and others over the organization of the German Institute in Cairo and Borchardt's failure to secure a successor who would continue his own strong emphasis on architectural research.[54]

Although Borchardt was Jewish and Hermann Junker (1877–1962) a German-born Catholic and an ordained priest, their careers had some remarkable similarities. Both earned PhDs under Adolf Erman at Berlin, contributed to his Berlin Egyptian dictionary, began their fieldwork at Philae, excelled at excavation, were offered posts at the University of Vienna, and directed the German Archaeological Institute in Cairo. Borchardt surveyed the temples of Philae ahead of flooding by the Aswan Dam, and Junker surveyed them a few years later before the initial heightening of the dam. (Longevity and persistence across two world wars enabled Junker eventually to publish his study of the inscriptions on the first pylon of the Philae Temple of Isis in 1958, when he was eighty.) Borchardt's declining an offer from the University of Vienna in order to found the German Institute in Egypt presumably cleared Junker's way to take up the Vienna post a year later.[55]

Junker excavated several Nubian sites for the Vienna Academy of Science, then from 1912 to 1914 excavated and recorded mastaba tombs of courtiers beside Khufu's Great Pyramid at Giza. After the war, truncated Austria seemed harmless and was admitted to the League of Nations in 1920, five years ahead of Germany. Austria and Junker had no Nefertiti problem, and in 1925 he resumed work at Giza under the auspices of the Austrian Academy of Science. The Academy also sponsored his survey of prehistoric sites in the western Delta. He selected Merimde for intensive work. Junker's ambitious excavation and publication plans, however, outran meager Austrian resources, and in 1929 he seized the chance to revert to German colors as director of the DAI. Chapter 8 takes up his critical role in Egyptology in Egypt in the 1930s as well as the other side of the coin—Borchardt's tragic displacement in Cairo as a German Jew after the rise of Hitler.

American Excavators: George Reisner and Herbert Winlock

With six expeditions working in Egypt during the 1926–27 season, Americans were far out in front in Foucart's aforementioned tally, with Britain and France a distant tie for second at two each. This American prominence clashed with the image of interwar isolationism, which kept the United States out of the League of Nations and delayed the creation of a division of cultural relations in the State Department until 1938. However, "as though to protest Congress's rejection of the League, the US intellectual world struck out on its own."[56] James Goode has shown that American archaeological expeditions did benefit at times from diplomatic support, but it was the convergence of enterprising northeastern and midwestern museums and universities, millionaire philanthropy, and public fascination with the pharaohs that thrust American fieldwork in Egypt to the fore before and after World War I.[57] Most of the institutions and directors are familiar from before the war: Lythgoe and Winlock of the MMA, Reisner of Harvard–Boston MFA, Breasted of the University of Chicago, and Fisher of the University of Pennsylvania.[58] Chicago's Oriental Institute now greatly magnified Breasted's work. The University of Michigan expedition, an interwar newcomer, is taken up in chapter 8.

John A. Wilson, Breasted's eventual successor at the University of Chicago, would eventually dedicate his history of American Egyptology to the memory of three great founders of the discipline: his mentor Breasted, George Reisner, and Herbert Winlock.[59] After sustaining limited fieldwork through much of the war, the Harvard–Boston and Metropolitan expeditions were well placed to pick up the pace once the war was over. Reisner calculated that the Met's access to the huge wealth of New York City gave its expedition two to three times the financial resources of his Boston-based operation. He kept his expenses down by training Egyptians for photography and other tasks usually reserved for expensive "European" staff.[60] Writing home in 1919, he described his austere routine at Harvard Camp, Giza. He worked eight to nine hours a day seven days a week, rode for an hour every other day, and counted yearly trips to work in Nubia as his only vacations. Though he had not been home since 1912, he pleaded that Harvard's President Eliot not interrupt his productive routine: "I confess that I dread going back to live within the four walls of a house, and still more to face the New England winters."[61]

Reisner quickly came to resent living in the publicity shadow of Howard Carter and Tutankhamun's tomb. He dismissed Carter as an ill-trained, unscientific amateur. Excavating a deep shaft at Giza in 1925, Reisner's team discovered impressive funerary furniture in the secondary tomb of Queen Hetepheres, the mother of Great Pyramid builder Khufu. The blurb for one of Reisner's articles reveals his longing to alter the balance of popular perception:

> The patient twenty years of labor by the Boston–Harvard Expedition in Egypt, headed by Dr. Reisner, have been recently rewarded with the discovery of a tomb of the Fourth Dynasty, whose importance completely overshadows the Eighteenth Dynasty tomb of Tutankhamen.[62]

Tutankhamun, however, remains a household word; Hetepheres does not. In January 1920, Winlock returned to the Metropolitan House's work at Deir al-Bahari after five years away. Lythgoe, the Met's curator of Egyptian art until Winlock succeeded him in 1929, left field direction to his subordinate. Winlock's prewar work near Hatshepsut's and Mentuhotep II's Deir al-Bahari monuments had already helped clarify the history of the Theban Eleventh Dynasty, which brought the First Intermediate Period to an end, reunited the country, and launched the Middle Kingdom. In the 1920s, Winlock uncovered much more, both in museum prizes for Cairo and New York, and in knowledge. The ex-soldier "liked to wear his military leggings and campaign hat, which seemed to give him added authority."[63] Once he ran through the sugarcane fields to catch robbers who had hijacked his payroll. Winlock's imaginative stories based on archaeological findings brought ancient Egypt alive for the public. However, his concentration on cemeteries, massive clearing of debris with hundreds of diggers, and ruler-centered history have become less fashionable among scholars today.[64]

In contrast to the Metropolitan House and Chicago House at Luxor, Reisner's Harvard Camp west of the Great Pyramid at Giza seemed modest, temporary, and utilitarian. Urging Western archaeologists to keep the lowest possible political profile, he deplored public protests and diplomatic pressure on such matters as divisions of finds and Tutankhamun's tomb:

> The foolish conduct of Mr. Carter during the last year, the very reprehensible contract made with the "Times," and the manner in which Breasted, Lythgoe, Gardiner, and Newberry identified themselves with Carter and his acts,—all this has aroused a bitter feeling against archaeologists in Egypt. . . .
>
> We have kept ourselves absolutely clear of all connection with Carnarvon, Carter and the Tomb. I have never accepted Mr. Carter or Carnarvon as a scientific colleague nor admitted that either of them came within the categories of persons worthy of receiving excavation permits from the Egypt. Government.[65]

Reisner believed that as in Italy and Greece, and recently Turkey, foreign excavators in Egypt would not be allowed for much longer to take museum pieces home and should emphasize digging for knowledge. His solicitude for the welfare of his Egyptian workers was not unprecedented, but his training Egyptians as photographers and record keepers was unique in its day.

Academic Empire: James Henry Breasted, John D. Rockefeller Jr., and the Oriental Institute

In May 1919, James Henry Breasted's dream came true when John D. Rockefeller Jr. unexpectedly agreed to fund what became the University of Chicago's Oriental Institute. Three months later, Breasted made a sweeping reconnaissance through Egypt, Palestine, Iraq, and Syria searching for sites where his "laboratory for the study of the rise and development of civilization"[66] could work. A dozen years later, he could proudly survey an OI archaeological empire with ongoing expeditions spread through six countries of the Middle East.[67] (see fig. 23)

The OI had followed in the train of the British and French empires through the former Ottoman lands of Egypt, Palestine, Syria, and Iraq and spilled over the Taurus and Zagros mountains into the old-new countries of Turkey and Iran. Indeed, Breasted's OI empire had a foothold in almost every country where the Persian Achaemenid Empire

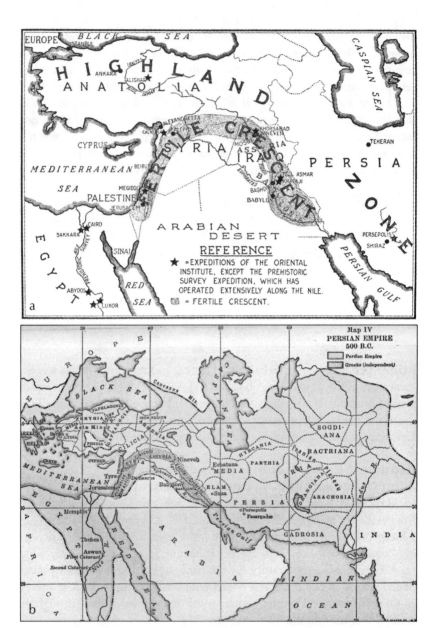

23 Breasted's empires. a: Map of Oriental Institute expeditions in the field, ca. 1931 (marked with stars). b: Breasted's map of the Persian Empire of the Achaemenids (500 BCE). Like the Achaemenids, the OI's archaeological empire stretched from Iran and Anatolia through Mesopotamia, Syria, Palestine, and Egypt. *a: Abt,* American Egyptologist, *355. Courtesy of the Oriental Institute, University of Chicago; b: Breasted,* Ancient Times, *Map IV.*

of Cambyses, Darius, and Xerxes—as mapped in Breasted's popular high school textbook *Ancient Times: A History of the Early World*—had once held sway.[68]

Ancient Times anchored the first part of the paradigm of Western Civilization which emerged in the 1920s as a mainstay of American liberal arts education and reigned with little challenge until the 1960s. Published in 1916, Breasted's *Ancient Times* and its companion volume on medieval and modern Europe by James Harvey Robinson reflected the world view expressed twenty years earlier in 1896 in Edwin Blashfield's painting *Evolution of Civilization* in the dome of the Library of Congress (see fig. 24).[69]

As already noted, the painting began with ancient Egypt and culminated in contemporary America. Its chronological-thematic-geographical progression runs as follows: Egypt (Written Records), Judaea (Religion), Greece (Philosophy), Rome (Administration), Islam (Physics), the Middle Ages (Modern Languages), Italy (Fine Arts), Germany (Art of Printing), Spain (Discovery), England (Literature), France (Emancipation), and America (Science). Except for Blashfield's omission of Mesopotamia, his first four phases match well the framework of Breasted's *Ancient Times*.

Two symbol-laden monuments and a third unbuilt one further reveal the sweep of Breasted's imperial dreams. The Oriental Institute in Chicago and its Chicago House in Luxor were architectural landmarks from their openings in 1931, while the unbuilt Rockefeller museum for Cairo points up the political blind spot in Breasted's scholarly vision. The Epigraphic Survey of the OI spent seven years in the 'old Chicago House' on the west bank of the Nile before moving to the new Chicago House across the river in Luxor in 1931. The "relative luxury" of even the temporary old Chicago House had probably been inspired by Breasted's visit to IFAO's premises in Cairo.[70]

Breasted's student Harold Nelson (1878–1954) was field director of the Survey from 1924 to 1947.[71] The Survey expressed Breasted's deep conviction that recording perishable inscriptions and scenes was far more urgent than excavation. He chose Ramesses III's Twentieth Dynasty temple at Medinat Habu, the most complete surviving mortuary temple of the pharaohs buried in the Valley of the Kings. Since later pharaohs quarried predecessors' monuments for building materials, the remains of Eighteenth and Nineteenth Dynasty mortuary temples are scanter. Ramesses III's weaker Third Intermediate Period successors did not build on so grand a scale at Thebes, so his temple survived largely intact.

Combining photography with meticulous on-the-spot collation by philologists, the Epigraphic Survey set new standards of epigraphic accuracy.[72] German architect and archaeologist Uvo Hölscher

24 Edwin Blashfield, *Evolution of Civilization,*1896, in the collar of the dome of the Thomas Jefferson Building, Library of Congress, Washington DC. Its vision of the progress of (Western) civilization (only partly shown here and in figure 10) runs: Egypt (Written Records), Judaea (Religion), Greece (Philosophy), Rome (Administration), Islam (Physics), the Middle Ages (Modern Languages), Italy (Fine Arts), Germany (Art of Printing), Spain (Discovery), England (Literature), France (Emancipation), and America (Science). This progression closely resembles that in Breasted's textbook *Ancient Times* (1916) and its companion volume by James Harvey Robinson covering medieval and modern European history. *Photo: Carol Highsmith, Library of Congress, public domain.*

(1878–1963) did an architectural survey of the temple to complement the epigraphic survey. Breasted sounded almost apologetic that excavations were necessary to complete the epigraphic and architectural surveys:

> The excavation of ancient buildings long ago ceased to be a search for museum treasures which might be brought home for the gratification of museum trustees and an interested public or for sensational exploitation in the daily press. The primary purpose of excavation is to discover every possible bit or fragment of evidence and . . . to record and publish it as a part of the assets available to science for all future time. Museum pieces are, of course, welcome, and they were not lacking in the course of this clearance; but they formed an incident, not the main object, of the work.[73]

Nevertheless, Breasted was pleased when Lacau—with whom he often crossed swords—awarded the OI an impressive monumental statue of

25 Imperial archaeology: The Oriental Institute's Chicago House, Luxor, completed 1931. Photo by James Henry Breasted Jr., 1933. *Wilson, Signs and Wonders, Plate 29b.* Courtesy of the Oriental Institute, University of Chicago.

Tutankhamun for its museum in Chicago.

Breasted wrote of Ramesses III's temple at Medinat Habu: "As architecture it proclaims in no uncertain terms the age of imperial conquest."[74] He might almost have been thinking of the Rockefeller museum he tried to build in Cairo or, on a lesser scale, the Chicago House he did realize in Luxor. In 1929, Breasted shepherded John D. Rockefeller Jr. on a tour of Egypt, Palestine, and Syria.[75] Rockefeller's ensuing gift financed the construction of the Chicago House at Luxor and the new OI headquarters in Chicago even as the Great Depression closed in.

The new Chicago House at Luxor cast even J.P. Morgan's Metropolitan House at Deir al-Bahari into the shade (see fig. 25).

Its low "California–Spanish style" buildings did not loom over the landscape like Ramesses III's temple but were a striking monumental statement at a time of global depression and ostensible American isolationism. The 3.5-acre complex occupied a prime Nile-side site between the temples of Luxor and Karnak. It had ample living quarters, photographic darkrooms and other workrooms, the best archaeological library south of Cairo, and beautiful gardens. Expropriation of a strip to expand the Corniche leading to Karnak soon diminished its effect, however.[76]

26 Ancient Egypt's gift of writing to modern Western man. Tympanum relief over the entrance to the Oriental Institute, University of Chicago. Conceived by Breasted and sculpted by Ulric Ellerhusen, ca. 1931. *Courtesy of the Oriental Institute, University of Chicago.*

At the turn of the twenty-first century, widening the Corniche for mass tourism cost Chicago House the rest of its front lawn, and a new wall hid the still flourishing center from passersby.

The OI's Chicago headquarters—offices, laboratories, lecture hall, classrooms, library, and museum—were also completed in 1931.[77] Breasted commissioned a bas-relief over the entrance to express his vision of "East Teaching West" (see fig. 26).

The name 'Oriental Institute' itself took for granted the great dichotomy of East and West, a concept so firmly rooted that even the storms following the publication of Edward Said's *Orientalism* half a century later failed to alter the institution's proud name. The relief captured Breasted's twin vision of an Egyptian-led ancient East and a progressive West culminating in modern America, with the two streams of civilization interacting to the benefit of both. Akhenaten's Aten sundisk beams down the blessing of life, symbolized by the ankh, on both worlds. A scribe from a Fifth Dynasty relief passes the gift of writing to a classically fashioned, white Western man. A lion modeled on those of Amenhotep III's temple of Soleb in Nubia is balanced by an American bison. The Giza Pyramids and Sphinx, a capital from the Temple of Sahure, and the Achaemenid palace at Persepolis balance the West's Parthenon, Cathedral of Notre Dame, and skyscraping Nebraska State Capitol.[78]

For the East, Djoser—of Step Pyramid fame—and empire-builder Thutmose III join Babylonian lawgiver Hammurabi, Assyrian Assurnasipal, and Chosroes of Sassanid Persia. The scene epitomizes the OI's geographical and chronological domain—the pre-Islamic history of Egypt, the Fertile Crescent, and Iran. The Western heroes are Herodotus, Alexander, Augustus, a crusader, a field archaeologist, and a museum archaeologist with a lens. The latter—perhaps a philologist like Breasted—has the power to make the ancient East live again. The relief sums up the powerful paradigm of Western Civilization which Breasted's textbook *Ancient Times* helped define and canonize. In keeping with racial theories of his day, Breasted's text folded the inhabitants of ancient Egypt and the Near East (despite their darker skins) into "the Great White Race." He credited the Great White Race with the rise of civilization, and saw

the eventual triumph of Greece and Rome in the Near East as evidence that the Indo-European branch of the white race triumphed over the southern Semitic branch—"the complete triumph of *our* ancestors."[79]

The Western-civilization paradigm held sway in American liberal education largely unchallenged until the 1960s, and it retains its grip on many minds today.

The Hebrews, whose Bible had started Breasted on his intellectual–spiritual pilgrimage, are notably absent from the OI tympanum relief, and the institution's Anatolian reach is not represented. Eighty years on, other absences cry out as well: this Orient of the Achaemenids and Alexander does not stretch beyond the Indus, the Muslim enemy who called forth the crusader is off stage, no Native American human accompanies the bison, and Africans and women are nowhere to be seen. The relief admirably captures Breasted's worldview of Western civilization originating in ancient Egypt and the Near East and progressing northward and westward to Europe and on to its culmination in the contemporary United States.

Imperial Overreach: Breasted and a Rockefeller Museum for Cairo

Constructing the OI's Chicago headquarters and expedition house at Luxor was simple compared to Breasted's attempt in 1926 to plant a magnificent Western-controlled antiquities museum in the heart of Cairo. Nothing about the undertaking was modest; Breasted boasted to King Fuad that it would be "the finest modern monument in Egypt."[80]

Sailing home in 1924 after failing as a mediator in Carter's dispute with the Antiquities Service, Breasted cast about for ways to reassert the

Western control over Egyptian archaeology that seemed to be slipping away, and to give it an American twist. He had shown George E. Vincent, president of the Rockefeller Foundation, the inadequacies of Cairo's Egyptian Museum. The building was only twenty-two years old, but the roof leaked, basement storerooms flooded, and it was already overstuffed. Adding Tutankhamun's treasures was about to tax its capacity even further.

In October 1925, John D. Rockefeller Jr. approved Breasted's proposal for a $10 million Cairo antiquities museum and research institute—$5.2 million for construction and $4.6 million for an operating endowment. A three-man American board under Breasted would oversee construction and installation. An Egyptian Archaeology Foundation to manage the endowment would have two members each from the United States, Britain, and France, and possibly two from another country or countries to be added later. (He was hoping to bring the Germans in.) An International Museum Commission to run the museum would include the board of the Foundation, Egypt's minister of public works, and the director general of Antiquities. Should the latter not be Egyptian (as currently with Lacau), Egypt's minister of education would take his place. After thirty-three years, the museum would revert to Egyptian control, but through the Foundation, Westerners would control a linked Institute of Archaeological Research for at least fifty years.

Breasted's dedication to Egyptology expressed both personal and national ambitions. The Rockefeller pledges which had created the OI had initially ruled out funds for a headquarters or endowment. If the Cairo museum could be realized, the future of both the OI and its director, Breasted, would be assured. He would chair the American board overseeing construction in Cairo and have a seat on the Foundation. (The National Academy of Science was to fill one seat on the Foundation, and Breasted was the only Egyptologist who belonged to the Academy.) And as director of the OI, he would also direct the Institute of Archaeological Research in Cairo.

Two scarcely concealed goals were to end French domination of the Antiquities Service and to delay an Egyptian takeover as long as possible. Breasted believed an Anglo–American alliance could accomplish both. Moving to secure his American base first, he could count on Lythgoe at the Metropolitan Museum; Breasted had worked with Met staff on Carter's Tutankhamun team and the Met was to nominate the second American to the proposed Cairo Foundation. Secretary of State Kellogg promised Breasted diplomatic support as needed.[81]

Crossing the Atlantic next, Breasted won support from Alan Gardiner (with whom he was copublishing Middle Kingdom coffin texts); director

of the British Museum Sir Frederick Kenyon; and head of the British
Academy Lord Balfour. At the Foreign Office's Egyptian desk, John Mur-
ray was encouraging, and High Commissioner Allenby expressed interest.
Murray confided to George Lloyd, Allenby's successor-designate, that
Breasted was "anxious to establish on the Board of Trustees an Anglo-
Saxon block of four, which would in effect constitute the majority."[82]
Breasted laid out to Foreign Secretary Austen Chamberlain his hope for

> Anglo–American co-operation in our Museum project. The control of
> Palestine and Mesopotamia, with its great ancient cities of Jerusalem,
> Babylon, and Ninevah, which have been recovered from Mohammedan
> rule, as they have been, by a great Christian nation:- all this, together
> with the extraordinary discovery of the tomb of Tutenkhamon, [h]
> as aroused universal interest, - caught the imagination of all civilized
> people, and centered their thoughts on the ancient Bible Lands where
> civilization was born. I urged that, just at this juncture, a combination
> of British influence and American resources in these ancient lands in
> its published results, would work far-reaching consequences among all
> English speaking peoples, and prove most effective in bringing together
> England and America.[83]

To Breasted's relief, the Foreign Office recommended keeping Lacau and
the French government in the dark until King Fuad was on board.[84] Britain's decision to postpone indefinitely its evacuation of the Qasr al-Nil
barracks—his preferred museum site—was disappointing, but Rockefeller agreed to southern Gezira, across the Qasr al-Nil Bridge, instead.
(Three decades later, it would be the American-operated Nile Hilton and
the Arab League headquarters instead that would inherit the site of the
British-occupied Qasr al-Nil barracks.)

In January 1926 Breasted laid the project before King Fuad at Abdin
Palace:

> The earliest of its [Egypt's] venerable monuments were erected at a time
> when all Europe was still shrouded in darkness and savagery . . . [and]
> modern peoples must regard Ancient Egypt as their cultural ancestor, to
> whom they naturally look back with gratitude and veneration. . . . .
> It may be of interest to your Majesty to know that a little over thirty years
> ago there was not a single teacher of the Ancient Egyptian language in any
> American university. We in America, like you in Egypt, are politically a
> very young nation; and culturally too, the higher development of America
> has been very recent. . . .

The period of thirty years is suggested because . . . America has itself required a period of about thirty years to develop a generation of Egyptologists capable of representing the American nation in the world of science.[85]

He presented to the king a printed brochure with plans drafted by Rockefeller architect Welles Bosworth (see fig. 27). The museum would face the Nile, like the Temple of Amun at Karnak. Unlike its Beaux Arts neoclassical predecessor of 1902, its façade would have a pharaonic aspect—fifteen-meter columns of Aswan granite. An inscription in Arabic, English, and French—not the imperial Latin of the old museum—would proclaim: "Erected in the Reign of His Majesty King Fuad I." A painting in the brochure imagined dignitaries arriving for opening day by regatta on the Nile. Breasted felt sure to

intoxicate the King and give him such a pipe-dream of the Arabian Nights . . . that we shall be able to stampede him and his whole group into it. . . . When he says the word [the brochure will be sent] to all the leading people and institutions of the world! If that doesn't get a vain and self-conscious Oriental, nothing else will.[86]

To Breasted's dismay, the king barely glanced at the brochure and launched a tirade about American meddling and the impracticality and underfunding of the project. The scheme had been in the making for months without Fuad or any Egyptian ever being consulted. At the very moment Egypt was bursting with hopes for full independence, the plan would lock the Antiquities Service into another thirty years of Western control. Regaining his composure, however, Fuad agreed to forward the project to the Ziwar cabinet to consider. The government's legal department requested changes, which Breasted forwarded for Rockefeller's consideration.

Breasted had also alienated two important compatriots. He dismissed American minister Morton Howell, who according to protocol had to present him to King Fuad, as a "pompous and stupid old country doctor, from Ohio, a small town product," and kept him in the dark as long as possible.[87] Breasted even fancied that President Coolidge might choose him to replace Howell.[88] Shutting out George Reisner was a bigger mistake. Getting wind of the project in February, Reisner spilled the news to Lacau, the French minister, and the press. "There was without any doubt a conspiracy of Breasted, Lythgoe, Gardiner and others to 'down Lacau,'" wrote Reisner, and make Breasted "dictator of antiquities."[89] Breasted clumsily lobbied for the Museum of Fine Arts to rebuke Reisner, their employee. He accused Reisner of "doing all in his power to undermine western influence," "from obviously very petty motives," in "publicly opposing a plan so magnificently endowed

27 Dazzling an Oriental monarch? Imagining inauguration day for the new Rockefeller/Breasted museum proposed for Cairo in 1926. "Suggested Treatment of Water Approach to the New Cairo Museum Buildings Seen from Mid-Nile as They Might Appear at Ceremonial Dedication." Drawing by William Walcot from designs by Welles Bosworth in a booklet for a proposed Rockefeller-funded museum in Cairo, presented to King Fuad by James Henry Breasted, in January 1926. *Courtesy of the Rockefeller Archive Center.*

by the generosity of a great American and one so valuable for science."[90]

In *al-Ahram*, nationalist lawyer Muhammad Lutfi Juma denounced this proposal

> to form a league of nations that would dispose of the antiquities . . . as if Egypt were a minor or a person who has attained his majority but is restrained from carrying on his own business owing to extravagance or stupidity or incapability of keeping this great wealth inherited from the forefathers. . . .
>
> If this Haroun [al-Rashid, fabled caliph of the Arabian Nights, i.e., Rockefeller] or any other thinks that by means of his money he can buy the Pyramids or Pharaoh's obelisk, as it is possible to buy anything in his country, then let me state, by virtue of my being the humblest heir of my forefathers, that I totally refuse to sell my share.[91]

British support came unraveled. One of Lord Lloyd's staff described his superior's attitude as one of "malevolent neutrality."[92] Foreign Secretary Austen Chamberlain wrote:

> it is strongly felt among a number of archaeologists here that the Lythgoe–Breasted clique are working to "down" Lacau and that the Rockefeller Museaum [sic] scheme and the modification of the Archaeological research permit proposal are a means to that end. . . . Moreover Breasted, with our knowledge rather went behind the back of the French Legation in the matter of the Rockefeller Museum.[93]

Breasted confided the scheme to Briton Cecil Firth of the Antiquities Service, who replied:

> I am quite convinced that the only straightforward course is to take M. Lacau into your confidence at the earliest possible moment, or, failing that, publish openly what you propose to do. This secrecy sounds a little like intrigue against a Government Department and will certainly be so interpreted in some quarters. . . .
>
> Put yourself in M. Lacau's position and try to realize what would be your feelings if a Frenchman came along backed by a huge sum of money and at a stroke proposed to sweep aside the work built up from small beginnings during more than half a century by a series of America[n] Directors General![94]

Breasted angered Firth by swearing him to secrecy, then spilling Firth's views to the British Residency. Firth warned that the project might look like an attempt to obtain antiquities for Europe and America, have its International Foundation take over divisions of finds, and obtain a quarter each of Tutankhamun's treasures for London and the Metropolitan.[95] Breasted suggested that Firth could win an attractive post in the new order, then thought better of sending the letter.[96]

When the story broke in February 1926, Lacau correctly perceived an assault on French dominance of the Antiquities Service, warned it would unleash American and German meddling, and lobbied King Fuad against it.[97] The French Legation stayed neutral, however, and Georges Bénédite of the Louvre even backed Breasted. Bénédite assumed that French control of the Antiquities Service would end in 1927 and that Breasted's scheme offered the best hope of perpetuating Western control. It had not escaped Bénédite that a French seat on the new Foundation was to go to the Louvre, but he died in Luxor in March 1926 before the denouement.[98]

Rockefeller's revised proposal reached Breasted in Cairo in April 1926. Charles Breasted's biography of his father claimed that the Egyptian government irrationally rejected revisions it itself had proposed. In fact, Rockefeller's advisers introduced two major changes: that the European vice president of the Museum Commission, not its Egyptian president, would be the effective head, and that the Commission would control museum appointments and salaries.[99]

With parliamentary elections looming, Prime Minister Ziwar rejected the amended proposal as an insult to national sovereignty. On Breasted's advice, Rockefeller withdrew the offer. Toying with reviving the project a few months later, Breasted thought of adding two Germans to the Foundation and conceding the Egyptians a third seat on the Museum Commission: "In the practical politics of the situation an Anglo–German–American combination of six votes could out-vote, if necessary, the possible Franco–Egyptian combination of five votes."[100]

The project was dead, however, and Breasted followed Petrie in seeking greener pastures over the border in the British mandate of Palestine. He drew up a far more modest proposal—$2 million compared to the $10 million for Egypt—for a Rockefeller museum and research institute in Jerusalem. The plan went through, and Petrie's *Ancient Egypt* wrote enviously:

> The activity and lavish expenditure of the many American enterprises in the East makes a melancholy contrast with the deadness of England. . . . The cause of our neglect is the blindness of our millionaires. One who was interested in Palestine work left over four millions to be swept into the Exchequer, instead of founding a body of research. All honour to the Rockefeller enterprises.[101]

An earthquake and the Palestinian revolt delayed the opening of the Palestine Archaeological Museum until January 1938. Breasted did not live to see it.[102]

The day had passed when Westerners could ignore or easily manipulate Egyptian politicians, scholars, and the public. Chapter 4 turns to the establishment of Egyptian Egyptology and wider public support for pharaonism in the wake of Tutankhamun.

4
Egyptian Egyptology and Pharaonism in the Wake of Tutankhamun, 1922–1930

The discovery of Tutankhamun's tomb gave a critical push to two developments already under way in Egyptians' relationship to their pharaonic past: it hastened the transformation of Egyptology into a scholarly profession open to Egyptians, and it accelerated the growth of pharaonism among the public. Selim Hassan, Sami Gabra, and Mahmud Hamza—the budding scant second generation of Egyptian Egyptologists—were rushed off to Europe for advanced degrees. At home, a durable university program to produce Egyptian Egyptologists was finally established in 1924. This had been the dream of Ahmad Kamal Pasha for fifty years; he died on the eve of its realization. In 1925, the program became the Department of Archaeology in the Faculty of Arts of the new state-run Egyptian University. The French and British would fight a long rearguard action in the Antiquities Service, but Egyptianization there and in the new career track in academia was only a matter of time.

Pharaonism—popular interest in, and identification with, ancient Egypt—was a prominent strand in Egyptian territorial nationalism, the dominant ideology of the 1920s. Saad Zaghlul and the Wafd, Liberal Constitutionalists, King Fuad, and others all enlisted pharaonism as they competed to occupy the political space opened up by Britain's declaration of Egyptian independence in 1922. Muhammad Husayn Haykal, editor of the Liberal Constitutionalist *al-Siyasa*, succeeded his mentor Lutfi al-Sayyid as the leading literary promoter of pharaonic-inspired nationalism. In the visual arts, the unveiling of Mahmoud Mukhtar's sculpture *Nahdat Misr* (Revival of Egypt) in 1928 marked the pharaonist high point of the decade.

Recruiting the Second Generation of Egyptian Egyptologists: Selim Hassan and Sami Gabra

Scarcely noticed in the tumult of the 1919 revolution, the tide began to turn in Egyptian Egyptology even before Tutankhamun burst onto the scene. In 1920, minister of public works Muhammad Shafiq asked his nominal subordinate Pierre Lacau to hire and train two Egyptians as assistant museum curators. Ahmad Kamal's lobbying with Sultan Fuad may have precipitated the action.[1] In August 1921, Selim Hassan and Mahmud Hamza were duly appointed.[2] By one account, the only European who welcomed the novices and provided some mentoring was Vladimir Golenischeff, the émigré Russian scholar then cataloguing the museum's hieratic papyri.[3]

The dual surprises of 1922—partial independence and Tutankhamun's tomb—increased pressure for an academic program to train Egyptian Egyptologists. Since it would take four years to graduate the first class of even BA Egyptologists, three young men already holding BAs were rushed to Europe for graduate study in the field. Secretary general of Antiquities Pierre Lacau was annoyed that the Ministry of Education did not consult him on their selection. Taha Hussein, professor of ancient history at the private Egyptian University and fresh from the Sorbonne, suggested the selection criteria—that candidates hold degrees from a higher school, be under twenty-six, and be familiarized with the Egyptian Museum's collection before being sent to Europe.[4]

Two of the three winning candidates are central to our story—Selim Hassan (1887–1961) and Sami Gabra (1892–1979). The third, Mahmud Hamza (1890–1980), will be brought in as the sparser information allows. The three became the core of the scant second generation of Egyptian Egyptologists (see table D).[5] Calling them "second generation" counts Ahmad Kamal and his obscure colleague Ahmad Naguib as the first generation and skips a shadowy "lost generation" of several of Kamal's early students and others without education in the field[6] (see table D). The birthdates of the second generation place them squarely in the "generation of 1919"—cultural and political leaders who came to the fore with the 1919 revolution. These three second-generation Egyptologists all interrupted other careers to go back for higher European degrees in Egyptology and returned to take up posts in the late 1920s.

Selim Hassan's and Sami Gabra's contrasting careers, attitudes, and personalities reveal a great deal about the politics of Egyptian archaeology from World War I to Nasser. Hassan denounced France's long colonization of the field, accused Western archaeologists of stealing antiquities, and tried unsuccessfully to replace the French director general of Antiquities. An unlikely alliance of Britain, France, and King Faruq drove

Hassan out of public life on corruption charges in 1939. In contrast, Sami Gabra extolled the French Antiquities directors and hailed the interwar years as the "golden age of Egyptology," during which "scholars of all countries of the university world flocked to Egypt, well equiped, and well financed; they were happy to live under the desert sky of Egypt."[7] With Hassan ostracized throughout the 1940s, Gabra became the first Egyptian to chair the Egyptology Department at Fuad I University and informal dean of the profession. He retired at sixty in 1952, three months before the revolution. The revolution partially reversed Gabra's and Hassan's fortunes. Why did the views and careers of the two contrast so sharply?

Selim Hassan and Sami Gabra were born five years apart in a colonized country over which Sir Evelyn Baring (later Lord Cromer) was slowly tightening control. Both were village born, Hassan in the Delta in Mit Nagi, Daqhaliya, on the Damietta branch of the Nile, and Gabra in Abnub, near Asyut in underdeveloped Upper Egypt (the Said). Springing from a family of prosperous landowners got Gabra off to a promising start.[8] Christiane Desroches (later Noblecourt), who met his family in Asyut on the eve of World War II, later wrote: "These opulent Coptic pashas, very Francophile, were accustomed, like most wealthy Egyptians, to spend their summer vacations at Vichy."[9]

Selim Hassan's father died early. With only 7 percent literacy in Egypt when Cromer retired in 1907, schooling offered a critical path up and out of the village. While the great literary leader Taha Hussein got his start at the village Quran school (*kuttab*) in Middle Egypt and followed the religious track on to al-Azhar University, Selim Hassan transferred from a *kuttab* to the state primary and secondary school track. Gabra followed a third track—private schools, run in his case by American United Presbyterian missionaries.

Proximity to a city facilitated critical access to education. Hassan's village was only seventy kilometers by rail from Cairo. Although Cromer instituted tuition fees at all levels of the state schools, both to economize and to discourage social climbing, Hassan's family managed to put him through state primary school, Cairo's elite Tawfiqiya Secondary School, and the Higher Teachers College. Already twenty-two when he entered the Teachers College in 1909, Selim Hassan immediately joined the College's Egyptology section when Ahmad Kamal opened it in 1910. One of his classmates was Mahmud Hamza, who would also win an Egyptology scholarship to Europe in 1923. Until the Faculty of Arts of the state-run Egyptian University opened in 1925, the Higher Teachers College provided critical training for a whole generation of future Egyptologists, historians, geographers, and—in the case of Prime Minister Mahmud al-Nuqrashi—politicians.[10] In a discouraging replay of Ahmad Kamal's travails forty years before, Maspero did

Table D. Early Generations of Egyptian Archaeologists

Egyptian Archaeologists			Contemporary Western Archaeologists	Contemporary Political and Cultural Leaders
Egyptologists	Islamic Archaeols.	Coptologists		
1st Generation Ahmad Naguib (1847–1910) Ahmad Kamal (1851–1923)	Ali Bahgat (1858–1924)	Murqus Simaika (1864–1944)	Gaston Maspero (1846–1916) Petrie (1853–1942) GUISEPPE BOTTI (1853–1903) Max Herz (1856–1919)	Lord Cromer (1841–1917) Muhammad Abduh (1849–1905) Saad Zaghlul (1859–1927) Lord Allenby (1861–1936)
Lost Generation of Egyptian Archaeologists		Claudius Labib (1868–1918)	Ludwig Borchardt (1863–1938) James Henry Breasted (1865–1935) George Reisner (1867–1942) Pierre Lacau (1873–1967) Howard Carter (1874–1939) EVARISTO BRECCIA (1876–1941) Junker (1877–1962) K.A.C. Creswell (1879–1974)	King Fuad (1868–1936) Ahmad Lutfi al-Sayyid 1872–1963 Ismail Sidqi (1875 –1950) George Lloyd (1879–1941) Mustafa al-Nahhas (1879–1963)
2nd Generation Selim Hassan (1886–1961) Mahmud Hamza (1890–1976) Sami Gabra (1892–1979) Mustafa Amer (prehistorian rather than Egyptologist) (1896–1973)		Georgy Sobhy (1884–1964) Aziz Atiya (1898–1988)	Herbert Winlock (1884–1950) Gaston Wiet (1887–1971) Étienne Drioton (1889–1961)	Miles Lampson (1880–1964) Salama Musa (1887–1958) Muhammad Husayn Haykal (1888–1956) Makram Ubayd (1889–1961) Taha Hussein (1889–1973) Mahmoud Mukhtar (1891–1934) Tawfiq al-Hakim (1898–1987

Egyptian Archaeologists			Contemporary Western Archaeologists	Contemporary Political and Cultural Leaders
Egyptologists	Islamic Archaeols.	Coptologists		
3rd Generation	Muhammad	Pahor Labib	John Wilson	Hassan al-Banna
Zaki Saad	Mustafa	(1905–1994)	(1899–1976)	(1906–1949)
(1901–1982)	(1903–87)		Jean-Philippe Lauer	Sayyid Qutb
Ahmad Fakhry		Togo Mina	(1902–2001)	(1906–1966)
(1905–1973	Muhammad	(1906–49)	ACHILLE ADRIANI	Fuad Sirag al-Din
Pahor Labib	Zaki Hassan		(1905–1982)	(1910–2000)
(1905–1994)	(1908–1957)	Mirrit		Naguib Mahfouz
Girgis Mattha		Boutros Ghali		(1911–2006)
(1905–1967)		(1908–1992)		
Labib Habachi				
(1906–1984)				
Abdel Moneim				
Abu Bakr				
(1907–76)				

Islamic archaeologists underlined. GRECO–ROMAN ARCHAEOLOGISTS IN CAPITALS

not hire any of the Teachers College Egyptology graduates, forcing the program to close. Hassan had to fall back on school teaching for a decade until Lacau finally hired him in 1921 at the Egyptian Museum.

Gabra's Abnub was only ten kilometers from Asyut, the Upper Egyptian city where the "American Mission" of the United Presbyterian Church had established its Egyptian headquarters. He attended the Mission's Asyut College (a primary and secondary school), then the Syrian Protestant College (now the American University in Beirut, AUB), which a different denomination of American Presbyterians had opened in 1866.[11] Some sources say that Gabra studied Egyptology with Ahmad Kamal,[12] and it could be that he attended Kamal's program at the Higher Teachers School before leaving for France in 1911. If that were the case, however, why would Gabra not have mentioned it—or Kamal—in his memoirs? Bent on practicing law—the most prestigious profession of the day—before Egypt's French-influenced Mixed Courts, Gabra earned a *licence* and doctorate in law from the University of Bourdeaux. In 1923, however, he abandoned his promising legal career to retool for Egyptology. Gabra recalled childhood days exploring Old and Middle Kingdom tombs near Asyut with a cousin during school holidays. He proudly noted that the name of his village Abnub meant "village of gold" in Egyptian, that Asyut (Lycopolis to the Greeks) was the capital of the Sycamore nome, and that funeral processions at its Mari Mina (St. Menas) Church followed rituals inherited from pharaonic times.

Selim Hassan taught English and history in Cairo's Khedival School and other schools before finding a path back to Egyptology. He also wrote Arabic textbooks—A History of Egypt since the Ottoman Conquest (1916), Modern Europe and Its Civilization (2 vols., 1920), and A Concise History of Egypt and the Arab States (2 vols.)—and cotranslated to Arabic a History of the Mamluks in Egypt (1923) and A Page from the History of Muhammad Ali.[13]

Taha Hussein's "under twenty-six" age criterion for the scholarships to Europe was set aside in view of the strengths of the three winners. Hassan turned thirty-six in 1923, Hamza thirty-three, and Gabra thirty-one. Hassan and Hamza already had Egyptology diplomas from Kamal's Higher Teachers College program and two years of museum experience. Hamza had also married Ahmad Kamal's daughter Nimat in 1919.[14] Gabra had more higher education—a French doctorate—but in the apparently irrelevant field of law. On closer inspection, however, his published University of Bordeaux doctoral thesis was on Egyptian land law in ancient and Islamic times.[15]

Educating the Second Generation: Liverpool and Paris

Although bypassed in selecting the scholarship students for Europe, Antiquities director Lacau did get to prescribe their program of studies: first a year at the University of Liverpool and then a year at the Sorbonne's École des hautes études. Beginning in Britain was a nod to its political primacy in Egypt; the second, more advanced year in Paris reflected not only the strengths of French Egyptology but also France's domination of Egypt's Antiquities Service.

Why Liverpool? Egyptology had come late to British universities.[16] It had taken root first in amateur circles of leisured gentlemen, like Gardiner Wilkinson, who lived on inherited wealth or patronage and read papers at learned societies, and in the British Museum, where the combined careers of Samuel Birch and his successor, E.A.W. Budge, stretched all the way from 1836 to 1924. Tradition-bound Oxford and Cambridge had slumbered as rural retreats of Anglican gentility until beginning serious reform in the 1850s, and it was University College London (UCL) which established the first chair of Egyptology in Britain in 1892. Amelia Edwards, a key founder of the Egypt Exploration Fund (EEF) in 1882, made her bequest establishing the chair at London because it was the only institution admitting women to higher degrees by examination. Her will implicitly selected Flinders Petrie as the first to occupy the chair.[17] Petrie's imperial and racial beliefs make it unlikely that he would have welcomed Egyptian students, and Lacau's poor relations with Petrie would not have inclined him to recommend UCL for the Egyptian students in any case.[18] In 1901, Oxford had followed UCL's lead, naming Francis Llewellyn Griffith Reader in Egyptology, but Oxford may have been too exclusive to admit Gabra and Hamza. Cambridge was not in the running; not until 1946 did it found the Egyptology chair, which Stephen Glanville became the first to occupy.[19]

Liverpool was one of the half-dozen "red brick" universities founded in the industrial midlands in the first decade of the twentieth century as secular, civic enterprises.[20] The port city was a booming gateway to the globe—not least for Egyptian cotton. In 1904 John Garstang mobilized merchant and shipowner funding for the university's Institute of Archaeology.[21] He excavated in Egypt and the Sudan before World War I and after it founded the Department of Antiquities in Britain's Palestine mandate. Garstang occupied Liverpool's chair of Archaeology and Percy Newberry its chair of Egyptology until 1919. As chair of the Egyptian University's Department of Archaeology (1929–33), Newberry would help foster Hassan's and Gabra's early careers.

Garstang being out of town when Gabra and Hamza arrived in 1923, it was Eric Peet, Newberry's successor in 1920, who welcomed them to Liverpool. Peet had read mathematics and classics at Queen's College Oxford. He came to Egyptology through fieldwork after graduation and in 1913 became lecturer in Egyptology at Manchester.[22]

Thomas Kelly's institutional history of the University of Liverpool neglects the imperial network so evident in its archives. Gabra's and Hamza's recruitment was no accident:

> Another student, an Egyptian, is reading for the Certificate and Diploma in Archaeology, his special area naturally being Egypt. It is hoped that more Egyptian students may be induced to come to Liverpool and take this course. It may well be that the future of the Department of Antiquities in Egypt rests with the Egyptians. If the Institute can train some of the rising generation, and so ensure that when they take over the Department they administer it efficiently, it will have rendered a signal service to Archaeology and to Egypt itself.[23]

In 1921–22, Egypt, with twenty-six students, trailed only South Africa's thirty-four in overseas enrollments at the university; India was a distant third with ten.[24] The South Africans were inscribed as 'white,' while classification as 'coloured' helped keep the Egyptians in their place.[25] After Saad Zaghlul and the Wafd swept to power back home in January 1924, their minister of public works, Murqus Hanna, overruled his subordinate Lacau and sensibly kept Gabra and Hamza at Liverpool for a second year

so they could complete diplomas.[26] Gabra studied with Garstang, Blackman, and Peet and heard guest lectures by Alan Gardiner and Francis
Griffith. Building on his expertise in law, Gabra wrote his thesis on "Justice under the Old and New Kingdom Egypt."[27] Hamza's thesis "Relations
of Nubia and Egypt in the Light of Recent Discoveries" emphasized finds
salvaged during the 1907–11 heightening of the Aswan Dam. His preface,
though perhaps accurate, sounded unduly self-deprecating:

> The present dissertation . . . is nothing more than a mere compilation
> of the most important facts which Egyptologists and Archaeologists have
> arrived at after hard scientific work for many years. Two or four years
> persevering study will certainly not enable me to write any original work
> or solve difficult problems. It is essential to spend many years in the exca-
> vation field.[28]

Geographer and prehistorian Mustafa Amer, who in 1953 would
become the first Egyptian to head the Antiquities Service, had earned a
Liverpool BA and MA before Gabra and Hamza arrived. Ahmad Fakhry
reportedly studied there briefly around 1930. Peet's successors at Liverpool, Aylward Blackman (1934–48) and H.W. Fairman (1948–74), both
considered applying for the Egyptology chair at Cairo after Newberry
vacated it in 1933. Most of the Egyptian historians and geographers
who studied at Liverpool between the wars are beyond our scope here.[29]
So too are the seventeen Egyptian architects who studied at Liverpool
from 1920 to 1940.[30] After World War II, Liverpool again drew Egyptian students in Egyptology and other fields; notable among these was
Gaballa A. Gaballa, secretary general of the Supreme Council of Antiquities in the 1990s.[31]

In 1925, Gabra and Hamza crossed the Channel to Paris, where Selim
Hassan had already been studying for two years. In the summer of 1923,
Hassan had neglected to stop by the Egyptian Museum for study instruc-
tions from James Quibell (Lacau being on leave). Skipping Liverpool,
Hassan went straight to Paris.[32] Hassan, Gabra, and Hamza all studied at
the École pratique des hautes études (ÉPHE), where Maspero had begun
teaching in 1869. When Maspero left in 1899 for his second term in Egypt,
his former pupil Alexandre Moret became director of studies. Moret was
still on hand to supervise Hassan, Gabra, and Hamza, and to welcome King
Fuad on his state visit to the Louvre in 1927. Moret obtained a chair at the
Sorbonne in 1920 and in 1923, like Champollion and Maspero, became
professor at the Collège de France.[33] Gabra also studied under Gustave
Lefebvre and Raymond Weill, both of whom became ÉPHE directors

of study in 1928.[34] Selim Hassan studied Egyptian with the young priest Étienne Drioton (1889–1961) at the École libre des langues orientales of the Institut catholique de Paris. Perhaps the seeds of enmity between the two, discussed in chapter 9, were planted in Paris.

Age alone would place Abbas Bayoumi (1904–1983) in the younger, third generation of Egyptologists. His studying in Paris in the 1920s, however, put him closer to the second generation of Hassan, Gabra, and Hamza than to his own age cohort. Bayoumi went straight to Paris after secondary school, skipping the new undergraduate Egyptology program in Cairo. He returned from France in 1931 to take up a career in the Antiquities Service.[35]

Pierre Lacau, a grizzled veteran of World War I, was also furious with Borchardt over the export of the bust of Nefertiti. No wonder he omitted from his study prescription for the Egyptians the German leg of the tripod of leading European schools of Egyptology. When Zaghlul and the Wafd came to power in 1924, however, minister of public works Murqus Hanna wanted to add a German stage to their studies. Embroiled with Carter over Tutankhamun, Hanna appreciated that Germany, unlike Britain and France, had no imperial stake in controlling Egyptian antiquities. Hanna went down with the Zaghlul government in November 1924, however, and nothing came of the proposed German year for the three students.[36] Hassan and Gabra nevertheless touched base in Berlin. Kurt Sethe and Wilhelm Spiegelberg welcomed Hassan's visit in the summer of 1924.[37] Arriving with an introduction from Hermann Junker, Gabra was warmly welcomed by Professor and Mrs. Erman and Heinrich Schäfer. Erman effused: "You are a Copt, he said, of the pure blood of Amenophis III, that dear Pharaoh whom I would like to meet in another life."[38]

The Third Generation: An Egyptian School of Egyptology on the Fifth Try

Ahmad Kamal, as noted above, had been involved in four attempts to establish a school of Egyptology in Cairo, all of which foundered on the reefs of the colonial age. He just missed savoring the success of the fifth try. He died on August 5, 1923, two days before his family received notice of his appointment as director of the Egyptology program about to open at the Egyptian University.[39] After fifty-four years in the field, his passing went unremarked in the *Annales* of the Antiquities Service. When Kamal had pleaded with Lacau—twenty-four years his junior—to hire Egyptians, Lacau retorted that few besides Kamal himself had shown any interest. "Ah, M. Lacau," he replied, "in the sixty-five years you French have directed the Service, what opportunities have you given us?"[40]

Two weeks after Zaghlul's Wafdist cabinet took power in January 1924, the Egyptology department of the private Egyptian University began shaping the third generation of Egyptian Egyptologists (see table D). For the first two years, the program met on the premises of the Higher Teachers College, holding classes in the evening to accommodate working students. Arabic and French were the languages of instruction. In the fall of 1925, the program became the Department of Archaeology in the Faculty of Arts of the new state-run Egyptian University.

Labib Habachi began in February 1924 as one of seventeen in the first class; twelve stayed the course to graduate in 1928 as the first class of BA Egyptologists. Reminiscing nearly fifty years later, Habachi regretted having missed meeting Ahmad Kamal. He praised the Europeans who stepped in to teach Egyptian in Kamal's stead—Russian émigré Vladimir Golenischeff (1856–1947), then sixty-eight, and young Charles Kuentz (1895–1978), secretary and librarian at IFAO.[41]

A pioneer of Egyptology in Russia, Golenischeff had read a paper at the Third International Congress of Orientalists (ICO) when it convened in Saint Petersburg in 1876. The city trailed only Paris and London and was ahead of Berlin in hosting the ICO. In 1886, Golenischeff became curator of the Egyptian Department of St. Petersburg's Hermitage Museum. In 1908, the collapse of gold mining in the Urals forced him to sell his collection of Egyptian antiquities to the state. A large Russian delegation—although none were Egyptologists—participated in the ICO at Athens in 1912, the last before World War I and the Russian Revolution. Stalin had not yet consolidated power in 1928, when a strong Soviet delegation attended the first post-war ICO at Oxford. The USSR boycotted the next five ICOs; only Stalin's death freed Soviet scholars to rejoin their capitalist colleagues at the ICO in Cambridge in 1954.[42]

Émigrés Golenischeff and Vladimir Vikentiev represented Russian Egyptology in interwar Egypt. Sixty-one years old in 1917, Golenischeff never went home after the Bolshevik Revolution. Dividing his time between Nice and Egypt, from 1924 to 1929 he chaired the Egyptology department he founded in Cairo. Although he never obtained a chair, Vikentiev, who came to Cairo in 1923, taught at the university until his death in 1960. Eccentric theories marred his later work. Another Russian émigré, Oleg Volkoff, taught French at the German school in Dokki (Cairo), presided over the Russian Immigrants Association, and published studies on European guidebooks to Egypt and Russian travelers to the country.[43]

Labib Habachi's other European professors at Cairo included Liverpool's Eric Peet for archaeology. He took French from Belgian dean of arts Henri Grégoire, English from Evelyn White, and Latin and Greek from IFAO librarian Father Saint-Paul Girard. Habachi considered the smattering of a year each of Greek and Latin of little use.

As for Egyptian teachers, Habachi learned Coptic from fellow Copts— Georgy Sobhy (professor at the School of Medicine) and Ahmose Labib. In the present author's interview with Habachi, he pointed out the latter's pharaonic name. Dr. Georgy Bey Sobhy (1884–1964), a medical doctor who taught Coptic on the side, presided over the Society of Egyptian Archaeology *(al-Jamiya al-athariya al-misriya)*, which a score of students in the BA Egyptology classes of 1928 and 1929 founded in 1925. Student members included journalist Hassan Sobhi, future Egyptologists Rizqallah Naguib Makramallah (treasurer) and Ahmad Fakhry (secretary), and Labib Habachi and Girgis Mattha. The Society brought out at least two issues of *al-Qadim: sahifa athariya* (Antiquity: An Archaeological Review) in 1925. The cover displayed the university's emblem—the god Thoth (Djehouty)—with pen and scribal palette. *Al-Qadim* reported on recent fieldwork—all by foreigners, including Reisner, Firth, IFAO at Edfu, Griffith, Petrie, and Carter. There was also a notice on Georgy Sobhy's Arabic-language grammar of Coptic.[44] The Society held a tea at the Continental Hotel to honor James Henry Breasted (see fig. 28), who

> expressed his pleasure at the fact that the young descendants of the Pharaohs were so keenly occupied with the history of their ancestors, with the assistance of foreign savants who are entirely disinterested.[45]

Breasted's insistence on his own scholarly disinterestedness is revealing: at that very moment, he was up to his neck in trying to steer his proposal for a Rockefeller museum for Cairo through the shoals of personal rivalries and Egyptian and international politics.

Habachi also had Sami Gabra and Selim Hassan, both fresh from Paris, for ancient Egyptian history and archaeology respectively. The famous Taha Hussein taught him Arabic literature. Berlin-educated Ali el-Enani, who unlike Golenischeff and Taha Hussein did not make the transfer from the private to the state-run Egyptian University, taught him Hebrew and comparative Semitics. Habachi did not mention Ali Bahgat, director of the Museum of Arab Art, who was to have taught Arab architecture but died the month after the department opened.

From his seat on the private university's board of directors, IFAO director George Foucart denounced the new Egyptology program as "a device for disorganizing our Egyptian University" and obtaining honoraria for certain lecturers. He pronounced Golenischeff the only recognized scholar involved and declared, mistakenly, that Golenischeff

28 The first class of Egyptian University Egyptology students at the Egyptian University, Garden of the Continental Hotel, March, 1926. Visiting luminary James Henry Breasted commands the center, with departmental chair Vladimir Golenischeff on his right and classical historian Paul Graindor on his left. *Wilson, Signs and Wonders*, plate 32a. Courtesy of the Oriental Institute, University of Chicago.

had declined to teach. Foucart warned that German-trained Egyptians—apparently Enani—might open the door to German influence. Egyptians enrolled would miss the true immersion in French education and culture, which only residence in France could provide. Even after classes had been under way for two months, Foucart still hoped that Zaghlul or another minister would quash the program.[46]

Pressure on Golenischeff to lecture in English rather than French[47] was in keeping with High Commissioner Lord Lloyd's campaign to Anglicize the university. Although Lloyd was no friend of Egyptianization, Selim Hassan's replacement of IFAO's Charles Kuentz in January 1928 gave him the satisfaction of checking off another departing Frenchman. That left Girard the lone Frenchman in the department.[48] Taha Hussein's patriotism overriding his cultural Francophilia, he welcomed Selim Hassan's arrival to teach Egyptology at the university.

Ahmad Fakhry, Labib Habachi, and Girgis Mattha stood out among the dozen BA graduates of 1928, the vanguard of the third generation. The classes of 1929 and 1930 included Ahmad Badawi, Abd al-Munim Abu Bakr, and Zaki Saad, as well as future Coptic Museum directors Togo Mina, Pahor Labib, and Victor Antun Girgis. These first three classes together totaled fifteen Christians and eleven Muslims, or 58 percent and 42 percent respectively.[49] Abu Bakr, Ahmad Badawi, and Pahor Labib went on to earn PhDs in Berlin and Girgis Mattha at Oxford. Togo Mina earned diplomas in Paris and Victor Girgis an Italian doctorate. Fakhry studied in Berlin, Brussels, and Liverpool but finished his doctorate at Cairo. Zaki Saad and Labib Habachi missed out on graduate study altogether but made the most of their Antiquities Service fieldwork, reading on their own, and learning from Western colleagues. Career prospects for these pioneers were bright; of twenty-seven graduates of the classes of 1928–30, twenty-four entered the Antiquities Service or academia.

Mlle Afifa Iskandar spoke at the retirement dinner hosted by Rector Lutfi al-Sayyid for Golenischeff in 1928. She had been allowed to attend classes as an exception, but not to earn a degree, and she seized the occasion to plead for coeducation.[50] The first women entered the state university the following year, though not in Egyptology. The first woman in Egyptology graduated in 1941, followed by three more in 1949.[51]

First Steps in Egyptianizing the Antiquities Service

Selim Hassan, Sami Gabra, and Mahmud Hamza came home in 1927 or 1928 with various diplomas, but not doctorates, and took up Antiquities Service posts under Lacau. They were eager to get on with long-delayed careers; Hassan was already forty and Gabra thirty-six. Both published maiden articles in the Antiquities Service's *Annales* (*ASAE*) in 1928, and Hamza followed in 1930. The Service sponsored the publication of Hassan's and Gabra's Paris theses. Earlier in the 1920s, four of the *ASAE*'s annual volumes had had no Egyptian contributors at all, and four other volumes had only short items by "lost generation" members who were about to retire.[52] Their retirements and Hassan's and Gabra's transfer to the university opened promising careers in the Service to the emerging third generation, some of whom also began contributing to the *ASAE*.

In 1928, Reginald Engelbach, assistant curator at the Egyptian Museum, reported a palpable change in atmosphere: any curator could now veto exporting an object, with final appeal to go over Lacau's head to the minister. With two Egyptian assistant curators looking over his shoulder, Lacau grew more cautious in dividing finds with foreign expeditions. Engelbach worried lest foreigners conclude that excavation was no longer worthwhile.[53]

In these changing times, Hassan and Gabra reacted in strikingly different ways to their senior European colleagues. Lacau assigned Hassan to the museum library to translate the museum guide into Arabic,[54] an unglamorous task earlier carried out by Ahmad Kamal. Hassan already had a list of grievances against colonial Egyptology: Maspero's failure to hire him back in 1912; the cool reception when Lacau finally took him on in 1921; having to pay his own way to Grenoble to attend the Champollion centennial; and Engelbach's attempt to deny him a visit to Tutankhamun's tomb. On his European trip in the summer of 1922, Hassan toured the major museums, asking pointed questions about how they had acquired Egyptian objects, including the bust of Nefertiti, and reporting the results in al-Ahram. This endeared him neither to Lacau nor to the Cairo museum's assistant curator, Gustave Lefebvre, who had made the controversial division involving the bust of Nefertiti. In January 1928, Hassan leapt at the chance to leave the Antiquities Service for better opportunities and a friendlier climate at the university.

Gabra, in contrast, fondly recalled his "five unforgettable years" in the Antiquities Service. With his fluent French and English, he escorted foreign dignitaries—including the Prince of Wales, the crown prince of Sweden, and the king of Afghanistan—through the Egyptian Museum. He wrote glowingly of the "pioneering genius" Champollion and "the noble line of his successors," Antiquities directors "Mariette, Maspero, Loret, Lacau, and Drioton. One cannot forget these noble figures, these men always ready to serve science and Egypt, with rectitude and modesty." Gabra praised Lacau's rebuff of foreign expeditions out to enrich their museums at Egypt's expense. Gustave Lefebvre was "my professor and guide." Engelbach, the hard-drinking Briton who had fought in the French army and could swear colorfully in French and Arabic, waved Gabra off to his first dig with a "Good luck for you Sami!"[55] Gabra's mentions of Egyptian colleagues in his memoirs are scantier, and he does not mention Ahmad Kamal or his own contemporaries Selim Hassan and Mahmud Hamza at all. Significantly, Gabra wrote his memoirs in French, and it was several years before they were translated into Arabic.[56]

Selim Hassan was never as at home as Gabra in English and French or in cosmopolitan circles. In Paris, a fellow student (Mme G. Gauthier) helped Hassan with French and typing his thesis,[57] but he did not find a mentor among his professors. Gabra came home with a French wife, Hassan with a French mistress who later sued him in the Mixed Courts.[58]

Sami Gabra and Mahmud Hamza got off to more promising starts with Lacau than did Selim Hassan. Lacau handpicked Gabra as a Copt to excavate near the Coptic village of Deir Tassa in 1929, and Gabra quickly established rapport with the villagers. In 1928, Hamza dug at Qanatir, in the northeastern Delta, north of Tell al-Daba. He decided that it was the site of Piramesse, the Biblical city named for Ramesses II. Labib Habachi later excavated west of Tell al-Daba and concluded that Hamza's identification of Qanatir as Piramesse was correct and that Tell al-Daba was the site of

Avaris, the capital of the Hyksos. However, the opinions of Pierre Montet, the excavator of Tanis, long overshadowed those of the junior Egyptians. Montet said that Tanis was the site of Avaris and later of Piramesse. After Manfred Bietak began excavating Tell al-Daba in 1966, he concluded that Montet had been wrong and the two Egyptians right.[59] Hamza also excavated a prehistoric site at al-Omari, which he left unpublished. From 1941 until his retirement in 1950, he directed the Cairo Museum.

In May 1929, Prime Minister Muhammad Mahmud transferred the Antiquities Service from the Ministry of Public Works to the Ministry of Education. University Rector Lutfi al-Sayyid, the leading prewar proponent of pharaonism, was minister of education at the time. Perhaps the shift implied that antiquities were no longer engineering problems to be managed but a precious national heritage about which the public needed to be educated.

Pharaonism after Tutankhamun

In the mid-1920s, while the second generation of Egyptian Egyptologists were off studying in Europe and the third were undergraduates in the new program at Cairo, pharaonism flourished among the public as never before. Its florescence coincided with the heyday of Egyptian territorial nationalism, the decade's dominant ideology. Wafdists, King Fuad, and Liberal Constitutionalists vied with each other in enlisting pharaonism to advance their respective agendas. In less political contexts too, pharaonism flourished in a range of different media.

Muhammad Nagi's painting *Nahdat Misr* (Revival of Egypt) and Mahmoud Mukhtar's sculpture of the same name were both conceived before the declaration of Egyptian independence and discovery of Tutankhamun's tomb in 1922 (see figs. 17 and 18). In 1924 and 1928 respectively, these works were enshrined in central national spaces as icons of independence and revival inspired by the great pharaonic past. Nagi's *Revival* decorated the new parliament building called forth by the 1923 constitution and inaugurated by Zaghlul's Wafdist government on March 25, 1924. The building's twenty-four-columned hall, with palm leaf capitals patterned on Fifth Dynasty granite columns from Abusir, complemented the pharaonism of Nagi's painting.[60]

There was nothing specifically Wafdist about Nagi's *Nahdat Misr*, the parliament's pharaonic columns, or the 1923 constitution. Planning for the parliament building dated to 1922, when non-Wafdists—including future Liberal Constitutionalists—were in power, and the Wafd boycotted the commission which wrote the constitution. However, the Wafd's presiding over the 1924 opening of the constitutional era, the newly elected parliament, and the parliament building gave the party a stake in their symbolism, including the pharaonic motifs.

Muhammad Nagi was an exact contemporary of Muhammad Husayn Haykal (1888–1956)—they were born and died the same years. Haykal became the leading literary exponent of pharaonism in the 1920s. In 1922, he joined his mentor Ahmad Lutfi al-Sayyid, a leading prewar exponent of Egyptian territorial nationalism and pharaonism, in founding the Liberal Constitutionalist Party. Haykal edited the new party's daily *al-Siyasa* and weekly *al-Siyasa al-usbuiya*. The winged sun disk on the masthead proclaimed a bold embrace of pharaonism.[61]

Lutfi al-Sayyid and Haykal were both sons of landowning *umda*s from Delta villages only six kilometers apart, near Simbalawin in Daqhaliya. Al-Sayyid was a personal friend of Haykal's father. Like al-Sayyid, Haykal studied at Cairo's Khedival Secondary School and School of Law, edited a newspaper for a reformist but socioeconomically conservative party of big landowners, and became minister of education. Haykal was homesick in Paris while studying for a law doctorate when he wrote his bucolic novel *Zaynab*. Al-Sayyid's *al-Jarida* published it in 1913 under the pseudonym "Egyptian Fellah." Like Nagi and Mukhtar, Haykal romanticized peasant women as embodying the authentic essence of Egypt.

Zaynab made only one explicit reference to ancient Egypt.[62] Haykal's pharaonism became more prominent in a series of articles in *al-Sufur* (The Unveiling), a magazine which al-Sayyid's younger associates published after *al-Jarida* closed in 1915. Ostensibly on the late feminist writer Qasim Amin, the series explored French critic Hippolyte Taine's ideas on environmental determinism. Haykal attributed the deep persistence of Egyptian traditions to the Nile valley's unique topography and climate, which enabled it to assimilate successive conquerors.[63]

Haykal's pharaonism emerged full-blown in the 1920s in a series of articles on "Ancient Egypt and Modern Egypt." He called for a "national literature" *(al-adab al-qawmi)* based on the enduring pharaonic legacy. Emphasis on successive foreign conquests, he complained, had artificially divided Egypt's past into pharaonic, Greek, Roman, Arab, and Ottoman eras. This obscured the persistence of a spirited people. The Persians and Romans were indeed exploitative foreigners, but under the Ptolemies, Fatimids, Ayyubids, and Mamluks, Egypt kept its independence by Egyptianizing its rulers. The Ptolemies made Alexandria a great world city, and Coptic Christianity thwarted the Roman–Byzantine exploiters. Egypt did adopt the language of its Arab conquerors, and the majority converted to Islam, but such features as pharaonic marriage and funerary rites, circumcision, and hair styles persisted among both Copts and Muslims. After Egypt's great achievements under the assimilated Tulunids, Fatimids, Ayyubids, and Mamluks, the Ottoman conquerors drained off Egyptian talent to distant Istanbul. In the eighteenth century, however, Mamluks led by Ali Bey allied with the ulama and the people to reassert Egypt's independence in all but name.[64]

As though answering Haykal's call, one of the contributors to his *al-Siyasa al-usbuiya*, Muhammad Gallab, published his University of Lyon doctoral thesis *Les survivances de l'Égypte antique dans le folklore moderne* (Survivals from Ancient Egypt in Modern Folklore) in 1929.[65] From an Upper Egyptian village near Mallawi in the province of Minya, Gallab later became a professor of philosophy at al-Azhar University. He seems not to have read Winifred Blackman's recent *The Fellahin of Upper Egypt: Their Religion, Social and Industrial Life To-Day with Special Reference to Survival from Ancient Egypt* (1927), but he drew on Maspero's collection of ancient and Yaqub Artin's collection of modern folklore. Omnia El Shakry suggests that while European anthropologists like Blackman perceived such continuities as "primitive" survivals in a still premodern Egypt, Egyptian nationalists like Gallab embraced "antique folk presences" as crucial to modern national identity. Egyptologists Selim Hassan and Moharram Kamal (1908–1966) were among those who later emphasized this theme of finding pharaonic survivals in modern folklife.[66]

King Fuad vigorously exploited pharaonic symbolism in his struggle against Liberal Constitutionalists and Wafdists. Sharing the Italian exile of his deposed father Khedive Ismail, he had studied in Geneva and the Turin military academy. He felt at home in Italian, French, and Turkish but less so in Arabic. Fuad had served as military attaché in Vienna, aide-de-camp to Khedive Abbas II, rector of the private Egyptian University, and in 1914 missed a chance at the throne of Albania. In 1917, he succeeded his brother Husayn Kamil as sultan of Egypt. Switching to the title of king in 1922, he pushed for as much royal autocracy as possible in the emerging semicolonial order. Having grown up in the land of Machiavelli, he could present himself—depending on the moment and audience—as a pious Muslim candidate worthy of the caliphal throne the Ottomans had vacated, as a European-style constitutional monarch, and as heir of the pharaohs.

Zaki Fahmi's Arabic biographical dictionary of 1926 was a carefully crafted instrument of royalist propaganda. It opens with a panegyric poem tying King Fuad to "the glory of the early pharaohs," then sketches Fuad's biography. Biographies of the dynasty's rulers back to Muhammad Ali, along with sketches of several other princes of the family, follow.

A twelve-page section then presents Fuad in the reflected glory of Tut-ankhamun's tomb (see fig. 21), a theme already noted in chapter 2. Next, a section discusses the new constitutional order and Western precedents of parliamentary government. The text of the king's March 1924 speech inaugurating the first parliament follows. The remainder of the work is a compilation of biographies of modern Egyptians, beginning with former prime minister Saad Zaghlul.[67]

Fahmi's Tutankhamun section extols Egypt's empire, military, wealth, arts, industries, and sciences when the rest of the world was still "in igno-rance" and links this heritage to King Fuad. (There is no hint of the troubles of the Amarna age of Akhenaten and Tutankhamun.)

In a minor key, postage stamps and coins also drove home Fuad's pharaonist and monarchist message (see figs. 29 and 30).

Breaking with Ottoman–Islamic tradition, he traded in the title 'Sul-tan' for 'King of Egypt,' and boldly put his portrait on stamps and coins as though he were a European monarch. Dropping the customary French or English as a second language on the postage stamps, he experimented at first with an Arabic-only set which showed him in coat, tie, and tar-boosh.[68] Egyptian stamps soon reverted to bilingualism, but the king took

29 Fuad's philatelic pharaonism (1923-1931). Top row: King Fuad broke with Ottoman/Islamic tradition by putting his portrait on postage stamps and coins. He took a slap at the British by first trying Arabic-only inscriptions on the stamps. When this proved impractical, he reverted to French rather than to English as the sec-ond language. Center: The scribal god of wisdom Thoth inscribes "Fuad" in hieroglyphs in a royal cartouche. Center row left and right, and bottom row: Pharaonic motifs on stamps commemorat-ing the international congresses which Fuad loved to host. *From the collection of D. Reid.*

Obverse   Reverse

30 Egypt's numismatic iconography from Ottoman Arabic calligraphy to royal portraits. Top row: *Tughra* of Ottoman Sultan Mehmed V (AH 1327/ 1909 CE), struck in Egypt. Second row: Husayn Kamil, Sultan of Egypt (AH 1333/1917 CE). Third row: Portrait of Fuad I, King of Egypt (AH 1352/1933 CE). Fourth row: Portrait of Faruq I, King of Egypt (AH 1357/1938 CE). *From the collection of D. Reid.*

a slap at Great Britain by restoring French rather than English as their European language.[69] Fuad wrote his pharaonism large in a striking 1925 stamp set commemorating the convening of the International Geographic Congress in Cairo.[70] The ibis-headed god of wisdom and writing, Thoth, inscribes "Fuad" in hieroglyphs in a royal cartouche. Fuad delighted in hosting such international congresses to burnish his image as a renaissance prince. His stamps for Cairo congresses of Navigation, Statistics, and Medicine also deployed pharaonic motifs, though those for Cotton, Railroads, and Aviation did not. An elaborate 1933 airmail set featured an airplane over the Pyramids of Giza.[71]

In another pharaonist gesture, Ali Mahir, minister of education in Ziwar's palace government, dispatched school groups to tour Upper Egyptian antiquities in January 1926. Thomas Cook & Son had taken students from the Arabic teachers college Dar al-Ulum on such a trip in the early 1890s, and even during World War I, students from Cairo's al-Saidiya School visited Luxor, posing for snapshots amidst the ruins. The scale and fanfare of Mahir's trips, however, was remarkable. Five groups of 150 students and teachers each traveled with a physician and two nurses. Students paid £E2 apiece. The minister himself saw them off at the railway station, and a series of articles by Ahmad Ali, one of the students, reported their progress in *al-Ahram*.[72]

Another royalist, Yusuf Qattawi (Joseph Cattaui) Pasha, went to the extreme of extending Manetho's thirty-dynasty scheme for pharaonic history to cover all Egyptian history down to the present. Long president of Cairo's Sephardic Jewish Council, Qattawi was an MP and cabinet minister whose wife was lady-in-waiting to Fuad's consort Queen Nazli. Imitating La Fontaine's dedication of his *Fables* to Louis XIV's son the crown prince, Qattawi dedicated *Coup d'oeil sur la chronologie de la nation égyptienne* (Paris, 1931) to crown prince Faruq. Qattawi reckoned that the ruling Muhammad Ali family, which he hailed for leading a "national renaissance," was Egypt's Forty-Fifth Dynasty.[73]

Europeans too were quick to flatter the pharaoh in King Fuad. Egyptologist Alexandre Moret welcomed him on a visit to the Louvre on October 22, 1927:

> Here you are still on the sacred soil of Egypt and you will receive there the homage of faithful subjects, who have freely chosen Egypt as a second fatherland. . . .
>
> The dead also greet you, Champollion, Mariette, de Rougé, Deveria, Revillout, Maspero. . . .
>
> Following the example of the great Pharaohs, you want to be the Guide, the father of your people. . . . Like the Amenemhats and the Ramses, you bring liberty through order, prosperity through work, and through consensual discipline.[74]

Kilyubatra (Cleopatra), like *Wadi al-muluk* (Valley of the Kings), a short-lived pharaonist magazine of the mid-1920s, hedged its bets. After presenting King Fuad in a pharaonic setting in its first issue, its second framed Prime Minister Saad Zaghlul in a pharaonic pylon[75] (see fig. 31).

After Tutankhamun, the greatest pharaonist political drama of the decade may have been the struggle over Mahmoud Mukhtar's sculpture *Revival of Egypt*.[76] Because Nagi's *Revival of Egypt* hung inside the parliament, it had only a limited direct audience. Mukhtar's *Revival*, in contrast, stood in Railway Station Square—then the hub for arrival of Egyptians from both Upper and Lower Egypt and for Westerners, as well as the main point

31 Pharaonism for the Wafd: Prime Minister Saad Zaghlul on the cover of *Kilyubatra (Cleopatra)* magazine, 1924. *As reproduced in Colla,* Conflicted Antiquities, *212.*

of departure for antiquities tours of Upper Egypt. The tortuous path of Mukthar's statue *Nahdat Misr*, which recapitulates the political vicissitudes of the era, strengthened the Wafd's association with pharaonism (see fig. 32). Adli Yakan's cabinet authorized the project in June 1921, and work on it began a year later. The £E3,000 initially appropriated ran out, stopping work for almost a year. When the Wafd came in in 1924, it appropriated £E12,000 more, but Ziwar's palace cabinets of 1924–26 harried the sculptor with petty obstructions. Cartoons in the pro-palace *al-Kashkhul* had Mukhtar lamenting, "Only God knows who has injected morphine into the revival," and despairing: "Every time I place the sculpture somewhere, someone comes and moves it. For God's sake, when I will finally despair, I will take it to Beirut and call it 'The Revival of Syria'" (see fig. 32).

In May 1926, the Liberal Constitutionalist–Wafd cabinet under Adli Yakan broke the impasse, appropriating £E8,000 more. Prime Minister Mustafa al-Nahhas, Zaghlul's successor as leader of the Wafd, gave the keynote address when the unveiling finally arrived, on May 20, 1928.

32 Mahmoud Mukhtar's dismay at political obstruction of his sculpture *Nahdat Misr (Revival of Egypt)*. Caption: "Every time I place the sculpture somewhere, someone comes and moves it. For God's sake, when I will finally despair, I will take it to Beirut and call it 'The Revival of Syria.'" Al-Kashkul, *April 24, 1925, 10; as shown in Gershoni and Jankowski,* Commemorating the Nation, 64.

Al-Nahhas lauded the statue's linking of pharaonic greatness with modern artistic and political progress, hailed Zaghlul and the Wafd as leaders of national revival since 1919, and tried to box King Fuad in by saluting him as Egypt's "first constitutional monarch." Both neoclassicist Ahmad Shawqi and modernist Ahmad Zaki Abu Shadi, who had titled his 1926 anthology of poems The Land of the Pharaohs, wrote odes for the occasion.[77] Though the statue represented modern Egypt as a woman raising her veil, Queen Nazli was still in seclusion and Fuad banned Egyptian women from attending.[78] To the king's embarrassment, the curtain resisted his tug at the climactic moment, and firefighters had to step in to execute the unveiling.

Liberal Constitutionalists Lutfi al-Sayyid and Haykal extolled the sculpture for linking ancient glory to modern achievements and aspirations. Mustafa Sadiq al-Rafii, an Islamist opponent of westernization and pharaonism, criticized the statue on aesthetic grounds. *Al-Khashkul* castigated the Wafdist government for embarrassing the king with the curtain. It ran a cartoon of people, mostly in galabias, milling around after the ceremony, with the caption: "In the gloom after the event, the statue *Nahdat Misr* says: How can I appear in the limelight when al-Nahhas is doing his utmost to kill the revival? It is a shameful act, a decline."[79]

33 Pharaonic-style mausoleum, Cairo cemetery of Sayyida Nafisa. *Photo: M. Volait Volait, Architectures de la décennie pharaonique en Égypte, 179. Courtesy of CEDEJ.*

Beyond party politics, pharaonic architectural styles were pressed into service in several mausolea in Cairo cemeteries (see fig. 33).

In the press, the independent magazine *al-Hilal*'s crescent moon name and symbol seemed to suggest Islamic affinities (though its owners were Christians of Lebanese origin). For a number of months in 1923–24, however, striking pharaonic columns boldly framed its covers (see fig. 34).

Egyptian theater also caught the pharaonist tide. Tutankhamun's tomb revived interest in his father, Akhenaten, a fascinating figure since his rediscovery in the nineteenth century. Ankhenaten's reputed monotheism and attack on the old gods and priesthoods attracted both Muslims and Christians eager to make ancient Egypt seem less alien. Ahmad Zaki Abu Shadi's 1927 play Akhenaten, Pharaoh of Egypt depicted a heroic revolutionary fighting reactionary priests and palace officials. Abu Shadi's Akhenaten is a modern hero fighting for peace, brotherhood, and social welfare, and his death is a tragic loss. Ahmad Sabri's *Kahin Amun: Masrahiya firawniya* (The High Priest of Amun: A Pharaonic Drama, 1929) praised Akhenaten's idealism and imagines that despite the reaction after his death, his religious tolerance influenced later pharaohs.[80]

الهلال

١٩٢٤

محتويات هذا الجزء

الله ـ قصيدة لاحمد شوقي بك
من اب الى ابنه ـ رسالة لجرجي زيدان
اساس الملك ـ بقلم امين الريحاني
حياة مرآتها ـ قصيدة لمصطفى صادق الرافعي
وراثة النبوغ والعبقرية ـ بقلم سلامه موسى
قيصرة روسيا ـ بقلم ملكة رومانيا
دولة لا فردٌ : هوغوستينس
سهم الى القمر
صور من حياة المتوحشين
علي بهجت بك ـ بقلم توفيق اسكاروس
الخ ... الخ ...

الهلال لسان حال النهضة المصرية

34 *Al-Hilal* goes phara-
onic. Cover format used by
al-Hilal for some months in
1923–1924. The slogan at
the bottom translates: "*Al-
Hilal*, voice of the Egyptian
revival." Al-Hilal, *May, 1924.*

Ramesses II, a mighty builder often depicted in battle, had a different appeal for still British-occupied Egypt. Popular composer Sayyid Darwish set Mahmud Murad's play The Glory of Ramses (1923) to music. As will be seen in chapter 10, their production enthralled Ahmad Husayn and his fellow students at the Khedival Secondary School. Darwish and Murad followed up with the musical play *Tutankhamun* in 1924.[81] In 1923 Yusuf Wahbi (1898–1982), pioneering actor and producer for stage and screen, named his theatrical troupe the Ramses Company.[82]

Like Ramesses II, and unlike Akhenaten and Tutankhamun, Cleopatra VII—*the* Cleopatra—had never been forgotten. Pharaonists of the 1920s renewed Cleopatra's appeal to Egyptians. Muhammad Husayn Haykal and women's magazines published biographical sketches, and Ahmad Shawqi's play The Fall and Death of Cleopatra (1927) caught the public eye.[83] Returning from exile after the 1919 revolution, Shawqi had become a national, not just a royalist, poet. Shakespeare's *Antony and Cleopatra* had reflected Roman denigration of her as the Oriental "viper of the Nile" who corrupted Roman purity. Shawqi's Cleopatra, in contrast, is a devoted mother, a cultured ruler of a prosperous Hellenized Egypt, and a patriot fighting for her country against Octavian's Roman imperial aggression. The parallel with British imperialism in Egypt is clear. In Shawqi's 1931 play *Cambyses (Qambiz)*, it is Persian aggressors who resemble the British as enemies of Egypt and its religion.[84]

Western and Egyptian Egyptology, Western Egyptomania, and Egyptian pharaonism all did much to shape, and were shaped by, tourism. It is to the history of tourism in Egypt that chapter 5 now turns.

Part Two

**Tourism and Islamic,
Coptic, and Greco–Roman
Archaeologies**

5

Consuming Antiquity: Western Tourism between Two Revolutions, 1919–1952

The history of Egyptian tourism over the long nineteenth century to 1914 has received significant attention in recent years, as has postcolonial tourism under Nasser, Sadat, and Mubarak. Nineteenth-century tourism began with the excitement of rediscovering ancient Egypt in the dual wakes of Napoleon and Champollion, reached its stride after midcentury with the industrialized tourism of Thomas Cook and John Murray's and Karl Baedeker's guidebooks, and culminated in the romantic haze of the Edwardian belle époque.[1] Tourism since Nasser has been analyzed from varying perspectives of mass marketing, consumerism, gender, Orientalism, and postcolonialism.[2] The period from 1914 to 1952—during which British predominance in Egypt gradually gave way in the face of Egyptian nationalism and growing American influence—has received less attention.

As 1952 opened, it might have seemed that little had changed politically in Egypt since 1914. British troops still occupied the Suez Canal Zone, full independence was still a dream, an ineffectual monarch still occupied the throne, and big landowners still dominated state and society. Although World War II had killed off the Nile cruise, tourists continued to arrive mainly by sea in Alexandria or Port Said and followed the beaten paths to the same sites and most of the same hotels. The discovery of Tutankhamun's tomb did draw a rush of tourists, but otherwise these had been difficult decades for tourism. World War I, Egypt's 1919 revolution, the Great Depression, World War II, the 1948 Arab–Israeli war, and the January 1952 riots had delivered blow after blow to hopes for a stable and flourishing tourist trade.

The burning of Shepheard's Hotel in the riots of January 26, 1952, rang down the curtain on colonial-era tourism. The old Shepheard's replacement as Cairo's premier hotel by the Nile Hilton in 1959 proclaimed the arrival of postcolonial tourism, which would flower under Sadat and Mubarak. (The new Shepheard's, opened in 1957, perpetuated the legendary name but was less iconic.) This chapter examines the tourism of this unsettled era from 1914 to 1952 with respect to hotels, transportation, guidebooks, tourist promotion, and relations with dragomans. It also discusses Hassan Fathy's utopian village of New Qurna (or New Gourna) across the Nile from Luxor.

From the standpoint of British tourism, after the end of the Napoleonic wars reopened the continent, middle-class tourism increasingly overshadowed the seventeenth- and eighteenth-century tradition of the aristocratic grand tour. Spurred by industrialization and urbanization, a growing segment of the middle classes traveled for enlightenment and relaxation. In the 1830s, railroad and steamship travel took off, and John Murray and Karl Baedeker published the first modern guidebooks, brimming with practical advice and authoritative prescriptions on sights to be seen.[3] Temperance evangelist Thomas Cook led his first local excursion by rail in the English Midlands in 1841. He followed up with trips to London's Great Exhibition in 1851, the Paris Exposition in 1855, and over the Alps to Italy in 1864. Cook & Son made leisure travel more available to women, whether accompanied by male relatives or with the company standing in as chaperone. After the interruption caused by the US Civil War, Americans seeking the validation of "old world" high culture surged back across the Atlantic and into the Mediterranean.[4]

Ancient Roman and Renaissance Italy retained their drawing power, but nineteenth-century tourists also headed south in search of health, relaxation, and fun in the Mediterranean sun. By midcentury, steamships were extending excursions into the eastern Mediterranean, where Greece, the Holy Land, and Egypt beckoned with diverse but often overlapping appeals.[5] The opening ceremonies of the Suez Canal in 1869 elicited Thomas Cook's first excursion to Egypt. Over the next three decades, Thomas's son John Mason Cook built up a tourist empire on the Nile that worked hand in glove with British imperial expansion. Cook's Nile steamers carried the failed Gordan relief expedition to Khartoum in 1884–85, facilitated Kitchener's conquest of the Sudan in 1896–98, and were requisitioned for imperial forces during both world wars.[6] Wealthy travelers on private *dahabiyas* (sailing Nile houseboats) sneered at the "Cookites" herded onto steamers, but John Mason Cook astutely expanded into the luxury market as well. James Buzard perceptively treated "the formation of modern tourism *and* the impulse to denigrate tourists as a single complex phenomenon."[7]

Table E. Visitors to Egypt's Four Antiquities
Museums in Selected Years

Year	Egyptian Museum	Museum of Arab Art	Greco-Roman Museum	Coptic Museum
1913	29,718	5,166	4,977	
1922	37,470	4,156	9,497	1,135
1926	143,162	11,682	11,336	3,725
1929	100,485	9,553	11,403	2,738
1938	81,483	7,751	12,540	3,730
1941–43	Closed	Closed	Closed	Closed
1948	70,389	5,085	2,087	5,680

Compiled from *Annuaire statistique de l'Égypte 1914*, 6me année, Département de la statistique générale, Ministère des finances (Cairo: Imprimerie nationale, 1914), 104, and later volumes through *Annuaire statistique de l'Égypte 1947, 1948, et 1949* (Cairo, 1952), 258–59. After 1922, an Arabic title (*al-Ihsa al-sanawi al-amm*) is added.

Tourists disembarking in Alexandria or Port Said before World War I quickly boarded the train for Cairo, where the fashionable hotels included Shepheard's, the nearby Grand Continental, the Nile-side Semiramis, and the Mena House out by the Pyramids.[8] The prescribed pharaonic sights of this "antique land" formed the backbone of the standard tour, with glimpses of "Oriental" life presented as "straight out of the *Arabian Nights*" thrown in. After doing the pyramids of Giza and perhaps Saqqara, the Egyptian Museum, Khan al-Khalili, and the Citadel with its Muhammad Ali Mosque, the parade went south for the temples and tombs of Upper Egypt, either by Cook's steamer or by overnight train. At Luxor, the Winter Palace became *the* place to stay, at Aswan, the Cataract Hotel (see figs. 35 and 36).

Attendance statistics for Egypt's four main museums confirm the outsized draw of pharaonic antiquities (see table E). On the eve of World War I, the Egyptian Museum was hosting three or more times as many visitors as the other three museums combined, a ratio it maintained or bettered at least down to the 1952 revolution.

World War I: "The Season in Egypt: Tourists Replaced by Soldiers"

This *Times* headline of February 4, 1915, summarized the blow the war delivered to Egypt's tourist trade. Shortly before the war, seven to eight thousand Western tourists, mainly British and American, were arriving each year. Most stayed for at least three weeks of a "season" that began in December and ended in April.[9] The guns of August changed all that:

> And so the Cairo season is one of the victims of the war. Most of the chief hotels are closed. The two great hotel groups are represented only by the "Grand Continental" and "Shepheard's." Savoy, Semiramis, Ghezireh Palace will not open this season. Helouan is an abomination of desolation, with one hotel and pension alone open out of at least a dozen. . . . The Luxor Hotel at Luxor and the Grand Hotel at Assuan are open for the benefit of a few old habitués, of invalids, and of occasional officers on short leave or Anglo–Egyptian officials in need of a brief rest. . . .
>
> Yet if the season is non-existent there is animation enough in the European life of Cairo. The city has become militarized. . . . Shepheard's and the Grand Continental Hotel swarm with officers of every rank and every branch in the Imperial service—British, Indian, Colonial, and Egyptian. . . .
>
> The military have amply made up for the absence of tourists as far as Cairo is concerned. The dragomans, guides, and vendors of every species of rubbish from inefficient fly-whisks to stuffed crocodiles have thriven exceedingly. . . .
>
> It is only in Upper Egypt that the cessation of the tourist traffic has really been felt. [10]

In *Through Egypt in War-Time*, Martin Briggs reported that although photography shops in Luxor were servicing an "amazing number of Kodaks" in the armed forces, the town painfully felt "the substitution of a handful of military officers for a small army of millionaires."[11] Ten of Cook's Nile steamers were requisitioned, mainly for the Mespotamian campaign,[12] and Luxor's Winter Palace was turned into a military hospital.[13] In 1915, three out of every four visitors to the Egyptian Museum were imperial troops, pushing its total attendance to an unprecedented high of 44,261. In contrast, the closure of the museums during World War II would plunge attendance to zero for over three years (see table E).

That guidebook production on Egypt all but ceased during World War I underlines the abnormality of this military tourism. From 1900 to 1914, thirty-one editions of English-language Egyptian guidebooks had poured out, along with fifteen in French, nine in German, and one in Russian. For 1915–1919, Volkoff—the standard reference—does not list a single Egyptian guidebook.[14] He missed, however, the Macmillan Guides seventh edition (1916, reprinted 1918). In it, "references to enemy firms have been deleted" and temporary tent cities and the requisitioning of hotels and schools for military hospitals were ignored.[15]

Fragile Recovery: Thomas Cook, "Independence," and Tutankhamun's Tomb

In Egypt, as in Europe, hopes for a quick return to normalcy in 1919 were disappointed. With the war over, martial law could no longer keep the lid on protest. Resentment against foreign troops, conscription for labor battalions, market shortages, and inflation boiled over. The Egyptian uprising of March 1919 caught everyone off guard. A mix of British military repression and concessions finally restored order.

In December 1920, Thomas Cook announced the resumption of the Nile steamer service—along with the luxury hotels, the quintessential symbol of belle époque Egyptian tourism—and the reopening of Luxor and Aswan hotels after a six-year interruption[16] (see figs. 35, 36, and 37).

In Luxor and Aswan, the Winter Palace and the Cataract respectively resumed their unchallenged preeminence as luxury hotels. Of Cook's thirty-five Nile steamers with a known construction date, all but one were built before 1914. Steamers that had survived the war were refurbished, but the only capital Cook risked on new construction between the wars was on the eighty-berth *Sudan*, built in 1921.[17]

35 Thomas Cook & Son's Nile Flotilla. *Courtesy of Thomas Cook Archives (UK).*

36 The Edwardian "golden age of travel:" Winter Palace Hotel, Luxor, opened 1907. Gaddes. *As reproduced in Humphreys,* Grand Hotels of Egypt, *181.*

37 Twin pillars of the golden age of travel: Cook's steamer "Thebes" beneath the Cataract Hotel at Aswan, built 1899. *Courtesy of Thomas Cook Archives (UK).*

In 1922, Great Britain's declaration of limited Egyptian independence and the discovery of Tutankhamun's tomb paved the way for a tourist boom. The November discovery so thrilled the world that by late December, Thomas Cook, American Express, and three other agencies were advertising chartered cruises from the United States that, if filled, would draw a record 3,500 Americans. Another two thousand were expected to stop off on around-the-world cruises, and others would arrive by Italian steamers from Trieste, Genoa, Naples, and Venice.[18] In Luxor hotels, cots spilled over into halls and lobbies.

The lure of Tutankhamun pushed attendance at the Egyptian Museum to 143,162 in 1926 (a pre-1952 record), and the spillover effect of "Tut" also sent a record 11,682 visitors to the Museum of Arab Art (see Table E, p. 139). (Egyptian visitors, many of them schoolchildren coming with their classes, as well as Western tourists, accounted for the surge.) Visitors to the Egyptian Museum in 1926 outnumbered those to the other three museums combined by more than five to one, driving home the overwhelming preference for pharaonic antiquity which would persist throughout the semicolonial era and beyond.

Tutankhamun gave heart to shipping companies and hotel investors. The French company Messageries Maritimes added the *Champollion* to its Mediterranean steamer fleet in 1925 and the *Mariette Pacha* the year after.[19] In Cairo, Shepheard's, Semiramis, and the Continental-Savoy hotels all added rooms during the 1920s. To a considerable extent, however, the hotel industry coasted on pre-World War I capital. Alexandria's Cecil Hotel (1930) was the only new first-class hotel built in Egypt between 1914 and 1952.[20]

The hoteliers were a multinational lot. Samuel Shepheard, who arrived in 1842 and created the legendary hotel that bears his name, as well as the couple who founded the Mena House, were English. Most hoteliers, however, were not. Ferdinand Pagnon, who developed hotels in Luxor and Aswan, was French. George Nungovich, who arrived at age fourteen in 1870, was Greek-Cypriot. By his death in 1908, Nungovich Hotels Co. ran the Grand Continental (Shepheard's main rival), the Mena House, two other Cairo hotels, Alexandria's San Stefano Hotel-Casino, and two hotels and the thermal baths at Helwan. Charles Baehler, a Swiss who arrived at age eighteen in 1889, flourished despite being interned during World War I on charges of being pro-German. By 1925, Baehler's empire controlled Shepheard's and nearly all other first-class hotels in Egypt with four thousand beds.[21]

Compared to at least fifty-six editions of Western guidebooks to Egypt from 1900 through 1914, the 1920s limped along with only four or five, and the 1929 editions of Baedeker's and Cook's detailed guidebooks proved to be the last of their kind. Only five countrywide Egyptian guides, locally produced and poor in quality, came out from 1930 through 1949.[22]

As before 1914, constraints of time and money still severely limited the segments of the Western middle classes who undertook Egyptian tours. In 1929, Baedeker still declared "A glimpse of the country may be obtained in 4 or 5 weeks (exclusive of the journey out)."[23] With the rail-steamer journey from England still taking at least six days each way, the winter excursion was out of reach unless one could spare six weeks—or seven or eight if coming from America. In 1929, roundtrip fare from Britain by first-class rail sleeper and steamship cost £80 (£45 for second class)—not very different from the prewar £50 and £28 respectively if inflation is factored in. Sailing from Britain direct via the Straits of Gibraltar in 1929 was slightly cheaper but added five or six days to the trip. Luxury tourists could indulge in nostalgia for the age of sail: "The most attractive, but also the slowest and most expensive method of ascending the Nile is by Dahabiya." A surprising option opened up between the world wars—but never before or since: an excursion by first-class sleeping car from London to Cairo. This took a week each way and cost £86 roundtrip. Ferries across the Channel, Bosphorus, and Suez Canal, and a motor car from Tripoli (Lebanon) to Haifa or Jaffa (Palestine) filled in the missing rail links.[24]

The 1929 Baedeker signaled a growing trend—Americans bypassing both Britain and British mediation in visiting Egypt. Pre-1914 editions of Baedeker had listed "Steamship lines from England direct"; in 1929 this section became "Steamship lines from England and America direct."[25] The 1929 edition also revealed the rapid expansion of American Express, which now listed offices in London, Cairo, Luxor, and Aswan; these offices also served as agents for the Anglo–American Nile & Tourist Co., Thomas Cook's main rival in Egypt.[26] American Express's parent company, Wells Fargo Co., dated back to 1841, the same year which had seen the founding of Thomas Cook, Cunard (later British and North American Royal Mail Steam Packet Co.), and Bradshaw (Britain's national railroad timetable).[27]

Cook & Son had recruited Americans for its Egyptian tours since the later nineteenth century. For many years, American Express offered no competition; the offices it opened in Europe in the 1890s only begrudgingly began expanding from shipping and communication into tourism shortly before World War I.[28] In 1908, American Express's Express Nile Steamer Co. was running Cairo–Luxor cruises on the *America* and the *Virginia* in competition with Cook.[29] The war impelled the Hamburg & Anglo–American Nile Company to change its name to Anglo–American

Nile & Tourist Company and rename its ship the *Germania* the *Britannia*.[30] Cook, however, kept its lead in Nile cruises. In 1929, its large steamers (the *Sudan*, *Arabia*, *Egypt*, and *Thebes*), each with a physician aboard, left Cairo on a twenty-one-day round trip to Aswan every week from November 7 to March 6 for a fare of £70.[31] Although American ships regularly sailed from New York to Alexandria, not until World War II did the United States begin a serious challenge to Britain's economic predominance in Egypt.[32]

Advertisements in *The Egyptian Gazette* of January 1, 1924, drive home the idea of empire as a transportation network. Like those of its model, the London *Times*, the *Gazette*'s advertisements covered the front page. The thirty ads on the page are mostly for British firms. A dozen are for steamship lines (including Cook's Nile Steamers and Anglo–American Nile), four for railroads, and one for a telegraph company. Four offer shipping and related services, four insurance, and two are two asphalt contractors. Three supply drinks for thirsty travelers or workers—Lipton, White Horse Whiskey, and (Egyptian) Spathis mineral water.

Building on Edward Said, Timothy Mitchell, and Thomas Urry, Derek Gregory analyzed how Western tourists on Nile steamers behaved as "Emperors of the Gaze." Safely ensconced on their "secure viewing platform," they could savor the "Oriental" landscape drifting by and at times taste the pleasure of spying on intimate aspects of peasant life. Distance somewhat obscured poverty and filth and spared the viewers unpleasant backlash from the objects of their imperial gaze. Binoculars pulled in details of the passing exhibition, while camera, sketchbook, watercolors, or pen recorded the traveler's impressions.[33]

Air passenger service hardly began cutting in on steamships in transporting tourists to Egypt until after World War II. Beginning in 1929, for £104 roundtrip, the adventurous rich could try the London-to-Alexandria leg of Imperial Airways' service to Karachi, hopping via Paris, Genoa, Rome, Naples, Corfu, Athens, Crete, and Tobruk. (It took four additional days to continue on to Karachi).[34] In 1933, Misr Airwork, a joint venture of Egypt's Misr Bank and Britain's Airwork, began air passenger service within Egypt. That same year, Egypt issued airmail stamps featuring a plane over the Giza Pyramids and hosted an Aviation Congress. In 1939, Pan Am and Imperial Airways inaugurated regular mail and passenger flights across the Atlantic, and Imperial merged with British Airways to form British Overseas Airways Corporation (BOAC).[35] Meanwhile, Misr Airwork had begun service to neighboring countries. World War II interrupted international service worldwide. Egypt nationalized Misr Airwork during the war and subsequently changed its name to Misr Airlines, then to MisrAir.[36]

Toning Down the Guidebooks

The 1921 edition of E.A.W. Budge's *Cook's Handbook for Egypt and the Sudan* continued previous editions' arrogant, demeaning assaults on Egyptians and Islam:

> The religion which he [the Prophet Muhammad] preached was, and is, intolerant and fanatical, and, although it has made millions of men believe in one God, and renounce the worship of idols, and abhor wine and strong drink, it has set the seal of approval upon the unbridled gratification of sensual appetites, and has given polygamy and divorce a religious status and wide-spread popularity.[37]
>
> The Egyptian knows that the possession of money will enable him to keep wives, to dress well, to gratify his desires for pleasure. . . .[38]
>
> The destructive fanaticism peculiar to the Muhammadan mind, so common in the far east and parts of Mesopotamia, seems to be non-existent in Egypt; such fanaticism as exists is, no doubt, kept in check by the presence of Europeans, and all different peoples live side by side in a most peaceable manner. It should always be remembered that waves of fanaticism pass over all Muhammadan peoples at intervals, and it must be confessed that the Pan-Islamic propagandists in Egypt are producing a feeling of unrest in the country, and that disaffection in the army is likely to be the result.[39]

Compromising the portability expected in a "handbook" or "field guide," Budge's 1921 guide had ballooned to 946 pages, not counting advertisements. Sections packed with statistics from Cromer's reports were nearly unreadable. Did no one dare tell the eminent director of the British Museum's Department of Egyptian and Assyrian Antiquities that pruning and reworking were badly needed? In 1929, Cook jettisoned Budge—now retired from the British Museum—for a more concise guide by R. Elton.[40] Elton did not even mention Budge in his preface. He avoided Budge's smears on Islam but had mixed views on Copts, stating that they

> are said, even by their own people, to be sullen in temper, greedy and avaricious, and to pursue modern education merely for the love of personal gain. Against this view must be set the fact that until the rule of the British in Egypt they never enjoyed real freedom. . . . Many competent authorities consider the Copts to be the ablest and most intellectual of all the natives of Egypt.[41]

It took a decade after Germany's defeat in World War I for Leipzig-based Baedeker to bring out a new English-language edition of its classic Egyptian guide. This proved to be the last. Egyptologist Georg Steindorff had edited the Egyptian Baedeker since 1897. He revisited the country in 1928–29, and the new edition's scholarly authority was as impressive as ever. K.A.C. Creswell's chapter "Islamic Architecture in Egypt" was an improvement over Franz-Pasha's earlier "Buildings of the Mohammedans," and Ugo Monneret de Villard's section on Christian art introduced a new field.

Not being in the business of organizing tours like Cook, the 1929 Baedeker still sniffed:

> It is as well for the independent traveller to avoid as far as possible coming into contact with the large parties organized by the tourist agents, for otherwise circumstances are apt to arise in which he is pushed to the wall, without any redress.[42]

The 1929 Baedeker was slightly more tolerant on Islam than the 1908 edition, which had cautioned on the mosque-university of al-Azhar:

> This being one of the fountain-heads of Mohammedan fanaticism, the traveller should, of course, throughout his visit, be careful not to indulge openly in any gestures of amusement or contempt.[43]

In 1929, this was toned this down to: "cameras are forbidden and the visitor should carefully abstain from any manifestation of amusement or contempt."[44] The 1908 edition's section on Islam had declared:

> The doctrine of the resurrection has been grossly corrupted by the Koran and by subsequent tradition, but its main features have doubtless been borrowed from the Christians.[45]

C.H. Becker's 1929 chapter on Islam merely says:

> We are no longer surprised by the profound inner relationship between the mental outlook of mediaeval Christianity and that of Islam; both systems are based upon the common foundation of the Greek–Oriental civilization of Christian antiquity. The Arabs consistently stressed the oriental elements in this civilization; while on the other hand, on European soil, the Germanic spirit turned away from these and elaborated from its inner consciousness the typical western forms of the middle ages.[46]

Becker concedes that Islamic civilization is "based upon the same general principles as the civilization of mediaeval Europe," but goes on to declare that Islamic civilization "differs mainly in being represented by other peoples and other races, to whom the brilliant intellectual development of Europe has been denied."[47] In retrospect, Becker's speaking of "race" and "Germanic spirit" in the context of 1929 Germany are unsettling.

The Great Depression and Tourist Promotion

Published in the year in which the Wall Street crash touched off the Great Depression, Baedeker's and Cook's comprehensive Egyptian guides of 1929 were the last of their kind. As late as 1933, however, Egypt's Ministry of Finance hailed tourism's "invisible export" as "Egypt's second greatest economic asset," and the 1934–1935 figures—broken down in table F—were slightly better. Even without the "quick trip" passengers going through the Suez Canal, the 12,500 remaining annual visitors considerably outnumbered the seven to eight thousand of the prewar era.[48]

Well over 40 percent of the clients on Cook's Nile voyages in the late 1920s and early 1930s were British, with Americans at 26–38 percent a strong second. Over three-fourths of the clients came from English-speaking countries. German speakers were a distant third (6–8 percent), behind Britons and Americans, and Francophones ranked slightly behind that.[49]

Shortly before the Great War, Shepheard's, Wagon-Lits Co., Cook, and the Savoy Group of hotels in Egypt came together to form a Travel

Table F. Tourists of Various Means and Their Expenditures in Egypt, 1934–35

	Individuals of	Number	Value of invisible export	Value per head
A	Unlimited means	500	£E100,000	£E200
B	Adequate means	1,000	£E100,000	£E100
C	Cruise passengers	7,000	£E210,000	£E30
D	Quick trip passengers (passing through the Suez Canal)	8,000	£E56,000	£E7
E	Independent visitors of moderate means	2,000	£E100,000	£E50
F	Independent visitors on pension	2,000	£E50,000	£E25
	Total	**20,500**	**£E616,000**	

TCA, Box: Steamer Contracts, Folio 123, Tourist Development Association of Egypt, "Reporton the Publicity and Propaganda Campaign for the Season 1934–1935," p.7.

Association, and Lord Kitchener had the Egyptian State Railways match the largest private subscription.[50] Otherwise, tourist promotion was largely left to the private sector until the mid-1930s. In 1929, the foreign-dominated Tourist Development Association had offices in the Cairo railway station, London, and Paris, and the Egyptian State Railways had an enquiry office in London.[51] In 1929, the Association's magazine *Egypt and the Sudan* roughly divided its seventy-odd pages between peppy accounts of tourist attractions and advertisements for hotels, steamship companies, banks, and travel agencies. In 1937, the magazine became *Egypt: A Travel Quarterly*, with at least some numbers bilingual in French.

By 1933, I.G. Lévi, secretary of the Egyptian Federation of Industries (with which the Tourist Development Association was affiliated), was arguing that the slump in tourism had become deep enough to call for state intervention. He cited precedents in the French Maghreb, Italian Libya, and British Palestine. Except for the Nile steamers, he deplored the poor tourist infrastructure in Upper Egypt. Unlike in the past, he asserted, most tourist revenues now stayed in Egypt, to the benefit of both Egyptians and resident Europeans.[52]

In the summer of 1935, Egypt's Ministry of Finance, with High Commissioner Lampson's approval, set up the Egyptian Tourist Bureau, with Ahmad Sadiq Bey as director. Formerly director general of the Municipality of Alexandria, Sadiq happened to be out of favor with the king but was appointed through a loophole which bypassed the need for the royal signature.[53] Sadiq cut red tape in issuing visas, cracked down on beggars and "undesirables" who pestered tourists, and promoted Mediterranean summer beach tourism as a complement to winter antiquities tourism. Student–police clashes in the anti-palace demonstrations of the fall of 1935 scared away tourists, but the trade recovered with the restoration of the 1923 constitution and the Wafd's return to power in 1936. The Tourist Bureau, transferred to the new Ministry of Commerce and Industry, budgeted £E40,000 for tourist promotion through Cook & Son. The Bureau would grow into the Ministry of Tourism in the 1960s and commemorate its fiftieth anniversary with a postage stamp in 1985.[54]

Cook lost some of its edge in Egypt after 1928, when the founder's grandsons Frank and Ernest Cook sold the firm to Wagon-Lits (International Sleeping Car) Company.[55] For a dozen years, Belgian, Italian, and French interests in turn controlled Wagon-Lits and its Cook subsidiary. A 1933 proposal to eliminate British employees in Egypt elicited a protest that only they could keep British clients satisfied, and that:

Thomas Cook & Son, Ltd. in Egypt occupies a unique position. It is the leading industrial enterprise in that country and is so essentially British that, arising out of 60 years of existence, it has assumed something of the character of an official British undertaking.[56]

Playing the Dragoman Game

This chapter draws mainly from Western sources, which—even if read against the grain—reveal only glimpses of the relationships of Egyptians to antiquities tourism, whether as upper- and middle-class consumers or as producers—from donkey boys to felucca crews, and antiquities peddlers to dragomans. *Aboudi's Guide to the Antiquities of Egypt* offers a rare glimpse through subaltern eyes. Mohamed Aboudi was a dragoman, or local guide/translator. Being an Egyptian and practitioner of a maligned occupation during the colonial age made him a subaltern, though his success in parlaying his family's dragoman business into stores for photos, souvenirs, and books in Luxor and Cairo also turned him into a prosperous effendi member of an entrepreneurial elite[57] (see figs. 38 and 39).

Guidebooks to Egypt were steeped in cross-cultural, cross-national, and cross-class anxieties regarding dragomans. In 1908, Baedeker's section "Intercourse with Orientals. Dragomans" prescribed:

Travellers about to make a tour of any length may avoid all the petty annoyances incident to direct dealings with the natives by placing themselves under the care of a Dragoman (Arab. *Turgumân*). [58]

But a stern warning followed:

The dragomans are inclined to assume a patronizing manner towards their employees, while they generally treat their own countrymen with an air of superiority. The sooner this impertinence is checked, the more satisfactory will be the traveller's subsequent relations with his guide.

Macmillan's 1911 guide insisted that:

Travellers must remember that the dragoman, whether Egyptian or Syrian, dressed in European, Turkish, or Arab dress, is merely a servant, and should always ride on the box and not *in* the carriage. They are quick to take advantage of the slightest familiarity.[59]

The 1929 Baedeker started off boldly: "For the tours described in this book the services of a Dragoman . . . may be easily dispensed with,

38 From dragoman to effendi: Two portraits of Mohamed Aboudi. *Aboudi, Aboudi's Guide Book (Luxor, 1931), frontispiece;* Aboudi's Guide Book *(1954), frontispiece.*

even by those less accustomed to traveling," but conceded that "They are sometimes useful, however, for visiting mosques." If travelers hired "well-recommended dragomans . . . preferably those for whom the hotels assume some responsibility," "[t]hey must be treated from the first as servants and all familiarity should be discouraged."

The 1908 Baedeker had insisted:

> Above all, travellers should never permit their dragoman to "explain" the monuments. These men are without exception quite uneducated, without the least knowledge of the historic or aesthetic significance of the monuments; and their "explanations" are merely garbled versions of what they have picked up from guide-books or from the remarks of previous travellers.

Twenty years on, the warning softened slightly to: "dragomans are with few exceptions quite uneducated," and "their 'explanations' of them [antiquities] are only too often merely garbled versions," then added non-commitally, "Special schools for dragomans, however, are to be established by the government at Giza and Luxor."

The 1929 Baedeker retained its predecessors' parting warning:

> On the successful termination of the journey travellers are too apt from motives of good nature to write a more favourable testimonial for their dragoman than he really deserves; but this is truly an act of injustice to his subsequent employers. The testimonial therefore should not omit to mention any serious cause for dissatisfaction.

Aboudi's Guide Book gives us glimpses of how an unusually successful dragoman negotiated this highly charged field. Mohamed Aboudi's father had guided tourists to the Valley of the Kings as far back as the 1870s. In 1905 Aboudi began escorting tourists from Cook's steamers. Aboudi's portrait in the 1931 edition shows him a resplendent "oriental" in dragoman's robes and turban; the photo in the 1954 edition transforms (or promotes?) him to a modern effendi in coat, tie, and tarboosh[60] (fig. 38). By 1909 Aboudi had parlayed his Cook connections at Luxor into ownership of a tourist shop in the arcade of the new Winter Palace Hotel,[61] and by 1931 he had another store in Cairo just across the street from Shepheard's (fig. 39). The two stores' signs suggest different marketing ploys. Deep in Egypt's interior at Luxor (albeit in a major tourist hub), large lettering reassuringly advertises "English Photo Stores" and "Kodaks," while in cosmopolitan Cairo, the sign peddles exotic allure: "M. Aboudi & Co. Oriental Store."

Aboudi's Guide Book made no pretense of academic authority. Baedeker sneered at "garbled versions of what they [dragomans] have picked up from guide-books or from the remarks of previous travelers,"[62] but Aboudi was proud of what he had distilled from learned visitors he had accompanied. During summer off-seasons, Aboudi honed his skills in six foreign languages as a private courier to Europe.[63]

He patched into his guide brief summaries gleaned from other guide-books: a smattering of history through the reign of King Fuad; the religion, language, and hieroglyphs of ancient Egypt; cartouches of a few pharaohs; Muslim and Coptic beliefs and customs; birds and trees; and Arabic vocabulary. His information is sometimes oversimplified, misleading, or wrong: "Most of the mosques are made of the best Saracinic architecture"; "The Coptic language is derived from old Greek"; "The Fellahin are the Egyptian farmers and peasants in general. They are the descendants of the early Arab settlers, or, in the case of the Copts, of the ancient Egyptians"; and

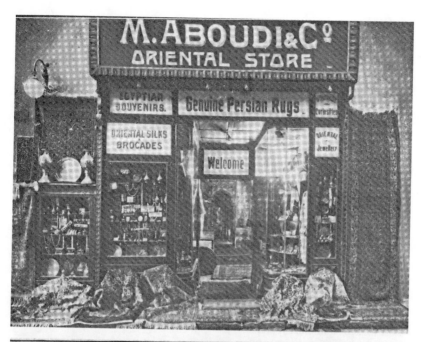

39 Flexible marketing: Mohamed Aboudi's "English Photo Stores" (Luxor) and "Oriental Store" (Cairo, opposite Shepheard's Hotel). Aboudi's Guide Book, *(1931), 38, 165.*

There are many people in the world and specially in America and other countries who are envolved in the wrong belief emanating from many false sources that Mohamed the Prophet is the God of all the Moslems.[64]

Aboudi obliged his clients with a "curse of the mummy" story from his father, who had guided the son of a Lord Harrington in 1879. The young man purchased a mummy and coffin and came to a gruesome end. After an elephant trampled him to death during an African safari, a curse on violators was deciphered on the coffin.[65]

Aboudi played the buffoon with Biblical allusions and orientalist stereotypes:

Who took Cook's tourists by the hand?
Who led them through the Pharaohs' land?
Who all things for their comfort planned?—
                    ABOUDI!

At all the Tomb and Temple gates
A wicked Arab thereby waits
Remember, therefore, at the wicket
You must produce your Temple Ticket.

O East is East, and West is West, in Luxor or in London town,
But Aboudi, our faithful Aboudi, he will never let us down.
Through all the plagues of Egypt; donkey-boys, the flies, the sand.
This trusty modern Moses leads us towards the Promised Land.

I want to go to Egypt, I want to do the Nile.
I want to ride the donkey, and see a crocodile.
I want to see the Pyramids, the Sphinx and all the Tombs;
I want to see the rock-hewn shrines, and all the painted rooms;

I want to be a tourist, with helmet made of cork;
And when I've seen Old Egypt, I'll go back to Old New York.
But I shall sure come back again, as soon as e'er I can,
And do the same Old Nile trip with the same Old Dragoman.[66]

When it came to the bust of Nefertiti in the Egyptian Museum in Berlin, however, Aboudi dropped his eager-to-please dragoman patter and spoke as an effendi nationalist. He recounted how he had visited the Berlin Museum in 1927 and angered "Professor Burchart" (Borchardt) by questioning the circumstances under which he had taken the bust out of Egypt. Aboudi "left the Museum with a broken heart at seeing this unique piece in Berlin and not in its proper place at the Egyptian Museum where it should be." [67]

Aboudi breached the defensive perimeter which Baedeker so sternly prescribed for keeping dragomans in their place. Whether his doggerel elicited chuckles or groans, he worked assiduously to subvert the prescription that dragomans "must be treated from the first as servants and all familiarity should be discouraged." [68] Baedeker's very insistence suggests the difficulty of maintaining the prescribed aloofness. The roughness of Aboudi's prose suggests that a native English speaker might have helped with the poems. Aboudi kept some dignity even when playing the clown, and as in many tourist–host encounters, it was not always clear who was using whom and who was calling the tune.

World War II and After

The fall 1939 issue of *Egypt: A Travel Quarterly* was as oblivious to the looming catastrophe as the September 1939 issue of Cook's *Traveller's Gazette*. Advertising hotels in Germany, the *Gazette* declared: "You will like Poland and Poland will welcome you." [69] This was the last issue of both magazines; World War II obliterated normal tourism that September as abruptly as had World War I in 1914. The influx of tens of thousands of British and imperial troops during World War I brought prosperity to some Egyptians but hardship, disruption, and degradation to many others. Except for catering to military tourists, Luxor and Aswan again lost their winter job opportunities in tourism and excavation. To make things worse, a malaria epidemic ravaged Upper Egypt from 1942 to 1945.

The absence after 1929 of up-to-date guidebooks from European metropolitan firms—Murray, Baedeker, Cook, Macmillan, and Hachette—opened the door for local attempts to fill the gap. Like the initial edition of *Aboudi's Guide*, Egyptian Museum curator A. Hamada's guidebook limited its geographical scope: *Visit Pharaonic Egypt. Guide-Book to the Egyptian Museum, Giza, Saqqara, Luxor and Aswan* (Cairo, 1948?). Two guidebooks catered to soldiers: M. Brin and R.A. Biancardi, *Say It in Arabic and See Egypt: Manual and Guide Book for the British and Imperial Forces* (Cairo, 1942), and the Co-ordinating Committee for the Welfare of H.B.M. Forces in Alexandria, *Service Guide to Alexandria* (2nd ed., 1940?). [70]

The several countrywide guides to Egypt attempted in the 1930s and 1940s were superficial. All but one were local productions, one by a resident Greek and two by Egyptians. The prefatory poem to Condopoulo's guide was hardly promising:

Good friends, who want a trusty guide,
Please turn these leaves and look inside,
And read about the famous Dam,
Which can be seen at Assouan.[71]

Riad Gayed, who had published Arabic guides to Europe, wrote *Egypt from Mena to Fouad: A Practical Guide Book and a Manual of Egyptian History* (Cairo, [1936–37]).[72]

No longer British-owned or in the Egyptian guidebook business, Thomas Cook & Son was repatriated to Britain in 1940 after Germany overran France. The Custodian of Enemy Property assigned Cook's assets to Hay's Wharf Cartage Co. Ltd., a subsidiary of Britain's four main railway companies.[73] Reincorporated in Britain after the war, Cook was nationalized along with the British railways in 1948. Becoming a state-owned company left Cook ill equipped to compete with the free-swinging entrepreneurs who pioneered cheap Mediterranean vacations via charter flights from Britain in the 1950s.

By 1944, Thomas Cook's chief administrator in London, Stanley Adams, was looking ahead toward rebuilding in postwar Egypt. Recalling the cozy ties of old between empire and company, he sent the British Foreign Office a copy of his memo to King Faruq. He proposed to refurbish Cook's Nile steamers—currently requisitioned for military hospitals and rest centers—after the war. He also envisioned a fleet of "first class cars as well as Motor Coaches" for Cook's clients. He requested that Egypt put up £E50,000 for tourist promotion in Western Europe and the United States and suggested that Egypt rent space for publicity offices in Cook's London and New York headquarters. He asked for a five-year tax exemption on Nile steamers and permission—despite pressure to Egyptianize companies—to keep enough European staff to keep European clients happy.[74]

It was 1944, however, not 1900, and Cook's future on the Nile was as murky as that of the Empire itself. British Ambassador Killearn (the former Miles Lampson) asked the Foreign Office to what extent he should support Adams's proposal. A Foreign Office clerk replied that the question could not be answered until Egypt's attitude was known. Since Egypt was tightening requirements for Egyptians on company staffs and boards, Cook was advised to set up a local subsidiary.[75] Adams asked if Ali Shamsi Pasha would be a suitable local liason; Ambassador Killearn recommended another well-connected politician instead—Hafiz Afifi Pasha.[76] In 1947, Thomas Cook & Son (Egypt) Ltd. duly took over locally from Thomas Cook & Son (Continental & Overseas Ltd.).[77] In 1950, Cook's manager in Egypt, a Mr. Hislop, diplomatically declined the presidency of a committee representing the Chamber of the Hotel and Tourist Industry of Egypt. Instead he recommended an Egyptian, the director of Wagon-Lits, and only accepted the vice presidency for himself.[78]

Once the war was over, Cook received a rush of British inquiries about holiday travel, but in August 1947 the sterling crisis led the Attlee government to ban foreign holidays for some months. The nationalization of Cook in Britain along with the railroads in 1948 tied the company's hands in competing with freewheeling competitors in the 1950s.[79] Nationalist demonstrations in Egypt heated up after the war, and the 1948 Arab–Israeli war frightened off tourists. Concluding that its clients no longer had the time or inclination for Nile cruises, Cook sold off its last seven Nile steamers between 1948 and 1950. Wafdist strongman Fuad Sirag al-Din and past and future prime minister Ali Mahir were among the buyers.[80] Cook ran the *Arabia* as a floating hotel moored at Zamalek for another decade.[81] In the end, it was not Cook but the Eastmar Company which revived Nile cruising in 1955, testing the waters first by sending the formerly Cook-owned *Sudan* on a twelve-day trip to Aswan.[82] Over the next several decades, Nile cruises would grow into a massive industry, dwarfing its Victorian, Edwardian, and interwar antecedents.

After the long hiatus on authoritative Egyptian guidebooks since 1929, Hachette published Marcelle Baud's *Égypte* in its *Guides Bleus* series in 1950. A student of Belgian Egyptologist Jean Capart, Baud was about to publish her guide in the summer of 1939 when the war intervened. Baud's acknowledgements in 1950 are almost a who's who of French Egyptology; she also thanked Egyptian Egyptologists Zakariya Ghoneim and Henri Riad.[83] Hotel recommendations had changed little since 1929, but Nile cruises were now gone, and air transport was becoming more common.[84]

The present author's father, W. Malcolm Reid, an American, sailed with his family for Egypt in 1951 carrying a 1908 Baedeker—a family heirloom—and Baud's 1950 *Guide Bleu* in French. Even for years after Reid returned home in 1955, nothing in English equaled the *Guide Bleu*'s *Égypte*. Despite the considerable volume of American travel writing on Egypt since the mid-nineteenth century, there seems to have been no Egyptian guidebook by and primarily for Americans until the 1970s.[85]

Tourism, National Heritage, and Local Resistance: Hassan Fathy's New Qurna

Egyptologist Sami Gabra wrote that "The poor villages of Egypt, near the excavations, have never forgotten the solicitude of these great foreign masters [Western archaeologists] so humane to the peasants and their off-spring."[86] Gabra was a romantic; Western archaeology and tourism were also immensely destructive of local customs and economies. Benedict Anderson remarked of colonial archaeology that:

> the reconstructed monuments, juxtaposed with the surrounding rural poverty, said to natives: Our very presence shows that you have always been, or have long become, incapable of either greatness or self-rule.[87]

As Aboudi's life story suggests, the modern histories of Aswan, Luxor, and villages like Qurna (opposite Luxor), Mit Rahina (by Memphis and Saqqara), and Nazlat al-Samman (at the foot of the Sphinx and Pyramids of Giza) would have been vastly different without the rise of tourism and archaeology. Stephen Quirke's *Hidden Hands* has restored the names of Flinders Petrie's archaeological laborers to history, and Wendy Doyon is researching the history of archaeological labor relations.[88]

Qurna, shorthand for a cluster of villages nestled among the Tombs of the Nobles along the western flood plain at Thebes, is a promising site for subaltern history of tourism and archaeology, as Timothy Mitchell and Kees Van der Spek have shown.[89] A multigenerational biography of the Abd al-Rasul family, who found the cache of royal mummies at Deir al-Bahari about 1871 and mined it for years before being caught, would make a revealing counterpoint to Maspero's account of the find. Maspero was in Europe when a quarrel within the Abd al-Rasul family enabled the Antiquities Service to crack the case. Émile Brugsch, assisted by Ahmad Kamal, hurriedly dispatched the cache by steamer to Cairo amidst funereal wails from village women.[90]

Qurna villagers had stoned eighteenth-century European travelers, and Bonaparte's savants sometimes had to make their archaeological surveys at bayonet point. To many nineteenth-century Egyptians, archaeology meant unpaid forced labor (corvée) for European consul collectors and the French-directed Antiquities Service. Excavation and tourism at Luxor and Edfu came at the cost of evicting villagers from homes in or atop the great temples. The uneven personal and regional benefits and costs of archaeology and concomitant tourism, the tensions between insensitive tourists and conservative villagers, folk beliefs about the fertility-inducing power of antiquities, and the antipharaonism of Islamist purists are all pieces of an as yet inadequately explored complex.

Westerners and urban Egyptian nationalists—so often at odds with each other—tended to agree on what both saw as enlightened state intervention to explore, conserve, and display antiquities—in which marginalized and exploited Upper Egypt was particularly rich. Qurnawis benefited from selling services to expeditions, the Antiquities Service, and tourists but also suffered wrenching seasonal disruptions and state intrusions into their lives and livelihoods with little local consultation or consent.[91]

Egyptologist Ahmad Naguib's 1895 Arabic guide to antiquities for "cultured, modern Egyptians" poured out Cairene contempt for uneducated Saidis (Upper Egyptians):

> Among the reasons which pressed me to write this book is that when I was appointed to the Antiquities Service to protect historical monuments throughout Egypt, I went to Upper Egypt to perform my duty [and there] I found ignorant people—uncultured mobs—attacking monuments to destroy them. Nothing can prevent them from doing this, and nothing can protect the antiquities from those people who listen not to sound advice and who have no shame. . . . They meddle with the dead and scatter their bones. They rip up towering monuments, they pull apart the joints [of mummy bodies] and sell them. They deface papyri. They lay their hands on the tombs of kings, now unknown, as if these were not the remains of their forefathers. I searched for reasons [why they do this]
> . . . . and realized that they are a people who do not know the difference between ugly wretchedness and beautiful value. They know neither science nor the general good.[92]

He rhetorically addressed Saidis directly:

> You people of Upper Egypt . . . don't you realize that once you have completely robbed Upper Egypt of its antiquities, visitors will stop coming? . . . In a few years, with so few visitors, you will grow rebellious, rant and rave, send delegations and claim "economic depression" and the spread of "corruption" and "poverty." . . . Whenever there are hordes of foreigners in your neighborhood, you destroy monuments and sell them away. You're like the one who cuts down the tree to pluck its fruit!

Half a century after Naguib wrote, disruptions associated with World War II brought tensions between Qurna villagers and national authorities to a head. Tourism had collapsed in wartime Luxor, and Antiquities Service surveillance flagged. From his British embassy post in Cairo, H.W. Fairman lamented to fellow Egyptologist Alan Gardiner back home that antiquities were being stolen from provincial magazines and reliefs hacked out of Theban tombs. Embassy adviser Robert Greg "deplored the Professor's [Gardiner's] tendency to believe cock and bull stories about the administration of antiquities in Egypt while refusing to come and do anything about it himself."[93] In April 1943, however, Gardiner and

British Museum director Sir Frederick Kenyon persuaded the Foreign Office to press the issue with the Egyptian government.

Antiquities director Drioton replied that his inspectors were demoralized and that the death in 1941 of Norman de Garis Davis, who with his wife Anna (Nina) had long copied Theban tombs for the Metropolitan Museum, had removed a restraining presence. A dozen watchmen were arrested but quickly released.[94] Drioton hired French artist Alexandre Stoppelaëre (1890–1978), who worked at restoring the damaged tombs until some months after the 1952 revolution.[95]

The collapse of tourism was not Qurna's worst wartime crisis. Raising the Aswan Dam in the 1930s supplied more water for sugarcane but also brought more mosquitoes. In 1942, a virulent strain of malaria spread north from the Sudan. Wartime censorship delayed recognition of the virulence of the epidemic. The opposition blamed the Wafd government. Up to a third of Qurnawis may have died from 1942 to 1945.[96]

Against this grim background, the government appropriated £E50,000 in 1945 to move seven thousand Qurnawis from hillside hamlets among the tombs down to a model village among the fields. Intended to preserve the tombs and make them more accessible to tourists, Fathy's "New Gourna" [Qurna] was also part of an old urban discourse on controlling and improving peasant life. Since the late nineteenth century, the growth of sugarcane plantations in the region had reduced many to landless laborers. Some found seasonal work as archaeological laborers and vendors of antiquities to tourists. With landlord interests in parliament blocking land redistribution until the 1952 revolution, paternalistic schemes for hygienic model peasant villages seemed the only possibility. Stoppelaëre and Osman Rostem, head of the Antiquities Services's engineering and excavations section, persuaded Drioton to award architect Hassan Fathy the commission.[97] Fifty acres were purchased from local magnate Boulos Hanna Pasha, and Fathy set to work.[98]

Born in Alexandria to a family of absentee Delta landowners, Fathy (1900–89) graduated from Cairo's Khedival Secondary School and in 1925 received an architecture degree from the School of Engineering (see fig. 40). He earned a diploma at the École des Beaux Arts, Paris, then taught at Cairo's School of Fine Arts.[99] His mother was Turco-Circassian,[100] and he married the sister of Oxford-educated Ahmad Hassanein Pasha, an adviser to kings Fuad and Faruq who explored the Western desert. When Hassanein died in an auto accident in 1946, Fathy designed a prominent neo-Mamluk tomb for him in Cairo's City of the Dead.[101]

Fathy was twenty-seven before he got his first glimpse of rural life—on one of his family's farms. He explained that his

40 Hassan Fathy on the roof of his Cairo house, with the mosques of Sultan Hassan and al-Rifai in the background. © Christopher Little / *Aga Khan Award for Architecture.*

father avoided the country. To him it was a place full of flies, mosquitoes, and polluted water, and he forbade his children to have anything to do with it. Although he possessed several Estates in the country, he would never visit them, or go any nearer to the country than Mansoura, the provincial capital, where he went once a year to meet his bailiffs and collect his rent.

Fathy's mother, however,

told us [childhood] stories of the tame lambs that would follow her about. . . . She told us how the people produced everything they needed for themselves in the country, how they never needed to buy anything more than cloth for their clothes, how even the rushes for their brooms grew along the ditches in the farm. I seemed to inherit my mother's unfulfilled longing to go back to the country, which I thought offered a simpler, happier, and less anxious life than the city could.

These two pictures combined in my imagination to produce a picture of the country as a paradise, but a paradise darkened from above by clouds of flies, and whose streams flowing underfoot had become muddy and infested with bilharzias and dysentery. This image haunted me and made me feel that something should be done to restore to the Egyptian countryside the felicity of paradise.[102]

Fathy took sun-dried mud brick, with which peasants had built for millennia, and showed them how to build cheap, modern houses true to authentic tradition. Mud brick provided good insulation, summer and winter, and was much cheaper than cement, steel rods, and baked bricks. Pharaonic stone temples, which did not use arches, had outlasted the mud brick houses in which ancient Egyptians lived. The Ramesseum, however had vaulted storage rooms which provided impressive examples of mud brick arches in the Qurnawis' own backyard. Local mud brick houses did not use arches, however, and villagers popularly associated domes not with houses but with the tombs of saints.

Fathy's brother, an engineer, called his attention to the village of Gharb Aswan, where Nubians still used mud brick vaults to roof their homes. Fathy believed that such construction, which dispensed with expensive wood scaffolding, was a pharaonic technique that had survived only in Nubia. Thus, he said,

the true pharaonic Arab identity of the Nubian soul was revealed: This live indigenous art which stems from a deep-rooted tradition of the land is the cornerstone in the hope of reviving the rural domains of this ancient country with its traditional architecture and technology which predate history.[103]

Reviving the technique would enable Qurna villagers to build their own affordable houses while returning to their pharaonic heritage. Fathy also incorporated features of Cairene Islamic and Coptic design in New Qurna: irregular streets, interior courtyards, latticework for privacy, and wind scoops for cooling by the prevailing north wind. Hassan Fathy's writings, plans and sketches, and buildings themselves reveal the mix of pharaonic, Islamic, and other influences on his architecture.

In October 1945, Fathy and a Nubian master mason from Aswan began training a local crew by building his New Qurna headquarters. A mosque, khan, market, village hall, theater, and exhibition hall were to cluster around a central square. There were to be separate primary schools for boys and girls as well as a crafts school, public bath, dispensary, small Coptic church, and police station. Fathy quizzed both sheikhs and ordinary families about what they wanted in a house. Four residential quarters were to accommodate the nine hundred families from five clans from the hamlets of Old Qurna.

Except for a children's weaving school, Fathy's plan for how seven thousand Qurnawis would support themselves was underdeveloped. One night during the third year, unknown villagers cut the dykes and flooded the site. The damage was minor, but a combination of local resistance and Antiquities Service infighting aborted the project, only 20 percent complete. Qurnawis stayed on in their hillside homes. Eventually, squatters from Aswan moved in and altered New Qurna in ways at odds with Fathy's vision.

Fathy produced two allegories of New Qurna:[104] a gouache and a short story. Fathy's disciple Ahmad Hamid described the gouache (fig. 41):

> The surfaces of the elevations, the lines of the plans, the depiction of the different flora and fauna, Gourna Mountain, and even the goddess Hathor peeping from behind the mountain, evoke a rural idyll, at once ancient and contemporary, an Egypt we dream of.[105]

Tellingly, Fathy published his rueful "Land of Utopia" not in Arabic but in French in *La revue du Caire*. A wise man and a beautiful woman flee the city in search of simple life in tune with nature and peasant neighbors. Their bucolic dream is frustrated, however, and they have to leave their green would-be paradise.[106] After the failure of New Qurna, Fathy found that "even teaching brought little reward. I felt I was trying to teach something that I had failed to do myself." When bureaucrats thwarted even building a prototype of a peasant mud brick house for which he won a state prize, "I understood that there was no place for me in Egypt; it was evident that mud brick building aroused active hostility among important people there."[107] In 1957 he left to work for five years in Greece with the architectural firm Doxiadis Associates.

Fathy Ghanem's (1923–1999) 1959 novel *al-Jabal* (The Mountain) offered another take on New Qurna. An inspector is sent from Cairo to find out why villagers have rejected a model village in the plain. A sheikh's wife says:

> in her view, only the tomb of a holy man is topped with a dome—but that's a tomb! Why does the architect insist on housing them in graves? She's not dead yet. . . . If the government wants to move her to the engineer's house, it can take her corpse after she dies and bury it in one of the houses.

Losing faith in his mission, the inspector resigns, leaving the file empty.[108] An unfinished novel by Lawrence Durrell transposed the New Qurna project to a fictional Greek village.[109]

In *Gourna: A Tale of Two Villages* (1969), republished as *Architecture for the Poor: An Experiment in Rural Egypt* (1973), Fathy blamed both

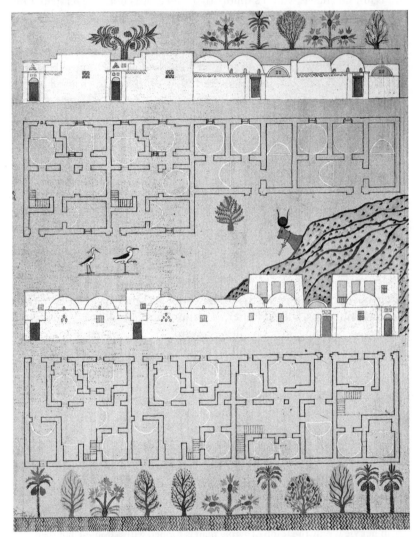

41 Hathor blesses Hassan Fathy's plans for New Qurna: The cow-headed goddess emerges from the Qurna cliff; depictions of the birds, trees, and the Nile draw on pharaonic conventions. *Gouache by Hassan Fathy.* © Gary *Otte /* AgaKhan Trust for Culture.

the villagers and the architectural and construction establishments. The architects and builders rejected both mud brick as a modern construction material and Fathy's plan for cooperative labor. The Qurnawis he denounced as inveterate tomb robbers, whose leaders

> had no intention of giving up their nice, profitable squalid houses in the cemetery with treasure waiting to be mined under their floors, to move to a new, hygienic, beautiful village away from the tombs.[110]

Egyptologist Labib Habachi maintained that Fathy never understood the differences between Nubians, fellahin, and Arabs of Bedouin stock. The Qurnawis were Arabs who would never consent to live among the peasants in the agricultural plain.[111]

Ironically, this champion of Egyptian folk authenticity won acclaim abroad, with projects in Saudi Arabia, Oman, India, and New Mexico. Fathy's only successful project at Qurna was the domed house perched above the entrance road to the Valley of the Kings, which he built in 1950 for restorer Alexandre Stoppelaëre and the Antiquities Service[112] (see fig. 42). The champion of *Architecture for the Poor* built country "rest houses" and urban villas for rich landowners, his own natal class. Fathy-style domes and ornaments, divorced from his philosophy, proliferated in seaside resorts. The mud bricks he championed were banned after the High Dam ended topsoil replenishment downstream. *Architecture for the Poor* was not translated into Arabic until the 1980s. In 1994, the prophet was belatedly honored in his own country with a commemorative postage stamp. By then, pressures of archaeology and tourism were again building toward the tragic displacement—now accomplished—of Qurnawis from their hillside homes.[113]

42 Alexandre Stoppelaëre house and Antiquities Service office, Qurna. Architect: Hassan Fathy. *Photo: D. Reid.*

After the flood, the fire. Four years after Qurnawis turned the Nile's waters against the utopia pressed on them by Cairo, alienated Cairenes burned down Shepheard's Hotel, department stores, movie theaters, and other businesses perceived to be European-owned or associated with European luxury or decadence.[114] The riots of January 26, 1952, were the beginning of the end for the monarchy, the Wafd and its rivals, and the British occupation. In 1869, Thomas Cook & Son had arrived simultaneously with the Suez Canal. In 1952, just as fittingly, its Cairo Shepheard's Hotel office went up in smoke. So did the Shepheard's Hotel office of a newer American symbol of global travel and imperial reach—TWA. Revolution soon followed, and before the decade was out, tourism had recovered and President Nasser presided over the opening of the prime tourist symbol of the emerging postcolonial age—the American-run Nile Hilton on the site of the old Qasr al-Nil barracks.

6

In the Shadow of Egyptology:
Islamic Art and Archaeology to 1952

Ali Bey Bahgat told me himself that he could not find a single native friend
to talk to on the subject of the Museum over which he presides so admirably. He stands, as yet alone. Where is the native architect to be found with
suitable sentiments? He does not exist.

—Somers Clarke, 1917[1]

Amr [ibn al-As, the Arab general who conquered Egypt] founded al-Fustat
under the banner of Islam. Ali Bahgat discovered al-Fustat under the banner of Science.

—Mustafa Abd El-Razeq, 1924[2]

At the height of British colonial control, British architect and archaeologist Somers Clarke presented Ali Bahgat as alone among Egyptians
in his love for Islamic antiquities. Only a few years later, however,
Mustafa Abd El-Razeq hailed his late compatriot for enlisting modern science to illuminate Egypt's proud past since the Arab-Islamic conquest.

Ali Bahgat (1858–1924), the founder of Islamic archaeology among
Egyptians, belonged to the same generation as Ahmad Kamal, the founder
of Egyptian Egyptology, and Saad Zaghlul, hero of the 1919 revolution.
Born in the 1850s, Bahgat and Kamal spent most of their careers in the
heyday of British imperial rule from 1882 to 1922. Both benefited greatly
from European mentors but also spent a lifetime struggling to win professional respect in the colonial order. Kamal, Bahgat, and Zaghlul all
died, still struggling, in the 1920s just as Egypt was passing into its semicolonial era. The British occupation had another three decades to run.

This chapter focuses on cultural and political aspects of Egypt's Comité
de conservation des monuments de l'art arabe (hereafter, the Comité),

Museum of Arab Art, and Department of Islamic Archaeology at the Egyptian (Fuad I, then Cairo) University. It examines these institutions mainly through the careers of Ali Bahgat, Gaston Wiet, K.A.C. Creswell, and Zaki Muhammad Hassan. Although Max Herz left Egypt in 1914 and died in 1919, he is also important here because of his centrality to the development of the Comité, Museum of Arab Art, and Bahgat's early career. Despite hopes aroused by partial independence in 1922, Bahgat died under a cloud in 1924, just a few months before a political assassination brought down Zaghlul's nationalist government. The Museum of Arab Art soon reverted to European control under Gaston Wiet, a Frenchman; K.A.C. Creswell, a Briton, later founded the Islamic archaeology program at the university. This talented pair, whose disciplinary backgrounds and personalities clashed dramatically, long survived the vicissitudes of semicolonial politics. When the independence struggle finally forced them out of office in 1951, their Egyptian successors, Zaki Muhammad Hassan and Muhammad Mustafa, found filling their shoes a tall order indeed.

Twenty years ago, the present author published an article on the Comité and Museum of Arab Art in imperial and national context.[3] Since then, István Ormos has published an authoritative biography of Max Herz Pasha, Philipp Speiser has explored Comité history from the perspective of a preservationist practicing in Cairo, and Mercedes Volait has studied architects and other Europeans who became "crazy for Cairo." Paula Sanders, Nezar AlSayyad, Irene Bierman, and Nasser Rabbat have examined the invention of the idea of "medieval Cairo," and Alaa El-Habashi has studied Egyptian–European interaction in architecture and historic preservation.[4] Much more is now understood about transnational schools of architecture and historic preservation, preservation histories of individual monuments, cosmopolitanism and hybridity, and the proximity or marginality of various actors to their respective national elites.

Several of these studies have suggested that my 1995 article overemphasized imperialism and nationalism in the dynamics of the Comité. Certainly, no individual is simply "an agent of imperialism," or of nationalism. This writer remains convinced, however, that British, French, and transnational European imperialism, as well as various strands of Egyptian nationalism, are indispensible to understanding the workings of the Comité, the Museum of Arab Art, and Islamic archaeology thoughout this era. It was no coincidence that the Comité was created in 1881 just as European imperialism was closing in on Egypt, nor that the Comité vanished from public view in the 1950s, just as the semicolonial era was giving way to the postcolonial one.

As this chapter's title "In the Shadow of Egyptology" suggests, Egyptology, far more than Islamic art and archaeology, captured the imagination of Westerners. Western fascination with ancient Egypt seems divided between a search for the roots of one's own imagined 'European' or 'Western civilization' and the attraction of an exotic 'Oriental' other. Westerners drawn to ancient Egypt through Biblical and classical sources were often seeking their own perceived roots. Western approaches to Arab or Islamic civilization, on the other hand, often envisioned an encounter with an alien other, either hostile and threatening or romantically alluring. The handful of European romantics who promoted the Comité and Museum of Arab Art in Cairo in the 1880s were drawn to an exotic legacy valued for qualities perceived as missing or lost in their own industrializing societies back home.

In Cairo as in Istanbul, interest in Islamic archaeology was overshadowed throughout the nineteenth century by other archaeologies, pharaonic in the case of Egypt and Hellenistic and Byzantine in the central Ottoman Empire. The value which Europeans accorded these heritages powerfully stimulated local appreciation of them as well. Toward the close of the nineteenth century, museums in both Cairo and Istanbul began paying more attention to Islamic antiquities. In founding a museum dedicated to Islamic art in 1883, Cairo was thirty years ahead of Istanbul; the latter's Museum of Pious Foundations (Evkaf Müzesi) was not established until 1914. However, the Ottomans did add an Islamic section to their Imperial Museum in 1889, and they were far ahead of colonized Egypt in having their own nationals, rather than Europeans, direct their museums.[5] Just as modern Greeks faced the challenge of connecting their Byzantine and Greek Orthodox heritage to the ancient Greece so beloved of Western philhellenes in a continuous national narrative down to the present,[6] Egyptian nationalists needed a historical narrative which embraced not only the pharaohs of Western imagination but also the Islamic heritage so meaningful to most Egyptians.

The intensification of Arabic and Islamic themes in Egyptian public discourse in the 1930s and 1940s seems not to have translated very directly into support for the Museum of Arab Art or the preservationist activities of the Comité. Most Egyptians were more attracted to the religious associations of holy sites than to the artistic or historical value of particular structures. People from many walks of life poured out their devotion at the shrines of al-Azhar, Sayyidna Husayn, Sayyida Zaynab, Imam al-Shafii, and (in Tanta) Sayyid Ahmad al-Badawi. Devotion to the text and message of the Quran and lesser religious classics outshone attachment to the specific architecture or decoration of any building, however old or beautiful it might be. Egyptians valued mosques as living centers of worship and study and sometimes resisted preservationist drives to aestheticize, historicize, and monumentalize them as desired by historic preservationists and tourists.

In mosques, as in European cathedrals, demolition, addition, and reconstruction had been going on for centuries. Why freeze a structure in time after it had outgrown the historical moment, purpose, and style it had originally expressed? The water jugs, textiles, mashrabiya latticework, and jewelry enframed in the cases of the Museum of Arab Art were once the stuff of everyday life for rich or poor. Now, as Western fashions in architecture, furniture, and dress swept Egypt's upper and middle classes, Europeans—both empowered and unsettled by industrial and political transformations back home—were intervening to preserve 'Arab art' they thought beautiful, exotic, or 'traditional.' Perhaps historic preservationism, not its converse, cried out for explanation.

On the official level of Egyptian banknotes and postage stamps, Arab and Islamic themes under kings Fuad and Faruq were not as strongly represented as might have been expected. The 1930 one-pound banknote of the National Bank of Egypt featuring a bust of Tutankhamun did balance it out on the reverse with the hospital-madrasa-mausoleum of al-Mansour Qalawun in Bayn al-Qasrayn (fig. 43),[7] but such representations of medieval Islamic monuments on the currency were rather sparing at first. Indeed, when the portrait of King Faruq briefly shouldered Tutankhamun aside on the one-pound note in 1950, the Temple of Philae—not a mosque or other Islamic symbol—was chosen for the reverse.[8]

The terminology used in this chapter remains problematic. Egypt's Museum of Arab Art was renamed the Museum of Islamic Art in 1952 shortly before the Free Officers' coup.[9] Back in the 1890s, Stanley Lane-Poole opted for speaking of 'Saracenic' over 'Arabian,' 'Mohammedan,' and 'Moorish' art—all obsolete terms today.[10] Terms like 'Arab art' risk perpetuating discredited beliefs in distinct Arab, Turkish, Persian, Berber, and Negro races. Even as ethnic or linguistic rather than racial terms, they obscure the multiethnic, polyglot character of the Ottoman and other Islamic empires. 'Islamic art,' on the other hand, raises questions like those which troubled Marshall Hodgson: Could Christians or Jews produce Islamic art? Hodgson's distinction between 'Islamic' and 'Islamicate' has not caught on.[11] 'Arab art' is used in this book when reflecting pre-1952 usage; 'Islamic art' is preferred for more recent contexts. There was a two-decade overlap in Egypt in switching the official terminology, however. Creswell named the program he established at the Egyptian University in 1933 'Islamic archaeology,' but the museum did not change its name from 'Arab' to 'Islamic' until 1952. The term 'archaeology' in

43 Balancing off the pharaonic: Islamic Hospital/Madrasa/Mausoleum of Sultan al-Mansur Qalawun in Bayn al-Qasrayn, Cairo, shown on the reverse of the one-pound Tutankhamun banknote shown in figure 63, 1930. *From the collection of D. Reid.*

Cairo University's Department of Islamic Archeology and Faculty of Archaeology is also confusing since the program emphasizes the history of Islamic art and architecture more than archaeology in the strict sense.[12]

Ali Bahgat and the Comité de Conservation des Monuments de l'art arabe[13]

Ali Bahgat, like Ahmad Kamal, was of Turkish extraction (see fig. 44). His grandfather served under Muhammad Ali and settled in Bahat al-Ajuz, Beni Suef province, Upper Egypt, on land received as a pension. Bahgat's father, a government clerk and a bey, married the daughter of a Turkish official from a nearby village. Ali Bahgat was sent to Cairo's elite state schools—Nasriya primary, Tajhiziya preparatory, the School of Engineering, and the School of Languages. He learned Arabic, French, German, and Turkish, and later added enough English for research. In 1881, he began a twenty-year career teaching and translating in the Ministry of Education.

In December of that same year, 1881, Khedive Tawfiq gave in to European lobbying to found the Comité. In some ways, the founding seems tailor-made for Edward Said's hostile view of Orientalism.[14] French journalist Gabriel Charmes was among the European romantics promoting the Comité. In keeping with the times, he associated Arabs, Turks, and other Oriental 'races' with stereotypical attitudes toward the arts and civilization. Turks, he declared, were one of the least artistic races that ever existed. . . . May the curse of the god of arts be on them! Mehmed Ali, Abbas Pasha, Said Pasha, Ismail Pasha have built more walls than almost all of their predecessors together, but what walls, good God! If one of them had only had the inspired idea to build an Arab palace!

That which Ismail Pasha, in particular, took for the most refined art was a disgraceful compound of the most vulgar European style and of the most grotesque Turkish style.[15]

Tawfiq created the Comité at the very moment he desperately needed European support to resist the Urabi revolution. Col. Ahmad Urabi was challenging Tawfiq's authority, Turkish domination of the army, and European encroachment. Nine months later, Britain crushed Urabi, occupied Egypt, and nominally restored Khedive Tawfiq. The Comité began work in earnest under the umbrella of British occupation.

Three Europeans joined eight Egyptians as founding members of the Comité: French architect Ambroise Baudry, British former consul E.T. Rogers, and German-born architect Julius Franz, who had studied in Vienna.[16] Behind the three lay diverse traditions of nineteenth-century Orientalism, including scholarly and popular texts, painting, and architecture. Edward W. Lane had documented *The Manners and Customs of the Modern Egyptians*, and he and his adventurous compatriot Richard Burton both translated the *Arabian Nights*. Antoine Galland's French translation had first popularized the *Arabian Nights* in Europe a century earlier. It was a rare nineteenth-century tourist who wrote home from Cairo without exclaiming that street scenes in its old quarters were straight out of the *Arabian Nights*. Eugène Delacroix, Jean-Léon Gérôme, and David Roberts famously painted visions of this Arab Orient, while books by Pascal Coste and Prisse d'Avennes documented the romantic splendors of Cairo's Islamic architecture.

44 Ali Bahgat, pioneer of Islamic archaeology. Al-Hilal *32, no. 8 (May 1, 1924): 856.*

The Suez Canal was nearing completion when Khedive Ismail met Baron Haussmann at the Exposition Universelle in 1867 and saw firsthand the latter's remaking of Paris with grand boulevards, parks, formal buildings, and sewers. By the time Ismail and his engineer and urban planner Ali Mubarak hosted Europeans at the opening of the Suez Canal in 1869, they could display at least a preview of modern European-style quarters being rapidly developed in Cairo. The phrase "Paris on the Nile" captures this inspiration, but colonial Algerian and other city models also came into play.[17]

Several new streets driven straight through what was beginning to be seen as "medieval Cairo"[18] so shocked Gabriel Charmes that he hailed Egypt's bankruptcy—a catastrophe that led to Ismail's deposition, the Urabi revolution, and British occupation—because it had interrupted the destruction of architectural masterpieces. Only European control could preserve Cairo's monuments, he declared, and a country that neglected its antiquities does not deserve independence.[19]

Before Haussmann, destruction during the French revolutionary age had provoked the founding of France's Commission of Historic Monuments in 1837. The Commission's chief architect, Viollet-le-Duc, led the historic preservationist school which reconstructed monuments in their presumed original ideal form. Laissez-faire Britain lacked a comparable state agency, but in 1887 William Morris and other followers of John Ruskin founded the Society for the Protection of Ancient Monuments. Ruskinists attacked Viollet-le-Duc, advocating instead the stabilization of ruins in their existing state. France's Commission became a prime model for Egypt's Comité and French its working language, but Ruskin as well as Viollet-le-Duc echoed later in Comité debates.[20]

Unlike Egyptologists, the Comité dealt with monuments of a living culture, Islamic and Coptic Christian (the Comité added Coptic monuments to its purview in 1896), many of which were still in active use. Most Islamic monuments belonged to the Ministry (reduced for some years to an "administration") of Awqaf (sing. waqf, meaning religious endowments). Officials from the Ministry of Awqaf and the Ministry of Public Works constituted most of the Comité. The minister of awqaf chaired the Comité, but until 1922 successive European architects in chief—Julius Franz, Max Herz, and Achille Patricolo—had a powerful say in setting the agenda. Europeans long kept the Comité's minutes, but it is possible to learn a good deal about Egyptian views by reading this record against the grain.

In pharaonic, Coptic, and Islamic times, Egyptians had their own deep traditions of maintaining, staffing, and restoring religious and other monuments. In the Islamic era, this was largely accomplished through awqaf. Muhammad Ali confiscated many awqaf, some of which had fallen into decay or had their income diverted to other purposes, and began bringing the rest under state control. Alaa El-Habashi emphasizes maintenance and preservation through awqaf as an indigenous precedent long before the Comité, a theme that merits further investigation.[21]

The Comité drew up a list of structures worthy of preservation, repair, and sometimes reconstruction. Mosques, mausolea, and a few houses were included. The buildings selected were historicized, aestheticized, and—by definition—monumentalized. The Comité preferred to isolate them in lonely splendor, stripping away shops and dwellings that had engulfed their exteriors. Tourists appreciated easy access and vistas for photography, but the price was tearing monuments out of the living social fabric into which they had been woven. Preserving entire historic districts and assuring neighborhoods a stake in preservation was not yet part of the vision.

In the 1890s, the British Museum's Stanley Lane-Poole, grandnephew and Orientalist heir of E.W. Lane, persuaded Lord Cromer to allocate supplementary funds to the Comité.[22] Under Max Herz, it followed a policy of stabilizing in their current state early and rare buildings such as the mosques of Ibn Tulun and the Fatimids, whereas the more numerous Mamluk buildings could be more freely reconstructed to accord with their presumed original appearances.[23]

The interlocking of imperialism and Orientalism in Comité affairs was neither simple nor all-pervading. The two able architects who unofficially led the Comité down to 1914 hailed not from the main European powers in Egypt—Britain and France—but from countries with only modest imperial leverage there. Julius Franz (1831–1915) grew up in Germany and Max Herz (1856–1919) in Hungary.[24] Both studied architecture in Vienna; hence Franz is sometimes counted as Austrian. Neither owed his Egyptian career to home-country support. Edward Said's *Orientalism*, as often noted, largely ignored the rich tradition of German-language Orientalism.

Did Franz and Herz envision the Comité and Museum of Arab Art as something of an Austro–Hungarian cultural enclave—as the French did the Antiquities Service, the Germans the Khedival Library (five German Orientalist directors in a row), and the Italians who directed Alexandria's Greco–Roman Museum?[25] Herz's biographer Ormos thinks not, but did Herz's being Austro–Hungarian never cross the mind of Vienna-educated Julius Franz when hiring him in 1881? On the eve of World War I, Joseph Strzygowski clearly viewed the museum and Comité as an Austro–Hungarian sphere of influence. Ormos's discounting Stryzgowski's view on the matter because of the latter's notorious racism is unconvincing.[26]

Ali Bahgat's winding path to Islamic archaeology illustrates the serendipity of cultural and political relationships under British imperial rule. On one level, an Armenian Christian official of the Egyptian government (Yaqub Artin) opened the world of Islamic art and archaeology to a Muslim Turkish one (Bahgat).[27] Like the khedival dynasty itself, Artin's and Bahgat's immigrant families slowly Egyptianized over the decades. As undersecretary of education, Yaqub Artin, an industrious scholar and collector of Islamic art, worked well under Husayn Fakhri, the long-serving "Turkish"[28] minister of education under Cromer. Working together in the Ministry, Bahgat, Artin, and Fakhri had Turkish, Arabic, and French in common. Turkish was a diminishing and Arabic an appreciating asset, but it was French—the working language of the Comité, Antiquities Service, Mixed Courts, Institut égyptien, Geographical Society, and cosmopolitan high society—which opened most doors for Bahgat. Egyptian nationalist historiography tends to dismiss people like Fakhri and Artin as colonial collaborators. Yet it was they who rescued Bahgat when educational adviser Douglas Dunlop was about to ruin his career, and it was they who brought him into elite cultural institutions—the Comité, Institut égyptien, Geographical Society, and Egyptian University.

An assignment in 1887 to translate the Comité's minutes from French into Arabic was Ali Bahgat's first encounter with that body. Equally critical was Artin's recommendation of him to assist IFAO scholars with Arabic manuscripts and inscriptions. This introduced Bahgat to Max van Berchem (1863–1921), who encouraged him in Arabic scholarship. Van Berchem, the Swiss founder of Arabic epigraphy, would be made an honorary member of the Comité in 1907. In Van Berchem's corpus of Arabic inscriptions, he acknowledged that

> I owe a great deal to my friend and collaborator Ali Effendi Bahgat. He has devoted many days to revealing and deciphering the inscriptions of Cairo with me. His constant goodwill, his erudition and his practice of archaeology, together with a naturally superior feel for his native language, have been a great help to me during my research.[29]

A recent Arabic edition of correspondence between these two calls Van Berchem the 'student' (*tilmidh*) of Ali Bahgat.[30] Westerners have been inclined to see Bahgat as Van Berchem's research assistant or Arabic tutor. In 1899 Bahgat read a paper at the International Congress of Orientalists in Rome. From 1898 to 1901 he contributed articles to the magazine *Mawsuat*, sometimes signing them '*athari*' (archaeologist).[31] Over the years, he presented ten scholarly papers at the Institut égyptien.

In 1896, Bahgat joined Ahmad Lutfi al-Sayyid, Abd al-Aziz Fahmi, Talaat Harb, and four others in a secret society dedicated to liberating Egypt from British rule. Harb became founder of Bank Misr, Fahmi a leading jurist, and Lutfi al-Sayyid editor of *al-Jarida* as well as university rector, minister, and mentor to a generation. Bahgat's Turkish background was no barrier, as Ormos believes, to his being an Egyptian nationalist.[32] Fellow 'Turks' included Prime Minister Mahmud Sami al-Barudi, a leader of the Urabi revolt, and Muhammad Farid, Mustafa Kamil's successor as leader of the fiercely Egyptian nationalist Watani Party. Becoming a patron of a secret nationalist society, Khedive Abbas II sent Lutfi al-Sayyid to Switzerland in 1897 to become a Swiss citizen. The intention was to provide him with legal immunity so that he could publish a nationalist paper in Egypt. (The plan fell through.) One of al-Sayyid's incidental errands was to deliver books from Bahgat to Van Berchem and to Egyptologist Edouard Naville in Geneva.[33]

Bahgat's patriotism nearly ruined his career. Artin had Bahgat, chief translator of the Ministry of Education, draft a letter which minister Husayn Fakhri signed. Fakhri, however, signed without first consulting the Ministry's Scottish adviser, Douglas Dunlop. Dunlop forced Fakhri to retract his signature. Bahgat attacked Dunlop and defended Fakhri and Artin in unsigned articles in Sheikh Ali Yusuf's newspaper *al-Muayyad*. Dunlop found out and would have taken revenge on Bahgat had Fakhri and Artin not rescued him with a transfer to the Comité's Service des monuments.[34]

Ali Bahgat, the Museum of Arab Art, and the Excavation of Fustat

Fakhri and Artin got Bahgat onto the Comité in 1900, but they failed in their attempt also to make him curator of the Museum of Arab Art. Herz had already been running the museum for a decade and presumed that if anyone were to be named official curator, it should be he. In November 1901, Herz was appointed curator and Bahgat assistant curator, at £E25 a month.[35]

The decree establishing a Museum of Arab Antiquities (or Arab Art, Antikhana Arabiya, Musée Arabe) in 1869 on the initiative of French archaeologist Auguste Salzmann tuned out to be a dead letter. In 1880, Julius Franz, director of the technical bureau of the Ministry of Awqaf, began collecting relics in a makeshift structure in the the courtyard of the ruined Fatimid Mosque of al-Hakim. In 1884 the Musée Arabe opened there.[36] The museum drifted after Franz retired in 1887, but in 1892 Herz was delegated to run it. In 1895 Herz published a catalogue in French, which Stanley Lane-Poole translated into English. Lane-Poole doubted whether one tourist in a hundred had heard of the museum; those who thought they had, had usually confused it with the Egyptian Museum.[37]

As budgetary pressures finally eased in the 1890s, Cromer approved a new museum for pharaonic antiquities and a new building to house jointly the Museum of Arab Art and the Khedival Library. Italian architect Alfonso Manescalo,[38] who joined the Comité in 1897, designed the latter in the neo-Islamic (specifically neo-Mamluk) style, in keeping with its contents and mission. Islamic revival architecture in turn-of-the-century Cairo was as much fashionable import from Europe, where world's fairs' pavilions had popularized it, as a direct offshoot of local traditions. Coste's and Prisse d'Avenne's studies of Cairo's Islamic monuments had laid foundations for a Mamluk revival in Khedive Ismail's Egypt. Unlike Muhammad Ali's Ottoman-style mosque in the Cairo Citadel, the neo-Mamluk style—patronized by both Egyptian and European elites—would come to be appropriated as an Egyptian national style. Paris-educated architect Husayn Fahmi designed the al-Rifai Mosque facing the Mosque of Sultan Hassan for the mother of Khedive Ismail in neo-Mamluk style. Max Herz took up the interrupted project in 1905, modified it, and completed the edifice in neo-Mamluk style.[39]

Manescalo's museum/library exterior had massive portals, pointed arches, stalactites, crenellations, and stripes of alternating color (ablaq). The Khedival Library (Dar al-Kutub) had its own upstairs entrance on the opposite side from the ground-floor Museum of Arab Art.[40] The location in Midan Bab al-Khalq, where Ismail's new Abdin quarter met the old city, seemed fitting. Khedive Abbas II opened the "handsome new building in the Arabic style"[41] in 1903 in the presence of Cromer and other dignitaries. In 1906 Herz brought out a new guide to the museum in French. Bahgat translated it and another installment of the Comité's minutes into Arabic, reflecting both an effort to reach out to Egyptians and Bahgat's centrality to that effort. In 1907 he carried out a mission which was off limits to non-Muslims—photographing monuments in Mecca and Medina.[42] In 1910, he attended a pioneering exhibition of Islamic art in Munich.[43]

Several comparisons drive home the general priority given to pharaonic over Islamic antiquities. The new Museum of Egyptian Antiquities cost £E220,000, the Khedival Library/Museum of Arab Art £E50,000.[44] Since the Museum of Arab Art occupied only half of its building, its £E25,000 cost was only one-ninth that of the Egyptian Museum. The Museum of Arab Art was off the beaten tourist track, the Egyptian Museum at the emerging center of modern Cairo—today's Tahrir Square. The 1908 Baedeker devotes twenty-four pages and a foldout plan to the Egyptian Museum and only two and a half pages to the "Arabian Museum."[45] The former's 29,879 visitors in 1913 were nearly six times the latter's 5,166.[46]

Bahgat's report on a trip to Upper Egypt in May 1910 reveals the limitations of the Comité's conception of archaeology on the eve of its excavation of Fustat. Discovering that tourists had depleted the stocks of antiquities dealers at Luxor and Sohag, Bahgat proposed returning in November, after fertilizer (*sebakh*) diggers' finds had replenished the shops but ahead of the next winter season's tourists.[47]

Most previous Western excavations of Islamic relics had been the byproduct of digging for the pre-Islamic antiquities which so enthralled the West. In 1911, the year before Bahgat began at Fustat, the Imperial Museum of Berlin began a major dig at Samarra, the ninth-century Abbasid caliphate's short-lived alternative capital north of Baghdad. Friedrich Sarre organized and Ernst Herzfeld directed the work. Germany's alliance with the Ottomans, Kaiser Wilhelm II's courting of Sultan Abdulhamid II, and the Berlin-to-Baghdad railway provided the imperial context. German archaeologists also undertook excavations in Iraq at the pre-Islamic sites of Babylon and Assur.[48]

Although the Comité may have been spurred by the German example at Samarra, little if any European imperial motivation seems to have been behind the excavation of Fustat. In July 1912, the government turned archaeological surveillance there over to the Comité. Herz had his hands full with other work, so Bahgat took charge of Fustat. It had grown out of the Arab Muslim tent city which Amr ibn al-As founded for his army in 641 beside the walled fortress of Babylon, the inland Roman–Byzantine capital. Like Samarra, Fustat was a capital known from literary sources and easily accessible to archaeologists because of the paucity of later settlement. Mostly abandoned since the eleventh century, it had become a rubbish heap, quarry for fertilizer and building materials, center for pottery manufacture, and home for squatters. The lack of major pharaonic remains underneath had spared the Islamic levels from Egyptological excavation, but fertilizer diggers were ravaging the site.

With no budget at all for excavation, the best Bahgat could do was to tighten surveillance over the fertilizer diggers. He explained that his system offered something for everyone: the museum obtained Arab antiquities (mostly potsherds), the Egyptian Museum got any stones with hieroglyphs, scholars learned about the layout of Fustat, fertilizer companies made profits, cultivators could buy fertilizer, and the state obtained leveled land useful for other purposes.[49] Appalling as this sounds today, it does show that Bahgat's vision extended beyond acquiring museum pieces to exploring building and street remains for reconstructing the city's topography.

The Ottoman Empire's entry into World War I on the German and Austro–Hungarian side impelled Britain to sever Egypt's nominal Ottoman tie, depose Khedive Abbas II, and declare a protectorate. This turned Herz into an enemy alien, and he was forced to flee. He left for Italy, leaving most of his papers and possessions behind. He settled in Switzerland and died in Zurich in 1919.

Comité member Harry Farnall, a Briton, regretted that "circumstances external to art have deprived [the Comité] of the valuable services of this eminent architect and archaeologist" (Herz). Murqus Simaika, of the Coptic Museum, hoped that Herz would still complete the third edition of the guide to the Museum of Arab Art and only reluctantly postponed a motion to make him a corresponding member of the Comité.[50] Herz welcomed "heart-warming words from friends and appreciative gestures from the Ministry" but added

> The only person who wanted to return falsehood for the good he had received was the great patriot Ali Bey Bahgat. I am (not) surprised. The sentiment of gratitude is not a widespread human attribute, and he is by no means the only person to give me experience of this.[51]

Evidence on Bahgat's personal relations with Herz through a dozen years of service under him is scant, but the colonial power structure of the age is clear. The bid in 1900 to make Bahgat curator had failed, and one well-qualified European had succeeded another as curator of the museum. On one occasion, Bahgat wrote to Herz's and his mutual friend Max van Berchem:

> Monsieur Herz, who is busy with the catalogue now, asked me to stay here in order to supervise the printing of the catalogue. I gladly accepted this request because he had greatly improved his behavior towards me after he had considered me at my appointment to the Museum even if not an enemy, at least not a friend. Well, I gladly accepted because, as you know, I like to live quietly in peace, far away from problems.[52]

Upstairs in the museum/library building in late 1914, Arthur Schaade, the fifth German Orientalist to direct the Khedival Library, also had to flee as an enemy alien. That Egyptians took over the top posts both upstairs and downstairs seems at odds with Britain's tightened control under the declared protectorate and martial law, but because of the war no obvious European candidates were available. Noted editor and future university rector and cabinet minister Ahmad Lutfi al-Sayyid stepped in to become director of the library. The Comité's Italian assistant architect,

Achille Patricolo (1867–?) pronounced that combining architectural preservation and museum administration was an anomaly unknown in Europe.[53] Taking over only Herz's preservation duties and later his title as architect in chief, Patricolo left the museum to Bahgat.[54]

The Last Years of Ali Bahgat

In April 1918, the Comité obtained a law protecting antiquities dating from the Arab conquest to the death of Muhammad Ali. Sultan Fuad's visit to the Fustat excavations that same month raised their profile.[55] Bahgat knew Fuad from serving on the board of the Egyptian University. Now he boasted to the sovereign of filling the museum with treasures and laying bare 750,000 square meters of houses, palaces, public baths, mosques, workshops, sewers, and streets. The museum raised money by selling duplicate antiquities to collectors and debris to construction contractors. Fertilizer contractors had moved 3,750,000 cubic meters of dirt at no cost to the state, provided work for one thousand men, and produced essential fertilizer at a time when the war had cut off imports.

A month after the royal visit, however, an article in *The Egyptian Gazette* signed only "S" attacked the excavations. "S" declared that with proper excavations at Fustat,

> instead of filling our museums with fragments of undated and unclassified pottery, we could have had a nearly complete history of the development of pottery from the Roman era to the end of the Middle Ages.[56]

Instead of allowing fertilizer diggers to ravish Fustat, excavators should have charted the level of each piece of pottery and tied the stratigraphic evidence to two historically known burnings of the city. "S" soon revealed himself as the Rev. A.H. Sayce, an Assyriologist and well-known popularizer of Egyptology who regularly wintered in his *dahabiya* on the Nile.[57]

Captain K.A.C. Creswell of the Royal Air Force—soon to be an authority on Islamic architecture—leapt to defend "the capable and energetic Director of the Arab Museum," who had managed to wrest "marvelous results" from the fertilizer diggers without any budget for scientific excavation. If anyone was to blame, declared Creswell, it was "the savants who have known for years the importance of the site and have done nothing."[58] In reply, Sayce conceded that Bahgat had salvaged a fragment of architectural history and denied attacking him personally.

The Comité's Harry Farnall, a British diplomat who later served on Egypt's *Caisse de la dette publique*, called Bahgat an "eminent archeologist" and claimed that—unlike Hissarlik (the site of Troy), Rome, and London—Fustat's mounds were unstratified rubbish heaps.[59] Sayce regretted that "my friend Farnall" had not consulted him before writing; even if Fustat was unstratified, one did not need an archaeologist of the caliber of George Reisner or Flinders Petrie to sort out the relative age of the different mounds.[60] Farnall offered another consideration:

> If there is a conflict between the interests of science and something else, which in my opinion is not the case, it is a conflict between science and the necessity, in time of war, in the absence of imported fertilizers, to find local ones for the plants which provide human nourishment. In my opinion, it is science which must give way, if there is a conflict, just as it had to give way in the case of the dam at Aswan and the temple of Philae.[61]

In March 1920, the charges against Bahgat shifted from incompetence to financial corruption. After Murqus Simaika, director of the Coptic Museum, audited the books, the Comité affirmed its confidence in Bahgat.[62] That June, however, a report by Patricolo led to the dismissal of assistant conservator Muhammad Khalil for grave irregularities and the transfer of a museum secretary accountant due to "incompatibility with his superior." "While recognizing the services of Ali Bahgat Bey, conservator of the Museum, to science and to Egypt from an archaeological point of view," the Comité censured his supervision of accounting and excavation personnel. The Comité hired Albert Gabriel (1883–1972), a veteran of the French archaeological school in Athens, at six thousand francs to coauthor a book with Bahgat on the architecture of Fustat. Bahgat was sent to Paris on unpaid leave for four and a half months to work on the book. Paying him £E5 a month to resume translating the Comité minutes into Arabic hardly softened the blow. Meanwhile, Patricolo oversaw an inventory of the museum and investigated other complaints.[63]

Early in 1921, Bahgat returned from Paris with a book contract. Resuming museum and excavation duties, in June he toured Fustat with Farnall, Lacau, and two other Europeans to take in Patricolo's new arrangements.[64] Bahgat and Gabriel's *Fouilles d'al-Foustat* was published that year. An Arabic translation and album of photos eventually followed in 1928, after Bahgat's death.[65] *Fouilles*'s preface emphasized the necessity of working through fertilizer diggers, affirmed that the rubbish heaps were unstratified, and said that the traces of burning had not established clear stratigraphic benchmarks. The authors declared

> We freely recognize that the extraction of sabakh, which would be done under supervision, does not accord well with scientific research. However,

we do not believe that, in this particular case, any other method of excavation could furnish more complete documentation and we can affirm that, from the day that the Museum assumed direction of the excavations, no architectural element, however minimal, has been destroyed.[66]

No evidence of the earliest Arab settlement was found. The authors speculated that their house remains were from prosperous Abbasid and Tulunid times. Six years after Bahgat's death, his other coauthor, Félix Massoul, brought out *La céramique musulmane de l'Égypte* (Cairo: Museum of Arab Art: IFAO, 1930). It asserted that the metallic faience of Tulunid pottery grew out of a local tradition with pharaonic antecedents. For many years after Bahgat's death, desultory excavations at Fustat yielded hardly any published results. George Scanlon, who began systematic excavations at Fustat in 1965, decided that Bahgat's houses were probably Fatimid. Whether luster decoration on ceramics and glass descended from local Coptic–Byzantine tradition or was a technique imported later, and whether to call it 'Coptic,' remain disputed.[67]

In 1922, Bahgat reported on his excavations at a history of art congress in Paris and stopped in Grenoble with Ahmad Kamal Pasha and Selim Hassan for the centenary celebration of Champollion's decipherment.[68] The following year, the French legation in Cairo urged Marseilles customs officials to facilitate Bahgat's arrival to work with his printer on plates for *La céramique égyptienne de l'espagne musulman*. He was a great savant, and his writing works in "our language" and publishing them in France made excellent propaganda for "our culture."[69]

In 1922, the Comité complained that the curator of the Museum of Arab Art (Bahgat) earned only £E800 a year compared to £E1,100–1,300 for the director general of the Antiquities Service (Lacau).[70] One of the first acts of Saad Zaghlul's Wafdist government in January 1924 was to promote Bahgat from curator to director of the Museum of Arab Art. In February, he joined Wafdist dignitaries at the opening of Tutankhamun's sarcophagus. Two months later, Bahgat died in Cairo in his "Arab-style" villa at Matariya.[71] Prime Minister Saad Zaghlul himself, Ahmad Lutfi al-Sayyid, and Murqus Simaika—all pashas—were among the attendees at the memorial service, at which an ode by Ahmad Shawqi was recited.[72] Mustafa Abd El-Razeq delivered a eulogy at the Institut égyptien. In sharp contrast to their praise of Herz upon his departure from Egypt, the Comité's minutes only mentioned Bahgat's death in passing.[73]

Death spared Bahgat a final humiliation. In 1925, Muhammad Khalil, who had been fired as assistant curator of the Museum of Arab Art back in 1920, petitioned for reinstatement. Khalil testified that in 1920 he had taken the rap for Bahgat's late son Mahmud, the museum's secretary accountant, who had died in 1918. Mahmud had illegally worked a Fustat fertilizer concession under the name of a maidservant. Now, in 1925, Khalil's appeal for reinstatement split the Comité's technical section rather ominously on European-versus-Egyptian lines. Lacau and Farnall suspected Khalil of peculation as well as covering up. Simaika, Sayed Mitwelli, and Ahmad al-Sayyid all argued that Khalil had lied only to save the honor of his patron Ali Bahgat and deserved reinstatement. Simaika praised Khalil as an excellent museum man and "one of the rare Egyptians who love archaeology."[74]

Gaston Wiet, the Comité, and the Museum of Arab Art

Two personnel changes on the Comité in the aftermath of Britain's 1922 declaration of Egyptian independence illustrate the unpredictable paths of the semicolonial era. Late in 1922, Ahmad al-Sayyid Bey abruptly replaced Achille Patricolo, the last European architect in chief. Hundreds of European officials of the Egyptian government had to retire by 1927 in return for guaranteed pensions. Yet, imperial and national politics permitting, European officials could stay on for years on periodically renewable contracts. In 1926, the Museum of Arab Art reverted to European control under Gaston Wiet, who would cling to the post for a quarter of a century. And in 1929, Frenchman Edmond Pauty was hired as 'expert architect' alongside the Comté's Egyptian architect in chief.

Back in 1917, when Farnall annotated an earlier printed list of Comité members, two had already died and nine others (including three European Egyptologists) rarely attended meetings. Britons Harry Farnall, Oriental Secretary Ronald Storrs, and architect Somers Clarke were regulars, as were Bahgat, Simaika, and four other Egyptians. Patricolo had inherited Herz's preservationist duties, but at only a fraction of his salary and without his seat on the Comité or his title of architect in chief. Farnall worried lest some incompetent replace Patricolo or that the Comité might not have the spine to block a proposal such as that of Prince Muhammad Ali "to destroy the venerable mosque of 'Amr and to build in its place something that should eclipse the temple of Karnak."[75] Patricolo's position was accordingly firmed up by promoting him to architect in chief and according him a seat on the Comité. In 1921, Patricolo had two European assistant architects (apparently Italians) and three Egyptian engineers working under him.[76]

The declaration of Egyptian independence in February 1922, however, suddenly cut the other way. Patricolo returned from summer leave that October to find that Ahmad al-Sayyid had replaced him as architect in chief. The press blamed Patricolo for a roof collapse at the Abu Ayla Mosque in Cairo's Bulaq district; fifteen had died and twenty were injured.[77] A British memo claimed that Patricolo "possessed an 'infortunate [sic] manner' to 'go up against nearly every one he had to work with,'" and that King Fuad "had quite made up his mind to be rid of him."[78] Somers Clarke, however, resigned from the Comité in protest at the new appointment:

> I entirely decline to place myself under the direction of the gentleman who is now forced to act as architect to the Comité de Conservation. It would be ridiculous. There are few positions held in higher esteem in Great Britain than that to which I have had the honour of being elected, namely that of Architect in charge of St. Paul's Cathedral, London.[79]

Upon Ali Bahgat's death a letter to the editor of *al-Ahram* raised the question of who would follow him.[80] Britain's ouster of Zaghlul's government in November 1924, the strong hand of King Fuad, and Ahmad al-Sayyid's poor showing in combining Patricolo's and Bahgat's duties reopened the door to European hires—first Gaston Wiet and later Edmond Pauty as well.[81] King Fuad rarely met a European scholar he didn't prefer to an Egyptian.

King Fuad's caliphal ambitions after Turkey abolished the Ottoman caliphate in 1924 encouraged the revival of Prince Muhammad Ali's proposal to rebuild the Mosque of Amr in its imagined full splendor. Back in 1914, Lord Kitchener, pressed by London's Society of Antiquaries, had quashed the Prince's original proposal. In 1926–27, the Ministry of Awqaf held an international competition to restore the mosque to its state "at the time of its greatest splendor." Several Comité members were among the international jury of six foreigners and five Egyptians. Europeans won the first three places (Creswell and a partner came in second), though none was recommended for implementation because of the archaeological heritage they would destroy. All four entries by Egyptians were rejected. An anonymous "wondering architect" denounced the results in the newspaper *al-Balagh al-yawmi*. The author may have been Mahmud Ahmad (1880–1942), director of the Ministry of Awqaf's bureau of monuments. Ironically, this coauthor of one of the rejected projects became Comité architect in chief from 1934 to 1942.[82]

During the unsettled times from the spring of 1923 until January 1926, the Comité never met.[83] In January 1926, King Fuad had Ahmad Ziwar's palace government summon the Comité into session. Nine Egyptians and five Europeans attended.[84] European membership was now down to the wartime Allies: two Britons, two Frenchmen, and an Italian. Architect in chief of royal palaces Ernesto Verucci, a confidant of King Fuad's, had replaced Patricolo as the Italian voice. Farnall's presidency of the Comité's technical section and Lacau's election as Comité secretary assured assertive European input. Former minister of public works Abd al-Hamid Sulayman proposed making an Egyptian still in his thirties director of the Museum of Arab Art and assigning a European specialist to do the catalogue and other 'technical' tasks. No one seconded this nationalistic proposal, and Sulayman walked out. The Comité endorsed the hiring of Gaston Wiet.[85]

King Fuad was feeling pleased with himself for outmaneuvering the British by slipping Francophone European professors into the new state university. Now he asked the French legation for Arabists who could head the Museum of Arab Art and the National Library. The French moved quickly, "for foreign appointments will certainly be suspended if a nationalist ministry comes in as expected at the end of spring."[86] The king wanted Gaston Wiet, whom he knew from the prewar university, for director of the Museum of Arab Art.[87]

Times had changed, however, since 1896, when Herz had been advised to groom a European architect as a possible successor.[88] Now Lacau carefully regretted the lack of qualified Egyptians, said that Wiet must recruit and train them, and observed that the museum curatorship need not remain in foreign hands for long.[89] In fact, the brilliant and nimble Gaston Wiet (1887–1971) locked up the post for twenty-five years. He held a law *licence* and Arabic, Persian, and Turkish diplomas from the École national des langues orientales. After three years in Egypt as an IFAO fellow, he had taught at the University of Lyon. He married a woman from the prominent Egyptian Jewish Nahum family. In 1938 Wiet would found *La revue du Caire*. Jean-Paul Sartre was a contributor, and Wiet hosted André Gide and Jean Cocteau on their visits to Egypt.[90] At home in Arabic as well as French literary circles, Wiet translated Taha Hussein, Tawfiq al-Hakim, and Mahmud Taymur into French.[91]

Ali Ibrahim—physician, university rector, and cabinet minister—declared of Wiet

> My admiration of his enthusiasm and zeal for Moslem Art is boundless. He has infused this zeal into all who have come into contact with him. The great talent and scientific spirit which he exhibited as Director of the Arabic Museum during the past ten years, is fully appreciated by all of us. . . . I express the gratitude felt by all his friends in Egypt.[92]

In 1920, Lacau complained that the Comité had published only two scholarly works in forty years, unlike his own prolific Antiquities Service.[93] By 1939 the Museum of Arab Art had published ten volumes of its catalogue and thirteen other volumes, including five in Arabic.[94] One was Wiet's new guide to the museum (1939), which Zaki M. Hassan translated into Arabic. In keeping with his emphasis on scholarly publication, one of Wiet's first acts had been to raise the museum library's acquisitions budget from £E10 to £E500 a year.

Like Ali Bahgat, Wiet had learned Arabic epigraphy from its founder, Max van Berchem. Wiet contributed a volume to Van Berchem's *Corpus Inscriptionum Arabicarum* and helped organize a *Répertoire chronologique d'epigraphie arabe* (16 vols., Cairo, 1931–1954). He edited part of al-Maqrizi's history of Egypt and translated Ibn Iyas and al-Yaqubi on Egypt. He coauthored a book on Cairo mosques[95] with Louis Hautecoeur (1884–1973), director general of fine arts in Egypt (1927–30) and later author of a *Histoire de l'architecture classique en France* (9 vols., 1943–57). Their collaboration is notable in view of their contrasting post-1939 politics. Hautecoeur served as secretary general of fine arts under President Pétain at Vichy,[96] while Wiet rallied to General de Gaulle in 1940 and became vice president of Cairo's Comité de la France libre.

Wiet was instrumental in recruiting Edmond Pauty (1887–?) in 1929 as 'expert architect' to the Comité.[97] Pauty had served as head of historic monuments under Gen. Lyautey in Morocco. In Cairo he emphasized neglected Ottoman-era mosques and was forward-looking in advocating conserving whole neighborhoods, not just isolated monuments.[98]

In May 1936, the month al-Nahhas and the Wafd returned to power, the Ministry of Awqaf lost its long bureaucratic battle to rein in the autonomous Comité, which was transferred to the Ministry of Education. Two years later, Wiet rebuffed the Ministry of Awqaf's attempt to reclaim the Comité's Service des monuments de l'art arabe. He declared that the Commission des monuments historiques in France had finally escaped clerical control in 1906, and that now

in all countries where art occupies a preponderant place, the services of historic monuments, which include numerous churches and cathedrals, are linked to the ministry of national education, where their activity is pursued without prejudice from interested religious authorities. It should be the same for Egypt, where Muslim art attained its apogee, [and] all the more so because the Comité des monuments arabes, in the course of its long career has contributed to the revival of worship in several mosques which time had [otherwise] condemned.[99]

In August 1939, a Conseil supérieur pour le service de conservation des monuments de l'art arabe, under the minister of education, replaced the Comité. The old Technical Section was renamed the Comité permanent; its veteran president Simaika welcomed the change but stepped down.[100] These name changes seem to have had little effect, and the Conseil informally continued to be called simply "the Comité."

K.A.C. Creswell and Islamic Art and Archaeology at the Egyptian University

In keeping with this chapter's title "In the Shadow of Egyptology," the founding of the Comité and Museum of Arab Art in the early 1880s trailed the founding of the Antiquities Service and Egyptian Museum by over two decades. With Islamic art and archaeology coalescing as a field in Europe between the world wars, the program in Islamic archaeology at the Egyptian University was founded only a decade after the Department of Egyptology. Independence and Tutankhamun had spurred the breakthrough to university Egyptology. The far less heralded inauguration of a university program in Islamic archaeology in 1933 came in the context of Prime Minister Ismail Sidqi's strong-arm palace government, and the program's founder, K.A.C. Creswell (1879–1974), was an outspoken British imperialist.

Creswell was acutely sensitive to being neither an Orientalist nor a university graduate. After studying electrical engineering at City and Guilds Technical College, he worked for an electrical manufacturing firm. Inspired by *The Thousand and One Nights* and Rawlinson's *Seven Oriental Monarchies*,[101] he had by 1910 made Islamic art his hobby. Two years later he began noting references for what would become his *Bibliography of the Architecture, Arts, and Crafts of Islam to 1960*.[102] Royal Air Force service took him to Egypt in 1916, and in 1919–20 Captain Creswell was inspector of Monuments in Occupied Enemy Territory in greater Syria.

In 1920, Sultan Fuad awarded him a grant of £E800 a year for three years for a proposed history of Muslim architecture. He settled into a bachelor routine—October to June in a flat near Abdin Palace and July to September in England or traveling on the Continent.[103] In 1923, his compatriot Harry Farnall encouraged the Comité to take over funding of Creswell's project at £E400 year for two years. Creswell won a two-year extension in 1925 and another in 1927, but at only £E300 a year. The Comité ended its subsidy in 1929 but promised a £E100 bonus upon the publication of each volume.[104] In 1931 the Egyptian University rescued Creswell with a post teaching Islamic art, and in 1933 he founded the Islamic archaeology section in the university's graduate

Institute of Archaeology. Oxford University Press brought out volume 1 of *Early Muslim Architecture* in 1932. It and the second volume (1940) covered the Islamic world for its first three centuries. The next two volumes (1952, 1959) narrowed the focus to *The Muslim Architecture of Egypt*, carrying the story to 1326, short of his intended cutoff with the Ottoman conquest of 1517.

Creswell dedicated *Early Muslim Architecture*, vol. 2:

> To His Majesty Farouk I, King of Egypt, thanks to whose father's enlightened generosity this work was conceived and carried out and the second volume finally brought to completion in the reign of his son who has already shown his great interest in Art and Archaeology. [105]

Volume 1 of *Muslim Architecture of Egypt* again thanked the king, but it came out in 1952—the year of the revolution and the end of the line for such royal patronage. The Gulbenkian Foundation stepped in to subsidize the publication of volume 2.[106]

With iron discipline, Creswell did most of the measuring, photography, and drafting himself. His organization was "strictly chronological, for chronology is the spinal column of history."[107] Relentlessly chronicling the appearances of each architectural feature, he refused to speculate about influences, ignored aesthetics, and depended on others to translate Arabic for him.[108] Grateful to Max van Berchem, like Bahgat and Wiet, he dedicated his *Bibliography of the Architecture, Arts, and Crafts of Islam* "To the Memory of Max van Berchem, perfect friend and perfect scholar."[109] Creswell's prejudices were as evident as his magisterial achievement:

> All who travelled with him, who had enjoyed his high spirits or relished his often entertaining displays of inveterate prejudice, would agree that Creswell had a vein of eccentricity. He was something of a dandy ... moving with military swagger in impecably tailored close-fitting suits and hat jauntily set just right. His starched white collars, in whatever desert of climate or cramped conveyance he might be travelling. . . .
>
> He was the master of casual encounters in the streets, of which his stick was the symbol if not the instrument. He would not be obstructed by lesser breeds.[110]

Creswell's admiration of Germans extended to "the racialist aims of National Socialism"[111] in the 1930s, and he deeply disliked the French. He berated Georges Marçais, who had sent him a complimentary publication, for failing to cite him adequately. He raged on:

It is quite clear to me that citing a foreign scholar causes real agony to a Frenchman, who obviously likes to think that French scholarship is self-sufficing; so that there should never be any need to cite a sacré boche or a sacré anglais [damned German or damned Englishman]. . . .

I have often heard people talk of French chauvanism [sic]; now I know what it is.

Yours,
absolutely "fed up."[112]

Although nominated in 1932 and again in 1936, it was not until 1939 that Creswell finally made it onto the Comité.[113] He blamed the delay squarely on a Frenchman—Gaston Wiet. Creswell

was convinced during his time at Fuad University that a conspiracy against him, and against the appointment of English staff generally, existed among French academics in Cairo, led by one [Gaston Wiet] who owed his own appointment to Creswell. He embodied his grievance in a four-page typed memorandum detailing the evidence going back to 1931, when the person in question was instrumental in getting the post offered to Creswell reduced from Professor to Lecturer.[114]

Creswell wrote:

Since then he [Wiet] has done all he can to down me, to keep me off committees, to prevent my students from filling openings in his museum, to get control of the Arabic Monuments, although he knows nothing about architecture, to control my activities at the University by means of a committee chosen by himself and T.H. [Taha Hussein], and finally to boost F as a candidate for my post. Tuesday's outrageous incident [unidentified] is simply the culmination of ten years of underground hostility against an interloper in a field which he thinks ought to be entirely French. [He] is the spearhead of French anti-British influence here, and he is helped by numerous Egyptians with French wives.[115]

Some officials at the British embassy were similarly down on Wiet:

In more specifically cultural matters he is less friendly to the British, being an heir to the tradition of Anglo–French cultural rivalry. He has a flair for intrigue and is the nigger in many a cultural wood pile. His activities are viewed with some misgivings by the Ambassador's Advisory Committee on British culture.[116]

In the mid-1930s, Creswell also drew the ire of the former and future dean of the Faculty of Arts, Taha Hussein. A British diplomatic dispatch conceded that the dismissal of Hussein as dean and Lutfi al-Sayyid as rector of the Egyptian University by Ismail Sidqi's dictatorial palace government had been unjust, but

> Unfortunately Taha Hussein, after his dismissal, joined the editorial staff of the Wafdist 'Kawkab-esh-Sharq' and, in the course of a prolonged journalistic campaign against the Governments of Sidky and Abdel Fat-tah Yehia Pashas, indulged in much xenophobia and anti-British attacks. He even made an attack on the book on Islamic Architecture by Captain Cresswell [sic], Assistant Professor of Muslim Architecture in the Faculty of Letters, on the ground that it contained anti-Islamic passages.[117]

Creswell's hope that Taha Hussein would not regain the deanship proved to be in vain.

In November 1938, Sir Robert Greg (1876–1953),[118] a former diplomat who had succeeded Harry Farnall on the Caisse de la dette publique and as an amateur on the Comité, nominated Creswell to replace their late compatriot Sir John Home. In 1939 "The Professor of Muslim Archeology at Fouad I University"—Creswell—at last took his overdue seat on the Comité.[119]

Training the Second Generation: Zaki Muhammad Hassan and Muhammad Mustafa

Although Wiet and Creswell relished the semicolonial age which afforded them such rich careers, they did fulfill their mandate to train Egyptian successors. As in Egyptology, a "lost generation" or two intervened between the Egyptian founding pioneer in the field and the second generation, led in this case by Zaki Muhammad Hassan (1909–1957) and Muhammad Mustafa (1903–1987). They were too young to have learned directly from Ali Bahgat.[120] Like second-generation Egyptologists Selim Hassan and Sami Gabra, Zaki Hassan and Mustafa were sent to Europe before the Egyptian University had a program in their field. In 1927 Wiet examined thirty-six applicants for two scholarships for study in Europe. The applicants had to write essays on historians of Muslim Egypt and on Egyptian governments from the Arab to the Ottoman conquests; they also had to translate a passage from al-Maqrizi on the Sultan Hassan Mosque. Wiet judged the winners as worthy of a French *baccalaureat* but wanted to raise them to *licence ès lettres* level before sending them to Europe. He appointed them assistants at the museum and enrolled them in medieval Egyptian history at the Egyptian University.[121]

Zaki Muhammad Hassan was studying at the Higher Teachers College when he won one of Wiet's slots.[122] After finishing both a history BA and a Higher Teachers College degree in Cairo in 1931, he went on to the Sorbonne. He wrote his doctoral thesis on the Tulunids and earned a certificate in Islamic and Asian Archaeology from the École du Louvre. For seven months, he assisted Ernst Kühnel (1882–1964), director of the Islamic department of the Berlin State Museums from 1931 to 1951.[123] Muhammad Mustafa (1903–87) also worked under Kühnel. Mustafa lectured at the University of Bonn's Institute of Oriental languages (1927–35) and wrote his doctoral dissertation on the chronicler Ibn Iyas.[124]

Zaki Hassan and Muhammad Mustafa both married German women[125] and came home in the mid-1930s to assistant curatorships under Wiet. Hassan was seconded to the Egyptian University to teach Islamic history, and in 1939 he transferred to join Creswell in the Institute of Archaeology. His 'minor arts' specialization complemented Creswell on architecture, and they got along well. Zaki Hassan began attending Comité meetings in 1939 and quickly became an active participant.[126] Publishing in French, English, and Arabic, he became a full professor in 1946, and in 1948, at age forty, dean of the Faculty of Arts. In 1945 Wiet and university rector Ali Ibrahim, an avid collector of Islamic art, helped Zaki Hassan set up an Islamic section in the university museum.[127]

Meanwhile, Muhammad Mustafa continued at the Museum of Arab Art while earning a diploma in Islamic archaeology from Fuad I University in 1940. This improved his chances of succeeding Wiet, whose tutelage he resented.[128] The three-year graduate diploma required Islamic history, architecture, and minor arts; history of art (Western); Persian; and German. Knowledge of English was presumed, and many students would have had some French.[129] The absence of a Turkish requirement reflected the hostility of Europeans and many Egyptian nationalists to Egypt's Ottoman era before the advent of Muhammad Ali.

The German requirement reflected the prominence of such scholars as E. Herzfeld, F. Sarre, and E. Kühnel. Earlier, Egyptian-based Comité architects Julius Franz and Max Herz had also belonged to the vigorous German-language scholarly community of central Europe. In building his university program, Creswell refused to hire Frenchmen, there were no British candidates in the field, and the British Residency was trying to oust the few Germans then teaching in the university. Creswell recruited C.J. Lamm, a Swedish specialist in Islamic glass who taught from 1934 to 1937. In 1937 and again after the war (1948–50), Kühnel visited the university from Berlin.

"Really, we couldn't understand very well his pronunciation," recalled a former student of Creswell's, "but we could read his books."[130] A British scholar wrote:

> Creswell was not a born teacher, his lectures consisted largely of readings from his own books or articles, replete with facts but too magisterial to encourage independent inquiry in his audience. It is hard to say how far he may have instilled in his Egyptian students, many of whom would later seek appointment in the archaeological service, a scientific or disinterested approach to archaeology; probably not far. But they respected and may have liked him. He worked hard for their interests and careers, and some remained his staunch admirers. But a bulky recent work in Arabic on Arab Architecture by a former "best pupil" contains no acknowledgement of debt to Creswell.[131]

Cairo's first seven Islamic archaeology graduates in 1936 became the vanguard of the third generation. In contrast with the Institute of Archaeology's Egyptology section, with its high proportion of Christians, all, or nearly all, the graduates in Islamic archaeology were Muslims.[132]

Wiet recommended hiring two of the new graduates at the museum and two at the Comité's Service des monuments arabes.[133] Hiring Muhammad Abd al-Fattah Hilmi, the Service sent him to England for three months to study historic preservation. He returned an advocate of the British school, which favored consolidating rather than reconstructing monuments.[134] Hilmi served as the Comité's architect in chief for a decade (1943–53) and in 1957 became the first non-Egyptologist Egyptian to direct the Antiquities Service.[135]

World War II's closure of Europe to foreign students accelerated the growth of doctoral programs in Egypt. Cairo awarded its first Islamic archaeology PhD in 1943, three more by the 1952 revolution, and four from 1953 to 1957. These homegrown PhDs—including Farid Shafii, Jamal Mihriz, Hassan al-Basha, and Suad Mahir—would lead the field in the Nasser years and after.[136]

The Changing of the Guard

By the 1940s, European representation on the Comité was down to two Frenchmen: Wiet and the Antiquities Service's Drioton, and two Britons: Creswell and Sir Robert Greg.[137] The first three were great scholars, while Greg was the last of the Comité's assertive European amateurs. Cultural adviser to the British embassy, Greg served as vice president, then president of the Comité's Comité permenante. Although Mirrit

Boutros Ghali of the Society of Coptic Archeology and irrigation engineer Kamal Osman Ghaleb carried on Simaika's tradition as wealthy amateurs,[138] Egyptians on the Comité were also becoming more professionalized. Zaki Hassan had a PhD and Abd al-Fattah Hilmi and Col. Abd al-Rahman Zaki graduate diplomas in the field. Simaika's successors at the Coptic Museum Togo Mina and Pahor Labib both had doctorates. Egyptianization of the Comité finished with a rush in 1951–52. Soon after his last Comité permanent meeting in February 1951,[139] Wiet was forced to leave Egypt. He took up a chair at the Collège de France. Claude Cahen said that Wiet left for political reasons but did not spell them out.[140] Upon Wiet's death in 1971, an Egyptian compared him to the encyclopedic fifteenth-century writer al-Suyuti, but it was Israelis who organized and published a volume to Wiet's memory.[141]

No mystery surrounds Creswell's dismissal a few months after Wiet's. In October 1951, al-Nahhas's Wafdist cabinet abrogated the Anglo–Egyptian Treaty, which al-Nahhas himself had signed in 1936. Guerillas attacked the British in the Suez Canal Zone, demonstrations proliferated, and few university classes met that fall. Creswell attended a Comité meeting on October 31.[142] On December 9, 1951, the Egyptian government fired him and 162 other Britons—mostly teachers and professors.[143] On January 25, 1952, British troops slaughtered Egyptian auxiliary policemen in their barracks at Ismailiya, provoking the Cairo riots the next day which burned down Shepheard's Hotel and many other establishments and toppled the Wafdist government. Only Egyptians showed up for the Comité meeting of March 12, 1952, which sent Creswell an appreciative, if not frank, farewell:

> The mandate of Professor Creswell having terminated by the resignation of his functions as Professor at the Fuad I University, the Comité charges Mr. Abdel Fattah Bey to send him a letter in its name to express its appreciation for the numerous services which he has rendered to the Comité and to the cause of Arab monuments in a spirit of perfect collaboration with the members of the Comité, through the whole time of his mandate.[144]

Four months later, the July 1952 revolution swept Drioton away along with his patron King Faruq. Greg was neither a state employee who could be fired nor a royal protégé, but in April 1952 he resigned the presidency of the Comité permanent due to poor health. He died in Cairo in 1953.[145] There was a postscript. Creswell fought unsuccessfully for reinstatement at Cairo University,[146] but he did regain membership on the body which succeeded the Comité.[147] He remained an outspoken member even after the Suez War of 1956 turned him into an enemy alien and forced him to find a new academic home at the American University in Cairo.[148] He died in 1974 at ninety-five.

Wiet's, Creswell's, and Drioton's departures suddenly opened top cultural posts to Egyptians just as Egypt was entering the final stages of its struggle for independence. The unexpected loss of Zaki Hassan—to postrevolutionary politics, voluntary exile in Baghdad, and an early death—was a sharp blow to the field of Islamic art in Egypt. In April 1951, he had succeeded Wiet as director of the Museum of Arab Art, adding the post to his university deanship. He renamed the museum "Museum of Islamic Art"[149] to reflect better its Turkish and Persian aspects. In December 1952, for unclear reasons, the Free Officers dismissed him. He took refuge as professor of Islamic art at the University of Baghdad, where he died in 1957, not yet sixty.

Muhammad Mustafa had resented Zaki Hassan's return to direct the museum after Wiet's departure and may have fed the new regime the alleged minor misdeed used to dismiss him.[150] In 1953 Mustafa succeeded Hassan as director of the Museum of Islamic Art. Mustafa's publications were sparse,[151] but in his decade as director he trained the next generation, who would run the museum for many years.

The Comité and Museum of Arab Art were initially primarily products of a transnational European initiative, with French, Austro–Hungarian, and British components. Although not directly created by the British, these institutions flourished under their imperial umbrella. Julius Franz, Max Herz, and other Europeans largely drove the Comité's agenda throughout Ali Bahgat's lifetime. Bahgat learned historic preservation from Europeans, fought to convince his countrymen of its value, and struggled to prove that Egyptians could satisfactorily run their own cultural institutions. During the high tide of British imperialism, he worked with European colleagues in such institutions as the Institut égyptien, Geographical Society, and private Egyptian University. Never very gregarious, he felt more at home in upper-class than in popular circles. Although not an outspoken nationalist like Mustafa Kamil or the later Saad Zaghul, he helped to lay cultural foundations upon which the generation of 1919 could later build.

After the Wafd's failure to achieve full independence through the 1919 revolution, the British regrouped and found Egyptian allies in the palace, upper-class 'minority' parties, and eventually in the evolving Wafd as well. This helped sustain British influence through the ensuing three decades of semicolonial rule and made possible Wiet's, Creswell's, and Drioton's remarkable Egyptian careers even as they trained Zaki Hassan, Muhammad Mustafa, and others as their eventual postcolonial successors.

In the denouement at midcentury, national/imperial politics converged with the rarified world of Islamic art and archaeology as dramatically as at the beginning of the story in the early 1880s. European direction of the Museum of Arab Art, university program in Islamic archaeology, and Antiquities Service outlasted neither the monarchy nor the British occupation. Nationalist currents intensified by the 1948 Arab–Israeli War, abrogation of the Anglo–Egyptian Treaty, Black Saturday riots, and 1952 revolution swept away Wiet, Creswell, and Drioton along with the king, parties, and parliament of the old regime. By the time Suez rang down the final curtain on British empire in Egypt in 1956, the Egyptian successors of Wiet, Creswell, and Drioton were already immersed in the old-new challenges of the emerging postcolonial age.

7

Copts and Archaeology: Sons of Saint Mark / Sons of the Pharaohs

C alling on Patriarch Kyrillus (Cyril) V one winter day in 1908, vice president of the Coptic Community Council Murqus (Marcus) Simaika found him supervising while a silversmith weighed out old silver gospel covers and church vessels to be melted down for reworking. The objects bore fourteenth- and fifteenth-century Coptic and Arabic inscriptions. Simaika offered to raise the £E180 value of the bullion if he could preserve these in an annex of al-Muallaqa Church as a start toward a museum. Kyrillus agreed, and the Coptic Museum was born.[1] This dramatic foundation story from Simaika's unpublished memoirs has been challenged and is an oversimplification at best. Nevertheless, it captures a shift in worldviews in keeping with far-reaching changes then percolating through Coptic and Egyptian society. Worn-out cult objects were transvalued into priceless antiquities to be revered in a new type of shrine—a museum.

Simaika's career and the Coptic Museum provide central narrative threads for this chapter. His passion for Coptic archaeology developed in the context of the quest of an emerging Coptic elite of educated and prosperous laymen seeking a proud past to legitimate their challenge to the clergy for communal leadership and provide a critical link in the long chain of Egypt's national history. Upper-class lay reformers depicted the contemporary Coptic clergy as poorly educated, superstitious, and often corrupt. Drawing on the heritages of both early Christianity and the pharaonic era, Simaika and other Coptic officials, professionals, and landowners aspired to lead a Coptic and Egyptian awakening. European-style schools were key instruments of this envisioned revival. The Coptic Community Council (al-Majlis al-Milli), which was instituted in 1874 in keeping with the Tanzimat reforms emanating from Istanbul,

197

opened an arena in which the laity could challenge clerical control of Coptic endowments (awqaf), schools, and personal status law. In Europe and America, Protestant clergymen and laymen alike were turning to archaeology as a means of vindicating the Bible in the face of skepticism and the higher criticism.[2] In Egypt, however, Coptic popes, priests, and monks were slower to develop much interest in either the Coptic Museum or the pharaonic heritage.

Like Ahmad Kamal in Egyptology and Ali Bahgat in Islamic archaeology, Simaika struggled to kindle enthusiasm for antiquities as an instrument of national revival. Although Simaika was fifteen years younger than Kamal and six younger than Bahgat, they shared something of a generational consciousness. All three completed their schooling before the British conquest, spent most of their careers during the heyday of colonial occupation (1882–1922), lived through the hopes and disappointments of the 1919 revolution, and helped shape the ensuing semicolonial period.

Mirrit Boutros Ghali (1908–1992) and the Society of Coptic Archeology he founded in 1934 provide an additional narrative thread for the latter part of this chapter. Like Simaika, he drew support from upper- and upper-middle-class laymen and emphasized Coptic rather than pharaonic antiquity. Mirrit was two generations younger than Simaika, however, and his proposed socioeconomic reforms had a national rather than a Coptic communal focus. Finally, the chapter examines the idea of Copts as "modern sons of the pharaohs."[3] The very word 'Copt' came from the Greek *Aegyptos*—Egypt—and the language still used in Coptic scriptures and liturgy descends from that of ancient Egypt. European Orientalist perceptions of Copts as "sons of the pharaohs" influenced Coptic self-perceptions, and Copts stood out in both the new profession of Egyptology and in popularizing pharaonism.

Murqus Simaika and the Nineteenth-century Coptic Community

The Coptic community into which Murqus Simaika was born in 1864 attributed its origin to St. Mark's mission to Egypt in the first century CE. After inspiring contributions by martyrs, church fathers, and pioneers of monasticism, what would become the Coptic Orthodox Church parted with Rome and Constantinople over Christological doctrines at the Council of Chalcedon in 451 CE. The ensuing persecution of anti-Chalcedonian Egyptians by the Chalcedonian Byzantine establishment of Constantinople helped soften Egypt up for the Arab Muslim conquest of 640–42. Recent scholarship, however, has challenged assumptions that the theological dispute ran along Greek-versus-Coptic linguistic or ethnic lines and the idea that Egyptians welcomed the Muslims as deliverers from Byzantine Greek oppression.[4] After several centuries of Muslim rule, conversion tipped the population balance in favor of Islam, and Arabic gradually displaced Coptic except as a scriptural and liturgical language.[5]

In 1798, a few Copts threw in their lot with the French invaders under General Bonaparte, but most did not.[6] A century later, the 1897 census counted 608,000 Copts, 6.2 percent of Egypt's 9,734,000 residents.[7] Twentieth-century census figures range up to just over 8 percent Copts, but Copts claim to be undercounted because of census-taker bias or informants' fear of taxation or conscription. Copts are often estimated at 10 percent of the population, with other Christians totaling less than 1 percent. Copts were most concentrated in the Upper Egyptian provinces of Minya and Asyut. In the nineteenth century, most were peasants and in many ways undifferentiated from their Muslims neighbors.[8] Urban Copts were drawn to crafts, finance, and tax collection. Lacking networks of wealthy coreligionists abroad, they were less active in commerce than the Greek Orthodox, Armenians, and Jews.[9]

Murqus Simaika attended the Patriarchal School which Kyrillus IV, "the Father of Reform" (r. 1854–61), had founded a decade before his birth. Partly to win European support, Muhammad Ali had discarded restrictions on dhimmis (protected but inferior Christian and Jewish subjects in Islamic states) in dress, horseback riding, religious processions, and erecting churches. He did not, however, recruit Copts into his new army, schools, study missions to Europe, translation bureau, printing press, or official journal. His grandson Said Pasha (r. 1854–63), who came to power the same year as Kyrillus IV, abolished the poll tax (jizya) on non-Muslims and began drafting Copts into the army. Said refused, however, to open state schools to Copts, and Kyrillus founded schools for his own flock. Kyrillus was also influenced by schools which Anglicans of the Church Missionary Society (CMS) operated in Cairo in the 1830s and 1840s.[10]

Europeans were of several minds about Copts. Orientalist Edward Lane was scathing:

> One of the most remarkable traits in the character of the Copts is their bigotry. They bear a bitter hatred of all other Christians, even exceeding that with which the Muslims regard the unbelievers in El-Islám. . . . They are, generally speaking, of a sullen temper, extremely avaricious, and abominable dissemblers; cringing or domineering according to circumstances.[11]

Lane's friend Gardiner Wilkinson, on the other hand, found something to admire in the clergy:

There is an air of respectability and mildness, in the deportment of the superiors, and most of the aged fathers, which is characteristic of the Christian, and . . . [contrasted with] the arrogance of the ulemas of Islam, cannot fail to leave a pleasing impression on the Christian stranger, and to call up in his mind the conviction that these people, though ignorant and prejudiced, are united with Him in a common bond of union, and have ideas that sympathize with His own.[12]

The Church Missionary Society's John Lieder believed that Copts were redeemable through education. He ran schools with the cooperation of Coptic Patriarch Boutros (Peter) VII (r. 1809–52) and eschewed superficial conversion from Coptic to Anglican Christianity. Seeking a deeper transformation, Lieder used the monitorial educational system which Joseph Lancaster had elaborated in England to inculcate discipline, industry, and learning in the lower classes. Educators in Muhammad Ali's state schools also showed interest in Lancastrianism as a means of internalizing discipline in students.[13]

Kyrillus IV opened schools, imported a printing press, cracked down on priestly ignorance and corruption, and reached out ecumenically to Greek Orthodox and Armenian Christians. Coptic elementary schools (*kuttabs*), like their Muslim counterparts, emphasized rote memorization and recitation of scriptures, often with blind instructors. There was no Coptic al-Azhar for higher learning. Kyrillus IV's new Patriarchal School (Madrasat al-Aqbat al-Kubra) shaped a generation of lay leaders at a time when missionary and state schools had only begun to make education more widely available to Copts. Simaika boasted that his alma mater produced three prime ministers.[14] Khedive Ismail and minister of education Ali Mubarak opened state schools to all religions in 1867. Two of Simaika's brothers transferred to the state law school.[15]

St. Mark's Cathedral, the Patriarchate, and the Patriarchal School were in the heavily Coptic quarter north of Ezbekiya,[16] just two hundred meters from the house of Simaika's maternal grandfather, where Murqus grew up. Slave girls did their housework. Simaika's mother was born in Damascus, where her father was secretary to Muhammad Ali's son Ibrahim Pasha. Simaika's paternal forebears had donated manuscripts to al-Muallaqa Church. He studied Arabic, Coptic, Greek, and English at the Patriarchal School and French at the École des frères chrétiens. Muslim families often sent one son to al-Azhar; Simaika's father tried to save him for the church by forbidding him to learn English. The boy rebelled, however, and after a hunger strike was allowed to join the English class taught by Mikhail Abd al-Sayyid, founder of the Coptic daily *al-Watan*.[17]

Missionaries from what in 1858 became the United Presbyterian Church of North America arrived "to occupy" Egypt—the military metaphor was theirs—in the same year that Said and Kyrillus IV ascended their thrones: 1854. The "American Mission" denounced the Coptic Church as heretical, corrupt, and superstitious and tried to lure away its flock.[18] Protestant ideas echo in Simaika's denunciation of the Coptic clergy as lazy and corrupt refugees from the world of work who neglected religious duties, sold justice, and enriched relatives with church funds.[19]

Decade after decade, Kyrillus IV's successors Demetrius II (r. 1862–1870), Kyrillus V (r. 1874–1927), and Yuannis (John) XIX (r. 1928–1942) defended clerical prerogatives against both foreign missionaries and Coptic lay reformers. Popes, bishops, and monks mostly came from poor, provincial Upper Egyptian families, spent years in monastic isolation, and were revered for piety and asceticism, not education or worldly knowledge. "It is a shameful confession," wrote Simaika, "but we must acknowledge that very few of the existing bishops belong to respectable families."[20] Mikhail Abd al-Sayyid's *al-Watan*, founded in 1878, defended clerical authority against reformist laymen. From the 1890s until 1923 it also backed the British occupation.[21]

Educated in the new schools, officials, professionals, and landowners in the Majlis al-Milli demanded a say in administering Coptic schools, awqaf, and personal status law. In the seventeenth and eighteenth centuries, Coptic lay notables (archons) had prospered as financial agents for Muslim military households and overshadowed the popes as patrons of church renovations, manuscript copying, and icon painting.[22] Voting rights for the Majlis al-Milli were limited to office holders and wealthy landowners; in 1891, the body's twelve laymen included seven beys and Boutros Ghali, a pasha.[23] As with Saad Zaghlul, Ahmad Lutfi al-Sayyid, and Muhammad Husayn Haykal, the secularizing reforms which young Simaika advocated never threatened his social class. In 1891, Simaika was also among the founders of the Copts' Tawfiq Society, which promoted education.[24]

The patriarch's presidency of the Majlis al-Milli frustrated lay reformers.[25] About once a decade, discontent forced the election of a new Majlis al-Milli, whose lay leaders soon clashed with the patriarch. Kyrillus V refused even to convene the second Majlis al-Milli, elected in 1882. In 1892–93, the third Majlis colluded with Khedive Abbas II, Prime Minister Mustafa Fahmi, Lord Cromer, and notable Boutros Ghali to exile Kyrillus to a desert monastery. This provoked a popular outburst, however, and the patriarch returned in triumph to rule without the Majlis al-Milli. Paul Sedra has critiqued the "enlightenment" or "awakening" narrative prevalent in both Coptic and Western accounts. It lionizes Kyrillus IV as "the

Father of the Reform" and denigrates his successors until Kyrillus VI (r. 1959–71) and Shenuda III (r. 1971–2012) as either reactionary or weak.[26]

Simaika and Tadrus Shenuda al-Manqabadi (1857–1932) stood out as anticlericals in the Majlis al-Milli of 1892–93.[27] Al-Manqabadi had attended both American and Coptic schools in Asyut. He founded a Society for the Preservation of Coptic History there in 1883 or 1884, translated E.L. Butcher's *Story of the Church in Egypt*[28] into Arabic, and was one of the founders of the Asyut Benevolent Society. In 1895 he launched the newspaper *Misr* to counter the propatriarchal *al-Watan*. *Misr* backed the British occupation until 1918, then switched to support the Wafd.[29]

Kyrillus V soon suppressed the Coptic Clerical College of 1874–75, which he had been pressed into founding. After he reopened it under pressure in 1893, it became the base of Claudius Labib, a friend of Simaika's.[30] Labib (1868–1918), born to a scribal family in Asyut, had entered the Patriarchal School in Cairo at age seven. He taught Coptic in Ahmad Kamal's short-lived Egyptology school at the Egyptian Museum, learned ancient Egyptian, and entered the Antiquities Service as an inspector. He left the Service to teach in Coptic and American schools, then settled in to teach Coptic at the Clerical College. The College's press—imported from Germany—had Latin, Arabic, Coptic, and hieroglyphic fonts. Labib used it to publish Arabic hymnals and Coptic liturgical works. He published a magazine, *Ain Shams* (Arabic for Heliopolis) in Arabic and Coptic and installments of a Coptic–Arabic dictionary. Labib gave his six children pharaonic names and insisted that they speak Coptic—a language as dead as Latin in the West—at home. Claudius's son Pahor Labib followed him into Egyptology and became director of the Coptic Museum.[31]

Another activist layman, Habib Girgis (1876–1951), became director of the Clerical College in 1918 after twenty years on its staff. He founded the Sunday School Movement, which by midcentury spearheaded a sweeping spiritual and educational revival and in 1971 produced one of the great Coptic popes, Shenuda III.[32]

Simaika, the Comité, and the Coptic Museum

Copts seeking a golden past could look back either to the Roman/Byzantine era of the early church or to the pharaonic era. The clergy and common folk were drawn to Saint Mark, Saint Antony, and the early Christian martyrs, while by the late nineteenth century some of the lay elite were also showing a growing interest in the pharaohs. Similarly, nineteenth-century Greeks looked to either their Byzantine/Greek Orthodox heritage, which appealed to the clergy and common people, or to the classical past idealized by northern Europeans and some Greek merchants and lay intellectuals. One contrast with Greece was that Byzantine/Greek Orthodox enthusiasts could celebrate either martyrs and saints or the worldly glory of Christian emperors like Constantine, Theodosius, and Justinian. Copts, however, had no worldly glory to remember. Their calendar dated from neither the birth of Christ nor St. Mark's mission to Alexandria but from the accession of Diocletian (284 CE), whose persecution began the Copts' "era of martyrs." Muslims, in contrast, could take pride in the simultaneous spiritual and worldly triumphs of Islam beginning in the lifetime of the Prophet himself.

Roger Bagnall notes that the terms 'Coptic' and 'Byzantine' applied to Egypt in late antiquity are problematic. Art historians tend to use 'Coptic,' while more classically minded papyrologists and historians often use 'Byzantine.' Papyrologists even stretch the term 'Byzantine' back to Diocletian's accession in 284, and Egypt's church, including Greek-speaking clergy, is often called 'Coptic' well before the 451 doctrinal split at the Council of Chalcedon.[33]

Because it survived as a sacred language, Coptic never had to await a Champollion. The Vatican's Coptic College began training Catholic missionaries in the seventeenth century. German Jesuit Athanasius Kircher's (1602–1680) fanciful hieroglyphic researches came up dry, but he laid the foundation for Coptic studies in Europe.[34] Beginning with Champollion, Coptic studies became an auxiliary to Egyptology as well as a branch of Biblical and patristic studies. In the 1830s, Robert Curzon and Henry Tattam obtained Coptic manuscripts from Egyptian monasteries for the British Museum. Tattam shared missionary John Lieder's goal of shifting the teaching of Coptic in Egypt from memorization to textbook-based grammatical instruction. At the Patriarchal School, Simaika used Tattam's Coptic–Arabic New Testament, and his teacher Barsum al-Rahib wrote the first modern Coptic grammar in Arabic.[35]

Hired in 1880 to tutor the sons of Khedive Tawfiq, Oxford classicist Alfred Butler was shocked to discover that

> day by day they [Christian antiquities] are perishing, unknown to western travellers, and little regarded by the Copts themselves; and nothing, absolutely nothing, has been done or is doing to rescue them from oblivion, or to save them from destruction.[36]

Butler wrote *Ancient Churches of Egypt* (1884) and *The Arab Conquest of Egypt* (1902). Antiquities director Gaston Maspero promoted the excavation of Coptic sites, displaying the results in the Egyptian Museum. Somers Clarke, the retired architect of St. Paul's Cathedral, London, came to Egypt in 1902 to work on his *Christian Antiquities in the Nile Valley* (1912). Jean Clédat excavated half a dozen Coptic sites before 1914.[37] In 1903, Butler, Clarke, Clédat, Max Herz, and Khedival Library director B. Moritz founded an ephemeral Society of the History of Coptic Antiquity in Egypt.[38]

When the British marched into Cairo in 1882, eighteen-year-old Murqus Simaika immediately put his English to work. Viscountess Stranford set up a volunteer hospital for wounded officers and hired him as her secretary. In 1883, Simaika began his career in the state railways. Copts had an inside track in the railways department, where British influence was strong; in 1911 Copts made up 48 percent of railway and telegraph officials.[39] For Simaika, unlike for Ahmad Kamal and Ali Bahgat, antiquity was an after-hours hobby.[40]

Simaika reported that Butler's *Ancient Churches* inspired him to lobby for placing Coptic monuments under the Comité de conservation des monuments de l'art arabe and to found the Coptic Museum. Visiting Butler in Oxford in 1890, Simaika met Somers Clarke and informed him that Coptic notables were remodeling churches in "modern Greek style" with Italian marble, and that neither the patriarch nor lay leader Boutros Ghali had made any objection. Clarke fired off a protest letter, and 1891 found Simaika showing Sir Evelyn Baring (soon to be Lord Cromer) Cairo's old churches. Although Kyrillus V consented in 1896 to put these under the surveillance of the Comité, Simaika reported that the pope "blamed" this arrangement on him and retaliated by keeping him off the Comité.[41] Nakhla Bey al-Barati and Hanna Bey Bakhum were appointed instead.[42]

István Ormos points out that Comité records say nothing of Simaika's claim to have instigated putting Coptic monuments under the mandate of the Comité.[43] Simaika blamed al-Barati for starting to demolish a Roman tower of the fort of Babylon in order to enlarge the entrance to al-Muallaqa Church (the Hanging Church). Baring himself intervened to halt the project. Simaika's deploring al-Barati's jumbling of screens and icons of various eras together in refurbishing the Church of St. George[44] suggests a clash between a traditional devotional and an emerging art historical approach.

Ormos also challenges Simaika's claim to have founded the Coptic Museum. Max Herz, architect in chief of the Comité, proposed in December 1897 collecting objects for a museum: "Arab Art has its museum; Coptic art now awaits one of its own."[45] Comité chairman Husayn Fakhri, minister of public works and education, obtained the patriarch's consent, and Nakhla al-Barati was assigned to coordinate the collecting. Ormos notes that Simaika first recounted the museum foundation story which opens this chapter only decades later in his memoirs and that he ignored earlier efforts.[46] What became of any items collected in al-Muallaqa's annex before Simaika took over, however, is unknown, and denying his claim to be the museum's founder seems to go too far.

Three victories of Simaika's between 1905 and 1908—appointment to the Comité and to the Legislative Council and founding the museum—were scarcely noticed in Egypt's rush of national events: the execution of peasants who clashed with British troops at Dinshaway, the financial crash, Cromer's retirement, the founding of political parties, the deaths of Mustafa Kamil and Qasim Amin, the opening of the Egyptian University, and Boutros Ghali's appointment as Egypt's first Coptic prime minister. Back in 1892–93, Simaika had been one of only two members of the Majlis al-Milli who refused to sign Boutros Ghali's petition to recall the patriarch from monastic exile.[47] Simaika soon came to realize, however, that he would never win a seat on the Comité or direct the Coptic Museum unless he made up with the patriarch. He recanted his early radicalism:

> Unfortunately, instead of showing some consideration for the wishes of the Patriarch by avoiding the controverted points and devoting ourselves to other much-needed reforms, we pursued a rather violent policy. A serious struggle ensued between the Council, supported by the mass of the people, and the Patriarch, who had on his side the bishops, most of the clergy and a certain section of the Community.[48]

By the turn of the century, as a British observer remarked: "Occasionally the Patriarch can by gentle and tactful persuasion of such a man as Murqus Simaika Pasha be wooed a little into the way of reform."[49] Simaika, however, had largely sacrificed reform on the altar of his beloved archaeology.

Nakhla al-Barati's death in 1905 cleared the way for Simaika's appointment to the Comité.[50] By then, papal administration had become so corrupt that even bishops and *al-Watan* joined *Misr* and lay reformers in demanding a Majlis al-Milli. Simaika's vice presidency (under the patriarch) of the resulting Majlis staved off a showdown until October 1909, when Kyrillus dissolved the body.

In 1906, Simaika's appointment to the Legislative Council thrust him beyond Coptic into national politics. The Council and a rarely convened General Assembly were the closest the British allowed to a parliament. In 1914, Simaika became one of four Copts appointed to the Legislative Assembly which superseded the Legislative Council and General Assembly.[51] He associated there with the landowners and intellectuals of Ahmad Lutfi al-Sayyid's Umma Party.[52] Simaika's parliamentary contacts helped him raise over £E300 to launch the Coptic Museum. Prince Husayn Kamil (president of the Legislative Council and from 1914 to 1917 sultan of Egypt, Prime Minister Boutros Ghali, other ministers, and consul general Sir Eldon Gorst chipped in. So did Simaika's Comité colleagues Boghos Nubar and Yaqub Artin, both Armenians. Kyrillus V contributed nothing in cash, but the archbishop of Alexandria and the abbot of Deir al-Muharraq monastery did.[53] Sometime between 1914 and 1918 Simaika was made a pasha.[54]

The museum's setting was truly historic—next to al-Muallaqa Church in Old Cairo (Misr al-qadima / Fustat), near the Church of St. Sergius (a legendary refuge of the Holy Family). Armed with a papal mandate, Simaika scoured churches and monasteries "from Rosetta in the north to Khartoum in the south,"[55] paying nominal prices for relics for the museum. The museum's first budget (1910) listed £E266 in donations and a £E50 state subsidy. The state began an annual subsidy of £E200 in 1913 and raised it to £E300 in 1918.[56] Baedeker lists 1910 as the museum's founding date.[57] A visit by ex-president Theodore Roosevelt that March drew attention to the fledgling institution. In a speech at the Egyptian University, Roosevelt had decried the assassination of Prime Minister Boutros Ghali, berated the nationalists, and lauded British rule. Approving Coptic notables invited Roosevelt to the museum, and but for Simaika's veto might have presented the ex-president its most precious manuscript.[58]

By World War I, elite Coptic laymen were better educated, wealthier, and more in touch with the outside world than ever before.[59] Simaika's embryonic museum and the churches the Comité had repaired were a source of growing pride. Few Coptic clergymen, however, yet shared in this awakening to antiquity. S. Leeder lamented: "I wish I could say that the Patriarch himself had anything like a proper appreciation of the treasures still left to his sadly depleted church."[60]

Copts, Interwar Politics, and the Nationalization of the Coptic Museum

Bringing Coptic monuments under the Comité in 1896 was a step toward recognizing Coptic membership not just in a sectarian millet but also in the national community. Simaika's Comité and parliamentary seats drew him into national affairs, and in 1931 the Coptic Museum was transformed from a communal into a national institution. The Wafd Party and lay reformers in the Majlis al-Milli would have preferred a more democratic way of nationalizing the museum, but in fact it was autocratic actors who accomplished the deed—King Fuad, Yuannis XIX, Prime Minister Ismail Sidqi, and Murqus Simaika.

In 1910, a Muslim youth assassinated Prime Minister Boutros Ghali in the belief that he had sold out to the British. In reaction, a Coptic

Congress in Asyut in 1911 boldly asserted Coptic rights. Muslim notables countered with an "Egyptian Congress"—a pointedly nonsectarian, national label—convened in Heliopolis.[61] Thereafter, Muslims and Copts gradually pulled back from the abyss of communal strife. In 1919, they rose together against the British. *Misr* jettisoned its support for the occupation, added Muslims to its staff, and transformed itself into a Wafdist newspaper.[62] Lobbying by the Wafd helped keep a provision for minority representation out of the 1923 constitution. The late prime minister's son Wasif Boutros Ghali, Murqus Hanna, Wisa Wasif, and Makram Ubayd (Ebeid) rose to national leadership through the Wafd.[63] There were six Copts out of fourteen on the Wafd's executive committee in 1923,[64] and Zaghlul pointedly put two in his 1924 cabinet of ten.[65]

From the 1920s into the 1940s, whenever parliamentary elections were free, the Wafd won and Copts obtained 7–9 percent of the seats in the Chamber of Deputies. Copts were less represented in other parties and so did poorly when elections were rigged against the Wafd. In Ismail Sidqi's rigged election of 1931, Copts won only 2.6 percent of Chamber seats.[66] Coptic support for the Liberal Constitutionalists—never strong—dwindled in the late 1920s, when the party began accusing Mustafa al-Nahhas, Zaghlul's successor as head of the Wafd, of being under undue Coptic influence. The accusers had the Wafd's powerful secretary general Makram Ubayd primarily in mind.[67] Former Liberal Constitutionalist Tawfiq Doss had gone over to the palace, where he joined Qallini Fahmi as a key Coptic "fixer" for King Fuad.[68]

Two months before the 1919 revolution, Simaika confided that he had no faith in Muslim justice and preferred the British yoke.[69] The British Residency's secret file on Simaika reported:

After a brief disappearance under the waves of the Independence movement, he emerged to try to form a Moderate party, to oppose the chauvinism of Zaghlul. He has been helpful at various times to the Residency.[70]

Soon after ascending the throne in 1917, Sultan Fuad began angling for an invitation to visit the Coptic Museum. Simaika's plea for more time provoked Fuad's retort: "Yoummak Bi Sana [Your day is a year]." Fuad used his visit, accomplished on December 21, 1920, to open a royal campaign to nationalize the museum (see fig. 45). The monarch donated £E500 on the spot, and his entourage chipped in another £E1,500.[71]

Wooing the museum suited Fuad's campaign to present himself as a renaissance prince—an enlightened patron of international congresses, historical publications, and cultural institutions generally. The cultural

45 Murqus Simaika welcomes King Fuad (with cane) to the Coptic Museum, 1920. Simaika (holding folded paper with both hands) is on his left. *Simaika,* Guide sommaire du musée copte et des principales églises du Caire, *second frontispiece.*

campaign was an integral part of his drive to build a strong monarchy in the political space which the British evacuated in 1922.[72] The Coptic Museum served his purposes as a site for impressing Europeans with his solicitude for his Christian subjects. In 1923 he came by with Victor Emanuel III of Italy and his queen.[73] Cautious old Kyrillus V, however, preferred keeping the museum a communal institution in the millet tradition and kept putting the king off.

The Coptic Museum did not cross the horizon of the travel industry until the 1920s. Neither the 1914 Baedeker nor the 1916 Macmillan guide mentioned it. The 1929 Baedeker gave it a single page compared to twenty-three and a foldout plan for the Egyptian Museum, three for the Museum of Arab Art, and four for the Greco–Roman Museum.[74] In 1927, George Sobhy (Sobhi) lamented the museum's low profile:

> The tourists are dazzled by the monuments of pagan Egypt, to the neglect of the Coptic churches, yet the name of the Copts is in itself but an echo of the word of Egypt. The ancient tongue of the Pharaohs is still being spoken every day in divine service within the walls of those neglected and hidden buildings. May it continue forever![75]

Simaika knew how to deal. He long held his own as the only Copt on the Comité, even chairing its vital executive arm—the "technical section."[76] In 1928, while lobbying parliament for £E40,000 for Comité repairs on the Mosque of Ibn Tulun, he slipped in a request for £E4000 for a new roof for the Church of St. Barbara. When minister of finance Muhammad Mahmud balked, Simaika invited Makram Ubayd, the Coptic minister of communications who had shown little interest in Coptic affairs, for a tour. On his way out, Ubayd offered a £E10 donation. Simaika pressed him instead to use his influence to obtain the £E4,000 for St. Barbara. Ubayd did, and won the grant.[77]

The Wafd's coalition cabinets (1926–28) under Liberal Constitutionalists Adli Yakan and Abd al-Khaliq Tharwat, and the death of Kyrillus V, presented an opportunity to reform both al-Azhar and Coptic affairs. Reformist Mustafa al-Maraghi was made sheikh of al-Azhar over Fuad's objection, and a law stipulated that the Majlis al-Milli, elected by universal male suffrage, would have a say in administering Coptic awqaf, personal status law, and schools.[78] It all unraveled, however. In 1928, Fuad installed an authoritarian cabinet under Muhammad Mahmud, replaced Sheikh al-Maraghi at al-Azhar, and thwarted the Majlis al-Milli by installing Yuannis XIX (John, r. 1928–42) as pope. The British Residency reported that Simaika had "often rendered good services in the past as arbiter between the Coptic reformers, with whom his sympathies lay, and the reactionary patriarchate," but now

> he ratted from the Coptic reforming party in December 1927 and favoured the reactionary cause in the matter of succession to the Patriarchal Throne—probably with the good of his beloved museum in view. His was a notable defection.

The British Residency's secret file called the new pope "the evil genius of the Coptic Church" and claimed that he stood "for all that is reactionary and corrupt in the Coptic Church. His exploitation of certain rich monastery Wakfs [awqaf] is a scandal."[79]

Royal and clerical authoritarianism converged again when Ismail Sidqi's palace government appointed Yuannis XIX to the Senate in 1931 over the protests of *Misr* and the Majlis al-Milli.[80] Murqus Simaika had kept up with Sidqi through the years when the latter presided over annual dinners of "old boys" of the Frères School,[81] and one of the pope's fellow Senate appointees was Murqus's brother Abdallah Simaika.[82] Another brother, Wasif Simaika, had served in the 1922 cabinet of Abd al-Khaliq Tharwat.[83]

Three popes in a row after Kyrillus V were installed only after divisive communal wrangling. All were uninspiring leaders who continued to clash with Majlis al-Milli laymen.[84] After Yuannis XIX (1928–42), Simaika again backed a traditionalist (the future Yusab II, r. 1946–55), who lost to the reformist who became Makarius III (r. 1942–44). Makarius's brief reign disillusioned his reformist backers, however, and Yusab II's reign turned into a disaster that ended in his deposition.

Simaika's temporizing on nationalizing the museum had angered Fuad: "His Majesty was offended by the way I acted in this matter and from that day to my great grief, has refused to see me." Even Yuannis XIX's debt to the king for his papal throne did not yield immediate nationalization of the museum. Escorting King Albert I of Belgium to the museum in 1930, Fuad snapped at Simaika: "The State is above individuals, so why do you not hand over the Museum as I asked you to do?"[85] In 1931 Prime Minister Ismail Sidqi's dictatorial cabinet, with minister of communications Tawfiq Doss as broker, finally closed the deal: the Antiquities Service would administer the museum, Simaika would remain its director, the patriarch would appoint four members to the museum board, and church waqf rights would be respected.

The Majlis al-Milli protested, though in vain. So did one clergyman, Higumanus Hanna Shanuda. He and his brother had minded the museum for Simaika; now he wanted his son Wadi Hanna, a 1928 graduate in Cairo's first class of BA Egyptologists, appointed director. Angry at having been bypassed in appointments to the museum board, the Majlis al-Milli ordered Shanuda to lock the museum and transfer its records to the patriarchate, beyond government reach. Simaika admitted that many, "especially ladies," agreed with the Majlis al-Milli's accusation blaming him for selling communal property to the state. He countered that he had built up the museum with private donations alone; the patriarchate had contributed "not a penny." Never one for half measures, Prime Minister Sidqi dispatched an undersecretary of education with a truckload of soldiers, changed the locks, and installed Simaika as director of the museum. The patriarch acquiesced and named a new curator[86] who got along with Simaika. Simaika replaced the missing records with a new inventory. In January 1932, Prime Minister Sidqi savored his triumph with a visit to the museum, and in 1935 crown prince Faruq and his sisters followed[87] (fig. 46).

Attendance at the Coptic Museum remained a distant fourth among the four antiquities museums throughout the interwar period. After the post–World War II museum reopenings, however, it vied for third or second place (far behind the first-place Egyptian Museum) with the Museum of Arab Art and the Greco–Roman Museum.[88]

With Tutankhamun's treasures crowding the Egyptian Museum beginning in 1923, Simaika lobbied for transferring its Coptic collection to the Coptic Museum. Antiquities director Lacau refused, maintaining that Coptic antiquities illustrated a necessary stage in the evolution of Egyptian art, and King Fuad backed him up. In 1936, however, Fuad died and Lacau retired, and Lacau's successor Drioton approved the transfer. Simaika wrote that a new wing added to the Coptic Museum now

46 Crown Prince Faruk and his sisters with Murqus Simaika (right) at the Coptic Museum, ca. 1935. *Simaika,* Guide sommaire du musée copte et des principales églises du Caire, *first frontispiece.*

has made possible the grouping together of the antiquities pertaining to the four main periods of Egyptian history: The Pharaonic in the Great Egyptian Museum in Cairo, the Graeco–Roman in Alexandria, the Christian in the Coptic Museum and the Arabic and Moslem in the Museum of Arab Art.[89]

In 1937 Simaika published *Guide sommaire du musée copte et des principales églises du Caire*.

A theme, more than an era, defined the scope of the Coptic Museum. Passing from pharaonic to Hellenistic to Roman/Byzantine to Islamic rule, Egypt had never experienced Coptic sovereignty. The 1953 guide gave a rather narrow description of the museum's chronological reach: "Coptic Antiquities roughly date from the IIIrd Century AD to the Xth Century of the Christian Era."[90] It thus overlapped in time with the contents of the museums of Greco–Roman and Arab/Islamic antiquities.

Simaika also worked hard to catalogue and conserve manuscripts in the patriarchate, monasteries, and churches. A visit in 1912 to Wadi al-Natrun monasteries with Johan George, crown prince of Saxony, gave him a sense of urgency. They found dusty manuscripts strewn through cells and churches. A calligrapher himself, Kyrillus V loved manuscripts and backed Simaika's campaign. Yassa Abd al-Masih (1898–1959), librarian of the Coptic Museum from 1922 to 1957, did much of the work. After schooling in Beni Suef, he had graduated from the Coptic Clerical College in 1922 and later studied Coptic at the Egyptian University. In each monastery at Wadi al-Natrun, Simaika and Abd al-Masih designated a room as the library, put the "most enlightened" monk in charge, and shelved and catalogued the manuscripts. The two coauthored the *Catalogue of the Coptic and Arabic Manuscripts*. Abd al-Masih later helped edit and translate Sawirus ibn al-Muqaffa's *History of the Patriarchs of the Egyptian Church* and assisted the Library of Congress in microfilming manuscripts at Saint Catherine Monastery.[91]

Sons of the Pharaohs? Copts and Ancient Egypt

Although Simaika and Abd al-Massih were among the Coptic laymen drawn primarily to Christian antiquity, others emphasized the pharaonic legacy. During the colonial age, European belief that Copts were the truest heirs of ancient Egypt became a powerful validation, although other Europeans complained about how far these 'sons of the pharaohs' had fallen. Like European philhellenes who judged modern Greeks unworthy of their idealized ancestors, eighteenth-century Danish traveler Karsten Niebuhr wrote that Copts are descended from the ancient Egyptians; and the Turks, upon this account, call them in derision, the posterity of Pharaoh. But their uncouth figure, their stupidity, ignorance, and wretchedness, do little credit to the sovereigns of ancient Egypt.[92]

Over the course of the nineteenth century ideas of civilization and progress became increasingly entangled with theories of race.[93] An 1890s guidebook even described Copts as follows:

Complexion yellow, oval face, forehead flat, nose large, longish eyes, large mouth, lips very thick, hair curly and black. The Copts are the most ugly of men. They are also exceedingly dirty and very disgusting in their habits.[94]

Assyriologist clergyman A.H. Sayce swung to the opposite extreme:

It is with the Copts, that is to say the Christian Egyptians, that our hope for the future well-being of Egypt must lie. Egyptian Mohammedanism is hopeless; it is only among the Copts that we find the same fundamental principles of morality and action as among ourselves. It is, moreover, only among the Copts that we find the pure strain of the ancient Egyptian race; elsewhere the people are descended from Arabs, or contaminated by Arab blood. And it is the Copts, accordingly, who have inherited the cleverness and abilities of their Pharaonic forefathers.[95]

Maspero lent his scholarly authority to the belief that Copts were the purest descendants of the ancient Egyptians. In 1908 he spoke at the Copts' aptly named Ramses Club. He said that Egyptian Muslims were mostly of the same stock but lacked "racial purity" because of marriage to outsiders.[96] Characteristically, Maspero's English colleague Petrie was more blunt:

A Coptic village is clean and well swept, the women sitting at work in the doorways and chatting across the street. It is on the level of a civilised Mediterranean land, and not like the filthy confusion of a Moham-medan village. . . . Egypt will never be a civilised land til it is ruled by the Copts—if ever.[97]

Rev. S.H. Leeder's *Modern Sons of the Pharaohs* deplored such bigotry:

Such ill-informed views as those of Dean Stanley, that the Coptic Chris-tians of Egypt are "the most civilised of the natives," views which have been re-echoed again and again by those who know little or nothing of the Egyptian people, their wish as Christian writers alone being father to the thought, is resented by the Moslem section of the community, not merely as a libel upon themselves but as a misstatement of facts which they suspect has been cunningly fostered.[98]

The phrase "sons of the pharaohs" of course betrayed an elitist as well as a patriarchal bias. Europeans applied it more readily to Copts than to their other main candidates for pharaonic descent—the peasantry or fellahin. They depicted fellahin as stolid, with "coarser" features, less self-consciousness, and subordinated to the unchanging agricultural rhythm in the Nile landscape. Physical descriptions of Copts, in contrast, stressed their "Pharaonic eyes" and long toes and fingers—inherited indicators of a capacity for leadership and civilization.[99]

Conflation of race and culture receded somewhat in scholarly circles after the excesses of the Nazis, but a lively interest in 'survivals' or cultural continuities from ancient Egypt persists. Some continuities do seem certain—persisting place names, the Coptic calendar's origin in the ancient Egyptian solar and agricultural calendar, and the early Christian rein-terpretation of the hieroglyphic ankh—a symbol of life—as a form of the cross. Folk practices at funerals, pilgrimages, and mulids (birthdays of saints) still fascinate observers as possible pharaonic survivals.[100] The truth or falsity of such continuities is of less interest, however, than the uses to which both Egyptians and Westerners have put the idea.

Whether influenced more by indigenous traditions or Western ideas, both Muslims and Copts since the late nineteenth century have emphasized special Coptic ties to ancient Egypt. Copts got an early start in modern Egyptology. In 1882, the minister of public works proposed adding ten students to the five already attending Ahmad Kamal's Egyptology school at the Egyptian Museum. Four of the ten could be chosen, he suggested,

from among the notables of the Coptic sect, which is particularly inter-ested in the hieroglyphic language because it was the language of their ancestors and they still retain a number of expressions which will facilitate their study.[101]

A little-known Copt, Marc Kabis, briefly joined the Europeans on Mariette's staff in the 1860s as assistant conservator and inspector of exca-vations.[102] Two of the "lost generation" of Egyptologists between Ahmad Kamal and the second generation of Selim Hassan and Sami Gabra were Copts. Sobhi Yusuf (Sobhi Joseph) Arif (1870–1905) became secretary to

Antiquities director Jacques de Morgan in 1892 and, in 1897, an Antiquities Service inspector. Tawfiq Bulus (Tewfik Boulos) learned English at the Americans' Asyut College, became Howard Carter's secretary, held Antiquities inspectorships, served as chief inspector at Thebes in 1923, and attended the unwrapping of Tutankhamun's mummy.[103] Arif and Bulus each contributed four items to the *ASAE*. In 1921, three of ten Egyptians who were inspectors in the Antiquities Service were Copts.[104]

The titles of Coptic-run journals often referred to ancient Egypt or to territorial patriotism compatible with it. The Taqla brothers, Greek Catholic immigrants from Syria, preempted "The Pyramids" (*al-Ahram*) for their paper in 1876. Coptic-edited journals included *Ramsis* (1893), *Firawn* (Pharaoh, 1900), *Ain Shams* (Arabic for Heliopolis, 1900), *al-Athar al-Misriya* (Egyptian Antiquities, 1909), and a second *Ramsis* (1911).[105] The names of the Coptic papers *al-Watan* (The Homeland, 1877) and *Misr* (Egypt, 1896) implied Egyptian territorial patriotism. Although its title did not reveal the fact, the Coptic-edited magazine *al-Samir al-Saghir* founded in 1897 was also pharaonist.[106]

In 1893, Yusuf Manqariyus equated the Coptic nation with ancient Egyptians, whom he credited with populating Greece, founding Athens, and spreading civilization across Europe. The Coptic nation preserved the scriptures, pioneered monasticism, produced great theologians, and was now leading modern Egypt toward progress. Two decades later, Ramzi Tadrus saw Copts as pure descendants of ancient Egypt, survivors of persecution, and especially receptive to European modernity.[107]

Coptic editor Malaka Saad pushed Coptic exceptionalism to a dangerous degree in her magazine *al-Jins al-latif* (The Gentle Sex) in 1908. "Egyptian women used to study science, speak from pulpits, and govern the empire when women in other countries were still in a state of slavery and misery." With Christianity, the woman "did not lose a thing of freedom, for the Christian religions did not decrease her due and did not prevent her learning." It was only after the Arab conquest that Muslim rulers "enforced the rule of the veil on the Egyptian woman."[108]

Although Simaika emphasized Coptic over pharaonic heritage, he insisted on their continuity:

> The Egyptians were among the first nations to adopt Christianity, which offered great similarities to their old religion. The Redeemer Christ recalled the old legend of the good and generous Osiris who had also died as a victim of evil, and who rose again to enter Eternal Life. The Holy Trinity, the judgement of the dead, are similarly familiar to ancient Egyptian religious traditions.[109]

"All enlightened Muslims," he wrote, citing Qasim Amin, now agreed that most Egyptian Muslims had descended from Copts. "All Egyptians are Copts," Simaika later put it. "Some are Muslim Copts, and others Christian Copts, but all are descendants of the ancient Egyptians."[110]

The career of Salama Musa, a leading interwar promoter of pharaonism, will be taken up in chapter 10.[111] Georgy Sobhy (Jurji Subhi, 1884–1964), whose career like Musa's stretched from Cromer's day to Nasser's, took an early interest in both Coptic issues and pharaonism. Georgy's father had directed a state gunpowder factory. Georgy's mother having died at his birth, an English doctor (Harbor) and his wife raised him for nine years. Sobhy graduated from the Cairo School of Medicine in 1904, joined its faculty, and dissected mummies there with his former professor, Australian Grafton Elliot Smith (1871–1937). While professor of anatomy at Cairo from 1900 to 1909, Smith seized the opportunity to study skeletons excavated in Nubia in the regions to be flooded by the Aswan Dam as well as the royal mummies in the Cairo Museum. Smith later became Petrie's colleague at UCL. The two were personal enemies but shared the era's common belief in races as driving forces of culture. Smith is remembered for his hyperdiffusionist thesis that Egypt was the original source of all world civilizations.[112]

In addition to his medical courses, Sobhy later taught Coptic and Demotic part time at the Egyptian University and Coptic and Egyptian at the Coptic Clerical College and the Institute of Coptic Studies. In 1925, the Ministry of Education published his Arabic grammar of Coptic. He was also active in the Coptic Archeological Society and published in its *Bulletin*.[113]

Two article titles suggest Sobhy's ideological agenda: "Notes on the Ethnology of the Copts considered from the point of view of their descendance from the Ancient Egyptians" and "Survivals of Ancient Egyptian in Modern Dialect."[114] Like Elliott Smith and Petrie, he emphasized craniometry—measuring skulls to establish racial identities. He published in Petrie's *Ancient Egypt*. After claiming to Smith that he could tell Muslims from Copts by appearance, he sought out "anthropometric and biological facts" to prove it. On one point, Sobhy disagreed with his former professor:

> There is another series of Coptic skulls in our museum with a very suspicious negroid element in them according to Professor Elliott-Smith, particularly shown in the coarse elevated eyebrows and short flat noses. I am afraid I cannot concur with him in his opinion.[115]

Sobhy did not object to Smith's racism but to his association of Copts with Negroes.

In a variation on Mariette's report that his workmen had hailed a wooden statue found at Saqqara as "shaykh al-balad"—their contemporary village chief, Oriental Secretary Ronald Storrs claimed that

The Prime Minister, Būtros Pasha Ghāli seemed a reincarnation of the Pharaonic Grand Vizier. In appearance he strikingly resembled the Fourth Dynasty wooden statue in the Cairo Museum known as the "Shaikh al-Balad", the burgomaster. He had been born in his ancestral village of Kemān in Upper Egypt (the birthplace of St. Antony).[116]

Sobhy and his "friend and collaborator" Claudius Bey Labib found hundreds of ancient Egyptian words surviving in colloquial Arabic. Unlike Ahmad Kamal, and later Abd al-Munim Abu Bakr, who emphasized the Semitic affinities of ancient Egyptian, Sobhy tied it to the Berber languages of Libya and northwest Africa.[117] He noted

the common saying among their compatriots that the Copts are of "gins pharaoni," or genus pharaonicus: this tradition alone would prove that there is some truth in the assertion that the Copts are of ancient Egyptian blood. Even the fellahin are never designated 'gins pharaoni,' nor do they accept it, for they are always proud to assert that they are Arab sons of Arabs.[118]

He affirmed that

the Copts of the present day, considered from the ethnological, philological and anthropological points of view, are not only the direct descendants of the ancient Egyptians, but are the actual representatives of the ancient civilization.[119]

Sobhy sometimes expanded his assertions on pharaonic resemblances from Copts to Egyptians in general. He was struck by the resemblance of one of his patients to Akhenaten (see fig. 47).[120]
Rejecting Asiatic as well as negroid racial affinities, he declared

The bulk of the Egyptian population presents the characteristics of the white races which have been found established from all antiquity on the Mediterranean slope of the Libyan Continent; this population is of African origin and came to Egypt from the west or south-west.[121]

For decades, Cairo University's Egyptology program attracted Copts far out of proportion to their representation in Egypt's population. Copts made

47 Sons of the Pharaohs? Medical doctor and Coptologist Georgy Sobhy juxtaposes one of his patients and a statue of Akhenaten. *GPG Sobhy, "1. The Persistence of Ancient Facial Types amongst Modern Egyptians,"* Journal of Egyptian Archaeology *16, nos. 1 & 2 (1930): plate 3.*

up over half of the first three graduating Egyptology classes (1928–30) and over 40 percent of graduates from 1928 to 1950.[122] Coptic Egyptologists Sami Gabra and Girgis Mattha successively chaired the Cairo University department from 1939 to 1965. Delving more deeply into language than his first teacher, Sobhy, Mattha became a demotic specialist.[123]

Sami Gabra's memoirs, as already seen, stress Coptic affinity with the pharaohs. Church funerals near his village reminded him of pharaonic customs. German Egyptologist Adolf Erman hailed him as a Coptic descendant of the pharaohs, and Lacau handpicked him as a Copt to dig near a Coptic village. Upon retiring from the university in 1952, Gabra's alienation from the Free Officers regime and his directorship of the Institute of Coptic Studies propelled him more deeply into Coptic affairs.

Two recent signs among many illustrate the continuing lure of pharaonism for Copts: the translation of Leeder's *Modern Sons of the Pharaohs* into Arabic after ninety years, and the title of Jill Kamil's *Christianity in the Land of the Pharaohs: The Coptic Orthodox Church.*[124]

Mirrit Boutros Ghali, Political Reform, and the Société d'archéologie copte

In April 1934, Mirrit Boutros Ghali (1908–1992), not quite twenty-five, founded what soon became the Société d'archéologie copte (see fig. 48).

Two generations younger than Simaika, he was born in the year the Coptic Museum was founded. Both men were aristocrats and proud of the heritage of the pharaohs but chose to emphasize Coptic archaeology instead. Sprung from the first family of the Coptic aristocracy, Mirrit was two when his grandfather Prime Minister Boutros Ghali was assassinated. Mirrit's father, Naguib Boutros Ghali, became a cabinet minister, and his uncle Wasif Boutros Ghali was a Wafdist foreign minister who wrote poetry in French. Mirrit's cousin Boutros Boutros-Ghali would become secretary general of the United Nations in the 1990s. Mirrit attended the Collège de la Sainte Famille in Cairo and in Paris earned a law *licence* and a diploma from the École des sciences politiques. He married a Swiss woman, became a bey, and was twice elected to parliament. He belonged to all the right clubs: Gezira Sporting, Muhammad Ali, Royal Automobile, Royal Hunting, and Royal Fencing.[125]

In keeping with the cosmopolitan milieu in which he moved, Mirrit originally named his society in French—Société des amis des églises et de l'art copte. This "friends of Coptic churches and art" designation reveals the group as a Coptic variation on the Société des amis de l'art founded in Cairo a decade earlier under the presidency of Prince Yusuf Kamal.[126] Mirrit later sat on the board of the Société des amis de l'art. Muhammad Mahmud Khalil, one of its presidents, assembled the collection of European paintings now in the national museum which bears his name. A year or two after Mirrit Boutros Ghali founded his own society, he renamed it the Société d'archéologie copte. Charles Bachatly, the Society's secretary general from 1936 until his death in 1957, helped define research as its main mission, founded its library, and organized the Exhibition of Coptic Arts which King Faruq inaugurated in 1944. Bachatly also directed the Society's excavation of the Monastery of Phoebammon near Luxor in 1947–48.[127]

The Société's over one hundred founding members included two emirs, ten pashas, a score of beys, a few judges, and several European noblemen. There were five Muslims, about thirty Europeans, and most of the rest Copts. About a score of the founding members were women. Six Copts, three Europeans, and a Muslim made up the initial board. Murqus Simaika accepted a seat on the board but probably had misgivings about a newcomer organization in the field he had long dominated.[128] His son Yusuf Murqus Simaika—a pasha, irrigation

48 Mirrit Boutros Ghali, founder of the Société d'archéologie copte. *Le mondain égyptien et du moyen orient*, ed. E.J. Blattner, 293.

engineer, and expert on the Nile—long served the Société as treasurer. Kamal Osman Ghaleb (1882–1963), also an irrigation engineer, was the first Muslim to serve on the board. Most members were amateurs, but professional scholars included Egyptologists Hermann Junker, Selim Hassan, Sami Gabra, and Étienne Drioton; Islamic art historians Creswell and Zaki Hassan; classicist Pierre Jouguet; and modern historian Shafiq Ghurbal. Gaston Wiet's absence, given his Islamic art specialty and Francophonia, is noteworthy and may have had to do with the presence of his rival Creswell.[129]

Mirrit Boutros Ghali ran the society as a personal fief for over fifty years. Its headquarters were in his family's Garden City villa until 1950, then in one of his properties in Giza. In the 1940s and 1950s, Simaika's successors as director of the Coptic Museum continued to represent that institution on the Comité de conservation des monuments de l'art arabe, and the addition of Mirrit Boutros Ghali to the Comité added a second Coptic member.[130] As with the Coptic Museum, the pope extended his blessing to the Société d'archéologie copte, but it was lay elites who gave it its impetus and financing. Eschewing religion and politics, its bylaws proclaimed its mission "purely aesthetic, archaeological, and historic."[131] For Mirrit as for Simaika forty years earlier, archaeology and modern revival went hand in hand:

> It is a good omen that the beginning of the reign of our noble king has coincided with the dawn of our national independence, after centuries of expectancy. The reign of Farouk I is the connecting link between the greatness of Ancient Egypt and the hopes we entertain for Modern Egypt.[132]

Like Simaika in his youth, Mirrit Boutros Ghali fervently campaigned for social reform. But times had changed since the 1890s. Simaika had directed his reformism to fellow Copts, as the Majlis al-Milli's lay notables challenged church control of awqaf, schools, and personal status law. Secularism, liberalism, efficiency, and honesty were at issue, not the social distribution of wealth. Coming of age after the 1919 revolution and during the Great Depression, Mirrit addressed the whole Egyptian nation and called for the redistribution of wealth. In 1938 he published *Siyasat al-Ghad* (Policy for Tomorrow), dedicating it to his Muslim friend Ibrahim Bayumi Madkur.[133] It outlined the program of what in 1944 became the National Renaissance Society (Jamaat al-nahda al-qawmiya), with Ghali, Madkur, and a dozen other members.[134] Its well-to-do young men had connections to older, anti-Wafdist politicians—Ahmad Lutfi al-Sayyid, Bahi al-Din Barakat, the Saadists, and Ali Mahir. Mirrit's wife Gertrude had joined other wives of politicians in exposing rural misery in Upper Egypt in 1944, when the ruling Wafd was trying to keep the malaria epidemic there out of the news.[135]

In 1946, fearing that socioeconomic crisis threatened the whole existing order, Mirrit Boutros Ghali and Ibrahim Madkur published their manifesto as *al-Islah al-zirai* (Agrarian Reform). "Some dozens of families were living in luxury while most were mired in poverty."[136] After the treaty with Britain in 1936, the tract declared, the Wafd had missed a prime chance for socioeconomic reform. Education, agriculture, health, industry, and housing all needed urgent attention. In 1947, Mirrit Boutros Ghali proposed a progressive income tax to assist inheritance law in breaking up landed estates over one hundred feddans.[137] In 1944, a senator had lost his seat for merely proposing a cap on *future* large land acquisitions except by inheritance,[138] but Mirrit hoped that fear of upheaval might force parliament to act.

Although the National Renaissance Society disbanded in 1949, it had helped put land reform on the national agenda. On July 22, 1952, Mirrit became minister of municipal and rural affairs in Ahmad Naguib al-Hilali's one-day cabinet, which the Free Officers' coup swept away. On September 6, Ali Mahir invited Mirrit back as minister of rural affairs, but again, General Naguib's cabinet swept the ministry away the next day. Too radical for the old regime, Mirrit's land reforms were too conservative for the new.[139] Mirrit Boutros Ghali and his class were forced out of public life. He later denounced Nasser's pan-Arabism as a futile dream.[140] He retreated into the solace of his Coptic Archeological Society. In 1963, its move into new quarters in the compound of his family's "Butrusiya" Church, next to the new St. Mark's Cathedral and papal headquarters, became an apt symbol of Mirrit's forced retreat from national into Coptic communal affairs.

After Simaika: The Coptic Museum and the Nag Hammadi Codices

The most famous development at the Coptic Museum after Simaika's death in 1944 was the acquisition and eventual publication of the Nag Hammadi manuscripts. These third- and fourth-century Coptic translations of Greek originals were mostly heterodox Christian theological tracts, usually described as Gnostic. As with the contemporaneous discovery of the Dead Sea Scrolls, political upheaval and scholarly rivalries delayed making these fascinating texts widely available for decades. Much of the Nag Hammadi story runs beyond the 1952 cutoff of this book and will not be pursued in detail here.[141]

Having nearly finished expanding and rearranging the exhibits in 1939, Simaika reported his dismay when World War II

> broke out and I received orders from the Government to pack up every-
> thing and move the cases to a safe place in the Serapeum at Sakkara. I shed
> tears of griefs [sic] and disappointment for at my age I do not know if I
> shall live long enough to bring them back again.[142]

He did not. His death in 1944 left it to his successor, Togo Mina (1906–49), to reopen the museum in 1947. Mina was born in Asyut to a pharmacist father (a popular profession among Copts) and named for Admiral Togo, who sank a Russian fleet in the Russo–Japanese War of 1904–1905. Mina's father saw Slavic Russia as a threat and rejoiced in its defeat. One of Mina's secondary school teachers at Asyut was Shafiq Ghurbal, later a noted modern historian. After an Egyptology BA from Cairo, Mina studied in Paris under Lefebvre, Drioton, and Moret, and briefly in Berlin with Kurt Sethe. His Paris doctoral thesis was not in Egyptology proper but on a Coptic topic.[143] Drioton welcomed Simaika's hire of Togo Mina as assistant curator of the Coptic Museum. In 1942 Mina published *Inscriptions coptes et greques de Nubie* (Cairo, IFAO).

King Fuad would not have missed the chance to preside over the opening of the renovated Coptic Museum, but in February 1947 King Faruq delegated the honor to minister of education Abd al-Razzaq al-Sanhuri.[144] The Coptic pope, Drioton, Tawfiq Doss, and undersecretary of education Shafiq Ghurbal joined Togo Mina at the ceremony. A bust of Simaika and a plaque in Arabic, Coptic, and English (the absence of the French usually associated with the Antiquities Service is notable) were unveiled (see figs. 4 and 49).

The façade of the museum's new wing featured a fluted radiating hood over the door and keel-arched niches, early Coptic motifs which had been echoed in the Fatimid Mosque of al-Aqmar.[145] Under Togo Mina, the Coptic Museum excavated the Monastery of St. Menas, west of Alexandria. Mina was busy trying to acquire the Nag Hammadi man-uscripts for the museum when he died in Asyut in October 1949, aged only forty-three.

Already nervous about declining Coptic influence in national poli-tics, Copts were alarmed that a Muslim—Antiquities Service architect Osman Rifky Rostem, 1895–?)—succeeded Mina as director of the Coptic Museum.[146] Since 1928, the Muslim Brothers had been campaigning for further Islamization of society and state, threatening Coptic aspirations for full equality. The Wafd's relative secularism weakened in the 1940s, and the party lost considerable legiti-macy when it returned to power in 1942 as a result of the British coup against King Faruq. Makram Ubayd's break with the Wafd several months later weakened Cop-tic influence in the party.[147] In 1950, when the Wafd won parliamentary elections for the last time, only 2.5 percent of Chamber seats went to Copts. Ibrahim Faraj, a minis-ter in al-Nahhas's Wafd cabinet (1950–52), had dropped his obviously Christian last name 'Masiha,' rather as Makram Ubayd had decided not to campaign under his first name 'William' thirty years before.[148]

Copts were relieved when Pahor Labib's (1905–94) appointment in 1951 returned the directorship of the Coptic Museum to Coptic hands.[149] Pahor's speaking Cop-tic at home at the insistence of his father, Claudius Labib, has already been noted. Pahor attended the Khedival Secondary School and the Faculty of Law, but rec-tor Lutfi al-Sayyid agreed to let him also

49 A new Rosetta Stone? Trilingual dedicatory plaque (Arabic, Coptic, English) at the Coptic Museum. The conventional Latin line at the bottom adds a fourth language. Photo: D. Reid.

attend afternoon lectures in Egyptology. With the encouragement of department chair Percy Newberry, Pahor Labib earned an Egyptology BA in 1930 and went on for a Berlin doctorate under H. Grapow. He lec-tured at the universities in Cairo and Alexandria before being appointed a curator at the Egyptian Museum in 1947. Junker at the university and Drioton at the museum encouraged him to pursue his Coptic interests. His predecessor, Togo Mina, had studied Greek in Paris and wrote his thesis on a Coptic topic; Pahor Labib, however, did not know Greek and had worked on the Hyksos and other topics in Egyptology proper. [150]

At the Coptic Museum, Pahor Labib picked up administratively on the Nag Hammadi codices, where Mina had left off. A peasant, Muhammad Ali al-Sannam, had uncovered the twelve leather-bound codices and a few leaves from a thirteenth in a pot in December 1945 while digging for fertilizer near Nag Hammadi, Upper Egypt. The family happened to be in the midst of a blood feud, and fearing a police raid, sold the codices cheaply to neighbors. A Coptic priest showed one to his brother-in-law, a history teacher. It was taken to Cairo, where George Sobhy saw it and informed Togo Mina and Drioton. In October 1946, the Coptic Museum bought it for £E250.[151]

50 Director of the Coptic Museum Togo Mina (left) and Jean Doresse examine a leaf from one of the Nag Hammadi codices. Fortunately, the fashionable cigarette appears to be unlit. *The Secret Books of the Egyptian Gnostics: An Introduction to the Gnostic Coptic Manuscripts Discovered at Chenoboskion by Jean Doresse, translated by Philip Miaret, copyright © 1958, 1959 by Librairie Plon; translation copyright © 1960, renewed © 1988 by Hollis & Carter, Ltd. Used by permission of Viking Penguin, a division of Penguin Group (USA) LLC.*

Mina showed the codice to Jean Doresse, a young IFAO scholar whose wife, Marianne, had been a classmate of Mina's in Paris (see fig. 50).

Doresse and his academic supervisor Henri-Charles Puech announced the discovery at the Académie des inscriptions et belles-lettres in Paris in February 1948, and Mina and Doresse coauthored an article on it that June. In June 1949, Doresse reported to the Académie on eight more codices, which Cypriot-born dealer Phokion Tano had bought on behalf of Marika Dattari. One included the Gospel of Thomas, previously only fragmentarily known. Deposited in the Coptic Museum for security pending purchase, the Tano-Dattari codices were later nationalized. The Jung Institute of Zurich bought one smuggled-out codex. After publication in 1975, this "Jung Codex" was returned to Egypt.

After years of scholarly squabbling over publication rights, James M. Robinson played a key role in coordinating UNESCO's facsimile edition of the Nag Hammadi codex (1972–1977). Robinson's separate English translation also appeared in 1977. The interaction in Cairo of Coptic specialists led to the First International Congress of Coptic Studies in Cairo in 1976. The Congress in turn created the International Association of Coptic Studies, which named Mirrit Boutros Ghali and Pahor Labib, along with Egyptologists Gamal Mokhtar and Labib Habachi, among its original "permanent honorary presidents."[152]

The 1952 revolution drastically altered the milieu in which the Coptic Museum, Coptic Archeological Society, Coptic Orthodox Church, and the Majlis al-Milli operated. Weak and corrupt, Pope Yusab II was so discredited that radical youths of al-Umma al-Qibtiya (the Coptic Nation), whose organization resembled that of the Muslim Brothers, attempted to kidnap him and force him to resign. In 1955 the Majlis al-Milli, Holy Synod, and the government came together to exile him to a monastery, where he died in 1956. The election of his successor, Kyrillus VI, in 1959 finally brought an inspiring pope to the throne of St. Mark. President Nasser brought Coptic schools, awqaf, and personal status law under state supervision, depriving laymen in the Majlis al-Milli of the prerogatives over which they had for so long battled the clergy. Land reform and later nationalization of big business undercut the old lay elite, and the parliament and later the Majlis al-Milli which they had dominated disappeared for some years.[153]

National politics ruled out a vigorous program of Coptic studies in the state universities, so in 1954, with the blessings of the Majlis al-Milli and the church, a group of scholars founded the (Higher) Institute of Coptic Studies. To the disappointment of the talented lay scholars who founded it, however, chronic underfunding and church affiliation cramped its development. Its first director, medieval historian Aziz Atiya, soon left to immigrate to the United States. He founded the Middle East Center at the University of Utah and from this base in the diaspora realized his dream of *The Coptic Encyclopedia* (8 vols., New York, 1991).[154] Retired Cairo University Egyptologist Sami Gabra succeeded Atiya as director of the Institute. Another of the Institute's founders, Semiticist Murad Kamil (1907–75), stayed on unhappily at Cairo University until retirement. Kamil's initial espousal of German critical theory on the Pentateuch had angered the church,[155] and the Nasser regime alienated him from the state. Mirrit Boutros Ghali's remark in the obituary of Murad Kamil was as much autobiographical as biographical:

Despite the considerable services he rendered the State, he didn't escape the humiliating vexations, as with so many worthy Egyptians, under the totalitarian and obscurantist government of President Nasser.[156]

51 The ankh—hiero-
glyphic symbol
of life—as Coptic
Christian Cross. Coptic
Catholic Archbishop-
ric, Luxor. Early Coptic
Christians adopted the
sign as a form of the
cross. *Photo: D. Reid.*

Meanwhile, Coptic spiritual and educational renewal had been building in another quarter for decades—Habib Girgis's Sunday School
Movement. As with the Muslim Brothers, it attracted young people of
modest origins who saw no future in the old parties, parliament, or monarchy. After Sadat loosened constraints on Islamist movements in the
1970s, Muslim–Coptic tensions intensified and sometimes turned vio-
lent. Popes Kyrillus VI under Nasser and Shenuda III under Sadat and
Mubarak reemerged as key spokesmen for the Coptic community, and
the voices of secular-minded laymen in the Majlis al-Milli and elsewhere
correspondingly weakened. Saints and martyrs took on new luster for
Copts in trying times, and monastic life blossomed anew.

The revival of clerical leadership did not come at the expense of
Coptic identification with the pharaohs, which now became evident in
clerical as well as lay circles. The building of the archbishopric of the

Coptic Catholic Church on the Luxor Corniche is topped by an ankh—
the hieroglyphic sign for life which had been adapted as one form of
the Christian cross in early Coptic iconography (see fig. 51). Medieval
depictions of the Holy Family's flight into Egypt had not included such
pharaonic signposts as the pyramids; modern ones usually do.

Thus Egyptians wrestled, and go on wrestling, with how Islamic and
Coptic archaeologies and their respective museums relate to the ancient
Egyptian heritage for which their country is so renowned. Chapter 8
turns to a fourth major archaeological field which has exercised a powerful claim on both Westerners and modern Egyptians—the classical legacy
of Greece and Rome.

8

Alexandria, Egypt, and the Greco–Roman Heritage

Muhammad Nagi's (Naji, 1888–1956) mural-scale *School of Alexandria*, a manifesto of the city's legendary cosmopolitanism, hangs in Alexandria's city hall (fig. 52).

Like its model, Raphael's *School of Athens*, Nagi's painting centers on Aristotle and Plato. The Pharos Lighthouse, the harbor, and an equestrian statue of Alexander the Great establish Nagi's Alexandrian setting. Archimedes hands a scroll representing the classical heritage to Ibn Rushd (Averroes), the Muslim Aristotelian who also figured in Raphael's painting. Martyred St. Catherine brings in the city's prominence in early Christianity. Modern Alexandrians include Greek poet Constantine Cavafy, Italian poet Giuseppe Ungaretti (Nagi's schoolmate at the city's Swiss school), and painter Mahmud Said. Muhammad Abduh, Ahmad Lutfi al-Sayyid, Ali Abd al-Raziq, and Taha Hussein represent Muslim liberal modernity. Taha Hussein's Mediterraneanist manifesto *Mustaqbal al-thaqafa fi Misr* (The Future of Culture in Egypt), which similarly emphasized the Greco–Roman strand of Egypt's heritage, was published in 1938, just as Nagi was about to begin work on *School of Alexandria*.[1]

Another symbol of the country's Mediterranean face is the Greco– (or Graeco–) Roman Museum (see fig. 2). It stands apart in Alexandria, Egypt's capital during its Greco–Roman millennium. From their inland locations in Cairo, the Egyptian Museum, Museum of Islamic Art, and Coptic Museum all tug in other directions. Nagi's, Taha Hussein's, and the Greco–Roman Museum's Mediterraneanism came under vigorous challenge from champions of Egypt's Arab and Islamic identity. Egyptian visions of Mediterranean cosmopolitanism, however, survived decolonization and made a striking recovery around the turn of the millennium. In 2002, Bibliotheca Alexandrina superseded the Greco–Roman Museum as the leading

52 *The School of Alexandria*, 1952, by Muhammad Nagi. With an equestrian statue of Alexander the Great in the background, Plato and Aristotle pass a scroll to Muslim philosopher Ibn Rushd (Averroes). The painting hangs in the Alexandria Municipal Hall. *Naghi et al, eds,* Mohamed Naghi (1888–1956), *unnumbered plates between pp. 44–45.*

modern institutional expression of the city's Hellenistic–Roman heritage and expressed the hopes of many Egyptians for a cosmopolitan future.

In 1798, Napoleon Bonaparte imagined himself reenacting in Egypt the oriental conquests and civilizing mission of Alexander the Great. A century later, Lord Cromer fancied himself a Roman proconsul imposing European order and justice on an oriental land long fallen from pharaonic greatness. The intensity of such European classical dreams made it more difficult for Egyptians to weave the Greco–Roman millennium into the tapestry of their long past. Islamic, Arab, Coptic, and pharaonic themes are more prominent in Egyptians' struggles to construct modern identities, yet people as varied as Mustafa Kamil, Taha Hussein, Ahmad Shawqi, King Fuad, and Muhammad Nagi refused simply to abandon Egypt's Greco–Roman heritage to Western interpretation and appropriation.

Under Muhammad Ali in the first half of the nineteenth century, Alexandria revived as a naval base and entrepôt for trade with Europe. Greeks, Italians, Frenchmen, Syro–Lebanese, Maghrebis, and immigrants from all over Egypt poured in to seek their fortunes. The city's second cosmopolitan era flourished—despite all its exploitation and exclusions—from the mid-nineteenth century to the end of the colonial age in the 1950s. This chapter examines the Greco–Roman Museum, Société archéologique d'Alexandrie, and Alexandria (Faruq I) University as sites of classical memory. Looking beyond Alexandria, it also brings in Cairo and Ain Shams universities and the Egyptian Museum, Antiquities Service, and Royal Papyrological Society as foci of classicism. Europeans initially dominated most of these institutions, but a small number of Egyptians were determined to reclaim their Greco–Roman heritage for their own purposes.

Europeans, Classics, and the Revival of Alexandria

In 1798, Napoleon exhorted his troops: "The first city we shall see was built by Alexander. At every step we shall find traces of deeds worthy of being emulated by the French."[2] The shrunken town of eight thousand which the French found disappointed them, but Napoleon clung to his classical dreams. On this campaign he carried the *Iliad*, Xenophon's *Anabasis* (with its Greeks fighting their way home through Asiatic hordes), and Plutarch's *Parallel Lives* for its exemplary biographies of Greeks and Romans.[3] With hieroglyphs still a closed book, his savants viewed Egypt through the eyes of Herodotus, Strabo, Diodorus Sicilus, and Pliny; the expedition's *Description de l'Égypte* quoted them in parallel Greek and Latin texts. Alexandria's "Pompey's Pillar" and "Cleopatra's Needle" framed the *Description*'s frontispiece—an antiquities-packed Nilescape from the Mediterranean to Aswan (see fig. 53).[4] In the top frame, Mamluks go down in Oriental confusion before Napoleon's charging chariot. In his wake, the Muses disembark from a French ship to return the arts to the land of their legendary origin. Roman eagle battle standards trail down the sides of the frame.

Four years after the defeated French evacuated in 1801, Ottoman officer Muhammad (Turkish: Mehmet) Ali seized power in Cairo. Building up for an eventual challenge to his overlord, the sultan in Istanbul, he linked Alexandria to the Nile with the Mahmudiya Canal, built a naval arsenal and fleet, exported cotton in exchange for European manufactured goods, and erected a palace by the sea at Ras al-Tin.[5] After a breathing space under Abbas I, digging the Suez Canal under Said Pasha and Khedive Ismail again cost the peasants immense suffering. The Canal project quickened the flow of Europeans, Levantines, and Egyptians into Alexandria. Its population reached 231,000 by the British conquest (1882), 403,000 by Cromer's retirement (1907), and 573,000 in 1927. In 1917, Europeans made up 16 percent of Alexandria's population. At 25,000, Greeks were the most numerous Europeans (36 percent), with Italians second at 25 percent, Britons (including Maltese) third (14 percent), and the French (including their North African subjects) fourth (12 percent).[6]

53 Classicizing frontis-
piece of the *Description
de l'Égypte,* 1809. In the
top frame, Napoleon
Bonaparte, in the guise
of Alexander or perhaps
Apollo, defeats the Mam-
luks. In the wake of the
hero, the Greek Muses
disembark to return
the arts to Egypt, the
land of their legendary
origin. In the side frames,
standards with Roman
eagles commemorate
French victories. Des-
cription de l'Égypte, *vol
1,* Antiquités: planches,
*(Paris, 1809), frontispiece
engraving by Cécile.*

The Suez Canal—Britain's lifeline to India via Gibraltar, Malta, Cyprus, and Aden—sealed Egypt's fate: it led to British occupation in 1882. France's Maghrebi and West African empire only partly assuaged its dismay at losing Egypt. Italians could dream of reviving ancient Rome's Mediterranean empire, but as a weak sixth among modern European powers, Italian imperialists captured only Libya and Eritrea—whose classical names it revived—and part of Somalia. Greek dreams of reconstituting the Byzantine or Hellenistic empires were even more fantastic and came to a rude end in 1922 with the Turkish victory over the Greeks in Anatolia.

European nationals and other minorities in Alexandria and Cairo each had their own schools, clubs, hospitals, places of worship, and cemeteries. Some kept mostly to themselves, while others thrived on cosmopolitanism, hybridity, and ambiguity. The Capitulations and Mixed Courts protected Westerners and their protégés. Nostalgia for this "second golden age" of Alexandria still flourishes among Westerners and some upper-class Egyptians. This golden glow, however, elides the colonial and class exploitation which most Alexandrians suffered throughout the era.[7]

During the nineteenth century, few tourists lingered in Alexandria. After Americans carted off "Cleopatra's Needle" in 1879, "Pompey's Pillar" was the only striking standing antiquity. David Hogarth of the British School at Athens excavated at Kom al-Dikka in 1894, reached only Roman levels, and concluded: "There is nothing to hope for at Alexandria: you classical archaeologists, who have found so much in Greece or Asia Minor, forget this city."[8] Stephen Dyson's history of classical archaeology omits Alexandria altogether.[9]

In contrast to winter antiquities tourism in Cairo and Upper Egypt, Alexandria developed as a summer resort for Europeans resident in Egypt and for Egyptians. The Alexandria–Cairo railway of 1858 accelerated this development. The San Stefano Hotel-Casino, opened in 1887 in Ramla, became a fixture of the coastal resort industry, and the Hotel Cecil, a late arrival opened in 1930, another. Montaza Palace, dating from 1892, gave the royal court a second Alexandrian palace to supplement Ras al-Tin.[10]

"Founded upon cotton with the concurrence of onions and eggs," wrote E.M. Forster, "modern Alexandria is scarcely a city of the soul."[11] The city's main mosque never rivaled Cairo's al-Azhar as a center of learning. The Institut égyptien, a European-dominated learned society established in Alexandria in 1859, decamped for Cairo in 1880. The newspaper *al-Ahram*, founded in Alexandria by Syrian Christian immigrants in 1876, also succumbed to Cairo's gravitational pull in 1898. The capital established Egypt's first state university in 1925; Alexandria had to wait until 1942 for one of its own.

Alexandria was sixty years ahead of Cairo, however, in obtaining a municipal government, which Europeans long dominated. In Renaissance Italy, princely, clerical, and bourgeois elites had enhanced their status by donning the mantle of classical Rome, and European elites elsewhere followed suit. Now Europeans brought classical fashion to Alexandria. In 1891, British consul general Sir Charles Cookson (1829–1906) and Admiral of the Port Blomfeld and Lady Blomfeld were active in founding the Atheneum, modeled on London's Atheneum Club of 1824. Cookson had a classics BA from Oriel College Oxford.[12] Invoking Alexandria's famed ancient Museum and Library, the Atheneum persuaded the new Municipality to found the Greco–Roman Museum and a Municipal Library in 1892.[13] The Egyptian Antiquities Service administered the museum, but with city funds. Two Swiss librarians in a row directed the European section of the library until 1943.[14]

Classically minded modern Greeks might have coveted the directorship of an institution with MOYΣEION (Museum) over its portal in the
city which Alexander had founded and where modern Greeks were the
largest European colony. Greeks flourished in Egypt as cotton brokers,
money lenders, grocers, and tavern keepers. Athens-born medical doctor
Tassos Neroutsos Bey (1826–92) had studied classics as well as medicine
at the University of Munich. Active in the Institut égyptien, he wrote on
Greek and Latin inscriptions, vases, topography, and statues.[15] Sir John
Antoniadis (1818–95) settled in Alexandria in 1833, made a fortune in
trade, donated to the museum, and bequeathed his palace and garden to
the city.[16] Classical accounts inspired tobacco magnate Nestor Gianaclis—
like Cardinal Lavigerie's White Fathers in Algeria—to revive viticulture.[17]
Two of Gianaclis's wines were Crue des Ptolémés and Reine Cléopatre.
Constantine Cavafy became the great Greek poet of modern Alexandria.[18] At the other end of the social spectrum, a bigoted British guidebook
declared that "of criminals in Egypt, the large majority are Greeks."[19]

It was Italians, however, who won control of the museum as a sphere
of influence. "The Greco–Roman Museum of Alexandria," boasted
Angelo Sammarco, "is an entirely Italian glory."[20] Julius Caesar, Marc
Antony, Octavian, Hadrian, and Diocletian had walked these streets.
Italians—the second largest of the modern foreign colonies—excelled
as architects, builders, craftsmen, mechanics, and confidants of the royal
family from Khedive Ismail to King Faruq. On the left, Italian socialists
and anarchists stood out in international trade unions and Alexandria's Free Popular University (1901).[21] Guiseppe Botti (1853–1903),
the founding director of the Greco–Roman Museum, had headed the
city's Italian school and helped found the Atheneum.[22] Khedive Abbas
II presided at the museum's founding in 1892 and its inauguration in
1895. Botti excavated tombs outside the Ptolemaic walls[23] and founded
the *Bulletin* of the Société archéologique d'Alexandrie. Evaristo Breccia
(1867–1967) happened to be digging in Egypt when Botti died in 1903,
and his succession as museum director confirmed the post as an Italian
sphere of influence.[24]

The museum and Société archéologique d'Alexandrie, however, were
also cosmopolitan or European transnational ventures. In 1893, Société
membership consisted of five Britons, two Italians, a Swiss, a Frenchman,
a Greek, and Baron Charles Menasce (a Jew, probably of Syrian origin,
and an Austro–Hungarian citizen).[25] This was cosmopolitanism without
Egyptians: there were no Muslims or Copts. As in the Mixed Courts,
Antiquities Service, and European high society, the Société's main
working language was French.[26] Over the course of sixty years, the Société

had Italian, French, British, Spanish, American, and Greek presidents, three of whom were judges on the Mixed Courts. Westerners often denigrated the Hellenistic age compared to 'classical' Athens of the fifth and fourth centuries BCE, but late Victorians and Edwardians credited Alexander and his Hellenistic successors with spreading Greek rationalism, benevolent administration, and economic efficiency to a stagnant Orient. This benign view of Macedonian/Greek and Roman imperialism closely resembled Britons' own imagined civilizing mission around the globe.

Alexandria's Greco–Roman Museum may be compared with two other contemporary museums which evoked the heritage of Greece and Rome—the Egyptian Museum in Cairo and the Imperial Museum in Istanbul. Alexandria's museum was provincial, a product of the seaport's powerful European communities. Cairo's Egyptian Museum and Istanbul's Imperial Museum, in contrast, were the main state antiquities museums of Egypt and the central Ottoman Empire respectively. In colonized Egypt, Europeans directed the Cairo Museum until 1941; in independent Istanbul, Osman Hamdi reclaimed direction of the Imperial Museum from Europeans in 1881 and ran it until his death in 1910. Emphasizing pharaonic antiquities, the Egyptian Museum reached deep into Egypt's territorial past. Istanbul's Imperial Museum, however, highlighted Hellenistic and Byzantine antiquities and only belatedly began to take an interest in the earlier Hittite and Mesopotamian remains of the sprawling Ottoman Empire. (Between the wars, the Turkish Republic would elevate the Hittites to cherished ancestors.) Istanbul had not forgotten that it had once been Constantinople, and nineteenth-century Europeans' relentless quest for classical antiquities spurred the Imperial Museum's counterclaims to these as part of the Ottoman heritage. The Imperial Museum was a product of Tanzimat reformers who borrowed from Europe while elaborating an alternative Ottoman modernity.[27]

All three museums had European architects. The Egyptian Museum (constructed 1897–1902) was in Beaux-Arts neoclassical style. The façades of Alexandria's Greco–Roman Museum (founded in 1892 and inaugurated in 1895, with the façade finished in 1900) and Istanbul's Imperial Museum (1891) displayed the Doric columns and pediment of a Greek temple. They deployed, however, a significantly different imperial language on their façades. In Alexandria, "ΜΟΥΣΕΙΟΝ" (Museum) in Greek over the portal evoked the legendary institution of the Ptolemies. In Cairo, classics-loving Lord Cromer and Antiquities Service director general Gaston Maspero could agree on Latin for the Egyptian Museum, even though no state school in the colonized country then taught the language. Istanbul's Imperial Museum, in contrast, proclaimed Ottoman independence with Arabic-script inscriptions over the portal—Sultan Abdulhamid II's official signature (*tughra*) and "Museum of Antiquities."

Beyond Alexandria: Cromer and Maspero, Oxyrhynchus and Papyrology

Flattered as "one in whom the Greek lucidity of intelligence is combined with the Roman faculty of constructive administration,"[28] Cromer was as proud as any Roman that he could toss off a Greek epigram. A dazzling display of Latin got Oriental Secretary Ronald Storrs off on the right foot with Cromer.[29] Storrs rose at six thirty to read Homer before breakfast. After retiring in 1907, Cromer was elected president of London's Classical Association. He gave his inaugural address on *Ancient and Modern Imperialism* and larded his *Modern Egypt* with untranslated quotations in Greek and Latin.[30]

Maspero took more interest than had his predecessor Mariette in classical antiquity. He made the Cairo Museum Egypt's main repository of Greco–Roman papyri. He helped organize the first International Congress of Classical Archaeology in Athens (1905) and brought the second one to Cairo (1909).[31] Just as his French compatriots imagined themselves reenacting Roman history in the Maghrib,[32] he was thrilled by a Latin stela at Philae recounting how Augustus's governor Cornelius had subdued Egypt. Cornelius had been born on "Gallic soil," and Maspero was

> reminded immediately of the other, more recent inscription, which is prominently displayed on the inner jamb of the great gate at Philae. Eighteen centuries after the Gaul Cornelius, other Gauls, brought to Nubia by chance and wanting to leave a souvenir of their presence, recorded in stone how in Year VI of the Republic, the 12th of Messidor, a French army, commanded by Bonaparte, disembarked at Alexandria. Twenty days later, the army, having put the Mamluks to flight at the Pyramids, Desaix, commandant of the first division, pursued them beyond the cataracts, where he arrived the 18th of Nivôse of the Year VII.
>
> . . . One must see, in the *Voyage* of Denon or in the volumes of the *Description*, how greatly they were nourished by reminders of classical antiquity, and what a thrill they felt to fly their banners over the rocks where the Legions had carried out in a few weeks, an enterprise which had seemed almost impossible.[33]

IFAO, which Maspero founded in 1880, often hosted classicists. In 1905 Maspero hired two Hellenists for the Antiquities Service: C.C. Edgar

(1870–1938), who published half a dozen volumes on Greek antiquities in the *Catalogue* of the Egyptian Museum, and Gustave Lefebvre (1879–1957), who was also an Egyptologist and published a standard grammar of Egyptian. Maspero's son Jean became a Byzantinist; he catalogued Greek papyri in the Cairo Museum before dying at age thirty on the western front.[34]

Papyrology came of age after Maspero's arrival in 1880. Egypt's dry climate preserved papyri which would have perished elsewhere. The Greek papyri from Crocodilopolis (Kiman Faris) in Fayoum which turned up in the market in the 1880s ended up in Vienna. Flinders Petrie found a roll of Homer at Hawara in 1888 and Ptolemaic mummy cases made of Greek waste papyri at Gurob in 1889. Wallis Budge found a copy of Aristotle's lost *Constitution of Athens* on the antiquities market and bought it for the British Museum.[35]

The champion papyrus hunters were Bernard Grenfell (1869–1926) and Arthur Hunt (1871–1934), classics graduates of Queens College Oxford, who began digging at Oxyrhynchus—the city of "the sharp-nosed fish"—(Bahnasa) in 1896 and kept at it for a decade. The EEF set up its Graeco–Roman Branch to support their work. E.G. Turner later defended their tight focus on papyrus hunting: they were digging trash heaps with few foundation blocks or walls in situ, salvaging papyri from rapid destruction at the hands of *sebakh* (fertilizer) diggers. In 1922, Petrie reported that up to 150 tons of *sebakh* were being hauled off daily by rail from Oxyrhynchus. In 1914, the Graeco–Roman Branch stopped digging for papyri to focus on publication. At Oxford, Edgar Lobell worked on Oxyrhynchus papyri for over sixty years.[36] In 1908, Girolamo Vitelli founded the Italian Society for the Research of Greek and Latin Papyri in Egypt, which became the Papyrological Institute at the University of Florence.[37] Evaristo Breccia dug for papyri at Oxyrhynchus and Antinoe for Alexandria's Greco–Roman Museum from 1927 and, after 1931, for the University of Pisa.

Egyptians and the Greco–Roman Legacy to 1914

Arabic translations from Greek (often via Syriac) underlay Islamic philosophy, science, medicine, and mathematics, and Aristotelian logic was fundamental to Islamic theology. Muslims burst onto the world with their own religion, folklore, and pre-Islamic poetry, however, and did not inherit Greek and Latin drama, poetry, mythology, or the histories of Herodotus and Thucydides.[38] The *Iliad* was not translated into Arabic in 804 in the Baghdad of Harun al-Rashid but in 1904 in the Cairo of Cromer.[39] Al-Tabari's (d. 923) history of the Ptolemies and Caesars was little more than a king list. Greek and Latin literature were not "the classics" to Muslims, and Napoleon saved his masquerading as Alexander and Caesar for European audiences. Similarly, Europeans were deaf to Amr ibn al-As as a great conqueror and Abu Nuwas as a timeless poet. Pious Muslims looked back with nostalgia to the Prophet and the Rashidun Caliphs, and worldly ones to Harun al-Rashid's Baghdad, Umayyad Cordoba, or Ayyubid Cairo.

Studying in Paris in the 1820s, however, al-Azhar-educated Rifaa al-Tahtawi encountered Greece and Rome at every turn. The translation bureau he later directed in Cairo translated several French works on classical topics to Arabic.[40] Al-Tahtawi's history of pre-Islamic Egypt, *Anwar al-tawfiq al-jalil* (1868) is remembered for its pioneering coverage of pharaonic history in Arabic, but it devoted twice as many pages to Egypt's Greco–Roman millennium. He praised ancient and modern Greeks alike as benefactors of Egypt. Muhammad Ali's birthplace in Kavala was only a hundred miles from Alexander's Pella; al-Tahtawi praised both as foreign conquerors who nevertheless ruled Egypt tolerantly and well.[41]

Mahmud al-Falaki (1815–85) even won the respect of European classicists. Like his pupil Ali Mubarak, al-Falaki was a French-educated engineer of indigenous descent who reached the cabinet at a time when most ministers were still Turco-Circassians. His work in meteorology, terrestrial magnetism, chronology, and cartography touched on pharaonic, Greco–Roman, and Islamic archaeology. The map from al-Falaki's 1865–66 excavations became a baseline for the ancient topography of Alexandria.[42]

Lebanese writers in Beirut and Cairo also wrote in Arabic on the classics. Boutros al-Bustani, his sons, and their kinsman Sulayman al-Bustani compiled an encyclopedia which included significant coverage of Greek and Roman topics.[43] Jurji Zaydan, who founded the magazine *al-Hilal* in Cairo after emigrating from Beirut, published the last two volumes of the Bustanis' encyclopedia as well as a History of the Greeks and Romans in Arabic.[44] Sulayman al-Bustani's Arabic translation of the *Iliad*, printed on Zaydan's *al-Hilal*'s press, was feted at Shepheard's Hotel by Syrian Christian journalists (Zaydan, Faris Nimr, Yaqub Sarruf, and Jibrail Taqla), poets (Ahmad Shawqi, Hafiz Ibrahim, and Khalil Mutran), future prime ministers (Saad Zaghlul and Abd al-Khaliq Tharwat), and Muhammad Abduh's disciple Rashid Rida.

The lawyer leaders of the Watani Party tried to turn the West's classics against the British. Mustafa Kamil compared Islamic slavery favorably with Roman slavery. His successor Muhammad Farid's History of the Romans (1912) in Arabic exhorted Egyptians to emulate Roman patriotic unity against foreign aggressors. Covering only through the Punic Wars, Farid omitted the late republic and empire (when Egypt fell to Roman imperialism) which Cromer found so congenial.[45] Ahmad Lutfi al-Sayyid, of the Umma Party, praised the Greeks for clinging to Hellenic pride throughout centuries of "Turkish" rule until regaining independence—an unusual view for a Muslim in still nominally Ottoman Egypt.[46]

Despite such forays into classics, few Egyptians besides Khedive Abbas could read the Latin inscribed in his name over the Egyptian Museum's portal (see fig. 5). As a student at Vienna's Theresianum, Abbas had had not only to read but also to speak Latin. No Egyptian state school yet taught the language. When Maspero brought the International Congress of Classical Archaeology to Cairo in 1909, only one Egyptian read a paper.[47] Until Taha Hussein in the 1920s, classical studies lacked an Egyptian champion comparable to Ahmad Kamal in Egyptology, Ali Bahgat in Islamic archaeology, and Murqus Simaika in Coptic archaeology.

Imperial Tremors: Shifting Registers of European Classical Discourse

In 1922, High Commissioner Allenby's Oriental Secretary Robin Furness quoted Aeschylus, in Gilbert Murray's translation, to clinch an argument for Egyptian independence. Furness later recalled:

> It was that sort of dispatch. When reading the draft, the High Commissioner grunted in recognition of the Aeschylus, and said: "I think we might have this in the original Greek," which he proceeded to inscribe.[48]

Unlike in Cromer's day, however, classics were now being deployed to cover a tactical imperial retreat.

Classics continued to crop up in odd corners of officialdom. Mining engineer and geologist John Ball (1872–1941) of Egypt's Geological Survey wrote *Egypt in the Classical Geographers* (1942).[49] Oriental Secretary Robin Furness "abused his official position in the name of culture by having his translations of these [selections from the Greek Anthology] printed, in parallel Greek and English, by the Alexandria police press."[50] When L.A. Tregenza came to Qena in 1927 to teach secondary school:

> My knowledge of Egypt was still of the distant past. I had been reading Herodotus and had a vague mental picture, pervaded by the dreamlike atmosphere of his stories, of a great river movement hidden somewhere in this famous valley, with temple ruins on either side.
>
> I spent a lot of time, year after year, in uninterrupted study under this [mosquito] net, confining myself chiefly to Greek and Latin authors. I was in the right atmosphere for this kind of reading for the world I was living in was not so very different in many ways from that of Homer or Virgil.[51]

British officers had marched off to war in 1914 reciting the *Iliad*. As the Great War dragged on, Thucydides's tragic view of beleaguered Athens during the Peloponnesian War came to seem more "philosophically contemporary," as Arnold Toynbee put it.[52] On the eve of World War II, Ronald Syme's *Roman Revolution* presented the empire of Augustus—much admired in Britian several decades earlier—as sadly tarnished. Syme had seen too much of Mussolini's Roman imperial posturing.[53]

In Cairo during World War I, Oriental Secretary Ronald Storrs encountered another imperial classicist very different from his old superior Lord Cromer—T.E. Lawrence.

"I would come upon him in my flat," wrote Storrs,

> reading always Latin or Greek, with corresponding gaps in my shelves. . . . We had no literary differences, except that he preferred Homer to Dante and disliked my preference for Theocritus before Aristophanes.[54]

Lawrence's imperial vision was as tortured as Cromer's had been assured. Before burying himself as a private in the Royal Air Force, Lawrence attempted the impossible task of squaring British imperialism in the postwar mandates with Arab self-rule. As classically minded in obscurity as he had been while in the limelight, Lawrence translated the *Odyssey*.

Classical visions at odds with Cromer's also flowered in the cafes of Alexandria, where Palestinian George Antonius, author of *The Arab Awakening*, is said to have introduced Greek poet Constantine Cavafy to E.M. Forster. Cavafy looked not to the golden Athens of Pericles but to the Hellenistic and Byzantine eras [55] and to themes often dismissed as decadent or perverse—homoerotic love and loss. Forster's *Alexandria: A Guide* drips with disillusionment. Of the Greco–Roman Museum, he writes:

> The collection was not formed until 1891, by which time most of the antiquities in the neighbourhood had passed into private hands. It is consequently not of the first order and little in it has outstanding beauty. Used rightly it is of great value, but the visitor who "goes through" it will find afterwards that it has gone through him, and that he is left with nothing but a vague memory of fatigue. The absence of colour, the numerous small exhibits in terra cotta and limestone, will tend to depress him, and to give a false impression of a civilization which, whatever its defects, was not dull. He should not visit the collection until he has learned or imagined something about the ancient city, and he should visit certain definite objects, and then come away—a golden rule indeed in all museums. He may then find that a scrap of the past has come alive.[56]

Not long after, *A Passage to India* laid bare Forster's disenchantment with British imperialism, a conviction remarkably suppressed in his classic Alexandrian guide. Lawrence Durrell's much later *Alexandria Quartet* (1957–60), in which Muslims barely figure as a backdrop and Coptic aristocrat Nessim improbably conspires with Zionists, was also a far cry from Cromer. This canonical literary trio of Alexandria—Cavafy, Forster, and Durrell—have recently been creatively reread by Hala Halim.[57]

Back home in Britain, classical languages were in retreat. Cambridge dropped its Greek matriculation requirement in 1919, Oxford in 1920.[58] Harvard had already done so in 1886. Even Gilbert Murray, Regius Professor of Greek at Oxford, refused to defend the Greek requirement.[59] Latin quotations faded out in the House of Commons in the 1930s. In 1960, Oxford and Cambridge finally abolished their Latin matriculation requirement. No longer *the* gateway to the humanities or a passport to gentility, Greek and Latin retreated to the specialist's study, and most students took their classics watered down—in translation—if at all.

Planting Classical Studies in the Egyptian University

Even as classical languages were fading in Europe, Taha Hussein insisted that Egyptians emphasize them. At al-Azhar, he had heard of Aristotle only in logic and theology and was thus thrilled to discover Ahmad Lutfi al-Sayyid's Aristotle: "One heard strange new words—democracy, aristocracy, oligarchy."[60] Becoming rector of the new state-run Egyptian University in 1925—in the wake of qualified independence and the 1923 constitution—Lutfi al-Sayyid argued that Aristotle could set Egypt's awakening on the same rational foundations which had underpinned Europe's Renaissance. He translated *Nicomachaean Ethics* to Arabic in 1924 and followed up with Aristotle's *Physics*, *Politics*, and other works. Taha Hussein's only complaint was that his mentor translated from French instead of the Greek originals.[61]

Taha Hussein's fundamentalism on classical languages grew out of his own personal ordeal with them. He had graduated from al-Azhar and earned the Egyptian University's first doctorate. Going on to study in France, however, he was dismayed to discover that Latin was required for matriculation for the *licence*. His French peers had already had six years of lycée Latin. Grimly, he set to work with a tutor and eventually learned enough Latin to write his secondary doctoral thesis at the Sorbonne on Tacitus. He also studied Greek.[62]

Few remember that Taha Hussein began teaching not Arabic literature but "History of the Ancient East" at the private Egyptian University in 1919. His syllabi for 1922–25 emphasized Greek and

Roman history—Greece from the Peloponnesian War to Alexander; Alexander, the Hellenistic era, the early Roman Republic and its Greek conquests; "Egypt in the Macedonian Age"; and "Roots of the Roman Republic, Rome, and Greece."[63] Three of his Arabic books grew out of these courses: Selected Pages from Greek Dramatic Poetry, Leaders of Thought, and The Political System of the Athenians.

Taha Hussein's The Future of Culture in Egypt, published in Arabic in 1938, emphasized Egypt's Mediterranean ties to European Greece and Rome. He continued the campaign in al-Katib al-Misri, the review he founded in 1945. He declared Latin and Greek as fundamental to the humanities as mathematics and laboratories are to science.[64] Sayyid Qutb, though not yet the Islamist radical which Nasser's prisons would make him in the 1950s, attacked Taha Hussein's Mediterraneanism and reaffirmed Islam as the core of Egypt's identity.[65] Historians Muhammad Rifat and Husayn Munis later also emphasized Egypt's Mediterranean aspects, although in a less liberal framework than Taha Hussein's.[66]

The private Egyptian University had offered neither Latin nor Greek, and the British-dominated University Commission of 1917 in Egypt prescribed only modern languages. Presumably Greek and Latin were judged appropriate only for imperial masters, not the docile 'native' clerks the British envisioned. The 1919 revolution derailed the Commission, and not until 1925 did King Fuad finally open the state-run Egyptian University. A British adviser lamented that Fuad—who was fluent in Italian and French—was "genuinely unaware of the very existence of a British cultural civilisation."[67] Catching Britain between high commissioners in the summer of 1925, Fuad, Prime Minister Ziwar, and minister of education Ali Mahir seized the moment to hire Belgians and Swiss as Francophone stand-ins for French professors. Among them were Belgian classicists Henri Grégoire (1881–1964), the dean of arts, and Paul Graindor (1877–1938), professor of Greek and Roman history. The two had just cofounded the journal Byzantion.[68]

Upon reaching Cairo in October 1925, High Commissioner George Lloyd was furious to find only one British dean out of four. The Faculty of Arts had five French, four Belgian, and two French-educated Egyptian professors—and only two Britons. The French, Belgians, and Italians lectured in French and were all just "Latins" to Lloyd. Lloyd's memoirs—Egypt since Cromer—left no doubt about his hero. As with Cromer, Indian service had brought out Lloyd's authoritarianism.[69] At Cairo, newly arrived professor of English Robert Graves—novelist, poet, classicist—was embarrassed to be told that he "must keep the [British] flag flying in the faculty of letters." Lloyd, remarked Graves, "believed in his job more than I did in mine. He used to drive through Cairo in a powerful car, with a Union Jack flying from it, at about sixty miles an hour."[70]

Ali Mahir had also recruited forty-one French, seven Belgian, and two Swiss classicists in a remarkable project to introduce Greek and Latin into the secondary schools. Lloyd protested—not the subject matter but the fifty Francophone "Latins"—and the project soon foundered.[71] Taha Hussein blamed Mahir only for a tactical error—not recruiting British schoolmasters instead.[72] Students already overburdened with English and French were no doubt relieved, but the failure did mean that Egypt's few future classicists might enter university innocent of Latin and Greek. How could they compete with someone like Orientalist A.J. Arberry, who briefly taught classics at Cairo? He casually remarked: "Before going up to Pembroke College, Cambridge in 1924 I had read everything worth reading in Greek and Latin."[73]

An Egyptian medal commemorating King Fuad's state visit to Italy in 1927 captured his official classicism at full flood (see fig. 54). The king's profile portrait is on the obverse. On the reverse, the Sphinx and Pyramids are balanced by the Coliseum, while in the foreground two nude women empty jugs to mingle the waters of the Nile and the Tiber. A more jarring image for the conservative subjects of the Egyptian king who had lately been campaigning to become caliph could scarcely be imagined. This was no coin for common circulation, however, but a luxury commemorative medal struck for a radically different section of King Fuad's constituency.

54 Mingling the Nile and the Tiber: Classicizing medal commemorating King Fuad's visit to Italy in 1927. *Norman D. Nicol, Raafat el-Nabarawy, Jere L. Bacharach,* Catalog of the Islamic Coins, Glass Weights, Dies and Medals in the Egyptian National Library, Cairo, *American Research Center in Egypt / Catalogs (Malibu, CA: Undena Publications, 1982),* 6234. Collection of the Egyptian National Library. Courtesy of the Egyptian National Library.

With George Lloyd's arrival in 1925, the British proconsulship in Egypt passed from graduates of military academies (Cromer and Kitchener—Woolwich; McMahon and Allenby—Sandhurst) to Etonians. Cromer and Allenby had struggled mightily to acquire the Greek and Latin that military schooling had denied them. Of the Etonians, Lloyd dropped out of Cambridge, Percy Lorraine out of Oxford, and Miles Lampson skipped university altogether to enter the Foreign Office directly.[74] Lampson made no pretense of classical scholarship, but he chose the Greco–Roman ruins of Karanis in Fayoum as a favorite weekend retreat.

To Taha Hussein's dismay, a French professor—himself a good Latinist—joined French-educated Egyptians in voting down a Latin requirement in the Faculty of Law: Egyptian professors of Roman law, civil law, and legal history who could not read a simple Latin text would be the laughing stock of Europe.[75] With Grégoire and later Taha Hussein as dean, the Faculty of Arts required a classical language of all its students, and history and philosophy majors had to take four years of either Latin or Greek.

Egypt's first classics graduate, Muhammad Salim Salem, recalled Grégoire's first Greek class:

> For two hours we took notes while the famous Grégoire lectured on the letter alpha in all known dialects. We didn't know a word of Greek, and we left determined never to return. I still have the notes and I still don't understand the lecture.[76]

A Belgian assistant of Grégoire's stepped in to save the day, teaching beginning Greek from scratch. Of the class of 1929, only Salem made it through to emerge with a classics BA.

Dean Grégoire's reported observation that the university was "of a very low standard, about on the level of an English University" elicited from Lloyd: "This illuminating remark alone leaves us no room for doubt that M. Grégoire must go."[77] In 1928 Gustave Michaud, professor of French literature but also a classicist who had written his Sorbonne thesis in Latin and published a three-volume history of Roman comedy, succeeded Grégoire as dean of arts.[78] In 1929, Lloyd finally turned the tide on the "Latins." A faculty vote to hire a senior Italian classicist was overruled in favor of William Waddell (1884–1945), a Scot with MAs from Glasgow and London.[79] Prime Minister Muhammad Mahmud was an Oxford graduate, and King Fuad was pressured into conceding chairs in classics, medieval history, ancient oriental history, and geography to Britons.[80] Lloyd had no time to savor his victory, however. Britain's incoming Labour cabinet replaced him as high commissioner with the less stridently imperialist Percy Lorraine.

Taha Hussein's fellow Liberal Constitutionalists Lutfi al-Sayyid and jurist Abd al-Aziz Fahmi, who translated part of Justinian's code into Arabic, took to heart Aristotle's warning against mob rule.[81] Sometimes they even preferred royal despotism to Wafdist populism. Hussein's humbler roots perhaps encouraged his switch to the Wafd in the early 1930s and his criticism of Lutfi al-Sayyid and Fahmi for elitism.

In 1930, Taha Hussein became the first Egyptian dean of arts.[82] When Ismail Sidqi's palace government dismissed him in 1932, Rector Lutfi al-Sayyid resigned in protest. Sidqi vengefully downgraded Latin and Greek from major to auxiliary subjects, and Waddell went home to teach in Britain. A.J. Arberry filled in as classics instructor (1932–34) while waiting for an Arabic or Persian appointment back home.[83] Cairo graduated one classics BA in 1932 and two in 1933, then no more until 1938.[84]

After popular demonstrations contributed to the fall of palace government in 1934, Taha Hussein regained his chair and Lutfi al-Sayyid returned as rector. The Wafd's triumph in 1936 restored Hussein to the deanship. Classics was reinstated as a major subject, and Waddell agreed to return to his Cairo chair. He published classical works on Egypt—Herodotus Book II, Manetho's pharaonic king list, and Diodorus Sicilus.[85] After Waddell retired in 1944, E.M. Forster declined to stand as a possible successor.[86] Douglas Drew took the post and ran the department with a mainly British staff until 1951.[87] In other departments, A.H.M. Jones (1904–70) taught ancient history (1929–34) before rising to fame back in Britain.[88] Sami Gabra and Girgis Mattha, who between them directed the Institute of Archeology from 1939 to 1965, were also Greco–Roman era specialists, Gabra as an archaeologist at Tuna al-Gebel and Mattha as a demoticist.

Private schooling gave Taha Hussein's daughter Amina and son Munis Claude (Moënis Taha-Hussein) strong starts in languages, and both majored in classics.[89] Hussein dedicated a memoir of Paris student days to Munis:

And now you too, my son, young as you are, will be leaving your home, your birthplace, your country, and parting with your family and friends to journey across the sea and live a student's life alone in Paris.

Let me present you with this story. From time to time, when you are worn out with study and tired of Latin and Greek, it may perhaps bring you some comfort and relaxation.[90]

Munis earned an agrégation in Paris in 1949 and came home to teach in Cairo University's French department until leaving for a UNESCO post.[91]

Outside the university, Ahmad Shawqi (1868–1932) and Ahmad Zaki Abu Shadi (1892–1955) explored classical themes. Shawqi's play *Masra Kilyubatra* (The Death of Cleopatra, 1929) presented her not as the Oriental seductress of Roman slander but as an Egyptian patriot who died rather than surrender to Roman imperialism.[92] In 1922, Abu Shadi returned from England with a medical degree and an English wife. Although he later chaired the bacteriology department at Faruq I University, he won fame as a poet. His review *Apollo* (1932–34) introduced Apollo as god of the sun, poetry, music, and prophecy. A statue of Apollo, nude but for a fig leaf, adorned the cover. Shawqi's "Apollo! Welcome, Oh Apollo" and a poem by Khalil Mutran led off the first issue.[93] Abbas Mahmud al-Aqqad grumbled that Abu Shadi should have chosen the Chaldean–Arab god of poetry Utarid instead. Ancient historian Abd al-Latif Ahmad Ali deplored al-Aqqad's aversion for classics, comparing him unfavorably with Tawfiq al-Hakim.[94] Novelist Edwar al-Kharrat was thrilled to discover Shelley's "Ozymandias" in a school anthology, liked *Apollo*, and worked briefly at the Greco–Roman Museum.[95]

Return to Alexandria: Museum, Société archéologique, and Princely Patronage[96]

Evaristo Breccia's absence in Italy for a time during World War I slowed activity at the Greco–Roman Museum.[97] In 1925, the Société archéologique d'Alexandrie became the Société royale d'archéologie d'Alexandrie, reflecting King Fuad's active patronage.[98] Europeans flattered Fuad as a Maecenas (Roman literary patron in the age of Augustus). Italian–Egyptian diplomacy and classical history converged in 1928, when Breccia escorted the king to the oasis of Siwa, where the oracle of Zeus Ammon had hailed Alexander as a god. Breccia effused:

> In spite of immense differences and of the lapse of twenty-three centuries that lie between the two kings who have travelled 600 kilometers across the desert to visit this small group of their subjects, yet a comparison can be made between the two expeditions. Alexander the Great came to the Oasis in search of an incalculable service to himself and to gain an immense personal advantage; King Fuad has come hither moved by the most disinterested affection for this neglected part of his realm and with the sole purpose of promoting its economic development and its moral elevation.[99]

Italian officers saluted Fuad at the Libyan border, and an Italian destroyer met him at the coast. Fuad invited Italian officers aboard his yacht the *Mahrusa* and sent greetings to Victor Emmanuel III and Mussolini.

Fuad's great-grandfather Muhammad Ali had also evoked Alexander: "I too am a Macedonian!"[100] Like the Ptolemies and Muhammad Ali, Fuad carefully courted both European and Egyptian clienteles. The Ptolemies lived as Greeks in Alexandria and inland showed themselves as pharaohs offering to Egyptian gods. One day Fuad would play the urbane European, attending the Cairo Opera and chatting in Italian and French; the next he might present himself at al-Azhar as a pious Muslim worthy even of the caliphate.

In 1930, the year Egyptologist Jean Capart convened the Brussels meeting later counted as the First International Congress of Papyrologists,[101] IFAO director Pierre Jouguet (1869–1949) persuaded King Fuad to establish the Société royale égyptienne de papyrologie. After founding an Institute of Papyrology at the University of Lille, Jouguet had moved to the Sorbonne. In 1929, he came to Cairo as director of IFAO after George Foucart had lost the favor of King Fuad. Most of the fourteen members Jouguet proposed for the Egyptian papyrological society were French. Waddell was the lone Briton, and there were three Egyptians (Sami Gabra, George Sobhi, and Mahmud Hamza).[102] Only Europeans published in the Society's monograph series until 1945 and in its journal until 1948, when Sami Gabra and Zaki Ali respectively broke the ice.[103] During the lean 1930s, the Société's secretary intoned:

> The Auguste Founder of our Society, whose solicitude has never ceased to be extended to us, remains our eternal refuge, The One through whom the impossible suddenly becomes realizable.[104]

Omar Toussoun (1872–1944), "Prince of Alexandria" and grandson of Said Pasha,[105] was honorary president of the Société archéologique d'Alexandrie for decades. Although Swiss educated, Toussoun was so conservative that "he had never forgiven King Fuad for disobeying the Koranic injunction against copying natural forms, by allowing his image to appear on Egyptian currency."[106] Keen on desert exploration and historical geography, Toussoun published a dozen scholarly volumes through the Société archéologique.[107] He also presided over the Royal Agricultural Society. He owned much of the Abuqir peninsula, east of Alexandria. In 1933, a diver he hired discovered the lost towns of Menouthis and Herakleion. Toussoun presented most of the finds to the Greco–Roman Museum.[108] Underwater exploration at Abuqir and Alexandria did not resume until the 1960s, and dramatic discoveries followed. Prince Toussoun aside, Egyptian participation in the Société was long minimal. Of 212 articles in its *Bulletin* from 1898 to 1934, only two (by Toussoun) were by an Egyptian.[109] Mahmud Bey Said—son of former prime minister Muhammad Said—served on the Société's board from the 1930s into the 1950s. An advocate before the Mixed Courts, he won fame as a painter, and his house in Alexandria is now a museum.

In 1931, Breccia left the Greco–Roman Museum for the University of Pisa, where he later became rector.[110] He dismissed Gilbert Bagnani as a possible successor at Alexandria: "a snob who affected to speak English, married to a Canadian, presumptuous and antifascist."[111] Young Achille Adriani (1905–1982), a graduate of the University of Rome who had dug in Athens and inspected antiquities in Naples, won the post.[112] Breccia and Botti had debated Hellenistic versus Roman influences in Ptolemaic art; Adriani emphasized interaction between Greek and pharaonic styles instead.[113]

Greeks, Italians, and the Gathering Storm

After fighting on the victorious Allied side in World War I, both Italy and Greece emerged from the peace settlement disappointed. Mustafa Kemal (Atatürk) thwarted Greece's expansionist designs on Anatolia, shattering the Megale Idhea (Great Idea) of reviving the Byzantine Empire. Italy's retention of Rhodes and the Dodecanese also angered the Greeks, a tension which spilled over to their respective communities in Egypt.[114]

Over Egypt's Libyan border, the collapse of Sanussi resistance in 1931 cleared the way for intensive Italian settlement on the Libyan portion of the "fourth shore" of Mussolini's "Italian lake." The Roman cities of Leptis Magna (the birthplace of Emperor Septimius Severus) and Sabratha were excavated and restored. Mussolini's Libyan coastal road from the Tunisian to the Egyptian border recalled the triumphs of Roman road engineering. Putting the roads to good use, the Libyan Tourism and Hotel Association (1935) promoted guidebooks, tours, and exhibits and managed a network of eighteen hotels.[115] Back in Italy too, "the new Augustus" exploited archaeology to the hilt. He excavated and displayed the Ara Pacis—an ancient monument to Augustan peace—celebrated the bimillenary of Augustus in 1938, and had Rome's seaport at Ostia excavated for a major exposition planned for 1942.[116]

Mussolini's conquest of Ethiopia in 1935–36 prodded Britain and the Wafd into the Anglo–Egyptian Treaty which had long eluded them. Omar Toussoun denounced Italy's invasions of Libya in 1911 and Ethiopia in 1935, but King Faruq, Ali Mahir, General Aziz al-Misri, and a young Anwar al-Sadat hoped that Italy might liberate them from Britain. In

December 1938, the Italians of Alexandria unveiled a marble monument with a statue of Khedive Ismail on the Corniche. Ismail's grandson King Faruq, Prime Minister Muhammad Mahmud, and Ali Mahir attended the inaugural ceremonies, which featured the Fascist anthem and salute and marching black-shirted Italian youth.[117]

Pursuing Romanità (Roman-ness), the Italian Foreign Ministry funded Carlo Anti's University of Padua excavation of the Greco–Roman town of Tebtunis in Fayoum. Tebtunis trailed only Oxyrhynchus in its yield of Roman-era papyri. The site lacked showy monumental remains, however, and Fascist funding for its excavation dried up. Anti's field director Gilbert Bagnani, who had an English or Canadian wife and mother-in-law, immigrated to Canada in 1936.[118] Breccia, formerly of the Greco–Roman Museum, dug at al-Hibeh and then Antinoe until 1937. His successor at the Alexandria museum, Achille Adriani, and Breccia's student Sergio Donadoni dug at Antinoe in 1939. Donadoni continued into May 1940, the month before Italy's plunge into the war put an end to Italian papyrological digging in Egypt until 1964.[119]

Nazi Germany exploited archaeological symbolism as well. The Dorian invaders of ancient Greece were lionized as Aryans, for example, and Hitler resumed German excavations at Olympia, Greece, in preparation for the 1936 Berlin Olympic Games.[120]

Classics in the Storm: Alexandria and World War II

When Italy joined Germany in invading France in June, 1940, Sir Miles Lampson ordered Faruq to dismiss his Italian advisers and the Ali Mahir cabinet. The king had a clever, if futile, retort:

> Referring to the Italian origins of Lady Lampson and the fact that her father was now serving Mussolini as chief physician to Il Duce's armies, Farouk said, "I'll get rid of my Italians if he gets rid of his."[121]

Sir Aldo Castellani had earlier stopped in Cairo to visit his daughter on his way to Italy's war in Ethiopia; Lampson had done his best to keep his embarrassing father-in-law out of sight.[122]

Stiff resistance to Mussolini's invasion of Greece in 1940 brought Germany in to aid the Italians, and in May 1941, British troops had to flee Greece for Egypt and Cyprus. Italy's failed invasion of Egypt from Libya in 1940 also drew the Germans in to aid the Italians. Bracing for a second Axis drive on Egypt, Lampson forced Faruq in February 1942 to install a pro-Allied Wafdist cabinet under al-Nahhas. After the fall of France, Pierre Jouguet resigned as director of IFAO and headed a

Free French committee in Cairo. His *Révolution dans la défaite: études athé-niennes* looked for hope in the failure of attempts by reactionary ancient Athenians to abolish democracy while under Spartan occupation.[123]

The British interned Greco–Roman Museum director Achille Adriani in Alexandria's Italian School until 1944.[124] British-born Alan Rowe (1890–68) replaced Adriani as curator. Rowe had immigrated to Australia as a young man and excavated in Palestine and Egypt. Alongside his intelligence work during the war, he dug in Alexandria at Kom al-Shuqafa and the Serapeum.[125] The wartime influx swelled the ranks of the Société royale d'archéologie d'Alexandrie (about 130 in 1930) to 256 in May 1940.[126]

One of the new arrivals was Lawrence Durrell, who escaped Greece by sailboat as the Germans poured in. Durrell had little love for the city which inspired his *Alexandria Quartet*. The fiction of Alexandrians Ibrahim Abdel Maguid and Edwar al-Kharrat gives a far better sense of what the war was like for most residents of the city. Both emphasize Egyptian community across Muslim–Coptic lines.[127]

Harry Tzales, future founder of the Hellenic Institute for Ancient and Medieval Alexandrian Studies, recalled hiding in Alexandrian air raid shelters while his Greek and Italian grandmothers rooted for opposite sides.[128] In June 1942, Rommel reached al-Alamein, seventy miles away. Mussolini arrived in Libya, hoping to enter Alexandria on a white charger.[129] Axis supply lines across the desert were overextended, however, and in October, General Montgomery began driving the Germans and Italians back across North Africa. In December 1943, the Société royale d'archéologie felt secure enough about the military situation to stage a dramatic celebration of their fiftieth anniversary in the catacombs of Kom al-Shuqafa. Alan Rowe and American Jasper Brinton, the Société's president from 1935 to 1949 and a judge on the Mixed Courts,[130] addressed the gathering. The Société also organized an exhibit of Ptolemaic, Hellenistic, and Roman Art at the city's Atelier.[131]

Remarkably, Faruq I University opened in Alexandria in October 1942, the same month the British began their al-Alamein offensive. (See table G for the confusing name changes of Egypt's universities.) The new university awarded its namesake an honorary doctorate, and a medal was issued juxtaposing Faruq's profile with that of Alexander the Great. Faruq was twenty-two; Alexander had conquered Egypt at twenty-four (see fig. 55).

Taha Hussein's appointment (the Wafd was in power) as founding rector assured classics and Mediterraneanism a prominent place in the new university by the sea. Abdel Hamid El-Abbadi (1891–?), the first dean of arts, had grown up in Alexandria, then attended Cairo's Higher

Table G. Name Changes of Egypt's First Three State Universities (excluding al-Azhar)

Cairo University	Alexandria University	Ain Shams University
The Egyptian University (private), 1908–25		
The Egyptian University (public) 1925–38		
Fuad (Fouad) I University, 1938–1953	Faruq (Farouk) I University 1942– Sept. 1952	Ibrahim Pasha University 1950–54
Cairo University, 1953–	Alexandria University, Sept. 1952–	Ain Shams University Sept. 1954–

Teachers College and—like Taha Hussein—the private Egyptian University. Although a professor of Islamic history (at Cairo and then Alexandria), El-Abbadi urged his son Mostafa (later a prominent Greco–Roman historian) to study Greek and Latin because the Arabic sources for early Islamic history were scanty and had to be supplemented from outside.[132] Dean El-Abbadi's speech persuaded Daoud Abdou Daoud—later a pillar of the Société archéologique—to major in classics.[133] The elder El-Abbadi and his students recovered the neglected history of Islamic Alexandria, which Europeans had dismissed as a dark age.[134]

The Alexandrian journal *La reforme* hailed the new university in Hellenistic idiom:

> In 1943, a little over a century after its glorious rebirth, it is in a city of 750,000 inhabitants, that, under the reign of King Farouk I, following in the footsteps of the Ptolemies and taking up again the torch from the hands of [Ptolemy I] Soter, a University was founded at Alexandria, the institution of which promises our city the best future.[135]

For its official seal, the university chose the famous Pharos Lighthouse (see fig. 73). A university catalog effused: a "centre of international commerce, she [the city] was at the same time a cradle of civilisation whose fame has left a luminous trace in the history of human progress." Evoking the Museum and Library, it boasted of Eratosthenes's estimate of the

55 Alexander Fantasies: Alexander's profile is juxtaposed on that of King Faruq on a medal commemorating the founding of Faruq I (Alexandria) University, 1942. Greek and Arabic on obverse: Alexandros Basileus (King Alexander) / Faruq al-Awwal Malik Misr (Faruq I King of Egypt). *Norman D. Nicol, Raafat el-Nabarawy, Jere L. Bacharach,* Catalog of the Islamic Coins, Glass Weights, Dies and Medals in the Egyptian National Library, Cairo, American Research Center in Egypt / Catalogs *(Malibu, CA: Undena Publications, 1982), plate 27, no. 6250. Courtesy of the Egyptian National Library.*

earth's circumference, Aristarchus's heliocentric theory, Euclid's geometry, Archimedes's physics, Apollonius's trigonometry, and Theophrastus's botany. It made a bow to Clement's and Origen's "Christian School of Alexandria" and to "ecclesiastical controversies between Arius and Athanasius which resulted in the Monophysite creed throughout Egypt." Then an astonishing sentence erased fifteen centuries of Byzantine and Islamic history: "The ancient university stayed in existence from the 3rd century BC to the 4th century AD, and after a long period of lethargy and decadence its rightful heir came into being in 1942."[136]

Faruq I University's first chairman of classics, Alan Wace (1879–1957), had dug at Mycene. Because of his disagreement over the Mycenaeans with Sir Arthur Evans, the excavator of Knossos, "Evans saw that he never held a proper position in England and had to spend many years as a professor in Cairo."[137] Wace's test pits at Kom al-Dikka, like Hogarth's half a century before, disappointed classicists by yielding mainly Islamic remains.[138] Daoud Abdou Daoud, secretary of the Société archéologique, fondly recalled Wace's small Greek classes, which often met at the museum. Daoud was Alexandria's lone classics graduate of 1948, and one of only six in the 1940s.[139]

Egyptians and Classics in the 1940s

Zaki Ali (Aly) taught classical history and Latin at Alexandria under Wace from 1942 to 1950. A graduate of the Higher Teachers College (1926) with a Liverpool BA and MA, he taught at the Egyptian University before transferring to Alexandria. In 1950 he returned to Cairo when Ibrahim Noshy left for the ancient history chair at the new university soon to become Ain Shams. Zaki Ali later chaired the Cairo University history department, and after retirement taught at Ain Shams.[140]

Ancient historian Abd al-Latif Ahmad Ali vividly recalled the difficulty of pursuing his rarified specialty. He was born in 1918 in Alexandria—"like Nasser"—and attended the Ras al-Tin secondary school, as had the future president briefly.[141] At the Egyptian University, Abd al-Latif Ali took Greek from Waddell and Greco–Roman history from Jouguet. Three of the six initially in Ali's class survived to graduate in classics in 1940. Tuition waivers helped attract the university's twenty-four classics graduates of the 1940s.[142] Upon graduation, Ali "was at a loss. What was I to do?" Egypt had no posts for Greek or Latin schoolmasters and no graduate programs, and Waddell would write "unfit" on applications for assistantships.[143] Taha Hussein, however, persuaded dean of arts Ahmad Amin to create the assistantship which enabled Ali to work on an MA. Later, Ptolemaic historian Ibrahim Noshy persuaded Hussein to send Ali to the United States for a doctorate in classical papyrology. He arrived in January 1946 on an American warship with the first contingent of Egyptian students sent to the United States instead of Europe for graduate studies. Ali chose the University of Michigan; its excavation of Karanis in Fayoum (1924–1935) had given it the best papyrus collection in the United States. Unlike Grenfell and Hunt, expedition director Francis Kelsey and field director Enoch E. Peterson had investigated the town site in its entirety.[144] Ali wrote his dissertation under A.E.R. Boak on "The Roman Veterans in Egypt" and returned in 1951 to teach ancient history at Fuad I University.[145]

In 1950, Taha Hussein once again happened to be strategically placed to emphasize classics when Egypt opened its third state university—Ibrahim Pasha (soon to be Ain Shams), in Cairo. Hussein was minister of education in al-Nahhas's last Wafdist cabinet. Although a medical doctor, the new university's first rector, Muhammad Husayn Kamil (1901–77), had literary interests. He praised al-Sayyid's translations of Aristotle but wanted Egyptians now to move on to Descartes.[146] The new university raided Fuad I University across town for its first dean of arts, Ptolemaic historian Ibrahim Noshy, and for its chair of classics, Muhammad Salim Salem. Salem had earned the Egyptian University's first classics BA (1928) and a Liverpool doctorate (1937) and until leaving in 1950 was the only

Egyptian on Cairo's classics staff. He frankly declared that classics had gone downhill in Egypt since "the famous Grégoire": "I am responsible for the drop in standards." "I say half an Egyptian is better than an Englishman."[147] Ain Shams, unlike Cairo and Alexandria, taught Greek and Latin in Arabic, not English, and welcomed large enrollments.

Ibrahim Noshy (1907–2004), like Salem, began in classics at the Egyptian University in 1925. Before finishing his BA, however, Noshy left to study ancient history at Liverpool. After earning his PhD at University College London, he followed A.H.M. Jones in the Egyptian University's History Department.[148] Noshy's *Arts in Ptolemaic Egypt: A Study of Greek and Egyptian Influences in Ptolemaic Architecture and Sculpture* challenged colonialist belief that Hellenistic rulers had bestowed rational administration on a backward East and fostered hybrid culture. Despite some intermarriage and a few high Egyptian officials, Noshy saw little mixing in art or language:

> With the population of Egypt so sharply divided in the third century into Greeks who believed themselves worthy masters, equipped with higher civilization . . . and Egyptians, who felt themselves reduced to an undignified position, robbed of the riches of their country but preserving their traditional mode of life and still cherishing the memory of their past glory, any intercourse between the two must have been reduced to a minimum. Even though the Greeks had no racial prejudice, Egyptian hearts must have throbbed with national pride and burning grievance.[149]
>
> The Ptolemaic artists who attempted a fusion of styles find a parallel among some modern Egyptian dramatists, who found to their own cost the futility of Egyptianizing Western plays, because the characters, although called by Egyptian names, dressed in Egyptian dress, and introduced into Egyptian surroundings felt strange and uneasy, and imparted their discomfort to the audience, who would applaud purely Egyptian or purely Western plays as readily as they hiss a confused medley.

Noshy's detailed History of Egypt in the Age of the Ptolemies (in Arabic)[150] emphasized culture and society over war and diplomacy. It praised "the latent force of the Egyptian nation *(umma)*" and its pride in clinging to its traditions. Revolts made Egypt "the graveyard of tyrants who oppressed it." Publishing this magnum opus in Arabic was patriotic, but it also made the work invisible to most of Noshy's fellow specialists.

Muhammad Awad Husayn, a generation younger, was one of the first classicists to earn all his degrees in Egypt. His PhD dissertation at Cairo, published in Arabic in 1949, was also patriotic: "The Movement of National Resistance in Ptolemaic Egypt."[151] He joined Alexandria's

Department of Greco–Roman Civilization. He and Noshy may have read too much nationalism back into Ptolemaic times, but seeing juxtaposition more than fusion anticipated postcolonial skepticism of the melting pot thesis for the Ptolemaic era.[152] In modern Egypt too, most Greeks kept to their own churches, schools, and clubs and sent their children to university in Greece or Western Europe.[153] Greeks were more endogamous than other European residents in Egypt—only 2 percent of Greek marriages in Egypt in the 1930s were to Egyptians.[154]

Modern nationalists could either Egyptianize the Ptolemies, as with Shawqi's Cleopatra, or emphasize indigenous resistance to the Greeks. For the Romans, however, foreign exploitation seemed clearer. As Egyptologist Fayza Haikal put it, "Egypt under the Ptolemies was Egypt, not a province as under Rome. . . . I would end the history of [pharaonic] Egypt with the Roman, not the Greek invasion."[155] Coptic Egyptian resistance to pagan Rome and then to Orthodox Christianity as defined by Constantinople and Rome became standard themes for modern Egyptian nationalists.

At the Egyptian Museum, assistant curator Octave Guéraud (1901–1987), a papyrologist, was in charge of the Greco–Roman section from 1931 to 1947. In 1942, he was joined by Abd El-Muhsin El-Khashshab (1906–?), who entered the Egyptian University in 1925 and in 1937 went on to the Sorbonne. Forced home by World War II, El-Khashshab researched Greek coinage in Egypt for his Cairo PhD under Jouguet. He directed the Egyptian Museum library and founded its numismatics department.[156]

Zaki Najib Mahmud and Louis Awad were also classicists. Mahmud, a logical positivist philosopher, translated four of Plato's dialogues. He asserted that the cultural peaks of Pericles's Athens, al-Mamun's Baghdad, the Medicis' Florence, and Voltaire's Paris all had rationality in common, but that modern Arabs only paid lip service to it.[157] Louis Awad (1915–1990) read translations of Marcus Aurelius and Epictetus in his father's library. He earned a BA from Cairo, an M.Lit. from Cambridge, and a PhD from Princeton (1953) with a dissertation on "The Theme of Prometheus in English and French Literature." He translated to Arabic Horace's *Ars Poetica*, Shelley's "Prometheus Unbound," Shakespeare's *Antony and Cleopatra*, Aeschylus's *Oresteia*, Aristophanes's *Frogs*, and Plato's *Ion*.[158]

Outside the academy, Tawfiq al-Hakim's classical plays included *Praxa or: How to Govern* (1939, 1954), *Pygmalion* (1942), and *King Oedipus* (*al-Malik Udib*, 1949). *Praxa* was a variation on Aristophanes's *Lysistrata*, with women boycotting war-loving men. *Praxa*'s Athens resembled Cairo in 1939, with corrupt politicians potentially opening the door to military dictatorship. His *Oedipus* sidestepped Greek themes alien to Muslims— humans defying gods, gods plotting against humans, and inexorable fate.[159]

56 Indian Summer of Classicism: The Alexandria Municipal Stadium and an ancient Roman statue personifying the Nile. The stadium hosted the First Mediterranean Games in 1951. Its classical portico featured Olympic-style athletes and was shown on a stamp commemorating these Games. An ancient Roman statue (now in the Vatican Museum) representing the fecund Nile as a human male was featured on a commemorative stamp set in 1949 and on the reverse of the five-pound banknote of 1946 and 1952. Stadium photo by D. Reid. Stamps and banknote from collection of D. Reid.

Physician Husayn Fawzi dedicated his autobiographical *Sindibad Misri* (An Egyptian Sindbad) to al-Hakim. He visited the Pyramids as a boy and was fascinated by scenes from the *Iliad* in a Greek barbershop: "Since that remote day I bear in my memory and cherish deep in my heart the love of early Egyptian civilization and that of the ancient Greeks." Like Shawqi, he praised the Ptolemies despite their foreign blood.[160]

Indian Summer: Classics, Europeans, and Postwar Alexandria

The Société royale d'archéologie d'Alexandrie flourished for several years after 1945, moving to premises behind the Greco–Roman Museum and boasting 248 members in 1949.[161] The Société conserved the Temple of Abusir; Kamal al-Mallakh, soon to discover Cheops's boat at Giza, supervised the work.[162] Judge Brinton was still president, and Alan Wace and Étienne Combe, who lectured at the university on Islamic history and Arabic epigraphy after retiring from the Municipal Library, provided scholarly input.[163] Having a university in the city brought energetic new members onto the board: Abd al-Munim Abu Bakr (Egyptology), Aziz Atiya (medieval history), Zaki Ali (Greco–Roman history), and Rector Mustafa Amer.[164]

In a flourish of midcentury Mediterranean classicism, Egyptian postage stamps depicted the Vatican museum's statue of a reclining male figure of the Nile from the temple of Serapis and Isis in Rome (see fig. 56).[165] Three years earlier, in 1946, a £E5 banknote had shown the Vatican's Nile statue on its reverse, balancing it off with the portrait of King Faruq and the Citadel's Muhammad Ali Mosque on the front side. Another stamp set celebrated Alexandria as the site of the first Mediterranean Games in 1951; it showed a Roman triumphal arch—the entrance to the Alexandria Municipal Stadium which hosted the Games—and the seal of Alexandria, with the Pharos Lighthouse and a seaborne goddess.[166] In a final flurry of classicism before the tide went out, in 1952 Muhammad Nagi completed his aforementioned painting which had been commissioned for the city hall.

The immediate postwar years were difficult for the Greco–Roman Museum, however. It reopened in March 1945,[167] but then was long closed with a damaged roof. Curator Alan Rowe requested a transfer in order to excavate Cyrene, Libya. The Embassy begged him to "stay on at Alexandria since his successor would certainly not be British and probably not even a foreigner (so that Monsieur Drioton would regret Mr. Rowe's departure as much as we)."[168] In 1949, however, he left for the University of Manchester, which undertook to sponsor his excavation of Cyrene. Achille Adriani then made a remarkable comeback. Freed from internment in 1944, he had taught at the University of Palermo and inspected antiquities in Rome. After Rowe left, he leapt at the chance to resume direction of the Greco–Roman Museum, and in 1950 he reopened it to the public.

Time was running out, however, on the colonial and semicolonial "liberal age" during which classical discourse had so flourished.[169] In 1947, Prince Pierre of Greece tried to set up an Institut international de recherches hellénistiques in Egypt led by Pierre Jouguet. The prince's ambitions outran his means in struggling postwar Greece, however. The Institute had only £E701.940 in the bank when Jouguet died in 1949. Giving up in 1951, the prince signed the balance over to the Société royale d'archéologie d'Alexandrie.[170] Alan Wace's eulogy of Jouguet in 1949 praised him for realizing that ancient Greeks in Egypt had remained essentially foreign and that Rome had impoverished the land. Was this also a veiled commentary on contemporary colonialism and the storm that was about to break?

The closing of the Mixed Courts in 1949 undercut privileges which had helped Westerners to flourish through the colonial age. Judge Brinton and Judge Poly Modinos, the Greek who succeeded him as president of the Archeological Society (1949–51), thus lost their Alexandria livelihoods. Brinton moved to Cairo as legal adviser to the American Embassy. In 1951, Modinos resigned the Society's presidency and emigrated to work for the Council of Europe. After editing the Société's *Bulletin* for a decade, Étienne Combe moved to Cairo to direct the Swiss Institute.[171]

In the December 1951 purge of Britons following the abrogation of the Anglo–Egyptian Treaty, the Classics and English departments at Cairo and Alexandria suffered most. Alexandria lost Wace and several others, and Cairo lost D.L. Drew, L.A. Tregenza, and D.S. Crawford. Crawford and his wife were killed a few weeks later in the January 26, 1952 riots.[172] At the Greco–Roman Museum, Adriani's not being British spared him in 1951, but the Société had to lobby to get him more than a six-month renewal. Sometime after June 1952,[173] he returned to Italy, where he successively held chairs at Palermo, Naples, and Rome. Sixty years later, the Università della Tuscia in Viterbo would revive the Italian tie with an agreement to help renovate Alexandria's Greco–Roman Museum.[174]

Royal patronage, in classics and other fields, was swept away in 1952. King Faruq and Cleopatra seem an unlikely pair, yet both traced their dynasties to a founder from Macedonia, were the first of their line to feel at home in the language of most of their Egyptian countrymen, and were the last of their family to rule. Both took leave of Egypt from Alexandrian palaces by the sea, Cleopatra by suicide and Faruq on the yacht *Mahroussa* bound for Italian exile. Both left behind a city headed for drabber times, a provincial appendage to Rome after Cleopatra, and, after Faruq, a second city overshadowed by Cairo and about to lose much of its European and upper-class Egyptian cosmopolitan glitter. In Naguib Mahfouz's *Autumn Quail* and *Miramir*, the desolation of off-season Alexandria suits the melancholy of old regime figures cast aside by Nasser's revolution.[175] After the Suez War rang down the curtain on the old colonialism, nationalizations hastened the flight of most of Alexandria's—and Egypt's—remaining resident Europeans, and the Arab–Israeli conflict forced out most Egyptian Jews.

The 1950s and 1960s called into question the very existence of classical studies in Egypt, but the Greco–Roman Museum, Alexandria

Archeological Society, and classical studies at Cairo, Alexandria, and Ain Shams universities survived. By the 1990s, French-led underwater explorations were revealing lost sections of ancient Alexandria. In 2002, the improbable dream launched by Egyptian professors at Alexandria University came true: with the help of UNESCO, Bibliotheca Alexandrina opened its doors. What this glittering tribute to Egypt's classical, Mediterranean, and cosmopolitan heritage means, however, is still being worked out in a city that had also become a stronghold of Islamist movements.

Part Three

Egyptology and Pharaonism to Nasser's Revolution

9

Contesting Egyptology in the 1930s

Two voices, both Egyptian:

"We live in the heart of French archaeology!" proudly exclaimed my
father, for Mariette Pasha Street [where our apartment faced the Egyptian
Museum] was perpendicular to Maspero, Champollion, and Antikkhana
streets, the latter word meaning 'antiquities museum' in Turkish.
                                                —Midhat Ghazalé[1]

With foreigners wanting to monopolize Egyptian antiquities, the former
students of the School of Hieroglyphs had to enter teaching like Ahmad
Bey Najib and Muhammad Effendi Ismat or teach calligraphy like Ibrahim Effendi Najib. . . .

All these Egyptians passed like shadows. Unfortunately they were Egyptians.
    —"An Egyptian instead of a Foreigner for the Antiquities Service,"
                                        —*Rose-al Youssef*, March 21, 1936[2]

E
gypt's politics in the 1930s were as unsettled as those of much of
the globe, and Egyptian archaeology did not stand aloof. Globally,
the League of Nations had been handicapped from the start by the
American refusal to join the international body which Woodrow Wilson
had worked so hard to establish. Germany was excluded from the League
until 1926, and the Soviet Union until 1934. For the League's first dozen
years, Persia was the only Middle Eastern member. Turkey and Iraq joined
in 1932, almost passing Japan and Germany on their way out (1933). Not
until May 1937—in the wake of the 1936 Anglo–Egyptian Treaty and
the ensuing Montreux Convention—was Egypt considered independent

enough to join. It proved, however, to be the last country to do so. Six months later, Italy followed its emerging allies Germany and Japan out of the League. In the cultural sphere, Taha Hussein took up his seat on the League-affiliated International Committee on Intellectual Cooperation only in 1939, the year the war struck the League its mortal blow.

As the United States retreated into isolationism during the Great Depression, Britain struggled to regain its pre-1914 financial and commercial preeminence in its empire and the larger sterling area. From 1929 to 1937, the sterling area also included the Scandinavian and Baltic countries, Portugal, Thailand, and formerly British Eire, Iraq, and Egypt. In 1938, however, the abandonment of the convertibility of the pound sterling opened the door for emerging American financial global dominance.[3]

In Egypt, King Fuad's last bid for autocratic rule through prime ministers Ismail Sidqi and Abd al-Fattah Yahya unraveled in 1934, beginning the slow transition toward the restoration of the 1923 constitution and the return of the Wafd to power in the spring of 1936. The Anglo–Egyptian Treaty which al-Nahhas signed a few months later eased, but did not resolve, the tensions between Britain and Egyptian nationalists. The treaty tarnished the Wafd in the eyes of some nationalists. Early hopes for handsome young King Faruq, who succeeded Fuad in April 1936, soon faded. The Depression had devastated the price of Egyptian cotton on world markets, and unemployment rose sharply. Outside and below the palace and the landlord-dominated parliamentary parties, the Muslim Brotherhood, Young Egypt, Marxists, and other radicals voiced the disillusionment of aspiring effendis—educated but often underemployed middle-class (or would-be middle-class) youths.

In the Antiquities Service, the agile cleric Étienne Drioton took over the rearguard defense of France's archaeological protectorate from ailing Pierre Lacau in 1936. British High Commissioner (from 1936, Ambassador) Sir Miles Lampson's occasional reluctant cooperation with the French only temporarily slowed the inevitable Egyptianization of the Service. Meanwhile, Egyptians began climbing a newly opening second career ladder in Egyptology—university positions. Europeans still chaired the university's archaeology department, but the chairmanship shifted from a Briton to a German. Hermann Junker succeeded Percy Newberry as head of the Egyptian University's Department of Egyptology while continuing to direct the reorganized German archaeological institute. Being Jewish, Junker's displaced predecessor at the German Institute, Ludwig Borchardt, had to scramble to save his property from the Nazis. In 1939, the British finally forced Junker out of his Egyptian University chair, but they were slow to resign themselves to an Egyptian successor—Sami Gabra. In

1939 too, an improbable alliance of Britain, France, and King Faruq drove Selim Hassan from the Antiquities Service and out of public life. From the mid-1930s, Western excavations in Egypt dwindled; they would not recover until the Nubian campaign of the 1960s.

European Mentors and Egyptian Egyptologists in the Egyptian University

Succeeding émigré Russian Vladimir Golenischeff in the Egyptian University's chair of Egyptology in 1929, Briton Percy Newberry presided over an impressive commitment of university resources to archaeology before retiring in 1933. Even as the Depression deepened, the Faculty of Arts under Rector Lutfi al-Sayyid and Dean Taha Hussein sponsored *three* major excavations, elevated Egyptology to a graduate-level program, and added a new program in Islamic archaeology. Newberry was sixty-one upon arrival, with forty-five years in Egyptology behind him. He had begun assisting the EEF with secretarial work at sixteen, studied botany and archaeology at King's College London, learned field archaeology under Petrie, and occupied the Egyptology chair at Liverpool from 1905 to 1919.[4] A senior scholar with independent means, he had no need to worry that the Cairo salary was modest, that he might miss a critical career step back home, or that Egyptianization might squeeze him out.

High Commissioner Lord Lloyd may have had a hand in Newberry's appointment. Lloyd dedicated his four years in Cairo (1925–29) to a crusade to reestablish British influence, sadly diminished since the days of his hero Lord Cromer. Determined to roll back French influence at the university, he kept a tally of British versus "Latin" professors. He dismissed the Francophone Belgians and Italians favored by King Fuad as mere surrogate Frenchmen. Though no friend of Egyptianization, Lloyd could at least cross off another Frenchman when Selim Hassan replaced Charles Kuentz, an instructor from IFAO, at the university in 1928.[5] Lloyd was no longer around in the fall of 1929 to welcome Newberry, however; Ramsey MacDonald's incoming Labour government favored a less abrasive brand of imperialism and forced him out in July.[6]

In 1930, Newberry formulated a plan to replace undergraduate Egyptology with a postgraduate Institute of Archaeology.[7] Students entering with BAs, perhaps in history or classics, would be presumed to know English, French, and Latin as well as their native Arabic, and be ready to take Egyptian, Coptic, Greek, German, ancient Egyptian history and archaeology, and Greco–Roman history. The shift to graduate-level archaeology suited Rector Lutfi al-Sayyid's and Dean Taha Hussein's drive to emulate European research universities. Pierre Lacau, however, saw the university's Institute of Archeology as a ploy by Newberry to subvert French control of the Antiquities Service and install Selim Hassan as director of the Egyptian Museum.[8]

Selim Hassan and Sami Gabra came into their own in the early 1930s, both at the Egyptian University and in the excavations which its Faculty of Arts sponsored (see fig. 57).

The university had lured Selim Hassan away from the Antiquities Service in 1928. He felt welcome at the university as he never had at the Service under Lacau. Three successive department chairs—Goleniescheff, Newberry, and Junker—helped Hassan climb the academic ladder. The Faculty of Arts sponsored publication of his Sorbonne thesis by the Government Press at Bulaq. He dedicated it to "my master, Professor Golenischeff" and later dedicated another volume to his memory.[9] Taha Hussein would have appreciated that the work's dedication to King Fuad was in Latin as well as in Arabic.

Unlike Selim Hassan, Sami Gabra loved his stint in the Antiquities Service. In 1931, however, Gabra too left for the university. In the teeth of the Great Depression, Taha Hussein committed the Faculty of Arts to two more long-term excavations in addition to Hassan's at Giza—Sami Gabra's at Tuna al-Gebel and Mustafa Amer's at Maadi. Egyptians had hitherto lacked universities, research institutes, and learned societies outside the Antiquities Service which could sponsor excavations. Ahmad Kamal and his little-known Egyptian contemporaries in the Service had had only brief chances to excavate, often salvaging sites turned up by accident or by illicit digging. Except for Asyut notable Sayyid Bey Khashaba—whose ventures ended on a sour note—and Prince Omar Toussoun, Egypt had lacked wealthy archaeological hobbyists like Lord Carnarvon, Theodore Davis, Robert Mond, and James Simon. Just as Maspero had recommended Howard Carter to Lord Carnarvon as a field archaeologist, he arranged for Kamal to dig privately for Khashaba at Meir, Deir Dronka, and Asyut (1912–14) and report the results in the *ASAE*. Khashaba sold some of his share of the finds, but then Kamal persuaded him to establish a provincial museum in Asyut. Maspero arranged for a founding decree, but Khashaba died, his heirs sold off part of the collection, and the concession was revoked.[10] Antiquities secretary general Daressy, whose animosity toward Kamal has already been noted, scathingly declared in 1921: "There is no museum in Asyut." Up to now, he added, there was "not a single one [Egyptian] capable of conducting a large-scale excavation in a scientific manner."[11]

No wonder Egyptians felt proud when Selim Hassan began his Faculty of Arts excavations at Giza in 1929. His future department chair

Le Prof. Sélim Hassan
Professeur de Philologie et d'Egyptologie
à l'Université Egyptienne

a

b

57 Second-generation Egyptologists Selim Hassan and Sami Gabra a: *Raul Fargeon, Silhouettes d'Égypte (lettrés et mondains du Caire) (Paris?: Éditions de "Orient," 1931), 157; b:* Le mondain égyptien et du moyen orient, *ed. E. J. Blattner, 293.*

Hermann Junker, who was working the nearby Austrian concession, gave him a three-month crash course in field archaeology. George Reisner's Harvard–Boston expedition at Menkaure's third pyramid was also close at hand for consultation.[12] Hassan dug out the Sphinx and its temple completely for the first time and excavated tombs near the causeway of Khafre's (Chephren's) second pyramid. He investigated the palace-façade tomb of Queen Khent-kawes, popularizing it as "the fourth pyramid;" the *New York Times* was among the newspapers that picked up the story.[13] Over nearly thirty years, Hassan's ten-part *Excavations at Giza* (1932–1960) laid out his results in large format. Newberry lined up the publisher—Oxford University Press—and helped edit volume 1, but Hassan proudly noted that his field staff were all Egyptians. Volume 2 (1934) brought the publishing venture home to the Government Press at Bulaq; Selim Hassan claimed that this was the first time a "purely Egyptian press" had printed inscriptions in hieroglyphic font.[14]

With equal energy, if less fanfare, Sami Gabra began digging at the necropolis of Tuna al-Gebel (Hermopolis West) in February 1931. Tuna was some 180 miles south of Cairo in Minya province and sixty miles north of Gabra's native Abnub. In the early 1920s, his mentor Gustave Lefebvre had excavated the Persian-era tomb-temple of Petosiris at this Late Period / Greco–Roman site. Lacau had no funds for Gabra to dig there but backed up his protégé's Faculty of Arts expedition with an experienced inspector, trained diggers, and a Décauville mining cart and rails. Gabra followed Reisner's method—digging section by section, level by level, down to virgin soil. After the expedition had roughed it in tents for three seasons, Lacau rewarded them with a brick excavation house.[15]

Taha Hussein's transfer in 1925 from ancient history to the chair of Arabic literature in no way diminished his zeal for classical civilization, and as dean of arts he enjoyed visiting Gabra's site at Tuna. Their wives, both French, enjoyed each other's company. Despite the Depression, the Faculty's budget for Tuna rose from £E500 in 1931 to £E8,000 by 1937.[16] No wonder Gabra looked back on 1935–1939 as "the golden age of archaeology and the apogee of our site."[17] Hermopolis had been the cult center of the god of scribes and wisdom, Thoth—Djehuty to ancient Egyptians and later Hermes Trismegistos to Greeks. Thoth was chosen for the official seal of the Egyptian University. Gabra uncovered tombs in both pharaonic and Greco–Roman styles and galleries of the mummies of the ibises and baboons sacred to Thoth. Like Selim Hassan, he took great pride in his Egyptian professional team. Gabra's assistant Naguib Mikhail helped explore the Tuna galleries and set up a museum at nearby Mallawi. The lead article in a 1933 issue of al-Ahram hailed Gabra's Hermopolis excavations as having uncovered "another Pompeii in Egypt."[18]

Gabra consulted often with Newberry, Junker, William Waddell of the classics department, Pierre Jouguet of IFAO, and Lacau's successor, Drioton. He brought his work to the attention of Western colleagues with presentations at congresses in Europe. The last of the decade was the International Congress of Archaeology which convened in Berlin in late August, 1939. Welcomed in the name of "our Führer Adolf Hitler," the attendees were assured that "Germany would continue to be the land of freedom of knowledge." Gabra co-chaired a panel and on August 26 read his paper "Récent découvertes à Hermopolis Ouest." Six days later, Hitler's invasion of Poland touched off general war in Europe, and Gabra had to scramble to catch a steamer home from Marseilles.[19]

The third Faculty of Arts excavator of the 1930s was geographer and prehistoric archaeologist Mustafa Amer, who had preceded Gabra and Mahmud Hamza in studying at Liverpool.[20] Amer and fellow Liverpool geography graduate Muhammad Awad, who took his PhD at the University of London, welcomed their Liverpool mentor P.M. Roxby to the Egyptian University's geography department in 1930 as visiting professor.[21] That same year, Amer and Oswald Menghin, a German, began codirecting excavations at a Neolithic site at Maadi, just south of Cairo. Menghin left after three seasons; Amer kept on at Maadi and later at nearby Wadi Digla.

During the 1940s, however, university administration in Cairo and Alexandria took up most of his time. Amer was rector of Alexandria University in January 1953, when the Free Officers tapped him to become the first Egyptian director general of the Antiquities Service.

Associate professors Hassan and Gabra made debuts at the eighteenth International Congress of Orientalists (ICO) in Leiden in 1931 with reports on their excavations. The ICOs have received surprisingly little attention in the debates touched off by Edward Said's *Orientalism*. For a century after the first ICO met in Paris in 1873, Egyptologists dominated one of its sections. In the two decades before 1914, Egyptians read half a dozen papers on Arabic or Islamic subjects at ICOs, but none on Egyptology. At the first postwar ICO, at Oxford in 1928, Taha Hussein was the only Egyptian to present.[22] Such Arabic/Islamic scholars as Ahmad Amin and Mustafa Abd al-Raziq joined him at later ICOs into the 1950s. In Egyptology, Selim Hassan presented again at the nineteenth ICO in Rome (1935), and Gabra at the twentieth in Brussels (1938).[23]

Cairo's BA Egyptology graduates of 1928–1933 and MAs of 1934–1940 may be considered, respectively, the first and second cohorts of the third generation of Egyptian Egyptologists. Both cohorts studied with both European and Egyptian professors, usually including Selim Hassan and Sami Gabra. Ahmad Fakhry, Abdel Moneim Abu Bakr, Labib Habachi, Zaki Saad, and Girgis Mattha stood out in the first cohort of this third generation, and Abdel Mohsin al-Bakir, Anwar Shukri, Iskandar Badawi, Zakariya Ghoneim, and Naguib Mikhail in the younger cohort. This third generation interacted with European professors more intensively than the fourth generation, graduates of the 1940s who encountered Europeans at Egyptian universities mainly as adjunct or visiting professors.

The Return of the Germans: Hermann Junker, "Archaeological Ace"

In 1933, the year Hitler came to power, the British Foreign Office rebuked the Cairo Residency for allowing Junker to succeed Newberry in the Egyptology chair:

> I do not remember in four years' experience a case where our interests in Egypt have been so inexcusably let down. . . . the Residency are altogether too slack on the subject of these University posts. . . . The Residency ought to have known that Professor Newberry who is violently anti-French and cares only for keeping out Frenchmen, is not a person who should be allowed to have any say as to the selection of his successor. We drew attention to this aspect of Newberry's character over a year ago.[24]

Junker had been affiliated with the Egyptology Department at the Egyptian University since 1930.

In 1934, the British and the French were still hoping to claim the chair for one of their own. Francis Griffith, retired from Oxford, was not interested. Aylward Blackman declined to gamble on a precarious three-year Cairo contract at mediocre pay and soon found a permanent post at Liverpool.[25] The Residency toyed with bringing Reginald Engelbach or Guy Brunton over from the museum, but the salary was too low.[26] Frenchman Raymond Weill dismissed the Cairo salary as two steps below what he would consider.[27]

The university salary posed no problem for Junker, however, because he was concurrently director of the Deutsches Archäologische Institut-Abteilung Kairo (German Archaeological Institute, Cairo Department, DAI). Declining a chair at Bonn in his native Rhineland, Junker had directed the DAI since replacing Ludwig Borchardt at the helm of German Archaeology in Egypt in 1929. Junker's previous sponsor, the Vienna Academy of Sciences, lacked the resources to fully support his ambitious publication and excavation plans.[28] Since the old German Institute's Zamalek premises were Borchardt's private property, in 1931 Junker set up new quarters for the DAI in the Zamalek villa which later housed the Canadian Embassy.[29] The offices were on the lower floor and living quarters on the top two floors. In 1930, the DAI began competing with the IFAO's well-established publication program by launching *Mitteilungen des Deutschen Instituts für Ägyptische Altertumskunde*.

With Egypt's ban on German excavations finally lifted, Junker dug throughout the 1930s at the Neolithic site of Merimde on the western edge of the Delta. Günther Roeder (1881–1966) excavated the temple of Thoth at al-Ashmunein/Hermopolis. From 1915 to 1945, he directed the Pelizaeus Museum, which German businessman Wilhelm Pelizaeus (1851–1930) had founded at Hildesheim, Germany in 1911. During the war years from 1940–45, Roeder also directed the Egyptian Museum in Berlin. Allied denazification purged him from both posts in 1945.[30] At Hermopolis, he excavated the city for the cemetery which Gabra was excavating six miles away. Both read papers, sometimes on the same panel, at ICOs in 1931 and 1938, and in 1939 at the International Congress of Archaeology.[31] Probably due to political reasons, however, Gabra made no mention of Roeder in his memoirs.

Junker's dual directorships at DAI and the Egyptian University situated him ideally to influence young Egyptian Egyptologists through the 1930s. In the 1920s, the second generation had studied in Liverpool, Paris, or both, with only side visits to Berlin. In the 1930s, two of the Egyptian

University's Faculty of Arts excavations involved Germans or Austrians—Junker as mentor to Hassan at Giza and Oswald Menghin as codirector with Mustafa Amer at Maadi. Junker also helped guide Selim Hassan to his University of Vienna doctorate in 1935 at the age of fifty-one.

Like Mustafa Amer, Junker's Vienna colleague Oswald Menghin (1888–1973) was not an Egyptologist but a prehistoric archaeologist. While excavating with Amer at Maadi (1930–33), Menghin was also professor in residence at the Egyptian University. Menghin had become professor of prehistoric archaeology at Vienna in 1918 at age thirty, edited an influential journal, and served as dean of the philosophical faculty before going to Cairo. His Vienna culture-historical school of ethnography espoused hyperdiffusionist theories and opposed the materialist evolutionist school. Menghin had been active in the radical right Deutschen Gemeinschaft in the 1920s, and in 1933 he lectured to a Nazi Party chapter in Cairo. In a 1934 book, he denounced Jews as a racial threat to German culture and advocated their immigration to Palestine. He became rector of the University of Vienna in 1935 and in March 1938 was minister of culture and education in the cabinet which welcomed anschluss—Austria's absorption into Germany. As a pious Catholic, however, Menghin did not fully subscribe to Nazi doctrine on Aryan supremacy or become a full member of the party. Interned in 1945 but not tried for war crimes, he immigrated in 1948 to Argentina, where he had an influential second academic career.[32]

German Egyptology greatly influenced the rising third generation of Egyptian Egyptologists. Abd al-Munim Abu Bakr, Ahmad Badawi, and Pahor Labib, who would hold prominent posts after 1952, earned PhDs in Germany in the 1930s. Medieval historian Aziz Suriyal Atiya earned his PhD at the University of London, then taught at the University of Bonn until 1939.[33] Abd al-Muhsin Bakir, Anwar Shukri, and Ahmad Fakhry studied Egyptology in Germany in the 1930s but finished their doctorates at Oxford (Bakir) and Cairo (Shukri, Fakhry). The war's interruption of Shukri's studies at Göttingen under Hermann Kees forced him to finish his doctorate at Cairo. Junker's ouster from his Cairo chair in 1939 and the outbreak of the war interrupted the flow of Egyptian students to Germany.

It took more than half a century after 1945 before Germans began serious examination of the impact of Nazism on Egyptology, and Nazism's effects on Egyptians who studied in Germany in the 1930s have yet to be systematically explored. At Leipzig, senior Egyptologist Georg Steindorff, a Jew, was forced out and in 1939 fled to the United States. In June 1945, Steindorff sent Chicago's John Wilson an "I accuse" list categorizing the politics of individual German Egyptologists.[34] Steindorff called

Walther Wolf, the former student who had replaced him at Leipzig, "a terrible Nazi," but Hermann Grapow of Berlin topped the list, followed by Grapow's associate Alfred Hermann. Steindorff said that Grapow had been

> a pupil and collaborator of Erman. So long as Erman lived, he posed as a democrat. Later however, especially after Sethe passed away, he showed his true colors as an arch-Nazi. . . . He persecuted everybody who did not say "Heil Hitler!" and did not follow the Nazi flag.

Hermann Kees of Göttingen ranked third on Steindorff's list:

> a member of an old Saxon land-owning family, a militarist and junker. He was an army officer in the First World War, and fought later by all means in his power, openly and secretly, the Weimar Republic. He is antidemocratic from the bottom of his soul. A conservative, he at first opposed Hitlerism, but afterwards became a Nazi. Though I do not know whether he actually joined the party, I would not trust him, even if he should say that he became a Nazi only from compulsion.

Kees condemned Akhenaten for undercutting the ideal of a master race and hailed other pharaohs for anticipating Nazi ideas of leadership. Kees had initiated a call to purge Jewish scholars, and in 1945 denazification cost him his university chair.[35]

Anwar Shukri studied under Kees until the war intervened, and Ahmad Badawi took his second doctorate (habil) at Göttingen with Kees after his first under Grapow at Berlin. Shukri's attitude toward the Nazis is unknown, but Badawi continued to praise Hitler long after his death.[36] After Egypt's 1952 revolution, Badawi invited Kees, his old professor, to lecture at Ain Shams University.[37] Badawi rose during the Nasser years to become rector of first Ain Shams and then Cairo University.

Although Junker came fourth on Steindorff's list, his condemnation was qualified:

> It is very difficult to describe the character of this man because he has none. I have heard that it was rumored in England that Junker acted as a spy in Egypt. I do not believe it. He was too clever to compromise himself by such activity. He played safe. However, he used his position and the State Institute to promote Nazi propaganda. . . . Every Nazi found a cordial reception in the German Institute in Cairo. I appreciate Junker as a scholar of the first order. More than that, I am sorry I cannot say. At best, his actions and opinions have always been ambiguous.

Chapter 3 discussed how German-born Junker finessed Egypt's postwar ban on German excavations by digging at Giza under Austrian auspices. In 1929, the lifting of the ban cleared the way for him to direct the DAI and dig in its name. In 1938, Hitler's annexation of Austria rendered the question of Junker's German or Austrian citizenship moot for a time. Ambassador Lampson warned that Junker was trying to place German lecturers in the university and suspected the DAI of spreading Nazi propaganda.[38] When minister of propaganda Joseph Goebbels visited Cairo in April 1939, Junker showed him around Giza, Saqqara, and the Egyptian Museum.[39] British–French rivalry still ran deep enough, however, that Miles Lampson worried lest Junker's ouster from the university enable the French to capture his chair.[40] By early 1939, two German lecturers had been forced out of the university, and Dean Taha Hussein promised to terminate Junker's appointment at the end of term.[41] A British official warned that this could not be justified on academic grounds: Junker was "an archaeological ace."[42] Walter Bryan Emery speculated that Junker might have a hand in selling antiquities to Germany, for which Selim Hassan was being investigated.[43]

Like Borchardt in 1914, Junker was summering in Europe when war broke and the German Institute in Cairo was sequestered. Its library was eventually divided between Faruq I University (Alexandria), Fuad I University (Cairo), and the Documentation Center which was founded in 1955–56. Antiquities Service officials also took over the (second) German House at Qurna until 1958, when it was returned to the Germans.[44] During the war, reused blocks in Amarna style which Roeder had excavated at al-Ashmunein/Hermopolis were looted from the site warehouse and turned up on the Cairo market.[45] After the war Junker, like many others, took great trouble to cover the tracks of his association with the Nazi former regime.[46]

A German Patriot Loses His Country:
Borchardt and the Swiss Institute

Although a great Egyptologist, Ludwig Borchardt's imperious manner alienated many. Emigré German Egyptologist Louis Keimer—one of the "men of honor" on Steindorff's list—spat: "this 'prussian' [Borchardt]—if he had not been a Jew, he would certainly have been a militant nazi."[47] Under Hitler, the world grew dark for Borchardt. Ironically, it was he who had brought home to Berlin the bust of Nefertiti which Hitler so admired. After Junker replaced him at the German Institute in Cairo in 1929, Borchardt drew on his wife's fortune to found his own Institute for Architectural and Archaeological Research in adjoining villas in Zamalek.[48]

58 Old enemies meet: Germans Hermann Junker (far left) vs. Ludwig Borchardt (far right), and Americans George Reisner (center left) vs. James Henry Breasted (center right). Garden of the Continental Hotel, Cairo, Nov. 1935. *Photo by Leslie F. Thompson. Wilson,* Signs and Wonders, *Plate 32b. Courtesy of the Oriental Institute, University of Chicago.*

Adolf Hitler had been chancellor for eight months when Adolf Erman published a tribute to his former student Borchardt on his seventieth birthday, and Borchardt responded with a privately printed selection of his recent work.[49] In his memoirs published four years earlier, Erman had defied the rising racism and chauvinism in the Weimar Republic. Of Swiss Protestant origin, he said he did not claim "pure Aryan" descent. His forebears included three Frenchmen and a Jew, and he repudiated the idea of a "pure race." He had studied in a French Gymnasium and praised a Jewish mentor—Julius Friedlaender of the coins and medals section of the Berlin Museum library. Erman was a German patriot but also proud of having had French, British, Swiss, Scandinavian, and Egyptian students and proud that Berlin Egyptology circles included Jews, Catholics, and Copts as well as Protestants.[50]

A photo taken about 1935 in the garden of the Continental Hotel shows an awkward meeting of Borchardt with his adversary Junker and another set of old rivals, Americans Breasted and Reisner (see fig. 58). The facial expressions and body language of the four signal anything but reconciliation.

Even as the Nazi noose tightened, Borchardt in his Cairo refuge dreamed of grandiose projects. In 1937, after the Anglo–Egyptian Treaty, the British considered evacuating the Qasr al-Nil barracks next to the Egyptian Museum. Borchardt had his assistant Otto Königsberger draw up plans for a "Cité des Musées" on the site.[51] It would incorporate the existing museum and add other buildings around a plaza where three Paris-style avenues converged on Mariette Pasha Street. Behind, a park would stretch to the Nile. A mausoleum would house the mummies of the New Kingdom pharaohs and Tutankhamun's treasures, with four flanking buildings for prehistoric and Old Kingdom, Middle Kingdom, New Kingdom, and Late Period relics. Offices, laboratories, a library, and a director's residence rounded out the plan. Borchardt sent the proposal to Antiquities director Drioton, Prime Minister al-Nahhas and other ministers, and—anonymously—to the press. Like the Breasted–Rockefeller project a decade earlier, it came to nothing. Borchardt had no Rockefeller, lobby of scholars, or even a country behind him. The Qasr al-Nil barracks would stand until the 1950s. When they finally gave way during the early Nasser years, it was not to a museum complex but to the Nile Hilton and the headquarters of the Arab League.

By July 1938, Borchardt was desperately pleading with friends for help in obtaining American, British, Swiss, or other citizenship. George Reisner explained:

> I have tried all my life to get an endowment of a million dollars for historical research in Egypt. I was in sight of success with the help of an American millionaire when the Depression broke in 1929 and the scheme went to pieces. Now the political events in Germany and the persecution of the Jews has brought again a possible hope of an endowed American Institute for Egyptian Architecture and Archaeology. . . . preferably Harvard or the Boston Museum of Fine Arts.
>
> At the present time the German Government is canceling all German passports held by Jews and making an attempt to confiscate all their possessions both in Germany and in foreign lands. Thus Borchardt anticipates the wiping out of his private research institute, the total impoverishment of his wife and himself (they have no children). He is now 75 years old.[52]

With $700,000 invested in America, Holland, and Switzerland, and with his land, buildings, and library in Cairo, Borchardt's fortune came to nearly a million dollars. In return for citizenship, he was prepared to leave—after his and his wife's deaths—his institute and money to an institution in the rescuing country. "I fear so greatly for him and the Institute," wrote Reisner, "that I have advised him to seek British or Egyptian citizenship immediately."

Reisner warned Borchardt of a problem with having his German assistant Herbert Ricke succeed him: "If the Director remains German and has the appointment of all members of the staff, how is any American to be introduced into the staff?" American appointments, however, "would possibly result in the complete Americanisation of the proposed Institute." Borchardt wrote reassuringly from Zurich: "I did not in the least think to create a 'national German Institute.' On the contrary, it should serve the science of all nations." Were Harvard to take over the Institute, the board would consist of a lawyer and a banker, probably Americans, and three specialists

> who have somewhere professorships of Egyptian Architectural History, and among them there could be the Director.
>
> The board would therefor (sic.) be at first nearly wholly American, later on most likely totally American. Especially as Ricke, who is to be retained, as he would be the best Director, would later on be replaced by an American Director and he would also be elected as a member of the board.[53]

The Institute's mission would be "to further research on Egyptian Architecture and Archaeology in the widest sense." Borchardt insisted: "ability in our science is the chief demand." Architectural expertise would take precedence over philology. With this "scientific" or "technical" requirement satisfied, hiring priorities would be:

1. Descendants of the grandparents of himself and his wife
2. German Jewish exiles
3. Persons speaking German as their family language
4. "Every student of architecture" "of any nation"

Borchardt assured Reisner that the first three priorities were unlikely to count: none of his relatives knew Egyptology, the Nazi ban on Jews studying architecture made a German Jewish candidate unlikely, and hardly anyone in the third group—mainly German–Americans or German–Swiss—had the required specializations. There was one more stipulation: "No so-called Aryan German is to be employed in the Institute until twelve years after the restoration of equal rights to Jews in Germany, de jure and de facto." Until then,

> no "Aryan" German—I would even exclude with them the Germans of Bohemia (and Danzig)—could be a member of the board or have an appointment in the Institute, save those that now are in it.

The last phrase cleared the way for Borchardt's "Aryan" assistant Herbert Ricke. Borchardt explicitly ruled out another German former assistant, Uvo Hölscher.

Reisner's German background and study in Berlin commended him to Borchardt. Though not an architect himself, Reisner appreciated Borchardt's stress on architecture over philology. Reisner's work at Menkare's third pyramid at Giza built on Borchardt's study of the pyramid of Sahure at Abusir, and Reisner's *Development of the Egyptian Tomb down to the Accession of Cheops* (1936) stressed architecture. Reisner's emphasis on excavation contrasted with the philological and epigraphical priorities of his rival Breasted. Rockefeller funding had enabled Breasted to institutionalize his priorities through Chicago's Oriental Institute; Reisner was still searching for his millionaire.

While trying to interest Harvard and the MFA in Borchardt's proposal, Reisner arranged for the American Embassy in Paris to interview the Borchardts. The State Department, however, ruled that there was no way around the requirement for US residence prior to citizenship.[54] Borchardt's feeler to Britain through Alan Gardiner and Norman de Garis Davies also fell through,[55] and he died in Paris on August 12, 1938. His desperate widow sent Reisner in Cairo power of attorney to transfer her property to a Swiss corporation. Late in September 1938, as the world held its breath to see if Hitler's dismemberment of Czechoslovakia would touch off general war, Reisner wrote

> It appears that Mrs. Borchardt cannot get any citizenship anywhere with the possible exception of Egypt. The poor woman is worried to death. It would have been an irony of fate if war had been declared and she had been interned somewhere as a German subject.
>
> I think that we must give up the idea of taking over the Borchardt institute.[56]

Frau Borchardt and her late husband's assistant Herbert Ricke rode out the war in Zürich. After her death in Switzerland on October 31, 1948,[57] her husband's institute in Cairo became the Swiss Institute of Architectural and Archaeological Research on Ancient Egypt (Schweizerisches Institut für Ägyptische Bauforschung und Altertumskunde). The history of this remarkable institution is at last receiving the scholarly attention it deserves.[58] Ricke returned to Egypt as scientific expert at the new Swiss institute in 1950, became scientific director in 1952, and director from 1963 until his retirement in 1971. From 1950 to 1963, Étienne Combe, an Arabist and Orientalist who had retired from the Alexandria

Municipal Library, served as the institute's administrative director. One intriguing theme is the Swiss Institute's close collaboration with the German Archaeological Institute in Cairo after the latter's reopening in 1957. A block of pink Aswan granite marks Ludwig Borchardt's grave in the garden of the Swiss Institute in Zamalek on the street formerly named "Swiss Institute Street."[59]

Contesting the Antiquities Directorship: "God the Father" versus Selim Hassan

With his contract set to expire in March 1933, Director General Pierre Lacau seemed almost resigned to an Egyptian successor, probably Selim Hassan.[60] From the university, Newberry lobbied for Hassan, first as director of the Egyptian Museum and then as successor to Lacau. Cultural adviser Sir Robert Greg reported that Newberry "pleaded very hard for Selim Hassan and suggested that after he had trained up a suitable Egyptian for the post it was rather unfortunate that he should not be utilized." Greg and Oriental Secretary Walter Smart, however, preferred an "Egyptian administrator without archaeological experience . . . to an Egyptian archaeologist"—a way to keep "scientific authority" in European hands.[61]

"God the Father"—Lacau's nickname because of his beard and formidable exterior—discounted three possible French successors. Secretary general of the Service Henri Gauthier, an authority on the names and titles of the pharaohs,[62] lacked tact and was unpopular with Egyptians. Alexandre Moret was five years older than Lacau himself and happy at the Collège de France. Lacau judged Raymond Weill of the École des hautes études unsuited to cope with the inevitable intrigues.[63]

In 1933, Britons Reginald Engelbach and Guy Brunton pressed for renewal of their French superior's contract. A Residency official demurred:

> Are we justified in suggesting to the Egyptian government that they should agree to the renewal of a contract of a French archaeologist of no special distinction on conditions unusually advantageous to him and of dubious advantage to Egyptian archaeology? Presumably Mr. Engelbach and Mr. Brunton have more or less got M. Lacau under their thumb and prefer a Frenchman (a sick, inactive one into the bargain) they know to Frenchmen they know not of. . . . I would prefer that he and the French Legation were left to fight their own battles.[64]

The Foreign Office, however, insisted on standing by its 1904 commitment that the director should be French. Engelbach and Gauthier worked out a compromise on Lacau's summer leaves which still gave him six months away—five in Europe and one in Upper Egypt researching architecture.[65] Lacau's contract was renewed for three years.

In May 1935, *al-Ahram* and *al-Balagh* raised a cry over the theft and sale of papyri and other relics from Bernard Bruyère's IFAO dig at Deir al-Medina. In 1928 Alan Gardiner had bought a papyrus in Cairo from the dig on behalf of mining magnate Chester Beatty, who donated it to the British Museum. Gardiner's publication of the papyrus called attention to its theft. The Arabic press blamed Lacau as well as Bruyère and IFAO; *al-Jihad* demanded that Lacau resign.[66] IFAO director Pierre Jouguet was attending a papyrological congress in Italy when the story broke. Lacau launched an investigation, and the French concessions at Deir al-Medina and Edfu were suspended. Jouguet speculated on who might be feeding the story to the press: Selim Hassan, Junker, Newberry, former IFAO director Chassinat, or Mme. Gauthier-Laurent, who had helped Selim Hassan with his Paris thesis.[67] Suspecting Chassinat, Lacau and Jouguet tried to make sure that he never again received a state grant. In January 1936, Jouguet and Bruyère were cleared of blame, and IFAO was allowed to resume work at Deir al-Medina and Edfu.

In the fall of 1935, Jouguet speculated that perhaps the furor was cooling because Selim Hassan was preoccupied with a suit his French former mistress had brought against him in the Mixed Courts. An art collector's secretary, she had met Hassan in a Paris café, become his mistress, and given up her livelihood. In 1928 she followed him to Cairo. She claimed to have paid restaurant, theater, and travel bills for him and his Egyptian contacts in Paris and Cairo. She charged that he had advised her to buy antiquities which turned out to be fake and had undercut her attempt at a couture business in Cairo. She sought the protection of the French consulate and sued him for £E8,000 and various expenses.[68] Absent a record of the disposition of the case, her allegations remain just that.

Selim Hassan's Challenge to the Imperial Order[69]

From June 1936, when Abbé (or Chanoine) Étienne Drioton became director general of Antiquities and Selim Bey Hassan assistant director, until Hassan was forced into retirement in September 1939, the two fought an epic battle for control of the Antiquities Service. Nationalists mostly backed the bey, but the abbé won in the end due to an unlikely triangular alliance of the French, British proconsul Miles Lampson, and Faruq, the teenage king. Drioton had previously taught Egyptian and Coptic at the Catholic Institute, Paris, and been assistant curator at the Louvre. To minimize Egyptian objections to his clerical status, he was given dispensation to wear lay dress and the tarboosh of Egyptian officials. His religious calling freed him from worldly distractions, ran the argument, so he could dedicate himself solely to his work.[70]

High Commissioner Sir Miles Lampson (1880–1964, Lord Killearn from 1943) had taken up his post in Cairo in 1934, two years before Drioton. After growing up on an estate in Killearn, Scotland, and in a house in Mayfair, London, Lampson had entered diplomatic service straight out of Eton. Six feet five and 250 pounds, he had served as British minister to Peking and had his sights set on being viceroy of India. He arrived in Cairo a widower with two young daughters. Hosting a niece and her girl friend, the fifty-four-year-old Lampson "found his little dream girl in the seventeen-year-old barely five-feet-tall Jacqueline Castellani, one of London's debs of the year,"[71] and married before the year was out. The ties of the bride's father, Italian physician Sir Aldo Castellani, to Mussolini's Fascist regime soon became an embarrassment for his son-in-law Lampson.

Wrestling with the issue of succession to Antiquities director Lacau, whose retirement was set for March 1936, Lampson opined:

> My own inclination is to get such things [the directorship of the Antiquities Service] for our own people whenever we properly can! It's always a little galling to me that the Antiquities here should be French run.[72]

In the absence of a strong French candidate, he wondered about Egyptian Museum curator-in-chief Reginald Engelbach, a Briton. The Foreign Office, however, insisted on Britain's 1904 commitment to a French director. Lampson toyed with naming a Frenchman for only a year or two, leading the French to suspect he might be preparing the way for Selim Hassan.[73]

Nothing committed Egypt to Britain's 1904 agreement to reserve the Antiquities Service directorship for a Frenchman. In March 1936, the Wafdist al-Balagh came out for an Egyptian to succeed Lacau, and other papers took up the cause.[74] A local French journal suggested Sami Gabra. His old classmate Mahmud Hamza pressed his own case, claiming a degree that antedated Gabra's and discoveries in the Delta.[75] Selim Hassan's well-publicized Giza discoveries and new Vienna doctorate, however, made him the national favorite. He was close to the wing of the Wafd that would break away in 1937 under Ahmad Mahir, Mahmud al-Nuqrashi, and Ahmad Abd al-Wahhab to form the Saadist Party.[76] Abd al-Wahhab, finance minister in the transitional cabinets before the Wafd's 1936 victory, had been Hassan's classmate in Ahmad Kamal's pre-1914 Egyptology classes.

Lampson warned of a "drive to appoint an Egyptian, possibly Selim Hassan, though no Egyptian is really qualified,"[77] but as late as March 1936, he had not ruled Hassan out: "Took Godfrey out to see the Sphinx," reads his diary. "We were met there as usual by Selim Hassan," who had just cleared out the courtyard in front of the Sphinx and was arguing that the Sphinx represented not a pharaoh but the Sun God himself. 'Maybe he is right!'"[78] Howard Carter and Lt. Col. Percival Elgood told Lampson they were glad to see the last of Lacau,

> but what interested me particularly was that they both also seemed to think that there was much to be said for letting Selim Hassan have the job. I questioned them in turn pretty closely but they didn't shake in their opinion. Howard Carter, incidentally, was very contemptuous of Engelbach's qualifications.[79]

Engelbach backed his colleague Henri Gauthier for director general, with Mahmud Hamza as his deputy, and noted that it was Egyptians who had blocked Selim Hassan's election to the Institut égyptien. Over tea at the Residency, Lacau maintained that no Egyptian was qualified, Egyptians were resigned to a foreign director, and Gauthier and Drioton were strong candidates. Lampson declined to lobby for a Frenchman, however, and Drioton suspected that Newberry had persuaded Lampson that Hassan was pro-British.[80]

Al-Balagh came out for Selim Hassan on April 6, 1936, but with King Fuad's backing, Ali Mahir's caretaker cabinet decided for Drioton on April 23. Fuad died five days later, before a decree had been issued. Mahir was content to leave the unpopular announcement to the ensuing Wafdist government which emerged from the May 7 elections.

A decree combining the appointment of Drioton as director general and Selim Hassan as assistant director of the Antiquities Service on June 8, 1936, pleased no one. "The Abbé Drioton to the Antiquities Service: A Perpetual French Colonization," blared *Rose al-Youssef*; why would the [Wafdist] "Government of the People" name "this French priest," a mere assistant conservator at the Louvre with credentials inferior to Hassan's?[81] Haykal's Liberal Constitutionalist *al-Siyasa*, however, defended the choice of Drioton as a triumph of merit over nationality. Dismissing attacks on Drioton as infantile polemic, the French minister denigrated Hassan's education as "strictly primary" and "merely elementary" and called him "a rather mediocre student of the Abbé Drioton." "One has a hard time imagining an epigraphist ignorant of Greek and Latin;" the Rosetta Stone would have done him no good. In contrast, "l'Abbé Drioton himself, knows—like Champollion—besides Greek, Hebrew, Chaldean, Arabic, Syriac, and Coptic."[82]

Drioton arrived in Cairo to find the living room of the director's residence packed with royal mummies awaiting reinstallation in the museum. Ismail Sidqi had mockingly moved the mummies to Saad Zaghlul's neo-pharaonic mausoleum. One of the first acts of al-Nahhas's government was to send them back to the museum and to bury Zaghlul in state in the mausoleum built for him. For a time, Drioton had to conduct morning mass among the mummies, with his mother the only other living soul in the congregation.[83]

Drioton, with Engelbach in tow, called on Lampson, who took to the

> attractive, jovial sort of cove with a cherubic countenance and, I should think a strongly developed sense of humour. I imagine he will prove to be an improvement on his predecessor, Lacau.[84]

Yet Hassan might have driven Drioton out, wrote the French minister,

> if archeological science and its representative in Egypt [Drioton] had not found an unexpected, determined, and persistent champion, in the person of King Farouk.... He inherited from his father the conviction that Egyptian antiquity is one of the key sources of modern Egyptian brilliance, and that without foreigners, Egyptians are not yet capable of conserving and bringing it to light.[85]

Lampson too noted sixteen-year-old Faruq's

> keenness in antiquities and archaeological research, and he jestingly threw across the table a telegram which he had just received from London informing him of the purchase on his behalf of a series of "lots" at a sale just held at Sotheby's. These were all Egyptian antiquities. He also spoke most appreciatively of the Abbé Drioton. He continued that at his age they must not expect it to be all work and no play.[86]

"The Sovereign of Egypt and the able Canon of the Nancy Chapter [Drioton], successor of Mariette and of Maspero," wrote the French minister, hit it off on a tour of Upper Egypt. One of the stops was at Tuna al-Gebel, where Sami Gabra showed the young king the results of the university's excavations (see fig. 59).

By Drioton's account, Faruq tired of Selim Hassan's recommendations that he buy mediocre antiquities at high prices and turned for advice to himself instead. Drioton became the young king's antiquities mentor in a relationship that would last until the end of the reign (see fig. 60).

At Karnak, Faruq's sisters had trouble with Hassan's poor English and turned with relief to Drioton's French. (That Arabic was not employed for this Egyptian-to-Egyptian communication speaks volumes about the semicolonial age). Drioton said that Hassan had confused the sacrificial bull at Abydos with the Apis bull, and that at Asyut he pronounced genuine a fake antique necklace presented to the king.[87]

King Fuad had already enlisted ancient Egyptian props in presenting Prince Faruq as the heir to a would-be absolutist throne presumed to date back to the pharaohs. In 1933, the government had proclaimed the thirteen-year-old prince Grand Scoutmaster of Egypt. Four years later in 1937, after Faruq had already been on the throne for a year, a scouting magazine still showed him as Grand Scoutmaster in front of a Greco–Roman era temple relief (see fig. 61).

59 Sami Gabra (center) shows King Faruq (left) the ruins of Hermopolis West (Tuna al-Gebel) on the royal tour of Upper Egypt. *Al-Hilal 45, no. 4, Feb. 1937*, 410.

60 Young King Faruq (left) and his antiquities mentor Étienne Drioton, director general of the Antiquities Service. *Courtesy of Keystone Press Agency.*

The tarbooshed youth blocks out the figure of the pharaoh on the scene behind, so two goddesses with the respective crowns of Upper and Lower Egypt appear to be installing Faruq in office instead.[88]

The Liberal Constitutionalist *al-Siyasa al-usbuiya* had a different slant on Faruq's Upper Egyptian antiquities tour. After Drioton and Howard Carter had shown the king the sites of Thebes and explained the ankh as the "key of life" and the scarab as "the key of happiness," he produced a Quran from his pocket. Retorting "This is the key of happiness; it is the key of life," he kissed it and left.[89]

Engelbach from the museum and Walter Bryan Emery from Saqqara plied Lampson with anti–Selim Hassan stories. Drioton believed Hassan was bent on driving Europeans out of the Antiquities Service through bureaucratic harassment and scurrilous attacks in the press. In September 1936, IFAO director Pierre Jouguet reported that Hassan, wanting Saqqara to himself, had shaved two months off Emery's and Jean-Philippe Lauer's expected ten-month contracts and canceled the concession of Swiss archaeologist Gustave Jéquier.[90]

Accusations in the Arabic press in May 1937 that Lampson was digging illegally in Fayoum turned him irrevocably against Hassan. Lampson had taken over the old University of Michigan dig house at Kom Aushim (Karanis) as a weekend retreat.[91] A year and a half earlier, he had written in his diary:

> When we were groping about in the ruins last night I thought it would be rather interesting to get in a few local men to clear out one of the old houses for us, so this morning 2 diggers and 5 boys were turned on to the job to remove the rubbish. It suddenly occurred that this might be breaking some law or other, so I summoned Engelbach in order to ask him. He was frankly horrified! I explained that the whole thing was merely amusement and not serious digging in any shape or form. Furthermore, if so be we did find anything of the slightest interest they could of course most willingly have it. He said that was not the point. It was true that Kom Aushim was comparatively modern and contained nothing of any real interest to the Department of Antiquities, nothing being older than 250 AD, but there was a very strict law which had just been tightened up, to prevent digging anywhere in Egypt save under the most strict conditions. No doubt if I chose to dig no one would be able to stop me, but he was afraid that if it got out mountains would be made out of mole-hills. . . . Seeing that there was nothing to be done I said "Very Well," and then and there told Flower to telephone at once to Kom Aushim and tell them to call off the diggers! But maybe I may be able to wangle something, for it is really quite absurd that with a mass of ruins at one's very door one should not be allowed to poke about amongst them for one's own amusement.[92]

Lacau hurried to the Residency, Lampson went on,

> with a vigorous appeal to me not to create difficulties for him by starting digging operations at Kom Aushim! I told him he really need not be uneasy. All that I proposed to do was rummage about on my evening walks with a stick amongst the ruins. I had never contemplated anything in the nature of serious diggings. He said they had to be terribly careful. For years they had struggled to get a good law regarding unauthorized

diggings in Egypt, and he might mention to me confidentially that one of the worst transgressors had been Lord Kitchener who had had several private diggings of his own. . . .

I assured him once more that he need not be uneasy; at the same time I certainly could not give him any promise that I should not continue my evening perambulations amongst the ruins in Kom Aushim, or indulge in gentle proddings of the dump heaps with my walking stick.[93]

Now, in May 1937, Lampson wrote that Drioton had reported

a perfect deluge daily of telegrams coming to the Department from their ghaffir [watchman] out at Kom Aushim; all sorts of suggestions that I was removing valuable objects and bringing them to Cairo, and so on. Clearly all this was the greatest nonsense and it was an example of the mischief-maker that Selim Hassan was.[94]

Lampson showed Drioton his few recent finds, declaring

that of course the Museum could have the whole lot with the greatest joy; indeed if he thought it better I was more than prepared to stop all digging operations. Drioton said that that would be quite unnecessary, but what he would like to do would be to come out one day and see what we were doing so that no one could in the future suggest that anything irregular or not entirely above board was being done. . . . And in order to make the thing completely watertight he would force Selim to come out with him. I said I thought that would be an excellent scheme. . . .[95]

The Abbé Drioton, Selim Hassan, Hamilton and Gayer Anderson came out to tea. First of all I showed them all the [?] we had found which interested them mildly; then after tea I took them up to see the actual house we had emptied amongst the ruins. I had made a point of explaining that the moment I had heard rumors that all was not regarded as being properly in order, I had stopped the "dig" and, looking meaningly at Selim Hassan, I told him that I had become aware that reports containing all sorts of ridiculous allegations had been circulating in the Department of Antiquities. . . . Selim Hassen was evidently uneasy about this, for he was profuse in professions of willingness to help in every possible way.[96]

In the end, Prime Minister al-Nahhas made special arrangements to cover Lampson's digging.[97]

Lampson confided to Amin Uthman, an Oxford- and Paris-educated confidant of the British:

61 "His Majesty the Beloved King of Egypt and Grand Scoutmaster": Boy Scout Faruq against a pharaonic backdrop. Faruq's then still-slim figure blocks out the figure of the pharaoh, so the flanking goddesses wearing the crowns of Lower and Upper Egypt seem to be blessing the tarbooshed young monarch. *Cover of the scouting magazine* al-Dalil fi al-kashf, *April 15, 1937, as reproduced in Wilson Chacko Jacob,* Working Out Egypt: Effendi Masculinity and Subject Formation in Colonial Modernity, 1870–1940 *(Durham: Duke University Press, 2011), 120.*

I thought the man [Selim Hassan] was a public danger to Egypt. By intriguing he had had himself pushed into the Museum though his technical qualifications were sadly wanting. It was deplorable that a man of his poor caliber should be in a position of not only Egyptian but world responsibility. I could imagine what a figure of fun Egypt would cut if she were, for example, to be represented by Selim Hassan at some international scientific conference on antiquities. The man would be shown up to be an ignoramus and a buffoon at once. . . . When I had finished he said "it's time the man's neck was twisted" and indicated that he would proceed to see that his neck was so twisted. I hope that he may succeed—but one never knows with a slippery eel like Selim Hassan! Incidentally I warned Amin that Selim Hassan was under high protection. There had been a curious story just about the time when he was appointed of some not particularly reputable incident in which Selim Hassan and Abdel Wahab had become mixed up in the affairs of some not too virtuous lady. But this was scandal and I only mentioned it to him just to indicate that Selim Hassan had enjoyed protection in high places.[98]

Drioton complained to Lampson that

Selim Hassan was quite intolerable. He was upsetting everything, was a complete ignoramus and, in short, was proving absolutely perdition to the antiquities department. He would give anything to get rid of him; in fact the thought had passed through his mind that if at any time we were organizing a Museum or Service of Antiquities up in the Sudan it would be a blessed opportunity to take Selim over and put him in charge of it.[99]

It would hardly have been the first time an out-of-favor Egyptian official had been banished to the Sudan.

Drioton blamed Selim Hassan for press attacks in August 1937 holding European officials responsible for thefts from the museum. In the fall, Drioton reported that Hassan was trying to get rid of Gauthier and Engelbach at the museum and Lauer and Emery at Saqqara. Emery and Engelbach added that Hassan's mentor Junker might be plotting to bring in German replacements. Under pressure from the British and French embassies, Emery's and Lauer's contracts were renewed in April 1938.[100] The retirement of Secretary General Gauthier, who had been leapfrogged by Hassan's appointment, weakened French influence in the Antiquities Service.[101]

Unless more sources vindicating Hassan come to light, there is little to weigh against the views of his European detractors, who were struggling to perpetuate the colonial order. In addition to Newberry's early support for Hassan, George Reisner's views, at least as late as 1938, offer a partial antidote to scathing depictions of Hassan. Reisner had Hassan join a radio broadcast to America in February 1938, with Hassan speaking on the stela in front of the Sphinx.[102] Three months later, Reisner reported that

Selim Bey is composing a book on his excavations at the Sphinx and has sought my advice and assistance. He came himself and we talked for over an hour. He showed a very real friendliness.[103]

Reisner thought favorable publicity in the Arabic press for his own work at Giza was "probably generated by Selim Bey Hasan."

A photo of the division of antiquities at Harvard Camp, Giza, in 1937 conceals the Drioton–Hassan enmity but provides a revealing study of hierarchies of power (fig. 62). Expedition director George Reisner stands in the center, separating two mortal enemies—Selim Hassan and Antiquities director general Drioton. Moving outward and down the social scale,

62 Hierarchies of power and peripheries: Seasonal division of the finds at Harvard Camp, Giza, 1937. Director of the Harvard–Boston Museum of Fine Arts Expedition George Reisner (floppy hat) is in the center, with director general of the Antiquities Service Étienne Drioton on his left. Reisner separates Drioton from his adversary, Selim Hassan, assistant director of antiquities. Next come antiquities inspector Abd es Salam Effendi (on Hassan's right) and Reisner's assistant Evelyn Perkins (on Drioton's left). On the far left is *rais* (foreman) Mahmud Said, and on the far right an unidentified Egyptian chauffeur. *Photograph by Mohammedani Ibrahim. Courtesy of the Museum of Fine Arts, Boston, as shown in Goode,* Negotiating for the Past, *123.*

Antiquities inspector Abd es Salam Effendi is on Hassan's right and Reisner's assistant Evelyn Perkins on Drioton's left. Further out and down, Reisner's *rais* Mahmud Said and an unidentified chauffeur in effendi dress occupy the peripheries. Except for the *rais*, no manual laborers are included.

By May 1938, with King Faruq's support, Drioton felt ready for a showdown.[104] In October 1938, Selim Hassan's superior, minister of education Muhammad Husayn Haykal, set up a commission of inquiry and warned him to hire a lawyer. Hassan's assistant on excavations at Saqqara, Zaki Saad, had saved the account books "which Hassan wanted to burn."[105] Emery had a seat on the commission and kept Lampson informed. The commission accused Hassan of embezzling £E10,000 in excavation funds and hosting parties at the Antiquities Service rest house at Giza which compromised the reputations of politicians and women from well-known families. In January 1939, the commission sent its report to the parquet (prosecutor's office), and Hassan was put on leave.

Lampson blamed Prime Minister Muhammad Mahmud, other ministers, and Ali Mahir (chief of the palace cabinet) for protecting Hassan, partly out of fear of blackmail. Lampson also blamed Hassan for an Arabic press campaign that began in February 1939, four months before Drioton's contract came up for renewal. Curator-in-chief Engelbach was blamed for thousands of objects allegedly being missing from the Egyptian Museum.[106] Drioton urged the Foreign Office to bolster Engelbach with an honorary degree from a British university. Liverpool University quickly awarded Emery an honorary MA, but it was too late in the year for Engelbach.[107]

In June 1939, minister of education Haykal drafted a decree dividing the Antiquities Service into administrative and scientific sides, to be headed respectively by an Egyptian and by Drioton. The decree also unified the Egyptian, Greco–Roman, Coptic, and Arab Art museums under the Antiquities Service. Faruq, however, refused to sign and assured Drioton that his contract would be renewed for a year.[108]

Once he had his own contract in hand, Drioton suspended Hassan, only to have Haykal make him inspector of history teaching in the schools. Lampson protested to Prime Minister Muhammad Mahmud, who replied that the parquet had cleared Hassan of wrongdoing. Lampson observed that Hassan had powerful protectors; Mahmud agreed and dropped the subject. King Faruq forced Haykal to annul the history inspectorship and told Drioton that Hassan would soon be arrested. In August 1939, however, Ali Mahir returned as prime minister. Mahmud al-Nuqrashi, a Saadist friend of Hassan's, became minister of education and made Hassan an adviser; again Faruq blocked the appointment. On September 3, 1939—as Europe plunged into war—Faruq, Lampson, and Drioton settled for partial victory: the cabinet censured Hassan and retired him on pension. This shielded him from further prosecution, but it also drove him from public life for a dozen years.[109] The evidence against him reported in British and French archives seems strong, but no court convicted him of a crime. His opponents were fighting to preserve the colonial order, and Egyptian sources which might favor his case have yet to come to light.

In one last twist, Drioton survived what he assumed was a plot by Selim Hassan to frame him in a scandal. One day at the museum, a woman screamed for help from behind Drioton's closed office door. Rescuers found her with clothing torn, but Drioton was sitting calmly behind his desk, smoking. Forewarned, he had hidden guards, who attested to his innocence. Christiane Desroches Noblecourt, who had the story from Drioton, identified the woman as Omm Seti. Omm Seti was Dorothy

Eady, Selim Hassan's eccentric British assistant. She had married an Egyptian and given birth to a son who was named Seti; following popular Egyptian custom, she became known henceforth as Omm Seti (the mother of Seti). Omm Seti believed she was a reincarnated pharaonic priestess and lover of Nineteenth Dynasty pharaoh Seti I.[110]

King Faruq was now able to arrange a three-year contract for Drioton and renewals for other European Antiquities officials. He was amenable to Sami Gabra's succeeding Hassan as assistant director of the Antiquities Service. Nothing came of it, probably, thought Drioton, because Gabra was a Copt. The post lapsed.[111]

The interplay of Western and national archaeology in interwar Iraq was both similar to and different from that in Egypt. Iraq too had major French, British, German, and American archaeological expeditions, both before World War I and between the wars. Iraq did not fall under British colonial control until World War I, and it trailed Egypt by six decades in establishing a museum and antiquities department (the 1920s instead of the 1850s). Nevertheless, Iraq was ahead of Egypt in winning enough independence to join the League of Nations (1932 vs. 1937), and it appointed its first national (rather than European) director of antiquities in 1934 instead of 1953. Iraq's first Arab director of antiquities was Arab nationalist Sati al-Husri. He shifted the emphasis from Sumerian, Babylonian, and Assyrian to Islamic-era monuments, excavating the Umayyad provincial capital of Wasit and establishing a Museum of Arab Antiquities. Al-Husri was forced out when the British reconquered Iraq in 1941, reinstating a pro-British order which lasted until the 1958 revolution. Iraqis continued to run their own antiquities department, but until 1958 the emphasis again reverted to pre-Islamic archaeology.[112]

In Egypt, Selim Hassan's challenge in the 1930s to European direction of the Antiquities Service failed. Even had his nationalist campaign succeeded, there would have been no swing from pre-Islamic to Islamic archaeology as with al-Husri in Iraq; Hassan was a proud Egyptologist. In the 1930s, both countries debated a stricter law on the division and export of archaeological finds. Iraq passed such a law in 1936, but foreign pressure derailed the effort in Egypt. The practical effects may not have been very different, however. As the Depression deepened and World War II closed in, foreign excavations in both Iraq and Egypt fell off sharply for two decades.

The Dwindling of the Foreign Expeditions

Despite uncertainties after the quarrels over Tutankhamun, the proposed Rockefeller museum, and the ending of excavators' presumed entitlement to 50 percent of their finds, the 1930s opened with American, French,

British, and German expeditions busily at work. Reisner's Harvard–Boston MFA expedition fared well in Lacau's divisions of finds, and even Lacau's old adversary Breasted obtained a colossal statue of Tutankhamun for the Oriental Institute's museum. In 1931, the OI's splendid Chicago House on the east bank at Luxor seemed a vote of confidence in the future of Western archaeology in Egypt.

There was even some backwash to Egypt from British-controlled Palestine, whence Petrie and Breasted's proposed Rockefeller museum had fled. Alan Rowe, director of the University of Pennsylvania's Beisan expedition, complained that John Garstang's successor at the Palestine Antiquities Department was retaining an unfair share of finds in order to fill the nascent Jerusalem museum. Rowe left Palestine in protest, and Lacau welcomed him back to Egypt with a concession at Meidum. Rowe reported

> Now that the Nationalist party no longer exists in Egypt, and the country is ruled by a purely business government, the anti-foreign feeling has died down, with the result that the divisions of antiquities are much better than in the past. I know for a fact that Dr. Reisner had a very good division last year. . . .
>
> Owing to the fact that we refused to take sides in the Howard Carter controversy over the tomb of Tut-ankh-Amen, our relationship with the Cairo Museum are of the friendliest nature, and M. Lacau has often asked me when we are going to excavate in Egypt. The divisions are certainly much fairer than in Palestine, for there is none of that grab-all spirit which unfortunately exists in Jerusalem. Lacau passed a very good division.[113]

In 1935, pressed by Alan Gardiner and Britain's Joint Archaeological Committee, Lampson persuaded Egypt to abandon plans for a more restrictive Antiquities law.[114]

Nevertheless, the tide turned in the mid-1930s against Western hopes for liberal export of finds. Palace governments inclined to collude with foreign interests gave way to a Wafdist one in 1936, and Selim Hassan launched his bid to take over the Antiquities Service. The prolonged depression in the West cut into private and public resources for overseas archaeology. Nicholas Reeves wrote that tightening regulations on the export of finds induced the EEF in 1936 and the Metropolitan Museum of Art to leave Egypt. Gady points out that no new antiquities legislation was actually passed,[115] but with Selim Hassan looking over his shoulder, Drioton had to be cautious in clearing items for export.

In 1935, two decades after Petrie launched *Ancient Egypt* and a decade after he decamped for Palestine, the magazine (which had changed its title to *Ancient Egypt and the East*) breathed its last.[116] In 1936, Robert

Greg lamented that the EES was quitting Tell al-Amarna and abandoning Egypt for the Sudan. Robert Mond's expedition at Armant continued, but his "wife hates his activities in Upper Egypt and he has not been out here for some time past."[117] Americans were leaving too, said Greg. The Metropolitan had stopped digging at Lisht in 1934 and, after twenty-four seasons, at Thebes in 1936.[118] Only photographer Harry Burton and his wife stayed on in the Metropolitan House at Deir al-Bahari.[119] At Giza, "Old Reisner is nearly blind and occupies himself entirely in getting on with his belated publications." Greg might have added that the OI stopped digging at Medinat Habu in 1932, Pennsylvania wound up at Meidum in 1932, and Michigan left Karanis in 1935.

Breasted's death in December 1935 spared him the news that staggered his successor John Wilson a few weeks later—drastic budget cuts and staff reductions for the Oriental Institute. Battered by the Depression, John D. Rockefeller Jr. and the Rockefeller boards awarded a terminal grant to the OI. With his annual budget slashed by two-thirds, Wilson had to drop from nine OI expeditions to two—the Epigraphic Survey at Luxor and a small expedition in one other country focused on a clearly delineated problem.[120] Perhaps the only silver lining was that the pause in fieldwork for nearly a quarter of a century gave scholars like Wilson, Dows Dunham of the MFA, and William Hayes of the Metropolitan a chance to work on materials and records accumulated from several active decades in the field. Their students and successors in Chicago, Boston, and New York are still continuing the task.[121]

Had Greg surveyed beyond "Anglo-Saxon" archaeologists, he would have found that the French, Germans, and Italians—with better government funding—were still digging. Indeed, Kaimierz Michalowski and Jean Capart, founding fathers respectively of Polish and Belgian field Egyptology, began their first major excavations in 1937. Michalowski excavated jointly with IFAO at Edfu, while Capart, making his headquarters in the landmark villa Somers Clarke had built in 1906, began exploring al-Kab. Capart made up for Belgium's belated start in Egyptology. In 1923 he escorted the queen of Belgium on a visit to Tutankhamun's tomb and persuaded her to set up the Fondation Égyptologique Reine Élisabeth. Under its auspices, he began bringing out the influential Egyptological review *Chronique d'Égypte* in 1925–26.[122]

World War II, however, soon interrupted all this. The German onslaught of Poland on September 1, 1939, ended all prospects for Egyptian fieldwork for Junker and Roeder. As the world waited through the winter for the German invasion of France, the thinned ranks of French and Italian excavators eked out a last Egyptian season. Pierre

Montet of the University of Strasbourg kept on at Tanis and Bernard Bruyère at Deir al-Medina. IFAO also sponsored Alexandre Varille's and Christiane Desroches's 1940 season at the temple of Montu at Karnak. Mussolini's delaying entry into the war until June 1940 enabled Italians to dig at Arsinoe (Sheikh Ibada) into the spring of that year.[123]

Montet's first decade at Tanis climaxed with discoveries in March 1939 and again in the winter-spring season of 1940. Irregularities in an enclosure wall led him to the intact royal tombs of the Twenty-First and Twenty-Second Dynasties. Groundwater and humidity had destroyed the organic material, unlike in Tutankhamun's tomb, but the objects of stone, jewels, and precious metals would have made a worldwide sensation had war news not crowded them out. Montet's assistant Georges Goyon (1905–96), who had been born in Egypt and learned Arabic growing up in the Canal Zone, was mobilized in the French Army of the Orient in Syria. During the winter-spring lull of 1940, however, General Weygand seconded him to Tanis to help excavate the royal necropolis before war closed in. Drioton kept his eager pupil King Faruq abreast of the finds. Faruq visited Tanis twice in 1940, urging Montet to continue digging there later than usual into the spring.[124] Hearing that Goyon was an expert marksman, the young king challenged him to a competition on the spot. The two hit it off, and Faruq later personally commissioned archaeological investigations by Goyon, as will be seen in chapter 11. Goyon later vigorously defended the much-maligned king: "He was the first king who had known, not without pain and sacrifices, how to make Egypt really independent since the time of the Ptolemies."[125]

Before pursuing Egyptian archaeology into the war years and beyond in chapter 11, chapter 10 revisits the 1930s to examine debates over pharaonism among Egyptian nonspecialists and to follow this theme through to the 1952 revolution.

10

Pharaonism and Its Challengers
in the 1930s and 1940s

> This is an ancient people. If you take one of these peasants and remove
> his heart, you'll find in it the residue of ten thousand years of experiential
> knowledge one layer on top of the other, but he's not aware of it.
> —fictional archaeologist Monsieur Fouquet in Tawfiq al-Hakim's
> *Return of the Spirit* (*Awdat al-Ruh*)

Facts bore out the French archaeologist's opinion: "A nation which at the
dawn of humanity brought forth the miracle of the pyramids will be able
to bring forth another miracle . . . or several. They claim this nation has
been dead for centuries, but they have not seen its mighty heart reaching
toward the sky from the sands of Giza. Egypt has created her heart with
her own hands in order to live eternally." Perhaps the archaeologist who
lived in the past saw the future of Egypt better than anyone else. [1]

The immediately preceding and following chapters of this book
concentrate on Egyptology as practiced by Egyptians and Westerners in Egypt. This chapter turns to expressions of pharaonism
among the wider Egyptian public in the 1930s and 1940s, as well as to
Egyptians who opposed turning to pharaonic history and antiquities for
contemporary inspiration. There is something of a scholarly consensus
that in the 1930s, the territorial Egyptian nationalism of the 1920s—and
the pharaonism usually associated with it—retreated under challenges
from proponents of Islamic and Arab aspects of Egyptian national identity.
The pharaonist cultural landmarks of the 1930s—Saad Zaghlul's tomb,
Mukhtar's Alexandria and Cairo statues of Zaghlul, and al-Hakim's *Return
of the Spirit*—were to some extent belated expressions conceived in the
pharaonist heat of the 1920s. In the 1930s, the literary leaders of "the

generation of 1919"—Muhammad Husayn Haykal, Mahmud al-Aqqad, and Taha Hussein—shifted to writing biographies of the Prophet Muhammad, the Rashidun caliphs, and early Islamic heroes. The excitement over Tutankhamun also receded, and no archaeological discovery of the 1930s and 1940s came close to rivaling the sensation of finding his tomb.

Without contesting that pharaonism receded and was thrown on the defensive in the 1930s and 1940s, however, this chapter argues that its retreat was not the rout that is often assumed. Salama Musa, for example, continued to champion pharaonism. Others deplored pitting pharaonism against Arabism and Islam as a false dichotomy and insisted on embracing the entire Egyptian past. Even those uninterested in ancient Egypt appreciated that the country was now producing its own Egyptologists, that Selim Hassan and Sami Gabra—not just foreigners—were making significant finds, and that Egyptians were gradually replacing Europeans in the Antiquities Service. Among the younger generation, Ahmad Husayn of Young Egypt was captivated by pharaonic history, King Faruq became an avid collector of antiquities, schoolboy Gamal Abdel Nasser thrilled to al-Hakim's *Return of the Spirit*, and Naguib Mahfouz set his first three novels in ancient Egypt.

Chapter 10 opens with Tawfiq al-Hakim's pharaonist masterpiece *Return of the Spirit* and examines Salama Musa's championing of pharaonism. It analyzes Islamist and Arabist challenges to pharaonism, primarily as played out in the press, and notes the partial fading of Tutankhamun in national consciousness. Next, it examines the dedications of Saad Zaghlul's tomb and Mukhtar's Cairo and Alexandria statues of him as cases of "belated monumental pharaonism," then two cases of youthful "pharaonic mania" in the 1930s—Ahmad Husayn of Young Egypt and Naguib Mahfouz in his first three novels. The chapter concludes with the assessment that the assumption that pharaonism had nearly vanished by the late 1940s is wide of the mark.

Tawfiq al-Hakim's *Return of the Spirit (Awdat al-Ruh)*

Return of the Spirit came out in a discouraging year. In 1933 Hitler came to power, and the Great Depression was in full swing. In Egypt, Abd al-Fattah Yahya followed Ismail Sidqi at the head of the repressive palace regime of King Fuad, which had swept aside the 1923 constitution. The Liberal Consitutionalists and the Wafd Party both seemed locked out. Outside and below parliamentary politics, radical groups like the Muslim Brothers (al-Ikhwan al-Muslimin) and Young Egypt (Misr al-Fatah) attracted underemployed, educated youths fed up with the status quo. Such was the milieu in which al-Hakim's *Return of the Spirit* was published. However, it had been written five years earlier in Paris, when pharaonism was still riding high.

Al-Hakim's Mr. Black, the obtuse English irrigation engineer who serves as foil to the sensitive French archaeologist in *Return of the Spirit*, has no inkling of the pharaonic heritage coursing through the veins of the fellahin or of the approaching climactic upheaval:

> In the month of March [1919], at the beginning of spring, the season of creation, resurrection, and life, the trees turned green with new leaves. Their branches conceived and bore fruit.
>
> Egypt too, in the same manner, conceived and bore in her belly an awesome child. The Egypt that had slept for centuries in a single day arose to her feet. She had been waiting, as the Frenchman said, waiting for her beloved son [Zaghlul], the symbol of her buried sorrows and hopes, to be born anew, And this beloved was born again from the body of the peasant.
>
> By sunset that day Egypt had become a fiery mass. Fourteen million people were thinking of only one thing: a man who expressed their feelings, who arose to demand their rights to freedom and life. He [Zaghlul] had been taken and imprisoned and banished to an island in the middle of the seas.
>
> Osiris, who had brought reconciliation to the land of Egypt, who gave it life and light, was also taken, imprisoned in a box, and banished, in scattered pieces, in the depths of the waters.
>
> Cairo was turned head over heels. Stores, coffee shops, and residences were closed. Lines of communications were disrupted. Demonstrations were widespread. The same agitation arose in all the regions and throughout the countryside. The farm workers were even more vigorous than the city dwellers in their protests and anger. They cut rail lines to prevent military trains from arriving. They set fire to police stations.[2]

Tawfiq al-Hakim (1898–1987) is usually grouped with Taha Hussein, Muhammad Husayn Haykal, and Salama Musa as one of the literary lights *(udaba)* of the generation of 1919, who experienced that critical upheaval in their late twenties or early thirties.[3] However, because al-Hakim was a few years younger and slow to complete his formal schooling, he experienced 1919 as secondary school student. His grandfather, a classmate of Muhammad Abduh's at al-Azhar, had settled on a rural Delta estate near Damanhur. Al-Hakim's father had coedited a magazine at the Cairo School of Law with fellow students Ismail Sidqi and Ahmad Lutfi al-Sayyid. Al-Hakim's mother, Asma al-Bustami, was of proud her Turkish lineage, looked down on her husband's peasant roots, and tried in vain to make their son a Turkish aristocrat.

His father's transfers as a state official disrupted al-Hakim's schooling, and his passion for the theater slowed his academic progress. Living
with uncles in Sayyida Zaynab, Cairo, he graduated from the Muhammad
Ali Secondary School in 1921. His father insisted that he go on to the
School of Law, from which he graduated in 1925. His father was furious
to discover that he had been writing plays for a theatrical troupe under
a pseudonym. His juvenile plays included a never-performed pharaonic
comedy, *Aminosa* (1922), an adaptation from Alfred de Musset's *Carmo-
sine*. Aminosa, the daughter of a court physician, falls in love with a man
she mistakes for the pharaoh.[4]

Naively hoping to get him away from the theater, al-Hakim's father
followed Lutfi al-Sayyid's advice to send him to Paris for a doctorate
in law. In Paris, al-Hakim plunged into theatrical life instead. In 1928,
with a doctorate nowhere in sight, his father ordered him home. Al-
Hakim's ensuing work in the legal service in Tanta and Dissuq provided
rich material for his satirical *Yawmiyat naib fi-l-aryaf* (Diary of a Country
Prosecutor, Cairo, 1937).[5] In 1943 he left state service to concentrate on
writing. In 1951, minister of education Taha Hussein lured him back as
director of the Egyptian National Library. Al-Hakim treated the post as a
sinecure which enabled him to write.

Like Haykal a quarter of a century earlier, al-Hakim had been homesick in Paris when he wrote a landmark novel romanticizing Egyptian
rural life. He sprinked quotations from the *Book of the Dead* through
Return of the Spirit and treated Saad Zaghlul's exile and triumphant return
in 1919 as a recapitulation of the murder and resurrection of Osiris. Al-
Hakim's alter ego, Muhsin, is a schoolboy living with relatives in Sayyida
Zaynab. He and his uncles compete for the attention of a beautiful neigh-
bor, Saniya, the daughter of a medical doctor: "Her hair was cut short too
and was a gleaming black as well . . . and rounded like an ebony moon:
Isis!"[6] On a visit to the family estate, Muhsin meets French archaeologist
Monsieur Fouquet[7] and Mr. Black, a British irrigation engineer. A mysti-
cal Russian writer influenced al-Hakim's belief, voiced by Fouquet, in the
fellahin as unconscious heirs of pharaonic ancestors.[8] In the end, Muhsin
and his uncles sublimate their longing for Saniya into the 1919 uprising.
The pharaonist patriotism of *Return* inspired a new generation, not least
Gamal Abdel Nasser.[9]

Al-Hakim's law school contemporary Yahya Haqqi (1905–93) also
wrote pharaonist fiction in the 1930s. Like al-Hakim, he was struck by
the gulf separating a young lawyer from Cairo from the peasants—Upper
Egyptians from near Manfalut in Haqqi's case. Haqqi too suggested that
the fellahin had an "uncontaminated connection with the great pharaonic

past."[10] He did not publish his Upper Egyptian short stories until the 1950s, however, and is mainly remembered for his short story "The Lamp of Umm Hashim" ("Qandil Umm Hashim," 1944). Set in Sayyida Zaynab, it treats the clash of scientific medicine with popular belief in the healing power of lamp oil from a saint's tomb. Although of Turkish stock like al-Hakim's mother, Haqqi's family mingled with working-class neighbors in Sayyida Zaynab. Haqqi himself left for a career in the foreign service.

Salama Musa, Champion of Pharaonism

If Haykal's articles constituted the leading pharaonist manifesto of the 1920s, and al-Hakim's *Return of the Spirit* was the leading pharaonist literary work published in the early 1930s, Salama Musa (1887–1958) was the most persistent pharaonist writer throughout the interwar era.[11] His birth in 1887 situates him squarely in the generation of 1919 with Haykal. Haykal's "Islamic turn" in the 1930s seemed to call his earlier pharaonism into question, whereas Musa—a Copt—continued to defend the pharaonism and the Fabian socialism he had settled upon years earlier in Edwardian England.

Born in Zaqaziq, Sharqiya, in the Delta, Musa studied in both a Muslim and a Coptic *kuttab* before switching to a state primary school. He remembered the Khedival Secondary School, from which he graduated in 1907, as "a succession of punishments" by English school masters "who took pleasure in our suffering." The early death of his father, a government clerk, left him an inheritance in land which yielded £E25–30 a month— three times the salary of a government official with a secondary degree. This enabled Musa to spend a year studying in Paris and four years in London. Challenged in Paris by questions about pharaonic Egypt he could not answer, he signed on for a Cook's tour of Upper Egypt and plunged into two months' reading on ancient Egypt. Eighty years earlier, it had also been in Paris that Rifaa al-Tahtawi had first discovered the pharaohs.

Both the socialist magazine Musa founded in 1913 and the socialist party he cofounded in 1920 soon foundered. As editor from 1923 to 1929 of *al-Hilal*, which Syrian Christian immigrant Jurji Zaydan had founded in 1892, Musa strengthened the magazine's pharaonist tint. The late founder's son Émile Zaydan gave Musa scant credit, and Musa thought Zaydan too favorable to the king. In 1929 Musa broke away to issue his own *al-Majalla al-jadida*, which imitated *al-Hilal*'s popular picture-rich format. He attacked Syrian immigrants like the Zaydans, who had been so prominent in Egypt's early Arabic press. He briefly joined Fathy Radwan, coleader with Ahmad Husayn of the Piastre Plan and Young Egypt, in calling for a Gandhi-style boycott of British goods. In 1931, Prime

Minister Ismail Sidqi closed Musa's magazine for attacking the king. It reappeared in 1933, after Sidqi stepped down.

In 1935 Musa published *Misr asl al-hadara* (Egypt, the Source of Civilization), basing it on the work of Sir Grafton Elliot Smith. Smith (1871–1937), as already noted, had dissected numerous mummies while professor of anatomy at the Cairo School of Medicine (1900–1909) before leaving for Manchester and then the University of London. Musa recounted how Smith had shown him the skulls of an ancient Egyptian and a modern Englishman to demonstrate homology between the two races.[12] Musa also drew on William James Perry's *Children of the Sun*, which expanded Smith's diffusion theory that all civilization had spread out from Egypt into a "Heliolithic" theory that sun worship and mega-lithic monuments across the world reflected Egyptian influence.[13]

"If you want honor and respect when you are traveling in Europe," pronounced Musa, "then say that you are Egyptian of Pharaonic descent."[14] He blamed his countrymen for neglecting this proud heritage. Champollion had opened the door, but with Muslim religious leaders denouncing the pharaohs as infidels *(kuffar)*, "we in Egypt remained ignorant of these antiquities. There was little on it in our schools, few books were written on it, and our magazines and newspapers didn't treat it. . . . No Egyptian knew the language of the ancient Egyptians."[15] Overlooking Rifaa al-Tahtawi and Ahmad Kamal, Musa associated Egypt's awakening to pharaonism with the 1919 revolution, independence, and Tutankhamun's tomb. Now Arabic papers were proudly reporting on the discoveries of Selim Hassan and Sami Gabra. Musa complained, however, that since Hassan's major publications were in English, they were easier for Londoners, Berliners, and New Yorkers to read than for Egyptians, "even though we are the sons of the pharaohs."

Musa asserted that both Muslim and Christian families were giving their children pharaonic names: Ramsis, Isis, Khufu, and Ahmus. He named his own son Khufu. Though in fact pharaonic names were far more popular among Copts than Muslims, pharaonism was indeed afoot. He might have cited Ali Pasha, the Ottoman governor of Epirus, who observed of Greeks on the eve of their war of independence: "You have something big in your head: you do not give your children names like Yannis, Petros, Kostas any more, but Leonidas, Themistocles, Aristides! You are planning something for sure."[16]

Musa noted that Coptic liturgy had preserved the ancient language and cited Lutfi al-Sayyid's assertion that modern Egyptians are racially closer to ancient Egyptians than to the conquering Arabs. Arabs, Turks, Circassians, and Britons had successively constituted only ruling classes in Egypt. Since many fellahin had converted to Islam, Muslim Egyptians had more pharaonic blood than did Copts, who had intermarried with Greeks. Musa called for committees in every town to distribute books on ancient Egypt. There was a film on Cleopatra; why not films on Akhenaten, Thutmose, and Ramesses? He hoped Zaghlul would soon be buried in the neo-pharaonic mausoleum intended for him. Paris, London, Washington,[17] and Istanbul all boasted Egyptian obelisks; Cairo should at least erect pharaonic statues in a few squares.

A year after *Misr asl al-hadara*, Musa contributed to a special issue of *al-Muqtataf* on "Turath Misr al-qadima" (The Heritage of Ancient Egypt). This was based on an American University in Cairo lecture series cosponsored by the Royal Papyrological Society. Contributors included Sami Gabra (Egyptologist), Mustafa Amer (geographer and prehistorian), Hassan Kamal (medical doctor), George Sobhy (physician and lecturer in Coptic), graduate students Husayn Munis and Gamal el-Din el-Shayyal (both later history professors), and several Egyptology graduates working in the Antiquities Service. *Al-Muqtataf*, which was edited by Christians of Lebanese origin, was careful to follow up this pharaonic issue with one on Islamic civilization.[18]

Deploring the retreat of secularism, Musa quoted Ahmad Lutfi al-Sayyid:

Egypt is the homeland of all Egyptians, Muslims, Christians, and Jews, non-believers and atheists, and there is no place for religion in patriotism. But Lutfi al-Sayyid is no longer writing. Muhibb al-Din al-Khatib [a proponent of Islamic revival] is writing. Thus the new generation does not know Lutfi al-Sayyid and *al-Jarida* in which Lutfi al-Sayyid fought the proponents of the Ottoman state and Islamic unity.[19]

Musa's influence waned as the 1940s wore on. Pharaonism had passed its peak, his Fabian socialism was too tame for Egypt's few Marxists, and he had nothing to say to the burgeoning Muslim Brothers. He tried to draw a veil over his youthful support of the British occupation and his later enthusiasm for the Nazis. In 1942, he turned *al-Majalla al-jadida* over to young Marxists, George Hunayn and surrealist painter Ramsis Yunan. Its offices became a meeting place for "Trotskyists" until the British had it closed in 1944.[20]

After having steered clear of Coptic communal issues most of his life, in 1942 Musa became editor of the Coptic daily *Misr* and began voicing Coptic grievances in the increasingly assertive Islamic atmosphere. His pharaonism would likely have appealed to *Misr*'s Coptic readers, but he wisely published his more politically radical articles elsewhere. In 1947 he endorsed an unsuccessful project for a Coptic-run Pharaonic Bank.[21] After the 1952 revolution, Musa edited the science section of *Akhbar al-yawm* until his death in 1958.

Challenges to Pharaonism and Territorial Nationalism: Easternism, Islamism, and Arabism

Israel Gershoni and Jim Jankowski have shown how Egyptian territorial nationalism, often tinged with pharaonism, was challenged in the 1930s by Easternism, Islamism, Arabism, and "Integral Egyptian nationalism." ("Integral Egyptian nationalism"—mainly Young Egypt—will be treated later in this chapter.) Easternism, Arabism, and Islamism all looked beyond Egypt's borders, reflecting a yearning to reconnect with a larger community such as that lost with the demise of the Ottoman Empire.

Easternism—like Orientalism and Western overseas imperialism—assumed a dichotomy between "East" and "West," however defined. Egypt's Arabic press liked to contrast a spiritually minded East with a materialist and imperialist West. Taha Hussein and Musa were among the minority of Egyptians in the 1930s who insisted that Egypt was an integral part of the Mediterranean world and therefore belonged on the Western side of any civilizational divide. It had nothing in common with China, for example.[22]

Islam, of course, had continued prominently in Egyptian discourse throughout the 1920s. It was central to calls to renew the caliphate after Kemal Atatürk's Turkish Republic deposed the last Ottoman caliph in 1924. King Fuad's caliphal dreams, however, never got much traction. Rashid Rida's *al-Manar* carried a torch for Islam through the 1920s. Muhibb al-Din al-Khatib, a Syrian immigrant like Rida, also carried on Jamal al-Din al-Afghani's and Muhammad Abduh's tradition of Islamic Salafi reform. Al-Khatib's magazine *al-Fath* did not last long, but his influence continued through the Young Men's Muslim Association. As its name suggests, it was founded in Cairo (1927) partly to counter the Young Men's Christian Association (YMCA). Appreciating the power of print, al-Azhar began publishing *Nur al-Islam* in 1931; in 1935–36 it became *Majallat al-Azhar*. In 1933 Ahmad Hassan al-Zayyat (1885–1968) added his Arab and Islamic-oriented magazine *al-Risala* to the scene. Like Taha Hussein, al-Zayyat had attended both al-Azhar and the private Egyptian University. Unlike Hussein, however, he had not gone on to study in Europe, and in the 1930s he emerged as a conservative, religious voice of the generation of 1919.[23]

The turn of Taha Hussein, Haykal, al-Aqqad, and Ahmad Amin from

Egyptian territorial nationalism in the 1920s to writing on the Prophet Muhammad and the Rashidun Caliphs in the 1930s reflected either personal shifts in belief or practical accommodation to a popular mood. Haykal's *Hayat Muhammad* (The Life of Muhammad), published serially and then in 1935 as a book, was very popular. He continued with biographies of the first three caliphs and reflections on a pilgrimage he made to Mecca. Haykal delegated editing *al-Siyasa al-usbuiya* to Mahmud Azmi, and the pharaonic winged sun disk on its masthead disappeared as it pursued a more Arab–Islamic appeal.[24] Taha Hussein published three volumes of stories on the early Islamic community (*Ala hamish al-sira*, 1933–43), al-Aqqad wrote biographies of the Prophet and first four caliphs, and Tawfiq al-Hakim wrote a play about the life of the Prophet. In 1939 Ahmad Amin's *al-Thaqafa* joined *al-Risala* as yet another forum for Arab and Islamic literary discussion.[25]

By the 1930s, this generation of 1919 was firmly entrenched as the establishment, and a younger generation was pushing onto the scene. The most influential young Islamist was Hassan al-Banna, the founder of the Muslim Brotherhood. Both he and Sayyid Qutb, who did not emerge as a controversial Brotherhood leader until after al-Banna's assassination in 1949, were born in 1906, attended Dar al-Ulum teachers college, and came of age in the 1920s. Al-Banna's father was a small landowner on the Rosetta branch of the Nile, ran a watch and clock repair shop, served as a part-time imam and muezzin in a mosque, and belonged to the Shadhili order of Sufis (Islamic mystics). Hassan thus grew up acquainted with both Sufism and the usually anti-Sufi Salafism of Muhammad Abduh and Rashid Rida. He graduated from Dar al-Ulum, a hybrid institution influenced both by the religious al-Azhar and the European-inspired state schools and later the Egyptian University. Al-Banna's Muslim Brotherhood movement has been called the Islam of the effendis, in contrast to that of the Azhar-trained sheikhs. The Brotherhood especially appealed to young immigrants to the cities whose secular schooling had left a spiritual void.

Al-Banna was only a twenty-one-year-old primary school teacher in the Suez Canal Company town of Ismailiya when he founded the Muslim Brothers in 1928. Four years later, he moved its headquarters to Cairo. Al-Banna's Brotherhood soon grew into the leading Islamist movement of the century. Like al-Afghani, Abduh, and Rida, it addressed not only Egyptians or Arabs but Muslims everywhere. Al-Banna set out to purify Islamic society, expel Western imperialism, and Islamize society and state.[26]

As for Arabism, Gershoni and Jankowski speak of "Egyptian Arab nationalism" to emphasize that Arab nationalism was not merely an import from Arab neighbors to the east. The language, culture, and history of the

Arabs provided the common denominators. Arabness was projected back not only onto Semites (Babylonians, Assyrians, Canaanites, Aramaeans, Hebrews, and Phoenicians) but sometimes even onto ancient Egyptians, Sumerians, and Hittites. Moses, Jesus, and Muhammad were hailed as Arab national heroes.[27] Cairo's Arab Language Academy, founded in 1932 under King Fuad's patronage, championed classical Arabic as a unifying force and denounced the promotion of vernacular Arabic literature as a Western imperialist plot to divide and conquer.

Across Egypt's Sinai border in Palestine, the general strike and revolt of 1936 drew Egypt deeper into the politics of its Arab neighbors. In 1945, the choice of Cairo for the headquarters of the League of Arab States and of Egyptian Abd al-Rahman Azzam as its first secretary general affirmed Egypt's centrality to Arabism. Arab nationalism in Egypt has been described as appealing broadly to

> Native Egyptians and Arab émigrés living in Egypt; Christians and Muslims; established politicians and radicals from the new extraparliamentary movements; older figures and the new effendiyya emerging in the 1930s and 1940s; Wafdists and Liberals; Palace and *"ulama."*[28]

Arab nationalism's appeal to Egypt's Copts, however, was severely limited compared to its attraction for Christians of the Fertile Crescent, especially the Greek Orthodox. Makram Ubayd (1889–1961) was one of the few Copts who emphasized Egypt's Arabness. Born in the same year as Taha Hussein and al-Aqqad, he was also, like them, a Saidi (Upper Egyptian) who came to the fore in the wake of the 1919 revolution. Unlike them, Ubayd was not a litterateur or scholar but a politician. He was born in Qena to a family from Asyut. His father prospered as a contractor when the railroad was extended south to Luxor and invested in land sold off from the royal estates. Ubayd inherited 150 feddans. His education was diverse—the American "college" in Asyut; Tawfiqiya Secondary School in Cairo; New College, Oxford (law, class of 1908); and the University of Lyons, where he studied for a doctorate in law. After five years' work in the Ministry of Justice, he resigned in 1918 in a dispute with judicial adviser William Brunyate. In 1919, William Makram Ubayd dropped the politically inconvenient "William" from his public persona and embraced Zaghlul and the 1919 revolution. Ubayd married the daughter of fellow Copt Murqus Hanna, the Wafd's first minister of justice. Chosen secretary general of the Wafd in 1927, Ubayd became right-hand man to Zaghlul's successor, Mustafa al-Nahhas. He served as al-Nahhas's finance minister in 1930, 1936–37, and 1942, then broke with the party and exposed its corruption in his "Black Book." Founding his own Wafdist Bloc (al-Kutla al-wafdiya), he served in several cabinets after the Wafd fell in 1944.[29]

Ubayd's embrace of Arab nationalism was designed to blunt Haykal's charge that undue Coptic influence made the Wafd excessively pharaonist. Speaking in Lebanon in 1931, Ubayd insisted that Egyptians and Arabs had a common origin and urged solidarity against the Zionist drive for a Jewish state.[30] In *al-Hilal* in April 1939, he proclaimed, "Egyptians are Arabs!" Egyptians had originated from "the Semitic stock which immigrated to our land from the Arabian Peninsula," and "We, the Egyptian community, came from Asia. Since antiquity we have been closely related to the Arabs in regard to color, language, Semitic character traits, and nationalism."[31]

Literary Wars over Pharaonism
Salama Musa's leaving *al-Hilal* in 1929 facilitated its shift to a more Arab emphasis. That same year Mahmud Azmi wrote in *al-Hilal*:

> I was personally liberated from the bondage of "Egyptianist Pharaonic" theory after I traveled to Palestine, Lebanon, and Syria and discovered the reality of the feelings of the people there towards Egypt and the extent of the relationship of all the regions which speak the Arabic language and are linked by Arab history.[32]

In 1930, the Egyptian University staged a debate: was Egypt's culture pharaonic or Arab? Muhammad Lutfi Juma argued for pharaonism and Egyptian uniqueness. Rashid Rida, seconded by law student Ahmad Husayn, carried the audience for Arabism and Islam by a vote of 187 to 103.[33] Some months later, Arabism won again when *al-Hilal* polled prominent Egyptians as to whether Egypt was "Pharaonic or Arabic or Western."[34]

In 1933, Taha Hussein's inclusion of the Arabs in a list of invaders who had inflicted "injustice" and "aggression" on Egypt provoked a storm of protest. Hassan al-Banna defended Arab rule in Egypt as "a spiritual, enlightening cultural imperialism," Abd al-Rahman Azzam asserted that "most of the blood of its [Egypt's] people is traceable to Arab veins," and Hassan al-Zayyat wrote: "as for the culture of papyrus, it has no connection with Arab Egypt, neither with the Muslims nor with the Copts." Taha Hussein's defenders emphasized Egypt's uniqueness and its distance from Arab culture, but in summing up, Azzam told a British official that Hussein felt defeated. Haykal, a Liberal Constitutionalist, and Abd al-Qadir Hamza, a Wafdist, rejected such polarizing debates, insisting that

Egypt was both pharaonic and Arab.[35]

In 1940, Abd al-Qadir Hamza (1880–1941) bucked the Arab and Islamic tide with a collection of essays *Ala hamish al-tarikh al-misri al-qadim* (On the Margins of the History of Ancient Egypt). Born in the Delta province of Buheira and educated at Alexandria's Ras al-Tin Secondary School and the Cairo School of Law, Hamza practiced law and assisted Lutfi al-Sayyid on *al-Jarida*. He edited *al-Ahali* in Alexandria (1910–23) and then the Wafdist *al-Balagh* in Cairo. In 1924, a visit to Tutankhamun's tomb awoke his interest in ancient Egypt. Like his mentor Lutfi al-Sayyid, Hamza lamented having learned nothing of the pharaohs in the schools in the 1890s:

> Thus it is for the educated among us; they know no more of the history of ancient Egypt than they know of Japan in Asia or of Canada in America. And they know more about past and present-day England or France than of Egypt. Thus the connection between ancient and modern Egypt is broken.[36]

"Advanced countries"—England, France, and Germany—taught patriotic national history in every grade. Taking stock, Hamza noted Ahmad Kamal's and Ahmad Naguib's Arabic works on ancient Egypt and a recent volume by Egyptian Museum officials. Kamal's son Dr. Hassan Kamal had translated Breasted's *History of Egypt*. The university taught Egyptology and sent graduates on to Germany. But why were there not hundreds of works in Arabic on the subject? Hamza did concede that in religion, ancient Egyptians had been only in "the stage of childhood," "believing things now known to be wrong."[37]

In 1938, an Arabic magazine asked how Arab culture could be revived. Husayn Fawzi retorted that Arab culture had died out with the Middle Ages and could not be revived. He admitted, however, that even among Egyptians, he was swimming against an Arab tide.[38]

Forgetting Tutankhamun

Tutankhamun had made too big a splash to be forgotten, but after Howard Carter finished work in the tomb in 1932 and published his third volume on the discovery in 1933, the pharaoh receded considerably in British and Egyptian collective memories for nearly thirty years.[39] The disputes over the tomb left a sour taste in both countries. The sixth earl of Carnarvon turned away from his father's Egyptian obsession, and Carter's projected six-volume scientific report never got off the ground. Like Coleridge's "Ancient Mariner," Carter haunted the terrace of the Winter Palace Hotel at Luxor, telling his tale to passing tourists for a few more seasons. In 1939 *The Times* punctured its near silence on Tutankhamun with a report on

BBC's broadcast of notes played on a trumpet from the tomb and with a notice on Carter's sparsely attended funeral.[40] With only minimal formal education, acutely sensitive to the social chasm separating him from his aristocratic patron, an embarrassment to British diplomats seeking an accommodation with Egyptians at a time of imperial retrenchment, the man who made the most sensational find in the history of archaeology died without imperial or academic honors from his own country.

During World War II, Tutankhamun listings in the quarterly indexes of *The Times* often plunged to zero. Still fearing diplomatic complications, the Foreign Office even declined to help Carter's executors discretely return a few pieces which Carter or Carnarvon had spirited out of the tomb. Other channels had to be found—the Egyptian Embassy in London, King Faruq, and his antiquities mentor Étienne Drioton.[41]

Egyptologists had their own reasons for steering clear.[42] T.G.H. James wrote:

> For someone like myself who grew up before the Second World War, and became a professional Egyptologist after the war, Tutankhamun and Howard Carter have been constant symbols of the popular appeal of Egypt, although for much of the time it would have been thought slightly *de trop* to show professionally too active an interest in them.[43]

James waited until retirement to publish his authoritative biography of Carter. The British Library listed only three books on Tutankhamun published between 1934 and 1960. The *Annual Egyptological Bibliography* averaged only two scholarly books or articles on him a year in the late 1940s and only 3.5 for 1950–56.[44] John Romer claimed that even in the 1960s, his frequent visits to the Valley of the Kings surprised older Egyptologists: "royal tombs were out of fashion."[45]

In Egypt, Tutankhamun, although no longer in the headlines, remained the central attraction in the Egyptian Museum and the Valley of the Kings. Until the 1960s, however, only Egyptians and the modest number of foreign tourists had access to these. The Depression, World War II, the 1948 Arab–Israeli War, the riots and revolution of 1952, and the 1956 Suez War all took their toll on tourism to Egypt.

Beginning in 1930, the £E1 banknote did keep Tutankhamun's portrait in the public eye, except when King Faruq's image briefly replaced it near the end of his reign (see fig. 63).[46]

What the pharaoh on the banknote meant to Egyptians, however, is elusive. Few people reflect on—or even notice—the images on their money, the issuing National Bank of Egypt was still British-controlled in the 1930s,[47] and

63 Remembering and forgetting Tutankhamun: Banknotes and postage stamps. Top row: £E1 banknote with portrait of Tutankhamun, design first issued 1930, National Bank of Egypt. First row of stamps: Tutankhamun's funerary mask, 1947. Second row of stamps: Lotus vase from his tomb, 1959. Third row: Three stamps out of a larger set show objects from his tomb, 1964. *From the collection of D. Reid.*

Islamic monuments often balanced off pharaonic images on the banknotes. The portrait, based on a statue of Tutankhamun rather than the iconic funerary mask, may have been seen as merely that of a generic pharaoh. The first Egyptian postage stamp to depict an object from his tomb did not appear until 1947, and it was on a semipostal stamp which few besides philatelists and the art world would likely have noticed (see fig. 63). Nor would many have recognized a lotus vase on a second stamp in 1959 as coming from the tomb. Only in 1964, when interest in Tutankhamun was beginning to revive worldwide, did a larger set with three items from the tomb, including one of the easily recognizable coffins, make something of a splash. Objects from the tomb have been popular on Egyptian stamps ever since.[48]

Belated Monumental Pharaonism: Commemorating Saad Zaghlul

The neo-pharaonic vogue in official architecture in Egypt lasted little more than a decade. The pharaonic columned hall in the parliament building inaugurated in 1924 was an early example. The French firm which designed a Cairo high court building in 1923 chose classical Roman style, as though in reference to the Roman-influenced law applied within. The pylon-like façade and bulk, however, did suggest the grandeur of a pharaonic temple. The pavilion of Cairo's *Exposition agricole et industrielle* of 1926, with a sphinx-lined entry, may have been Egypt's first entirely neo-pharaonic edifice. A garden created in Gezira in Cairo (1928–35) with pharaonic statuary ended up being incongruously named "al-Andalus Garden."[49]

Pharaonism was riding high when Mukhtar's statue *Revival of Egypt* was inaugurated at the Railway Station in 1928, but the dedication of pharaonist monuments to the late Saad Zaghlul was long delayed by politics—his mausoleum until 1936, and his statues in Cairo and Alexandria until 1938 (see figs. 64, 65, and 66).

After Zaghlul's death in 1927, the Liberal Constitutionalist–Wafd coalition cabinet turned his home ("the house of the nation," *bayt al-umma*) into a museum and planned a mausoleum for across the street. The Wafdist committee raising funds for monuments to commemorate him issued fancy receipts for those who contributed as much as £E100. Saturated with pharaonic symbolism, these were issued in the name of

64 Pharaonic fundraising: Receipt from Mustafa al-Nahhas for £E100 contribution to a fund for a monument to commemorate Saad Zaghlul. Al-Hilal *36*, no. 4 (Feb. 1, 1928): 392.

65 Saad Zaghlul's neo-
pharaonic mausoleum,
Munira, Cairo. Architect:
Mustafa Fahmi. Inaugurated
1936. *Photo: D. Reid.*

Zaghlul's successor, Mustafa al-Nahhas Pasha
(see fig. 64). A dispute broke out in the press
as to whether Zaghlul's tomb should be in
Arab/Islamic style, in European style like
Napoleon's tomb, or in 'national' (pharaonic) style. Wafdist minister of public works
Uthman Muharram had versatile architect
Mustafa Fahmi (1886–1972)[50] draw up both
Islamic and pharaonic plans. Muharram
and Zaghlul's widow, Safiya, settled on
pharaonic style as appropriate for a national
shrine that could appeal to Christians as well
as Muslims (see fig. 65). Fahmi's eclectic
neo-pharaonic tomb looked to the Ptolemaic temples of Edfu and Philae, though
the outward-leading front steps recalled the
European Renaissance.[51]

A campaign raised £E60,000 toward Cairo and Alexandria statues of Zaghlul, but sculptor Mahmoud Mukhtar had not yet signed the
commission in 1928 when al-Nahhas's Wafdist cabinet gave way to a pal-
ace-dominated one under Muhammad Mahmud. Detesting Zaghlul, King
Fuad obstructed plans for both his tomb and statues, ostensibly because
of high costs. Hypocritically ignoring his own pharaonist record, Haykal
denounced the twenty-seven-meter height and pharaonic style proposed
for the tomb as un-Islamic and blamed its pharaonic style on undue Coptic
influence in the Wafd.

Upon returning to power for six months in January 1930, al-Nahhas
rushed both projects ahead. The two bronze statues which Mahmoud
Mukhtar executed in his Paris atelier owed more to Rodin than to
Ramesses (see fig. 66). Both depicted an aging Zaghlul in frock coat, tie,
and tarboosh. In Alexandria, the pasha strides toward the Mediterranean;
in Cairo he faces the Qasr al-Nil Bridge, his right hand raised as though
to address the nation. Pharaonism comes through mainly in the pedestals, plaques, and accompanying figures. Papyrus cluster columns of pink
Aswan granite form the imposing pedestal at Cairo. Plaques depict rural
Nile life and a peasant woman with palm branches, sword, and a broken
chain. On the pedestal plaques in Alexandria, pharaonic goddesses represent Upper and Lower Egypt, Zaghlul confronts High Commissioner
Wingate, and a crowd bears their hero aloft.[52]

In June 1930, King Fuad's palace coup installed a cabinet under
Ismail Sidqi, and work on the Zaghlul memorials again bogged down.

The mausoleum was completed in 1931, but his widow Safiya Zaghlul rejected Sidqi's proposal to bury other politicians there alongside her husband.[53] The cynical Sidqi then packed the tomb with the mummies of New Kingdom pharaohs, mocking the Wafd's alleged pharaonism. *Rose al-Youssef* countered with a cartoon of Zaghlul shaking out the mummies. Mukhtar shipped the two statues from Paris in 1932, but they were still in storage when the sculptor died two years later.

Train stations planned in 1926 were also in neo-pharaonic style (fig. 67). They too were delayed and opened with little fanfare at Edfu, Kom Ombo, and Giza in 1932, 1933, and 1935 respectively.[54]

While waiting out Sidqi's palace dictatorship, Wafdist Uthman Muharram built a unique villa on Pyramids Road in Giza (see fig. 67). Villas sometimes balanced 'Egyptian' (pharaonic) and 'Arab' reception rooms, but Uthman used pharaonic style throughout. A dozen tombs in Cairo cemeteries provide further interwar examples of private pharaonic architecture (see fig. 33).[55]

66 Mahmoud Mukhtar's Cairo statue of Saad Zaghlul. Raised on a monumental pharaonic-columned pedestal of pink Aswan granite at the Qasr al-Nil / Tahrir Bridge, Cairo. Inaugurated 1938. *Photo: D. Reid.*

Continuing the palace dictatorship after Ismail Sidqi stepped down, Prime Minister Abd al-Fattah Yahya shed no tears when Mahmoud Mukhtar died in March 1934, aged only forty-three. Wafdists Taha Hussein and Abbas Mahmud al-Aqqad eulogized him as the artistic leader of the 1919 revolution and lamented that although hailed in Europe and Egypt in the 1920s, he was now disgracefully neglected at home by the hostile government. Liberal Constitutionalist Haykal's eulogy raised a pointed question: "The Revival of Ancient Egyptian Art: Will It End with Mukhtar's Death?" Would young artists now "find in their hearts that same strong belief [which Mukhtar] had in ancient Pharaonic art and in the vital need to revive it as modern Egyptian art?"[56]

The following year, two young sculptors—Mansour Faraj and Ahmad Uthman—seemed to answer Haykal's question in the affirmative (see fig. 68).

They drew on both pharaonic and Nubian African art in designing the entrance to the Cairo Zoo. Faraj's (1910–?) father had painted as a hobby and sent his son to the School of Art and Embellishment (later

67 Architectural phara-
onism of the 1930s.
Above: Art Deco doors
of Uthman Muharram's
villa, Giza. Below: Giza
Railway Station, 1935.
Photo: Haycham Labib.
Mercedes Volait, Archi-
tectures de la décennie
pharaonique en Égypte,
179. Courtesy of CEDEJ.

Cairo University's Faculty of Applied Art). After studying in England, France, and Italy, Faraj imbibed Nubian and African inspiration while working for a year in Aswan. He became a professor in his alma mater's sculpture department.[57]

In May 1936, the return of the Wafd under al-Nahhas broke the impass on the Zaghlul monuments. The royal mummies were sent back to the museum, and Zaghlul was finally buried in state in his mausoleum. By the time the pedestals for his statues were ready, however, the Wafd had already fallen. Muhammad Mahmud's palace government scheduled the unveilings for August 27, 1938, when al-Nahhas was away on his summer holiday in Europe. Denied a seat on the dais, Safiya Zaghlul boycotted the ceremonies. King Faruq unveiled the statue in Alexandria, the unofficial summer capital. Deputy Prime Minister Abd al-Fattah

68 Pharaonic/African-style pylon relief at entry to the Cairo Zoo. Sculptors: Mansur Faraj and Ahmad Uthman, 1935. *Photo: D. Reid.*

Yahya's speech mockingly depicted Zaghlul as a faithful servant of King Fuad and spotlighted the still popular young King Faruq.[58]

In a further royalist swipe at Zaghlul's memory, Prime Minister Ali Mahir unveiled the statue of National Party (Watani) hero Mustafa Kamil on May 14, 1940, in the Cairo square renamed for him (see fig. 13). Kamil had had to wait even longer than Zaghlul for monumental commemoration. Upon Kamil's death in 1908, Watanists had commissioned a statue of him by French sculptor Leopold Savine. It was delivered early in 1914, but erecting it in a public square in Kitchener's Cairo was out of the question. It was relegated to the courtyard of the Watani Party's Mustafa Kamil school. It anticipated Mukhtar's *Revival* in juxtaposing a sphinx and a modern figure—in this case Kamil—to symbolize the pharaonic roots of modern Egypt's awakening. As the Wafd's reputation dimmed somewhat in the 1940s, Mustafa Kamil's burned brighter, and a campaign was launched for a national shrine. By now there was no question that it would be in Arab/Islamic style. Kamil was a hero for the Free Officers. In 1953 they reburied him and his deputy Muhammad Farid in a new mausoleum on Salah al-Din Square beneath the citadel. [59]

"Pharaonic Mania": Ahmad Husayn and Young Egypt

Among the younger generation who came of age a decade or more after the 1919 revolution, Ahmad Husayn (1911–1982) and later Naguib Mahfouz stood out. The two were born in the same year in the quarter of Gamaliya, the heart of "medieval" Cairo. Both experienced the 1919 revolution as primary school students, and both were later seized by "pharaonic mania." At the Khedival Secondary School, Ahmad Husayn and the drama club hailed the pharaonist nationalism of Mahmud Murad's plays The Glory of Ramsis (1923) and *Tut-Ankh-Amon* (1924), which Sayyid Darwish set to music. On their school's trip to Luxor in December 1928, Husayn and his classmates burst into song at Karnak Temple:

> Suddenly we realized that we were repeating the entire script, melody after melody and word for word. We spent three hours at the gates of Karnak, chanting [the play's] songs of glory and pride.[60]
>
> I no longer gazed at the pillars and monuments at Karnak with the feeling that they were relics, but as though they were a living thing speaking [to me]. I stood before the soaring obelisk and the pool and the hundreds of statues scattered all about. . . . I was envisioning the armies massed behind Thutmose and Ramses, armies which conquered the whole [known] world of the time. I was listening to their songs of victory and imagining the light which radiated from this spot. In short, I was resurrected, yes resurrected; I became a new man.[61]

Ahmad Husayn exhorted his fellow students:

> The grandeur surrounding you is not foreign to you. Those who erected all this have bequeathed their power and firmness of will. Egypt which once carried the banner for all humanity is obligated to revive itself in order to return to its previous position. Finally, we must shake off the dust of our apathy and laziness. It is our duty to fill our souls with faith and determination. It is our duty to utilize our courage and strength. It is our duty to strive until we resurrect Egypt in all its power, glory, and greatness. . . .
>
> Since that night [at Karnak], I devoted my life to the revival of the glory of Pharaonic Egypt. I joined the partisans of Pharaonicism, and did

even too much in this regard through appealing to people to take Pharaonic names—starting with myself. I took the name Ahmas . . . a shortening of my name Ahmad Husayn. I became obsessed with Pharaonicism. I became famous for my Pharaonic mania [*majnun al-fir'awniya*].[62]

Borrowing French terminology for the fascist-style youth movements of Europe in the 1930s, Gershoni and Jankowski see Ahmad Husayn's Young Egypt (Misr al-Fatah) as an expression of "integral Egyptian nationalism." Husayn and his Young Egypt co-leader Fathy Radwan were both born in Cairo in 1911 to government official fathers with modest landholdings in the Delta. The boys met in primary school and again in the Faculty of Law in 1929.[63]

Ahmad Husayn catapulted to fame at twenty-one in 1932 as secretary general of a university student committee when it launched the "Piastre Plan" to promote Egyptian-owned industry. They collected donations to establish a tarboosh (fez) factory. The signature red hat of both the burgeoning effendi and the pasha class had hitherto been imported from Austria and Czechoslovakia. Mustafa Fahmi, the architect who designed Zaghlul's tomb, steered the youths to an architect recently back from studies in England. The discrete pharaonic details of Muhammad Abd al-Halim's design—a cornice and *palmiform* capitals at the entrance—were in keeping with the tarboosh factory's patriotic character. Production began in 1933. The factory prospered and diversified, surviving into the 1960s on Factory of the Tarbooshes Street, which still bears the name.[64]

In 1933 Ahmad Husayn founded the Young Egypt Society, with Fathy Radwan as secretary general. Toasting "God, Fatherland [Watan], King," they aimed to reestablish "Egypt over all *(Misr fawqa al-jami)*," "a mighty empire of Egypt and Sudan, allied with the Arab states, and leading Islam."[65] Challenging the gradualism of the Wafd, Young Egypt joined Watanists in demanding total independence. From the palace, Ali Mahir clandestinely subsidized Young Egypt. Until the government banned paramilitaries in 1938, Young Egypt's Green Shirts brawled in the streets with the Wafd's Blue Shirts and the Muslim Brotherhood's Rovers. Like other fascist-like youth movements, Young Egypt promoted chauvinism, will over reason, and a cult of its leader. The salute was a raised right arm, palm open and fingers pointing up. Its pharaonist flag showed the three Giza pyramids outlined in white on a green field, and the Society held its annual convocation at the Pyramids.[66]

Magazine advertisements of the day also assumed the appeal of pharaonism to the young. A 1934 ad featured a youth in Boy Scout uniform with the Egyptian flag and the Giza Pyramids and holding a pair of socks (fig. 69).

مجد مصر القديم
يتجلى فـى بنـاء الأهرام
ومجدها الحديث
يتجلى فى مصنع جوارب الشوربجى

متينة كالأهرام
قوية كالشباب
تلك هى
جوارب الشوربجى

69 Pharaonic advertise-
ment for Shurbaji socks.
Uniformed Boy Scout with
pyramids and flag, and
Shurbaji socks factory with
protective winged sun disk
over the door. "Egypt's
ancient glory is expressed in
building the pyramids. Her
modern glory is expressed
in al-Shurbaji's hosiery
factory. Durable like the
pyramids; strong like boys
[al-shabab]—Shurbaji's
socks." *Rose al-Youssef*, no.
349, Oct. 29, 1934 (special
issue), 27, as shown in
Nancy Y. Reynolds, A City
Consumed, fig. 13.

Pharaonic falcon wings protect the door of the Shurbaji factory. The
caption reads:

> Egypt's ancient glory is expressed in building the pyramids. Her modern
> glory is expressed in al-Shurbaji's hosiery factory. Durable like the pyra-
> mids; strong like boys [al-shabab]—Shurbaji's socks.[67]

Bank Misr factories boasted that locally made clothes of long-staple cotton
lasted far longer than competing imports. Such pharaonist advertisements
were not limited to youth. In 1936 tycoon Ahmad Abbud renamed the
Khedival Mail Line the Pharaonic Mail Line to imply that it was no longer
foreign controlled and therefore eligible for a government subsidy.[68]
    The ad for Shurbaji socks with its references to pharaonism and the
Boy Scouts was an expression of the continuing attempt to work out
"effendi masculinity" in the context of "colonial modernity."[69] A cartoon
on the cover of the magazine *al-Matraqa* expressed anxieties about the
implications of changing times and values for Egyptian women (fig. 70).

70 Gender Anxieties: Modern Egyptian woman in pharaonic headdress, high heels, and loincloth: "The truth that one who loses his past is lost and that everything goes back to its origins has shaped me accordingly: A union of the ancient and modern." *Cover of the magazine* al-Matraqa, *Feb. 12, 1928, as shown in Wilson Chacko Jacob,* Working Out Egypt: Effendi Masculinity and Subject Formation in Colonial Modernity, 1870–1940 *(Durham NC: Duke University Press, 2011), 214.*

A topless woman, with a temple pylon and palm trees in the background, wears only pharaonic headdress, Western-style high heels, and a loincloth. The caption reads:

The Modern Egyptian Woman: "The truth that one who loses his past is lost and that everything goes back to its origins has shaped me accordingly: a union of the ancient and modern."[70]

In 1933, Fathy Radwan denounced debates pitting pharaonism against Arabism as "a shame and a disgrace." Pharaonic Egypt had been closely tied to Sumeria, Babylonia, and Assyria. All Arabs shared the pharaonic legacy, so any attack on Egypt's pharaonic heritage was an attack on the heritage of all Arabs.[71] Ahmad Husayn never abandoned his Egyptian focus, but he did move beyond narrow pharaonism. In 1936, he wrote:

I used to believe . . . that civilization in Egypt, in other words the golden age of Egypt, was limited to the Pharaonic age. . . . Suddenly I became aware of my mistake. . . . The golden age has repeated itself two and three and four times. Indeed, Egypt through most of the phases of its history has always been as it was in the age of the Pharaohs, the home of science, knowledge, and religion.[72]

Egypt had Egyptianized its Greek conquerors, declared Ahmad Husayn, and the Library of Alexandria was a wonder of the civilized world. Under Rome, Egyptian martyrs transformed Christianity into a universal religion which conquered Rome itself. Under Islam, Egypt was again in the vanguard under the Tulunids, Fatimids, Ayyubids, and Mamluks. It repelled both the Crusaders and the Mongols. Muhammad Ali's Egyptian army so frightened Europeans that they had to band together to defeat him. Recovering from the blow of the British occupation, Egypt, inspired by its glorious past, was now rising again toward independence and greatness.[73]

In 1938, Ahmad Husayn intensified the cult of his own personality, praised Mussolini and Hitler, and denounced parliamentary systems and parties. Moving with the times, Young Egypt radically changed its name twice: in 1940 to the Islamic Nationalist Party (al-Hizb al-Watani al-Islami) and in 1949 to the Socialist Party of Egypt. Vying with the Muslim Brothers in the 1940s, it denounced Zionism and British imperialism in Palestine, boycotted Egyptian Jewish companies, and called for a ban on prostitution and alcohol. Yet in neither its Islamic nor its socialist phase did Young Egypt abandon the Pyramids as the site of its annual rally.[74]

The imprisonment of its leaders from May 1941 to mid-1944 paralyzed the party. It reverted to its "Young Egypt" name until 1949, when it rebranded itself as Socialist. In 1950 Ibrahim Shukri became its only member ever elected to parliament. The United States came in for condemnation now along with Britain as an imperialist and capitalist enemy. The party called for closer ties to the USSR, though it carefully insisted that its own socialism was Islamic. It advocated a fifty-feddan limit on landownership. In late 1951, it organized guerilla raids on the British in the Canal Zone. Ahmad Husayn and two others were tried for arson after the Cairo riots of January 26, 1952, but were released after the July revolution. Nasser had belonged to Young Egypt in the 1930s, and Sadat and other Free Officers were said to have been members. The Free Officers picked up on some of Young Egypt's themes, although the party had no monopoly on them.[75]

In the 1970s, Ahmad Husayn chronicled over 1,600 pages on Egyptian history from the pre-Cambrian era to 1921. Only some 130 pages were devoted to the pharaohs, but Husayn declared their era central to "the Spirit of Eternal Egypt to which I devoted my entire life and health." He dedicated the tome to "the martyrs who fell across the ages to realize the Glory of Egypt, including my son Airman Samih Mari Abd al-Raziq."[76]

Naguib Mahfouz's Pharaonism and Sayyid Qutb

Remarkably, given the emphasis on Arab and Islamic themes in the 1930s, four out of eighteen novels submitted to Egypt's Arabic Language Academy in a 1941 literary competition had pharaonic settings, and the three co-winning books were all "pharaonic."[77] In a flurry of pharaonism in 1939–40, the venerable *al-Hilal* featured one pharaonic cover after another, ran regular articles by Egyptologist Moharram Kamal (Ahmad Fakhry's and Labib Habachi's classmate from the class of 1928), and reported Montet's discoveries at Tanis. Nor was pharaonism merely a leftover fancy for old-timers; the authors of the three prize-winning novels of 1941—Adil Kamil, Ali Bakathir, and Naguib Mahfouz (1911–2006)—all sprung from the rising generation.

Adil Kamil's (1916–?) King of Rays (*Malik min shuʻaʻ*), published in 1945, imagined Akhenaten as a revolutionary inspired by his love for a girl of humble origins. Five years younger than his friend Mahfouz, Kamil came from a lower-middle-class Coptic family in the Abbasiya district to which Mahfouz had moved as a boy. Kamil earned a law degree, practiced law, and cofounded the Harafish circle of friends which Mahfouz made famous. Kamil, however, gave up writing early.[78]

Ali Ibrahim Bakathir (1910–69) was not even Egyptian; he was born in Indonesia to Arab parents and raised in Arabia in the Hadramawt. Settling in Egypt in 1934, he earned a BA in English from the Egyptian University in 1939. After teaching for fifteen years, he took up posts in the Ministry of Culture. His *Ikhnatun wa Nafartiti* (Akhenaten and Nefertiti), a verse drama published in 1940, depicted Akhenaten's religion of love and peace as disastrous for the state. Bakathir's prose play *al-Firʻawn al-Mawʻud* (The Promised Pharaoh, 1945) featured a corrupt king and treacherous women. In keeping with his Arabian background, however, Bakathir set more of his historical works in the Arab than in the pharaonic past.[79]

Another writer not remembered for pharaonism also dabbled in it at this time—poet Ali Mahmud Taha (1901–49). In 1943 he adapted an ancient Egyptian poem which Drioton had translated in *La revue du Caire*.[80] A decade older than Mahfouz and Kamil, Mahmud Taha had belonged to the *Apollo* circle and is recognized especially for his Arab nationalist convictions.

Naguib Mahfouz's early pharaonist phase had been nearly forgotten in 1988, when he won the Nobel Prize for Literature for his social realist Cairo trilogy set in the first half of the twentieth century. His three first novels—all pharaonist—have since been republished, translated, and closely studied.[81] The three co-winners of the Arabic Language Academy prize of 1941 were a generation younger than the Taha Hussein–Haykal–Musa generation of 1919. Mahfouz was seven in 1919, when he saw British troops shoot down demonstrators near al-Azhar and the Mosque of Sayyidna Husayn in his neighborhood. Saad Zaghlul became Mahfouz's hero, and the boy grew into a lifelong Egyptian territorial nationalist. Mahfouz was ten when Carter discovered Tutankhamun's tomb. He recalled chanting "Tutankhamun is our father" at demonstrations.[82] His father was a civil servant turned copper merchant, but it was his mother, the illiterate daughter of an Azhari sheikh, whose stories awakened him to history and archaeology. She plied him with folk tales and took him to the Egyptian Museum, the Pyramids, and old mosques and churches. He also devoured Arabic translations of Sir Henry Rider Haggard's pharaonic-themed adventure stories.

Entering the Egyptian University in 1930, Mahfouz studied philosophy with Sheikh Mustafa Abd al-Raziq, was drawn to ancient Greek literature, and audited afternoon lectures on Egyptology. He found his main mentor, however, outside the university—pharaonist and Fabian socialist Salama Musa. Frequenting Musa's Thursday salons, Mahfouz took up his mentor's conviction that the Nile Valley had shaped an enduring Egyptian identity still alive in folk customs shared by Muslims and Copts:

> The most important element of this heritage may be the deep religious belief that characterizes the Egyptian people. Ancient Egypt raised religion to a level unparalleled by any of the other ancient civilizations. Egypt through Akhenaten, was the first civilization to call for monotheism.[83]

"The master," who edits a progressive review in Mahfouz's Cairo trilogy, is modeled on Salama Musa.[84]

Mahfouz's first book was an Arabic translation of Rev. James Baikie's *Ancient Egypt* (*Misr al-qadima*, 1932). Inspired by Sir Walter Scott's *Ivanhoe*, Mahfouz envisioned writing a multivolume sequence of novels set in ancient Egypt. Between 1936 and 1945 he published four short stories and three novels with pharaonic themes. Although two won prizes, they found few readers and he long refused to reprint these immature works. His sources included works by Egyptologists Ahmad Kamal, James Breasted, Heinrich Brugsch, Flinders Petrie, and Arthur Weigall.[85]

Abhath al-aqdar (Mocking the Fates, 1939, translated as *Khufu's Wisdom*), *Radubis* (1943), and *Kifah Tiba* (1944, *The Struggle of Thebes*) are set, respectively, in the Fourth and Sixth Dynasties of the Old Kingdom, and at turn of the Eighteenth Dynasty—the dawn of the New Kingdom. *Khufu's Wisdom* is a variation on a Fifth Dynasty tale of the futile attempt of the builder of the Great Pyramids to thwart a prophecy that the sons of a priest of Ra would displace his own line. Ironically, although Mahfouz's mentor Musa named his own son Khufu, he persuaded the fledgling author to change his title from "The Wisdom of Khufu" to "Mocking the Fates." Musa's *al-Majalla al-jadida* published it as a special issue in 1939.[86] *Radubis* drew on Herodotus's tale of a courtesan who seduced an ephemeral pharaoh at the end of the Sixth Dynasty. Priests led a people's revolt in which the pharaoh is slain. *The Struggle of Thebes* tells of the war of liberation which expelled the Hyksos intruders and ushered in the New Kingdom. Seqenra Tao II's mutilated mummy in the Egyptian Museum had captivated Mahfouz; the pharaoh had presumably died in battle with the Hyksos.

In Mahfouz's short story "The Mummy Awakens" (1939), Egyptologist Professor Dorian (likely a variation on the name of director general of Antiquities Drioton) visits the Upper Egyptian estate of Mahmud Pasha al-Arnauti, an Albanian contemptuous of Egyptians who wants to donate his collection of paintings to Paris. A magician recommends to them a spot where Dorian and they might dig. They uncover a mummy, which rises up to rebuke them. As Dorian translates, the pasha dies of fright. Mahfouz denied having read Western mummy stories—Edgar Allan Poe's *Some Words with a Mummy* or Rider Haggard's *She*—or having seen Boris Karloff's 1932 movie *The Mummy*.[87] Mahfuz may well have been influenced by "Pharaoh Awakes," a story published anonymously in the Arabic magazine *Ramsis* in 1923 (12:10). In this case, the mummy Tutankhamun is warned that Westerners are about to discover and desecrate his tomb. Rather than flee, he decides to surrender and puts on his finery to dazzle the discoverers.[88]

What were the contemporary implications of Mahfouz's pharaonic novels? In the first, written in 1939, Mahfouz was not yet ready to challenge popular young King Faruq. Four years later, critics assumed that *Radubis* satirized Faruq's dalliance with a dancer, and his publisher worried about Mahfouz's reference to a "playboy king."[89] In *The Struggle for Thebes*, celebration of Egypt's liberation from light-skinned northern invaders targeted both the British and Egypt's Turco-Circassian aristocracy, including the Muhammad Ali dynasty of King Faruq. Mahfouz associated blond hair, blue eyes, and light skin with treachery and vice and the dark skins of Egyptian peasants with virtue. He usually depicted people from

Sinai and greater Syria (Bedouin or Arabs) as non-Egyptians and, like blacks to the south, as having undesirable character traits.[90]

In 1945, Mahfouz abandoned pharaonic themes for nearly forty years. Unlike the generation of 1919, however, he turned not to early Islamic but to modern times. *Al-Qahira al-jadida* and *Khan al-Khalili* convinced him that he could criticize contemporary corruption without bringing down the censor's wrath. By the eve of the 1952 revolution he had finished writing the Cairo trilogy which would make him famous. In the 1980s, in his old age, Mahfouz would return to his youthful pharaonic themes in *Amama al-arsh (Before the Throne)* and *Aish fi-l-haqiqa* (translated as *Akhenaten: Dweller in Truth*).[91]

The Struggle of Thebes received scant critical attention, but none other than future radical Islamist Sayyid Qutb praised it lavishly in *al-Risala* in October 1944.[92] Qutb urged every young Egyptian of both sexes to read its attack on "rapacious foreigners" who had occupied Egypt "from the Shepherd Kings [Hyksos], to the Romans, to the Arabs, to the European Turks." Egyptian peasants, agreed Qutb, were "nobler and with longer lineages than all of them."[93] Qutb's appreciation fit the tenor of his early work, when liberal nationalist writer Abbas Mahmud al-Aqqad was his main model.

In the later 1940s, Qutb turned toward Islamic topics. He returned from two years' study in the United States (1948–50) appalled by American vices, support for Zionism, and anti-Arab prejudice. He joined the Muslim Brothers, whose Supreme Guide Hassan al-Banna had recently been assassinated. Al-Banna had written:

> There is nothing in any of this preventing us from being interested in the ancient history of Egypt, and all that the ancient Egyptians possessed in the way of knowledge and science. We welcome ancient Egypt as a history containing glory, science and learning. But we resist with all our strength . . . the program that seeks to recreate [ancient] Egypt after God gave Egypt the teaching of Islam . . . and rescued her from the filth of paganism, the rubbish of polytheism, and the habits of the Jahiliyya.[94]

Young Qutb had hailed the positive pharaonism suggested by al-Banna's first two sentences. Imprisonment and torture as a Muslim Brother in Nasser's jails from 1954, however, turned Qutb toward the dark vision of al-Banna's last sentence. The pharaonist dream which had inspired Haykal, Musa, al-Hakim, Mahfouz, and the young Qutb, had turned into nightmare.[95] Qutb's Nasser came to resemble the blasphemous, tyrannical pharaoh of the Quran, who oppressed Moses and the worshipers of the true God. Qutb no longer limited the *Jahiliya*—the age of pagan darkness—to the pre-Islamic past; it now included contemporary society and state. True believers must fight it with all their might. Nasser's execution of Qutb in 1966 made him a martyr, and his later works became foundational for radical Islamists. In 1994, a would-be assassin inspired by Qutb's legacy stabbed Naguib Mahfouz in the neck for the supposed blasphemy of one of his novels.

The Fading of Pharaonism? 1945–1952

From the end of World War II until the 1952 revolution, pharaonism in literature, architecture, politics, and art seemed at low ebb. In 1947, *al-Hilal* posed a question to cultural leaders and artists which would have been unthinkable twenty years earlier: "Should we destroy the sculpture *Nahdat Misr*? [Mukhtar's *Revival of Egypt*]." No one took the question literally, but *al-Risala* summed up the most frequent responses: some suggested demoting the sculpture from its public square to a museum, and many thought its pharaonist symbolism no longer adequately represented the modern revival. [96]

The lack of headline-making discoveries in the decade after 1940 facilitated this fading of pharaonism. Excavations, whether by foreigners or Egyptians, were sparse. An unpublished index of articles in *al-Ahram* on archaeological topics shows a striking drop-off in coverage between 1936–39, with an average of twenty-six articles a year, and 1941–49, when the average plunged to four. [97]

Nicholas Reeves's year-by-year chronicle of "great discoveries" points in a similar direction. He mentions only the Nag Hammadi codices (1945), Greek-era silver coins and vessels from Tell al-Maskuta (1947), and Queen Takhut's Late Period funerary furnishings from Tell Atrib (1950). None of these was found by an archaeologist, and the partial dispersal of the codices and Takhut relics on the market delayed publicity and appreciation of their significance. Eventual awareness of the significance of the Nag Hammadi codices was stronger in the West than in Egypt. Reeves also mentions Zakariya Ghoneim's discovery on January 29, 1952, of what would prove to be Sekhemkhet's unfinished step pyramid at Saqqara. However, the press was then riveted on the "burning of Cairo" three days before, and Ghoneim had to wait for his day in the sun until he opened the pyramid in 1954. [98]

In official architecture, only King Faruq's rest house at the Pyramids (treated in the following chapter) and the Faculty of Engineering at Faruq I University (Alexandria) carried neo-pharaonic style into the 1940s (see fig. 71).

71 Pharaonizing pylon entrance, Faculty of Engineering, Faruq I (Alexandria) University, 1940s. *Photo: D. Reid.*

Once again, there was an apparent Wafdist connection with pharaonism. As minister of public works in 1927, Uthman Muharram had suggested pharaonic style for Egyptian University buildings. Rejecting this on grounds of cost[99] may have merely provided cover for detractors of the Wafd. The Wafd happened to be back in power when the Faruq I University was founded in Alexandria in 1942. Thus Wafdist Taha Hussein became its first rector, and Minister of Public Works Uthman Muharram commissioned the pharaonic-style building for the Faculty of Engineering.[100] The Wafd fell in 1944, but the building, with grandiose pharaonic columns, went ahead from 1946 to 1951. Mustafa Fahmi, the architect of Zaghlul's pharaonic tomb, oversaw the design for the Alexandria campus. Pharaonic style was only one arrow in Fahmi's quiver, however, and the rest of the campus was in modern style.

Playing on the Wafd's supposed pharaonism, an Iskandar Saroukhan cartoon depicted al-Nahhas's January 1950 cabinet in pharaonic guise (fig. 72).[101]

The aging pharaoh on the throne is al-Nahhas, and strongman Minister of Interior Fuad Sirag al-Din wields a sword. Blind Minister of Education Taha Hussein (in dark glasses) appears as the Louvre's Fifth Dynasty statue of a seated scribe, discovered by Mariette at Saqqara. In 1946, Taha Hussein had chosen this statue for the masthead of his monthly *al-Katib al-misri* (The Egyptian Scribe). His inaugural editorial sounded familiar themes: Egyptians had been the first to write with a pen, and Egypt was a Mediterranean crossroads of East and West. Salama Musa helped edit *al-Katib al-misri*, and Ahmad Naguib al-Hilali, Muhammad Rifat, Suhayr al-Qalamawi, Sulayman Huzayin, and Husayn Fawzi were among the intellectuals who contributed to its first issue.[102] The General Egyptian Book Organization (GEBO) later picked up the seated scribe as its own symbol.

When Ibrahim Pasha University (soon to become Ain Shams) was founded in Cairo in 1950, Ahmad Badawi came over from Fuad I University to head up its Egyptology program. Badawi later became rector of Ain Shams (1956–61) and then of Cairo University (1961–64). While at Ain Shams, he invited his old Göttingen professor Hermann Kees, who had been dismissed in Germany in 1945 for his Nazi activities, to teach as visiting professor from 1951 to 1956.[103] Badawi must have had a hand in designing the new university's seal—the obelisk of Heliopolis (On to the ancient Egyptians, Ain Shams to the Arabs) flanked by two falcons of Horus (see fig. 73).

72 The Wafd's last cabinet, in pharaonic guise. Iskandar Saroukhan cartoon, 1950. Prime Minister al-Nahhas sits on the throne. Blind minister of education Taha Hussein is the scribe in the dark glasses. Sword-wielding minister of interior Fuad Sirag al-Din is on Hussein's left. *Haranat Kashishiyan, ed., Iskandar Saroukhan: Nabdha an hayatihi wa fannihi wa ijazatihi (Cairo: Jamiyat al-Qahira al-Khayriya al-Armaniya al-Amma, 1978), 110. Courtesy of the Armenian General Benevolent Union, Cairo.*

73 Evoking antiquity in university seals: right to left: Cairo University, the scribal god of wisdom Thoth (Djehuty); Alexandria University, the Pharos Lighthouse of the Ptolemies; Ain Shams University, the obelisk of On (Heliopolis or Ain Shams), flanked by falcons representing Horus. *Reid,* Cairo University, *117.*

Thus Egyptian universities closed out the semicolonial era as they had begun it, with a pharaonic flourish in their official seals. In the 1920s, the Egyptian University (Cairo) had chosen the scribal god of wisdom Thoth. In between, Faruq I University (Alexandria) had opted for the Pharos Lighthouse of the Ptolemies.

Sulayman Huzayin's "Egypt, the connecting link between East and West" in the December 1945 issue of *al-Katib al-misri* echoed editor Taha Hussein's call for blending the best of Egypt's Pharaonic, Hellenistic, Arab, and Islamic heritage with modern Western culture in a new cultural synthesis for the world.[104] Huzayin emphasized "Unity of the Nile Valley," a popular slogan which reflected Egyptians' fear that Britain would repudiate Egypt's claims to the Sudan. All of Egypt's vital upstream water ran through the Sudan. In Britain's 1922 declaration of Egyptian independence, the Sudan was one of four fields reserved for British freedom of action. Two years later, in retaliation for the assassination of the sirdar, Sir Lee Stack, in Cairo, the British expelled Egyptian troops and civil officials from the Sudan, threatening to turn the Anglo–Egyptian condominium there into a fiction. The Anglo–Egyptian Treaty of 1936 was possible only because it sidestepped the Sudanese question. As decolonization pressures built up after 1945, Egyptians across the political spectrum feared that Britain might sever Sudan from Egypt. In addition to diplomats, the government in 1947 mobilized Egyptologists, historians, and geographers to make the case in print for "Unity of the Nile Valley." The Egyptian–Sudanese unity they perceived down through history amounted to a racially charged Egyptian civilizing mission to the Sudanese, the progress of which the British had rudely interrupted.[105]

An October 1951 stamp set celebrating the abrogation of the 1936 Anglo–Egyptian Treaty proclaimed Faruq "King of Egypt and the Sudan." A classically robed, winged female "Egypt" in pharaonic headdress stands before a Nile Valley map stretching deep into Africa.[106] "Unity of the Nile Valley" was an expansionist version of Egyptian territorial nationalism, with various possible mixtures of pharaonist, Islamic, and Arab components. Eve Trout Powell has explored Egyptians' frequent blindness to the colonial implications of their racial and cultural attitudes toward the Sudanese.[107]

To sum up, by the eve of the 1952 revolution, the intense pharaonism of the 1920s among Egyptian elites had faded, and Islamic and Arab themes were more prominent. Yet identification with pharaonic greatness, linked to hopes for modern revival, still cropped up frequently in quests to express Egyptian national identity. Short-story writer Yahya Haqqi, a diplomat stationed in Paris from 1949 to 1951, felt torn between resentment of Europe's imperial arrogance and love for its culture. He turned

> to Egypt's past for comfort. No monuments, he claims, are the subject of as much research. The Egyptian collections are the pride of all museums—their statues and mummies still retain the perfume of "our" valley. Haqqi writes of his visits to the Musée de l'Homme [in Paris] "to greet my fellow countryman—a skeleton in a glass case."
>
> How little does the west understand of this skeleton that it has encapsulated, but whose greatness is still clearly visible! While looking at the relic Haqqi sensed its dynamism, as though he were seeing himself for the first time.[108]

This chapter has examined pharaonism among the wider Egyptian public. Pharaonism had retreated in the 1930s and 1940s, but it was by no means dead. Chapter 11 returns to the politics of specialist Egyptology from 1939 to 1952—the twilight of both British empire and Egyptian monarchy.

11
Egyptology in the Twilight of Empire and Monarchy, 1939–1952

In the dozen years from the outbreak of World War II to the July Revolution of 1952, sweeping global and internal Egyptian changes greatly affected the practice of Egyptology in Egypt. Invasion by Italian and then German troops from Libya threatened the Nile Valley and the Suez Canal, making Egypt a critical front through the first half of the war. A British coup in February 1942 forced King Faruq to install a Wafdist government to support the Allied war effort (at considerable cost to the party's nationalist credentials). The war also brought the United States in as a major player in Egyptian affairs for the first time.

After the Allied victory, the emerging Cold War forced the United States to temper its opposition to the old-style European colonialism of their British and French allies, but the British suspected that their superpower ally was increasingly playing its own game in the Middle East. With the Wafd back in opposition from 1944 to 1950, King Faruq and the politicians of the smaller parties, which lacked a mass base, made little progress toward either full independence or alleviation of mounting socioeconomic problems. Large landowners of all parties blocked even modest land redistribution. Israel's defeat of Egypt and other Arabs in 1948 shook the whole political order. Outside and below parliamentary politics, the Muslim Brothers mobilized a mass following but wavered between peaceful preaching and violence. The assassination of Prime Minister al-Nuqrashi in 1948 provoked the retaliatory assassination of Hassan al-Banna, the Brothers' Supreme Guide.

Al-Nahhas's last Wafdist government of 1950–52 drifted into unilateral abrogation of the 1936 Anglo–Egyptian Treaty but then had to deal with guerilla raids it could not control on British bases in the Canal Zone. The British slaughter of Egyptian auxiliary police at Ismailiya on January

25, 1952, triggered the Cairo riots the next day, which brought down the Wafd. Feckless ensuing cabinets could not contain the crisis, and on July 23, 1952, Nasser's small group of junior army officers moved in to overthrow and exile King Faruq.

In Egyptology, World War II and the turmoil of the postwar years severely curtailed field archaeology. Egyptianization of the profession continued in the Antiquities Service and universities. With Selim Hassan sidelined, Sami Gabra presided as the dean of Egyptian Egyptology, while behind him the third and fourth generations moved up the Antiquities Service and university ladders. Hassan Fathy, Egypt's most famous architect since Imhotep, designed the utopian village of New Qurna but could not persuade the villagers to abandon their hillside homes among the Tombs of the Nobles. King Faruq took a personal interest in Egyptology, and his embrace of Étienne Drioton as his mentor enabled colonial archaeology to fight a rearguard defense down to 1952. Finally, on the eve of the revolution, two separate crises of decolonization brought both French and British archaeology in Egypt to a standstill in 1951.

European Egyptology in Wartime Egypt

In the summer of 1942, Britons relived their nightmare of the spring of 1918, when it looked as though Germany might dominate continental Europe, cut the British Empire in two at the Suez Canal, and bring Britain to its knees.[1] Axis troops were only seventy miles from Alexandria and closing in on the oil fields in the Caucasus, while the Japanese in Burma were driving toward India. On February 4, 1942, the British secured their Egyptian base by surrounding Abdin Palace with tanks to force King Faruq to appoint a Wafdist cabinet under al-Nahhas. During World War I, they had keenly felt the absence of a broad-based Egyptian ally to deflect resentments born of political repression under martial law, conscripted labor, and economic hardship. Contrary to frequent interpretation, outright pro-Axis sentiment among Egyptians was thin.[2] The Wafd paid a price in popular legitimacy, however, for riding to power on British tanks. The Wafd had hardly settled into office when it was weakened by its last major schism—the defection of Makram Ubayd, al-Nahhas's right-hand man and minister of finance. On the battlefield, the tide turned in North Africa in October 1942, when General Montgomery began his drive westward from al-Alamein to eventual rendezvous with the Americans in Tunisia.

Even the Sphinx went to war. The cover photo of *Life* magazine for October 19, 1942, showed the Sphinx up to its chin in protective sandbags (see fig. 74).

74 The Sphinx goes to war. Cover photo on *Life* magazine, Oct. 19, 1942 issue. *Photo: Bob Landry / Life Picture Collection / Getty Images.*

That same year the United States joined the Middle East Supply Centre, which Britain had set up in 1941 to manage regional economies during the war. Americans' hostility to European imperialism often irritated their British ally. Britons in Cairo also noted that the American military camp insisted on huts instead of tents and forty gallons of water a day per man; British soldiers got twenty. American privates earned twice the pay of Britons, and PX luxuries such as nylons gave them an edge in competition for local women. Americans suspected the British of fighting for empire instead of for freedom and democracy.[3] Roosevelt and Stalin talked over Churchill's head at the 1943 Tehran conference,[4] but the Cold War later compelled the United States to keep paying at least lip service to British primacy in Egypt.

In Egyptology, the war abruptly terminated the expeditions of Hermann Junker and Günther Roeder. The German Archaeological Institute and German expedition house at Qurna were again sequestered. Mussolini's entry into the war in June 1940 cut short Italian excavations in Egypt. Achille Adriani, the director of the Greco–Roman Museum, was interned in the Italian school in Alexandria, and Briton Alan Rowe took over his post. Back in Germany, Hitler dreamed of renaming the Third Reich's capital Germania and building a new museum highlighting the bust of Nefertiti. Georg Steindorff and Bernard Bothmer fled to the United States, while Ludwig Keimer and Joseph Leibovitch rode out the war in Cairo. Others, such as Günther Roeder, flourished under Hitler. Roeder not only continued to direct the Pilizaeus Museum in Hildesheim but also received the prize of directing the Egyptian Museum in Berlin. Junker directed the German Archaeological Institute–Cairo from Berlin until 1943, when he returned to Vienna. After the war, denazification stripped Roeder, Hermann Grapow, and Hermann Kees of their chairs. The Cold War, however, enabled some purged professors to make a comeback.[5]

Egypt's Egyptian Museum and other museums were closed through most of the war. Of the Europeans in the Antiquities Service, Director General Drioton—forty-nine and a clergyman—stayed at his desk. His British subordinates Reginald Engelbach and Guy Brunton, veterans of World War I and fifty-one and sixty-one respectively, also stayed on the job. Emery, thirty-six, left the Antiquities Service for military intelligence work in Cairo. Among the French, Henri Chevrier and Jean-Philippe Lauer, directors of works at Karnak and Saqqara respectively, and Octave Guéraud, assistant curator of the Egyptian Museum, were mobilized. Drioton and the consul general pleaded with French military authorities that their posts might be lost to France, but only Guéraud was released from service. Chevrier and Lauer were fortunate to reclaim their Antiquities Service posts in 1945.[6]

All five male fellows (pensionnaires) at IFAO in 1939 were mobilized, leaving only Mlle. Christiane Desroches (later Mme. Noblecourt). In 1937, at age twenty-four, she had become IFAO's first female pensionnaire, despite the grumbling of male colleagues. Disembarking from the *Champollion* in Alexandria, she had been welcomed at the Cairo railroad station by her former professor from Paris—Étienne Drioton, now director general of Antiquities.[7]

While France awaited German invasion after the fall of Poland, its Egyptologists kept digging into the spring of 1940—Bernard Bruyère at Deir al-Medina, Alexandre Varille and Christiane Desroches at Karnak

North, and Pierre Montet at Tanis. In February 1939, after ten years at Tanis, Montet discovered the first of a series of Twenty-First and Twenty-second Dynasty royal tombs. King Faruq visited Tanis three times for sarcophagus openings between March 1939 and April 1940. Montet's January–May 1940 season became a race against the calendar of war. On March 1, he opened the silver coffin of Psusennes I, the only pharaoh's burial ever found intact, and found a fine golden funerary mask. Germany's annihilation of the rump of Czechoslavakia days later, however, crowded news of Tanis out of the French press. The funerary treasures of Amenemopet reached the Cairo Museum on May 3. A week later, Germany's onslaught on France and the Low Countries derailed *L'Illustration*'s planned feature on Tanis. It fell to the London *Times* to spread news of some of the spectacular French discoveries.[8]

Christiane Desroches made it home on the last French steamer to cross the Mediterranean before Italy joined Germany in invading France. Her ship carried antiaircraft guns and was shadowed by Italian planes. In Paris, she threw herself into evacuating the Louvre's Egyptian treasures for safekeeping in country castles, joined the resistance in response to de Gaulle's radio appeal from London, and married, becoming Mme. Desroches Noblecourt. Seventeen members of her resistance circle were shot, and she was once detained for several days. After liberation, she served on a committee which censured collaborators in the cultural sector.[9]

British-occupied Egypt became one of several colonial arenas where General Pétain's Vichy regime and General de Gaulle's *France libre* fought it out. Consul General Jean Pozzi held much of the resident French *haute bourgeoisie* for Vichy until Egypt broke off relations in January 1942. The Free French included many scholars and teachers: "You can tell them easily," sniffed a society lady, "the Gaullists don't know how to dance."[10]

The fall of France in June 1940 cut IFAO off from Paris until liberation in 1944. When Egypt severed relations with Vichy, the Free French took over the consulate and tapped blocked funds for IFAO and other cultural institutions. Visiting Egypt in August 1942, de Gaulle predicted that Britain would soon turn the tide at al-Alamein.[11] From October 1943 until the liberation of Paris, a commission of *France libre* in Algiers oversaw IFAO. In 1945, France raised its Cairo consulate to embassy status. The Resistance was well represented in the new Fourth Republic's foreign service; Jouguet stayed on for a year as cultural adviser to the Cairo embassy.[12]

After Desroches went home in 1940, Alexandre Varille (1909–51) dug on alone at Karnak North until 1943, IFAO's only excavation between the fall of France and the end of the war.[13] In 1943, Charles Kuentz cut off Varille's IFAO fellowship, probably partly because he suspected him of

Vichyist sympathies. Drioton, however, stepped in to rescue Varille with an Antiquities Service post. Drioton and Varille long sat on the fence between Pétain and de Gaulle. As Gaullists, Jouguet and Kuentz were marked men when Rommel nearly broke through in 1942; they fled to Beirut. Drioton stayed on, and the Swiss minister representing Vichy's interests had contingency plans for him to direct IFAO. Probably for political reasons, Desroches Noblecourt did not mention Varille, her coexcavator at Karnak North, by name in her memoirs. Of her mentor Drioton's fence sitting, she wrote only that he was "a proud man from Lorraine [who] remained an Egyptian official and did not take part openly but used his influence at the palace to greatly help us all."[14] Drioton took his time in registering at the consulate after the Free French takeover, and de Gaulle's cultural aide Claude Schaeffer, a Near Eastern archaeologist, considered having him replaced.[15]

Drioton's solicitude for Joseph Leibovitch (1898–1968) shows his broad political tolerance. An Alexandria-born Jewish Egyptologist, Leibovitch had studied with Golenischeff in Cairo and Junker in Vienna and worked as Borchardt's secretary. From 1937 to 1949, Drioton took Leibovitch under his wing as librarian of the Egyptian Museum. An active Zionist, Leibovitch immigrated to Israel in 1949.[16]

Wartime Egyptianization: the Antiquities Service and the University

Drioton's difficulties with Egyptians did not end with Selim Hassan's dismissal in 1939. In June 1941 minister of education Haykal tried to shift Drioton to a position as scientific adviser to the Antiquities Service, with geographer and prehistoric archaeologist Mustafa Amer taking over the role of director general.[17] When the jewels of King Psusennes I, which Montet had discovered at Tanis the year before, were stolen from the Egyptian Museum in September 1941, a British official warned that the theft was "deliberately framed in order to discredit and expel all Europeans from the Service."[18] Drioton scoffed at Selim Hassan's further charge that twenty-six thousand objects were missing from the museum. It was probably Drioton's patron King Faruq who blocked Amer's appointment. Haykal did, however, make Sadiq Jawhar (Gohar) administrative director of Antiquities. Drioton maintained his scientific authority by insisting that the appointee be someone without Egyptological credentials. Haykal also succeeded in replacing Engelbach as director of the Egyptian Museum with Mahmud Hamza, the first Egyptian to hold the post. Engelbach stayed on as a scientific adviser.[19]

Any nationalist satisfaction at Hamza's appointment was dimmed by Drioton's hostility toward him. From his wartime embassy post, H.W.

Fairman advised on how I.E.S. Edwards should go about applying for permission to study Third Dynasty materials in the museum:

> Hamza is the man to approach, and Edwards should not on any account give Hamza any reason to suspect that he has approached Drioton first, or vice versa. If Edwards goes direct to Hamza and asks permission, he will probably get it. . . . Hamza at present makes it a matter of principle to refuse any request concerning the Museum that has first been referred to Drioton.[20]

Diplomacy was not Fairman's strength. He declared:

> Egyptology has been built up by the efforts of scholars of all nations and has been a truly international science, with the exception that the Egyptian contribution has been nil.

He denounced Mahmud Hamza as a "lazy" and "ignorant" "intriguer." Engelbach, however, defended the Egyptian who replaced him as chief curator at the museum. Hamza was perhaps "mediocre, but honest, a fair scholar," who turned anti-French only because of Drioton's "hatred." Unlike the "scoundrel" Selim Hassan, Engelbach considered Hamza pro-English and predicted he "will give little trouble." Engelbach also praised Abbas Bayoumi and another Egyptian colleague, stressing that he corrected their manuscripts only for English.[21] Ambassador Lampson wondered about slipping Fairman into the museum as an understudy to Guy Brunton, but without Lampson's guarantee of support in any tangle with Hamza, Fairman declined.[22]

While Selim Hassan paced the sidelines in forced retirement through the 1940s, the Egyptianization of Egyptology continued. Though the British were slow to accept an Egyptian head of the university's Egyptology program, Junker's removal in 1939 cleared the way for Sami Gabra as both department chair and dean of the Egyptian profession.

Back in 1933, Aylward Blackman had shied away from the uncertainty of the Cairo chair and gone to Liverpool instead. He did not forget Cairo, however. In 1942, he urged the Foreign Office to turn the German Institute of Archaeology into a British institute, with himself as director. Herbert W. Fairman also mused:

> I often find myself wishing that when the war is over we could take over the German Institute—which had forfeited all right to continue as a scientific institution—and make it the centre of a British School of Archaeology out here.[23]

Nothing came of it, but the British Council—founded privately in 1934 to promote British culture abroad and taken over by the government during the war—did become a fixture in Cairo. Former High Commissioner Lord Lloyd, the old cultural crusader, became president of the British Council in 1937. Although far behind the Continent in state promotion of culture abroad, the British were slightly ahead of the Americans. The State Department's Bureau of Cultural Affairs dates only from 1938, and at first it dealt only with Latin America. In 1943 it extended its work to the Middle East.[24]

Stephen Glanville of University College London was suggested for Cairo's Egyptology chair and may have visited for a term in 1943.[25] An attempt in 1944 to make him visiting professor there at £E1,200 with a British Council supplement of £E800 fell through, partly because Glanville's wartime reports on damage to Theban tombs had angered Drioton. By January 1946, the Foreign Office had grudgingly accepted that an Egyptian—Sami Gabra—had permanently occupied the Egyptology chair. As late as 1947, Blackman, nearing retirement at Liverpool, lobbied for a visiting professorship at Cairo at £E1,500. He warned that Junker might try to wangle reappointment. The Foreign Office agreed that "We must certainly do what we can—while we can—to prevent this unprincipled time-server from being reappointed" and that Blackman's appointment should be pushed "before we altogether lose our hold on the teaching of Egyptology."[26] Blackman volunteered that his sister Winifred, author of *The Fellahin of Upper Egypt* (1927), could come too and continue her ethnological research. He promised that he would gladly leave administration to Gabra, but a Foreign Office comment suggested that Blackman's temperament made this unlikely.[27]

Western Egyptology in Postwar Egypt

After World War I, the return of foreign expeditions to Egypt had been robust. After 1945, in contrast, Western excavation remained sparse for another decade and a half. The resources of the Antiquities Service were also cramped. As already noted, the only "great discoveries" between 1945 and 1952 were accidental or illegal finds, the most important being the Nag Hammadi Coptic papyri of a Christian Gnostic community.[28]

In postwar Europe, reconstruction preoccupied victor and vanquished alike. Britain emerged victorious but nearly bankrupt. In the fall of 1945 the Labour government agreed, in return for an emergency $3.5 billion US loan, to dismantle the sterling bloc and open it to American exports by mid-1947. The Cold War, however, gave the British and French a reprieve from US expansionist and anticolonial pressure. Rallying support against Soviet communism, the United States propped up the sterling area and tolerated continued British imperial tariff preferences.[29] In 1947, Britain's withdrawal from India and Pakistan removed the keystone of the imperial arch. Israeli independence followed, with disastrous results for Palestinians, Egyptians, and other Arabs. Where did that leave the Suez Canal, the British imperial artery the control of which had cost Egypt so dearly?[30]

Shortages and inflation during World War II hit Egyptians hard. The cost-of-living index nearly tripled from 1939 to 1945 before leveling out for a decade.[31] Some Egyptians made fortunes by provisioning the Allied armies, and in 1943, Egypt paid off the national debt which had shackled it since the days of Khedive Ismail. In 1947, Egypt severed its tie to the pound sterling, and British troops withdrew from the Cairo Citadel and Qasr al-Nil barracks to bases in the Suez Canal Zone. The closing of the Mixed Courts in 1949 removed another instrument of foreign privilege. The shattering defeat in Palestine in 1948, however, overshadowed these achievements, dispossessed the Palestinians, and left Egypt and other Arab regimes reeling. The future of the Sudan and British occupation of the Canal Zone remained roadblocks to a British–Egyptian settlement. The drive to Egyptianize big businesses was slow, and landlord-dominated parties, including the Wafd, blocked land reform. There was nothing left to hope for from the increasingly dissolute king.

None of these circumstances facilitated field archaeology in Egypt. It took the defeated German and Italian archaeologists years to work their way back into Egypt. Squeezed between financial austerity at home and Egyptian nationalism abroad, British field Egyptology in the late 1940s was limited to minor epigraphic projects. As for the Americans, nothing about the Oriental Institute's quiet resumption of epigraphic work at Medinat Habu suggested the global reach of the new superpower. Battered France's leverage in Egypt was a far cry from the days of Mariette and Maspero, but its twin bases in the Antiquities Service and IFAO enabled it to bounce back until a new crisis from an unexpected quarter undercut it in 1951.[32]

In 1942, Alan Gardiner wistfully wrote to the Foreign Office recalling David Hogarth's and Sir John Maxwell's futile urging after World War I that Britain take over the Egyptian Antiquities Service and officially support Petrie's British School of Archeology in Egypt. Gardiner continued:

To be preeminent in Egyptology was part and parcel of France's notion of prestige; hence the large sums of money expended by that country on its Institute and on its professorial chairs at home. Germany, of course, took the same line, and even Italy spent large sums of money on excavations in

Egypt. The very half-hearted attempt made by our own Government to help in these matters appears to me to have been due more to a desire for British prestige in Egypt than to any interest (even second hand) in the subject itself. Clearly, Egyptology as a national concern, cannot flourish if it is regarded merely as an instrument and not as an end in itself. . . .

With yourself at the Foreign Office and Mr. Eden, a scholar, at the head of it, the position should be more hopeful than in the past, but the tradition that minor sciences are individual interests, and no direct concern of the Government, seems so strong in Britain that I do not feel optimistic.

After the war, he hoped, America and Britain might join France and a reformed Germany to make it "clear to Egypt that its historic possessions from the past were not national, but a supra-national concern and that we insisted upon their being regarded as such."[33]

With the war over, Emery hoped to resume his Antiquities Service work at Saqqara. Without a salary supplement such as the French supplied some of their nationals, however, he could not make a go of it.[34] He continued nonarchaeological work for the Cairo embassy until 1951, when University College London rescued him for Egyptology by making him Edwards Professor. Concurrently, the EES appointed him its field director, and in cooperation with the Antiquities Service he resumed his work in the Early Dynastic cemetery at North Saqqara for four seasons (1953–56), until the Suez War.

The near absence of the American superpower from Egyptian excavations for fifteen years after 1945 is noteworthy. Even World War I had not completely choked off the American field Egyptology which had begun at the turn of the century, and in the 1920s it had flourished under private auspices despite the isolationism of US foreign policy. After 1945, no comparable millionaire patronage was forthcoming. In 1919–20, Breasted had surveyed archaeological prospects from Egypt to Iraq with John D. Rockefeller Jr.'s initial commitment in his pocket; Breasted's archaeological empire of the University of Chicago's Oriental Institute was the result. In contrast, three American post–World War II archaeological reconnaissances were modest indeed. In 1945–46, Breasted's successor, John Wilson, surveyed prospects from Egypt to Iraq, and in 1946–47 and 1950, Dows Dunham (1890–1984) and Bernard Bothmer respectively did so for the Boston MFA, for Egypt only.

Wilson's somber 1946 report found excavation prospects poor everywhere except in Iraq. He was taken aback when Egyptian Museum director Mahmud Hamza demanded that the Oriental Institute return ostraca lent years earlier for study or lose its welcome in Egypt. News of another blow reached Wilson by mail in Luxor: the University of Chicago had assimilated Rockefeller's terminal grant of $2 million to the Oriental Institute into the general university budget. Wilson resigned as director of the OI.[35]

Breasted's postwar mission had been to found an archaeological empire; Dows Dunham went out in 1946–47 to liquidate the Harvard–Boston expedition which Breasted's old rival George Reisner had established. Harvard graduate Dunham had learned field archaeology under Reisner in Egypt and Sudan, beginning in the spring of 1914, and spent much of 1925–27 as Reisner's chief assistant in excavating the tomb of Queen Hetepheres at the foot of Khufu's Great Pyramid at Giza.[36] Now, Dunham came to close the late Reisner's Harvard Camp at Giza, ship its archives home, and sort out the expedition's share of the antiquities in its storehouses. Drioton and Egypt's minister of education urged Dunham to resume fieldwork, but he noted that the positions of both these men were politically precarious. American ambassador Pinkney Tuck warned that "Recent statements from the Administration in Washington on the Palestine situation are seriously undermining our favorable standing with the Egyptians" and regretted that the closing of the Mixed Courts would remove a buffer against antiforeign passions. The only silver lining was Dunham's hope that American institutions would pool resources to found a research institute—the future American Research Center in Egypt (ARCE).[37]

In 1943, Britain's EES had about eighty-five Americans among its 391 members. Three years later the EES disbanded its American branch, though individual Americans remained as members.[38] In Egyptology, as in trade and diplomacy in Egypt, Americans were moving out of Britain's shadow. Thirty attendees at a luncheon in Boston on May 14, 1948, founded "an American Research Center in Egypt for Egyptian and other Near Eastern studies, from earliest times to the present day."[39] ARCE was "modest in its first formulation, but potentially like the American Schools in Rome and Athens." Edward W. Forbes, retired professor of art history and director of Harvard's Fogg Museum of Art, was elected chairman of the Board of Trustees and Chicago Egyptologist John A. Wilson chairman of the Center. Egyptologists Dows Dunham of the MFA of Boston and Richard A. Parker of Brown University also became officers. The bitter rivalry of founding giants Breasted and Reisner faded with their passing; their heirs were eager to collaborate in ARCE.

Incorporated in Massachusetts in 1950, ARCE established itself in Egypt in February 1951 with William Stevenson Smith of the Boston MFA as first Cairo director. Until 1963, when a contract with the State Department funded a dramatic expansion through Public Law 480,

ARCE was a shoestring operation with two fellowships a year at most. The Cairo director, who changed every year or two, usually held one. At times he ran ARCE out of his apartment with the help of his wife.[40]

In the winter of 1950, Bernard V. Bothmer's (1912–93) Egyptian tour documented how thin archaeological activity was on the eve of ARCE's arrival and the gradual return of British, German, and Italian excavators.[41] Bothmer had three months' leave from the Boston MFA to survey Egyptian archaeology on a small grant from the American Philosophical Society. Though not Jewish, Bothmer had

> left Germany of his own volition and, together with his brother, came to America because he would not live in a Nazi Germany. He is now a private in the United States Army, his greatest wish to fight and conquer Nazidom.[42]

Now he toured Egypt for the first time, Baedeker in hand. He visited sites from Aswan to Cairo, meeting most of the Western and Egyptian Egyptologists then in the field. American, British, German, and Italian excavators were absent from his diary; there were none. He encountered Aylward Blackman, resuming an interrupted EES epigraphic project at Meir, and the Belgian–Dutch team of Jozef Janssen and Arpag Mekhitarian, who were copying graffiti around al-Kab. Frenchmen, mostly working through IFAO or the Antiquities Service, were almost the only foreigners then excavating.

As for Americans, Chicago House, with its focus on epigraphy rather than excavation, was bustling. Bothmer met the French couple Jean Doresse and his wife, who were "living under primitive conditions in the old Metropolitan Museum House."[43] At Reisner's abandoned Harvard Camp at Giza, "An old-timer took me around and showed me the office; Dr. Reisner's study, his bedroom, his wife's and daughter's rooms, and the other wings, but it was a sad sight."[44] American Egyptologists being few, Bothmer socialized with other Americans of a vanishing world— Judge Brinton and his wife (the Mixed Courts had recently closed) and United Presbyterian missionaries, whose days in Egypt were numbered. Bothmer's other American contacts pointed toward the future—Ambassador Jefferson Caffery, the American Luncheon Club at the Semiramis Hotel, TWA, American Express, Fulbright scholars, and the fledgling American Research Center in Egypt. "Crowds of American tourists," he reported, "were descending on the Muski."[45] Bothmer's itinerary also anticipated the future in his bypassing of Alexandria—he arrived and departed through Cairo by air on TWA.

In contrast to the United States and Britain, war-battered France's deep tradition of state-supported culture, proud record in Egyptology, and dual bases in the Antiquities Service and IFAO quickly propelled it back into fieldwork in 1945. After five years away, Chevrier reclaimed his Antiquities Service post at Karnak. Lauer did the same at Saqqara. IFAO fellowships brought Bruyère back to Deir al-Medina and Montet to Tanis, where they worked until 1951. Georges Goyon had guarded isolated Tanis throughout the war and was disappointed with Montet's scant appreciation upon returning.[46] Drioton had promised Montet the sarcophagus and funerary objects of Prince Hornakht for the Louvre, but the political moment for collecting such prizes had passed.[47] Coptologist Jean Doresse's excavation under IFAO auspices at Deir al-Gazaz (1948–51) luckily put him on the spot in Egypt to recognize the significance of the Nag Hammadi codices when they surfaced.

By 1947, Jouguet had concluded that his handpicked IFAO successor, Charles Kuentz, was quarrelsome and a poor administrator. He lobbied the French ambassador to replace Kuentz with Gaston Wiet, director of the Museum of Arab Art. Wiet had excellent Arabic language skills and warm relations with Egyptians. The Quai d'Orsay, however, refused: "in a country where the memory of Champollion, of Mariette, and of Maspero remains so vivid," the IFAO director must be an Egyptologist ready to replace Drioton should he depart. Kuentz stayed on at IFAO's helm until 1953.[48]

Selim Hassan in the Wilderness

Forced retirement in 1939 at age fifty-three compelled Selim Hassan to watch both wartime and postwar developments from the sidelines. Barred from teaching, excavation, and museum work, he poured his immense energy into the only scholarly activity still open to him—publication. He dedicated the first volume of *Tarikh Misr al-qadima* (History of Ancient Egypt) to an influential friend in the Saadist Party but also defiantly "to those who wanted to abuse me and expel me from my job but actually assisted me and enhanced my productivity and service to science and the fatherland."[49]

His publication drive had two main prongs—specialized reports in English on his decade excavating at Giza and Saqqara, and an encyclopedic survey, in Arabic, of ancient Egyptian history and archaeology. The first targeted fellow Egyptologists (still largely foreign) and the second Egyptian archaeology students and the wider Arabic-reading public. The Government Press at Bulaq required no imprimatur from Hassan's enemies, King Faruq and Drioton. It published the third volume of *Excavations at Giza* in 1941 and seven volumes more by 1960, the year before he died. *Excavations at Saqqara 1937–8* came out post-humously.[50] Hassan would have cherished the later tribute of a British Egyptologist:

> Hassan's endeavours at Giza, like those of his mentor [Junker] not only achieved impressive results, but would be published in full, in several large and abundantly illustrated volumes which remain of great value to scholarship today.[51]

Hassan dedicated volumes of *Excavations at Giza* to the memories of Ahmad Kamal Pasha, "the first Egyptian Archaeologist and Founder of the Science of Egyptology among Egyptians," "my Professor V. Golénischeff," and "my friend" James Henry Breasted. He also honored a living scholar with a dedication: "My Professor Hermann Junker," who had helped him revise the volume in question (1953).

The preface to volume 3 (1941) thanked "My pupil Mrs. Dorothy Eady," for doing the drawing. As already noted, Eady (1904–81) was a British eccentric who came to Egypt in 1933, married Iman Abdul Meguid, and upon the birth of their son Sety, became known as Omm Sety "the mother of Sety." She believed that she had once been a temple attendant in Abydos, who at age fourteen had become the lover of Seti I, father of the famous Ramesses II. Divorced from Abdul Meguid in 1936, she became a student of Hassan's and personal assistant for his publications. She recalled him as a great, though stern and humorless, teacher. In 1951 the Antiquities Service hired her to assist Ahmad Fakhry at Dahshur. In 1956 she achieved her dream of settling at Abydos, where she worked for the Antiquities Service until retiring in 1969.[52] Omm Sety straddled two modern worlds with small patience for each other— that of scholarly Egyptologists and that of fanciful mystics entranced with ancient Egypt.

In writing for both specialists and also in Arabic for his countrymen, Hassan was following the example of his mentor Ahmad Kamal. In the very decade of the 1940s when pharaonism is assumed to have been eclipsed by Arabic and Islamic themes, Hassan was churning out a massive history of ancient Egypt in Arabic for his compatriots. The ten thousand pages of *Misr al-qadima* (Ancient Egypt, 16 vols., Cairo: 1940–62) covered from prehistoric through Ptolemaic times. At the time of his death, Hassan was planning a seventeenth volume on the age of Cleopatra. At a time when prefaces often fawned on the king, one of his prefaces hinted at defiance of the monarch who had brought him down:

I did not take the history of the pharaoh to show his people's history, as used to be in previous books. I did not take his life, traditions, systems, wealth, or beliefs as a measurement for the status of his subjects, as differences among them may be big enough. I took the status of ordinary people as a basis for what I wrote, and this draws us close to the truth and makes us avoid slipping into mistakes and misreadings.

Misr al-qadima was a mine of information for students whose English, French, or German was weak, but what nonspecialist would have had an appetite for such detail? Reissued in the 1990s, the massive work was a tribute to Hassan's memory but by then decades out of date.

Two of Hassan's Arabic translations may have found wider audiences. He translated Adolf Erman's *Literature of the Ancient Egyptians* while also updating it. He emphasized that Erman had revealed an authentic literature which antedated the Babylonians, the Bible, Homer, and the Greeks. He also translated Breasted's *Dawn of Conscience* (1956), a speculative work for a general audience.

Egyptianizing the Academy and Antiquities Service: Sami Gabra, Ahmad Fakhry, and Labib Habachi

Sami Gabra headed the Egyptology department of the university's Institute of Archaeology for a dozen years before retiring at sixty, as required by law, in the spring of 1952. Centering on his life's work at Tuna al-Gebel, his memoirs reveal little about his teaching or university administration. Although at the summit of the Egyptian profession through the 1940s, Gabra remembered the decade as a "painful stage" of hardship and austerity in contrast to his and archaeology's golden years in the 1930s. His student Naguib Mikhail assisted him in excavating Tuna's underground galleries, packed with the mummies of ibises and baboons sacred to the god Thoth, and in developing a provincial museum at nearby Mallawi. Promotion to bey in 1951 made Gabra the titular equal of Selim Hassan.[53]

In August 1947, Gabra and one of his students, Mustafa El Amir, represented Egypt in Copenhagen at a "brave attempt" to found an International Association of Egyptologists.[54] France, with six Egyptologists, was best represented at the conference. The Germans had not been invited, however, and Pierre Lacau, Alan Gardiner, and Oxford professor Battiscombe Gunn declined to join. Jean Capart, who had with difficulty kept *Chronique d'Égypte* going through the war, favored casting the participatory net broadly, with the exception of Nazified Egyptologists (Germans and Italians) and Egyptians who were too nationalistic. He wanted to include only those Egyptians "who guarantee that foreign

Egyptologists would not be considered and treated by them as intruders, as poachers on a hunting preserve which they jealously strive to guard."[55] In any event, the Copenhagen meeting failed, and it would be another thirty years before the International Association of Egyptologists would come into being. Dutch scholars did manage to salvage from the wreckage a project for a valuable *Annual Egyptological Bibliography*.

Behind Gabra and Hassan's second generation, Cairo's BA Egyptology graduates of 1928–33 and MA-level diploma holders of the classes of 1934–40 constituted the first and second cohorts of the third generation. The Antiquities Service and academia provided their two main career options. A fortunate few won fellowships for graduate studies in Europe until World War II cut them off and accelerated the development of graduate studies back home in Egypt. Anwar Shukri, for example, worked under Hermann Kees at Göttingen until the war intervened. In 1942, he earned Fuad I University's first doctorate in Egyptology. Four others—including Ahmad Fakhry, Alexander Badawi, and Naguib Mikhail—earned Egyptology doctorates at Cairo during the war. Two doctorates awarded in 1947 brought the pre-1952 total to seven.[56]

Third generation Egyptologists who became professors included Girgis Mattha (Cairo class of 1928), Abdel Moneim Abu Bakr and Ahmad Badawi (both 1930), Abdel Muhsin Bakir (1935), Naguib Mikhail (1936), Ibrahim Rizqana (1938), Alexander Badawi (1939), and Mustafa Muhammad El Amir (1940).[57] El Amir and Bakir worked briefly in the Antiquities Service before returning to school for graduate study; most of the others never left the academy. University excavations were critical to the careers of Abu Bakr, Badawi, Mustafa Amer's assistant Ibrahim Rizqana, Gabra's assistant Naguib Mikhail, and Alexander Badawi. Mattha, Bakir, and El Amir, on the other hand, were primarily philologists.

The opening of Faruq I (Alexandria) University in 1942 broadened opportunities in academia. Naguib Mikhail made his career there, and Abu Bakr and Rizqana taught there before returning to Cairo. Faruq I University, like Cairo, sponsored excavations. These included Abu Bakr's early work at Giza and—in partnership with classical archaeologist Alan Wace—at Ashmunayn, where the war had put an end to Roeder's fieldwork.[58] Alexandria lacked Cairo's depth in Egyptology but had strength in Greco-Roman studies.

Egyptology graduates of Fuad I/Cairo University's Institute of Archaeology from 1940 to 1957 constituted the fourth generation of Egyptian Egyptologists. Unlike the third generation, most of them had not studied or worked under Selim Hassan. The fourth generation straddles the 1952 revolution and comes to an end with the class of 1957. This was Cairo's last class of MA-level graduates in Egyptology before the reintroduction of the undergraduate BA. Seventy-three Egyptologists earned these graduate diplomas from 1940 to 1957, an average of four a year. Half a dozen were women, the first graduating in 1941 and three more in 1949. This number of fourth-generation graduates was modest compared to the ballooning numbers of the later Nasser years and after.[59]

In the third generation, Zaki Saad, Zakariya Ghoneim, and Labib Habachi worked their way up through the Antiquities Service despite missing the opportunity for graduate studies. Ahmad Fakhry combined the Antiquities Service and academic career tracks. He began graduate studies in Europe but earned his doctorate at Cairo while working for the Service. At age forty-seven in 1952, he left the Service for a chair at Cairo University.

Jill Kamil's biography of Labib Habachi perceptively compares his career with that of his friend and rival Ahmad Fakhry. They graduated together in 1928 in the first class of BA Egyptologists.[60] In 1929–32, Fakhry studied in Berlin, Brussels, and Liverpool—under Kurt Sethe, Jean Capart, and Eric Peet respectively. He learned field archaeology from Selim Hassan at Giza and worked twenty years in the Antiquities Service. In 1935 he published a monograph on seven tombs east of the Great Pyramid. Fakhry moved up quickly—chief inspector for Middle Egypt and the Oases in 1936 and for the Delta in 1938, curator at the Cairo Museum, and chief inspector of Upper Egypt (1942–44).

Coming from a landed family in Fayoum, Fakhry grew up hearing tales of the desert from Amm (Uncle) Said, a freed black slave from Siwa Oasis. Fakhry published two books on the oases before earning his Fuad I University doctorate in 1943. He directed desert researches at the Antiquities Service (1944–50) and did a pioneering archaeological survey in Yemen (1947). As director of pyramid researches from 1950, he dug at Dahshur and Saqqara. Upon Gabra's retirement in 1952, Fakhry left the Service for Cairo University's chair of the History of Ancient Egypt. He retired at sixty in 1965.

Jill Kamil maintains that social class rather than being a Copt slowed Labib Habachi's advancement.[61] Passed over for a fellowship to Europe, he had to wait two years after graduating before obtaining an Antiquities Service appointment as inspector at Aswan (1930). By the time he became chief inspector of Upper Egypt in 1944, he had been transferred fifteen times, from Aswan to Zagazig and Tanta in the Delta.

Habachi's early challenges to two theses propounded by European Egyptologists were long ignored. He argued that the Hyksos capital of Avaris was at modern Tell al-Daba, not Tanis, as Pierre Montet, excavator of the latter site, maintained. Habachi also argued that Rosetta, not Alexandria, was the main destination of inscribed blocks quarried from the temple of Sais. He was eventually proven right on both counts.[62]

Although Habachi won a state prize for his book on Tell Basta (Bubastis), in the Delta near Zagazig, the shrine and tombs associated with the cult of Heqaib at Aswan were his greatest discovery. Heqaib was a Sixth Dynasty governor of Aswan who was locally worshiped during the Middle Kingdom. His shrine was on Elephantine Island, and his tomb nearby on the west bank of the Nile. Fertilizer diggers hit on the shrine in 1932, shortly after Edouard Ghazouli succeeded Habachi as inspector there. Ghazouli's hurried excavations turned up Middle Kingdom statues, but these were stored away unpublished. When Habachi was posted back to Aswan in 1946, he persuaded Drioton to fund an excavation. He found a treasure trove of Middle Kingdom statues and stelae in the Elephantine sanctuary to Heqaib and was able to link them to associated tombs on the west bank.

Even after Belgian Egyptologist Constant de Wit announced the Heqaib discovery without permission at the International Congress of Orientalists in Paris in 1949, Habachi put off publishing a preliminary report. Alan Gardiner helped him with the texts, and Drioton urged him on. Drioton was gone by the time he finally turned in the manuscript to the Antiquities Service for publication. There it languished for years until Habachi managed to retrieve, revise, and publish it. It finally came out posthumously in 1985.[63]

A Moment Longer: King Faruq, Drioton, and Royal Archaeology

The sixteen-year-old king who would degenerate into a playboy and the jovial, scholarly French abbé who directed the Antiquities Service were an unlikely pair. Dissolute though he became, Faruq never lost the enthusiasm for antiquities he discovered as a teenager under Drioton's fatherly tutelage. As already noted, he traveled to Tanis three times in 1939–40 to watch Pierre Montet open royal sarcophagi.[64]

Beneath the Great Pyramid on the Giza plateau, Faruq replaced a kiosk from Ismail's day with a fantasy rest house in neo-pharaonic style (see fig. 75). Italian and Egyptian designers executed and furnished the structure. The gateway resembled a pylon, the main hall had hunting scenes of a nobleman with his wife, and the dining room ceiling reproduced the zodiac ceiling from the Temple of Dendera. Faruq's name in a hieroglyphic cartouche was found without and within.[65] Replica statues of Thutmosis III flanked the entry, and the furniture included a replica of

75 Faruq's pharaonism: Rest house at the Great Pyramid, Giza. *Photo: D. Reid.*

Tutankhamun's throne.[66] In the wake of the 1952 revolution, a disapproving army major wrote: "The bedroom is Louis XIV and it was prepared only after Farouk expressed his desire to turn this temple like building into a private night-club."[67]

Drioton adeptly channeled Faruq's antiquarian enthusiasm into "royal excavations" at Saqqara and Helwan, which were funded by the palace instead of the Antiquities Service. Faruq also underwrote Georges Goyon's research on graffiti on the Great Pyramid.[68] Faruq's "royal archaeology" helped make up somewhat for the sparseness of both foreign and Egyptian excavations in the dozen years leading up to the 1952 revolution.

Zaki Saad (1901–82) was the Egyptologist who benefited most from Faruq's largesse. He earned his Egyptology BA in 1930 and married the sister of Rizqallah Naguib Makramallah, an Egyptology classmate in Fakhry and Habachi's class of 1928. Saad learned field archaeology in the Antiquities Service under Walter Bryan Emery, two years his junior, on a Nubian survey (1931–34) and then at Saqqara (1934–39). After Selim Hassan was forced out and Emery left for wartime intelligence work, Saad moved up to become director of works at Saqqara (1940), chief inspector for Saqqara and Giza (1941), and a curator at the Cairo Museum (1944).

In 1941, Herbert W. Fairman charged that

> there are a crowd of Egyptian excavators working at Sakkara, ruthlessly
> opening tomb after tomb, and leaving no record of their work except the
> obvious, many will not be published, some will only be published inad-
> equately and all are rigorously prohibited to the Egyptologist to visit.[69]

Ambassador Lampson objected that only Zaki Saad was digging at
Saqqara, that his work was not bad, and that Drioton checked in on him
every week.[70] At Saqqara, Saad discovered Old Kingdom and Saite tombs
between the Step Pyramid and the causeway of Unas's pyramid. Moving
across the Nile to Helwan, he then excavated ten thousand Early Dynastic graves over a dozen seasons (1942–54). Saad's book dedications were
necessarily fulsome:

> Unto His Majesty Faruk the First, King of the Nile Valley, He who Revives
> and Protects the Ancient Civilization of Egypt, To whom the Science of
> Egyptology will be forever indebted, I humbly present this brochure.[71]

Even so, Saad complained about having to manage without an assistant
for seven years. Drioton finally provided him with one—Mohammed Abd
al-Tawwab al-Hitta.[72]

For Drioton, being a "royal archaeologist" became a liability overnight with the Free Officers' coup of July 23, 1952. It is not clear whether
this was the case with Saad, for he survived in the Antiquities Service
and in 1954 was promoted to director of inspectorates.[73] Be that as it
may, his new position cut him off from his excavations at Helwan. Saad
coauthored four popular Arabic books with restorer Ahmad Yusuf and
published a pharaonic novel.[74] In 1960, a clash with Anwar Shukri, the
director general of Antiquities "who fired Habachi,"[75] forced him to
retire. After working as a tourist guide, Saad immigrated with his family
to Raleigh, North Carolina. He published, "with J.F. Autry," the popular
Excavations at Helwan (1969) but never published preliminary reports on
his later seasons or a final report.[76]

Meanwhile, British representation in the Antiquities Service, never
a top priority for the embassy, withered away. When Engelbach died
in 1946, Robert Greg consulted the embassy's Advisory Committee on
British Culture under Oriental Secretary Walter Smart. Smart speculated about moving Guy Brunton to Engelbach's slot as scientific adviser,
replacing Brunton as assistant curator with Emery, and hiring a junior
Englishman such as Oliver Myers for Saqqara. Myers had dug with the

Robert Mond expedition at Armant and worked in wartime intelligence. Greg countered that Emery was a better excavator than museum man and asked if Herbert Fairman's "hasty temper and uncertain manners" must always rule him out. Drioton, however, warned that the poor state of British–Egyptian relations made a push for any British appointments inopportune. Brunton was ill; he retired in March 1948 and died in South Africa seven months later. Half a century of British work in the French-dominated Antiquities Service had come to an end.[77]

Drioton stood alone, the last European in the Antiquities Service's central administration and nearly paralyzed administratively. Neither France nor Britain retained the leverage and will to intervene on Egyptological matters, and it was King Faruq who got Drioton's contract renewed in 1949 despite attacks in the press.[78] Most of the few Frenchmen remaining in Egyptian service depended on Quai d'Orsay salary supplements of about £E30 a month.[79]

Outside Cairo, in 1945 Henri Chevrier resumed work at Karnak and Jean-Philippe Lauer at Saqqara. Varille worked at Saqqara and Karnak until his position was eliminated in 1950, ostensibly for reasons of economy.[80] In 1947 Greg reported that the contract of Alexandre Stoppelaëre, who had been restoring tombs, had not been renewed, adding, "If this holds, all Theban tomb work will be thrown away." Walter Smart commented: "There is nothing we can do with the present hostile regime. We can only hope that Drioton will be able to work the thing." Once again, King Faruq came through. He assured Drioton that the contracts of Stoppelaëre and other foreigners in the Service would be renewed but stipulated that no more foreigners could be hired. Like Faruq and Drioton, Stoppelaëre made it through until the 1952 revolution.

Like his father Fuad, King Faruq often deployed pharaonic motifs on his postage stamps. The young king was himself an avid stamp collector. In 1941–43, four additions to his father's 1933 airmail set kept to the same design of an airplane over the Giza Pyramids.[81] Stamps celebrating ophthalmological and telecommunications conferences (1937, 1938) and an agricultural and industrial exposition (1949) all deployed pharaonic motifs.[82] In 1947, a beautiful set of stamps for an International Exposition of Contemporary Art showed the Ramesseum, a triad sculpture of Menkaure and two goddesses, the bust of Nefertiti, and Tutankhamun's funerary mask.[83] For the Sixteenth Agricultural and Industrial Exposition (1949), another set showed the Roman sculpture (now in the Vatican) of the Nile as a reclining nude male with cherubs symbolizing fruitfulness.[84] Another stamp for the same exposition juxtaposed pharaonic-style male and female peasants with factory smokestacks.[85] A soldier looms over the scene, in retrospect an omen in a country whose loss of the 1948 war with Israel was already spurring young Free Officers into plotting their coup.

For all his personal interest in pharaonic antiquities, King Faruq was no narrow pharaonist. Both his postage stamps and the Museum of Egyptian Civilization opened on Gezira in 1949 project a vision, inherited from his father Fuad, of an enlightened monarch presiding over all phases of Egyptian history. In such symbolic assertions of royal sovereignty during the semicolonial age, evidence of the colonizing British, the king's Wafdist challengers, and the insurgent Muslim Brothers all remained out of sight.

In a stamp set of 1938, lightly redesigned for reissue in 1947–51, the resplendent monarch stands alone on the two highest denominations (see fig. 76). The other five stamps in the set all juxtapose his image with monuments, projecting an image of his benevolent protection over the full sweep of Egypt's national heritage. Rather like the modern Greeks, whose "indigenous Hellenism" embraced not only the classical past so idolized by

76 King Faruq, guardian of Egypt's heritage from the pyramids to Fuad I (Cairo) University. Postage stamp set, 1938. *From the collection of D. Reid.*

Western philhellenes but also medieval Byzantium and Greek Orthodox Christianity as bridges to modern times,[86] the official Egyptian nationalism promoted by King Faruq imagined an unbroken glorious past from the pharaohs to the present.

In contrast to Kitchener's colonial set of 1914, Faruq's 1938 set represents pharaonic Egypt on only a single stamp—the Pyramids of Giza. The next in the series features the imposing Sultan Hassan Mosque, representing the medieval Islamic age, which Kitchener's set had reduced to background. Then comes the Citadel's Muhammad Ali Mosque, as in the colonial set. This mosque takes on new meaning here, however, for it is juxtaposed with the portrait of Faruq, the great-great-grandson of the monument's builder. The Aswan Dam is also carried over from the 1914 set, but now the king's portrait distances the monument from its British associations, and it is no longer the climax of the set. A higher denomination stamp boasts a newer marvel—the Egyptian University, with which Faruq's father Fuad had been closely associated and which had just been renamed in Fuad's honor.

Like the stamps, the Museum of Egyptian Civilization, inaugurated in 1949, attempted to overcome the chronological and thematic fragmentation of the national heritage implied by the four antiquities museums and smaller museums on such themes as war, agriculture, ethnography, irrigation, railways, postal services, and education. The Museum of Egyptian Civilization stood on the fairgrounds on southern Gezira that are now part of the new Opera House cultural complex. Faruq was not yet twenty in 1939 when a proposal in his name was presented to the Royal Agricultural Society for a new museum to tell the story of Egypt's unbroken heritage from prehistory to the present. Paintings, dioramas, maps, and models would treat natural habitat, customs and beliefs, clothing, monuments, weapons and army organization, agriculture, crafts, communications, territorial extent, and conquests.[87]

If the new museum's prehistoric age is folded into the pharaonic, and its "Arab" and "Ottoman" periods are combined, the paradigm resembles the one implied by the creation between 1858 and 1908 of the Egyptian Museum, Greco–Roman Museum, Coptic Museum, and Museum of Arab Art. The Museum of Egyptian Civilization, however, added on a modern history section with four divisions: the French Expedition, Egyptian expansion into the Sudan, the Muhammad Ali dynasty to 1917 (highlighting Muhammad Ali and Ismail), and the climactic "Hall of King Fuad and King Faruq." Committees of experts recommended the displays for each period.[88] Undersecretary of education Shafiq Ghurbal, a distinguished modern historian who had once studied Egyptology under Ahmad Kamal at the Higher Teachers College, oversaw the project.[89]

The Museum of Egyptian Civilization opened in 1949 under the cloud of the defeat by Israel the year before and never drew much of an audience. Three years later, the 1952 revolution made its glorification of Faruq, Fuad, and the Muhammad Ali dynasty obsolete. Gathering dust and little visited in later years, the museum remained open at least into the 1980s.

An ambitious successor, the National Museum of Egyptian Civilization (NMEC) is currently under development in Fustat (Old Cairo) in cooperation with UNESCO. Minus the monarchism, the NMEC plans to carry on its predecessor's driving emphasis on Egyptian exceptionalism and continuity—"Egypt boasts of being the birth place of the most ancient central government in history," and "Egyptian civilization is characterized by consistency and stability since time immemorial."[90]

Toward Revolution: Archaeology and Two Crises of Cultural Decolonization

In the fall of 1951, less than a year before the overthrow of King Faruq, two separate crises of decolonization roiled British and French cultural relations with Egypt. That these erupted under a Wafdist government, with al-Nahhas as prime minister and Taha Hussein as minister of education, might seem surprising. Al-Nahhas himself had signed the 1936 Anglo–Egyptian Treaty, returned to power via Britain's 1942 coup against the king, and staunchly supported Britain in World War II. Taha Hussein —who spearheaded the 1951 cultural clash with France—had studied at the Sorbonne, married a French woman, given his children French as well as Arabic names, and sent his son Claude to the École normale supérieure in Paris. Decolonization was in the air in 1951, however, and more than the personal proclivities of cabinet ministers was driving relations with Britain and France. Egypt had left the sterling bloc in 1947. In 1951, it received only 13 percent of its imports from Britain—lower than at any time in the previous forty years—and it shipped only 19 percent of its exports (mainly cotton) there.[91]

It was the issue of Algeria which provoked a confrontation over French archaeology in Egypt.[92] Pointing out that France had long had an archaeological institute in Egypt (IFAO), independent Egypt proposed to open its own cultural institutes in the French Maghrib. In April 1951, Taha Hussein warned the French Embassy, Drioton, and IFAO director Kuentz that unless France approved the proposed Institut Farouk I in Algiers, Egypt would retaliate against IFAO. The Quai d'Orsay approved the Algiers institute in September 1951.

On October 31, 1951, however, the government promulgated Law No. 215, the first general regulation of antiquities since Law No. 14 of 1912. At a time when the director general of the Antiquities Service was still French, the new law required approval by the minister of education (not merely his subordinate the director general) for any export of antiquities.[93]

In November, al-Nahhas named Yahya al-Khashshab, professor of Persian at Fuad I University, founding director of the Algiers institute. The Algerian Revolution was still three years off, but France's minister of interior and the governor general of Algeria worried lest Egypt encourage independence movements in the Maghrib. Al-Khashshab was denied a visa.

Egypt struck back on November 29, 1951. Minister of education Taha Hussein summoned Drioton to announce the suspension of IFAO fieldwork and the sealing of its excavation houses. At Karnak, a friendly tip from inspector Zakariya Ghoneim enabled the French to spirit their records out overnight before the sealing.[94] IFAO became semi-paralyzed. Although its famous scholarly press did manage to carry on, regular publication of IFAO's *Bulletin* was interrupted for the only time except during the two world wars. Egypt began denying French citizens visas for cultural activities. In May 1952, the seals on the personal residences of Egyptologists Bernard Bruyère and his assistant Clément Robichon were removed—probably through Drioton's appeal to the king—but that was all. Two months later, the revolution made Drioton persona non grata, and prospects for renewing IFAO excavations were indefinitely postponed.

The crisis in Egyptian–British cultural relations in the fall of 1951 was less surprising, for it reflected a general breakdown in political relations. All attempts at a new "Anglo–Egyptian" treaty over the years had failed; the Sudan and the Suez Canal remained sticking points. In October, as Britain was struggling through a new sterling crisis, it joined the United States, France, and Turkey in inviting Egypt to join a military alliance— the Middle East Command (MEC). The United States was preoccupied with the Cold War, Britain and France with propping up their beleaguered empires. On October 8, al-Nahhas rejected MEC as a sham and repudiated the 1936 Anglo–Egyptian Treaty and the 1899 Anglo–Egyptian condominium on the Sudan.[95] Anti-British demonstrations ensued, and the government sanctioned guerilla raids on British bases in the Canal Zone. In December, as already noted, al-Nahhas dismissed all remaining British employees of the Egyptian government. No British Egyptologists were left in the Antiquities Service or universities to feel the sting, but K.A.C. Creswell (Islamic architecture), Alan Wace (classical archaeology), and other university staff in classics and English lost their jobs. Most of the rest were schoolteachers.

A few weeks later, on January 26, 1952, Jean-Philippe Lauer and Zakariya Ghoneim found Pyramids Road nearly deserted as they drove home together from work at Saqqara. They spotted smoke in the distance. Lauer dropped off Ghoneim and realized the scope of the crisis only when he neared his flat in Qasr al-Nil Street. The BOAC building, the Turf Club, and Groppi's pastry shop were in flames, and Ismailiya Square (now Tahrir) was full of demonstrators. Lauer took refuge with a friend in Zamalek, which like Garden City remained untouched.[96] The British killing of about fifty auxiliary police in the Canal town of Ismailiya the day before had provoked the Black Saturday riots in Cairo.[97]

While Cairo burned, King Faruq, cabinet ministers, and army and police officers were at Abdin Palace celebrating the birth of the crown prince. Not until late in the afternoon was the army sent in to restore order. Several hundred buildings in the Ismailiya district—the fashionable quarter between Ezbekiya and the Nile dating from Khedive Ismail's day—and along Pyramids Road in Giza were burned. British losses included the premises of the British Council, the Turf Club, Barclays Bank, BOAC, Thomas Cook, Shell Oil, W.H. Smith, and auto showrooms for Morris Motors, Standard, Jaguar, Studebaker, and Ford. The targets went far beyond British-owned institutions—movie theaters, bars, nightclubs, and department stores popularly associated with colonialism, vice, or luxury went up in flames. Shepheard's Hotel was the most famous casualty.

Members of Ahmad Husayn's Socialist Party (Young Egypt) and the Muslim Brothers were suspected of organizing the arson, but their responsibility was never proved. King Faruq seized the opportunity to dismiss al-Nahhas and the Wafd, but his own reputation was also irreparably damaged. Palace governments limped along for six more months until the Free Officers coup of July 23, 1952. Three days later, ex-King Faruq sailed from Alexandria into exile. Nasser's young Free Officers proved to be very different, and with a very different agenda, from the generals who had feasted with the king while Cairo burned.

12
Conclusion

A hmad Kamal's retirement from the French-run Egyptian Antiquities Service in 1914 went unremarked in *Annales du service des
antiquités de l'Égypte*. So did his death in 1923. Three decades
later in 1951, as the semicolonial era on which this book concentrates was
drawing to a close, the first edition of *Who Was Who in Egyptology* seemed
to confirm his consignment to oblivion. It left Kamal out altogether and
listed no other Egyptian Egyptologists. Had time stood still?

In fact, Egyptians had made great strides in both specialist Egyptology and public enthusiasm for pharaonic Egypt between 1914 and the
1952 revolution. No one did more than Ahmad Kamal to prepare the way
for this. Over the course of half a century, he had been involved in five
attempts to establish a durable school to train Egyptian Egyptologists.
Four attempts foundered on the circumstances of the colonial age. The
fifth, spurred in 1922 by both partial independence and the discovery
of Tutankhamun's tomb, was on the brink of success when Kamal died.
Had he lived six months longer, he would have become director of the
Egyptology program which began classes in February 1924 and eventually grew into Cairo University's Faculty of Archeology.

Nominally Ottoman until 1914 despite British occupation in 1882,
Egypt was a British protectorate *de jure* for only eight years, from 1914 to
1922. Britain's unilateral declaration of circumscribed Egyptian independence in 1922 and the constitution of 1923 turned Egypt from a colonial
protectorate into a semicolonial parliamentary monarchy. After the
Wafd's failure to win full independence in the 1919 revolution, the British
regrouped and found Egyptian allies in the palace, upper-class 'minority'
parties, and later the evolving Wafd itself. Three decades of semicolonial
rule were the result. The Free Officers' revolution of 1952 ushered in a

military-dominated regime, which took the form of a republic the following year. In 1956, President Nasser's diplomatic victory following the Suez War won the evacuation of foreign troops from Egyptian soil and brought the semicolonial period to an abrupt end.

In archaeology, two world wars punctuated the vigorous fieldwork which the French, British, Germans, Americans, and Italians pursued before 1914 and again after World War I. The Antiquities Service and IFAO furnished the French with two strong bases for Egyptological work. Pierre Lacau and then Étienne Drioton flourished in the Antiquities Service, while IFAO made possible the productive Egyptian careers of classicist Pierre Jouguet and excavators Bernard Bruyère and Pierre Montet. For the British, the EEF, Petrie, and independent excavator Lord Carnarvon had all been active before 1914. After the war, the EES dug at Tell al-Amarna, Petrie tentatively went back to work, and Howard Carter and Lord Carnarvon uncovered the tomb of Tutankhamun. All this British exacavation came to an end by the mid-1930s. Petrie abandoned Egypt in 1926 to work in British-controlled Palestine, Carter wound up his fieldwork on Tutankhamun's tomb in 1932, and in 1936 the EES abandoned Egypt for the Sudan.

For nearly a decade after World War I, the dispute over Berlin's possession of the bust of Nefertiti locked Germans out of excavations in Egypt. Hermann Junker, however, resumed work at Giza in 1925 under the Austrian flag. In 1929, Germany and Egypt sidestepped the Nefertiti dispute as Junker replaced Ludwig Borchardt—who had discovered the Nefertiti bust—at the helm of a reorganized German archaeological institute in Egypt. A decade of vigorous German excavations followed, until the outbreak of World War II.

In American Egyptology, private philanthropy funneled through museums and universities made up for the lack of state-funded archaeology. George Reisner's Boston Museum of Fine Arts–Harvard University expedition worked at the Giza Pyramids into World War II. The Metropolitan Museum of Art dug at Deir al-Bahari on the west bank at Luxor and at the Middle Kingdom pyramids of Lisht. With Rockefeller money, James Henry Breasted founded the Oriental Institute at the University of Chicago, launched its epigraphic project at Medinat Habu, and built its well-equipped Chicago House. At its peak in the early 1930s, Breasted's OI archaeological empire stretched from Egypt through Palestine, Syria, and Iraq into Turkey and Iran. He overreached, however, in his proposal for a lavish Rockefeller-funded museum and research institute in Cairo. It foundered on the objections of Egyptian nationalists and personal and national rivalries among Western archaeologists.

World acclaim for Tutankhamun's tomb invigorated Egypt's drive for full independence from both British rule and French colonial archaeology. Selim Hassan and Sami Gabra were rushed off to Europe for advanced study. They returned to lead a sparse second generation of Egyptian Egyptologists in the Antiquities Service and the new career track in academia. Hassan's and Gabra's excavations, at Giza and Tuna al-Gebel respectively, won recognition from both their compatriots and Western colleagues. Meanwhile, the Egyptian University's Department of Archaeology began turning out the third generation of Egyptian Egyptologists. Ahmad Fakhry and Labib Habachi were among their standouts.

As in the League of Nations mandates, Britain and Egypt were steering uneasily between the realities of European colonialism and the ideal of self-determination in 1922 as they entered the uncharted waters of the semicolonial era. In archaeology, as in political, economic, and military affairs, the transition to full independence stretched into the 1950s. Selim Hassan's challenge to French archaeological control in the mid-1930s proved to be premature, and an unlikely alliance of Britain, France, and King Faruq forced him out of public life. Sami Gabra, in contrast, worked smoothly with Western colleagues and flourished in the semicolonial milieu. In 1939, Hermann Junker was forced out of his Egyptian University chair, and with Selim Hassan on the sidelines, Gabra stepped up to preside as dean of the Egyptian profession for a dozen years.

Pharaonism, already catching on among educated Egyptian elites before World War I, found new inspiration in Tutankhamun's tomb. Politics and pharaonist art converged in Mahmoud Mukhtar's sculpture *Revival of Egypt*, his Cairo and Alexandria statues of Saad Zaghlul, Muhammad Nagi's paintings, and Saad Zaghlul's mausoleum. Writers Muhammad Husayn Haykal, Salama Musa, and Tawfiq al-Hakim turned to ancient Egypt for inspiration. Among the younger generation, so did Ahmad Husayn of Young Egypt and Naguib Mahfouz in his early pharaonic novels. In the 1930s and 1940s, greater emphasis on Islamic and Arab themes dimmed the pharaonist glow, but it endured in a lower key.

Overshadowed by Egyptology in both Egyptian and Western eyes, modern Islamic archaeology in Egypt grew up at the Comité and its Museum of Arab Art. As in Egyptology, Europeans took the lead at first. Yet here too, the quest for national independence intensified the demand for Egyptian specialists who could interpret and cultivate the heritage of Arab–Islamic art and archaeology. Max Herz's effective expulsion from the Comité and Museum of Arab Art as an enemy alien in 1914 enabled his assistant Ali Bahgat to become director of the museum, just as Ahmad Lutfi al-Sayyid replaced an expelled German Orientalist to become the first Egyptian to direct Dar al-Kutub (the National Library). Bahgat is remembered for his pioneering excavation of the early Arab city of Fustat. This Egyptianization of the Museum of Arab Art proved to be premature, however, and after Bahgat's death in 1924, its directorship reverted to a European. Gaston Wiet's brilliant career running the museum for a quarter of a century underlines the staying power of colonial interests. Founding a graduate program in Islamic art and architecture (*athar*, literally "antiquities" or "archaeology") in the early 1930s was also a European initiative. K.A.C. Creswell was soon joined, however, by Zaki Muhammad Hassan, the leader of the second generation of Egyptians in the field. Wiet and Creswell were remarkably productive, and—enabled by the semicolonial ethos—they dominated their fields in Egypt into the 1950s.

Because of its close involvement with the living Coptic community and church, Coptic archaeology evolved rather differently in Egypt than Egyptology and Islamic archaeology. The Comité's Max Herz had taken initial steps toward a Coptic Museum in the 1890s, but it was an Egyptian—Murqus Simaika—who made it a reality. This was thus the only one of the four antiquities museums to be founded by an Egyptian. A lay notable, Simaika found his main support in lay rather than clerical circles. He could not have succeeded, however, without winning at least the passive consent of Coptic Patriarch Kyrillus V. Egyptianization was never an issue at this Egyptian-run museum; nationalization became the issue instead. Should the Coptic Museum remain a community and church-sponsored institution or be transformed into a national one? After protracted maneuvering, the Coptic Museum became a national institution in 1931, albeit with special provisions for Coptic church and community rights.

In the year that Simaika turned seventy—1934—a new generation of amateurs led by Mirrit Boutros Ghali reinvigorated the field by founding the Société d'archéologie copte. Unlike Egyptology, Islamic archaeology, and Greco–Roman studies, Coptic studies could not flourish at Egypt's state universities; Muslim–Coptic politico–religious relations were too sensitive. Coptic studies thus had to develop mainly elsewhere—at the Coptic Museum, the Société d'archéologie copte, and—under clerical constraints—in Coptic schools, churches, and monasteries. By definition, the Coptic Museum and the Société concentrated on Christian antiquities, which straddled the Roman–Byzantine and Islamic periods.

In addition to their Christian heritage, many Copts came to feel a special affinity for ancient Egypt. The Coptic language of the scriptures and liturgy was, after all, the last stage of ancient Egyptian. Impressed by the admiration which so many Westerners felt for ancient Egypt, many Copts asserted that culturally and perhaps even racially they were the

truest "sons of the pharaohs." Throughout the semicolonial era, a dispro-
portionate number of Egyptology students were Copts.

Of the fields represented by the four museums, classics and classical
archaeology had the hardest time taking root among modern Egyptians.
Classical archaeology had no Egyptian founding father comparable to
Ahmad Kamal, Ali Bahgat, or Murqus Simaika. The very intensity with
which European colonialists from Napoleon to Cromer and Maspero
imagined themselves heirs of Alexander and the Caesars was part of the
story. Except for "Pompey's Pillar," Alexandria, Egypt's capital during its
millennium of Greek and Roman rule, lacked surviving standing monuments to compare with the Pyramids, Karnak, or the mosques of Ibn
Tulun and Sultan Hassan. Upper Egyptian temples like Edfu and Kom
Ombo might be of Ptolemaic date, but their pharaonic style tended to
assimilate them to the pharaohs in popular perceptions.

The influx of Greek, Italian, and other European settlers from the
reign of Muhammad Ali on encouraged the revival of classical memories.
Alexandria by the sea, not Cairo, seemed the natural location to the Europeans who took the lead in founding the Greco–Roman Museum in the
1890s. Italian classicists—Giuseppe Botti, Evaristo Breccia, and Achille
Adriani—monopolized its directorship until World War II. Yet Egyptians also had their own classical memories. Aristotle had been critical to
medieval Islamic philosophy, theology, and science, and Muslims had their
own Alexander legends. Already before World War I, a Lebanese Christian immigrant to Egypt had translated the *Iliad* into Arabic, and Egyptian
nationalists had tried to turn Europe's classics against European colonialism. After World War I, Taha Hussein championed classical studies in
Egypt's emerging universities. Ahmad Shawqi depicted Cleopatra as an
Egyptian nationalist queen, and classical references abound in the works
of Tawfiq al-Hakim. World War II battered the Italian communities in
Egyptian cities, British classicists in Cairo and Alexandria universities were
fired in 1951, and most Egyptian Greeks emigrated during the Nasser
years. Yet classics survived the decolonization of the 1950s in Egypt, and at
the turn of the twenty-first century—despite the strength of the Muslim
Brothers and other Islamists in Alexandria—Bibliotheca Alexandrina reasserted the city's proud commitment to its Greco–Roman heritage.

Although some Muslims wrote off pharaonic history and the Antiquities Service as European colonial distortions that might lead true
believers astray, nationalists generally embraced Tutankhamun's treasures, endorsed the demand that Germany return the bust of Nefertiti,
favored university programs to train their own Egyptologists, and supported Egyptianization of the Antiquities Service. The small but steady

output of Egyptology graduates enlarged the reservoir of Egyptian professionals with a vested interest in ancient Egypt, while numerous guides, hoteliers, boatmen, and craftsmen had a personal financial stake in the antiquities that drew tourists to the land of the Nile.

The denouement came at midcentury as national/imperial politics again spilled over into archaeology. Foreign direction of archaeology, classics, and history at the museums and universities outlasted neither the

77 Pharaonism without Faruq: Stamps, coins, and banknotes. In 1953–54, overprinted bars on stocks of existing stamps obliterated King Faruq's face. The pyramids, however, endured. The Sphinx replaced Faruq as the national symbol on coins in 1954. In 1950, King Faruq's portrait had briefly replaced Tutankhamun's on the one-pound (£E1) banknote. In May 1952, however—as though anticipating the July revolution—Tutankhamun's portrait returned instead of Faruq's. On the reverse of the 1950 banknote, the Temple of Philae replaced the monument of Mansur al-Qalawun. In the 1952 issue, the Sphinx watermark (not visible in illustration) in the blank circle, together with Tutankhamun and the Temple of Philae, made the bill triply pharaonic. *From the collection of D. Reid.*

78 Nasser's initial pharaonism: The Memphis statue of Ramesses II raised in front of the Cairo railway station in 1955. The square (hitherto Station Square / Bab al-Hadid Square) was renamed Ramsis Square, and the main artery leading into it (formerly Queen Nazli Street) became Ramsis Street. *Photo: D. Reid.*

monarchy nor the British occupation. Nationalism fanned by the 1948 Arab–Israeli War, abrogation of the Anglo–Egyptian Treaty, the Black Saturday riots, and 1952 revolution swept away the semicolonial world in which monarchy, parliament, and parties—and the careers of Drioton, Wiet, Creswell, and Adriani—had flourished. In little over a year, 1951–52, these four remarkable scholars were gone. By the time the Suez War rang down the curtain on British empire in Egypt in 1956, their Egyptian successors were already immersed in the old-new challenges of the emerging postcolonial age.

The retreat from the exaggerated pharaonism of some intellectuals and politicians in the 1920s made it easier for educated upper- and middle-class elites to keep in touch with pragmatic sheikhs from al-Azhar and the public at large. Perhaps because no old regime politicians identified with pharaonism to the extent that the Pahlavi shahs glorified ancient Iran, Egypt's revolutionaries of 1952—unlike Islamist Iranian revolutionaries in 1979—had no scores to settle with the pre-Islamic past. Indeed, Nasser and the Free Officers initially fostered something of a revival of pharaonism. The Sphinx, not Nasser's portrait, was chosen as the national symbol to replace King Faruq on the coins (see fig. 77).

Tutankhamun's portrait on the £E1 banknote had briefly been replaced by that of Faruq in 1950. In May 1952, however, as though in anticipation of the revolution two months later, Tutankhamun reclaimed the spot. The Temple of Philae was on the reverse side of the note, and a blank oval containing a watermark of the Sphinx (invisible in figure 77) made it triply pharaonic.

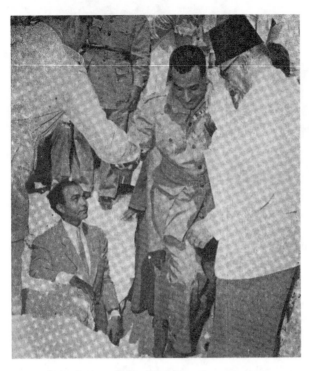

79 The archaeological wonders of 1954. Nasser visits the "Cheops boat." Discoverer Kamal al-Mallakh is below and Mustafa Amer, the first Egyptian director general of the Antiquities Service, is on the right. Les grandes découvertes archéologiques de 1954, special number of La revue du Caire, 33, no. 175 (Cairo, 1955), iii.

In 1955, the colossus of Ramesses II from Memphis went up before the railway station in renamed Ramses Square (hardly anyone remembered that this had originally been a colonial project of Kitchener's) (fig. 78). Nasser made a point of visiting the "Cheops Boat" at Giza and the pyramid of Sekhemkhet at Saqqara in 1954 to emphasize that Egyptians, not Westerners, had made these great discoveries (fig. 79).

Only after Suez in 1956 did Nasser's turn to Arab nationalism overshadow this pride in the pharaonic legacy. Just as Kitchener's stamp set of 1914 captured a British colonial view and Faruq's set of 1938 a monarchical vision of national heritage during the semicolonial age, a 1957 set catches the post-Suez moment of this Pan-Arabist turn (see figs. 7, 76, and 80).

Kitchener's set imagining Egypt as an "antique land" had pharaonic themes on six of its ten stamps and medieval Islamic monuments as only an afterthought on one stamp, concluding triumphantly with the colonial monument of the Aswan Dam. During the semicolonial era, Faruq's 1938 stamp set projected the king as the protector of all phases of the national past. The pharaonic legacy is reduced to more appropriate proportions— a single stamp with the Giza Pyramids. The Mosque of Sultan Hassan brings in medieval Islam, and the Mosque of Muhammad Ali, Faruq's

80 "Egypt Tomb of Aggressors" stamp set of 1957 in the wake of the Suez War and the pivot toward Arab nationalism. *From the collection of D. Reid.*

great-great-grandfather, is retained from the colonial set. The Aswan Dam is also kept, but the climax of the set is now the Egyptian University, which Faruq's father Fuad had been instrumental in founding and which was now renamed in his honor.[1]

Nasser's 1957 postcolonial set "Egypt Tomb of Aggressors" glorified military victories, though his victory at Suez was in fact diplomatic rather than military. Faruq's portrait had of course vanished with his deposition, and existing stamp stocks were overprinted with bars across his face. In the 1957 set, ancient Egypt is again reduced to a single stamp—pharaoh in his chariot driving out the Hyksos intruders at the dawn of the New Kingdom—"Avaris 1580 BC." The medieval Islamic era of the Ayyubids and Mamluks now takes pride of place, with three out of the five stamps in the set. Two celebrate victories over the Crusaders—Saladin at Hateen (1187) and the capture of St. Louis IX of France at Mansura (1250). A third cheers the Mamluks' defeat of the Mongols in Palestine ("Ein Galout 1260"). Nasser was often compared to Saladin in his victory over European aggressors, and his (admittedly brief) unification of Egypt and Syria became known as the United Arab Republic. That Saladin was Kurdish and that the Mamluks too were neither Egyptian nor Arab-born was forgotten or irrelevant. As Egyptian-based warriors, they carried on the "Egypt Tomb of Aggressors" tradition. The set climaxes with Egypt's "victory" over the invaders at Port Said in 1956.[2]

Even as Nasser was turning toward pan-Arabism and third-world nonalignment, the Valley of the Kings was still selected as an appropriate site for him to take President Sukarno of Indonesia in 1958 (see fig. 81). Labib Habachi, as chief inspector of antiquities for Upper Egypt, showed the two presidents the tombs. Ironically, it was not until after Nasser's pan-Arabist turn that prolific amateur historian Abd al-Rahman al-Rafii, a lawyer-politician of the Watani Party turned from his multi-volume history of nineteenth- and twentieth-century Egyptian nationalism back to project the same phenomenon on ancient Egyptians from the dawn of history to the Arab conquest.[3]

81 Labib Habachi (right), President Nasser (behind him), and President Sukarno of Indonesia (left) at the Valley of the Kings, 1958. *Jill Kamil*, Labib Habachi, *201*.

Revolutionary times are anything but predictable, and so it proved for the careers of Egyptian Egyptologists. After a dozen years in official disgrace, the revolution enabled Selim Hassan to re-emerge as a senior figure in Egyptian Egyptology, and he was posthumously honored with a commemorative stamp (see fig. 82).

For Labib Habachi, in contrast, influence in the inner circles of power eluded him under the new regime, as it had under the old. Despite his rapport with President Nasser on the several occasions they met, Habachi was unable to obtain a meaningful promotion, and in 1960 intrigues forced him out of the Antiquities Service. Some years after both Hassan and Habachi were dead, the busts of noted nineteenth-century European Egyptologists were brought out

82 Selim Hassan rehabilitated. Commemorative stamp, 1987. From the collection of D. Reid.

of the Egyptian Museum and arranged on the marble backdrop to Mariette's sarcophagus and statue. Not long after, the European busts in this panethon were rearranged to make room for those of five Egyptian Egyptologists (see fig. 83).

Ahmad Kamal of course headed the list, Sami Gabra and Selim Hassan represented the second generation, and Labib Habachi and Zakariya Ghoneim the third. The installation of the Egyptian busts was a ceremony not of revolutionary overthrow but one of evolutionary inclusion. None of the European founding fathers was ousted; they simply had to move over to accommodate Egyptian colleagues in the pantheon.

In the 1960s, the UNESCO-coordinated Nubian salvage campaign ahead of the flooding to be caused by the Aswan High Dam became the preoccupation of Egyptian and foreign archaeologists alike. Such intensive foreign involvement in Egyptian field archaeology had not been seen since the 1930s. The level of international cooperation was unprecedented and set the stage for the decades that followed, but the old tensions and conflicts of interest left over from the semicolonial period were never far beneath the surface.

The evolution of Egypt's ten-milleme or one-piaster coin over the course of the twentieth century epitomizes some of the themes developed throughout this study (see figs. 30 and 84). The century opened with nonpictorial coins minted in Egypt but bearing the name of Ottoman Sultan Mehmed V (written as a *tughra*). In keeping with Islamic tradition, these featured only calligraphic, geometric, and vegetal designs. During

83 Make way for Egyptians: Busts of Egyptians are added to those of European Egyptologists at the Egyptian Museum's monument to Mariette. Lower tier, left to right: Labib Habachi, Sami Gabra, Selim Hassan, Ahmad Kamal, Zakariya Ghoneim. Upper tier, left to right: J. Duemchin, C. Leemans, C. Goodwin, E. De Rougé, S. Birch. *Photo: D. Reid.*

Britain's brief formal protectorate, the coins continued the nonpictorial tradition but substituted the name of Egyptian Sultan Husayn Kamil and added an inscription in English and a CE date in Western-style "Arabic numerals" along with the Islamic AH date. Portrait busts of kings Fuad and Faruq followed on the coins during the semicolonial era, but after the 1952 revolution these gave way to the quintessentially pharaonic head of the Sphinx as a national symbol. In 1960, during the United Arab Republic, the Sphinx would bow out in favor of the eagle of Saladin, which gave way in turn in 1973 to the falcon of Quraysh. Under Husni Mubarak in 1984, Egypt fell back on its pharaonic heritage with the Pyramids of Giza on its one-piaster coin. This last was balanced on the reverse, however, with an Ottoman-style *tughra*, now reading—in the absence of a sultan— Jumhuriyat Misr al-Arabiya (Arab Republic of Egypt). The struggle to define Egypt's identity goes on.

Egyptian nationalism and Western neocolonialism still clash from time to time in archaeology as elsewhere, and some Islamists still shun anything to do with the pharaonic past. Yet a football-mad country with fans from

Obverse   Reverse

84 Egypt's one-piaster (ten millième)
coin: from Faruq to pharaonism to
Arabism, and back to pharaonism,
1938–1984. First Row: Portrait of King
Faruq, CE 1938 / AH 1357. Second Row:
The Sphinx replaces Faruq as national
symbol, CE 1954/ AH 1374, *Jumhuriyat
Misr* (the Republic of Egypt). Third Row:
Eagle of Saladin replaces the Sphinx.
Al-Jumhuriya al-Arabiya al-Muttahida,
(the United Arab Republic). AD 1960
/ AH 1380. Fourth Row: Falcon of
Quraysh replaces Eagle of Saladin. *Jumhuriyat Misr al-Arabiya* (Arab Republic
of Egypt). AD 1973 / AH 1393.
Fifth Row: Return to pharaonic symbolism with the Pyramids of Giza.
AD 1984 / AH 1404. Note, however,
that the *tughra* on the reverse reverts
to Ottoman tradition, though it now
reads Jumhuriyat Misr al-Arabiya (Arab
Republic of Egypt) rather than giving
the name of the sultan. *From the collection of D. Reid.*

all social classes which calls its team "the Pharaohs" in international com-
petitions seems unlikely to repudiate its pre-Islamic heritage anytime soon.

Perhaps Naguib Mahfouz deserves the last word, asserting as fact an
aspiration which still moves many of his countrymen as they reflect on
their variegated past and troubled present:

> My mother was an illiterate woman who could neither read nor write;
> nevertheless, I considered her a repository of folk culture. She adored
> Sayyidna Husayn and would visit [his mosque] regularly. . . .
>
> The strange thing is that my mother was also a regular visitor to
> the Egyptian Museum where she liked to spend most of the time in the
> Mummy Hall. I can find no explanation for this: her passion for Al-Husayn

and Islamic historical monuments should have made the statues of the pharaohs repugnant to her. And she would visit Coptic monuments with the same zeal, especially Mar Guirguis Convent, considering the whole matter a form of baraka [blessing]. She was such a frequent visitor that a friendship developed between her and the nuns, who loved her very much. . . .

In truth, I was influenced by this beautiful tolerance; Egyptians have never been sectarian, and this is the true spirit of Islam.[4]

Notes

Introduction

1   Following frequent usage, the first three museums are usually called here the Egyptian Museum, Greco–Roman Museum, and Museum of Arab Art. In 1952, the Museum of Arab Art became the Museum of Islamic Art.

2   Donald Malcolm Reid, *Whose Pharaohs? Archaeology, Museums, and Egyptian National Identity from Napoleon to World War I* (Berkeley: University of California Press, 2002).

3   Lutfi El-Khouli, "A Pharaonic Theory of Resistance," *Al-Ahram Weekly* (December 3–9, 1992).

4   The main collections of the Egyptian Museum, Greco–Roman Museum, and Museum of Arab Art roughly formed a chronological sequence, with breaks at the conquests by Alexander the Great in 332 BCE and the Arab Muslims in 640–42 CE. The Coptic Museum, however, is defined more by theme than by chronology. Its antiquities overlap in time with those of both the Greco–Roman Museum and the Museum of Arab Art.

5   For its first several decades, it was often called the Bulaq (Boulak) Museum after the Cairo district in which it was originally located. The Egyptian Museum on Tahrir Square will soon be superseded, but not entirely replaced, by the Grand Egyptian Museum (GEM) out near the Pyramids of Giza.

6   This committee is usually known by its French name: Comité de conservation des monuments de l'art arabe. The Museum of Arab Art was also sometimes called the Museum of Arab Antiquities, Arab Museum, or Arabian Museum.

7   Mercedes Volait, *Architectes et architectures de l'Égypte moderne (1830–1950): genèse et essor d'une expertise locale* (Paris: Maisonneuve et Larose, 2005), 427.

8   Donald Malcolm Reid, "French Egyptology and the Architecture of Orientalism: Deciphering the Façade of Cairo's Egyptian Museum," in *Franco–Arab Encounters: Studies in Memory of David C. Gordon*, ed. Matthew Gordon and L. Carl Brown (Beirut: American University in Beirut Press,

1996), 35–69.

9   Two of the 'pharaonic' monuments in the 1914 set—a portrait of
    Cleopatra and a temple pylon from Karnak—were actually Ptolemaic
    in date, but being in pharaonic style and context, they may have been
    perceived
    as such.

10 Sayed Desokey El Sharif, *Egyptian Paper Money/ al-Umlat al-misriya al-
    waraqiya* (Cairo: al-Faris lil-diaya wa-l-ilan, 2003), 77.

11 Albert Hourani ended his "Liberal Age" in 1939: *Arabic Thought in the Lib-
    eral Age, 1798–1939* (Oxford: Oxford University Press, 1962).

12 Although stripped of his Cairo University chair, Creswell stayed on in
    Egypt and in 1956 found a new academic home at the American University
    in Cairo.

13 Popular usage, however, often mistakenly dubs any specialist on Egypt an
    Egyptologist.

14 Alain-Pierre Zvie, "L'Égypte ancienne ou l'orient perdu et retrouvé," in *D'un
    orient l'autre*, ed. Jean-Claude Vatin (Paris: CEDEJ: CNRS, 1991), 1:38.

15 Edward Said, *Culture and Imperialism* (New York: Knopf, 1993), 162.

16 Morris L. Bierbrier, ed., *Who Was Who in Egyptology*, 4th ed. (London: The
    Egypt Exploration Society, 2012). Hereafter Bierbrier, *WWWE4*.

17 Elliot Colla, *Conflicted Antiquities: Egyptology, Egyptomania, Egyptian
    Modernity* (Durham: Duke University Press, 2007), 273, lists the multiple
    connotations of 'pharaonism.'

18 Edward Said, *Orientalism: Western Conceptions of the Orient* (New York:
    Pantheon, 1978); Benedict Anderson, *Imagined Communities: Reflections on
    the Origin and Spread of Nationalism* (London: Verso, 1983; rev. ed. 1991);
    Bruce Trigger, *A History of Archaeological Thought* (Cambridge: Cambridge
    University Press, 1989; 2nd ed. 2006). Daniel Varisco, *Reading Orientalism:
    Said and the Unsaid* (Seattle: University of Washington Press, 2007), pro-
    vides a voluminous review of critiques of *Orientalism*.

19 Timothy Mitchell, *Colonising Egypt* (Cambridge: Cambridge University
    Press, 1988), and "Heritage of Violence," Chapter 6, in his *Rule of Experts:
    Egypt, Techno-Politics, Modernity* (Berkeley: University of California Press,
    2002), 179–205; John MacKenzie, *Orientalism: History, Theory, and the Arts*
    (Manchester: University of Manchester Press, 1995); Jason Thompson,
    *Edward William Lane, 1801–1876: The Life of the Pioneering Egyptologist
    and Orientalist* (London: Haus, 2010); Mercedes Volait, *Fous du Caire:
    excentriques, architectes et amateurs d'art en Égypte 1863–1914*, (Montpellier:
    l'archange minotaure, 2009).

20 Israel Gershoni and James Jankowski, *Redefining the Egyptian Nation,
    1930–1945* (Cambridge: Cambridge University Press, 1995), and *Com-
    memorating the Nation: Collective Memory, Public Commemoration, and
    National Identity in Twentieth-Century Egypt* (Chicago: Middle East Docu-
    mentation Center, 2004); Ziad Fahmy, *Ordinary Egyptians: Creating the
    Modern Nation through Popular Culture* (Stanford: Stanford University
    Press, 2011). Fahmy extends the ranks of those imaging the nation beyond

literate elites. He emphasizes vernacular Cairene Arabic as the medium of a little known colloquial press and expands Benedict Anderson's "print capitalism" into "media capitalism" by including recording and broadcasting. See also Mostafa Vaziri, *Iran as Imagined Nation: The Construction of National Identity* (New York: Paragon House, 1993).

21 For example, Margarita Díaz-Andreu and Timothy Champion, eds. *Nationalism and Archaeology in Europe* (London: UCL Press, 1996); Neil Asher Silberman, ed., *The Oxford Companion to Archaeology*, 2nd ed. (Oxford: Oxford University Press, 2012); Charlotte Trümpler, ed. *Das Grosse Spiel: Archäologie und Politik zur Zeit des Kolonialismus (1860–1940)* (Cologne: Ruhr Museum, 2008); Philip Kohl and Clare Fawcett, eds. *Nationalism, Politics, and the Practice of Archaeology* (Cambridge: Cambridge University Press, 1995); Lynn Meskell, ed., *Archaeology under Fire: Nationalism, Politics, and Heritage in the Eastern Mediterranean and the Middle East* (London: Routledge, 1998); Margarita Díaz-Andreu, *A World History of Nineteenth-Century Archaeology: Nationalism, Colonialism, and the Past* (Oxford: Oxford University Press, 2007).

22 Wendy M.K. Shaw, *Possessors and Possessed: Museums, Archaeology, and the Visualization of History in the Late Ottoman Empire* (Berkeley: University of California Press, 2003); Magnus Bernhardsson, *Reclaiming a Plundered Past: Archaeology and Nation Building in Modern Iraq* (Austin: University of Texas Press, 2005). See also Ran Boynter, Lynn Swartz Dodd, and Bradley J. Parker, eds. *Controlling the Past, Owning the Future: The Political Uses of Archaeology in the Middle East* (Tucson: University of Arizona Press, 2010).

23 Reid, *Whose Pharaohs?*; Colla, *Conflicted Antiquities*; Jill Kamil, *Labib Habachi: The Life and Legacy of an Egyptologist* (Cairo: American University in Cairo Press, 2007); Éric Gady, "Le pharaon, l'égyptologue et le diplomate. Les égyptologues français en Égypte, du voyage de Champollion à la crise de Suez (1828–1956)" (2 vols., PhD diss., Université de Paris IV-Sorbonne, 2005). Jason Thompson's *Wonderful Things: A History of Egyptology*, 3 vols. (Cairo: American University in Cairo Press, 2015–2018) began coming out too late for me to consult.

24 Neil Asher Silberman, *Digging for God and Country: Exploration, Archaeology and the Secret Struggle for the Holy Land, 1799–1917* (New York: Knopf, 1982); Boynter, Dodd, and Parker, *Controlling the Past*; Israel Finkelstein and Neil Asher Silberman, eds. *The Bible Unearthed: Archaeology's New Vision of Ancient Israel and the Origin of Its Sacred Texts,* (New York: Free Press, 2002); Nadia Abu El-Haj, *Facts on the Ground: Archaeological Practice and Territorial Self-Fashioning in Israeli Society* (Chicago: University of Chicago Press, 2001).

25 Partha Chatterjee, *The Nation and Its Fragments: Colonial and Post-colonial Histories* (Princeton: Princeton University Press, 1993).

26 For example, Kees van der Spek, *The Modern Neighbors of Tutankhamun: History, Life, and Work in the Villages of the Theban West Bank* (Cairo: American University in Cairo Press, 2011); Stephen Quirke, *Hidden Hands: Egyptian Workforces in Petrie Excavation Archives, 1880–1924*

(London: Duckworth, 2010); Stephen Quirke, "Exclusion of Egyptians in English-directed Archaeology 1882–1922 under British Occupation of Egypt," in *Ägyptologen und Ägyptologien zwischen Kaiserreich und Gründen der beiden deutschen Staaten. . . .*, Beiheft 1, ed. Susanne Bickel, et al. (Berlin: Akademie Verlag Berlin: de Gruyter, 2013), 379–405; Wendy Doyon, "On Archaeological Labor in Nineteenth-Century Egypt," in *Histories of Egyptology: Interdisciplinary Measures*, ed. William Carruthers (London: Routledge, 2015), 141–56. Anne Clément, "Rethinking 'Peasant Consciousness' in Colonial Egypt: An Exploration of the Performance of Folksongs by Upper Egyptian Agricultural Workers on the Archaeological Excavation Sites of Karnak and Dendera at the Turn of the Twentieth Century (1885–1914)," *History and Anthropology* 21 (June 2010): 73–100.

27   Pransenjit Duara, *Rescuing History from the Nation: Questioning Narratives of Modern China* (Chicago: University of Chicago Press, 1995).

1. Egyptology and Pharaonism before Tutankhamun

1   Or refounding. In 1835 Muhammad Ali Pasha founded a rudimentary and ephemeral Antiquities Service and museum and put Rifaa al-Tahtawi in charge of the collection. Donald Malcolm Reid, *Whose Pharaohs? Archaeology, Museums, and Egyptian National Identity from Napoleon to World War I* (Berkeley: University of California Press, 2002), 55–56.

2   The early sections of this chapter, lightly footnoted, are largely summarized from Reid, *Whose Pharaohs?*. Éric Gady, "Le pharaon, l'égyptologue et le diplomate. Les égyptologues français en Égypte, du voyage de Champollion à la crise de Suez (1828–1956)" (2 vols., Phd diss., Université de Paris IV-Sorbonne, 2005), provides a detailed later survey. For the wider context of French archaeology around the Mediterranean and eastward through Iraq, Iran, and Afghanistan, see Gran-Aymerch, Ève, Jean Leclant, and André Laronde, *Les chercheurs de passé, 1798–1945: la naissance d' archéologie moderne: dictionnaire biographique d'archéologie* (Paris: CNRS, 2007) and Nicole Chevalier, *La recherche archéologique française au moyen-orient 1842– 1947* (Paris: Editions recherche sur les civilizations, 2002). Robert Solé, *L'Égypte, passion française* (Paris: Seuil, 1997), surveys French fascination with Egypt generally.

3   Three recent studies of French archaeology, architecture, and city planning in the nineteenth-century Ottoman Empire exclude Egypt: Uzi Baram and Lynda Carroll, eds., *A Historical Archaeology of the Ottoman Empire: Breaking New Ground* (New York: Kluwer Academic/Plenum, 2000); Zainab Bahrani, Zeynep Çelik, Edhem Eldem, eds., *Scramble for the Past: A Story of Archaeology in the Ottoman Empire, 1753–1914* (Istanbul: SALT, 2001); Zeynep Çelik, *Empire, Architecture, and the City: French-Ottoman Encounters, 1830–1914* (Seattle: University of Washington Press, 2008). Egypt's growing autonomy from the Ottomans, the Ottoman Empire's post-1918 fragmentation into separate states, and the disciplinary independence of Egyptology from other archaeologies of "the ancient Near East" have

contributed to such exclusion. Emphasizing Egyptian exceptionalism, however, forfeits opportunities for fruitful comparison and runs counter to the recent tendency in Egyptian historiography to emphasize the Ottoman Turkish context of Muhammad Ali's reign (1805–1848) by calling him Mehmed Ali.

4   On Wilkinson and Lane, see the biographies by Jason Thompson, *Sir Gardner Wilkinson and His Circle* (Austin: University of Texas Press, 1992), and *Edward William Lane, 1801–1876: The Life of the Pioneering Egyptologist and Orientalist* (London: Haus, 2010).

5   Margaret S. Drower, *Flinders Petrie: A Life in Archaeology* (Madison: University of Wisconsin Press, 1995), and David Gange, *Dialogues with the Dead: Egyptology in British Culture and Religion, 1822–1922* (Oxford: Oxford University Press, 2013).

6   These same decades, which coincided with the violence of imperial expansion in Egypt and around the world, also witnessed the intensification of theosophic, occult, and spiritualist cults which rejected secularist beliefs in reason and scientific progress. Egypt provided rich raw materials, ranging from Masonic visions of the "secret wisdom of the Egyptians" to "curse of the mummy" nightmares. See Roger Luckhurst, *The Mummy's Curse: The True History of a Dark Fantasy* (Oxford: Oxford University Press, 2012).

7   Gange, *Dialogues with the Dead.*

8   *Scott 2012 Standard Postage Stamp Catalogue, Vol. 2: Countries of the World C–F,* (Sidney, OH: Scott Publishing Co., 2011), Egypt, #50–59.

9   FO371/10070/E6861, Kerr to MacDonald, Aug. 1, 1924, suggests donating to some charity the £E2500 raised by public subscription toward Kitchener's Ramesses statue project; *Scott 2012,* Egypt #70–71. The colonial origin of this national project eluded the fine study of Israel Gershoni and James Jankowski, *Commemorating the Nation: Collective Memory, Public Commemoration, and National Identity in Twentieth-Century Egypt* (Chicago: Middle East Documentation Center, 2004), 123–26.

10   This section draws especially on Reid, *Whose Pharaohs?*, 114–18, 197–98. For a concise recent overview of German Egyptology in Egypt from the later nineteenth century to 1914, see Susanne Voss, "La representation égyptologique allemande en Égypte et sa perception par les égyptologues français du XIXe au milieu du XXe siècle," *Revue germanique internationale* 16 (Nov. 2012): 171–92.

11   A fundamental new work on German Egyptology in the nineteenth century and especially the first half of the twentieth century is Bickel et al., eds., *Ägyptologen.* On Simon, see Bernd Schultz, ed., *James Simon: Philanthrop und Kunstmäzen/Philanthropist and Patron of the Arts,* 2nd ed. (Munich: Prestel, 2007), and Matthes Olaf, *James Simon: Mäzen in Wilhelmischen Zeitalter* (Berlin: Bostelmann & Siebenhaar, 2000). On the DOG, see Wolfgang G. Schwanitz, ed., *Germany and the Middle East 1871–1945* (Princeton: Marcus Wiener, 2004), especially Stefan R. Hauser, "German Research on the Ancient Near East and Its Relation to Political and Economic Interests from the Kaiserreich to World War II," 155–79. Suzanne L. Marchand,

German Orientalism in the Age of Empire: Religion, Race, and Scholarship
(Cambridge: German Historical Institute, Washington, DC/ Cambridge
University Press, 2009), emphasizes the frequent disconnect between
imperial politics and Oriental studies. On German–Egyptian relations, see
Thomas W. Kramer, Deutsch-ägyptische Beziehungen in Vergangenheit und
Gegenwart (Tübingen: H. Erdmann, 1974).

12 Adolf Erman and Hermann Grapow, Wörterbuch der Ägyptischen Sprache, 5
    vols. (Leipzig: Von Quelle & Meyer, 1926–31) and later supplements.

13 Gady, "Pharaon," 579–84, 640–42.

14 On Erman, see B.U. Schipper, ed., Ägyptologie als Wissenschaft. Adolf Erman
    (1854–1937) in seiner Zeit (Berlin: W. du Gruyter, 2006); M.L. Bierbrier,
    ed., Who Was Who in Egyptology? 4th ed. (London: Egypt Exploration
    Society, 2012), 180–81. On Borchardt, see Susanne Voss, Die Geschichte der
    Abteilung Kairo des DAI im Spannungsfeld deutscher Interessen. Bd. 1 1881–
    1929 (Rahden/Westf.: Rahden, Westf.: Verlag Marie Leidorf, 2013) and
    Bierbrier, WWWE4, 68–69. For earlier institutional histories, see Günter
    Dreyer and Daniel Polz, eds., Begegnung mit Vergangenheit: 100 Jahre in
    Ägypten: Deutsches Archäologisches Institut Kairo 1907–2007 (Mainz: P. von
    Zabern, 2007), and Werner Kaiser, 75 Jahre Deutsches Archäologisches Institut
    Kairo 1907–1982 (Mainz: P. von Zabern, 1982).

15 On the Deutsches Institut für Ägyptische Altertumskunde in Kairo under
    Borchardt, see Voss, Geschichte; Nicole Kehrer, "100 Jahren am Nil: Die
    Geschichte des Deutschen Archäologisschen Instituts in Kairo," in Dreyer
    and Polz, 100 Jahre in Ägypten, 3–7; Daniel Poltz, "Das Deutsche Haus in
    Theben: 'die Möglichkeit gründlicher Arbeit und frischen Schaffens,'" in
    Dreyer and Polz, 100 Jahre in Ägypten, 25–31; Kaiser, 75 Jahre Deutsches
    Archäologisches Institut Kairo, esp. 1–8. See also the website of the Deutsches
    Archäologisches Institut, Cairo Department, http://www.dainst.org/en/
    print/38. Accessed 1/10/2014.

16 On early American interest in ancient Egypt, see Gerry D. Scott III, "Go
    Down into Egypt: The Dawn of American Egyptology," in The American
    Discovery of Egypt, ed. Nancy Thomas (Los Angeles: Los Angeles County
    Museum of Art and American Research Center in Egypt, 1995), 37–47;
    Bruce Trigger, "Egyptology, Ancient Egypt, and the American Imagina-
    tion," in American Discovery of Egypt, ed. Nancy Thomas, 21–35; and John
    A. Wilson, Signs and Wonders Upon Pharaoh: A History of American Egyptology
    (Chicago: University of Chicago Press, 1964).

17 For analysis of the painting, see Donald Malcolm Reid, "Representing
    Ancient Egypt at Imperial High Noon (1882–1922): Egyptological Careers
    and Artistic Allegories of Civilization," in From Plunder to Preservation:
    Britain and the Heritage of Empire, c. 1800–1940, ed. Astrid Swenson and
    Peter Mandler, Proceedings of the British Academy 187 (Oxford: Oxford
    University Press, 2013), 204–209. On Blashfield, including this painting,
    see Mina Rieur Weiner, Edwin Howland Blashfield: Master American Muralist
    (New York: Norton, 2009); Leonard N. Amico, The Mural Decorations
    of Edwin Howland Blashfield (1848–1936) (Williamstown, MA: Sterling

and Francine Clark Art Institute, 1978); and *The Works of Edwin Howland Blashfield*, introduction by Royal Cortissoz (New York: C. Scribner's Sons, 1937).

18   Bierbrier, *WWWE4*, 78–79, 344, 459–60.

19   The rest of this section draws on Nancy Thomas, "American Institutional Fieldwork" and "Archaeological and Research Expeditions to Egypt" in her *American Discovery*, 49–62, 249–55.

20   On America's awakening to Biblical and Mesopotamian archaeology, see Bruce Kuklick, *Puritans in Babylon: The Ancient Near East and American Intellectual Life, 1880–1930* (Princeton: Princeton University Press, 1996).

21   On Breasted, see Jeffrey Abt, *American Egyptologist: The Life of James Henry Breasted and the Creation of His Oriental Institute*, (Chicago: University of Chicago Press, 2011), and Charles Breasted, *Pioneer to the Past: The Story of James Henry Breasted, Archaeologist* (New York: C. Scribner's Sons, 1947).

22   Europeans, rather than German-trained Americans, led the initial Egyptian excavations of the Brooklyn Museum and the University of Pennsylvania's University Museum. Henri de Morgan (1854–1909), brother of Egyptian Antiquities Service director Jacques de Morgan, led Brooklyn's excavation of predynastic / early dynastic Upper Egyptian cemeteries (1906–1908), and Briton David Randall-MacIver (1873–1945) directed Pennsylvania's work in Nubia (1907–11). Bierbrieir, *WWWE4*, 385–86, 347–48.

23   On Winlock (1884–1950), see Geoffrey T. Hellman, "Herbert E. Winlock Egyptologist," *The New Yorker*, July 29, 1933, 16–19, and Bierbrieir, *WWWE4*, 584–85.

24   H.E. Winlock, *Excavations at Deir El Bahri, 1911–1931* (New York, 1942), vii, quoted in Dorothea Arnold, "The Metropolitan Museum of Art's Work at the Middle Kingdom Sites of Thebes and Lisht," in *The American Discovery of Egypt: Essays*, ed. Nancy Thomas (Los Angeles: Los Angeles County Museum of Art and the American Research Center in Egypt, 1996), 58.

25   John M. Adams, *The Millionaire and the Mummies: Theodore Davis's Gilded Age in the Valley of the Kings* (New York: St. Martin's, 2013); Bierbrier, *WWWE4*, 145–46.

26   Gady, "Pharaon," 713.

27   Calvin Tomkins, *Merchants and Masterpieces: The Story of the Metropolitan Museum of Art* (New York: E.P. Dutton, 1970), 92–103, 136–37.

28   Tomkins, *Merchants*, 138.

29   On Ahmad Kamal see Reid, *Whose Pharaohs?* 186–89, passim, and Luway Mahmud Said, "Ahmad Basha Kamal: raid al-tanwir al-athari," in *Kamal wa Yusuf: athariyan min al-zaman al-jamil*, edited by Luway Mahmud Said and Mahmud Abd al-Munim Qaysuni (Cairo: Supreme Council of Antiquities, 2002), 7 ff.

30   Anouar Louca, "Rifa'a al-Tahtawi (1801–1873) et la science occidentale," in *D'un orient l'autre*, ed. Jean-Claude Vatin (Paris: CEDEJ: CNRS, 1991), 2: 213.

31   Okasha El-Daly, *Egyptology: The Missing Millennium: Ancient Egypt in Medieval Arabic Writings* (London: UCL Press, 2005).

32   For tales collected in the 1980s, see Elizabeth Wickett, *Seers, Saints, and Sinners: The Oral Tradition of Upper Egypt* (London: I.B.Tauris Press, 2012).

33   Bierbrier, *WWWE4*, 223.

34   As quoted in translation in Reid, *Whose Pharaohs?*, 188.

35   Bierbrier, *WWWE4*, 386.

36   See the bibliography in *Kamal wa Yusuf*, 127–29.

37   This and the following two translated quotations are from Taha Hussein, *A Passage to France: The Third Volume of the Autobiography of Taha Husain*, trans. Kenneth Cragg (Leiden: E.J. Brill, 1976), 34–35.

38   For the syllabi of the History of the Ancient East course, 1910–15, see B6/F87, Cairo University Archives; Taha Hussein's syllabi for 1923 and 1924 are in B4/F170.

39   Reid, *Whose Pharaohs?*, 201–204, 211.

40   Ahmad Lutfi al-Sayyid, *Qissat Hayati* (Cairo: Dar al-hilal, 1962). Based on conservations with Tahir al-Tanahi in 1950.

41   Lutfi al-Sayyid, *al-Jarida*, December 8,1912, as quoted in French translation in Amal Hilal, "Les premiers égyptologues égyptiens et la réforme," in *Entre réforme sociale et movement national: identité et modernizations en Égypte (1882–1962)*, ed. Alain Rousillon (Cairo: CEDEJ, 1995), 349.

42   Ahmad Lutfi al-Sayyid, *al-Jarida*, December 12, 1912, as translated in Charles Wendell, *The Evolution of the Egyptian National Image from Its Origin to Ahmad Lutfi al-Sayyid* (Berkeley: University of California Press, 1972), 272.

43   Wendell, *Egyptian National Image*, 236–38.

44   Lucie Ryzova, *The Age of the Efendiyya: Passages to Modernity in National-Colonial Egypt* (Oxford: Oxford University Press, 2013).

45   Israel Gershoni and James Jankowski, *Egypt, Islam, and the Arabs: The Search for Egyptian Nationhood, 1900–1930* (New York: Oxford University Press, 1986), 12–13.

46   Ralph M. Coury, *The Making of an Egyptian Arab Nationalist: The Early Years of Azzam Pasha, 1893–1936* (Reading: Ithaca, 1998), 83–7.

47   Beth Baron, *Egypt as a Woman: Nationalists, Gender and Politics* (Berkeley: University of California Press, 2005), 65–66. Baron notes that although Kamil opposed unveiling, the peasant woman's face is uncovered. On the 1940 ceremony, see Gerhsoni and Jankowski, *Commemorating the Nation*, 158, 187–90.

48   *Al-Samir al-Saghir*, reproduced in Reid, *Whose Pharaohs?*, 8.

49   Irfan Shahid, "Ahmad Shawqi," in *Essays in Arabic Literary Biography 1850–1950*, ed. Roger Allen (Wiesbaden: Harrassowitz, 2010), 315.

50   Shahid, "Ahmad Shawqi," 304–307.

51   Marilyn Booth, *May Her Likes Be Multiplied: Biography and Gender Politics in Egypt* (Berkeley: University of California Press, 2001), 1, 28, 224.

52   Booth, *May Her Likes Be Multiplied*, 67, 82.

53   Beth Baron, *The Women's Awakening in Egypt: Culture, Society, and the Press* (New Haven: Yale University Press, 1994), 34–35, and dust jacket picture.

54   Gady, "Pharaon," 724–25.

55 "Manifesto of German University Professors," in *World War I and European Society: A Sourcebook*, ed. Marilyn Shevin-Coetzee and Frans Coetzee (Lexington, MA, 1996), 26–28.

56 Marie-Eve Chagnon, "The Power of Intellectual Judgment: From Eduard Meyer to Michael Ignatieff," *Le Panoptique Feeds*, No. 6, February 2008, http//: www.lepanoptique.com/page article.php?id=53&theme=histoire, accessed February 8, 2008.

57 Gady, "Pharaon," 743.

58 Gady, "Pharaon," 744–45.

59 On German archaeological interests in Egypt during the war, see Voss, *Geschichte*, 168–72, 177–78; Gady, "Pharaon," 703–10.

60 Dreyer and Polz, *100 Jahre in Ägypten*, 6–7.

61 FO 141/440/1206. First Secretary (Cairo) to Financial Adviser, April 30, 1920. Cf. Kaiser, *75 Jahre*, 6.

62 Gady, "Pharaon," 733.

63 *Ancient Egypt* (London magazine issued by W.M.F. Petrie), 1916, Part 4 (Dec.), 187; on Lacau, see Bierbrier, *WWWE4*, 305–306.

64 Gady, "Pharaon," 753–73.

65 FO371/3202/88356, April 30, 1918, Wingate to Graham, enclosing extracts from Grenfell to Wingate, July 19, 1917, and Sayce to Wingate, March 16, 1918.

66 On BSAE and competition between *Ancient Egypt* and *JEA*, see Drower, *Petrie*, 296–98, 326–27.

67 Bierbrier, *WWWE4*, 155.

68 *Ancient Egypt* 1915, Pt. 1 (March), 47.

69 *Ancient Egypt* 1917, Pt. 4 (December), 1.

70 Calculated from Gady, "Pharaon," tables 1158–1163, which are based on Maspero's annual *Rapports*.

71 Reisner to Grey, May 12, 1915. MFA, Reisner, Folder 3.

72 *Ancient Egypt*, 1917, Pt. 1 (March), 48.

73 Reisner to Grey, December 1, 1919. MFA, Reisner, Folder 4.

74 David O'Connor, "The American Archaeological Focus on Ancient Palaces and Temples of the New Kingdom," in *American Discovery: Essays*, ed. Nancy Thomas (Los Angeles: Los Angeles County Museum of Art, American Research Center in Egypt, 1995), 85; Arnold, "Metropolitan," 66–67.

75 Drower, *Petrie*, 334–35.

76 Ahmed Kamal Bey, "Le procédé graphique chez les anciens égyptiens, l'origine du mot Égypte," *BIÉ*, sér. 5, t. 10, fasc. 1, (1916): 133–76.

77 Georges Daressy, "Les noms de l'Égypte," *BIÉ*, sér. 5, t. 10, fasc. 2 (1917): 359–60.

78 Kamal Bey, *BIÉ*, sér. 5, t. 11, fasc. 1 (1917): 331, 325–38. See also fasc. 2 (1918): 421–23.

79 *Ancient Egypt* 1916, Pt. 1 (March), 36.

80 *Ancient Egypt* 1916, Pt. 1 (March), 39.

81 MAE, AMB Le Caire. C 140 (52) Université 1907–1940, D4/SD: École égyptienne d'archéologie, [Summer 1920], 1–4. Signed by Lacau, Kamal,

Foucart, and Abdel Hamid Mostafa.

82   FO 371/3714/50207 "Egyptian Unrest," April 1, 1919, "Translation of Song Now Popular in Egypt." Retranslated from Arabic by Ziad Fahmy, *Ordinary Egyptians: Creating the Modern Nation through Popular Culture* (Stanford: Stanford University Press, 2011), 134. Reginald Wingate was High Commissioner, 1916–1919.

83   Gershoni and Jankowski, *Egypt*, 100, quoting Salah al-Din Dhihni, *Misr bayna al-ihtilal wa-l-thawra*, 71–73.

84   Although the 1919 uprising did not win full independence or overturn the sociopolitical order, Egyptians call it a revolution (*thawra*). Similarly, the European risings of 1848 are called revolutions even though they largely failed.

85   Raymond T. Stock, "A Mummy Awakens: The Pharaonic Fiction of Naguib Mahfouz" (PhD diss., University of Pennsylvania, 2008), 13.

86   Gershoni and Jankowski, *Egypt*, 89–91, lists leading writers of this generation of territorial Egyptian nationalists: Ahmad Amin, Mahmud al-Aqqad, Abd al-Qadir Hamza, Muhammad Husayn Haykal, Taha Hussein, Ismail Mazhar, and Salama Musa—all born between 1880 and 1891. Their study also includes about fifty "secondary intellectuals," mostly born between 1900 and 1910.

87   On Mukhtar, see Gershoni and Jankowski, *Commemorating the Nation*, 27–140, which draws mainly on Badr al-Din Abu Ghazi, *al-Maththal Mukhtar* (Cairo, 1964 and 1994 eds.). See also Arthur Goldschmidt Jr., *Biographical Dictionary of Modern Egypt* (Boulder, CO: Lynne Rienner, 2000), 138. On Nagi, see Christine Roussilon, ed., *Un impressioniste égyptien: Mohamed Naghi (1888–1956)* (bilingual text with Arabic title *al-Fannan al-tathiri al-misri*, Les cahiers de Chabramant, 1988, esp. the biographical sketch, 27–30; Goldschmidt, *Biographical Dictionary*, 150; Liliane Karnouk, *Modern Egyptian Art* (Cairo: American University in Cairo Press, 2005), 26–31.

88   Elliot Colla, *Conflicted Antiquities: Egyptology, Egyptomania, Egyptian Modernity* (Durham, NC: Duke University Press, 2007), 226–28.

89   Gershoni and Jankowski, *Commemorating the Nation*, 60–61.

90   Shahid, "Ahmad Shawqi," 315.

91   Gershoni and Jankowski, *Egypt*, 185.

92   Fahmy, *Ordinary Egyptians*, 167.

93   Fahmy, *Ordinary Egyptians*, 33.

94   Margot Badran, *Feminists, Islam, and Nation: Gender and the Making of Modern Egypt* (Princeton: Princeton University Press, 1995).

95   On al-Mahdiya and Darwish, see Fahmy, *Ordinary Egyptians*, 112–14, 115, and Goldschmidt, *Biographical Dictionary*, 115, 47. Al-Mahdiya was the stage name of Zakiya Hassan Mansour.

96   Fahmy, *Ordinary Egyptians*, 163–64, 218n144.

97   Baron, *Egypt as a Woman*, 70.

98   *Al-Lataif al-musawwara*, Dec. 8, 1919, as reproduced in Lisa Pollard, *Nurturing the Nation: The Family Politics of Modernizing, Colonizing, and Liberating Egypt, 1805–1923* (Berkeley: University of California Press, 2005), 180–81.

99 *Al- Lataif al-musawwara*, March 29, 1920, 4. Beth Baron kindly supplied me copies of pharaonist illustrations and cartoons from *al-Lataif al-musawwara*.

100 *Al-Lataif al-musawwara*, July 11, 1921: 4.

101 Baron, *Egypt as a Woman*, 77.

102 Pollard, *Nurturing*, 190–91. *Al-Lataif al-musawwara*, Aug. 2, 1920.

103 Mona L. Russell, *Creating the New Egyptian Woman: Consumerism, Education, and National Identity, 1863–1922* (New York: Palgrave MacMillan, 2004), 73.

104 In the 1930s, with pharaonism on the defensive, Labiba Ahmad dropped Mukhtar's *Awakening* for a more Islamic cover design. Baron, *Egypt as a Woman*, 199.

105 *Al-Ahram*, October 4, 1922.

106 Jill Kamil, *Labib Habachi*, 55. On Hassan's tour and *al-Ahram* articles, see 52–55.

2. Nationalizing Tutankhamun

1 *Scott 2012 Standard Postage Stamp Catalogue.* 6 vols. (Sidney, OH: Scott Publishing Co., 2011). Vol. 2: *Countries of the World C–F*, Egypt, #50–59; and Vol 3: *G–I*, Great Britain, #669

2 Elizabeth Monroe, *Britain's Moment in the Middle East 1914–1971* (2nd ed., London: Chatto & Windus, 1981).

3 For Carter and the discovery, see especially T.G.H. James, *Howard Carter: The Path to Tutankhamun* (2nd ed., London: Kegan Paul International, 2001). Basic works include Howard Carter and Arthur C. Mace, *The Tomb of Tut.Ankh.Amen: discovered by the late Earl of Carnarvon and Howard Carter*, 3 vols., vols. 2 & 3 by Carter alone (London: Cassell, 1923–33); Nicholas Reeves, *The Complete Tutankhamun* (London: Thames and Hudson, 1990); Nicholas Reeves and John H. Taylor, *Howard Carter before Tutankhamun* (New York: H.N. Abrams, 1993); and H.V.F. Winstone, *Howard Carter and the Discovery of the Tomb of Tutankhamun* (London: Constable, 1991). Thomas Hoving, *Tutankhamun: The Untold Story* (New York: Simon and Schuster, 1978) is a sensationalist account. Joyce Tyldesley, *TutankhAmen: The Search for an Egyptian King* (New York: Basic Books, 2012) provides a recent overview. Zahi Hawass, *Discovering Tutankhamun: From Howard Carter to DNA* (Cairo: American University in Cairo Press, 2013) gives an Egyptian Egyptologist's perspective, and Muhsin Muhammad, *Sariqat Malik Misr* (Cairo: Markaz al-Ahram lil-tarjama wa-l-nashr, Muassasat al-Ahram, 1985) presents a popular account in Arabic. Drs. Fayza Haikal, Gaballa Ali Gaballa, and Nasry Iskander kindly answered queries on this topic in personal correspondence in 2006.

4 Robert Solé, *L'Égypte, passion française* (Paris: Seuil, 1997), 236.

5 Yunan Labib Rizk, "Al-Ahram: A Diwan of Contemporary Life," *Al-Ahram Weekly*, 20–26 July, 2000, 18. John Darwin, *Britain, Egypt and the Middle East: Imperial Policy in the Aftermath of the War, 1918–1922* (London: Macmillan, 1981), treats the postwar settlement. For Egypt's interwar politics, see Marius Deeb, *Party Politics in Egypt: The Wafd and Its Rivals* (London: Ithaca Press, 1979); Afaf Lutfi al-Sayyid Marsot, *Egypt's Liberal*

Experiment: 1922–1936 (Berkeley: University of California Press, 1977); James Whidden, *Monarchy and Modernity in Egypt: Politics, Islam and Neocolonialism between the Wars* (London: I.B.Tauris, 2013).

6   From 1917 to 1922, Fuad bore the title 'sultan,' which the British conferred on his predecessor, Husayn Kamil (r. 1914–1917), after deposing Khedive Abbas Hilmi II and declaring the British protectorate. After the February 1922 ending of the British protectorate and declaration of Egypt's independence, Fuad discarded the title 'sultan' in favor of 'king.'

7   C.W.R. Long, *British Pro-Consuls in Egypt, 1914–1929: The Challenge of Nationalism* (London: I.B.Tauris, 2005), treats the first four: Col. Henry McMahon (1915–16); Sir Reginald Wingate (1916–19); Field Marshal Edmund Hynman, Viscount Allenby of Megido (1919–25); and George Lloyd (1925–29). The next two were Sir Percy Lorraine (1929–33), and Sir Miles Lampson (later Lord Killearn, 1933–46).

8   Robert Tignor, *State, Private Enterprise and Economic Change in Egypt, 1918–1952* (Princeton: Princeton University Press, 1984), 15, 49, 156, 274–75. On the interwar economy, see also Eric Davis, *Challenging Colonialism: Bank Misr and Egyptian Industrialization, 1920–1941* (Princeton: Princeton University Press, 1983), and Robert Vitalis, *When Capitalists Collide: Business Conflict and the End of Empire in Egypt* (Berkeley: University of California Press, 1995).

9   Carter, *Tut.Ankh.Amen*, 1: xvii, xx; 2: xxiv.

10   FO371/6332/E4235, Spender to Ingram, April 20, 1921, enclosing the Milner Mission's "Memorandum by the Special Mission to Egypt on the Antiquities Department," Dec. 9, 1920; and FO371/6332/E5310, Spender to FO, May 4, 1921.

11   DWQ/ MMW/ Nazarat al-Ashghal/ Maslahat al-Athar 1908–23. 3/4. President of the Council of Ministers, Adli Yakan Pasha, "Note au conseil des ministres," May 5, 1921.

12   MAE, AMB Le Caire, Enseignement égyptien, Service des antiquités C174 Daressy to undersec. of state of Min. of Public Works (of Egypt), Aug. 28, 1921. *The Egyptian Directory: L'Annuaire égyptien (Égypte et Soudan)*, (Cairo, 1921), 193, lists the "Technical Service" of the Antiquities Service from Lacau down.

13   Howard Carter, *The Tomb of Tut.Ankh.Amen* vol. 2 (New York: Cooper Square Publishers, 1963; reprint of 1927 ed.) title page, xx, 65, 106, Plate 28; Appendix 1: Douglas E. Derry, "Report upon the Examination of Tut. Ankh.Amen's Mummy," 143–61. Another background figure in the photo is Muhammad Chaban (Shaban, 1866–1930), a nephew of Ahmad Kamal and alumnus of his Egyptology school at the Cairo Museum in the 1880s. Chaban held various antiquities inspectorships, published eleven items in *ASAE*, and attended the unwrapping of Tutankhamun's mummy. Two years after Kamal retired in 1914, Chaban had succeeded him as assistant curator. Zaki Fahmi, *Safwat al-asr fi tarikh wa rusum mashahir rijal Misr* (Cairo: Matbaat al-itimad, 1926), 701–705; Bierbrier, *WWWE4*, 112.

14   *Recueil d'études égyptologiques dédiées à la mémoire de Jean-François Champollion*

à *l'occasion du centenaire de la letter à M. Dacier relative à l'alphabet des hieroglyphs phonétiques lue à l'académie des inscriptions et belles-lettres le 27 septembre 1822*. Bibliothèque de l'école des hautes études, publiée sous les auspices du ministère de l'instruction publique. Sciences historiques et philologiques. Fasc. 234 (Paris: E. Champion, 1922), i–iii.

15 Hermine Hartleben, *Champollion, sein Leben und sein Werk*, 2 vols. (Berlin: Weidmann, 1906).

16 Rosalind C. Morris and Gayatri Chakravorty Spivak, *Can the Subaltern Speak? Reflections on the History of an Idea* (New York: Columbia University Press, 2010).

17 Muhammad Jamal Mukhtar, "Selim Hassan ka munaqqib wa alim al-athar," *al-Majalla al-tarikhiya al-Misriya* 19 (1972): 78.

18 Muhammad Jamal Mukhtar, "al-Alim al-athari al-awwal fi Misr," *al-Majalla al-tarikhiya al-misriya* 12 (1964–65), 51–53; Luway Mahmud Said, "Ahmad Basha Kamal: raid al-tanwir al-athari," in *Kamal wa Yusuf: athariyan min al-zaman al-jamil*, edited by Luway Mahmud Said and Mahmud Abd al-Munim Qaysuni (Cairo: Supreme Council of Antiquities, 2002), 91–92.

19 Ahmad Basha Kamal, *Mujam al-lugha al-misriya al-qadima*, vol. 1 (Cairo: Supreme Council of Antiquities, 2002).

20 See, however, the recent proposal, indebted to Kamal's dictionary, for teaching hieroglyphs through an Arabic rather than a Latin-based transcription system: Okasha El-Daly and Stephen Quirke, "Arabic Transliteration of Ancient Egyptian," in *Managing Egypt's Cultural Heritage: Proceedings of the first Egyptian Cultural Heritage Organisation Conference on Egyptian Cultural Heritage Management*, eds. Fekri A. Hassan, L. S. Owens, A. De Trafford, Egyptian Cultural Heritage Organisation (ECHO), Discourses on Heritage Management Series No. 1 (London: Golden House Publications, 2009), 15–26.

21 See Ahmad Kamal, *al-Ahram*, Jan. 1, 1923, *al-Muqtataf*, Jan. 1, 1923: 6–8; Selim Hassan, "Kanz," *al-Ahram*, Jan. 1, 1923, reprinted in *al-Ahram: shuhud al-asr 1876–1986* (Cairo: Matbaat al-Ahram, 1986): 80–88; Hassan Ahmad Kamal, *al-Muqattam*, Feb. 20, 1924: 2, *passim* in Feb. and March.

22 Hala Sallam, "Ahmed Kamal Pasha (1851–1923): A Family of Egyptologists," in *Proceedings of the Seventh International Congress of Egyptologists: Cambridge, 3–9 September 1995*, ed. C.J. Eyre (Leuven: Peeters, 1998), 1019. For Hassan [Ahmad] Kamal's articles on Tutankhamun, see *al-Muqattam*, Feb. 20, 1924, and later issues in February and March. He also published on ancient Egyptian medicine: *Kitab al-tibb: al-Misri al-qadim* (Cairo: Matbaat *al-Muqtataf wa-l-Muqatam*, 1922).

23 Hassan Kamal, "Athar al-Uqsur," *al-Muqattam*, Feb. 20, 1924, 2.

24 Mukhtar, "Selim Hassan," *al-Majalla al-tarikhiya al-misriya*, 19 (1972), 78.

25 W.R. Dawson, ed. *Who Was Who in Egyptology?* (London: Egypt Exploration Society, 1951).

26 *JEA* 9 (1923), 241; *BIÉ* 6 (1924), 171–72 (V.M. Mosséri); Gamal Mukhtar, *al-Majalla al-tarikhiya al-misriya* 12 (1964–65), 43–57; *ASAE* 64 (1981), 1–5, (D. Abou-Ghazi). On the rehabilitation, see also Luway Mahmud Said, in *Kamal wa Yusuf*, 69–74.

27 Wendy M.K. Shaw, *Possessors and Possessed: Museums, Archaeology, and the Visualization of History in the Late Ottoman Empire* (Berkeley: University of California Press, 2003).

28 I.A. Maalouff, "Faqiduna wa atharuhu," *Majallat majma al-ilmi al-arabi/La revue de l'académie arabe* 3 (9 & 10, 1923): 306.

29 Quoted in James L. Gelvin, "The Middle East Breasted Encountered, 1919–1920," in *Pioneers to the Past: American Archaeologists in the Middle East 1919–1920*, Geoff Embling, ed. (Chicago: Oriental Institute, University of Chicago, 2010), 25.

30 MFA, Reisner, Correspondence, Box: Reisner 1900–26, Folder 7, "Memorandum on the Alexandria Massacre of May 1921."

31 University of Pennsylvania, University Museum Archives, Expedition Records, Egypt—Dendereh, Box 7, Folder 3: Correspondence [Fisher–Gordon] #3, 1917–1918, Fisher to Gordon, p. 8. For analysis of this quarrel, see Wendy Doyon, "On Archaeological Labor in Nineteenth-Century Egypt," in *Histories of Egyptology: Interdisciplinary Measures*, ed. William Carruthers, (London: Routledge, 2015), 149–152. See also Joanne Rowland, "Documenting the Qufti archaeological workforce," *Egyptian Archaeology*, no. 44 (Spring 2014): 10–12, and in the same issue, David Jeffreys, "Egyptian colleagues at Saqqara (and elsewhere)," 13–14. Calling the Qufti *rais*es and their crews 'colleagues' would have been unthinkable in the old days.

32 Fisher to Reisner, 20 May 1917, University of Pennsylvania, University Museum Archives, Expedition Records, Egypt: Mitrahineh, Box 30, Folder 3.

33 This paragraph's quotations are from Grace Thompson Seton, *A Woman Tenderfoot in Egypt* (New York: Dodd, Mead & Co., 1923), 132–34.

34 For this theme, see Pierre Nora and Lawrence D. Kritzman, *Realms of Memory: Rethinking the French Past*, 3 vols (New York: Columbia University Press, 1996–98). Selected translations from Pierre Nora, ed. *Les lieux de mémoire*, 7 vols. (Paris: Gallimard, 1984–92).

35 Edwards, I.E.S. *From the Pyramids to Tutankhamun: Memoirs of an Egyptologist* (Oxford: Oxbow, 2000).

36 On Egyptomania, see National Gallery of Canada, *Egyptomania: Egypt in Western Art 1730–1930* (Ottawa: National Gallery of Canada, 1994); Sally MacDonald and Michael Rice, eds. *Consuming Ancient Egypt* (London: UCL Press, 2003); Bob Brier, *Egyptomania: Our Three Thousand Year Obsession with the Land of the Pharaohs* (New York: Palgrave Macmillan, 2013); Fayza Haikal "Egypt's Past Regenerated by Its Own People," in *Consuming Ancient Egypt*, eds MacDonald and Rice, (London: UCL Press, 2003),123–138, treats the Egyptian equivalent of Western Egyptomania.

37 Karl Baedeker, *Egypt and the Sudan*, 6th ed. (Leipzig: Baedeker, 1908), xiii.

38 *The Times Digital Archive 1785–1985.*

39 On the controversy over the press monopoly, see James, *Carter*, 277–82, 480–85; and Julie Hankey, *A Passion for Egypt: Arthur Weigall, Tutankhamun and the 'Curse of the Pharaohs'* (London: I.B.Tauris, 2001), 260–63, 328–29.

40 Hankey, *Passion for Egypt*, 260.

41 James, *Carter*, 320–25.

42 *The Egyptian Gazette* (hereafter *EG*) Feb. 26, 1923, 3.

43 *EG* Feb. 26, 1923, 4, quoted in *The Egyptian Gazette*'s summary of "The Native Press." Similar quotations from the Gazette's translated selections from the Arabic press follow.

44 *EG*, Feb. 22, 1923, 2.

45 Gady, "Pharaon," 630–34.

46 James, *Carter*, 475–77.

47 James, *Carter*, 245–47, discusses divisions on the eve of the Tutankhamun discovery.

48 Mond to Secretary, September 13, 1923, and Secretary to Mond, September 20, 1923. EEF Archives, Box: Correspondence: SRK Glanville, R. Mond, Folder: Mond.

49 James, *Carter*, 270–271, quoting Lythgoe to Robinson, December 23, 1922, MMA archives.

50 James, *Carter*, 328.

51 Elliot Colla, *Conflicted Antiquities: Egyptology, Egyptomania, Egyptian Modernity* (Durham, NC: Duke University Press, 2007), 221–22, translating Ahmad Shawqi, "Tut Ankh Amun," *al-Shawqiyat: al-amal al-shiriya al-kamila* (Beirut: Dar al-Awda, 2000), 1: 270–71. The last line blames the British for the deposition and exile of the last Ottoman sultan, Mehmet VI Vahideddin, in 1922.

52 J. Brugman, *An Introduction to the History of Modern Arabic Literature in Egypt* (Leiden: Brill, 1984), 56–62. Brugman, 59n25, lists the three poems as being in Mutran's *Diwan* I–IV (new ed. in 3 vols, Beirut: Dar Marun Abbud, 1975–77, from Cairo: Dar al-Hilal ed., 1948–49) I: 104; II: 175; III: 166.

53 Irfan Shahid, "Ahmad Shawqi," in *Essays in Arabic Literary Biography 1850–1950*, ed. Roger Allen (Wiesbaden: Harrassowitz, 2010), 315.

54 James, *Carter*, 475.

55 *EG*, Feb. 21, 1923, 4.

56 Fikri Abaza, "Ila Tutankhamun," *al-Ahram*, Feb. 20, 1924, as translated in Colla, *Conflicted Antiquities*, 172.

57 Magda Baraka, *The Egyptian Upper Class between Revolutions 1919–1952* (Reading, UK: Ithaca Press, 1998), 126, citing Abdalla Ahmad Abdalla, *Sittun Sana Sinama* (Cairo, 1988).

58 Colla, *Conflicted Antiquities*, 223–24.

59 James, *Carter*, 332.

60 Howard Carter, *Tut.Ankh.Amen: The Politics of Discovery* (London: Libri, 1998, originally published as *Tut.Ankh.Amen. Statement, with Documents. . . .* privately printed and publication suppressed, 1924), 103–104.

61 *EG*, Feb. 18, 1924, 3.

62 *EG*, Feb. 23, 1924, 4.

63 *EG*, Jan. 1, 1924, 4.

64 *EG*, Feb.16, 1924, 3. Feb 18, 1924, 3, points out *al-Siyasa* 's isolation in the Arabic press on this issue.

65   *EG*, Feb, 20, 1924, 4.

66   Carter, *Tut.Ankh.Amen: Politics*, 104.

67   Carter, *Tut.Ankh.Amen: Politics*, 106–107.

68   Hoving, *Tutankhamun*, 294–95. Undersecretary Muhammad Zaghlul (a relative of prime minister Saad Zaghlul) asked Carter sarcastically if some of his sixteen-man archaeological staff were Muslims (i.e., polygamists) since the request was to admit twenty-two women. Muhammad, *Sariqat*, 251–52.

69   *EG*, Feb. 27, 1924, 4.

70   "Majd Misr al-qadima wa-l-haditha," *al-Hilal* 32 (April 1, 1924), 676–83.

71   Christopher Frayling, *The Face of Tutankhamun* (London: Faber and Faber, 1992), 31.

72   Colla, *Conflicted Antiquities*, 220, as translated from *al-Shawqiyat*, 2: 159.

73   Colla, *Conflicted Antiquities*, 220, as translated from *al-Shawqiyat*, 1: 274.

74   Colla, *Conflicted Antiquities*, 221, as translated from *al-Shawqiyat*, 2: 159–60. After the 1952 revolution, an edition of Shawqi's works omitted, without any indication, twelve lines in praise of King Fuad. S. Somekh, "The Neo-Classical Poets," in *Modern Arabic Literature, The Cambridge History of Arabic Literature*, ed. M.M. Badawi (Cambridge: Cambridge University Press, 1993), 70, n. 52.

75   *EG*, Feb. 27, 1924, 4; Jan. 27, 1925, 6.

76   Quoted in James Goode, *Negotiating for the Past: Archaeology, Nationalism, and Diplomacy in the Middle East, 1919–1941*, (Austin: University of Texas Press, 2007), 81.

77   *EG*, Feb. 18, 1924, 4.

78   *EG*, Feb. 27, 1924, 4.

79   *EG*, Feb.19, 1924, 2.

80   *EG*, Feb 22, 1923, 4.

81   *EG*, Feb. 21, 1923, 4.

82   Muhammad, *Sariqat*, 147–48.

83   Henri Loyrette, "The Eiffel Tower," in Nora and Kritzman, *Realms*, 3: 350.

84   Michel Pastoureau, "The Gallic Cock," in Nora and Kritzman, *Realms*, 3: 406.

85   Evoe, "Pioneers of Empire, II: Pharaoh's Furniture," *Punch*, March 12, 1924, 264. On Tutankhamun at Wembley generally, see Frayling, *Face*, 32–36.

86   *Illustrated London News*, January 19, 1924, 104.

87   *Illustrated London News*, February 23, 1924, 310–11.

88   *Illustrated London News*, April 19, 1924, 702–703.

89   Hankey, *Passion for Egypt*, 287–88.

90   *Punch*, March 12, 1924, 264.

91   Gady, "Pharaon," 825–68.

92   *WWWE4*: 96, 346–47.

93   *New York Times*, Dec 22, 1922, cited in Frayling, *Face*, 31.

94   Charles Breasted, *Pioneer to the Past: The Story of James Henry Breasted, Archaeologist* (New York: Charles Scribner's Sons, 1947), 368–72.

95   James, *Carter*, 339–43, 380–81, Reeves and Taylor, *Carter*, 161.

96   Carter, *Tut.Ankh.Amen: Politics*; James, *Carter*, 316–17, 373–75.

97   Hoving, *Tutankhamun*, 344–45.

98   *EG*, Mar. 2, 1925.
99   Zaki Fahmi, *Safwat al-asr fi tarikh wa rusum mashahir rijal Misr*, (Cairo: Matbaat al-itimad, 1926), 105. On Tutankhamun, see 105–112.
100   On the symbolism of the museum's architecture and façade inscriptions, see Donald Malcolm Reid, "French Egyptology and the Architecture of Orientalism: Deciphering the Façade of Cairo's Egyptian Museum," in *Franco–Arab Encounters: Studies in Memory of David C. Gordon*, ed. Mathew Gordon and L. Carl Brown (Beirut: American University in Beirut Press, 1996), 35–69.
101   See Artemis Cooper, *Cairo in the War 1939–1945* (London: H. Hamilton, 1989), 36–38, for this paragraph's quotations and the colonial landmarks.
102   "Egyptology for the Masses," *EG*, Jan. 12, 1926, 3.
103   E.A. Wallis Budge, *Cook's Handbook for Egypt and the Sudan* (London: Cook & Son, 1921, 1925).
104   *Baedeker's Egypt 1929* (Leipzig: Baedeker, 1908; repr. London: David & Charles, 1985), 88–111, 301–16.
105   Observation based on a list of *al-Ahram* articles on archaeology kindly supplied by Paula Sanders.
106   See *al-Hilal*, May 1924.
107   Hassan Shawqi, *al-Durr al-maknun fi jadath al-malik Tut Ankh Amun: adab wa tarikh* (Cairo, 1929).

3. Western Egyptology in the Wake of Tutankhamun

1   Éric Gady, "Le pharaon, l'égyptologue et le diplomate. Les égyptologues français en Égypte, du voyage de Champollion à la crise de Suez (1828–1956)," 2 vols, PhD diss, Université de Paris IV-Sorbonne, 2005, 767–71.
2   Margaret S. Drower, *Flinders Petrie: A Life in Archaeology* (Madison: University of Wisconsin Press, 1995), 345.
3   Glanville to Dixon, September 16, 1946. FO 924/547/LC 4763, enclosing "The Future of British Egyptology in Egypt. Egyptian Exploration Society—Statement of Financial Needs – Sept. 1946"; EES Archives, Box: British Institute in Cairo: Negotiations 1970–74.
4   Drower, *Petrie*, 355–56; Gady, "Pharaon," 824–28; James F. Goode, *Negotiating for the Past: Archaeology, Nationalism, and Diplomacy in the Middle East, 1919–1941* (Austin: University of Texas Press, 2007), 94–95.
5   Gady, "Pharaon," 777–78, 824–29, and Goode, *Negotiating*, 95–97.
6   *Ancient Egypt* (Pt. 4, December 1925), 128.
7   Drower, *Petrie*, 355–57, 361–64.
8   Susanne Voss, *Die Geschichte der Abteilung Kairo des DAI im Spannungsfeld Deutscher Politischer Interessen. Bd. 1 1881–1929* (Rahden, Westf.: Verlag Marie Leidorf, 2013), 179–82.
9   Cyril Aldred, "El-Amarna," in *Excavating in Egypt: The Egypt Exploration Society 1882–1982*, ed. T.G.H. James (Chicago: University of Chicago Press, 1982), 89–106.
10   Gady, "Pharaon," 837–38.
11   Gady, "Pharaon," 943.

12   MAE to Gaillard, October 30, 1923, and Gaillard to MAE, November 19, 1923. MAE, AMB Le Caire, Enseignement égyptien, Service des antiquités 1892–1941, Carton 174 Bis, Dossier "Personnel français," Pres. du Conseil.

13   Sous-dir. of Afrique-Levant (Political Section) to Gaillard, October 27, 1928. MAE, AMB Le Caire, Enseignement égyptien, Service des antiquités 1892–1941, Carton 174 Bis, Dossier "Personnel français."

14   Gady, "Pharaon," 518–30, 734–36.

15   J.M. Mitchell, *International Cultural Relations* (London: Allen & Unwin, 1986), 23, mentions the Bureau des écoles et des oeuvres française à l'étranger under the MAE in 1910.

16   Gady, "Pharaon," 788–94.

17   On these organizations, see Jean-Jacques Renoliet, *L'UNESCO oubliée: la Société des Nations et la cooperation intellectuelle* (Paris: Publications de la Sorbonne, 1999). See also Akira Iriye, *Cultural Internationalism and World Order* (Baltimore: Johns Hopkins University Press, 1997), 63–65. Susan Pedersen, "Back to the League of Nations" (Review Essay), *American Historical Review* 112 (4 October 2007): 1091–1117, notes the revival of scholarly interest in interwar international institutions since the end of the Cold War.

18   Jeffery Abt, *American Egyptologist: The Life of James Henry Breasted and the Creation of His Oriental Institute* (Chicago: University of Chicago Press, 2011), 207–209; Charles Breasted, *Pioneer to the Past: The Story of James Henry Breasted, Archaeologist* (New York: Charles Scribner's Sons, 1947), 135–37, 224–26, 319, 382.

19   Gady, "Pharaon," 785–86. On the Geographical Society—successively the Khedival, Sultanieh, Royal, and Egyptian Geographical Society—see Donald Malcolm Reid, "The Egyptian Geographical Society: From Foreign Laymen's Society to Indigenous Professional Association," *Poetics Today*, 14: 3 (Fall 1993): 539–72.

20   Bierbrier, *WWWE4*, 88.

21   Gady, "Pharaon," 677–82.

22   T.G.H. James, *Howard Carter: The Path to Tutankhamun*, 2nd ed. (London: Kegan Paul International, 2001), 341–42, 380–81, 392.

23   Gaillard to MAE, September 7, 1925. MAE, AMB Le Caire, Enseignement égyptien, Service des antiquités (1892–1941), Carton 174 bis, Dossier 53, 3: Fouilles.

24   *Scott 2012*, Egypt # 105–107.

25   Gady, "Pharaon," 907–16.

26   Gady, "Pharaon," 889.

27   Gady, "Pharaon," 890–95, 902–03, 1137. Jaroslav Černý (1898–1970), a central figure in Czech Egyptology after founding father František Lexa (1876–1960), spent his later career at Oxford. *Jiřna Růžová, Písař Místa pravdy: Život egyptologa Jaroslava Černého/The Scribe in the Place of Truth: The Life of the Egyptologist Jaroslav Černý* (Prague: Libri, 2010). The English section of the text begins on p. 137.

28   Unander to Allenby, February 11, 1920. FO141/440/12060. See also Gady, "Pharaon," 749–51.

29 Firth to Greg, November 3?, 1921. FO141/440/ 12060, enclosing Lacau letter.
30 Firth to Greg, March 10, 1921. FO141/440/12060.
31 Reisner to Allenby, September 24, 1921. FO141/440/12060.
32 Voss, *Geschichte*, 174–75.
33 As quoted in Thomas L. Gertzen, "The Anglo-Saxon Branch of the Berlin School: The Interwar Correspondence of Adolf Erman and Alan Gardiner and the Loss of the German Concession at Amarna," in *Histories of Egyptology: Interdisciplinary Measures*, ed. William Carruthers (London: Routledge, 2015), 42.
34 Gertzen, "Anglo-Saxon Branch," in *Histories of Egyptology*, ed. Carruthers, 46.
35 Thomas W. Kramer, *Deutsch-ägyptische Beziehungen in Vergangenheit und Gegenwart* (Tübingen: H. Erdmann, 1974), 184.
36 Allenby to Curzon, May 22, 1923. FO141/440/12060.
37 Gady, "Pharaon," 751.
38 The 2012 centennial of the discovery of the bust of Nefertiti, accompanied by intensified demands for its return to Egypt, called forth much research on the circumstances of its secretive export to Germany. See the studies which accompanied a centennial exhibition on Nefertiti by Berlin's Egyptian Museum: Friederike Seyfried, ed., *In the Light of Amarna: 100 Years of the Nefertiti Discovery*, (Berlin: Ägyptisches Museum und Papyrussammlung, Staatliche Museen zu Berlin, 2012), esp. Olaf Matthes, "Ludwig Borchardt, James Simon and the Colourful Nefertiti Bust in the First Year after Its Discovery," 427–37; Susanne Voss, "The 1925 Demand for the Return of the Nefertiti Bust, a German Perspective," 460–68; and Hannelore Kischewitz, "The Thirties—the Trouble with Nefertiti," 474–78. Relevant archival documents were published in Bénédicte Savoy, ed., *Nofretete: Ein deutsch-französische Affäre, 1912–1931* (Cologne: Böhlau, 2011); and Friederike Seyfried, "Die Büste der Nofretete: Dokumentation des Fundes under der Fundteilung 1912–1913," *Jahrbuch Preussischer Kulturbesitz 2010* (2011), Band 46: 133–202. Earlier studies include Susanne Voss and Cornelius von Pilgrim, "Ludwig Borchardt und die deutschen Interessen am Nil," in *Das Grosse Spiel: Archäologie und Politik zur Zeit des Kolonialismus (1860–1940)* (Cologne: Ruhr Museum, 2008), 294–305; Rolf Krauss, "1913–1988: 75 Jahre Büste der Nofretete/Nefret-iti in Berlin," *Jahrbuch Preussischer Kulturbesitz* 24 (1987): 87–124: and Krauss's update "Why Nefertiti Went to Berlin," *KMT* 19 (3, Fall 2008): 44–53.
39 Letter by Warren R. Dawson, Hon. Treasurer, and H. R. Hall, Hon. Sec., EES, *The Times*, Feb. 22, 1923: 11. On the dispute in the mid-1920s, see Voss, *Geschichte*, 208–16; and Voss, "The 1925 Demand," 460–68.
40 Gady, "Pharaon," 888.
41 Arthur R. Hinks to G. Roncagli, May 31, 1922. DWQ/Mahafiz Abdin/ Box 201: "Jamiyat Ilmiya: al-Jamiya al-Jughrafiya 1916–50." Correspondance confidentielle.
42 Brigitte Schroeder-Gudahus, "Challenge to Transnational Loyalties: International Scientific Organization after the First World War," *Science Studies* 3 (1973): 101–103.

43 Elisabeth Crawford, *Nationalism and Internationalism in Science, 1880–1939: Four Studies of the Nobel Population* (Cambridge: Cambridge University Press, 1992), 56.

44 *Proceedings of the Seventeenth International Congress of Orientalists. Oxford 1928* (Oxford, 1929), 13, 15, 17, 20, passim.

45 Schroeder-Gudahus, "Challenge," *Science Studies* 3 (1973): 93–118.

46 Adolf Erman and H. Grapow, eds., *Wörterbuch der Ägyptischen Sprache* (Leipzig: Von Quelle & Meyer, 1926) vol. 1: iv; Adolf Erman, *Mein Werden und Mein Werken: Erinnerungen eines Alten Berliner Gelehrten* (Leipzig, 1929), 289, 291.

47 Erman to Breasted, May 22, 1926. Oriental Institute Archives (OIA), University of Chicago, Breasted Papers, Cairo Museum Project, Box 1: Correspondence A–M, Folder E; Breasted to Sethe, May 26, 1926. Box 2, Correspondence, Folder S.

48 Gady, "Pharaon," 752; *Archäologisches Institut des Deutschen Reiches: Bericht über die Hundertjahrfeier 21–25 April 1929* (Berlin: W. de Gruyter & Co., 1930).

49 "Nefertiti Bust Sought by Egypt," *NYT*, March 31, 1929. FO371/13878/J1230, H. Rumbold (Berlin) to Arthur Henderson, MP, July 3, 1929. Hannelore Kischewitz, "The Thirties—Trouble with Nefertiti," in *In the Light of Amarna*, ed. Seyfried, 474–78.

50 Undated cartoon from *Kladderadatsh*, clipping in archives of Swiss Institute of Architectural and Archaeological Research on Ancient Egypt, Cairo.

51 Louis Keimer, "Le musée égyptologique de Berlin," *Cahiers d'histoire égyptienne*, Sèrie III, fac. 1 (Nov. 1950): 41; Bierbrier, *WWWE4*, 291–92. A German, Keimer settled in Egypt in 1927 and took Czech, then in 1951, Egyptian citizenship.

52 Nicholas Reeves, *Ancient Egypt: The Great Discoveries: A Year-by-Year Chronicle* (London: Thames & Hudson, 2000), 136. Savoy, *Nofretete*, 151–215.

53 Kischewitz, "The Thirties—Trouble with Nefertiti," in *In the Light of Amarna*, ed. Friedericke Seyfried, 477–78.

54 Werner Kaiser, *75 Jahre Deutsches Archäologisches Institut Kairo 1907–1982* (Mainz: P. von Zabern, 1982); Günter Dreyer and Daniel Polz, eds., *Begegnung mit Vergangenheit: 100 Jahre in Ägypten: Deutsches Archäologisches Institut Kairo 1907–2007* (Mainz: P. von Zabern, 2007); Voss, *Geschichte*, 185, 188–94, 229–237.

55 On Junker, see Hermann Junker, *Leben und Werk in Selbstdarstellung. Österreichische Akademie der Wissenschaften. Philosophisch-historische Klasse. Sitzungsberichte*, 242: Band 5. Abhandlung (Vienna: H. Böhlaus, 1963), and Julia Budka and Claus Jurman, "Hermann Junker: Ein deutsch-österreichisches Forscherleben zwischen Pyramiden, Kreuz und Hakenkreuz," in Susanne Bickel et al., eds., *Aegyptologen und Ägyptologien zwischen Kaiserreich und Gründen der beiden deutschen Staaten....*, Beiheft 1(Berlin: Akademie Verlag Berlin: de Gruyter, 2013) 299–31; Susanne Voss, "Der lange Arm des Nationalsozialismus: Zur Geschichte der Abteilung Kairo des DAI im 'Dritten Reich,'" in Bickel et al., eds., *Ägyptologen und Ägyptologien*, 266–98; Bierbrier, *WWWE4*, 285–86.

56 Richard T. Arndt, *The First Resort of Kings: American Cultural Diplomacy in the Twentieth Century* (Dulles, VA: Potomac Books, 2005), 45.

57 Goode, *Negotiating*.

58 The interwar work of the University of Pennsylvania's University Museum—Clarence Fisher at Memphis and Dra Abu el-Naga (1921–23) and Briton Alan Rowe at Maidum (1929–32)—was brief and less publicized than that of the Met, Harvard–Boston, and Chicago. Thomas, *American Discovery of Egypt*, 55–56, 174; Bierbrier, *WWWE4*, 192, 477.

59 John A. Wilson, *Signs and Wonders upon Pharaoh: A History of American Egyptology* (Chicago: University of Chicago Press, 1964).

60 Reisner to Fairbanks, June 8, 1919. MFA, Reisner Correspondence. In Egyptian context, Americans were often considered Europeans.

61 Reisner to Grey, December 1, 1919. MFA, Reisner. For Reisner and his work generally, see the Giza Archives of the Giza Digital Library: http://www.gizapyramids.org.

62 Blurb for George A Reisner, "The Dead Hand in Egypt," *The Independent* 114, no. 3903: 318–20.

63 Calvin Tompkins, *Merchants and Masterpieces: The Story of the Metropolitan Museum of Art* (New York: E.P. Dutton, 1970), 141.

64 Nancy Thomas, "American Institutional Fieldwork in Egypt, 1899–1960," in *The American Discovery of Ancient Egypt*, ed. Nancy Thomas (Los Angeles: Los Angeles County Museum of Art and the American Research Center in Egypt), 57–66.

65 Reisner to Hawes of Museum of Fine Arts, Boston, October 9, 1924, as quoted in Nicholas Reeves and John H. Taylor, *Howard Carter before Tutankhamun* (New York: H.N. Abrams, 1993), 161.

66 J.H. Breasted, quoted in C. Breasted, *Pioneer*, 238. On the trip, see Abt, *American Egyptologist*, 228–48.

67 Abt, *American Egyptologist*, 355, shows a map of OI expeditions reproduced in fig. 23a.

68 James Henry Breasted, *Ancient Times: A History of the Early World* (Boston: Ginn & Co., 1916), map 4, between pp. 184–85.

69 On Blashfield and the painting, see the sources cited on p.374 n.17.

70 Geoff Emberling and Emily Teeter, "The First Expedition of the Oriental Institute, 1919–1920," in *Pioneers to the Past: American Archaeologists in the Middle East 1919–1920*, ed. Geoff Emberling (Chicago: Oriental Institute, University of Chicago, 2010), 50–51.

71 Bierbrier, *WWWE4*, 401.

72 Jeffrey Abt, *American Egyptologist*, 281–301.

73 James H. Breasted, *The Oriental Institute*, V. 12 of *The University of Chicago Survey* (Chicago, 1933), 174–76.

74 Breasted, *The Oriental Institute*, 169.

75 Abt, *American Egyptologist*, 341–44.

76 Breasted, *The Oriental Institute*, 100.

77 On the OI's Chicago headquarters building, see Abt, *American Egyptologist*, 348–58. On the tympanum relief, see 349–53 and Neil Silberman, "Sultans, Merchants,

and Minorities: The Challenge of Historical Archaeology in the Modern Middle East," in *A Historical Archaeology of the Ottoman Empire: Breaking New Ground*, ed. Uzi Baram and Lynda Carroll (New York: Kluwer Academic/Plenum, 2000), 246.

78 The thirty-four-story Nebraska Capitol may seem an odd choice, but it was designed by the same firm which did the OI's Chicago headquarters, Godhue Associates.

79 Lindsay Ambridge, "Imperialism and Racial Geography in James Henry Breasted's 'Ancient Times, A History of the Early World,'" *Journal of Egyptian History* 4, no. 2 (Fall 2011), 24. See also Steve Vinson, "From Lord Elgin to James Henry Breasted: The Politics of the Past in the First Era of Globalization," in *Marketing Heritage: Archaeology and the Consumption of the Past*, ed. Yorke Rowan and Uzi Baram (Walnut Creek, CA: Alta Mira Press, 2004), 57–65.

80 Breasted to King Fuad, November 3, 1925. OIA, Breasted Papers, Cairo Museum Project, Box 1: Correspondence A–M, Folder E. This section draws primarily on Abt, *American Egyptologist*, 317–36. See also Goode, *Negotiating*, 100–15; and Gady, "Pharaon," 868–84. Jeffrey Abt, with permission from the Oriental Institute Archives, kindly supplied me selected copies of Breasted's correspondence on the project.

81 Goode, *Negotiating*, 103.

82 Murray to Lloyd, June 27, 1925. FO371/10897/J1797.

83 Breasted to Fosdick, June 23, 1925, "Curtis, Fosdick and Belknap," OIA, Breasted Papers, Cairo Museum Project, Box 1: Correspondence A–M, Folder: Curtis, Fosdick, Belknap.

84 Goode, *Negotiating*, 104.

85 Breasted to King Fuad, November 3, 1925. OIA, Breasted Papers, Cairo Museum Project, Box 1: Correspondence A–M, Folder E.

86 Abt, *American Egyptologist*, 330–31, quoting Breasted letter to George Ellery Hale.

87 Quoted in Goode, *Negotiating*, 105.

88 Goode, *Negotiating*, 89.

89 Reisner, "Memorandum" (no recipient indicated), February 18, 1926. MFA Archives, Reisner, Folder 12 (February–December 1926). See also [Reisner] "General News:" February 16, 1926.

90 Breasted to Miss Lucy Aldrich, October 21, 1926. OIA, Breasted Papers, Cairo Museum Project, Box 1: Correspondence A–M, Folder A.

91 Translation of Mohammed Lotfy Gomaa letter to *al-Ahram*, February 24, 1926. OIA, Breasted Papers, Cairo Museum Project, Box 1: Correspondence A–M, Folder A.

92 C. Breasted, *Pioneer*, 381.

93 A. Chamberlain to Lloyd, March 4, 1926. FO141/487/7436.

94 Firth to Breasted, February 8, 1926. OIA, Breasted Papers, Cairo Museum Project, Box 1: Correspondence A–M, Folder G.

95 Firth to Breasted, March 17, 1926. OIA, Breasted Papers, Cairo Museum Project, Box 1: Correspondence A–M, Folder G.

96 Breasted to Firth, undated, marked "Not Sent." OIA, Breasted Papers, Cairo Museum Project, Box 1: Correspondence A–M, Folder G.

97 Gady, "Pharaon," 868–84; Gaillard to MAE, April 6, 1926.MAE, AMB
    LeCaire, Enseignement égyptien, Service des antiquités: C174, D: Don de
    Rockfeller [sic.].
98 "Memo of Conversation with Lythgoe," April 10, 1926, enclosing copy of
    Winlock to Lythgoe, March 23, 1926. USNA, State Dept. 571, Microfilm
    Roll 31, GW, LVD, on letterhead of Div. of N.E. Affairs.
99 Jeffrey Abt, *American Egyptologist*, 331.
100 "Curtis, Fosdick, and Belknap," Breasted to Fosdick, October 5, 1926, OIA,
    Breasted Papers, Cairo Museum Project, Box 1: Correspondence A–M,
    Folder: "Curtis, Fosdick, Belknap."
101 *Ancient Egypt*, Pt. 3, Sept. 1932: 96.
102 Abt, *American Egyptologist*, 332–35, and J.H. Iliffe, "The Palestine Archaeo-
    logical Museum, Jerusalem," *Museums Journal* 38 (No. 1, April 1938): 1–22.

4. Egyptian Egyptology in the Wake of Tutankhamun

1   *al-Muqtataf* 63, No. 3 (Nov. 1923): 276.
2   Dar al-Mahfuzat, 2/379/3917/40146. (Pension folder). Selim Hassan began
    working on Aug. 1, 1921 at £E18 monthly; Muhammad Gamal Mokhtar,
    "Selim Hassan ka-munaqqib wa alim al-athar," *al-Majalla al-tarikhiya
    al-misriya* 19 (1972): 78.
3   Mokhtar, "Selim Hassan," 78.
4   Taha Hussein to wakil of university, July 9, 1923. CUA, Université égypti-
    enne, C 5, D 296: Missions to Europe of Princess Fatimah Hanum.
5   The prime source on Gabra is his *Chez les derniers adorateurs de Trismegiste:
    la nécropole d'Hermopolis Touna El Gebel (souvenir d'un archéologue)* (Cairo:
    al-Haya al-misriya al-amma, 1971), hereafter Gabra, *Souvenir*. See also Dia
    Abou-Ghazi and Ramadan el Sayed, *Sami Gabra from Tasa to Touna*, Vies
    et Travaux 2, Organisation des antiquités de l'Égypte, service des musées,
    (Cairo: Dar al-maarif, 1984); *BSAC* 24 (1979–82): 128–30; Jamiat Fuad al-
    Awwal, *al-Kitab al-fiddi li-kulliyat al-adab 1925–1950* (Cairo: Matbaat Jamiat
    Fuad al-Awwal, 1951), 58–59; Bierbrier, *WWWE4*: 203. On Selim Hassan,
    see Mokhtar, "Selim Hassan," 73–87; Dia Abou-Ghazi, "Selim Hassan: His
    Writings and Excavation," *ASAE* 58 (1964): 62–84; [Madrasat al-muallimin
    al-ulya], *al-Kitab al-dhahabi li-madrasat al-muallimin al-ulya 1885–1935*
    (Cairo, 1935): 125–26; Bierbrier, *WWWE4*: 244–45; *Le mondain égyptien et
    du moyen orient.* (Cairo: Paul Barbey, 1951), 328; John A. Wilson, *Signs and
    Wonders Upon Pharaoh: A History of American Egyptology* (Chicago: University
    of Chicago Press, 1964), 193–94, 230. Birthdates cited range from 1886 to
    1893; 1886 is the most likely. On Hamza, see Bierbrier, *WWWE4*: 241, and
    Hala Sallam, "Ahmed Kamal Pasha (1851–1923): A Family of Egyptologists,"
    in *Proceedings of the Seventh International Congress of Egyptologists: Cambridge,
    3–9 September 1995*, ed. C.J. Eyre (Leuven: Peeters, 1998), 1018–19.
6   Donald Malcolm Reid, *Whose Pharaohs? Archaeology, Museums, and Egyptian
    National Identity from Napoleon to World War I* (Berkeley: University of Cali-
    fornia Press, 2002), 189; Bierbrier, *WWWE4*: 397. This "lost generation"
    included Sobhi Joseph Arif (1870–1905), Tewfik Boulos (fl. 1902–1947),

and Ahmad Kamal's nephew and student Muhammad Chaban (Shaban, 1866–1930). See *WWWE4*: 25, 74–75, 112.

7   Gabra, *Souvenir*, 14, 15.

8   Gabra described his family as *terriens* who lost most of their land in the 1930s. Gabra, *Souvenir*, 8, 54.

9   Christiane Desroches Noblecourt, *La grande nubiade ou le parcours d'une égyptologue* (Paris: Stock/Pernoud, 1997), 115.

10   [Madrasat al-muallimin al-ulya], *al-Kitab al-dhahabi li-madrasat al-muallimin al-ulya*.

11   On the United Presbyterian "American Mission" in Egypt, see Heather Sharkey, *American Evangelicals in Egypt: Missionary Encounters in an Age of Empire* (Princeton: Princeton University Press, 2008). On the AUB, see Betty S. Anderson, *The American University of Beirut: Arab Nationalism and Liberal Education* (Austin: University of Texas Press, 2011).

12   Mirrit Boutros Ghali, *BSAC* 24 (1979–82): 128; Bierbrier, *WWWE4*: 203.

13   Mokhtar, "Selim Hassan," 77.

14   Sallam, "Ahmed Kamal Pasha," 1018–19.

15   Sami Gabra, *Esquisse de l'histoire économique et politique de la propriété foncière en Égypte* (Bordeaux: F. Pech, 1919).

16   Timothy Champion, "Beyond Egyptology: Egypt in 19th and 20th Century Archaeology and Anthropology," in *The Wisdom of Egypt: Changing Visions through the Ages*, ed. Peter Ucko and Timothy Champion (London: University College London, 2003), 180.

17   Rosalind M. Janssen, *The First Hundred Years: Egyptology at University College London 1892–1992* (London: University College London, 1992), 1–7; Margaret S. Drower, *Flinders Petrie: A Life in Archaeology* (Madison: University of Wisconsin Press, 1995), 199–201. On Edwards, see B. Moon, *More Usefully Employed: Amelia B. Edwards: Writer, Traveller, and Campaigner for Ancient Egypt* (London: Egypt Exploration Society, 2006).

18   On Egyptology at Oxford, see Alice Stevenson, "The Object of Study: Egyptology, Archaeology, and Anthropology at Oxford, 1860–1960," in *Histories of Egyptology*, ed. William Carruthers (London: Routledge, 2015), 19–33.

19   Bierbrier, *WWWE4*: 214.

20   Bruce Truscot, *Red Brick University* (London: Faber & Faber, 1943).

21   Thomas Kelly, *For the Advancement of Learning: the University of Liverpool 1881–1981* (Liverpool: University of Liverpool Press, 1981), 107, 149, 224–25. On Garstang, see Bierbrier, *WWWE4*: 208, 402–403. On Peet, see Bierbrier, *WWWE4*: 420–21.

22   Bierbrier, *WWWE4*: 420–21.

23   University of Liverpool, Institute of Archaeology *Annual Report*, 1922, 19: 13.

24   University of Liverpool Archives, University of Liverpool, *General Statistics, Sessions 1919–1923*, p. 7: "Geographical Distribution of Homes of Students in Residence during Session 1921–1922." Aziz Atiya suggested that British official Robin Furness may have channeled Egyptian students to Liverpool. Interview, March 29, 1986, Salt Lake City, Utah.

25   For example, University of Liverpool Archives, *General Statistics, Session 1924–1925*, 66 ff.

26   Gady, "Pharaon," 815.

27   Gabra, *Souvenir*, 12; and University of Liverpool, Special Collections and Archives, S.G. Gabra, "Justice under the Old and New Kingdom in Egypt" (unpublished thesis, Institute of Archaeology, University of Liverpool, 1925).

28   University of Liverpool, Special Collections and Archives, M.A. Hamza, "The Relations of Nubia and Egypt" (unpublished thesis, Institute of Archaeology, University of Liverpool, 1925), 1.

29   Egyptian historians who studied at Liverpool include M.F. Shukry, M.M. Ziadeh, A.S. Atiyeh, M. Zaki, and I. Noshy. Geographers include: M. Awad, M. Mitwally, and A.S. Hozayen. Classicists include M.S. Salem.

30   Mercedes Volait, *Architectes et architectures de l'Égypte moderne (1830–1950): genèse et essor d'une expertise locale.* (Paris: Maisonneuve et Larose, 2005), 286.

31   Other Egyptologists of the post–World War II era from Liverpool included Said Gohary, Ashraf I. Sadek, Aly Omar Abdalla (Greco–Roman specialist), and Khaled Dawood. Interviews with Gaballa Ali Gaballa, June 7, 2005, Maadi; and Aly Omar Abdalla, May 19, 2005, Cairo.

32   Gady, "Pharaon," 814–15.

33   On the Collège, see http://www.college-de-france.fr

34   Gabra, *Souvenir*, 12; on Moret, Lefebvre, and Weill, see Bierbrier, *WWWE4*: 384–85, 318–19, 571.

35   Bierbrier, *WWWE4*: 47.

36   Gady, "Pharaon," 815–16.

37   Gady, "Pharaon," 814–16.

38   Gabra, *Souvenir*, 14.

39   *JEA* 9 (1923): 241–42.

40   Wilson, *Signs*, 149.

41   Interview with Labib Habachi, June 23, 1982, Cairo. Information below on his professors is from this interview. See also Jill Kamil, *Labib Habachi: The Life and Legacy of an Egyptologist* (Cairo: American University in Cairo Press, 2007). This first full-scale biography of an Egyptian Egyptologist by one of his former pupils is useful but lacks scholarly rigor in some places. On Golenischeff, see Bierbrier, *WWWE4*: 216; *KMT* 17 (4, 2006–2007): 75–84. On Kuentz, see Bierbrier, *WWWE4*: 304.

42   Observations based on the *Proceedings* (in various languages) of the International Congress of Orientalists, including the 3rd (St. Petersburg 1876), 16th (Athens 1912), 17th (Oxford 1928), and 23rd (Cambridge 1954).

43   On Vikentiev, see Bierbrier, *WWWE4*: 556. Fayza Haikal took his course just before he died (Interview, July 17, 2005, Cairo). On Volkoff, see *L'Égypte aujourd'hui* 35 (1996): 55; Oleg V. Volkoff, *Comment on visitait la vallée du Nil: les guides de l'Égypte* (Cairo: IFAO, 1967), and *Voyageurs russes en Égypte* (Cairo: IFAO, 1972).

44   *al-Qadim*, No. 1 (June 1925). On Georgy Sobhy, see *BSAC* 19 (1967–68): 315–16.

45   "Dr. Breasted Entertained by the Archaeological Society," *Egyptian Gazette*, March 15, 1926, enclosed in USNA, Records of the Dept. of State relating

to the Internal Affairs of Egypt, 1910–29, microfilm roll 25, 883.911.

46 Gady, "Pharaon," 24, 111–14.

47 Gady, "Pharaon," 818.

48 Gady, "Pharaon," 817–18.

49 Calculated Jamiat al-Qahira, Kulliyat al-athar, *al-Dalil al-dhahabi lil-asatidha wa-khariji al-athar mundhu sanat 1925* (Cairo: al-Haya al-misriya al-amma lil-kitab, 1975), 5–7. The percentages exclude one individual whose religion is unknown.

50 Tawfiq Habib, "Dars al-athar fi-l-jamia al-misriya," *al-Muqtataf* 72 (1928): 443.

51 Jamiat al-Qahira, *al-Dalil al-dhahabi*, 10, 12–13. These were MA-level diplomas.

52 Hakim Abou-Seif published four items in *ASAE* and Muhammad Chabaan one.

53 Englebach to the Residency, May 12, 1928. FO141/487/7436.

54 Mokhtar, "Selim Hassan," 79.

55 Quotations from Gabra, *Souvenir*, 14, 19, 26, 29.

56 Gabra, *Souvenir*, came out in 1971 and the Arabic translation in 1974: *Fi rihab al-mabud "Tut": rasul al-ilm wa-l-hikma fi-l-marifa: mudhakkirat athari* (Cairo: al-Haya al-misriya al-amma lil-kitab, 1974).

57 Gady, "Pharaon," 929.

58 "Liquidation amoureuse (Aff. Dame P . . . c. Prof. S)," *Journal des Tribunaux Mixtes*, July 15–16, 1935, p. 5. Photocopy kindly supplied by Éric Gady, from the archives of the Institut de France, Mss. 6338, Fo. 242 (2).

59 Interview with Labib Habachi, June 23, 1982, Cairo. On Hamza, see Bierbrier, *WWWE4*, 241.

60 On the pharaonic columns, see Volait, "Decennie," in *Images d'Égypte*, 167–68, 185, 8n, citing *Majallat al-handasa*, January 1923, 59. For more recent pictures of the hall, including a statue of Khafre, see "Mubarak Opens Parliament," *Al-Ahram Weekly*, November 11–17, 1993, 1, and Fayza Hassan, "Housing Hope," *Al-Ahram Weekly* December 14–20, 1995, 10–11.

61 On Haykal, see Carl D. Smith, *Islam and the Search for Social Order in Modern Egypt: A Biography of Muhammad Husayn Haykal* (Albany: State University of New York Press, 1983); J. Brugman, *An Introduction to the History of Modern Arabic Literature in Egypt* (Leiden: Brill, 1984), 234–43; Michelle Hartman, "Muhammad Husayn Haykal," in *Essays in Arabic Literary Biography 1850–1950*, ed. Roger Allen (Wiesbaden: Harrassowitz, 2010), 125–137. Haykal's daughter Faiza Haykal notes that he spelled his name Mohamed Hussein Haekel in English.

62 Muhammad Husayn Haykal, *Mohammed Hussein Haikal's Zainab: The First Egyptian Novel*, trans. John Mohammed Grinsted (London: Darf, 1979), 15.

63 Israel Gershoni and James Jankowski, *Egypt, Islam, and the Arabs: The Search for Egyptian Nationhood, 1900–1930* (New York: Oxford University Press, 1986), 33–39.

64 Gershoni and Jankowski, *Egypt, Islam, and the Arabs*, 148–63.

65 Muhammad Gallab, *Les suvivances de l'Égypte antique dans le folklore moderne* (Paris: P. Guenther) in 1929.

66 Omnia El Shakry, *The Great Social Laboratory: Subjects of Knowledge in Colonial and Postcolonial Egypt* (Stanford: Stanford University Press, 2007), 47–53; Selim Hassan, "Survivals of Ancient Egyptian Customs in Modern Egypt," *Bulletin of the Society of the Friends of Coptic Art*, 2 (1936: 47–71); and Moharram Kamal, *Athar hadarat al-fara'ina fi hayatuna al-haliya* (Remnants of the Civilization of the Pharaohs in Our Present-Day Lives), 1957. On Kamal (1908–66), a third-generation graduate in 1928 with Ahmad Fakhry, Labib Habachi, and Girgis Mattha, see Bierbrier, *WWWE4*: 288.

67 See the analysis of the work in James Whidden, *Monarchy and Modernity in Egypt: Politics, Islam and Neo-colonialism between the Wars* (London: I.B.Tauris, 2013), 56, 151–63. Zaki Fahmi, *Safwat al-asr fi tarikh wa rusum mashahir rijal Misr* (Cairo: Matbaat al-itimad, 1926).

68 *Scott 2012*, Egypt, #92–103.

69 French remained the second language on Egyptian stamps until 1956, when France joined Britain and Israel in the Suez War against Egypt. Since then, English has been the European language on the stamps.

70 *Scott 2012*, Egypt #105–107.

71 *Scott 2012*, Egypt #118–20, 150–52, 153–54 (pharaonic); #125–27, 168–71, 172–76 (non-pharaonic); #C5–C25 (airmail).

72 On the 1926 trips, see "Diaries of a Field Trip," *Al-Ahram Weekly*, August 12–20, 2001, 20. On the earlier trips, see Reid, *Whose Pharaohs?*, 206; "al-Shabiba al-misriya al-raqiya wa-l-athar al-misriya al-qadima, 'ud ala bud'," *al-Lataif al-musawwara*, February 26, 1917, 11. Beth Baron kindly supplied me with illustrations of pharaonic themes from *al-Lataif al-musawwara*.

73 Joseph Cattaui Pacha, *Coup d'oeil sur la chronologie de la nation égyptienne* (Paris: Plon, 1931). He counts Alexander's and the Ptolemies' dynasties as the thirty-first and thirty-second, the Romans through Theodosius as the thirty-third, and the Byzantines as the thirty-fourth. This was not unusual, but extending the framework through the Islamic era was remarkable. Cattaui's count progressed through the Rashidun caliphs, Umayyads, Abbasids, Tulunids, second Abbasid era, Ikhshidids, Fatimids, Ayyubids, Bahri Mamluks, and Burji Mamluks. The Ottomans were his forty-fourth dynasty.

74 Alexandre Moret, "À Sa Majesté le Roi Fouad," *Révue de l' Égypte ancienne*, V. 3 (fasc. 1–2, 1931): 1–3.

75 Elliot Colla, *Conflicted Antiquities: Egyptology, Egyptomania, Egyptian Modernity* (Durham, NC: Duke University Press, 2007), 211–13. The hieroglyphs are imaginary, and the crowned female on the sides of the pylon—presumably Cleopatra—faces the reader in nothing but a loincloth with her arms crossed on her chest, not to hold the pharaonic royal crook and flail, but to cover partially her breasts.

76 The following account of Mukhtar's *Nahdat Misr* relies on Israel Gershoni and James Jankowski, *Commemorating the Nation: Collective Memory, Public Commemoration, and National Identity in Twentieth-Century Egypt* (Chicago: Middle East Documentation Center, 2004), 58–86.

77 Ahmad Zaki Abu Shadi, *Watan al-faraina* (Land of the Pharaohs) (Cairo: al-Matbaa al-salafiya, 1926). See Gershoni and Jankowski, *Egypt, Islam, and*

the *Arabs*, 185.

78 Beth Baron, *Egypt as a Woman: Nationalists, Gender and Politics* (Berkeley: University of California Press, 2005), 1–2.

79 Gershoni and Jankowski, *Commemorating the Nation*, 80–81.

80 Gershoni and Jankowski, *Egypt, Islam, and the Arabs*, 183.

81 Gershoni and Jankowski, *Egypt, Islam, and the Arabs*, 183.

82 On Wahbi, see Arthur Goldschmidt Jr., *Biographical Dictionary of Modern Egypt* (Boulder, CO: Lynne Rienner, 2000), 224. Wahbi's father, an irrigation engineer and Fayoum landowner, sent his son to Cairo's School of Agriculture. Yusuf Wahbi switched to studying acting instead, in Cairo and then Milan. The Ramses Company later became the National Troupe, and in 1935, the Egyptian National Theatre.

83 Muhammad Husayn Haykal, *Tarajim misriya wa gharbiya* (Egyptian and Western Biographies) (Cairo: Dar al-maarif, 1980), 29–45. All the other biographies of Egyptians in Haykal's selection are of males from the age of Khedive Ismail forward.

84 M.M. Badawi, "Ahmad Shawqi," in his *Modern Arabic Drama in Egypt* (Cambridge: Cambridge University Press, 1987), 207–15; S. Somekh, "The Neo-Classical Poets," in *The Cambridge History of Arabic Literature, Modern Arabic Literature*, ed. M.M. Badawi (Cambridge: Cambridge University Press, 1993), 69–71; Irfan Shahid, "Ahmad Shawqi," in *Essays in Arabic Literary Biography 1850–1950*, ed. Roger Allen (Wiesbaden: Harrassowitz, 2010), 304–17.

5. Consuming Antiquity: Western Tourism

1 See Donald Malcolm Reid, "From Explorer to Cook's Tourist," chapter two of *Whose Pharaohs? Archaeology, Museums, and Egyptian National Identity from Napoleon to World War I* (Berkeley: University of California Press, 2002), 64–92; F. Robert Hunter, "Tourism and Empire: The Thomas Cook & Son Enterprise on the Nile, 1868–1914," *Middle East Studies* 40, No. 5 (September 2004): 28–54; Waleed Hazbun, "The East as an Exhibit: Thomas Cook and Son and the Origins of the International Tourism Industry in Egypt," in *The Business of Tourism: Place, Faith, and History*, ed. Philip Scranton and Janet F. Davidson (Philadelphia: University of Pennsylvania Press, 2007), 3–33; Andrew Humphreys, *Grand Hotels of Egypt in the Golden Age of Travel* (Cairo: American University in Cairo Press, 2011); and the following studies by Derek Gregory: "Colonial Nostalgia and Cultures of Travel: Spaces of Constructed Visibility in Egypt," in *Consuming Tradition, Manufacturing Heritage: Global Norms and Urban Forms in the Age of Tourism*, ed. Nezar AlSayyad (London: Routledge, 2001), 111–151; "Scripting Egypt: Orientalism and the Cultures of Travel," in *Writes of Passage: Reading Travel Writing*, ed. James Duncan and Derek Gregory (London: Routledge, 1999), 114–150; "Emperors of the Gaze: Photographic Practices and Productions of Space in Egypt, 1839–1914," in *Picturing Place: Photography and the Geographical Imagination*, ed. Joan M. Schwartz and James R. Ryan (London: I.B.Tauris, 2003), 195–225.

2 L.L. Wynn, *Pyramids & Nightclubs : A Travel Ethnography of Arab and*

Western Imaginations of Egypt, (Austin: University of Texas Press, 2007); Lynn Meskell, "Sites of Violence: Terrorism, Tourism, and Heritage in the Archaeological Present," in *Embedding Ethics,* ed. Lynn Meskell and Peter Pels, (Oxford: Berg, 2005), 123–46; Jessica Jacobs, *Sex, Tourism and the Postcolonial Encounter: Landscapes of Longing in Egypt* (Farnham, Surrey, UK: Ashgate, 2010); Donald P. Cole and Soraya Altorki, *Bedouin, Settlers, and Holiday-Makers: Egypt's Changing Northwest Coast* (Cairo: American University in Cairo Press, 1998); Waleed Hazbun, *Beaches, Ruins, Resorts: The Politics of Tourism in the Arab World* (Minneapolis: University of Minnesota Press, 2008); *Middle East Report,* No. 196 (1995), special issue on "Tourism and the Business of Pleasure."

3   Rudy Koshar, *German Travel Cultures* (Oxford: Berg, 2000), 3. Daniel R. Headrick, *The Tentacles of Progress: Technology Transfer in the Age of Imperialism, 1850–1940* (New York: Oxford University Press, 1988), emphasizes the steamship, railroad, and telegraph.

4   William W. Stowe, *Going Abroad: European Travel in Nineteenth-Century American Culture* (Princeton: Princeton University Press, 1994).

5   John Pemble, *The Mediterranean Passion: Victorians and Edwardians in the South* (Oxford: Clarendon Press, 1987).

6   Reid, *Whose Pharaohs?*; Hunter, "Tourism and Empire," *Middle Eastern Studies* 40, No. 5 (Sept. 2004), 28–54. Company histories include John Pudney: *The Thomas Cook Story* (London: M. Joseph, 1953); Edmund Swinglehurst, *Cook's Tours: The Story of Popular Travel* (Poole, UK: Blandford Press, 1982); Piers Brendon, *Thomas Cook: 150 Years of Popular Tourism* (London: Secker & Warburg, 1991); and Jill Hamilton, *Thomas Cook: The Holiday Maker* (Thrupp, UK: Sutton, 2005). Lynn Withey, *Grand Tours and Cook's Tours: A History of Leisure Travel, 1750–1915* (New York: W. Morrow, 1997), offers a broader context.

7   James Buzard, *The Beaten Track: European Tourism, Literature, and the Ways to Culture, 1880–1918* (Oxford: Oxford University Press, 1993), 4.

8   Humphreys, *Grand Hotels,* and Nina Nelson, *Shepheard's Hotel* (London: Macmillan, 1960), and *The Mena House: A Short History of a Remarkable Hotel,* 4th ed. (Cairo: Mena House Oberoi Hotel, 1997).

9   I.G. Lévi, "Le tourisme et la villégiature en Égypte," *L'Égypte contemporaine* 3 (1912): 255–281. Lévi worried that the twenty-seven thousand Egyptian residents who summered in Europe drained off far more money than the seven to eight thousand winter tourists Egypt brought in.

10   *The Times,* February 4, 1955, 11.

11   As quoted in Anthony Sattin, *Lifting the Veil: British Society in Egypt 1768–1956* (London: J.M. Dent, 1988), 232.

12   Henderson to Foley, May 19, 1919.UKNA/ MT 23/651.

13   F.H. Cook (?), Smith to India Office, June 8, 1916, UKNA/ MT 23/ 651, "Townsend Relief Expedition"; Brendon, *Cook,* 257.

14   Oleg V. Volkoff, *Comment on visitait le vallée du Nil: les guides de l'Égypte* (Cairo: IFAO, 1967), 103–119 lists Egyptian guidebooks from 1830 to 1964. Unlike Volkoff, I have not counted guidebooks to a single city,

region, or museum.

15 *Guide to Egypt and the Sûdân*, Macmillan's Guides, 7th ed. (London: Macmillan, 1916, reprinted 1918), vii, viii.

16 Thomas Cook & Son, *Traveller's Gazette*, December, 1920, 9. Brendon, *Cook*, 262.

17 Thomas Cook Archives, "Egyptian Steamers" (scrapbook) including 1. "The Nile Steamers," enclosed in letter with illegible signature, Cairo, to W.D.C. Cormack, London, March 1, 1952. 2. J.H. Price, "Cooks Nile Flotilla." Typed list with notation: "Edmund[,] Found this. I compiled it after my 1961 visit when I went through the ships [sic] ledger in Cairo office. J.H.P. [Price]."

18 *New York Times*, Dec.31, 1922, 32.

19 Robert Solé, *L'Égypte, passion française* (Paris: Seuil, 1997), 240.

20 Humphreys, *Grand Hotels*, 39, 73, 85.

21 Humphreys, *Grand Hotels* ,76–79, 86–87, 101–109, 119–24, 198–200.

22 Oleg V. Volkoff, *Comment on visitait la vallée du Nil: les guides de l'Égypte* (Cairo: IFAO, 1967), 113–16. In 1984 the Automobile Association's (UK & Ireland) *Baedeker's AA Egypt* traded on the famous name but was very different. In a sign of the times, the 2008 Baedeker, *Egypt*, (Ostfildern: Karl Baedeker Verlag) was printed in China.

23 Baedeker, *Egypt*, 1929, xiii–xiv, 1–6; Baedeker, *Egypt*, 1908, xiii–xiv, 1–4.

24 Baedeker, *Egypt*, 1929, 6.

25 Baedeker, *Egypt*, 1908, 1–2; 1929, 1–2.

26 The 1908 Baedeker, *Egypt*, p. 1, had only noted in small print that passengers from New York could change in Marseilles, Naples, or Genoa for Egypt.

27 Brendon, *Cook*, 12.

28 Alden Hatch, *American Express: A Century of Service* (Garden City, NY: Doubleday, 1950); American Express Co., *Promises to Pay: The Story of American Express* (New York: American Express Co., 1997).

29 Baedeker, *Egypt*, 1908, 198, 33; *New York Times*, August 16, 1906, 5.

30 Baedeker, *Egypt*, 1929, 214; 1908, 198.

31 Baedeker, *Egypt*, 1929, 213–14.

32 Pre–World War I Egyptian Baedekers, headquartered in Leipzig, colonized London by affiliating with Dulau & Co. and later Allen & Unwin and colonized New York through Charles Scribner's Sons. Macmillan's Egyptian guides, headquartered in London, had a subsidiary office in New York.

33 Derek Gregory, "Emperors of the Gaze: Photographic Practices and Productions of Space in Egypt, 1839–1914," in *Picturing Place: Photography and the Geographical Imagination*, ed. Joan M. Schwartz and James R. Ryan (London: I.B.Tauris, 2003), 195–225; Gregory, "Colonial Nostalgia and Cultures of Travel: Spaces of Constructed Visibility in Egypt," in *Consuming Tradition, Manufacturing Heritage: Global Norms and Urban Forms in the Age of Tourism*, ed. Nezar AlSayyad, (London: Routledge, 2001), 111–51; Edward Said, *Orientalism* (New York: Pantheon, 1978); Timothy Mitchell, *Colonising Egypt* (Cambridge: Cambridge University Press, 1988); and John Urry, *The Tourist Gaze*, 2nd ed. (London: Sage, 2002).

34 Baedeker, *Egypt*, 1929, xviii.
35 Alan P. Dodson, *Peaceful Air Warfare: The United States, Britain, and the Politics of International Aviation* (Oxford: Clarendon Press, 1991).
36 http://egyptair.com/English/Pages/Story.aspx
37 E.A. Wallis Budge, *Cook's Handbook for Egypt and the Sudan* (London: Thomas Cook & Son, 1921), 827; cf. Budge, *Cook's Handbook for Egypt and the Sudan*, 1911, 326.
38 Budge, *Cook's Handbook for Egypt*, 1921, 25.
39 Budge, *Cook's Handbook for Egypt*, 1921, 105–106; 1911 edition, 291.
40 Roy Elston, *Traveller's Handbook for Egypt and the Sudan*, Cook's Travellers' Handbooks (London: Simpkin, Marshall, 1929).
41 Elston, *Traveller's Handbook*, xcvii-xcviii.
42 Baedeker, *Egypt*, 1929, 212, slightly reworded from the 1908 edition, 196.
43 Baedeker, *Egypt*, 1908, 53.
44 Baedeker, *Egypt*, 1929, 58.
45 Baedeker, *Egypt*, 1908, lxiv.
46 Baedeker, *Egypt*, 1929, lxxxiv.
47 Baedeker, *Egypt*, 1929, lxxxii.
48 TCA, Box: Egypt: Steamer Contracts; 1930s, Folio 123, Tourist Development Association of Egypt, "Report on the Publicity and Propaganda Campaign for the Season 1934/1935."
49 TCA, Box: Egypt: Steamer Contracts; 1930s, Folio: Review of T. Cook, "Notes on Mr. René Margot's Report," September 5,1933, 18. Amalgamated percentages are for the seasons 1926/27, 1927/28, and 1930/31 without a yearly breakdown, and separate percentages for 1932/33. In the same Box, Folio 123: Tourist Development Association of Egypt, "Report on the Publicity and Propaganda Campaign for the Season 1934/1935," notes advertising in Great Britain, the United States, and Continental Europe (Holland, Switzerland, Norway, Czechoslavakia, Denmark, France, and Sweden); Germany and Italy are notably absent.
50 Nelson, *Shepheard's*, 62.
51 Baedeker, *Egypt*, 1929, xv, 40.
52 I.G. Lévi, "Pour une politique du tourisme," *L'Égypte contemporaine* 24 (1933): 573–577.
53 Miles Lampson, *Politics and Diplomacy in Egypt: The Diaries of Sir Miles Lampson 1935–1937*, ed. M.E. Yapp, (Oxford, published for the British Academy by Oxford University Press, 1997), 286.
54 Yunan Labib Rizk, "Selling Egypt," *Al-Ahram Weekly*, June 9–15, 2005, 24; *L'Égypte contemporaine* (1941): 174; *Scott's 2012*, Egypt #1296.
55 Brendon, *Cook*, 266.
56 TCA, Box: Steamer Contracts; 1930s, Folder: Review of T. Cook, "Notes on Mr. René Margot's Report," September 5, 1933, p. 2.
57 The work began as Mohamed Aboudi, *Aboudi's Guide Book to the Antiquities of Upper Egypt and Nubia* (Cairo: A. Safarowsky, 1931), reprinted in 1944. By 1950, the scope had expanded to *Aboudi's Guide Book to the Antiquities of Egypt Historically Treated* (Cairo: Costa Tsoumas, 1950), but the enlargement and

updating were superficial. The historical sketch in the 1954 edition mentions neither the reign of King Faruq nor the 1952 revolution. Alexandria is dismissed in half a page. Cairo and vicinity get in twenty-four pages, compared to over a hundred on Aboudi's Luxor-area home territory. Hotels and tourist services are listed only for Luxor and to a lesser extent Aswan. Volkoff, *Vallée du Nil*, 116–118, lists the different editions of Aboudi.

58   The Baedeker quotations in this and the next several paragraphs are from Baedeker, *Egypt*, 1908, xxiv–xxv, and Baedeker, *Egypt*, 1929, xxv.

59   *Guide to Egypt and the Sûdân*, Macmillan's Guides, 6th ed. (London, 1911), 5.

60   Mohamed Aboudi, *Aboudi's Guide*, 1954.

61   Aboudi Bookstore (Luxor) calendar, 2011. Photos of the two shops in *Aboudi's Guide*, 1931, 38, 165; photos of Aboudi, 1931, 1; 1954, 1.

62   Baedeker, *Egypt*, 1908, xxv.

63   Aboudi, *Aboudi's Guide*, 1931, 150.

64   Aboudi, *Aboudi's Guide*, 1954, 36, 48, 63, 67.

65   Aboudi, *Aboudi's Guide*, 1954, 220–24.

66   Miscellaneous verses from several poems. Aboudi, *Aboudi's Guide*, 1954, 269–72.

67   Aboudi, *Aboudi's Guide*, 1954, 88–89.

68   Baedeker, *Egypt*, 1929, xxvi.

69   *The Traveller's Gazette*, September 1939, 12–13.

70   As cited in Volkoff, *Vallée du Nil*, 115–17.

71   P. Condopoulo, *An Illustrated Guide Book on Egypt and Nubia* (Cairo: E. Menikidis, 1930), 5.

72   Not listed in Volkoff, *Vallée du Nil*. The other Egyptian-authored guide was Wassef Morcos Hanna, *Égypte. le compagnon du touriste* (Cairo: Costa Tsoumas, 1947), as listed in Volkoff, *Vallée du Nil*, 117.

73   FO371/ 45987/ J2939, August 21,1945.

74   Adams to Killearn, June 21, 1944, enclosed in Killearn to Eden, July 19, 1944. FO371/ 41374.

75   Killearn to Bevin, August 21, 1945. FO371/ 45987/ J2939.

76   Adams to Killearn, November 28, 1945; Killearn to Adams, December 22, 1945. FO371/ 53326.

77   Memorandum of Articles of Association of Thos. Cook & Son (Egypt) Limited. UKNA/ RAIL 258/209.

78   Campbell to Bevin, April 21, 1950. FO371/ 80564/ JE1633/1.

79   Swinglehurst, *Thomas Cook*, 175–176.

80   TCA, "Egyptian Steamers" (scrapbook), (signature illegible) [Cairo] to Cormack, March 1, 1952.

81   TCA, "Egyptian Steamers" (scrapbook), J. H. Price, "The Nile Steamers," printed list of forty-five Cook's steamers and *dahabiyas*, with dates of construction and disposition when available. No date [1960s].

82   *Egypt Travel Magazine*, No. 6 (February 1955): 49.

83   Marcelle Baud, *Égypte. Les guides bleus* (Paris: Hachette, 1950), v.

84   Philip Dawson, *The Liner: Retrospective and Renaissance* (New York: Norton, 2006), documents how air travel in the 1950s and early 1960s made ocean

liners obsolete.

85   Kay Showker, *Fodor's Egypt* (New York: David McKay, 1977), may be the first.

86   Sami Gabra, *Chez les derniers adorateurs de Trismegiste: la nécropole d'Hermopolis Touna El Gebel (Souvenir d'un archéologue)* (Cairo: al-Haya al-misriya al-amma, 1971), 15.

87   Benedict Anderson, *Imagined Communities: Reflections on the Origin and Spread of Nationalism*, 2nd ed. (London: Verso, 1991), 180.

88   Stephen Quirke, *Hidden Hands: Egyptian Workforces in Petrie Excavation Archives, 1880–1924* (London: Duckworth, 2010); Wendy Doyon, "On Archaeological Labor in Nineteenth-Century Egypt," in *Histories of Egyptology: Interdisciplinary Measures*, ed. William Carruthers (London: Routledge, 2015).

89   Kees van der Spek, *The Modern Neighbors of Tutankhamun: History, Life, and Work in the Villages of the Theban West Bank* (Cairo: American University in Cairo Press, 2011) and Timothy Mitchell, *Rule of Experts: Egypt, Techno-Politics, Modernity* (Berkeley: University of California Press, 2002), 179–205.

90   Gaston Maspero, *La trouvaille de Deir-el-Bahari* (Cairo: Impr. Française F. Mourès, 1881); *Les momies royales de Deir-el-Bahari* (Paris: E. Leroux, 1889).

91   van der Spek, *Modern Neighbors of Tutankhamun*. See also Elliot Colla, "The Stuff of Egypt: The Nation, the State and their Proper Objects," *New Formations* 45 (Winter 2001–2002): 89.

92   For this and the following quotation, see Ahmad Naguib, *Kitab al-athar al-jalil li-qudama Wadi al-Nil* (Bulaq, 1895), 5, as translated in Colla, "Stuff of Egypt," 88–89, 81.

93   Campell to Bevin, July 2, 1946, enclosing "Minutes on a Meeting of the Advisory Committee on British Culture in Egypt," chaired by Sir Robert Greg. FO924/414/ LC3350.

94   Gady, "Pharaon," 1003–1005.

95   On Stoppelaëre see Gady, "Pharaon," 1003–1009, and *WWWE4*: 406.

96   Nancy Gallagher, *Egypt's Other Wars: Epidemics and the Politics of Public Health* (Syracuse: Syracuse University Press, 1990), 32–35, 60–66; and Timothy Mitchell, "Can the Mosquito Speak?" in his *Rule of Experts: Egypt, Techno-Politics, Modernity* (Berkeley: University of California Press, 2002), 19–53.

97   Hassan Fathy, *Architecture for the Poor: An Experiment in Rural Egypt* (Chicago: University of Chicago Press, 1973), 16–17. Originally published by the Ministry of Culture as *Gourna: A Tale of Two Villages* (Cairo: Ministry of Culture, 1969).

98   Mitchell, "Heritage and Violence," in *Rule of Experts*, 179–205, examines the political economy of tourism and archaeology on the west bank at Luxor, including Fathy's project.

99   Autobiographical information is scattered through Fathy, *Architecture for the Poor*. James Steele's *Hassan Fathy* (London: Academy Editions, 1988) and Steele's *An Architecture for People: The Complete Works of Hassan Fathy* (New York: St. Martin's, 1997) are fundamental. See also Max Nobbs-Thiessen, "Contested Representations and the Building of Modern Egypt: The Architecture of Hassan Fathy" (MA thesis, Dept. of History, Simon

Fraser University, 2006); and American University in Cairo, "Guide to the Hassan Fathy Architectural Archives, 1900s." http://lib.aucegypt.edu/record=b1527062

100 Nobbs-Thiessen, "Contested Representations," 66.

101 Steele, *Architecture for People*, 191. On Hassanein, see Goldschmidt, *Biographical Dictionary*, 73–44.

102 Quotations from Fathy, *Architecture for the Poor*, 1–2.

103 Ahmad Hamid, *Hassan Fathy and Continuity in Islamic Architecture: The Birth of a New Modern* (Cairo: American University in Cairo Press, 2010), 59, 60, quoting Fathy, unp. document, Rare Books and Special Collections Library, American University in Cairo.

104 Steele, *Architecture for People*, 86.

105 Hamid, *Hassan Fathy*, Plate 3 (plate pages not numbered).

106 Steele, *Architecture for People*, 86.

107 Quotations in this paragraph are from Fathy, *Architecture for the Poor*, 183, 184.

108 Hana Taragan, "Architecture in Fact and Fiction: The Case of the New Gourna Village in Upper Egypt," *Muqarnas* 16 (1999): 169–78. Quotation on p. 172.

109 David Roessel, "The Tale of Two Villages," *Al-Ahram Weekly*, July 4–10, 1996.

110 Fathy, *Architecture for the Poor*, 176.

111 Kamil, *Labib Habachi*, 297–98.

112 Steele, *Architecture for People*, 193; http://www.tawy.nl/EN_dh_Stoppelaere_House.html. The Stoppelaëre/Antiquities Service House is often mistaken for Howard Carter's house, which is below and across the road.

113 Mitchell, *Rule of Experts*, 196–205; van der Spek, *The Modern Neighbors of Tutankhamun*; Qurna History Project, http://www.qurna.org

114 For a list of British firms targeted, see Stevenson to Eden, February 5, 1952. FO371/ 96957.

6. In the Shadow of Egyptology

1 Farnall to Wingate, February 4, 1917, enclosing extract of Clarke letter to Farnall. FO141/800/16.

2 Mustafa Abd El-Razeq, "Ali Bey Bahgat, 1854–1924," *BIÉ* 6 (1923–24): 113.

3 Donald Malcolm Reid, "Cultural Imperialism and Nationalism: The Struggle to Define and Control the Heritage of Arab Art in Egypt," *IJMES* 24 (1992): 57–76. See also Donald Malcolm Reid, *Whose Pharaohs? Archaeology, Museums, and Egyptian National Identity from Napoleon to World War I* (Berkeley: University of California Press, 2002) 212–57.

4 István Ormos, *Max Herz Pasha (1856–1919): His Life and Career*, 2 vols. (Cairo: IFAO, 2009); Philip Speiser, "Das 'Comité de conservation des monuments de l'art arabe,'" chapter 2 in his *Die Geschichte der Erhaltung Arabischer Baudenkmäler in Ägypten. Die Restaurierung der Madrasa Tatar al-Higāzīya* (Heidelberg: Heidelbergerverlag, 2001), 47–94; Mercedes Volait, *Architectes et architectures de l'Égypte moderne (1830–1950): genèse*

et essor d'une expertise locale (Paris: Maisonneuve et Larose, 2005), esp.
148–155; Volait, *Fous du Caire: excentriques, architectes et amateurs d'art
en Égypte 1863–1914* (Montpellier: L'archange minotaure, 2009); Paula
Sanders, *Creating Medieval Cairo: Empire, Religion, and Architectural
Preservation in Nineteenth-Century Egypt* (Cairo: American University in
Cairo Press, 2008); Nezar AlSayyad, Irene A. Bierman, Nasser Rabbat,
eds., *Making Cairo Medieval* (Lanham, MD: Lexington Books, 2005); and
Alaa El-Din Elwi El-Habashi, "*Athar* to Monuments: The Intervention of
the Comité de Conservation des Monuments de l'Art Arabe," (PhD diss.,
University of Pennsylvania, 2001), and El-Habashi, "The Preservation
of Egyptian Cultural Heritage through Egyptian Eyes: The Case of
the Comité de Conservation des Monuments des Monuments de l'Art
Arabe," in *Urbanism: Imported or Exported*, ed. Joe Nasr and Mercedes
Volait (Chichester, UK: Wiley-Academic, 2003), 155–75. See also Stephen
Vernoit, ed., *Discovering Islamic Art: Scholars, Collectors and Collections,
1850–1950* (London: I.B.Tauris, 2000), and Vernoit, "The Rise of Islamic
Archaeology," *Muqarnas* 14 (1997): 1–10.

5   For the Ottoman case, see Wendy M.K. Shaw, *Possessors and Possessed: Museums, Archaeology, and the Visualization of History in the Late Ottoman Empire*
(Berkeley: University of California Press, 2003), 173–74.

6   Yannis Hamilakis, *The Nation and Its Ruins: Antiquity, Archaeology, and
National Imagination in Greece* (Oxford: Oxford University Press, 2007), 27,
114–16, 292.

7   Sayed Desokey El Sharif, *al-Umlat al-misriya al-waraqiya/ Egyptian Paper
Money* (Cairo: al-Faris lil-diaya wa-l-ilan, 2003), 81–82, lists this monu-
ment as 'El-Mansour mosque at Bein El-Kasrian' [sic]; it is described in
Caroline Williams, *Islamic Monuments in Cairo: The Practical Guide*, 6th ed.
(Cairo: American University in Cairo Press, 2008), 185–89. Remarkably,
in 2014, the Egyptian tour company Rehla Khana found that "one of the
group's most popular trips that caused a stir on social media was Rehlet
Al-Omlat—a trip to all the famous mosques printed on Egyptian currency."
Lamia Hassan, "The Road Less Travelled: alternative tourism in Egypt,"
Ahram Online, 22 June 2014, http://english.ahram.org.eg

8   El Sherif, *al-Umlat al-misriya al-waraqiya*, 84–85.

9   See Ormos, *Herz*: 2: 313–14. In Arabic, the museum's original name,
Antikhana al-Arabiya, was changed to Dar al-Athar al-Arabiya in 1903. In
French and English, it was variously called Musée arabe / Arab (or Arabian)
Museum, Musée de l'art arabe / Museum of Arab Art, and (less frequently)
Museum of Arab Antiquities.

10   Stanley Lane-Poole, *Cairo: Sketches of Its History, Monuments, and Social Life*
(London: J.S. Virtue, 1898), 99–100.

11   Marshall Hodgson, *The Venture of Islam*, Vol. 1 (Chicago: University of
Chicago Press, 1974), 57–60, 95.

12   A point made by Salah El-Din Beheri, interview, Cairo, June 7, 2005.

13   The primary published source on the history of the Comité is its *Bulletins*,
available at http:// www.islamic-art.org/comitte/comite.asp. These include

the minutes of both the full Comité and its Deuxième commission (later Section technique), which constituted its executive body. Hereafter, citations are abbreviated as follows: Comité de conservation des monuments de l'art arabe. Exercice 1882–83, Fasicule 1, p. 1 = BComité 1882–83, 1: 1. On Bahgat, see Cheikh Moustafa Abd El-Razeq Pacha, *BIÉ* 6 (1923–24): 103–13; Tawfiq Iskarus, *al-Hilal* 32 (8) May 1, 1924, 856–61; Bahgat's pension folder: Dar al Mahfuzat, Millafat al-khidma wa-l-maash, Dulab 37/ Ayn 3/ Mahfaza 767/ Dusiya (dossier) 21175 (as copied in 1996 by Magdi Rashad and arranged by Abd al-Munim Jumayi); Anwar Luqa, *Ali Bahjat: raid al-bahth fi-l-athar al-arabiya bi-Misr: min rasailihi 1887–1919 li-tilmidhihi al-sawisiri wanbirkham* (Cairo: Dar al-hilal, 2003); and Dia Mahmud Abou Ghazi and Imad al-Din Abou-Ghazi, *Ali Bahgat 1858–1924* (Cairo, 1974). I have not seen the published version of the last item; references here are to a mimeographed version in the Egyptian Museum Library, Case 40, Book #171.

14   Edward Said, *Orientalism* (New York: Pantheon, 1978).
15   Gabriel Charmes, *Cinq mois au Caire et dans la Basse-Egypte* (Paris: G. Charpentier, 1880, 1880), 46–47.
16   BComité, 1882–83, 1: 5.
17   Mercedes Volait, "Making Cairo Modern (1870–1950): Multiple Models for a 'European-Style' Urbanism," in *Urbanism: Imported or Exported*, ed. Joe Nasr and Mercedes Volait (Chichester, UK: Wiley-Academic, 2003), 17–50; cf. C. Myntti, *Paris along the Nile: Architecture in Cairo from the Belle Epoque* (Cairo: American University in Cairo Press, 1999).
18   Two works elaborate this thesis: Paula Sanders, *Creating Medieval Cairo: Empire, Religion, and Architectural Preservation in Nineteenth-Century Egypt* (Cairo: American University in Cairo Press, 2008), and AlSayyad et al., eds., *Making Cairo Medieval*.
19   Gabriel Charmes, "L'art arabe au Caire," *Journal des débats*," Aug. 2, 1881.
20   Ormos, *Herz*, l: 77–79.
21   El-Habashi, "*Athar* to Monuments."
22   Lane-Poole, *Cairo*, viii–x.
23   Ormos, *Herz*, 1: 74.
24   The best source on Franz and Herz is Ormos's exhaustive study, *Herz*.
25   Reid, *Whose Pharaohs?*, 161, 234.
26   Ormos, *Herz* 2: 324–26.
27   On Artin, see Piot Bey, *BIÉ* 1 (1918–1919): 194–195; Arthur Goldschmidt Jr., *Biographical Dictionary of Modern Egypt* (Boulder, CO: Lynne Rienner, 2000), 25–26.
28   'Turkish' was popularly used in Egypt to describe the Turco-Circassian elite. Fakhri was the Paris-educated son of a Circassian general. Goldschmidt, *Biographical Dictionary*, 52–53.
29   Max van Berchem, *Matériaux pour un Corpus Inscriptionum Arabicum*, part 1: *Inscriptions de l'Égypte*, vol. 19 of *Mémoires de la mission archéologique français au Caire* (Cairo: IFAO, 1903), 17. On van Berchem, see Solange Ory, "Max van Berchem, orientaliste," in *D'un orient l'autre: les métamorphoses successive*

des perceptions et connaissances, ed. Jean-Claude Vatin, 2 vols. (Paris: CEDEJ, CNRS, 1991), 2: 11–24.

30   Anwar Luqa, *Ali Bahjat.*

31   Abd El-Razeq, *BIÉ* 1923–24, 109–11.

32   As asserted by Ormoz, *Herz* 2: 324. On Barudi and Farid, see Goldschmidt, *Biographical Dictionary,* 36–37, 53–54.

33   Ahmad Lutfi al-Sayyid, *Qissat Hayati* (Cairo: Dar al-hilal, 1962), 34–36.

34   Abd El-Razeq, *BIÉ* 1923–24, 105–106.

35   Abd El-Razeq, *BIÉ* 1923–24, 106; BComité 1900, 17: 72; 1902, 19: 3. On Bahgat's appointment and relations with Herz, see Ormos, *Herz* 2: 319–20.

36   Ormos, *Herz* 2: 313–16.

37   Lane-Poole, *Cairo,* 98.

38   Volait, *Architectes,* 435.

39   On the Neo-Mamluk as an Egyptian national style, see Nasser Rabbat, "The Formation of the Neo-Mamluk Style in Modern Egypt," in *The Education of the Architect: Historiography, Urbanism, and the Growth of Architectural Knowledge,* ed. Martha Pollak (Cambridge, MA: MIT Press, 1997), 363–86; Ormos, *Herz* 2:372, passim; and Volait, *Fous du Caire.* On the Rifai Mosque, see Ormos, *Herz,* 2:430–56.

40   Tarek Mohamed Refaat Sakr, "Early Twentieth-Century Islamic Architecture in Cairo," MA Thesis, American University in Cairo, 1993, 22–23.

41   Baedeker, *Egypt,* 1908, 88.

42   In December 1998 several of these photographs were hanging in the library of the Museum of Islamic Art.

43   Iskarus, *al-Hilal* 32: 8 (May 1, 1924): 860.

44   *Egyptian Gazette,* Sept. 14 and 19, 1900, as quoted in Roger Owen, "The Cairo Building Industry and the Building Boom of 1897 to 1907," in *Colloque international sur l'histoire du Caire, 27 Mars–5 Avril 1969* (Cairo: Ministry of Culture of the Arab Republic of Egypt, General Egyptian Book Organisation, 1972), 348.

45   Baedeker, *Egypt,* 1908, 58–60, 75–99.

46   *Annuaire statistique de l'Égypte: 1914* (Cairo: Impr. nationale), 104.

47   BComité 1909, 26: 94–95.

48   Charlotte Trümpler, ed., *Das Grosse Spiel: Archäologie und Politik zur Zeit des Kolonialismus (1860–1940)* (Cologne: Ruhr Museum, 2008), esp. Jens Kröger, "Friedrich Sarre und die Islamische Archäologie," 274–85. On Hertzfeld and Sarre, see Vernoit, *Discovering,* 210, 213–14. For the development of Islamic archaeology, see J.M. Rogers, *From Antiquarianism to Islamic Archaeology* (Cairo, 1974); Timothy Insoll, *The Archaeology of Islam,* (Blackwell: Istituto italiano di cultura per la R.A.E., 1999; and Marcus Milwright, *An Introduction to Islamic Archaeology* (Edinburgh: Edinburgh University Press, 2010).

49   BComité 1913, 30: 126.

50   BComité 1914, 31: 134–35.

51   Herz letter to Max van Berchem, July 1915, translated in Ormos, *Herz,* 1: 30. A report which Bahgat submitted to the Comité but which it suppressed apparently triggered this response. Ormos, *Herz,* 2: 320–22.

52   As translated in Ormos, *Herz*, 2: 320.

53   BComité 1915–1919, 32: 1–2.

54   Patricolo to Allenby, April 17, 1923, with c.v. enclosed. FO141/813/15401.

55   For the text of the law, see BComité 1915–1919, 32: 241–49; on the royal visit, 275–78, 620.

56   BComité, 1915–19, 32: 279. Harry Farnall, "Polémique de press au sujet des fouilles à Foustât," 279–300 (articles collected from *The Egyptian Gazette* and translated into French). My English translations of Farnall's French will necessarily differ slightly from the English originals.

57   BComité 1915–1919, 32: 284, A.H. Sayce, *EG*, May 20, 1918.

58   BComité 1915–1919, 32: 281–82, Creswell, *EG*, May 27, 1918.

59   BComité 1915–1919, 32: 284–85, Farnall, *EG*, June 14, 1918. On Farnall (1852–1929), see *Who Was Who, 1929–1940* (London, 1941), 3: 431.

60   BComité 1915–1919, 32: 288–89, Sayce, *EG*, June 18, 1918.

61   BComité 1915–1919, 32: 291–92, Farnall, *EG*, June 20,1918.

62   BComité 1920–24, 33: 1–2.

63   BComité 1920–24, 33: 10–13.

64   BComité, 1920–24, 33: 121–22.

65   List of museum publications in G. Wiet, *Musée national de l'art arabe. guide sommaire* (Cairo: Ministère de l'instruction publique, 1939), 75–76.

66   Ali Bahgat Bey and Albert Gabriel, *Fouilles d'al Foustât, Musée de l'art arabe* (Paris, 1921), 4–5. Gabriel later directed the Institut français d'archéologie in Istanbul (1930–55) and specialized in medieval Islamic architecture from Anatolia to Iran. Vernoit, *Discovering*, 209.

67   Donald Whitcomb, "Archaeology," *Encyclopaedia of Islam*, 3rd ed. (Leiden: Brill, 2009) 2009-4: 54, 58. In addition to Scanlon's specialized reports, see Wladyslaw B. Kubiak, *Al-Fustat: Its Foundation and Early Urban Development* (Cairo: American University in Cairo Press, 1987).

68   BComité 1920–24, 33: 159–64, gives the text of his Paris paper; for Grenoble, see Iskarus, *al-Hilal* 32: 8 (May 1, 1924): 860.

69   Cairo Legation to MAE, June 23, 1923. MAE, AMB. Le Caire, Carton 346: Voyages et missions. Dossier: Personages divers.

70   BComité 1920–24, 33: 317–18.

71   Abd El-Razeq, *BIÉ* 1923–24, 102.

72   Dia Mahmud Abou-Ghazi and Imad al-Din Abou-Ghazi, *Ali Bahgat: 1858–1924*, 50. Published version not seen; references here to mimeographed version in the Egyptian Museum Library, Case 40, Book No. 171.

73   BComité 1925–26, 34: 56; cf. Ormos, *Herz* 2: 333.

74   BComité 1925–26, 34: 23–28.

75   Farnall to Wingate, February 23, 1917. FO141/ 800/ 16. On Patricolo's tenure, see Speiser, *Geschichte*, 70–71.

76   *The Egyptian Directory: L'Annuaire égyptien (Égypte et Soudan)* (Cairo, 1921), 195.

77   Ormos, *Herz*, 101–103.

78   G.?A. to Allenby, December 26, 1922. FO141/ 800/ 16, Cairo Residency minute.

79   Clarke to Ahmed Ali Pasha. Archives of the Griffith Institute, Oxford University, Somers Clarke MSS 10 (Correspondence, 1922). 4.1.
80   Mustafa Munir Adham, *al-Ahram*, April 22, 1924, 8.
81   On al-Sayyid, see Speiser, *Geschichte*, 71–72.
82   El-Habashi, "Preservation," 155–75. On Mahmud Ahmad's tenure as chief architect, see Speiser, *Geschichte*, 72–73.
83   BComité 1925–26, 34: 55, 58.
84   BComité 1925–26, 34: 58.
85   BComité 1925–26, 34: 55–60.
86   Gailland to MAE, February 15, 1926. MAE, AMB Le Caire, Services ég. divers. Carton 175, Dossier 3: Enseignement publique, dossier "Arabisants attachés au musée arabe et à la bibliotheque royale." On Fuad's Francophone Egyptian University hires, see Donald Malcolm Reid, *Cairo University and the Making of Modern Egypt* (Cambridge: Cambridge University Press, 1990), 87–88.
87   Karim Thabit, *al-Malik Fuad: malik al-nahda* (Cairo: Matbaat al-maarif, 1944), 177–78.
88   BComité 1896, 13: 111.
89   BComité 1896, 13: 60–6.1
90   Jean Cocteau, *Maalesh: A Theatrical Tour in the Middle East*, trans. Mary C. Hoeck (London: P. Owen, 1956), 32.
91   On Wiet, see *Studies in Memory of Gaston Wiet*, ed. Myriam Rosen-Ayalon (Jerusalem: Institute of Asian and African Studies, Hebrew University, 1977), ix–xii; Daniel Reig, *Homo orientaliste: la langue arabe en France depuis le XIXe siècle* (Paris: Maiseonneuve et Larose, 1988), 115–16; *al-Majalla al-tarikhiya al-misriy*a 12 (1972): 89–110 (Ahmad Darraj); *Revue des études islamiques* 39, fasc. 2 (1971): 205–07 (H. Laoust); *Journal of the Economic and Social History of the Orient* 14 (1971): 223–26 (Claude Cahen); *Journal asiatique*, 249 (1971): 1–9 (Nikita Élisséeff).
92   Ali Ibrahim Pasha, "Early Islamic Rugs of Egypt or Fostat Rugs," *BIÉ* 17 (1934–35): 123.
93   BComité 1920–24, 33: 79.
94   BComité 1925–26, 34: 80; Wiet, *Musée national de l'art arabe: guide sommaire*, 75–76.
95   Louis Hautecoeur and Gaston Wiet, *Les mosquées du Caire*, 2 vols. (Paris: E. Leroux, 1932).
96   Hilary Ballon, "The History of Louis Hautecoeur: Classical Architecture aand Vichy Politics," in *The Education of the Architect: Historiography, Urbanism, and the Growth of Architectural Knowledge. Essays presented to Stanford Anderson*, ed. Martha Pollak, (Cambridge MA: MIT Press, 1997), 217–37.
97   El-Habashi, "Preservation," 180n62.
98   Volait, *Architects*, 438.
99   BComité 1936–40, 38: 135–36.
100   BComité 1936–1940, 38: 239–48.
101   *Studies in Islamic Art and Architecture in Honor of Professor K.A.C. Creswell* (Cairo: American University in Cairo Press, 1965), xi.

102 Biographical information on Creswell here draws primarily on the unusual obituary by R.W. Hamilton, "Keppel Archibald Cameron Creswell, 1879–1974," *Proceedings of the British Academy*, 60 (1974): 1–20.

103 Helen Gibson, "Knight of the Dead Stones," *Aramco World*, 23, No. 3 May/June 1972, 4, http://www.saudiaramcoworld.com/issue/197203/knight.of.the.dead.stones.htm.

104 BComité 1920–24, 33: 238–43, 264–66; 1925–26, 34: 1–4, 11–12; 1927–29, 35: 77–83, 145–49; 1930–32, 36: 187; 1941–45, 39: 2.

105 K.A.C. Creswell, *Early Muslim Architecture*, vol. 2 (Oxford: Oxford University Press, 1940); K.A.C. Creswell, *The Muslim Architecture of Egypt*, 2 vols. (Oxford: Oxford University Press, 1952–1959).

106 Creswell, *Muslim Architecture of Egypt* 1, vii.

107 K.A.C. Creswell, *Early Muslim Architecture*, vol. 1, part 1: *Umayyads*, AD *622–750*, 2nd ed. (1969; repr. New York, 1979), xxxv.

108 On Creswell's work, see Oleg Grabar, ed., *K.A.C. Creswell and His Legacy*, *Muqarnas* 8 (Leiden: Brill, 1991).

109 K.A.C. Creswell, *A Bibliography of the Architecture, Arts, and Crafts of Islam to 1st January 1960* (Cairo, 1961).

110 Hamilton, "Creswell," *British Academy* 60 (1974), 15.

111 J.M. Rogers, "Architectual History as Literature: Creswell's Reading and Methods," in *K.A.C. Creswell and His Legacy, Muqarnas* 8 (Leiden: Brill, 1991), 46. AUC's Creswell archive includes a box labeled "Anti-Semitic Literature." AUC Library, Rare Books and Special Collections, Creswell: Box 11.

112 Creswell to Marçais, May 29, 1951. AUC Special Collections, Creswell Papers, Correspondence Box 1, Folder 1950–1959.

113 BComité 1930–32, 36: 221; 1933–35, 37: 416; 1936–40, 38: 179.

114 Hamilton, "Creswell," *British Academy* 60 (1974), 16.

115 Hamilton, "Creswell," *British Academy* 60 (1974), 16.

116 "Egyptian Personalities Report. 1945," 45, enclosed in Farquhar to FO, August 19, 1945. FO371/ 45925/ J3027. By 1950, the racial slur had been edited out of the entry on Wiet: Campbell to Bevin, April 28, 1950, "Leading Personalities in Egypt," p. 55. FO371/ 80342.

117 Peterson to Simon, December 3, 1934. FO371/18006/J3069.

118 Bierbier, *WWWE4*, 225.

119 BComité 1936–40, 38: 179, 240.

120 Hassan Hawary and Hussein Rached worked at the museum under Bahgat and then Wiet but missed the chance for advanced studies and were overshadowed. Interview with Abdel Raouf Ali Yussef, Cairo, April 18, 1988; Hassan Hawary and Hussein Rached, *Stèles funéraires. Catalogue général du musée arabe du Caire* (Cairo: IFAO, 1932), vol. 1.

121 BComité 1927–29, 35: 31–32, 40.

122 BComité 1927–29, 32. On Zaki Hassan, see *al-Kitab al-dhahabi lil-ihtifal al-khamsini bil-dirasat al-athariya bi- Jamiat al-Qahira* (vol. 1 of *Majallat kulliyat al-athar*, (Cairo, 1978) 17–28; *BSAC* 14 (1950–57): 251–52 (by Mohamed Moustapha); Ernst Kühnel, *Kunst des Orients* 3 (1959): 95–96;

Interview with Abdel Raouf Ali Yussef, Cairo, April, 18, 1988; Interview with Abd El Rahman Abd Eltawab, Cairo, January 7 and 10, 1999.

123 Vernoit, *Discovering*, 211.

124 On Muhammad Mustafa, see Fouad I National Research Council, *Guide to Scientific and Technical Workers in Egypt* (Cairo, 1951), 390; interview with Abdel Raouf Ali Yussef, Cairo, April 18, 1988. Mustafa and M.A. Marzouk were the two Egyptians who contributed to Kühnel's Festschrift: *Aus der Welt der Islamischen Kunst: Festschrift für Ernst Kühnel zum 75. Geburstag am 26.10.1957* (Berlin: Geber. Mann, 1959), 89–92, 283–89.

125 Zaki Hassan later married one of his students, Sayyida Ismail al-Kashif, who became professor of Islamic history at the Women's College, Ain Shams University. Interview with Amal El Emary, Cairo, January 3, 1999.

126 BComité 1936–40, 38: 248.

127 Zaky M. Hassan, *Moslem Art in the Fouad I University Museum* (Cairo: I University Press, 1950), vol. 1. On Ali Ibrahim (1880–1947), see *The Egyptian Medical Association Golden Jubilee 1920–1970*. Special issue of the *Journal of the Egyptian Medical Association*, 71–84. On Ali Ibrahim's daughter Laila Ali Ibrahim's career in Islamic art, see Doris Behrens-Abouseif, ed. *The Cairo Heritage: Essays in Honour of Laila Ali Ibrahim* (Cairo: American University in Cairo Press, 2000).

128 Interview with George Scanlon, Cairo, October 18, 1998.

129 Université Égyptienne. *Décret approvant le règlement intérieur de la faculté des lettres*. pp. 17–18. Extract from *Journal Officiel*, No. 67, Lundi, Juillet 24, 1933.

130 Interviews with Abd El-Rahman Abd Eltawwab, Cairo, January 7 and 10, 1999.

131 Hamilton, "Creswell," *British Academy*, 13.

132 See the lists in Jamiat al-Qahira, Kulliyat al-athar, *al-Dalil al-dhahabi lil-asa-tidha wa khariji al-athar Jamiat al-Qahira mundhu sanat 1925* (Cairo, ca. 1975).

133 BComité 1933–35, 37: 320–21.

134 BComité 1936–40, 38: 96–7, 181–82, 187–97.

135 Speiser, *Geschichte*, 73–74.

136 Jamiat al-Qahira, *al-Rasail al-ilmiya li-darajatay al-majistir wa-l-dukturah 1932–1966* (Cairo, 1967), 71–72.

137 BComité 1940–53, 40: 234–35.

138 See membership list in 1946: BComité 1941–45, 39: 361.

139 BComité 1946–53, 40: 256.

140 Claude Cahen, "Gaston Wiet," *JESHO* 14 (1971): 223–26. Minister of education Taha Hussein would have had to have been involved in Wiet's departure. However, in November 1951, he read a communication from Wiet to a meeting of the Institut d'Égypte, congratulated him on honors received from King Faruq, and regretted that his election to the Collège de France had deprived the Institut of his presence in Cairo. *BIÉ* 34 (1951–52): 467.

141 Ahmad Darraj, "Gaston Wiet wa-l-amal al-ilmiya," *al-Majalla al-tarikhiya al-misriya* 19 (1972): 92; Myriam Rosen-Ayalon, ed. *Studies in Memory of Gaston Wiet*. Institute of Asian and African Studies, The Hebrew University of Jerusalem.

142 BComité 1946–53, 40: 314.

143 "Former British Officials of the Egyptian Government dismissed in 1951," received January 28, 1958. FO371/ 131390/ JE1487/7.

144 BComité 1946–53, 40: 317.

145 BComité 1946–53, 40: 368, 387, 402.

146 After a ten-year struggle, Egypt agreed to pay over £E165,000 in compensation to the "1951 officials." Derek Hopwood, *Tales of Empire: The British in the Middle East 1880–1952* (London: I.B.Tauris, 1989), 25.

147 The Permanent Committee for Islamic and Coptic Antiquities. In 1953, a law brought the Antiquities Service, Egyptian Museum, Coptic Museum, Museum of Islamic Art, and the Comité together under the Antiquities Service. Antoine Khater, *Le régime juridique des fouilles et des antiquités en Égypte* (Cairo: IFAO, 1960), 84–88.

148 *al-Karasa al-hadiya wa-l-arbaun min mahadir al-lajna al-daima lil-athar al-islamiya wa-l-qibtiya* (Cairo: al-Haya al-amma li-shuun al-matabi al-amiriya, 1963), e.g., 1–4, 106 (41).

149 Jamiat al-Qahira, *al-Kitab al-dhahabi lil-ihtifal al-khamsini bil-dirasat al-athar-iya bi-Jamiat al-Qahira* (vol. 1 of *Majallat kulliyat al-athar*, (Cairo, 1978) 19.

150 Interview with Abd El Rahman Abd Eltawab, Cairo, January 7, 1999, July 12, 2005.

151 Including two booklets on the museum's holdings: Mohamed Mostafa, *Turkish Prayer Rugs: Collections of the Museum of Islamic Art* (Cairo: Ministry of Education Press, 1953) and *Moslem Ceramics* (Cairo: Museum of Islamic Art, S.O.P. Press, 1956).

7. Copts and Archaeology

1 Marcus Simaika, "Excerpts from the Memoirs of Marcus H. Simaika Pasha, C.B.E., F.S.A. (1864–1944)," unpublished typescript, 42–43. "Patriarch" and "pope" are used interchangeably for the head of the Coptic Church.

2 David Gange, *Dialogues with the Dead: Egyptology in British Culture and Religion, 1822–1922* (Oxford: Oxford University Press, 2013) emphasizes the powerful Biblical resonances in British Egyptology.

3 S.H. Leeder, *Modern Sons of the Pharaohs* (London: Hodder and Stoughton, 1918, reprinted New York: Arno Press, 1973).

4 See, for example, Ewa Wipszycka, "Le nationalism a-t-il existé dans l'Égypte byzantine?," *Journal of Juristic Papyrology* 22 (1992), 83–128, and Jacques van der Vliet, "The Copts: 'Modern Sons of the Pharaohs'?," *Church History and Religious Culture* 89, 1–3 (2009): 279–90.

5 Overviews of Coptic history include Otto Meinardus, *Two Thousand Years of Coptic Christianity* (Cairo: American University in Cairo Press, 1999), and Christian Cannuyer, *Les coptes* ([Turnhout, Belgium]: Editions Brepols, 1990). For the understudied Ottoman period, see Febe Armanios, *Coptic Christianity in Ottoman Egypt* (Oxford: Oxford University Press, 2011); Muhammad Afifi, *al-Aqbat fi Misr fi-l-asr al-uthmani* (Cairo: al-Haya al-misriya al-amma lil-kitab, 1992); and Alastair Hamilton, *The Copts and the West, 1439–1822* (Oxford: Oxford University Press, 2006).

6   Modern histories include B.L. Carter, *The Copts in Egyptian Politics* (London: Croom Helm, 1986); Tariq al-Bishri, *al-Muslimun wa-l-Aqbat fi itar al-jamaat al-wataniya* (Cairo: al-Haya al-misriya al-amma lil-kitab, 1982); Magdi Guirguis and Nelly Van Doorn-Harder, *The Emergence of the Modern Coptic Papacy*, vol. 3 of *The Popes of Egypt* (Cairo: American University in Cairo Press, 2011); Doris Behrens-Abouseif, *Die Kopten in der ägyptischen Gesellschaft—von der Mitte des 19. Jahrhunderts bis 1923* (Freiburg im Breisgau: K. Schwartz, 1972); Vivian Ibrahim, *The Copts of Egypt: Challenges of Modernisation and Identity* (London: I.B.Tauris, 2011); and S.S. Hassan, *Christians versus Muslims in Modern Egypt: The Century-Long Struggle for Coptic Equality* (Oxford: Oxford University Press, 2003).

7   This includes a few Catholics and Protestants of Coptic background. Earl of Cromer, *Modern Egypt*, rev.ed. (London: Macmillan, 1911), 560, 616. E.J. Chitham, *The Coptic Community in Egypt: Spatial and Social Change*, Occasional Papers Series, no. 32 (Durham: University of Durham, Centre for Middle Eastern and Islamic Studies, 1986), surveys population estimates and census figures.

8   The Egyptian government and the Coptic Church both reject 'majority' and 'minority' as divisive terms in referring to Egyptian Muslims and Copts. Paul Sedra, "Class Cleavages and Ethnic Conflict: Coptic Christian Communities in Modern Egyptian Politics," *Islam and Christian-Muslim Relations* 10, no. 2 (1999): 219–35, analyses competing "national unity" and "persecution" discourses for Coptic history.

9   Bruce Masters, *Christians and Jews in the Ottoman Arab World: The Roots of Sectarianism* (Cambridge: Cambridge University Press, 2002), provides an overview of minorities but mentions Egypt only in passing. See also Benjamin Braude and Bernard Lewis, eds., *Christians and Jews in the Ottoman Empire*, 2 vols. (New York: Holmes & Meier, 1982).

10 Paul Sedra, *From Mission to Modernity: Evangelicals, Reformers and Education in Nineteenth Century Egypt* (London: I.B.Tauris, 2011).

11 E.W. Lane, *An Account of the Manners and Customs of the Modern Egyptians: The Definitive 1860 Edition*, Intro., Jason Thompson (Cairo: American University in Cairo Press, 2003), 546.

12 J.G. Wilkinson, *Modern Egypt and Thebes*, 2 vols. (London: J. Murray, 1843), 1: 387–88.

13 Sedra, *From Mission to Modernity*, 19–62. See also Timothy Mitchell, *Colonising Egypt* (Cambridge: Cambridge University Press, 1988) and Khaled Fahmy, *All the Pasha's Men: Mehmed Ali, His Army and the Making of Modern Egypt* (Cambridge: Cambridge University Press, 1998).

14 Boutros Ghali, Yusuf Wahba, and Yahya Ibrahim. Simaika, "Memoirs," 11. In fact, however, Ghali, studied at the similar school which Kyrillus IV founded in Harat al-Saqqayin. Arthur Goldschmidt Jr., *Biographical Dictionary of Modern Egypt* (Boulder, CO: Lynne Rienner, 2000), 61–62.

15 Simaika, "Memoirs," 10–11.

16 Doris Behrens-Abouseif, *Azbakiya and Its Environs: From Azbak to Isma'il 1476–1879* (Cairo: American University in Cairo Press,1985), 37–42, 68–78.

17   Simaika, "Memoirs," 1–6, 8–13.

18   Heather J. Sharkey, *American Evangelicals in Egypt: Missionary Encounters in an Age of Empire* (Princeton: Princeton University Press, 2008).

19   A Coptic Layman, "The Awakening of the Coptic Church," *Contemporary Review* 71 (1897): 737–48. The references to protecting Coptic monuments (738, 747) suggest that Simaika was the author; hereafter [Simaika], "Awakening."

20   [Simaika], "Awakening," 737; cf. Leeder, *Modern Sons of the Pharaohs*, 253, 254: "It is admitted that there is scarcely a single dignitary in the Coptic Church who can claim to be of good family" and "one desert recluse succeeds another."

21   B.L. Carter, *The Copts in Egyptian Politics* (London: Croom Helm, 1986), 46–47.

22   Armanios, *Coptic Christianity*; Afifi, *al-Aqbat*.

23   Samir Seikally, "Coptic Communal Reform: 1860–1914," *Middle East Studies* 6 (1970): 262.

24   Hilmi Ahmad Shalabi, *al-Aqbat wa-l-islah al-ijtimai fi Misr (dawr jamiyat al-tawfiq) 1891–1952* (Cairo: Maktabat al-anjilu al-misriya, 1992). On Simaika's participation, see pp. 38, 40. See also Riyad Suriyal, *al-Mujtama al-qibti fi (al-qarn 19)* (Cairo: Maktabat al-mahabba, ca. 1971), 201.

25   The foundational account of lay vs. clerical struggle in the Majlis al-Milli is Seikally, "Coptic Communal Reform."

26   Sedra, *From Mission to Modernity*, 131–151; Sedra, "Writing the History of the Modern Copts: From Victims and Symbols to Actors," *History Compass* 7, no. 3 (2009): 1049–1063.

27   Simaika, "Memoirs," 86–87.

28   E.L. Butcher, *The Story of the Church of Egypt: Being an Outline of the History of the Egyptians under their Successive Masters from the Roman Conquest until Now* (London: Smith, Elder & Co.), 1897.

29   On al-Manqabadi, see Ilyas Zakhura, *Mirat al-asr fi akabir al-rijal bi-Misr* (Cairo, 1897–1916), 1: 414–17; Ramzi Tadrus, *al-Aqbat fi-l-qarn al-ishrin*, 4 vols. (Cairo: Matbaat jaridat Misr, 1910–11) 3: 39–50. On *Misr*, see Carter, *Copts*, 43–46.

30   Mirrit Boutros Ghali, "Clerical College," *CE* 2: 563–64.

31   For Claudius Labib, I have drawn on an interview with his son Pahor Labib, Cairo, October 22, 1987; Tadrus, *al-Aqbat fi-l-qarn al-ishrin*, 4: 135–39; W.E. Crum, *JEA* 5, Pt. 3 (July 1918): 215; Munir Basta, "Iqladiyus Labib," *CE* 4: 1302; Simaika, "Memoirs," 64. For Pahor Labib, see also Martin Krause, ed., *Essays on the Nag Hammadi Texts in Honour of Pahor Labib* (Leiden: Brill, 1975), 1–3; Bierbrier, *WWWE4*: 305.

32   On the Sunday School Movement, see Wolfram Reiss, *Erneuerung in der Koptisch-Orthodoxen Kirche: Die Geschichte der koptisch-orthodoxen Sonntagsschulbewegung und die Aufnahme ihrer Reformansätze in den Erneuerungsbewegungen der Koptisch-Orthodoxen Kirche der Gegenwart* (Hamburg: Hamburg Lit, 1998). S.S. Hassan, *Christians versus Muslims*, offers an

insightful Muslim persepective.

33 Roger Bagnall, *Egypt in the Byzantine World, 300–700* (Cambridge: Cambridge University Press, 2007), 4–5.

34 Hamilton, *The Copts and the West*. On Kircher, see Bierbrier, *WWWE4*, 296–97.

35 Simaika, "Memoirs," 9.

36 Alfred J. Butler, *Ancient Churches of Egypt*, 2 vols. (Oxford: Clarendon Press, 1884), 1: 371.

37 W.H.C. Frend, *The Archaeology of Early Christianity: A History* (London: Geoffrey Chapman, 1996), 145–49.

38 Tawfiq Iskarus, "Maks Harts Basha," *al-Hilal* 27, 10 (1919): 925.

39 Simaika, "Memoirs," 71–78; Kyriakos Mikhail, *Copts and Moslems under British Control* (London: Smith, Elder & Co., 1911), 42.

40 Simaika, "Memoirs," 80.

41 Simaika, "Memoirs," 29–33.

42 BComité 1896, 13: 35. Several Egyptian members suggested that one Copt was enough but were overridden.

43 István Ormos, *Max Herz Pasha (1856–1919): His Life and Career.* 2 vols. (Cairo: IFAO, 2009), 95–101.

44 Simaika, "Memoirs," 31–33.

45 As quoted in English translation in Ormos, *Herz*, 2: 335.

46 Ormos, *Herz*, 2: 334–35.

47 Simaika, "Memoirs," 86–87.

48 "Simaika Bey's Statement," in Archdeacon Dowling, *The Egyptian Church* (London: Cope & Fenwick, 1909), appendix 3: 47.

49 Leeder, *Modern Sons of the Pharaohs*, 263. Montague Fowler, *Christian Egypt: Past, Present and Future* (London: Church Newspaper Co., 1901), viii, shows the patriarch already relying on Simaika's advice in 1901.

50 BComité 1905, 22: 104.

51 The others were Qallini Fahmi, ex-Watanist Sinut Hanna, and Kamil Sidqi. Muhammad Khalil Subhi, *Tarikh al-hayah al-niyabiya fi Misr: min ahd rukn al-jinan Muhammad Ali Basha*, vols. 4–6 and supplementary vols. 5 and 6 (Cairo: Dar al-kutub al-misriya, 1939–47) 6: 52, 81–82; B.L. Carter, *Copts in Egyptian Politics*, 133.

52 Ahmad Shafiq, *Mudhakkirati fi nisf al-qarn*, vol. 2, pt. 2 (Cairo: Matbaat Misr, 1936): 237.

53 Simaika, "Memoirs," 43.

54 Leeder, *Modern Sons of the Pharaohs*, v.

55 Simaika, "Memoirs," 42.

56 *Note historique sur le Musée Copte au Vieux Caire à l'occasion de la visite de Sa Hautesse Fouad Ier Sultan d'Égypte. Mardi, 21 Décembre 1920* (Cairo: Musée Copte, 1920), 9. (French and Arabic bilingual pamphlet).

57 Baedeker, *Egypt*, 1929, 117.

58 Simaika, "Memoirs," 52.

59 Seikally, "Coptic Communal Reform," *Middle Eastern Studies* 6 (1970): 268. *al-Hilal* 19 (1911): 104–5, based on 1907 census and taxation figures,

estimated Copts at 7 percent of Egypt's population but owning 16 percent of cultivated lands and buildings and—with other capital assets—25 percent of the wealth.

60 Leeder, *Modern Sons of the Pharaohs*, 173.

61 al-Bishri, *al-Muslimun wa-l-Aqbat*, 65–97.

62 Carter, *Copts in Egyptian Politics*, 44–45.

63 For Copts in politics from 1919 to 1952, see al-Bishri, *al-Muslimun wa-l-Aqbat*; Carter, *Copts*; and Yunan Labib Rizq, "Political Parties," *CE* 6: pp. 1986–1993.

64 Carter, *Copts in Egyptian Politics*, 60.

65 Ibrahim, *Copts of Egypt*, 185–90, has a table of the number of Copts in cabinets (1892–1954). Two Armenians and a Jew, however, are mistakenly listed as Copts.

66 Carter, *Copts in Egyptian Politics*, 143, gives a table of Coptic representation in the Chamber of Deputies.

67 Mustafa Fiqi, *Copts in Egyptian Politics, 1919–1952* (Cairo: General Egyptian Book Organisation, 1991), emphasizes Ubayd's career.

68 Carter, *Copts in Egyptian Politics*, 182–86.

69 FO371/3711/J12835/1180/16, as cited in Carter, *Copts in Egyptian Politics*, 61, 81, n. 20.

70 Lampson to Eden, April 16, 1937, enclosing list of personalities in Egypt, p. 45. FO371/20916/137118.

71 Simaika, "Memoirs," 45–47.

72 Karim Thabit, *al-Malik Fuad: malik al-nahda* (Cairo: Matbaat al-maarif, 1944).

73 *al-Ahram*, Feb. 23, 1923.

74 Baedeker, *Egypt*, 1929, 22–26, 66–69, 88–111, 117–18.

75 George Sobhy, "The Coptic Museum in Cairo," *Ancient Egypt* pt. 4 (December 1927): 12.

76 BComité 36, 1930–32, 184; BComité 38, 1936–40, 180.

77 Simaika, "Memoirs," 35–36.

78 al-Bishri, *al-Muslimun wa-l-Aqbat*, 382–415; Carter, *Copts in Egyptian Politics*, 28–30.

79 Quotations in this paragraph are from Lampson to Eden, April 16, 1937, "List of Personalities in Egypt," 50. FO371/20916/137118. On the patriarchal election, see Carter, *Copts in Egyptian Politics*, 31–32.

80 Carter, *Copts in Egyptian Politics*, 148.

81 Simaika, "Memoirs," 13.

82 Muhammad Khalil Suhbi, *Tarikh al-haya al-niyabiya fi Misr: min ahd rukn al-jinan Muhammad Ali Basha.* (Cairo: Dar al-kutub al-misriya, 1939) 6: 235–36.

83 Yunan Labib Rizq, *Tarikh al-wizarat al-misriya 1878–1953* (Cairo: Markaz al-dirasat al-siyasiya wa-l-istratijiya bi-al-Ahram, wahdat al-wathaiq wa-l-buhuth al-tarikhiya, 1974), 243, 338.

84 Guirguis and Van Doorn-Harder, *Modern Coptic Papacy*, 108–113, 120–25.

85 Simaika, "Memoirs," 47–50; "Fi-l-mathaf al-qibti," *al-Muqattam*, June 3, 1931.

86   Archpriest Abd al-Masih Mikhail, rector of St. Mary's Church, Faggala.
87   Simaika, "Memoirs," 47–49. On Sidqi's visit, see also "Ziyarat rais al-wuzara," *al-Misa*, Jan. 16, 1932. On Faruq's visit, see Marcus Simaika Pasha, *Catalogue of Coptic and Arabic Manuscripts in the Coptic Museum, the Patriarch-ate, the Principle Churches of Cairo and Alexandria and the Monasteries of Egypt.* 3 vols. (Cairo: Government Press, 1939–42), 1: xv–xvi.
88   See table E, p. 139.
89   Simaika, "Memoirs," 50. For this paragraph, see 49–51.
90   Pahor Labib, *The Coptic Museum and the Fortress of Babylon at Old Cairo* (Cairo: General Organisation for Govt. Print Offices, 1953), 3.
91   Simaika, "Memoirs," 61–63; Marcus Simaika Pasha, ed., assisted by Yassa Abd al Masih Effendi, *Catalogue of the Coptic and Arabic Manuscripts in the Coptic Museum, the Patriarchate, the Principle Churches of Cairo and Alexandria and the Monuments of Egypt,* 2 vols. (Cairo: Government Press, 1939– 42), esp. 1: xvii–xx. On Abd al-Massih, see *BSAC* 15 (1958–60): 191–92, and *CE* 7: 2353–54.
92   M. Niebuhr, *Travels through Arabia and other Countries in the East,* trans. Robert Heron, 2 vols. (Edinburg: R. Morrison and Son, 1792), 1: 104.
93   See Elizabeth E. Oram, "Constructing Modern Copts: The Production of Coptic Christian Identity in Contemporary Egypt," (PhD diss., Depart-ment of Anthropology, Princeton University, 2004), 32–53.
94   *Practical Guide to Alexandria, Cairo, Port Saïd and Neighbourhood* (London: Nilsson & Co., n.d. [ca. 1908], 33.
95   A.H. Sayce, preface to Dowling, *The Egyptian Church*, vi.
96   Seikally, "Coptic Communal Reform," *Middle Eastern Studies* 6, pt. 3 (1970): 269.
97   Flinders Petrie, *Seventy Years in Archaeology* (London: Sampson Low, Mar-ston, 1931; repr. New York: Greenwood, 1969), 223–24.
98   Leeder, *Modern Sons of the Pharaohs,* 309.
99   Oram, "Constructing Modern Copts," 35–38.
100 Jean Doresse, *Des hiéroglyphes à la croix: ce que le passé pharaonique a légué au Christianisme* (Istanbul: Nederlands Historisch-Archeologisch Insti-tuut in het Nabije Oosten, 1960); Saphinaz-Amal Naguib, "Survivals of Pharaonic Religious Practices in Contemporary Coptic Christianity," *UCLA Encyclopedia of Egyptology,* 2008, 1–6. http://repositories.cdlib.org/nelc/uee/1008.
101 DWQ/MMW/NA/MA 1/ 4: Matahif 1879–1886/ D: "Madrasat al-Athar, 1881–86," Ministry of Public Works, "Note au conseil des ministres," No. 99, April 17, 1882.
102 Éric Gady, "Le pharaon, l'égyptologue et le diplomate. Les égypto-logues français en Égypte, du voyage de Champollion à la crise de Suez (1828–1956)" (2 vols., PhD diss., Université de Paris IV-Sorbonne, 2005) 1: 251–52.
103 On Arif and Bulus, see Bierbrier, *WWWE4*: 25, 74–75.
104 *The Egyptian Directory: L'Annuaire égyptien (Égypte et Soudan)* (Cairo, 1921), 195.

105 Filib di Tarrazi, *Tarikh al-sihafa al-arabiya*, 4 vols. (Beirut, 1913–1933) 4: 279, 289, 301, 303, 305. The religion of the editor of *Abu al-Hawl* (The Sphinx) is uncertain.

106 Donald Malcolm Reid, *Whose Pharaohs? Archaeology, Museums, and Egyptian National Identity from Napoleon to World War I* (Berkeley: University of California Press, 2002) 6, 8, 312 n.5. See also p. 283.

107 Seikally, "Coptic Communal Reform," *Middle Eastern Studies* 6, pt. 3 (1970); 269–70, referring to Yusuf Manqariys, *al-Qawl al-yaqin fi masalat al-aqabat al- urthudhuksiyin* (Cairo, 1893), intro., and Tadrus, *al-Aqbat fi-l-qarn al-ishrin.*

108 As quoted in translation in Beth Baron, *The Women's Awakening in Egypt: Culture, Society, and the Press* (New Haven: Yale University Press, 1994), 109–110.

109 Marcus H. Simaika, *Guide sommaire du musée copte et des principales églises du Caire* (Cairo: Impr. nationale, 1937), xi.

110 [Simaika], "Awakening," 734.

111 Carter, *Copts in Egyptian Politics*, 296–98.

112 On Smith, see Bierbrier, *WWWE4*: 515–16; Gange, *Dialogues*, 307–17.

113 On Sobhi, see *BSAC* 19 (1967–68): 315–16; 20 (1969–70): 1–3. His grammar was Georgy Sobhy, *Kitab qawaid al-lugha al-misriya al-qibtiya* (IFAO: Cairo, 1925).

114 Georgy Sobhy, "Notes on the Ethnology," *Bulletin de l'association des amis des églises et de l'art copte* (counted as *BASC*) 1 (1935): 43–59; Geo. P.G. Sobhy [Georgy Sobhy], "Survivals of Ancient Egyptian in Modern Dialect," *Ancient Egypt* (1921), 3: 70–75.

115 Sobhy, "Notes on the Ethnology," 55.

116 Ronald Storrs, *The Memoirs of Sir Ronald Storrs* (New York: Putnam, 1937), 94.

117 Georgy Sobhy, "Turath Misr al-lughawi: al-lugha al-misriya al-qadima," in "Turath Misr al-qadima," special issue, *al-Muqtataf* (Sept. 1936), 41.

118 Sobhy, *BASC* 1 (1935): 46–47.

119 Sobhy, *BASC* 1 (1935): 57–58.

120 Sobhy, "Miscellanea," *JEA* 16 (1930) 3, plates 3, 6. Sobhy did not specify the patient's religion.

121 Georgy Bey Sobhy, "The Survival of Ancient Egypt," *BSAC* 4 (1938): 62.

122 Statistics on Egyptology graduates calculated from Jamiat al-Qahira, Kulliyat al-athar, *al-Dalil al-dhahabi lil-asatidha wa khariji al-athar, Jamiat al-Qahira mundhu sanat 1925* (Cairo: al-Haya al-misriya al-amma lil-kitab, 1975). Calculated on basis of names that are distinctively Christian, Muslim, or indeterminate. Through 1948–49, published official statistics often classified enrolled students as Muslims, Copts, or other. Gouvernement égyptien, Ministère de l'économie, Département de la statistique et du recensement, *Annuaire statistique 1947–1948 et 1948–1949* (Cairo, 1952), 246. In 1948–49, 28 percent of the fifty-eight students enrolled in Cairo's Institute of Egyptian and Islamic Archaeology were Copts. Since virtually no Copts enrolled in the Islamic archaeology section, their proportion in

the Egyptology section would have been much higher than 28 percent.

123   On Mattha, see Bierbrier, *WWWE4*: 362–63; Jamiat al-Qahira, *al-Athar al-ilimiya li-ada hayat al-tadris bi-Jamiat al-Qahira*, 1958, 75–76.

124   S.H. Leeder, *Abna al-faraina al-muhdithun: dirasa li-akhlaq aqbat Misr wa adatihum*, trans. Ahmad Mahmud (Cairo: Dar al-Shuruq, 2008); Jill Kamil, *Christianity in the Land of the Pharaohs: The Coptic Orthodox Church* (London: Routledge, 2002). Note, however, that the translator of *Abna al-faraina* is Muslim.

125   For Mirrit Boutros Ghali, I have drawn on an interview, Cairo, April 15, 1988; *BSAC* 32 (1993: 1–10); and *Le mondain égyptien et du moyen-orient. l'annuaire de l'élite*, ed. E.J. Blattner (Cairo: Paul Barbey, 1951), 300. On the family, see Arthur Goldschmidt Jr., "The Boutros-Ghali Family," *JARCE*, 30 (1993): 183–88.

126   On the Société des amis de l'art, see *Le mondain égyptien*, 94–95.

127   *BSAC* 14 (1956–57): 249–51; Mirrit Boutros Ghali, "Short History of the Society of Coptic Archeology," *BSAC* 26 (1984): 113–16; "Dayr Apa Phoibammon: History," *CE* 3: 779–80.

128   Author's interview question of Mirrit Boutros Ghali, Cairo, April 15, 1988: Did Murqus Simaika support the Coptic Archeological Society? Answer: No, because the aims of his museum were similar to ours.

129   *Bulletin de l'association des amis des églises et de l'art coptes* (counted as *BSAC*) 1 (1935): 64–68; 8 (1941): 30.

130   *BSAC* 23 (1976–78): 303–04; BComité 39 (1941–45), minutes of March 27, 1947, 361.

131   "Statuts," *BSAC* 1, 1935: 61–63.

132   Mirrit Boutros Ghali, *The Policy of Tomorrow*, trans. Ismail R. el Faruqi from 2nd ed., 1951 (Washington, DC: American Council of Learned Societies, 1953), vii.

133   On Madkur, see *Le mondain égyptienne*, 388.

134   On the Society, see Raouf Abbas, *Jamaat al-nahda al-qawmiya* (Cairo: Dar al-Fikr, 1986); Roel Meijer, *The Quest for Modernity: Secular Liberal and Left-Wing Political Thought in Egypt, 1945–1958* (London: RoutledgeCurzon, 2002), 37–65.

135   Nancy Elizabeth Gallagher, *Egypt's Other Wars: Epidemics and the Politics of Public Health* (Syracuse: Syracuse University Press, 1990), 43, 68.

136   Mirrit [Boutros] Ghali Bey, "Un programme de réforme agraire pour l'Égypte," *L'Égypte contemporaine* 38 (1947): 4.

137   Mirrit Boutros Ghali, *L'Égypte contemporaine* 38 (1947): 1–59.

138   Jacques Berque, *Egypt: Imperialism and Revolution* (London: Faber, 1972), 641.

139   Joel Gordon, *Nasser's Blessed Movement: Egypt's Free Officers and the July Revolution* (New York: Oxford University Press, 1992), 62, 66–67; Meijer, *Quest for Modernity*, 66–95.

140   Mirrit Boutros Ghali, "The Egyptian National Consciousness," *The Middle East Journal* 32 (1978): 60.

141   Michael Allen Williams, *Rethinking "Gnosticism": An Argument for Dismantling a Dubious Category* (Princeton: Princeton University Press, 1996), argues that "Gnosticism" is such a diffuse category that it should be abandoned.

142 Simaika, "Memoirs," 52.

143 Published as *Le martyre d'Apa Epima* (Cairo: Imprimerie nationale, Boulaq, 1937). On Mina, see the obituary by É. Drioton, *BIÉ* 32 (1949–50): 325–29.

144 "Iftah janah jadid bi-al-mathaf al-qibti," *Misr*, Feb. 20, 1947.

145 Tarek Mohamed Refaat Sakr, "Early Twentieth-Century Islamic Architecture in Cairo," (MA thesis, American University in Cairo, 1993), 2. There has been speculation that the relative tolerance of the Fatimid rulers (Caliph al-Hakim excepted) for Copts may have influenced this design choice for the Coptic Museum, but the question awaits further research.

146 Carter, *Copts in Egyptian Politics*, 215, 246, 37n; Interview with Pahor Labib, Cairo, October 22, 1987. On Rostem, see Volait, *Architectes*, 422.

147 One member of Ubayd's splinter party al-Kutla al-Wafdiya was young Nazir Jayid, future Pope Shenuda III. Hassan, *Christians versus Muslims*, 263.

148 Hassan, *Christians versus Muslims*, 49.

149 Information on Pahor Labib is from interviews with him, Cairo, Oct. 22, 27, 1987; Krause, *Essays*, 1–3; Pahor Cladios Labib, *Herrschaft der Hyksos in Ägypten und ihr Sturz* (Glückstadt: J.J. Augustin, 1936), 43; Bierbrier, *WWWE4*: 305. List of publications in *BSAC* 36 (1997): 1–4, and Krause, *Essays*, 4–8. In interviews, Labib pointed out that Simaika and Togo Mina had been curators of the Coptic Museum; he himself was the first officially titled 'director.'

150 Interview with Gawdat Gabra, Cairo, May 16, 2005.

151 James M. Robinson, introduction, *The Facsimile Edition of the Nag Hammadi Codices*, 12 vols. (Leiden: Brill, 1972–77), 1: vi–xxxi; Robinson, "The French Role in Early Nag Hammadi Studies," *Journal of Coptic Studies* 7 (2005): 1–12.

152 Two Europeans rounded out the roster of founding permanent honorary presidents—Egyptologists Torgny Säve-Söderbergh and Pierre du Bourguet. The latter was primarily a Coptic specialist. International Association for Coptic Studies, *Newsletter* No. 1 (March 1977), p. 3. On Säve-Söderbergh and du Bourguet, see Bierbrier, *WWWE4*, 488-89, 75.

153 J.D. Pennington, "The Copts in Modern Egypt," *MES* 18 (1982): 158–79; John H. Watson, *Among the Copts*, (Brighton, UK: Sussex Academic Press, 2002); Samira Bahr, *al-Aqbat fi al-haya al-siyasiya al-misriya* (Cairo, 1984); Hassan, *Christians versus Muslims*.

154 Interview with Aziz Atiya, Salt Lake City, Utah, March 29, 1986; *BSAC* 29 (1990): 1–7 (Mirrit Boutros Ghali); Sami A. Hanna, ed., *Medieval and Middle Eastern Studies in Honor of Aziz Suryal Atiya* (Leiden: Brill, 1972), 5–15 (Paul Walker). See also Atiya's article "Higher Institute of Coptic Studies," *CE* 4: 1230.

155 Watson, *Among the Copts*, 124.

156 Mirrit Boutros Ghali, "Murad Kamil," *BSAC* 23 (1976–78): 300. On Kamil, see also Jamiat al-Qahira, *al-Athar al-ilmiya li-ada al-tadris bi-Jamiat al-Qahira* (Cairo, 1958), 22–28.

8. Alexandria and the Greco-Roman Heritage

1 Robin Ostle, "Modern Egyptian Renaissance Man," *BSOAS* 57, Pt. 1 (1994): 184–92. For a color reproduction of *School of Alexandria*, see Effat

Naghi et al., eds., *Mohamed Naghi (1888–1956): un impressioniste égyptien / al-Fannan al-tathiri al-misri* (Cairo: Les cahiers de Chabramant, 1988), one of the unnumbered plates between p. 44 and p. 45.

2   J. Christopher Herold, *Bonaparte in Egypt* (New York: Harper & Row, 1962), 60.

3   Martin Bernal, *Black Athena* (London: Free Association Books, 1987–2006) 1: 185; Phiroze Vasunia, *The Gift of the Nile: Hellenizing Egypt from Aeschylus to Alexander* (Berkeley: University of California Press, 2001), 285.

4   Commission des sciences et arts d'Égypte, *Description de l'Égypte: ou receueil des observations et des recherche qui ont été faites en Égypte pendant l'expédition de l'armée française*, Volume 1, *Antiquités, Planches* (Paris, 1809–1828), frontispiece.

5   On the history of modern Alexandria, see Robert Ilbert, *Alexandrie 1830–1930: histoire d'une communauté citadine*, 2 vols. (Cairo: IFAO, 1996), and Michael J. Reimer, *Colonial Bridgehead: Government and Society in Alexandria, Egypt 1807–1882* (Boulder, CO: Westview, 1997). Khaled Fahmy, *All the Pasha's Men: Mehmed Ali, His Army and the Making of Modern Egypt* (Cambridge: Cambridge University Press, 1998), emphasizes the tragic cost to the common people of Muhammad Ali's ambitions.

6   Calculated from Ilbert, *Alexandrie*, 2: 756, 761–62.

7   For attempts to apply updated theories of cosmopolitanism to the Middle East, see Roel Meijer, ed., *Cosmopolitanism, Identity and Authenticity in the Middle East*, (Surrey, UK: Curzon, 1999), esp. Sami Zubaida, "Cosmopolitanism and the Middle East," 15–33, and Stéphane Yerasimos, "Cosmopolitanism: Assumed Alienation," 35–39; Derryl N. MacLean and Sikeena Karmali Ahmed, eds., *Cosmopolitanism in Muslim Contexts: Perspectives from the Past* (Edinburgh: Edinburgh University Press, 2012); and Carl W. Ernest and Richard C. Martin, eds., *Rethinking Islamic Studies: From Orientalism to Cosmopolitanism* (Columbia, SC: University of South Carolina Press, 2010). On the issue of cosmopolitanism in modern Alexandria, see Hala Halim, *Alexandrian Cosmopolitanism: An Archive* (New York: Fordham University Press, 2013); Deborah A. Starr, *Remembering Cosmopolitan Egypt: Literature, Culture, and Empire* (London: Routledge, 2009); Robert Ilbert and Ilias Yannakakis, Jacques Hassoun, eds. *Alexandria 1860–1960: the Brief Life of a Cosmopolitan Community*, trans. Colin Clement (Alexandria: Harpocrates, 1997); Anthony Hirst and Michael Silk, eds., *Alexandria, Real and Imagined* (Aldershot, UK: Ashgate, 2004), esp. Robert Mabro, "Alexandria 1860–1960: The Cosmopolitan Identity," 247–62, and Khaled Fahmy, "For Cavafy, with love and squalor: some critical notes on the history and historiography of modern Alexandria," 263–80; Khaled Fahmy, "The Essence of Alexandria," *Manifesta Journal*, nos. 14 & 16 (2012); Robert Mabro, "Nostalgic Literature on Alexandria," in *Historians in Cairo: Essays in Honor of George Scanlon*, ed. Jill Edwards (Cairo: American University in Cairo Press, 2002), 237–266.

8   Jean-Yves Empereur, *Alexandria Rediscovered* (New York: G. Braziller, 1998), 14–15, 21.

9   Stephen L. Dyson, *In Pursuit of Ancient Pasts: A History of Classical Archaeology in the Nineteenth and Twentieth Centuries* (New Haven: Yale University

Press, 2006).

10   Andrew Humphreys, *Grand Hotels of Egypt in the Golden Age of Travel* (Cairo: American University in Cairo Press, 2011), 32–45.

11   E.M. Forster, *Alexandria: A History and a Guide*, 3rd ed. (New York: Anchor Books, 1961), 91.

12   *Who Was Who 1897–1916* (London, 1920), 155.

13   E. Breccia, *Alexandrea ad Aegyptum: Guide de la ville ancienne et modern et du Musée Gréco–Romain* (Bergamo: Istituto italiano d'arti grafiche, 1914), 2–3. On the Municipal Library, see also Egypt, Ministère des finances, département de la statistique générale, *Annuaire statistique de l'Égypte 1924–1925* (Cairo, 1926), 94, 96.

14   On Étienne Combe (1881–1962), see R. Lackany, *La société archéologique d'Alexandrie à 80 ans* (Alexandria: Impr. Don Bosco, 1973), 161.

15   Athanase G. Politis, *L'hellénisme et l'Égypte modern: v. 1: Histoire de l'hellénisme égyptien de 1798 à 1927* (Paris: Alcan, 1929), 403–407; Bierbrier, *WWWE4*: 401.

16   Bierbrier, *WWWE4*: 23; Rev. A.H. Sayce, *Reminiscences* (London: Macmillan, 1923), 274–75.

17   J. Dean O'Donnell Jr., *Lavigerie in Tunisia: The Interplay of Imperialist and Missionary* (Athens, GA: University of Georgia Press, 1979), 169; Alexander Kitroeff, *The Greeks in Egypt, 1919–1937: Ethnicity and Class* (London: Ithaca, 1989), 114–15.

18   Constantine Cavafy, *C.P. Cavafy: The Poems of the Canon* (Cambridge, MA: Harvard Early Modern and Modern Greek Library, Harvard University, Dept. of Classics, 2011). See Halim, *Alexandrian Cosmopolitanism*, for a challenge to selective canonical readings of Cafavy.

19   *Guide to Egypt and the Sûdân*, 6th ed. (London: Macmillan, 1911).

20   Angelo Sammarco, *Gli Italiani in Egitto: il contributo italiano nella formazione dell'Egitto moderno* (Alexandria: Edizioni del Fascio, 1937). For other histories of Italians in Egypt, see L.A. Balboni, *Gl'Italiani nella Civiltà Egiziana del Secolo XIX*, vol. 3 (Alexandria, 1906); Vittorio Briani, *Italiani in Egitto* (Rome: Istituto poligrafico e Zecca dello Stato, 1982); and Marta Petricioli, *Oltre il mito: l'Egitto degli italiani (1917–1947)*, (Milan: B. Modadori, 2007). On archaeology, see Maria Casini, ed., *One Hundred Years in Egypt: Paths of Italian Archaeology* (Milan: Electa, 2001), esp. Nicola Bonacasa, "The Work of Italian Archaeologists toward an Understanding of Greco–Roman Egypt," 107–29; A. Evaristo Breccia, *Faraoni senza Pace*, 2nd ed. (Pisa: Nistri-Lischi, 1958).

21   Briani, *Italiani in Egitto*, 47–55, provides statistics on Italians in Egypt. On Italian radical, internationalist, and subaltern politics, see Anthony Gorman, "Foreign Workers in Egypt 1882–1914: Subaltern or Labour Elite?" in Stephanie Cronin, ed., *Subalterns and Social Protest: History from Below in the Middle East and North Africa* (London: Routledge, 2008), 237–59, and "Anarchists in Education: The Free Popular University in Egypt (1901)," *Middle Eastern Studies* 41 (May 2005), 303–20.

22   On Giuseppe Botti (not to be confused with the Egyptologist of the

same name), see Bierbrier, *WWWE4*: 73; Bonacasa, "Work of Italian Archaeologists," 108–109; E. Breccia, *Uominie e libri* (Pisa: Nistri-Lischi, 1959), 158–67; G. Botti, *Catalogue des monuments exposés au Musée Gréco–Romain d'Alexandrie* (Alexandria, 1900), iii–xiii. On the museum archives, see Éric Gady, "La découverte et le projet de mise en valeur des archives du Musée Gréco–Romain d'Alexandrie: project AMGRA," *EDAL, Egyptian and Egyptological Documents, Archives, Libraries*, 1 (Milan, 2009), 141–47.

23 See Empereur, *Alexandria Rediscovered* for a general history of Alexandrian archaeology.

24 On Breccia, see Bierbrier, *WWWE4*: 79; Bonacasa, "Work of Italian Archeologists," 109–110.

25 *BSAA* 4 (1902): 3. For Menasce, see Ilbert, *Alexandrie*, 2: 86.

26 Histories of the Société include: Ét. Combe, "Le cinquantenaire de la société royale d'archéologie 1893–1943," *BSAA* (1946): 104–119 (list of founders, 110); Lackany, *La société archéologique*; Colin Clément, *La société archéologique d'Alexandrie à 100 ans: 1893–1993* (Alexandria, ca. 1993). The *Bulletin* carried several series and fascicle numbers, but the easiest reference is to its consecutive issue numbers, with the date. Founded as the Société archéologique d'Alexandrie, it became the Société royale d'archéologie d'Alexandrie in 1925. After the 1952 revolution, it reverted to its original name.

27 For the Imperial Museum, see Wendy M.K. Shaw, *Possessors and Possessed: Museums, Archaeology, and the Visualization of History in the Late Ottoman Empire* (Berkeley: University of California Press, 2003), and Shaw, "From Mausoleum to Museum: Resurrecting Antiquity for Ottoman Modernity," in *Scramble for the Past: A Story of Archaeology in the Ottoman Empire 1753–1914*, ed. Zainab Bahrani, Zeynep Çelik, Edhem Eldem (Istanbul: SALT, 2011), 423–41. Osman Hamdi, the son of an Ottoman Grand Vizier, was also a noted Orientalist painter who had studied in Paris under Jean-Léon Gérôme and Gustave Boulanger.

28 J.W. Mackail, *Classical Studies* (London: J. Murray, 1925), 12.

29 Ronald Storrs, *The Memoirs of Sir Ronald Storrs* (New York: Putnam, 1937), 43.

30 The Earl of Cromer, *Ancient and Modern Imperialism* (London: J. Murray, 1910); *Modern Egypt*, revised ed. (London, 1911). The standard biography is Roger Owen, *Lord Cromer: Victorian Imperialist, Edwardian Proconsul* (Oxford: Oxford University Press, 2004). On the interweaving of classics, archaeology, and British imperialism, see C.A. Hagerman, *Britain's Imperial Muse: The Classics, Imperialism, and the Indian Empire, 1784–1914* (Houndsmill, UK: Palgrave Macmillan, 2013), Phiroze Vasunia, *The Classics and Colonial India* (Oxford: Oxford University Press, 2014), and Richard Hingley, *Roman Officers and English Gentlemen: The Imperial Origins of Roman Archaeology* (London: Routledge, 2000).

31 *Comptes rendu du congrès international d'archéologie. 1er session, Athènes 1905* (Athens: Impr. "Hestia," C. Meissner & N. Kargadouris, 1905). On the Cairo congress, see Éric Gady, "Le pharaon, l'égyptologue et le diplomate. Les égyptologues français en Égypte, du voyage de Champollion à la crise de Suez (1828–1956)," (2 vols., PhD diss., Université de Paris IV-Sorbonne, 2005), 666–74.

32 Dyson, *Pursuit of Ancient Pasts*, 60–62.

33 G. Maspero, "Une inscription trilingue de C. Cornelius," in his *Causeries d'Égypte* 2nd ed. (Paris: E. Guilmoto, 1907): 95–101.

34 On Edgar, see Bierbrier, *WWWE4*: 171, and O. Guéraud, in C.C. Edgar, *Zenon Papyri*, v. 5 (Cairo: IFAO, 1940), ix–xiv; On Lefebvre, see Bierbrier, *WWWE4*: 318–19; on Jean Maspero, Bierbrier, *WWWE4*: 361.

35 Eric Turner, "The Graeco–Roman Branch," in *Excavating in Egypt: The Egypt Exploration Society*, ed. T.G.H. James, (Chicago: University of Chicago Press, 1982), 161–176.

36 A.K. Bowman et al., eds., *Oxyrhynchus: A City and Its Texts* (London: Egypt Exploration Society, 2007). On Grenfell and Hunt, see also Bierbrier, *WWWE4*: 225–26, 269–70, and the Oxyrhynchus Papyrus Project website: http://www.papyrology.ox.ac.uk/POxy. On Lobel (1888–1982), see Hugh Lloyd-Jones's entry in *Oxford Dictionary of National Biography*, Oxford University Press, 2004; online edition, January 2013, http://www.oxforddnb.com/view/article/31374.

37 For Italian papyrology in Egypt, see Casini, ed., *One Hundred Years*, 124–26, 153–70, and Rosario Pintaudi, "The Italian Excavations," in *Oxyrhynchus: A City and Its Texts*, ed. A.K Bowman et al. (London: Egypt Exploration Society, 2007), 104–107. On Vitelli (1849–1935), see Bierbrier, *WWWE4*: 557–58.

38 Ahmed Etman, "Translation at the Intersection of Traditions: The Arab Reception of the Classics," in *A Companion to Classical Receptions*, ed. Lorna Hardwick and Christopher Stray (Malden, MA: Blackwell, 2008), 141–52; Franz Rosenthal, *The Classical Heritage in Islam*, trans. E. and J. Marmorstein (Berkeley: University of California Press, 1975); and Felix Klein-Franke, *Die Klassische Antike in der Tradition des Islams* (Darmstadt: Wissenschaftliche Buchgesellschaft, 1980).

39 Wajih Fanus, "Sulayman al-Bustani and Comparative Literary Studies in Arabic," *Journal of Arabic Literature* 17 (1986): 105–19.

40 Gamal el-Din el-Shayyal, *Tarikh al-tarjama wa-l-haraka al-thaqafiya fi asr Muhammad Ali* (Cairo: Dar al-fikr al-arabi, 1951), 125; el-Shayyal, *A History of Egyptian Historiography in the Nineteenth Century* (Alexandria: Alexandria University Press, 1962), 26–27, 31–36; Ibrahim Abu Lughod, *The Arab Rediscovery of Europe* (Princeton: Princeton University Press, 1963), 50–51.

41 Charles Wendell, *The Evolution of the Egyptian National Image: From Its Origins to Ahmad Lutfi al-Sayyid* (Berkeley: University of California Press, 1972), 128, 130.

42 Mahmoud Bey [al-Falaki], *Mémoire sur l'antique Alexandrie* (Copenhagen: Imp. de B. Luno., 1872).

43 *Dairat al-Maarif*, ed. Butrus Bustani et al., 11 vols. (Beirut: Dairat al-maarif, and Cairo: Dar al-Hilal, 1876–1900). Albert Hourani, "Bustani's Encyclopaedia," and "Sulaiman al-Bustani and the *Iliad*," in his *Islam in European Thought* (Cambridge: Cambridge University Press, 1991), 164–73, 174–87.

44 On Zaydan, see *The Autobiography of Jurjī Zaidān*, trans. Thomas Philipp (Washington, DC: Three Continents Press, ca. 1990).

45 Abd al-Rahman al-Rafii, *Muhammad Farid: ramz al-ikhlas wa-l-tadhiya:*

tarikh Misr al-qawmi min sanat 1908 ila sanat 1919 (Cairo: Maktabat al-nahda al-misriya, 1962), 30; review of Farid's *Tarikh al-Rumaniyyin*, in *al-Muqtataf* 27 (Aug. 1, 1902), 805–806.

46 Wendell, *Egyptian National Image*, 258–59.

47 Attia Wahby Bey, "Les affinités de l'art copte," *Congrès international d'archéologie classique, 2ème session, Le Caire, 1909*, 262–63, patriotically emphasized the pharaonic rather than Greek or Roman affinities of Coptic art.

48 Laurence Grafftey-Smith, *Bright Levant* (London: J. Murray, 1970), 83.

49 John Ball, *Egypt in the Classical Geographers* (Cairo: Government Press, Bulaq, 1942).

50 Grafftey-Smith, *Bright Levant*, 70–71.

51 L.A. Tregenza, *Egyptian Years* (London: Oxford University Press, 1958), xiii, 37.

52 William H. McNeill, *Arnold J. Toynbee: A Life* (New York: Oxford University Press, 1989), 93–94. However, Elizabeth Vandiver, "Homer in British World War I Poetry," in *A Companion to Classical Receptions*, ed. Lorna Hardwick and Christopher Stray (Malden, MA, 2008), 463, notes that "The appropriation of Homer for both praise and protest of the war continues until the Armistice and after."

53 Hingley, *Roman Officers*, 189, 54n.

54 Storrs, *Memoirs*, 202.

55 E.M. Forster, *Pharos and Pharillon*, 2nd ed. (Surrey, UK: Leonard Woolf and Virginia Woolf at the Hogarth Press, 1923), 94.

56 Forster, *Alexandria*, 115.

57 Halim, *Alexandrian Cosmopolitanism*.

58 A.J. Engel, *From Clergyman to Don: The Rise of the Academic Profession in Nineteenth-Century Oxford* (Oxford: Oxford University Press, 1983), 224; Christopher Stray, *Classics Transformed: Schools, Universities, and Society in England, 1830–1960* (Oxford: Clarendon Press, 1998), 1, 12, 163–65, 223–24, 264–70, 293.

59 C. M. Bowra, *Memories: 1898–1939* (London: Weidenfeld and Nicolson, 1966), 227.

60 Taha Hussein, "Kitab al-siyasa li-Aristutalis," *al-Katib al-misri* 7, No. 27 (Dec. 1947), 478–84.

61 Taha Hussein, "Kitab al-siyasa li-Aristutalis," *al-Katib al-misri* 7, No. 27 (Dec. 1947), 478–84. In the same issue, see also Muhammad Kamil Husayn, "Ahmad Lutfi al-Sayyid wa-l-dawa ila Aristu," 203–207. Wendell, *Egyptian National Image*, 216, 282, treats Lutfi al-Sayyid's attitude toward the classics. For his autobiography, see Ahmad Lutfi al-Sayyid, *Qissat Hayati* (Cairo: Dar al-hilal, 1962).

62 Taha Hussein, *A Passage to France: The Third Volume of the Autobiography of Taha Husain*, Kenneth Cragg, trans., (Leiden: Brill, 1976), 114–18. On Taha Hussein's involvement in education, see also Donald Malcolm Reid, *Cairo University and the Making of Modern Egypt* (Cambridge: Cambridge University Press, 1990); Abd al-Munim Ibrahim al-Dusuqi Jumayi, *Taha Husayn wa-l-jamia al-misriya* (Cairo, 1981); and Abdelrashid Mahmoudi,

Taha Husein's Education from the Azhar to the Sorbonne (Surrey, UK: Curzon, 1998). See also, Roger Allen, "Taha Husayn" in *Essays in Arabic Literary Biography 1850–1950*, (Wiesbaden: Harrassowitz, 2010), 137–49.

63 CUA, Box 14, Folder 170: "Qism al-Adab. Baramij mawadd al-dirasa fi-l-sana al-dirasiya 1923–24;"Ahmad Abd al Fattah Budayr, *al-Amir Ahmad Fuad wa nashat al-Jamia al-Misriya* (Cairo: Matbaat Jamiat Fuad al-Awwal, 1950), 178–79, 185.

64 Taha Hussein, *The Future of Culture in Egypt*, trans. Sidney Glazer (New York: American Council of Learned Societies, 1975), 73–82, treats the Latin requirements and the attempt to introduce Greek and Latin in secondary schools. On *al-Katib al-Misri*'s program, see "Barnamij," 1, no.1, (Oct. 1945): 1–3.

65 John Calvert, *Sayyid Qutb and the Origins of Radical Islamism* (New York: Columbia University Press, 2010), 92–96.

66 Shimon Shamir, "Radicalism in Egyptian Historiography," in *Islam, Nationalism, and Radicalism in Egypt and the Sudan*, ed. Gabriel R. Warburg and Uri Kuperschmidt (New York: Praeger, 1983), 218.

67 Lampson to Eden, June 11, 1937, enclosing "Memorandum by Sir Robert Greg on the General Cultural Position in Egypt," p. 7, FO395/ 550/ P2759.

68 *Byzantion* 1 (1924): v–viii. On Graindor, see Jamiat Fuad al-Awwal, *al-Kitab al-fiddi*, 23, 43; *Byzantion* 35, No. 1 (1965), v–xxv.

69 On Lloyd vs. the "Latins," see Reid, *Cairo University*, 87–91, and Lord Lloyd, *Egypt since Cromer*, 2 vols. (London: Macmillan, 1933; New York: AMS Press, 1970). See also John Chamley, *Lord Lloyd and the Decline of the British Empire* (London: Weidenfeld and Nicolson, 1987).

70 Robert Graves, *Good-bye to All That* (London: Jonathan Cape, 1929), 430.

71 Lloyd to Chamberlain, March 7, 1926, enclosing "List of Foreign Officials Employed by Egypt in Government." FO 371/ 11591 /J523.

72 Hussein, *Future of Culture*, 73–82.

73 A.J. Arberry, *Oriental Essays: Portraits of Seven Scholars* (London: G. Allen & Unwin, 1960), 234.

74 Eldon Gorst (Eton and Cambridge, consul general, 1907–11) was the exception to the military educations of the 1883–1925 era British proconsuls in Egypt. On Gorst, see Goldschmidt, *Biographical Dictionary*, 65–66.

75 Hussein, *Future of Culture*, 73–74.

76 Interview with Muhammad Salim Salem, Cairo, November 26, 1987; paraphrase reconstructed from interview notes.

77 Lloyd to Chamberlain, May 1, 1927. FO371/12382/ J1114.

78 Jamiat Fuad al-Awwal, *al-Kitab al-fiddi*, 43.

79 Hoare to Cushendun, October 27, 1928. FO371/13130/J3138. On Waddell (1884–1946), see also *BSAA* 36 (1943–44): 146–47; Bierbrier, *WWWE4*: 561; *WWW 1944–50*, 4: 1187.

80 Lloyd to Chamberlain, April 6, 1929, enclosing clipping Philippe Sagnac, "L'enseignement français en Égypte," *La semaine égyptienne*, March 16, 1929. FO371/13876/ J1015.

81   Wendell, *Egyptian National Image*, 282–83.

82   Hussein, *Future of Culture*, 75.

83   Arberry, *Oriental Essays*, 233–39.

84   Jamiat Fuad al-Awwal, *al-Kitab al-fiddi li-kulliyat al-adab 1925–1950* (Cairo, Matbaat Jamiat Fuad al-Awwal, 1951), 222.

85   *BSAA* 36 (1943–44): 146–47; Bierbrier, *WWWE4*: 561.

86   Wayment to Hedley, Febuary 26, 1945. FO924/ 167/ LC 781.

87   Jamiat Fuad al-Awwal, *al-Kitab al-fiddi li-kulliyat al-adab* (Cairo: Matbaat Jamiat Fuad al-Awwal, 1951), 72–73.

88   On Jones, see *Dictionary of National Biography* (Oxford: Oxford University Press, 1981): 594–96; Mostafa El-Abbadi, "In Memoriam Hugo Jones," *BSAA* 43 (1975): 5–7.

89   Interview with Henry Riad, Cairo, April 20, 1988.

90   Taha Hussein, *The Stream of Days: A Student at the Azhar*, Hilary Wayment, trans. (London: Longmans, Green, 1948), 133.

91   Jamiat Fuad al-Awwal, *al-Kitab al-fiddi*, 222. For Munis, I have relied on Jamiat al-Qahira, *al-Athar al-ilmiya li-ada hayat al-tadris bi-Jamiat al-Qahira* (Cairo, 1958), 106, and interview with Yahya al-Khashshab, Cairo, April 14, 1983.

92   Ali al Rai, "Arabic Drama since the 1930s," in M.M. Badawi, ed., *Modern Arabic Literature* (Cambridge: Cambridge University Press, 1993), 359; A.J. Arberry, *Aspects of Islamic Civilization as Depicted in Original Texts* (New York: G. Allen & Unwin, 1964), 370; Azza Karrarah, "Egyptian Literary Images of Alexandria," in Anthony Hirst and Michael Silk, eds., *Alexandria, Real and Imagined*, 308–309; Ahlam Fathy Hassan, "Cleopatra in Dramatic Work," *Classical Papers / Awraq Klasikiya* (Cairo University, Faculty of Arts, Dept. of Greek and Latin Studies, 1995) 4: 96–98; Interview with Ahmed Etman, Cairo, April 22, 1999.

93   *Apollo* 1, No. 1 (Sept. 1932). For al-Aqqad's complaint, see p. 54. On Abu Shadi, see Robin Ostle, in *Essays in Arabic Literary Biography 1850–1950*, ed. Roger Allen (Wiesbaden: Harrassowitz, 2010), 32–37; Salma Khadra Jayyusi, *Trends and Movements in Modern Arabic Poetry*, 2 vols. (Leiden: Brill, 1977), 2: 382–87; J. Brugman, *An Introduction to the History of Modern Arabic Literature in Egypt* (Leiden, 1984), 153.

94   Interview with Abd al-Latif Ahmad Ali, Cairo, October 18, 1987.

95   Edwar al-Kharrat, *City of Saffron*, trans. Frances Liardet (London: Quartet, 1989), vii, 70–71, 91, 102.

96   For the title of this section, see Beverley Butler's fine study of the Bibliotheca Alexandrina, *Return to Alexandria: An Ethnography of Cultural Heritage, Revivalism, and Museum History* (Walnut Creek, CA: Left Coast Press, 2007).

97   *BSAA* 16 (1918): 66. *BSAA* references are to the consecutive number series, not to the volume and fascicle numbers of the several series.

98   *BSAA*: 16 (1918): 66; 22 (1926).

99   Evaristo Breccia, *With King Fuad to the Oasis of Ammon* (Milan: Bestetti & Tumminelli, 1929), quotation from p. 22.

100 Gabriel Hanotaux, ed., *Histoire de la nation égyptienne* , 7 vols. (Paris: Société de l'histoire nationale, 1931–1940) "Introduction" by Hanotaux, 1: lxxxviii.

101 Association Internationale des Papyrologues/ International Association of Papyrologists, "Histoire - History," http://www.ulb.ac.be/assoc/aip/histor. htm. Updated 8/23/2014.

102 MAE, AMB. Le Caire, Services égyptiennes divers, Carton 175, Dossier 3: Enseign, publique, Folder: Société royale égyptienne de papyrologie, Jouguet note, April 22, 1930. On Jouguet, see *BSAC* 34 1949: 115–36; Bierbrier, *WWWE4*: 284–85.

103 Girgis Mattha, *Demotic ostraka from the collections at Oxford, Paris, Berlin, and Cairo*, Publications de la Société Fouad I de papyrology, Textes et documents, vol. 6. (Cairo: IFAO, 1945); and Zaki Ali, "A Dedicatory Stele from Naucratis," *Études de papyrologie* 8 (1948): 73–92.

104 O. Guéraud, *Études de papyrologie* 4 (1938): 213. On Jouguet, see *BSAA* 34 (1949): 115–19; Bierbrier, *WWWE4*: 284–85.

105 Sahar Hamouda, *Omar Toussoun, Prince of Alexandria* (Alexandria: Bibliotheca Alexandrina, 2005). On Toussoun, also *BSAA* 36 (1943–44): 98–103; *BSAC* 10 (1944): v–vi; *BIÉ* 26 (1944): 1–19; Bierbrier, *WWWE4*: 543–44.

106 Artemis Cooper, *Cairo in the War 1939–1945* (London: H. Hamilton, 1989), 28.

107 Toussoun's multivolume titles included *Mémoires sur l'histoire du Nil*, *Mémoires sur les anciennes branches du Nil*, and *La géographie de l'Égypte à l'époque arabe*.

108 Paolo Gallo, "The Penninsula and the Island of Canopus: A History of Water and Sand," in Casini, ed., *One Hundred Years*, 131, 133.

109 A. Adriani, *Société royale d'archéologie—Alexandrie, indici analitici dei fascicoli 1–29* (1898–1934), *Bulletin [BSAA]*, n.s. vol. 8, suppl. (1937): 5–13.

110 On Breccia, see Bonacasa, "Work of Italian Archaeologists," 109–111; C. Barocas, in *Dizionario biografico degli Italiani* (Rome: Istituto della Enciclopedia italiana, 1972), 14: 91–93.

111 D.J. Ian Begg, "Fascism in the Desert: A Microcosmic View of Archaeological Politics," in *Archaeology under Dictatorship*, ed. Michael L. Galaty and Charles Walkinson (New York: Kulwer Academic/Plenum 2004), 25. Another rejected candidate, Doro Levi, was Jewish and married to a Greek.

112 On Adriani, see *Dizionario biografico degli Italiani*. v. 34: Primo Supplemento, A–C (Rome: Istituto della Enciclopedia italiana, 1988), 17–18; Bierbrier, *WWWE4*: 8; Bonacasa, "Work of Italian Archaeologists," 111–112; S. Stucchi, "A.A.," in *Archeologica classica* XXII (1980): 1–11; N. Boncasa and A. di Vita, eds., *Alessandria e il mondo ellenistico-romano: studi in onore di Achille Adriani*, 3 vols. (Rome: " L'Erma" di Bretschneider, 1983), esp. 1: xv–xix.

113 Bonacasa, "Work of Italian Archaeologists," 111.

114 Ilbert, *Alexandrie* 2: 609–15. On Italians in Egypt in the interwar period, see especially Petricioli, *Oltre il mito*.

115 Brian McLaren, *Architecture and Tourism in Italian Colonial Libya: An Ambivalent Modernism* (Seattle: University of Washington Press, 2006); Claudio Segrè, *Fourth Shore: The Italian Colonization of Libya* (Chicago: University of Chicago Press, 1974).

116 Marla Stone, "A Flexible Rome: Fascism and the Cult of Romanità," in

Roman Presences: Receptions of Rome in European Culture, 1789–1945, ed. Catherine Edwards (Cambridge: Cambridge University Press, 1999), 205–20.

117 Yunan Labib Rizk, "Fascist Celebration," *Al-Ahram Weekly*, Aug. 31–Sept. 6, 2006, 24; Hala Halim, "Dance to the Music of Time," *Al-Ahram Weekly*, July 2–8, 1998, 13; Gordon P Merriam to Sec. State. USNA, Department of State/ T1251/ Roll 12/ Target 2 883. 41 History 883.413/4.

118 Begg, "Fascism in the Desert," 19–31. For Mussolini's idea of Romanità, see Joshua Arthurs, *Excavating Modernity: The Roman Past in Fascist Italy* (Ithaca, NY: Cornell University Press, 2012).

119 Gido Bastianini and Rosario Pintaudi, "Acquisitions and Excavations by the Società Italiana per la Recerca di Papiri Greci e Latini in Egypt," in Casini, ed., *One Hundred Years*, 167.

120 Dyson, *Pursuit of Ancient Pasts*, 196–98.

121 William Stadiem, *Too Rich: The High Life and Tragic Death of King Farouk* (New York: Caroll & Graf, 1991), 191.

122 Stadiem, *Too Rich*, 148–49; Barrie St. Claire McBride, *Farouk of Egypt: A Biography* (London: Hale, 1967), 106.

123 "Personalities Report. 1945," 45. FO371/ 45925/ J3027. Pierre Jouget, *Révolution dans la défaite: études athéniennes* ([Cairo]: Éd. de la *Revue du Caire*, 1942).

124 Interview with Daoud Abdo Daoud, Alexandria, March 14, 1988; Interview with Henri Riad, Cairo, April 20,1988.

125 Bierbrier, *WWWE4*: 477; Interview with Daoud Abdo Daoud, Alexandria, March 14, 1988.

126 *BSAA* 25 (1930: 218; 33 (1939): 410; 34 (1941): 138.

127 Kharrat, *City of Saffron*, and *Girls of Alexandria*, trans. Frances Liardet, (London: Quartet, 1993); Ibrahim Abd al-Majid, *Nobody Sleeps in Alexandria*, trans. Farouk Abdel Wahab (Cairo: American University in Cairo Press, 1999). On Kharrat, see also Karrarah, "Egyptian Literary Images of Alexandria," 309–12.

128 Harry E. Tzalas, *Farewell to Alexandria*, trans. Susan E. Mantouvalou (Cairo: American University in Cairo Press, 2007), 61–74.

129 John L. Wright, "Mussolini, Libya, and the Sword of Islam," in *Italian Colonialism*, ed. Ruth Ben-Ghiat and Mia Fuller (New York: Palgrave Macmillan, 2005), 121.

130 *BSAA* 43 (1975): 1–4.

131 Ét. Combe, "Le cinquantenaire de la société royale d'archéologie 1893–1943," *BSAA* 36(1946): 104–19.

132 Interview with Mostafa El-Abbadi, Alexandria, August 14, 2005; Hala Halim, "Mustafa El-Abbadi: Alexandreus," *Al-Ahram Weekly*, July 6–12, 1995, 16.

133 Interview with Daoud Abdou Daoud, Alexandria, March 14, 1988. On Daoud (1928–90), the Société's longtime secretary, see *BAAS* 45, 1993, ix–x.

134 Halim, *Alexandrian Cosmopolitanism*, 28–33.

135 Victor Adm, "De Ptolémé Soter à Farouk 1er," *50 ans de vie d'Égypte: le livre d'or du journal La Réforme* (Alexandria, 1945), 240.

136 *The University of Alexandria Bulletin 1981–1982. (40th Anniversary)*, 11–12.

137 C. M. Bowra, *Memories*, 247. Wace in fact taught in Alexandria, not Cairo. Bierbrier, *WWWE4*: 561.

138 University of London, SOAS Archives: MS 380428/1–6, typescript Alan J.B. Wace, Farouk lst University, Alexandria, "Excavations at Kom Ed Dika, Alexandria" and associated correspondence.

139 Interview with Daoud Abdou Daoud, Alexandria, March 14, 1988.

140 Faruq Hafiz al-Qadi, "al-Ruwwad al-awail fi dirasat al-tarikh al-yunani al-rumani," *al-Majalla al-tarikhiya al-misriya* 39 (1996): 278–79; Jamiat Fuad al-Awwal, *al-Kitab al-fiddi li-kulliyat al-adab* (Cairo: Matbaat Jamiat Fuad al-Awwal, 1951), 80–81; Zaki Ali, *Essays and Papers* (Athens, 1995).

141 Interview with Abd al-Latif Ahmed Ali, Cairo, October 18, 1987; Jamiat al-Qahira, *al-Athar al-ilmiya li-ada hayat al-tadris bi-Jamiat al-Qahira 1958*: 49–50; Faruq Hafiz al-Qadi, "al-Ruwwad," 280–81. Abdullatif Ahmed Aly, ed. "Some Michigan Papyri from Karanis (i)," *Annales de la faculté des lettres*, Ibrahim University Studies in Papryology, no. 1, preface.

142 Jamiat Fuad al-Awwal, *al-Kitab al-fiddi*, 222, passim; *Jamiat al-Iskandariya, sijl al-kharijin 1958* (Alexandria, 1959).

143 Interview with Muhammad Salim Salem, Cairo, November 26, 1987.

144 On Kelsey (1858–1935), see J.G. Pedley, *The Life and Work of Francis Willey Kelsey* (Ann Arbor: University of Michigan Press, 2012); Bierbrier, *WWWE4*: 293. On Peterson (1891–1978), see Bierbrier, *WWWE4*: 427. He later directed Michigan's Kelsey Museum of Art and Archaeology.

145 Although Stephen L. Dyson does not mention Karanis, Michigan's excavation there fits the "big dig" pattern he delineates for American classical archaeology in the interwar and immediate post-World War II eras. Stephen L. Dyson, "Brahmins and Bureaucrats: Some Reflections on the History of American Classical Archaeology," in *Assembling the Past: Studies in the Professionalization of Archaeology*, ed. Alice B. Kehoe and Mary Beth Emmerichs (Albuquerque: University of New Mexico Press, 1999), 103–16.

146 Muhammad Husayn Kamil, *al-Katib al-Misri* 7 (Nov. 1947): 203–207.

147 Interview with Muhammad Salim Salem, Cairo, November 26, 1987.

148 Interview with Ibrahim Noshy, Cairo, May 22, 1983. Abd al Munim Ibrahim al-Dusuqi Jumayi, *al-Jamiya al-misriya lil-dirasat al-tarikhiya wa-dirasa tarikhiya lil-muassa ilimiya 1945–1985* (Cairo: Matbaat al-Jabalawi, 1985), 159–63; Faruq Hafiz al-Qadi, "al-Ruwwad," 277–78.

149 This and the following quotations are from Ibrahim Noshy, *Arts in Ptolemaic Egypt: A Study of Greek and Egyptian Influences in Ptolemaic Architecture and Sculpture* (London: Oxford University Press, 1937), 11, 142. For recent views on hybridity in Ptolemaic state and society, see J.G. Manning, *The Last of the Pharaohs: Egypt under the Ptolemies, 305–30 BC* (Princeton: Princeton University Press, 2010).

150 Ibrahim Noshy, *Tarikh Misr fi asr al-batalima*, (1946; repr., Cairo: Maktabat al-anjilu al-misriya,1966).

151 Jamiat Fuad al-Awwal, *al-Kitab al-fiddi*, 133.

152 Roger S. Bagnall, *Egypt in Late Antiquity* (Princeton: Princeton University Press, 1993), 230–31; Alan E. Samuel, *The Shifting Sands of History: Interpretations of Ptolemaic Egypt* (Lanham, MD: University Press of America, 1989); E.G. Turner, "Ptolemaic Egypt," in *Cambridge Ancient History*, 2nd ed. (Cambridge: Cambridge University Press, 1984), 172; Naphthali Lewis, *Greeks in Ptolemaic Egypt: Case Studies in the Social History of the Hellenistic Period* (Oxford: Claredon Press, 1986), 4.

153 Interviews with Aziz Atiya, Salt Lake City, March 29, 1986, and Ibrahim Noshy, Cairo, May 22, 1983.

154 Kitroeff, *Greeks*, 14; Ilbert, *Alexandrie* 2: 820. Muhammad Awad, founder of the Alexandria Preservation Trust, however, is a prominent example of mixed heritage. One of his grandmothers was Greek, the other grandmother a Greek-speaker from Crete who was probably of Turkish origin. Interview, Alexandria, July 6, 2005.

155 Interviews with Fayza Haikal, Cairo, March 1 and June 2, 1999.

156 Interview with Abd El Muhsin El-Khashshab, Cairo, April 14, 1983; Fouad I National Research Council, *Guide to Scientific and Technical Workers in Egypt*, 388. On Guéraud, see Bierbrier, *WWWE4*: 230.

157 Mahmud, Zaki Najib, "The Crisis of Civilizational Development in the Arab Homeland," in *Trends and Issues in Contemporary Arab Thought*, ed. Issa J. Boullata (Albany: State University of New York Press, 1990), 17.

158 Interview with Louis Awad, Cairo, April 20, 1982; Louis Awad, "Louis Awad," *The Literature of Ideas in Egypt*, Part 1, *Arabic Writing Today*, vol. 3, ed. Louis Awad (Atlanta: Scholar's Press, 1986), 210–215; Jamiat Fuad al-Awwal, *al-Kitab al-fiddi*, 140.

159 Ali al-Raʻi, "Arabic Drama since the Thirties," in *Modern Arabic Literature*, ed. M.M. Badawi, The Cambridge History of Arabic Literature (Cambridge: Cambridge University Press, 1992), 372–75.

160 Quoted in Sasson Somekh, "A Romantic Rationalist: Dr. Husayn Fawzi," *The Jerusalem Quarterly*, no. 45 (Winter 1988): 112. See also pp. 119, 120, 122. Husayn Fawzi, *Sindibad Misri* (Cairo: Dar al-maarif, 1961).

161 *BSAA* 36 (1946): 95; 38 (1949): 155.

162 Lackany, *La société archéologique*, 22–23.

163 On Combe (1881–1962), see Lackany, *La société archéologique*, 161.

164 Interview with Mostafa El-Abbadi, Alexandria, August 14, 2005; *BSAA* 38 (1949): 159.

165 *Scott 2012*, Egypt #272; Rushdi Said, *The River Nile: Geology, Hydrology, and Utilization* (Oxford: Pergamon, 1993), 98–99.

166 *Scott 2012*, Egypt #292–94; International Committee of Mediterranean Games, History, "Les jeux méditerranéens." http://www.cijm.org.gr/index.php?option=com_content&view=article&id=19&Itemid=27&lang=en, updated January 2015. A notable absentee from the Games has been Israel.

167 *Annuaire statistique 1945–1946, 1946–1947* (Cairo, 1951), 242; *1947–1948,*

et 1949 (Cairo, 1952), 258.

168 Edmonds on Rowe to Oriental Secretary Walter Smart, Cairo, December 8, 1947. FO141/ 1153 Minute by L.H.G.

169 Albert Hourani, *Arabic Thought in the Liberal Age, 1798–1939* (Oxford: Oxford University Press, 1962), ends with the outbreak of World War II, but Egypt's "liberal age" is often extended to the 1952 revolution.

170 *BSAA* 38 (1949): 156; 39 (1951): 190–91.

171 On Brinton, Modinos, and Combe, see the obituaries by Radamès Lackany, in *BSAA* 43 (1975): 1–4; Lackany, *La société archéologique* (1973), 29–31, 52, 161.

172 D.S. Crawford, ed., *Papyri Michaelidae* (Aberdeen: Egypt Exploration Society, 1955), pref. by E.G. Turner, vii. Furness to Morisson, May 16, 1949, enclosing list of British technicians and advisers in education employed by the Egyptian government, UKNA/ BW29/34 [British Council], shows Drew and four others in classics at Fuad I, and Wace and four others at Faruq I University.

173 A. Adriani, *Annuaire du Musée Gréco–Romain* III (1940–50) (Alexandria, 1952), 1–2; Bonacasa and di Vita, *Alessandrie e il mondo ellenistico-romano* 1: vii.

174 Nevine El-Aref, "Alexandria's Graeco–Roman Museum to Reopen within 18 Months," *Ahram Online*, Oct. 30, 2013: http://english.ahram.org.eg/UI/ Front/Search.aspx?Text=alexandria's%20graeco-roman%20museum%20 to%20reopen, accessed 1/9/2015.

175 Naguib Mahfouz, *Autumn Quail*, trans. Roger Allen (Cairo: American University in Cairo Press, 1985); Karrarah, "Egyptian Literary Images of Alexandria," 312–19.

9. Contesting Egyptology in the 1930s

1 Midhat Ghazalé, *Pyramids Road: An Egyptian Homecoming* (Cairo: American University in Cairo Press, 2004), 40, quoting his father. Born into a Coptic family in 1929, the author grew up on Mariette Street and attended the nearby French lycée.

2 MAE, AMB Le Caire, Enseignement égyptien, Service des antiquités, Carton 174, Dossier 53, 2: Succession M. Lacau. Translated from the French translation of the Arabic original.

3 P.J. Cain and A.G. Hopkins, *British Imperialism*, 1688–2000, 2nd ed. (Harlow, UK: Longman, 2001), 463, 467, 483.

4 Bierbrier, *WWWE4*: 402–03.

5 Éric Gady, "Le pharaon, l'égyptologue et le diplomate. Les égyptologues français en Égypte, du voyage de Champollion à la crise de Suez (1828–1956)," 2 vols, PhD diss., Université de Paris IV-Sorbonne, 2005, 929–30.

6 On Lloyd's anti-French crusade at the Egyptian University, see Donald Malcolm Reid, *Cairo University and the Making of Modern Egypt* (Cambridge: Cambridge University Press, 1990), 87–91.

7 Griffith Institute Archives, Oxford University, Newberry MSS. 1: Correspondence 48/5. "Report on the Work of the Archaeological Institute," undated, but after Ocober 1, 1930. For Newberry's university contracts at Cairo, see Newberry MSS. 1: Correspondence 30/59–63 (1929–1932).

8   Gady, "Pharaon," 930. Lacau perceived echoes of Breasted's failed 1925 proposal for a Rockefeller-funded museum in Cairo, which would have undercut French control of the Antiquities Service.

9   Selim Hassan, *Le poèm dit de Pentaour et le rapport official sur la bataille de Qadesh* (1929); Selim Hassan, *Excavations at Giza*, 6, Pt. 2, (Cairo: Government Press, Bulaq, 1948).

10   Ahmad Kamal, in *ASAE* 15 (1916): 177–78; interview with Abdel-Aziz Sadek, Cairo, June 12, 1988. The Metropolitan Museum purchased two of the statues which Kamal found in the tomb of Yuny near Asyut. George Reisner, "Recent Purchases of Egyptian Sculpture," *The Metropolitan Museum of Art Bulletin* 29, no. 11, pt. 1 (November 1934): 184–85.

11   Daressy to Undersec of State of Ministry of Public Works (Egypt), August 28, 1921. MAE, AMB Le Caire, Enseignement égyptien, Service des antiquités, C174.

12   John A. Wilson, *Signs and Wonders upon Pharaoh: A History of American Egyptology* (Chicago: University of Chicago Press, 1964), 193.

13   Muhammad Jamal Mokhtar, "Selim Hassan," *al-Majalla al-tarikhiya al-misriya* 19 (1972): 84–5; Wilson, *Signs*, 193–94, 230; "Fourth Big Pyramid at Gizeh Examined," *New York Times*, Feb. 19, 1932, 21.

14   Selim Hassan, *Excavations at Giza*. vol. 1 (Oxford: Oxford University Press, 1932), esp. v–vi; Vols. 2–10, (Cairo: Government Press, Bulaq, 1934–1960), esp. vol. 2: v. Several letters from Selim Hassan to "My dear Newberry" discuss publication arrangements with Oxford University Press. Griffith Institute Archives, Oxford University, Newberry MSS. 1: Correspondence 40/1–4 (1930–1932).

15   Sami Gabra, *Rapport sur les fouilles d'Hermoupolis Ouest (Touna El-Gebel)*. Université Fouad Ier. (Cairo, 1941); Sami Gabra, *Chez les derniers adorateurs de Trismegiste: la nécropole d'Hermopolis Touna El Gebel (Souvenir d'un archéologue)* (Cairo: al-Haya al-misriya al-amma, 1971); Griffith Institute Archives, Oxford, Newberry MSS 1: Correspondence 17/2, Gabra to "Dear Professor Newberry," undated but shortly after Febuary 4, 1931, reported on beginning the excavation and invited a visit and advice.

16   Gabra, *Souvenir*, 16. He qualifies this, however, by saying that these sums included excavations at Maadi and those of the Museum of Islamic Art.

17   Gabra, *Souvenir*, 150.

18   *al-Ahram*, Feb. 10, 1933.

19   *Bericht über den VI. Internationalen Kongress für Archäologie. Berlin 21–26. August 1939* (Berlin: Walter De Gruyter, 1940), 6, 22, 25, 55, 251–54. Gabra, *Souvenir*, 151, mistakenly remembers this as an International Congress of Orientalists.

20   On Amer, see Bierbrier, *WWWE4*, 17–18; *Bulletin de la société royale de géographie d'Égypte* 43–44 (1970–71): 1; Jamiat Fuad al-Awwal, *al-Kitab al-fiddi li-kulliyat al-adab 1925–1950* (Cairo: Matbaat Jamiat Fuad al-Awwal, 1951), 31; R. Lackany, *La société archéologique d'Alexandrie à 80 ans* (Alexandria: Impr. Don Bosco, 1973), 155–56.

21   Jamiat Fuad al-Awwal, *al-Kitab al-fiddi*, 48.

22   Selim Hassan was a subscribing member of the Oxford ICO: *Proceedings of the Seventeenth International Congress of Orientalists. Oxford, 1928* (London: H. Milford, 1929), 15, 22–41, 85. For the history of the ICOs, see its proceedings, with the volume title usually in the language of the host country. In the early 1970s, the ICO jettisoned the "Orientalist" label hitherto at the core of its identity to become the International Congress of the Human Sciences in Asia and North Africa (later, the International Congress of Asian and North African Studies, ICANAS). Egyptologists seceded in 1976 to form their own International Association of Egyptologists (IAE).

23   *Actes de XVIIIe congrès international des orientalistes. Leiden 7–12 Septembre 1931* (Leiden: Brill, 1932), 79–80, 85. Gabra's abstract was published in the proceedings; Hassan's was listed as "not received." *Atti del XIX congresso internazionale degli orientalisti. Roma, 23–29 Settembre 1935 – XIII* (Rome: Bureau du muséon, 1938), 5, 7–9, 133–34. *Actes du XXe Congès international des orientalistes. Bruxelles. 5–10 Septembre 1938* (Louvain, 1940), 5, 65–68.

24   Peterson to Campbell, May 8, 1933. FO371/ 17023/ J1080.

25   Lampson to Simon, June 14, 1934. FO371/ 18006/ J1518; Blackman to Scrivener, April 24, 1942. FO 370/ 663/ L1714.

26   Cairo Chancery to FO, August 23, 1934. FO371/18006/ J2032.

27   Rector of Académie de Paris to MAE, June 4, 1934. MAE, Service des oeuvres françaises à l'étranger, Série D.—Levant, Carton 365: Égypte. Facultés égyptiennes, Dossier: Égypte. Facultés égyptiennes.

28   On Junker and his DAI directorship, see Susanne Voss, "Der Lange Arm des Nationalsozialismus," in *Ägyptologen und Ägyptologien zwischen Kaiserreich und Gründen der beiden deutschen Staaten. . . .*, Beiheft 1, Susanne Bickel et al., eds. (Berlin: Akademie Verlag: de Gruyter, 2013); Julia Budka and Claus Jurman, "Hermann Junker: Ein Deutsches-Österreichisches Forscherleben zwischen Pyramiden, Kreuz und Hakenkreuz," in *Ägyptologen und Ägyptologien*, ed. Susanne Bickel, 299–331; Hermann Junker, *Leben und Werk in Selbstdarstellung*, Österreichische Akademie der Wissenschaften, Philosophisch-historiche Klasse. Sitzungbsberichte 242, Band 5, Abhandlung (Vienna: H. Böhlaus, 1963); Bierbrier, *WWWE4*: 285–86. On Junker's "national Catholic" politics during the Nazi era, see Thomas Schneider, "Ägyptologen im Dritten Reich," *Journal of Egyptian History* 4, no. 2 (Fall 2011): 160–63. The last number of *Mitteilungen* to appear under Junker's directorship was vol. 13, pt. 1, 1943.

29   Samir Rafaat, "Pretty in Pink: Zamalek's Maison du Canada," *Cairo Times*, Nov. 16, 2000.

30   On Roeder, see Bierbrier, *WWWE4*: 470–71, and—on his politics—Schneider, "Ägyptologen," 169–70. On Pelizaeus, see Bierbrier, *WWWE4*: 421.

31   *Actes du XVIIIe congrès international des orientalistes. Leiden 7–12 Septembre 1931*, 77–80; *Actes du XXe congrès international des orientalistes. Bruxelles. 5–10 Septembre 1938* (Louvain, 1940), 52–53, 65–68; *Bericht über XI.Internationalen Kongress für Archäologie. Berlin 21–26. August 1939* (Berlin, 1940), 53, 251–55.

32 Philip L. Kohl and J.A. Pérez Gollán, "Religion, Politics, and Prehistory: Reassessing the Lingering Legacy of Oswald Menghin," *Current Anthropology* 43, no. 4 (August/October 2002), 561–86; Schneider, "Ägyptologen," 162–63.

33 Interview with Aziz Atiya, March 29, 1986, Salt Lake City.

34 Georg Steindorff (North Hollywood, CA) letter to John A. Wilson, June 1945, Oriental Institute Archives, University of Chicago. Included in online post by Charles E. Jones, "Nazism and ANE Studies," October 25, 1993, http://oi.uchicago.edu/research/library/ane/digest/v01/v01.n021, accessed 1/9/2015. Facsimile in Schneider, "Ägyptologen," 213–16. The following quotations and information come from this letter (hereafter, "Steindorff's list"). For the context of Steindorff's list, see Dietrich Raue, "Der 'J'accuse'-Brief an John A. Wilson: Drei Ansichten von Georg Steindorff," in Susanne Bickel et al., eds., *Ägyptologen und Ägyptologien zwischen Kaiserreich und Gründen der beiden deutschen Staaten. . . .*, Beiheft 1 (Berlin: Akademie Verlag Berlin: de Gruyter, 2013) 345–76.

35 Schneider, "Ägyptologen," 153–60; Henning Franzmeier and Anke Weber, "'Anderseits finde ich, dass man jetzts nich so tun soll, als wäre nichts gewesen'. Die deutsche Ägyptologie in den Jahren 1945–1949 im Spiegel der Korrespondenz mit dem Verlag J.C. Hinrichs," in Bickel et al., eds., *Ägyptologen und Ägyptologien*, 128–33.

36 Interview with Salah al-Aqqad, Cairo, April 17, 1983.

37 Interview with Gamal Mokhtar, Cairo, June 6, 1988. On Badawi, see Dia Abou-Ghazi, "Vie," in *Pages from the Excavations at Saqqarah and Mit Rahinah*, Organisation des antiquités de l'Égypte, Service des musées, Vies et travaux IV, ed. Ahmad M. Badawi (Cairo: Dar al-maarif, 1984), 7–24; Bierbrier, *WWWE4*: 31–32.

38 Lampson to FO, November 28, 1938. FO395/ 567/ P3361.

39 Samir Raafat, "When Doctor Goebbels Came to Town," *Egyptian Mail*, September 30, 1995, accessed at www.egy.com/historica.

40 Lampson to FO, November 28, 1938. FO395/ 567/ P3361.

41 Lampson to Halifax, January 28, 1939. FO371/ 23352/ J468.

42 Lloyd to Cadogan. February 1, 1939. FO371/23352/J731.

43 Lloyd to Cadogan. February 1, 1939. FO371/23352/J731.

44 Günter Dreyer and Daniel Polz, eds., *Begegnung mit Vergangenheit: 100 Jahre in Ägypten: Deutsches Archäologisches Institut Kairo 1907–2007* (Mainz: P. von Zabern, 2007), 9, 17, 28–29.

45 Nicholas Reeves, *Ancient Egypt: The Great Discoveries: A Year-by-Year Chronicle* (London: Thames & Hudson, 2000), 195.

46 Voss, "Der lange Arm," and Budka and Jurman, "Hermann Junker," in *Ägyptologen und Ägyptologien*, Susanne Bickel et al. eds., 267–98, 299–331.

47 Louis Keimer, "Le musée égyptologique de Berlin," *Cahiers d'histoire égyptienne*," Série III, fasc. 1 (November 1950): 40. Keimer (1892–1957) held various posts in Cairo beginning in 1928, became a Czech citizen while teaching at Prague in the 1930s, and in 1951 took Egyptian citizenship. Despite his anti-Nazi convictions, he was interned in Egypt as an enemy alien until 1942. Isolde Lehnert, "Ludwig Keimer," *KMT* 23, No. 1 (Spring

2012): 74–77; Schneider, "Ägyptologen," 140; Bierbrier, *WWWE4*: 291–92.

48   On Borchardt, see Susanne Voss und Cornelius von Pilgrim, "Ludwig Borchardt und die Deutschen Interessen am Nil," in Charlotte Trümpler, ed., *Das Grosse Spiel: Archäologie und Politik zur Zeit des Kolonialismus (1860–1940)* (Cologne: Ruhr Museum, 2008), 294–305; Cornelius von Pilgrim, "Ludwig Borchardt und sein 'Institut für ägyptische Bauforschung und Altertumskunde' in Kairo," in *Ägyptologen und Ägyptologien*, Bickel et al., eds., 243–66; Bierbrier, *WWWE4*: 68–69.

49   Adolf Erman, *Ludwig Borchardt: Bibliographie zum 70 Geburtstage Ludwig Borchardts Am 5. Oktober 1933 Zusammengestellt*; Ludwig Borchardt, *Allerhand Kleinigkeiten. Seinen Wissenschaftlichen Freunden und Bekannten zu Seinem 70. Gerburtstage am 5. Oktober 1933* (Leipzig, privately printed, n.d.).

50   Adolf Erman, *Mein Werden und Mein Werken: Erinnerungen eines Alten Berliner Gelehrten* (Leipzig: Von Quelle & Meyer, 1929), 41–43, 123, 283. On Erman, see also Bernd Ulrich Schipper, ed., *Ägyptologie als Wissenschaft: Adolf Erman (1854–1937) in seiner Zeit* (Berlin: W. de Gruyter, 2006); Bierbrier, *WWWE4*: 180–81.

51   Horst Jaritz, "The Extension of the Egyptian Museum: A Project of 1937 by Otto Königsberger," in *Egyptian Museum Collections around the World*, ed. Mamdouh Mohamed Eldamaty and Mai Trad, (Cairo: Supreme Council of Antiquities, 2002), 581–89.

52   Reisner to Harold [G. Harold Edgell, director of the MFA], July 15, 1938. MFA Archives, Director's Correspondence, Reisner, Box 1927–50, Folder 18 (1937–38). For a detailed account of Borchardt's final struggle against the Nazis and the posthumous transformation of the Ludwig Borchardt Institute into the Swiss Institute, see von Pilgrim, "Ludwig Borchardt," 243–66.

53   Reisner's translation of Borchardt to Reisner, July 21, 1938, enclosed in Reisner to Harold [Edgell], August 5, 1938. MFA Archives, Director's Correspondence, Reisner, Box 1927–50, Folder 18 (1937–38).

54   Undersecretary of State Nells (?) to Edgell, August 11, 1938. MFA, Director's Correspondence, Reisner, Box 1927–50, Folder 18 (1937–38).

55   Gardiner to Gaselee, August 12, 1938, and Harding to Gaselee, August 16, 1938. FO371/ 21997.

56   Reisner to Edgell, September 30, 1938. MFA, Reisner, Director's Correspondence, Box 1927–50, Folder 18 (1937–38).

57   *Chronique d'Égypte* 24, no. 47 (Jan. 1949): 94.

58   von Pilgrim, "Ludwig Borchardt," 243–66; and Schweizerisches Institut für Ägyptische Bauforschung und Altertumskunde, "Geschichte des Instituts," http://www.swissinst.ch/html, accessed 1/9/2015.

59   Bierbrier, *WWWE4*, 68–69; Miroslav Verner, *The Pyramids: The Mystery, Culture, and Science of Egypt's Great Monuments*. trans. Steven Rendall (Cairo: American University in Cairo Press, 2002), 383.

60   Gady, "Pharaon," 947.

61   Cairo Residency to FO, February 13, 1933. FO141/759/269, W.A.S.

62   Henri Gauthier, *Le livre des rois d'Égypte*, 5 vols. (Cairo: IFAO, 1907–17). Bierbrier, *WWWE4*, 209.

63 Gady, "Pharaon," 947.

64 Cairo Residency minute, March 1, 1933. FO141/759/269, W.A.S.

65 Minute from Cairo Residency "M. Lacau," R. S[tevenson], March 1, 1933, and minute W. Stevenson, March 14, 1933. FO141/759/269; Gady, "Pharaon," 948.

66 The following account of this controversy draws mainly on Gady, "Pharaon," 923–38.

67 MAE, Service des oeuvres françaises à l'étranger, Série D-Levant, Dossier: Instit. d'Archéologie [IFAO], Director of Higher Education, Min. Education National to Marx, Serv. oeuvres françaises, enclosing Jouguet remarks of May 25, 1935.

68 Gady, "Pharaon," 931, and an article kindly sent me by Gady: "Liquidation amoureuse (Aff. Dame P… c. Prof. S…," *Journal des tribunaux mixtes*, July 15–16, 1935, 5, clipping in Lacau's correspondence in the Institut de France, Mss. 6338, fo. 242, 2.

69 Gady, "Pharaon," 953–84, offers the fullest account. He kindly shared documents I had not seen.

70 Gady, "Pharaon," 956. On Drioton, see Bierbrier, *WWWE4*: 160–61, and Françoise d'Orival, "Étienne Drioton, prêtre et égyptologue (1889–1961). Sa vie, son oeuvre," mémoire de 3ème cycle d'égyptologie de l'École du Louvre, 1997. (thesis, not seen, cited in Gady, "Pharaon," 1212). Drioton was honorary *Chanoine* (Canon) of the Cathedral of Nancy. Christiane Desroches Noblecourt, *La grande nubiade ou le parcours d'une égyptologue* (Paris: Stock/Pernoud, 1992), 96.

71 William Stadien, *Too Rich: The High Life and Tragic Death of King Farouk* (New York: Caroll & Graf, 1991), 148; for Lampson, see also Goldschmidt, *Biographical Dictionary of Modern Egypt*, 109.

72 Lampson to Oliphant, July 15, 1935. FO371/ 19094/ J3355.

73 Gady, "Pharaon," 952.

74 Gady, "Pharaon," 954–55.

75 MAE, AMB Le Caire, Enseignement égyptien, Service des antiquités 1897–1941, Carton 17, Dossier 53, 2 "Succession M. Lacau," French translation of article from *al-Balagh*, May 26, 1936.

76 Hassan dedicated volumes to the memories of "my friend" Abd al-Wahhab and of assassinated prime minister Ahmad Mahir (both Saadists): *Misr al-qadima*, 1 (Cairo: Matbaat dar al-kutub al-misriya, 1940), and *al-Adab al-misri al-qadima, aw, adab al-faraina* (Cairo: Matbaat lajnat al-talif wa-l-tarjama wa-l-nashr, 1945).

77 Lampson to Oliphant, July 15, 1935. FO371/19094/J3355.

78 Lampson, Miles, *Politics and Diplomacy in Egypt: The Diaries of Sir Miles Lampson, 1935–1937*, ed. M.E. Yapp, (Oxford: Oxford University Press, 1997), 419–20, entry for Jan. 8, 1936, 419–20.

79 Lampson, *Diaries of Sir Miles Lampson*, 480, entry for March 19, 1936.

80 Gady, "Pharaon," 954–55, 959.

81 Author's translation of French translation from *Rose al-Youssef*, June 9, 1936, in MAE, AMB Le Caire, Enseignement égyptien, Service des antiquités 1897–1941, Carton 174, Dossier 53, 2 "Succession M. Lacau."

82 French minister Cairo to Delbos, June 8, 1936. MAE, AMB Le Caire, Enseignement égyptien, Service des antiquités 1897–1941, Carton 17, Dossier 53, 2, "Succession M. Lacau."

83 Robert Solé, L' Égypte, passion française (Paris: Seuil, 1997), 251–53.

84 Lampson, Diaries of Sir Miles Lampson, 610, entry for July 9, 1936.

85 Minister of France, Cairo, to Bonnet, June 27, 1939. MAE, Service des oeuvres françaises à l'étranger, Série D—Levant/ Carton 366: Égypte: Facultés ég. et insituts d'archéologie, Dossier: Instituts arch. [IFAO]. Author's translation.

86 Lampson, Diaries of Sir Miles Lampson, 888, entry for July 28, 1937.

87 Minister of France, Cairo, to Delbos, March 10, 1937. MAE, AMB Le Caire, Enseignement égyptien, Service des antiquités 1897–1941, Carton 17, Dossier 53, 2, "Succession M. Lacau." For another take on the royal Upper Egyptian tour, including photographs, see "Faruq al-Awwal fi Misr al-Ulya," al-Hilal 45, no. 4 (February 1, 1937), 409–13. Drioton is pictured showing Faruq the tombs at Beni Hassan. Selim Hassan is not mentioned.

88 The illustration was on the cover of al-Dalil fi al-kashf, April 15, 1937, as cited and shown in Wilson Chacko Jacob, Working Out Egypt: Effendi Masculinity and Subject Formation in Colonial Modernity, 1870–1940 (Durham, NC: Duke University Press, 2011), 119–20.

89 Israel Gershoni and James Jankowski, Redefining the Egyptian Nation, 1930–1945 (Cambridge: Cambridge University Press, 1995), 55, citing al-Siyasa al-usbuiya, Jan. 30, 1937, 1.

90 Gady, "Pharaon," 963–64.

91 On the history of this dig house, see "Beyt Sobek: History," Fayum Project, UCLA, RUG, GOA, http://www.archbase.com/fayum/visitors.htm, accessed 1/9/2015. For a project dedicated to studying archaeological dig houses in Egypt, see Marcel and Monica Maessen's t3.wy Foundation for Historical Research in Egyptology, Dig House Project, http:///www.t3.wy.org/, updated July 20, 2014.

92 Lampson, Diaries of Sir Miles Lampson, 328, entry for Nov. 4, 1935.

93 Lampson, Diaries of Sir Miles Lampson, 348–49, entry for Nov. 14, 1935.

94 Lampson, Diaries of Sir Miles Lampson, 816, entry for May 6, 1937.

95 Lampson, Diaries of Sir Miles Lampson, 816, entry for May 6, 1937.

96 Lampson, Diaries of Sir Miles Lampson, 822, entry for May 23, 1937.

97 Gady, "Pharaon," 966–67.

98 Lampson, Diaries of Sir Miles Lampson, 828–29, entry for May 9, 1937.

99 Lampson, Diaries of Sir Miles Lampson, 816, entry for May 6, 1937.

100 Gady, "Pharaon," 967–68.

101 Gady, "Pharaon," 962–63.

102 MFA, The Giza Archives, "Broadcast from the Pyramids." February 6, 1938, diaries, microfilm begin p. 612. http://www.gizapyramids.org/view/diaries/asitem/search@/2/objectNumber-asc?t:state:flo, accessed 1/10/2014.

103 Reisner to Edgel, May 25, 1938. MFA, Reisner Papers, Box: 1927–1950, Folder 18 (1937–38). For the following observation on the Arabic press, see Reisner to Edgel, December 6, 1938.

104 The following account relies mainly on the summary in Lampson to
    Halifax, June 15, 1939. FO371/23354/J2487. Muhammad Husayn Haykal,
    Mudhakkirati fi al-siyasa al-misriya, v. 2 (Cairo: Matabaat dar al-maarif,
    1953): 122–25, circumspectly offers his own perspective.
105 Interview with Aziz Atiya, March 29, 1986, Salt Lake City.
106 Lampson to Halifax, June 15, 1939. FO371/23354/J2487.
107 Gady, "Pharaon," 978–79.
108 Minister of France, Cairo, to Bonnet, June 27, 1939. MAE, Ser-
    vice des oeuvres françaises á l'étranger, Série D-Levant, Carton 366:
    Égypte: Facultés égyptiennes et institut d'archéologie, Dossier: Institut
    d'archéologique.
109 Minister of France in Egypt to Daladier, 6 November 1939, in Service des
    oeuvres françaises à l'étranger, vol. 348. Reference kindly furnished by Éric
    Gady. See also Selim Hassan's pension folder in Dar al-Mahfuzat, Folder
    40146/ 3917/ 379/ 2.
110 Noblecourt, *Nubiade*, 101. On Dorothy Eady / Omm Sety (1904–81), see Bier-
    brier, *WWWE4*: 169, and the popular biography Jonathan Cott, *The Search
    for Omm Sety: A Story of Eternal Love* (Garden City, NY: Doubleday, 1987).
111 Gady, "Pharaon," 980–81.
112 Magnus Bernhardsson, *Reclaiming a Plundered Past: Archaeology and Nation
    Building in Modern Iraq* (Austin: University of Texas Press, 2005); Seton
    Lloyd, *Foundations in the Dust: The Story of Mesopotamian Exploration*. 2nd
    ed. (London: Thames & Hudson, 1980).
113 Rowe to ?, March 22, 1928; and Rowe to Joyne, April 22, 1931.University
    of Pennsylvania, University Museum Archives, Egypt, Meydum, Corre-
    spondence, Box 16, Folder 6: "Excavations in Palestine and Egypt."
114 Gady, "Pharaon," 840–41.
115 Reeves, *Great Discoveries*, 166; Gady, "Pharaon," 839–41. A new antiqui-
    ties law was not issued until October 31, 1951 (Law No. 215). It left
    the award of objects to the excavator to the discretion of Egyptian
    authorities, as had been the case since an administrative decision in 1923.
    Antoine Khater, *Le régime juridique des fouilles et des antiquités en Égypte*
    (Cairo: IFAO, 1960), 171.
116 Petrie, "Vale se Ave," *Ancient Egypt and the East*, Supplement (1935), 149.
117 Greg to Lloyd, November 20, 1936. UKNA/ BW 29/1, O.H. Myers had
    a last season at Armant for Mond, concentrating on Paleolithic tools on
    desert plateaus. *JEA*, Dec. 23, 1937: 262. Cf. the list of expeditions for
    1935–36 in Petrie's *Ancient Egypt and the East* Pt. 2 (Dec. 1935), 93–94.
118 Wilson, *Signs*, 194–95.
119 Cf. H.W. Winlock, "The Egyptian Expedition 1935–1936," *BMMA (Bul-
    letin of the MMA)* (1937), 1–3. Norman de Garis Davies and Harry Burton
    continued copying and photographing Theban tombs. Davies retired from
    fieldwork in 1939 and died in November 1941, *BMMA* 37, no. 2 (Feb.
    1942): 43. Burton died in Asyut hospital in June 1940 following three years
    of poor health, *BMMA* 35, no. 8 (Aug. 1940): 165–6.
120 John A. Wilson, *Thousands of Years: An Archaeologist's Search for Ancient Egypt*

(New York: Charles Scribner's Sons, 1972), 74–78.

121 Nancy Thomas, ed., *The American Discovery of Egypt: Essays* (Los Angeles: Los Angeles County Museum of Art and the American Research Center in Egypt, 1995), 55–56, 63–64, 66.

122 On Capart and the Belgians, see *Ceci n'est pas une pyramide: un siècle de recherche archéologique belge en Égypte* (Leuven: Peeters, 2012); Jean-Michel Bruffaerts, "Bruxelles, capital de l'égyptologie. Le rêve de Jean Capart (1947)," in *Ägyptologen und Ägyptologien*, Bickel et al., eds., 193–41; Jean Capart, *Fouilles en Égypte: El Kab: impressions et souvenirs* (Brussels: Fondation égyptologique Reine Élisabeth, 1946); Bierbrier, *WWWE4*: 103–104. On Michalowski, see Bierbrier, *WWWE4*: 371–72.

123 *JEA* 26 (Feb. 1941): 161. With French excavations at Tanis and Deir al-Medina suspended after the spring of 1940, A. Varille's work in the Montu enclosure at North Karnak (1940–43) was the only IFAO excavation until after the war.

124 Georges Goyon, *La découverte des trésors de Tanis: aventures archéologiques en Égypte* (Paris: Persea, 1987). On the shooting match, see pp. 136–37. On Goyon, see also Bierbrier, *WWWE4*: 219.

125 Goyon, *Découverte*, 120.

10. Pharaonism and Its Challengers, 1930s and 1940s

1 Tawfiq al-Hakim, *Return of the Spirit: Tawfiq al-Hakim's Classic Novel of the 1919 Revolution*, trans. William M. Hutchins (Washington, DC: Three Continents Press, 1990), 179, 272.

2 al-Hakim, *Return*, 272–73.

3 On al-Hakim, see William Maynard Hutchins, *Tawfiq al-Hakim, A Reader's Guide* (Boulder, CO: Lynne Rienner 2003); Richard Long, *Tawfiq al-Hakim, Playwright of Egypt* (London: Ithaca Press, 1973); Paul Starkey, *From the Ivory Tower: A Critical Study of Tawfiq al-Hakim* (London: Ithaca Press, 1978); Dina Amin, "Tawfiq al-Hakim," in *Essays in Arabic Literary Biography 1850–1950*, ed. Roger Allen (Wiesbaden: Harrassowitz, 2010), 98–113 ; and J. Brugman, *An Introduction to the History of Modern Arabic Literature in Egypt* (Leiden: Brill, 1984), 276–88. Birthdates cited for al-Hakim range from 1897 to 1903; 1898 is perhaps most likely.

4 M.M. Badawi, *Modern Arabic Drama in Egypt* (Cambridge: Cambridge University Press, 1987), 9, 10, and Amin, "Tawfiq al-Hakim," 103.

5 Translated into English as *The Maze of Justice*, by Audrey (later Abba) Eban (London: Harvill, 1947).

6 al-Hakim, *Return*, 86. Isis, the goddess who resurrected her murdered husband Osiris, or Isis-like women, figure in several of al-Hakim's works. Hutchins, *Tawfiq al-Hakim*, 27–29, 99–102.

7 The name "Fouquet" was probably inspired by Georges Foucart, the Egyptologist who directed IFAO at the time al-Hakim was writing the novel.

8 Dmitrii Mérezhkovskii, *Les mystères de l'orient: Égypte—Babylone* (Paris: L'artisan du livre, 1927), 109–11, as cited in al-Hakim, *Return*, 181.

9   Israel Gershoni, "An Intellectual Source for the Revolution: Tawfiq al-Hakim's Influence on Nasser and His Generation," in *Egypt from Monarchy to Republic: A Reassessment of Revolution and Change*, ed. Shimon Shamir, (Boulder, CO: Westview Press, 1995), 213–49.

10 Miriam Cooke, "Yahya Haqqi," in *Arabic Literary Biography, 1850–1950*, ed. Roger Allen: 121. See also her *Anatomy of an Egyptian Intellectual: Yahya Haqqi* (Washington, DC: Three Continents Press, 1984).

11 On Musa, see his autobiography *Tarbiyat Salama Musa*, translated by L.O. Schuman, *The Education of Salama Musa* (Leiden: Brill, 1961), based on the Arabic edition of 1947, with additions from the 1958 edition (the original prerevolutionary edition having been been censored). The standard biographical study is Vernon Egger, *A Fabian in Egypt: Salamah Musa and the Rise of the Professional Classes in Egypt, 1909–1939*, (Lanham, MD: University Press of America, 1986).

12 Omnia El Shakry, *The Great Social Laboratory: Subjects of Knowledge in Colonial and Postcolonial Egypt* (Stanford: Stanford University Press, 2007), 60.

13 On Grafton Elliot Smith and William James Perry, see Bierbrier, *WWWE4*: 515–16, 425–26.

14 Salama Musa, "Misr asl hadarat al-alam," *al-Majalla al-jadida* 1: 2 (Dec. 1929): 256, unpublished translation by Terri de Young.

15 For this and the following two paragraphs, see Musa, *Misr asl al-hadara* (Cairo: Matbaat al-majalla al-jadida, 1935), 4–10, 100.

16 Quoted in Yannis Hamilakis, *The Nation and Its Ruins: Antiquity, Archaeology, and National Imagination in Greece* (Oxford: Oxford University Press, 2007), 77.

17 Musa's mistake: the Washington Monument of Washington, DC, is of course a modern monument; the United States' ancient Egyptian obelisk is in Central Park, New York, behind the Metropolitan Museum of Art.

18 "Turath Misr al-qadima," special issue, *al-Muqtataf* (Cairo, September 1936).

19 *al-Majalla al-jadida*, (April 1938), 2, as translated in Israel Gershoni and James Jankowski, *Redefining the Egyptian Nation, 1930–1945* (Cambridge: Cambridge University Press, 1995), 77.

20 Egger, *Musa*, 222. On Musa's initial support and later criticism of Nazi Germany, see Israel Gershoni and James Jankowski, *Confronting Facism in Egypt: Dictatorship vs. Democracy in the 1930s* (Stanford: Stanford University Press, 2010), 125–31, 148–53.

21 B.L. Carter, *The Copts in Egyptian Politics* (London: Croom Helm, 1986), 98–99, 211, 296–97.

22 On "Easternism" in Egypt, see Gershoni and Jankowski, *Redefining the Egyptian Nation*, 35–53, and Donald M. Reid, *The Odyssey of Farah Antun: A Syrian Christian's Search for Secularism* (Minneapolis: Bibliotheca Islamica, 1975), 98–101.

23 On Islamism in Egypt in the 1920s, see Israel Gershoni and James Jankowski, *Egypt, Islam, and the Arabs: The Search for Egyptian Nationhood, 1900–1930* (New York: Oxford University Press, 1986), 55–74.

24 Gershoni and Jankowski, *Redefining the Egyptian Nation*, 62–63.

25 On the increased emphasis on Islam in Egyptian discourse in the 1930s, see

Gershoni and Jankowski, *Redefining the Egyptian Nation*, 54–78.

26 On Hassan al-Banna and the Muslim Brothers, see Richard Mitchell, *The Society of the Muslim Brothers* (London: Oxford University Press, 1969); Bynjar Lia, *The Society of the Muslim Brothers in Egypt: The Rise of an Islamic Movement 1928–1942* (Reading, UK: Ithaca Press, 1998); and Gudrun Krämer, *Hassan al-Banna* (Oxford: Oneworld, 2010). To emphasize the Egyptian specificity of Banna's original Muslim Brotherhood, Gershoni and Jankowksi, *Redefining the Egyptian Nation*, 79–96, refers to their movement as "Egyptian Islamic Nationalism."

27 Gershoni and Jankowski, *Redefining the Egyptian Nation*, 121. For the chapter on "Egyptian Arab Nationalism," see 117–42.

28 Gershoni and Jankowski, *Redefining the Egyptian Nation*, 118.

29 The "Black Book" was Makram Ubayd, *al-Kitab al-aswad fi-l-ahd al-aswad* (Cairo: Dar al-maarif, 1943); Goldschmidt, *Biographical Dictionary*, 217.

30 Gershoni and Jankowski, *Redefining the Egyptian Nation*, 147.

31 Gershoni and Jankowski, *Redefining the Egyptian Nation*, 121.

32 Gershoni and Jankowski, *Redefining the Egyptian Nation*, 27.

33 Gershoni and Jankowski, *Redefining the Egyptian Nation*, 28.

34 Gershoni and Jankowski, *Redefining the Egyptian Nation*, 28.

35 Gershoni and Jankowski, *Redefining the Egyptian Nation*, 28–31.

36 Abd al-Qadir Hamza Basha, *Ala hamish al-tarikh al-misri al-qadim* (Cairo: Matbaat dar al-kutub al-misriya, 1940), 5. For his biography, see Goldschmidt, *Biographical Dictionary*, 70–71.

37 Hamza, *Ala hamish*, 6, 11.

38 Gershoni and Jankowski, *Redefining the Egyptian Nation*, 78.

39 Donald Malcolm Reid, "Remembering and Forgetting Tutankhamun: Imperial and National Rhythms of Archaeology, 1922–1972," in William Caruthers, ed., *Histories of Egyptology: Interdisciplinary Measures*, (London: Routledge, 2014). Cf. T.G.H. James, *Howard Carter: The Path to Tutankhamun*, 2nd ed. (London: Kegan Paul International, 2001), 467.

40 *The Times*, April 15, 1939, 14; James, *Carter*, 465–66, 468–69.

41 James, *Carter*, 469–71.

42 For a recent review with insights on the long lull in Tutankhamun studies, see Marianne Eaton-Krauss, "Impact of the Discovery of KV 62," *KMT* 25, No. 1 (Spring 2014): 29–37.

43 James, *Carter*, xii.

44 J.M.A. Janssen, *Annual Egyptological Bibliography, Index 1945–1956* (Leiden: Brill, 1960).

45 John and Elizabeth Romer, *The Rape of Tutankhamun* (London: Michael O'Mara, 1994), 19.

46 *Standard Catalog of World Paper Money*, vol 2: *General Issues to 1960*. Colin R. Bruce and Albert Pick, eds. 8th ed., (Iola, WI: Krause Publications, 1996), "Egypt."

47 Robert Tignor, *State, Private Enterprise and Economic Change in Egypt, 1918–1952* (Princeton: Princeton University Press, 1984), 195.

48 *Scott 2012*, Egypt, #B12, 481, 601, 602, 616.
49 Mercedès Volait, "Architectures de la décennie pharaonique en Égypte (1922–1932)," in *Images d'Égypte de la fresque à la bande dessinée* (Cairo, CEDEJ, 1991), 163–86.
50 Mercedès Volait, *Architectes et architectures de l'Égypte moderne (1830–1950): genèse et essor d'une expertise locale* (Paris: Maisonneuve et Larose, 2005), 418.
51 On Zaghlul's tomb, see Ralph M. Coury, "The Politics of the Funereal: The Tomb of Saad Zaghlul," *JARCE* 29 (1992): 191–200, and Volait, "Architectures," 169–73.
52 Gershoni and Jankowski, *Commemorating the Nation*, 87–102, studies the creation and reception of Mukhtar's monumental Cairo and Alexandria statues of Zaghlul.
53 Jardin to Sec. State, December 23, 1931. Sharif Pasha, Muhammad Abduh, Mustafa Kamil, and Abd al-Khaliq Tharwat were proposed. USNA, Records of the Dept. of State relating to Internal Affairs of Eg, 1930–39, Decimal File 883, Microfilm Publications T 1251, Roll 1, W.M.
54 Volait, "Architectures," 177, 182.
55 Volait, "Architectures," 169–73, 177.
56 Gershoni and Jankowski, *Commemorating the Nation*, 106–108; Galila El Kadi and Alain Bonnamy, *Architecture for the Dead: Cairo's Medieval Necropolis* (Cairo: American University in Cairo Press, 2007), 196, 233.
57 Doaa El-Bey, "Mansour Farag: A Hand in History," *Al-Ahram Weekly*, May 18–24, 1995, 16.
58 Gershoni and Jankowski, *Commemorating the Nation*, 87–102.
59 Gershoni and Jankowski, *Commemorating the Nation*, 157–58, 181–224.
60 Gershoni and Jankowski, *Egypt, Islam and the Arabs*, 183.
61 Gershoni and Jankowski, *Egypt, Islam and the Arabs*, 174.
62 Gershoni and Jankowski, *Egypt, Islam and the Arabs*, 175.
63 Gershoni and Jankowski, *Redefining the Egyptian Nation*, 97–116. Their chapter draws on James Jankowski, *Egypt's Young Rebels: "Young Egypt:" 1933–1952* (Stanford: Stanford University Press, 1975).
64 Volait, "Architectures," 173–76.
65 Jankowksi, *Egypt's Young Rebels*, 13.
66 Jankowksi, *Egypt's Young Rebels*, 15, 18, 80, 92.
67 Nancy Y. Reynolds, "National Socks and the 'Nylon Woman:' Materiality, Gender, and Nationalism in Textile Marketing in Semicolonial Egypt, 1930–56," *IJMES* 43 (2011): 56–58.
68 Eric Davis, *Challenging Colonialism: Bank Misr and Egyptian Industrialization, 1920–1941* (Princeton: Princeton University Press, 1983), 155–56.
69 Wilson Chacko Jacob, *Working Out Egypt: Effendi Masculinity and Subject Formation in Colonial Modernity, 1870–1940* (Durham: Duke University Press, 2011).
70 Jacob, *Working Out Egypt*, 119–20. That ancient Egyptian women were often bare-breasted in ancient depictions rarely seems to have entered the discussion.
71 Gershoni and Jankowski, *Redefining the Egyptian Nation*, 109–10.

72 Gershoni and Jankowski, *Redefining the Egyptian Nation*, 102.

73 Gershoni and Jankowski, *Redefining the Egyptian Nation*, 102–05.

74 Jankowski, *Egypt's Young Rebels*, 80, 92.

75 Jankowski, *Egypt's Young Rebels*, 121.

76 Ahmad Husayn, *Mawsuat tarikh Misr* (Cairo: Dar al-shab, 1972).

77 Brugman, *Modern Arabic Literature*, 291, 297–98.

78 Brugman, *Modern Arabic Literature*, 290–91, 298; Raymond T. Stock, "A Mummy Awakens: The Pharaonic Fiction of Naguib Mahfouz," (PhD diss., University of Pennsylvania, 2008), 22.

79 Brugman, *Modern Arabic Literature*, 315–20.

80 Brugman, *Modern Arabic Literature*, 173–84.

81 Stock, "A Mummy Awakens," is the fundamental work on Mahfouz's pharaonism. See also, Matti Moosa, *The Early Novels of Naguib Mahfouz: Images of Modern Egypt* (Gainesville, FL: University Press of Florida, 1994).

82 Stock, "A Mummy Awakens," 48.

83 Stock, "A Mummy Awakens," 60.

84 J. Jomier, "Les Coptes," in *L'Égypte d'aujourd'hui: permanence et changements 1805–1976*, ed. M.C. Aulas et al. (Paris, 1977), 82.

85 Stock, "A Mummy Awakens," 64–65.

86 Stock, "A Mummy Awakens," 153.

87 Stock, "A Mummy Awakens," 109–122.

88 Elliot Colla, *Conflicted Antiquities: Egyptology, Egyptomania, Egyptian Modernity* (Durham, NC: Duke University Press, 2007), 223; Stock, "A Mummy Awakens," 117–18.

89 Stock, "A Mummy Awakens," 160, 184. Naguib Mahfouz, *Before the Throne*, trans. Raymond Stock (Cairo: American University in Cairo Press, 2009), and Mahfouz, *Akhenaten: Dweller in Truth*, trans. Tagried Abu-Hassabo (Cairo: American University in Cairo Press, 2001).

90 Stock, "A Mummy Awakens," 114, 189, 204. On racial overtones in *Kifah Tiba*, see also Colla, *Conflicted Antiquities*, 257–60.

91 Stock, "A Mummy Awakens," 246–314.

92 See Colla's chapter "Pharaonism after Pharaonism: Mahfouz and Qutb," in his *Conflicted Antiquities*, 234–72. Recent studies of Qutb include John Calvert, *Sayyid Qutb and the Origins of Radical Islam* (New York: Columbia University Press, 2010), and James Toth, *Sayyid Qutb: The Life and Legacy of a Racial Islamic Intellectual* (Oxford: Oxford University Press, 2013).

93 Stock, "A Mummy Awakens," 206.

94 Colla, *Conflicted Antiquities*, 248.

95 The metaphor is Colla's: *Conflicted Antiquities*, 268.

96 Gershoni and Jankowski, *Redefining the Egyptian Nation*, 115–19.

97 Calculated from an unpublished list covering 1886–1949. Compiled by a research assistant for Paula Sanders, who kindly shared it with me. The list may well be incomplete.

98 Nicholas Reeves, *Ancient Egypt: The Great Discoveries: A Year-by-Year Chronicle* (London: Thames & Hudson, 2000), 195, 198–200.

99 Volait, "Architectures," 182.

100 It was designed by Kamal Ismail (1908–?) of the Royal Buildings Service. The son of the *umda* of Mit Ghamr, Daqahaliya, he graduated in architecture from the School of Engineering in 1927. In 1934 he earned a doctorate from the École des Beaux Arts, Paris. In the 1980s and 1990s, he played a major role in making over the enclosures of the Kaaba in Mecca and the mosque of the Prophet in Medina. Aziza Sami, "Kamal Ismail: Making Monuments," *Al-Ahram Weekly*, July 25–31, 1996, 14.

101 Harant Kashishiyan, ed., *Iskandar Sarukhan, Nabdha an hayatihi wa fannihi wa injazatihi* (Cairo: Jamiyat al-Qahira al-khayriya al-armaniya al-amma, 1998), 110. See also Ameera Fouad, "Saroukhan, All But Forgotten," *Al-Ahram Weekly*, Oct. 25–Nov. 1, 2012.

102 "Barnamij," *al-Katib al Misri*, 1: 1 (Oct. 1945): 1–25; Iskandar Asad, "Timsal al-katib al-misri," 1 (1945–46): 582–84.

103 On Badawi and Kees, see Bierbrier, *WWWE4*: 31–32, 290–91.

104 Gershoni and Jankowski, *Redefining the Egyptian Nation*, 108.

105 *The Unity of the Nile Valley: Its Geographical Bases and Its Manifestations in History* (Cairo: Egyptian Kingdom, Presidency of Council of Ministers, Government Press, 1947). The contributors included modern historian Shafiq Ghurbal, Egyptologist Ahmad Badawi, Greco–Roman historian Ibrahim Noshy, geographer Abbas Mustafa Ammar, and director of the Military Museum, Lt. Col. Abd al-Rahman Zaki. See the analysis in El Shakry, *Great Social Laboratory*, 74–81.

106 *Scott 2012*, Egypt, #296–98. Existing stamp stocks were overprinted, in Arabic only, "King of Egypt and the Sudan": #299–316.

107 Eve Troutt Powell, *A Different Shade of Colonialism: Egypt, Great Britain, and the Mastery of the Sudan* (Berkeley: University of California Press, 2003).

108 Cooke, *Haqqi*, 63.

11. Egyptology, 1939–52

1 John Darwin, *The Empire Project: The Rise and Fall of the British World-System, 1830-1970* (Cambridge: Cambridge University Press, 2009), 523–25. See George Kirk, *The Middle East in the War* (London: Oxford University Press, 1952), for a near-contemporary overview of World War II in Egypt and its neighbors.

2 Israel Gershoni and James Jankowski, *Confronting Fascism in Egypt: Dictatorship vs. Democracy in the 1930s* (Stanford: Stanford University Press, 2010).

3 Artemis Cooper, *Cairo in the War 1939–1945* (London: H. Hamilton, 1989), 223–26.

4 Darwin, *Empire Project*, 516.

5 Thomas Schneider, "Ägyptologen im Dritten Reich," *Journal of Egyptian History* 4, no. 2 (Fall 2011): 105–216.

6 Éric Gady, "Le pharaon, l'égyptologue et le diplomate. les égyptologues français en Égypte, du voyage de Champollion à la crise de Suez (1828–1956)," (2 vols., PhD diss., Université de Paris IV-Sorbonne, 2005), 985, 986.

7 Gady, "Pharaon," 985; Christiane Desroches Noblecourt, *La grande nubiade ou le parcours d'une égyptologue* (Paris: Stock/Pernoud, 1997), 61, 79.

8   Pierre Montet, *La nécropole royale de Tanis*, 3 vols. (Paris: Uden forlag, 1947–60); Gady, "Pharaon," 986–89, 1018–20; Nicholas Reeves, *Ancient Egypt: The Great Discoveries: A Year-by-Year Chronicle* (London: Thames & Hudson, 2000), 189–93.

9   Noblecourt, *Nubiade*, 88–95.

10   Robert Solé, *L'Égypte, passion française* (Paris: Seuil, 1997), 260.

11   Solé, *L'Égypte*, 260–61.

12   Gady, "Pharaon," 1014–1015.

13   Bierbier, *WWWE4*, 552–53.

14   Noblecourt, *Nubiade*, 102.

15   Gady, "Pharaon," 989–993, 1007–1008.

16   Bierbier, *WWWE4*, 321.

17   DWQ, Abidin, no. 296: Taqarir an matahif wa-l-athar, Ministerial decree 5469, Muhammad Husayn Haykal.

18   Fairman to Gardiner, December 27, 1941. FO371/31585/J678.

19   Gady, "Pharaon," 996, 1000.

20   Fairman to Miss Keeves, November 7, 1949. EES, Unmarked folder on Amarna 1947–1948.

21   Lampson to Eden, May 7, 1942, enclosing Fairman to Smart, April 23, 1942, and Engelbach's May 1, 1942 comments on Fairman's note. FO371/ 31585/ J2493.

22   Gady, "Pharaon," 997–1001. Gady cites one source saying that Hamza became director of the museum in 1941 (as does Bierbrier, *WWWE4*, 241) but notes that FO correspondence implies that it was 1942. On Fairman (1907–82), see Bierbrier, *WWWE4*, 185–86.

23   Fairman to Gardiner, December 27, 1941. FO371/31585/J678.

24   Emily Rosenberg, *Spreading the American Dream: American Economic and Cultural Expansion, 1890–1945* (New York: Hill & Wang, 1982), 204–208.

25   Jamiat Fuad al-Awwal, *al-Kitab al-fiddi li-kulliyat al-adab 1925–1950* (Cairo: Matbaat Jamiat Fuad al-Awwal, 1951), 49. On Glanville (1900–1956), see Bierbrier, *WWWE4*, 214.

26   Macdermot to Smart, July 22, 1947. FO141/ 1171.

27   Montgu-Pollock to Smart, May 16, 1947; Furness to Smart, February 7, 1947; Scrivener to Smart, January 25, 1947; Macdermot to Smart, July 22, 1947. FO141/1171.

28   Reeves, *Great Discoveries*, 195–204.

29   Darwin, *Empire Project*, 531–40. P.J. Cain and A.G. Hopkins, *British Imperialism, 1688–2000*, 2nd ed. (Harlow, UK: Longman, 2001), 624–25.

30   Peter Hahn, *The United States, Great Britain, and Egypt, 1945–1956: Strategy and Diplomacy in the Early Cold War* (Chapel Hill, NC: University of North Carolina Press, 1991); William Roger Louis, *The British Empire in the Middle East, 1945–1951: Arab Nationalism, the United States, and Postwar Imperialism* (Oxford: Clarendon Press, 1984).

31   Donald C. Meade, *Growth and Structural Change in the Egyptian Economy* (Homewood, IL: R.D. Irwin, 1967), 400–01.

32   In 1948 *Orientalia* reviewed excavation activities in Egypt since 1939 and

began an annual survey of archaeological fieldwork: Ursula Schweiter, "Archälogischer Bericht aus Ägypten," *Orientalia* 17, Nova Series (1948): 262–68, 387–89, 536–45, etc. Three years later, Jean Leclant took over this annual survey for *Orientalia*.

33 Fairman to Gardiner, June 3, 1942, encl. in Gardiner to Gaselee. FO371/31585/J3014.

34 Gady, "Pharaon," 1027, 1173.

35 John A. Wilson, *Thousands of Years: An Archaeologist's Search for Ancient Egypt* (New York: Charles Scribner's Sons, 1972), 80–83.

36 Dows Dunham, *Recollections of an Egyptologist* (Boston: Museum of Fine Arts, 1972).

37 Dows Dunham to G.H. Edgell, October 25, 1946. MFA, Box: Egyptian Department 1943–54, Folder 8/9 (folder 8 out of 9). On Dunham's 1946–47 mission, see also Dunham, *Recollections*, 37–44.

38 EES, Correspondence, Box: AH Gardiner 1937–1949, Folder: Gardiner to the Secretary 1939–1949, Gardiner to the Secretary (Miss W.A. Keeves), May 28, 1943; T.G.H. James, *Excavating in Egypt: The Egypt Exploration Society 1882–1982*, (Chicago: University of Chicago Press, 1982), 6.

39 For this paragraph and its quotations, see MFA, Box: Egyptian Department, 1943–54, Folder 9, unaddressed form letter by John A. Wilson, June 28, 1948.

40 Smithsonian Institution Archives, Accession no. 94–118: records of the American Research Center in Egypt, Box 13, and the retrospective in Box 21, Folder 5: Smith, Ray, William Stevenson Smith to Ray Winfield Smith, US Embassy, Cairo, March 23, 1965, 1–2. ARCE's *Newsletter*s, beginning in typed format on May 15, 1951, are also a rich source.

41 For this and the following paragraph, see Bernard V. Bothmer, *Egypt 1950: My First Visit*, ed. Emma Swan Hall (Oxford: Oxbow Books, 2003). On Bothmer, see Bierbrier, *WWWE4*: 72–73.

42 Georg Steindorff to John A. Wilson, June 1945, reproduced in Schneider, "Ägyptologen im Dritten Reich," *Journal of Egyptian History* 4, no. 2 (Fall 2011): 130.

43 Bothmer, *Egypt 1950*, 63.

44 Bothmer, *Egypt 1950*, 137.

45 Bothmer, *Egypt 1950*, 110.

46 Claudine Le Tourneur d'Ison, *Lauer et Sakkara* (Paris: Tallander, Historia, 2000); Georges Goyon, *La découverte des trésors de Tanis: aventures archéologiques en Égypte* (Paris: Persea, 1987). On Goyon (1905–96), see Bierbrier, *WWWE4*: 219.

47 Gady, "Pharaon," 986–89, 1018–20.

48 Gady, "Pharaon," 1022–23.

49 Selim Hassan, *Misr al-qadima*, 2nd ed. (Cairo: al-Haya al-misriya al-amma lil-kitab, 1992), vol. 1, dedication following title page.

50 Selim Hassan, *Excavations at Saqqara 1937–8*, ed. Zaki Iskandar, 3 vols. (Cairo: Department of Antiquities, 1975).

51 Reeves, *Great Discoveries*, 166.

52 Bierbrier, *WWWE4*: 169, and Jonathan Cott, *The Search for Omm Sety: A*

Story of Eternal Love (Garden City, NY: Doubleday, 1987).

53 Sami Gabra, *Chez les derniers adorateurs de Trismegiste: la nécropole d'Hermopolis Touna El Gebel (Souvenir d'un archéologue)* (Cairo: al-Haya al-misriya al-amma, 1971).

54 Wilson, *Thousands of Years*, 122. See also *Orientalia* 17, New Series (1948): 126; *Chronique d'Égypte*, 23, nos. 45–46 (April 1948): 102–105; William Edward Carruthers, "Egyptology, Archaeology and the Making of Revolutionary Egypt, c. 1925–1958." (PhD diss., Darwin College, University of Cambridge, 2014), 146–48.

55 Jean-Michel Bruffaerts, "Bruxelles, capital de l'égyptologie. Le rêve de Jean Capart (1947)," in Susanne *Ägyptologen und Ägyptologien zwischen Kaiserreich und Gründung der beiden Staaten. . . .*, Bickel et al., eds., Beiheft 1 (Berlin, 2013), 237.

56 Jamiat al-Qahira, Kulliyat al-athar, *al-Dalil al-dhahabi lil-asatidha wa khariji al-athar, Jamiat al-Qahira mundhu sanat 1925* (Cairo: al-Haya al-misriya al-amma lil-kitab, 1975), 62.

57 All except Rizqana (Rizkana) are listed in Bierbrier, *WWWE4*. Rizqana earned an Egyptology diploma from the Institute of Archaeology, but like his mentor Mustafa Amer took his doctorate in geography and specialized in prehistoric archaeology rather than Egyptology: Jamiat al-Qahira, *al-Athar al-ilmiya li-ada hayat al-tadris bi-Jamiat al-Qahira*, (Cairo, 1958), 39.

58 Abdel-Moneim Abu-Bakr, *Excavations at Giza 1949–1950*. The University of Alexandria, Faculty of Arts (Cairo: Govt. Press, 1953). On Abu Bakr, see Bierbrier, *WWWE4*: 4–5.

59 Jamiat al-Qahira, *al-Dalil al-dhahabi*, 10–15.

60 Jill Kamil, *Labib Habachi: The Life and Legacy of an Egyptologist* (Cairo: American University in Cairo Press, 2007). For a comparison of the two careers, see 177–87. On Fakhry, see also Bierbrier, *WWWE4*: 186–87.

61 Kamil, *Habachi*, 63–64.

62 Kamil, *Habachi*, 73–77, 169.

63 Kamil, *Habachi*, 95–175.

64 Reeves, *Great Discoveries*, 192.

65 Farouk resthouse website, http://www.tawy.nl/EN_dh_Farouk_resthouse.html.

66 Mercedes Volait, "Architectures de la décennie pharaonique en Égypte (1922–1932)," in *Images d'Égypte de la fresque à la bande dessinée*, ed. Jean-Claude Vatin, (Cairo: CEDEJ: IFAO, 1991), 182–83.

67 Major Mahmoud El-Gawhary, *Ex-Royal Palaces in Egypt from Mohamed Aly to Farouk* (Cairo: Dar al-maarif, 1954), 111–18.

68 Claudine Tourneur d'Isson, *Une passion égyptienne: Jean-Philippe et Marguertie Lauer* (Paris: Plon, 1996), 168; Georges Goyon, *Les inscriptions et graffiti des voyageurs sur la grande pyramide* (Cairo: Société royale de géographie, 1944).

69 Fairman to Gardiner, December 27, 1941. FO 371/31585/J678.

70 Lampson, March 20, 1942. FO371/31585/J1626.

71 Zaki Youssef Saad, *Royal Excavations at Helwan (1945–1947)*, Supplément

aux *ASAE*, Cahier 14, (Cairo: IFAO, 1951).

72 Zaki Youssef Saad, *Royal Excavations at Saqqara and Helwan (1941–1945)*, Supplément aux annales du service des antiquités, 3 (Cairo: IFAO, 1947); Saad, *Royal Excavations at Helwan (1945–1947)*, x.

73 Carruthers, "Egyptology," 38–39, argues that E. Christiana Köhler's interpretation of Saad's royal associations being a liability after the revolution underestimates continuity in state technocracy despite the political turnover. See also E. Christiana Köhler, "Zaki Y. Saad (1901–1982): A Life for Archaeology," *Archeo-Nil* 17: 107–14.

74 *Unas, aw al-shams al-ghariba* [Unas, or The Setting Sun] (Cairo: Matbaat lajnat al-talif wa-l-tarjama wa-l-nashr, 1958).

75 Interview with Dia Abou-Ghazi, Cairo, 12 January 1999. Habachi was pressured into resigning from the Service in 1960: see Kamil, *Habachi*, 205–07.

76 On Saad, see Bierbrier, *WWWE4*: 481. For later work on Saad's Helwan diary and seventy boxes of excavated material, see E. Christiana Köhler, *The Cairo Museum Collection of Artefacts from Zaki Saad's Excavations at Helwan*. Lecture at Armidale, (University of New England, New South Wales, Australia, November 1, 2004); Ali Radwan, "The National Museum of Egyptian Civilization: Samples from the Helwan Collection," *ASAE* 78 (2004): 211–21.

77 Gady, "Pharaon," 1027–9. Alan Rowe, conservator of the Greco–Roman Museum, stayed until 1949, but its administration had not yet been incorporated into the Antiquities Service. Dorothy Eady had become an Egyptian citizen after marrying an Egyptian in 1933.

78 Gady, "Pharaon," 1173, reports that Louis Christophe was editorial secretary of the *ASAE* from 1950 to 1955.

79 Gady, "Pharaon," 1025–28.

80 Varille attributed his dismissal to minister of education Taha Hussein's displeasure at an article he had published. Gady, "Pharaon," 1029–30. For the rest of this paragraph, see 1171–73.

81 *Scott 2012*, Egypt #C5–25, C34–37.

82 *Scott 2012*, Egypt #220–22, 225–27, 273–76.

83 *Scott 2012*, Egypt #B9–B12.

84 *Scott 2012*, Egypt #273–76.

85 *Scott 2012*, Egypt #277.

86 Yannis Hamilakis, *The Nation and Its Ruins: Antiquity, Archaeology, and National Imagination in Greece* (Oxford: Oxford University Press, 2007), 27, 115–16, 292.

87 Wizarat al-maarif al-umumiya, *Mathaf al-hadara al-misriya 1949* (Cairo: Matbaat wizarat al-maarif al-umumiya, 1949); "al-Mathaf al-Hadara al-Misriya," *al-Hilal* 53, no. 4 (September 1945): 517–24.

88 Prehistory: Sulayman Huzayin, Mustafa Amer, and Ibrahim Rizqana; Pharaonic: É. Drioton and Muharram Kamal; Greco–Roman: Pierre Jouguet, Sami Gabra, and Ibrahim Noshy; Coptic: Gaston Wiet, Togo Mina, and Mirrit Boutros Ghali; Arab: G. Wiet and Hassan Abd al-Wahhab;

Ottoman: Col. Abd al-Rahman Zaki and Wiet; Modern: Shafiq Ghurbal, Georges Douin, Muhammad Rifat, and Col. Zaki. This roughly echoes the framework used in Egyptian history textbooks from the 1920s to midcentury.

89 On Ghorbal and his school, see Yoav Di-Capua, *Gatekeepers of the Arab Past: Historians and History Writing in Twentieth-Century Egypt* (Berkeley: University of California Press, 2009), 186–218; Anthony Gorman, *Historians, State and Politics in Twentieth-Century Egypt: Contesting the Nation* (London: RoutledgeCurzon, 2003), 22–25.

90 National Museum of Egyptian Civilization (NMEC), http://www.nmed.gov.eg, accessed 1/13/2014.

91 Robert Tignor, *State, Private Enterprise and Economic Change in Egypt, 1918–1952* (Princeton: Princeton University Press, 1984), 197, 274–75.

92 On Taha Hussein and the IFAO crisis, see Gady, "Pharaon," 1031–38.

93 Antoine Khater, *Le régime juridique des fouilles et des antiquités en Égypte* (Cairo: IFAO, 1960).

94 Gady, "Pharaon," 1034–35.

95 Geoffrey Aronson, *From Sideshow to Center Stage: U.S. Policy toward Egypt 1946–1956* (Boulder, CO: Lynne Rienner, 1986), 25–32.

96 Claudine Le Tourneur D'Ison, *Une passion égyptienne: Jean-Philippe et Marguertie Lauer* (Paris: Plon, 1996). 193–94. Lauer mistakenly recalled the day as Thursday, not Saturday.

97 On the January 26, 1952 riots, see Nancy Y. Reynolds, *A City Consumed: Urban Commerce, the Cairo Fire, and the Politics of Decolonization in Egypt* (Stanford: Stanford University Press, 2012), 181–201; Anne-Claire Kerboeuf, "The Cairo Fire of 26 January 1952 and the Interpretations of History," in *Re-envisioning Egypt 1919–1952*, ed. Arthur Goldschmidt Jr., Amy J. Johnson, and Barak A. Salmoni (Cairo: American University in Cairo Press, 2005), 194–216.

12. Conclusion

1 *Scott 2012*, Egypt #234–38, 267–69.

2 A year later in 1958, Egypt's joining Syria in the United Arab Republic wiped the very name Egypt off the coins and stamps for some years. The eagle of Saladin replaced the Sphinx on the coins. After the pan-Arab enthusiasm of the 1960s, pharaonism and Egyptocentrism reemerged under Sadat. Yet at the same time, these were also the years of rising Islamism.

3 Abd al-Rahman al-Rafii, *Tarikh al-haraka al-qawmiya fi Misr al-qadima: min fajr al-tarikh ila al-fath al-arabi* (Cairo: Maktabat al-nahda al-misriya, 1963).

4 "Mahfouz on Mahfouz," *Al-Ahram Weekly*, August 31–September 6, 2006, quoting an interview with Mahfouz by Raja Naqqash: Naguib Mahfouz and Raja Naqqash: *Naguib Mahfouz: safahat min mudhakkiratihi wa adwa jadida ala adabihi wa hayatihi* (Cairo: Markaz al-Ahram lil-tarjama wa-l-nashr, 1998).

Selected Bibliography

Published Works

Abbas, Raouf. *Jamaat al-nahda al-qawmiya*. Cairo: Dar al-fikr, 1986.

Abd al-Majid, Ibrahim. *Nobody Sleeps in Alexandria*. Translated by Farouk Abdel Wahab. Cairo: American University in Cairo Press, 1999.

Aboudi, Mohamed. *Aboudi's Guide Book to the Antiquities of Upper Egypt and Nubia*. Cairo: Sarafowsky, 1931. (Title and publisher vary in later editions, e.g. *Aboudi's Guide Book to the Antiquities of Egypt...* Cairo: Costa Tsoumas, 1954.)

Abou-Ghazi, Dia. "Vie." In *Pages from the Excavations at Saqqara and Mit Rahinah*, by Ahmad M. Badawi, 7–24. Vies et travaux 4. Cairo: Organisation des antiquités de l'Égypte, Service des musées: Dar al-maarif, 1984.

Abou-Ghazi, Dia Mahmoud, and Imad al-Din Abou Ghazi. *Ali Bahgat: 1858–1924*. Cairo, 1974.

Abou-Ghazi, Dia, and Ramadan el-Sayed, eds. *Sami Gabra from Tasa to Touna*. Vies et travaux 2. Cairo: Organisation des antiquités de l'Égypte, Service des musées: Dar al-maarif, 1984.

Abt, Jeffrey. *American Egyptologist: The Life of James Henry Breasted and the Creation of His Oriental Institute*. Chicago: University of Chicago Press, 2011.

Abu Ghazi, Badr al-Din. *al-Maththal Mukhtar*. Cairo: Dar al-qawmiya lil-tibaa wa-l-nashr, 1964.

Abu El-Haj, Nadia. *Facts on the Ground: Archaeological Practice and Territorial Self-Fashioning in Israeli Society*. Chicago: University of Chicago Press, 2001.

Abu-Lughod, Ibrahim. *The Arab Rediscovery of Europe: A Study in Cultural Encounters*. Princeton: Princeton University Press, 1963.

Abu Shadi, Ahmad Zaki. *Watan al-faraina: mutul min al-shir al-qawmi*. Cairo: al-Matbaa al-salafiya, 1926.

Adams, John M. *The Millionaire and the Mummies: Theodore Davis's Gilded Age in the Valley of the Kings*. New York: St. Martin's Press, 2013.

Afifi, Muhammad. *al-Aqbat fi Misr fi-l-asr al-uthmani*. Cairo: al-Haya al-misriya al-amma lil-kitab, 1992.

Al-Ahram.

Al-Ahram Weekly.

Allen, Roger, ed. *Essays in Arabic Literary Biography 1850–1950.* Wiesbaden: Harrassowitz, 2010.

AlSayyad, Nezar, Irene A. Bierman, Nasser Rabbat, eds. *Making Cairo Medieval.* Lanham, MD: Lexington Books, 2005.

American Express Company. *Promises to Pay: The Story of American Express.* New York: American Express Co., 1997.

Ambridge, Lindsay. "Imperialism and Racial Geography in James Henry Breasted's 'Ancient Times: A History of the Early World.'" *The Journal of Egyptian History* 4, no. 2 (Fall 2011): 12–33.

Amico, Leonard N. *The Mural Decorations of Edwin Howland Blashfield (1848–1936).* Williamstown MA: The Sterling and Francine Clark Art Institute, 1978.

Ammar, Abbas Mustafa, et al. *The Unity of the Nile Valley: Its Geographical Bases and Its Manifestations in History.* Cairo: Egyptian Kingdom, Presidency of Council of Ministers: Government Press, 1947.

Ancient Egypt. London. Magazine issued by British School of Archaeology in Egypt (Flinders Petrie), 1913-17, 1920-32. Continued as *Ancient Egypt and the East,* 1933-35.

Anderson, Benedict. *Imagined Communities: Reflections on the Origin and Spread of Nationalism.* 2nd ed. London: Verso, 1991.

Anderson, Betty S. *The American University of Beirut: Arab Nationalism and Liberal Education.* Austin: University of Texas Press, 2011.

Annales du service des antiquités de l'Égypte (ASAE).

Armanios, Febe. *Coptic Christianity in Ottoman Egypt.* Oxford: Oxford University Press, 2011.

Arndt, Richard T. *The First Resort of Kings: American Cultural Diplomacy in the Twentieth Century.* Dulles, VA: Potomac Books, 2005.

Arnold, Dorothea. "The Metropolitan Museum of Art's Work at the Middle Kingdom Sites of Thebes and Lisht." In *The American Discovery of Ancient Egypt: Essays,* edited by Nancy Thomas, 57–77. Los Angeles: Los Angeles County Museum of Art and the American Research Center in Egypt, 1995.

Aronson, Geoffrey. *From Sideshow to Center Stage: U.S. Policy toward Egypt, 1946–1956.* Boulder, CO: Lynne Rienner, 1986.

Badran, Margot. *Feminists, Islam, and Nation: Gender and the Making of Modern Egypt.* Princeton: Princeton University Press, 1995.

Badawi, Ahmad M., *Pages from the Excavations at Saqqarah and Mit Rahinah.* Vies et travaux 4. Cairo: Organisation des antiquités de l'Égypte, Service des musées: Dar al-maarif, 1984.

Baedeker, Karl. *Egypt and the Sudan.* 6th, 7th, and 8th eds. Leipzig: Baedeker, 1908, 1911, 1929. 8th ed. reprint, London: David & Charles: Hipocrene, 1985.

Bagnall, Roger S., ed. *Egypt in Late Antiquity.* Princeton: Princeton University Press, 1993.

———. *Egypt in the Byzantine World, 300–700.* Cambridge: Cambridge University Press, 2007.

————, ed. *The Oxford Handbook of Papyrology*. Oxford: Oxford University Press, 2009.

Bahgat Bey, Ali, and Albert Gabriel. *Fouilles d' Al Foustât*. Musée national de l'art arabe. Paris: E. de Boccard, 1921.

Bahr, Samira. *al-Aqbat fi-l-haya al-siyasiya al-misriya*. Cairo: Maktabat al-anjilu al-misriya, 1984.

Bahrani, Zainab, Zeynep Çelik, and Edhem Eldem, eds. *Scramble for the Past: A Story of Archaeology in the Ottoman Empire, 1753–1914*. Istanbul: SALT, 2001.

Balboni, L.A. *Gl'Italiani nella civiltà egiziana del secolo XIX*. 3 vols. Alexandria, 1906.

Ball, John. *Egypt in the Classical Geographers*. Cairo: Government Press, Bulaq, 1942.

Baraka, Magda. *The Egyptian Upper Class between Revolutions 1919–1952*. Reading, UK: Ithaca Press, 1998.

Baram, Uzi, and Lynda Carroll, eds. *A Historical Archaeology of the Ottoman Empire: Breaking New Ground*. New York: Kluwer Academic/Plenum, 2000.

Baron, Beth. *Egypt as a Woman: Nationalists, Gender and Politics*. Berkeley: University of California Press, 2005.

————. *The Women's Awakening in Egypt: Culture, Society, and the Press*. New Haven: Yale University Press, 1994.

Bastianini, Gido, and Rosario Pintaudi. "Acquisitions and Excavations by the Società Italiana per la Recerca di Papiri Greci e Latini in Egypt." In *One Hundred Years in Egypt: Paths of Italian Archeology*, edited by Maria Casini, 163–69. Istituto italiano di cultura per la R.A.U. Milan: Electa, 2001.

Baud, Marcelle. *Égypte*. Les guides bleus. Paris: Hachette, 1950.

Bavay, Laurent, et al. *Ceci n'est pas une pyramide…:un siècle de recherche archéologique belge en Égypte*. Leuven: Peeters, 2012.

Behrens-Abouseif, Doris. *Die Kopten in der ägyptischen Gesellschaft—von der Mitte des 19. Jahrhunderts bis 1923*. Freiburg im Breisgau: K. Schwartz, 1972.

Begg, D.J. Ian. "Fascism in the Desert: A Microcosmic View of Archaeological Politics." In *Archaeology under Dictatorship*, edited by Michael L. Galaty and Charles Walkinson, 19–31. New York: Kulwer Academic/Plenum, 2004.

Bernal, Martin. *Black Athena: the Afroasiatic Roots of Classical Civilization*. 3 vols. London: Free Association Books, 1987–2006.

Bernhardsson, Magnus. *Reclaiming a Plundered Past: Archaeology and Nation Building in Modern Iraq*. Austin: University of Texas Press, 2005.

Berque, Jacques. *Egypt: Imperialism and Revolution*. London: Faber, 1972.

Bickel, Susanne, et al., eds. *Ägyptologen und Ägyptologien zwischen Kaiserreich und Gründen der beiden deutschen Staaten: Reflexionen zur Geschichte und Episteme eines altertumswissenschaftlichen Fachs im 150. Jahr der Zeitschrift für Ägyptische Sprache und Alteretumskunde*. Beiheft 1. Berlin: Akademie Verlag Berlin: de Gruyter, 2013.

Bierbrier, M.L., ed. *Who Was Who in Egyptology?* 4th ed. London: Egypt Exploration Society, 2012. (See also the 3rd ed., edited by M. L. Bierbrier, 1995; 2nd ed., edited by Eric P. Uphill, 1972; and 1st ed., edited by Warren R. Dawson, 1951.)

al-Bishri, Tariq. *al-Muslimun wa-l-aqbat fi itar al-jamaat al-wataniya.* Cairo: al-Haya al-misriya al-amma lil-kitab, 1982.

Bonacasa, Nicola. "The Work of Italian Archaeologists toward an Understanding of Greco–Roman Egypt." In *One Hundred Years in Egypt: Paths of Italian Archaeology,* edited by Maria Casini, 107–29. Istituto italiano di cultura per la R.A.U. Milan: Electa, 2001.

Bonacasa, Nicola., and A. di Vita, eds. *Alessandria e il mondo ellenistico-romano: studi in onore dei Achille Adriani.* 3 vols. Rome: "L'Erma" di Bretschneider, 1983.

Booth, Marilyn. *May Her Likes Be Multiplied: Biography and Gender Politics in Egypt.* Berkeley: University of California Press , 2001.

Bothmer, Bernard V. *Egypt 1950: My First Visit.* Edited by Emma Swan Hall. Oxford: Oxbow Books, 2003.

Boutros Ghali, Mirrit. "The Egyptian National Consciousness." *Middle East Journal* 32 (1978): 58–77.

———. *The Policy of Tomorrow.* Translated by Ismail R. el Faruqi. Washington, DC: American Council of Learned Societies, 1953.

———. "Short History of the Society of Coptic Archeology." *Bulletin de la société d'archéologie copte* 26 (1984): 113–16.

Bowman, A.K., R.A. Coles, N. Goris, and D. Obbink, eds. *Oxyrhynchus: A City and Its Texts.* London: Arts and Humanities Council: Egypt Exploration Society, 2007.

Bowra, C. M. *Memories, 1898–1939.* London: Weidenfeld & Nicolson, 1966.

Boynter, Ran, Lynn Swartz Dodd, and Bradley J. Parker, eds. *Controlling the Past, Owning the Future: The Political Uses of Archaeology in the Middle East.* Tucson: University of Arizona Press, 2010.

Breasted, Charles. *Pioneer to the Past: The Story of James Henry Breasted, Archaeologist.* New York: C. Scribner's Sons, 1947.

Breasted, James Henry. *Ancient Times: A History of the Early World.* Boston: Ginn, 1916.

———. *The Oriental Institute.* V. 12 of *The University of Chicago Survey.* Chicago University of Chicago Press, 1933.

Breccia, Evaristo. *Alexandrea ad Aegyptum: Guide de la ville ancienne et modern e du Musée Gréco–Romain.* Bergamo: Istituto ialiano d'arti grafiche, 1914.

———. *Faraoni senza pace.* 2nd ed. Pisa: Nistri-Lischi, 1958.

———. *Uomine e libri.* Pisa: Nistri-Lischi, 1959.

———. *With King Fuad to the Oasis of Ammon.* Milan: Bestetti & Tumminelli, 1929.

Brendon, Piers. *Thomas Cook: 150 Years of Popular Tourism.* London: Secker & Warburg, 1991.

Briani, Vittorio. *Italiani in Egitto.* Rome: Istituto poligrafico e zeecca dell stato, 1982.

Brier, Bob. *Egyptomania: Our Three Thousand Year Obsession with the Land of the Pharaohs.* New York: Palgrave Macmillan, 2013.

Bruffaerts, Jean-Michel. "Bruxelles, capital de l'égyptologie. Le rêve de Jean Capart (1947)." In *Ägyptologen und Ägyptologien zwischen Kaiserreich und Gründung der beiden Staaten: Reflexionen zur Geschichte und Episteme eines* altertumswissenschaftlichen Fachs im 150. Jahr der Zeitschrift für Ägyptische Sprache und Altertumskunde, edited by Susanne Bickel et al., 193–241. Beiheft 1. Berlin: Akademie Verlag Berlin: de Gruyter, 2013.

Brugman, J. *An Introduction to the History of Modern Arabic Literature in Egypt.* Leiden: Brill, 1984.

Budayr, Ahmad Abd al-Fattah. *al-Amir Ahmad Fuad wa nashat al-Jamia al-Misriya.* Cairo: Matbaat Jamiat Fuad al-Awwal, 1950.

Budge, E.A.W. *Cook's Handbook for Egypt and the Sudan.* London: Thomas Cook & Son, 1911, 1921, 1925 editions.

Budka, Julia and Claus Jurman, "Hermann Junker: Ein deutsch-österreichisches Forscherleben zwischen Pyramiden, Kreuz und Hakenkreuz." In *Ägyptologen und Ägyptologien zwischen Kaiserreich und Gründen der beiden deutschen Staaten: Reflexionen zur Geschichte und Episteme eines altertumswissenschaftlichen Fachs im 150. Jahr der Zeitschrift für Ägyptische Sprache und Alteretumskunde*, edited by Susanne Bickel et al., 299–331. Beiheft 1. Berlin: Akademie Verlag Berlin: de Gruyter, 2013.

Butler, Alfred J. *Ancient Churches of Egypt.* 2 vols. Oxford: Clarendon Press, 1884.

Butler, Beverley. *Return to Alexandria: An Ethnography of Cultural Heritage, Revivalism, and Museum History.* Walnut Creek, CA: Left Coast Press, 2007.

Buzard, James. *The Beaten Track: European Tourism, Literature, and the Ways to Culture, 1880–1918.* Oxford: Oxford University Press, 1993.

Cain, P.J., and A.G. Hopkins, *British Imperialism 1688–2000.* 2nd ed. Harlow, UK: Longman, 2001.

Calvert, John. *Sayyid Qutb and the Origins of Radical Islamism.* New York: Columbia University Press, 2010.

Cannuyer, Christian. *Les coptes.* [Turnhout, Belgium]: Éditions Brepols, 1990.

Capart, Jean. *Fouilles en Égypte: El Kab: impressions et souvenirs.* Brussels: Fondation égyptologique Reine Élisabeth, 1946.

Carruthers, William, ed. *Histories of Egyptology: Interdisciplinary Measures.* London: Routledge, 2015.

Carter, B.L., *The Copts in Egyptian Politics.* London: Croom Helm, 1986.

Carter, Howard. *Tut.Ankh.Amen: The Politics of Discovery.* London: Libri, 1998. Reprint of *Tut.Ankh.Amen. Statement, with Documents.* Privately printed and publication suppressed, 1924.

Carter, Howard, and Arthur C. Mace. *The Tomb of Tut.Ankh.Amen: discovered by the late Earl of Carnarvon and Howard Carter.* 3 vols. London: Cassell, 1923–33. (Vols. 2 & 3 by Carter alone). Reprinted New York: Cooper Square Publishers, 1963.

Casini, Maria, ed. *One Hundred Years in Egypt: Paths of Italian Archaeology.* Milan: Istituto italiano di cultura per la R.A.U.: Electa, 2001.

Cavafy, Constantine. *C.P. Cavafy: The Poems of the Canon.* Cambridge, MA: Harvard Early Modern and Modern Greek Library, Harvard University, Department of Classics, 2011.

Chamley, John. *Lord Lloyd and the Decline of the British Empire.* London: Weidenfeld & Nicoloson, 1987.

Champion, Timothy. "Beyond Egyptology: Egypt in 19th and 20th Century Archaeology and Anthropology." In *The Wisdom of Egypt: Changing Visions through the Ages*, edited by Peter Ucko and Timothy Champion, 161–85. London: UCL Press, 2003.

Charmes, Gabriel. *Cinq mois au Caire et dans la Basse-Egypte*. Paris: G. Charpentier, 1880.

Chatterjee, Partha. *The Nation and Its Fragments: Colonial and Postcolonial Histories*. Princeton: Princeton University Press, 1993.

Chevalier, Nicole. *La recherche archéologique française au moyen-orient, 1842–1947*. Paris: Éditions recherche sur les civilisations, 2002.

Clément, Anne. "Rethinking 'Peasant Consciousness' in Colonial Egypt: An Exploration of the Performance of Folksongs by Upper Egyptian Agricultural Workers on the Archaeological Excavation Sites of Karnak and Dendera at the Turn of the Twentieth Century (1885–1914)." *History and Anthropology* 21 (June 2010): 73–100.

Clément, Colin. *La société archéologique d'Alexandrie à 100 ans: 1893–1993*. Translated by Centre culturel français d'Alexandrie. Alexandria, 1993.

Colla, Elliott. *Conflicted Antiquities: Egyptology, Egyptomania, Egyptian Modernity*. Durham, NC: Duke University Press, 2007.

Combe, Ét. "Le cinquantenaire de la société royale d'archéologie, 1893–1943." *Bulletin de la société royale d'archéologie-Alexandrie* No. 26, 1946., 104–119.

Cooke, Miriam. *The Anatomy of an Egyptian Intellectual: Yahya Haqqi*. Washington, DC: Three Continents Press, 1984.

Cooper, Artemis. *Cairo in the War 1939–1945*. London: H. Hamilton, 1989.

Coptic Layman, A. "The Awakening of the Coptic Church." *Contemporary Review* 71 (1897): 737–48. Internal references strongly suggest that Murqus Simaika was the author.

Cortissoz, Royal, intro. *The Works of Edwin Howland Blashfield*. New York: C. Scribner's Sons, 1937.

Cott, Jonathan. *The Search for Omm Sety: A Story of Eternal Love*. Garden City, NY: Doubleday, 1987.

Coury, Ralph M. *The Making of an Egyptian Arab Nationalist: The Early Years of Azzam Pasha, 1893-1936*. Reading, UK: Ithaca Press, 1998.

———. "The Politics of the Funereal: The Tomb of Saad Zaghlul." *Journal of the American Research Center in Egypt* 29 (1992): 191–200.

Crawford, Elisabeth. *Nationalism and Internationalism in Science,1880-1939: Four Studies of the Nobel Population*. Cambridge: Cambridge University Press, 1992.

Creswell, K.A.C. *Early Muslim Architecture*. 2 vols. Oxford: Oxford University Press, 1932–40.

———. *The Muslim Architecture of Egypt*. 2 vols. Oxford: Oxford University Press, 1952–1959.

Cromer, Earl of. *Ancient and Modern Imperialism*. London: J. Murray, 1910.

———. *Modern Egypt*. Rev.ed. London: Macmillan, 1911.

Cuno, James. *Who Owns Antiquity? Museums and the Battle over our Ancient Heritage*. Princeton: Princeton University Press, 2008.

Curl, James Stevens. *The Egyptian Revival: Ancient Egypt as the Inspiration for Design Motifs in the West.* Abingdon, UK: Routledge, 2005.

Dairat al-maarif. Edited by Butrus Bustani et al. 11 vols. Beirut: Dairat al-maarif, and Cairo: Dar al-hilal, 1876–1900.

Daressy, Georges. "Les noms d'Égypte." *Bulletin de l'institut égyptienne,* 5 sér., t. 10, fasc. 2 (1917): 359–68.

Darraj, Ahmad. "Gaston Wiet wa-l-amal al-ilmiya," *al-Majalla al-tarikhiya al-misriya* 19 (1972): 89–110.

Darwin, John. *Britain, Egypt and the Middle East: Imperial Policy in the Aftermath of War, 1918–1922.* London: Macmillan, 1981.

———. *The Empire Project: The Rise and Fall of the British World-System, 1830–1970.* Cambridge: Cambridge University Press, 2009.

Davis, Eric. *Challenging Colonialism: Bank Misr and Egyptian Industrialization, 1920–1941.* Princeton: Princeton University Press, 1983.

Deeb, Marius. *Party Politics in Egypt: The Wafd and Its Rivals.* London: Ithaca Press, 1979.

Description de l'Égypte: ou recueil des observations et des recherches qui ont été faites en Égypte pendant l'expédition de l'armée française. Commission des sciences et arts d'Égypte. 9 vols of text and 11 vols of plates. 2nd ed. Paris: Pancouke, 1821-1829.

Díaz-Andreu, Margarita. *A World History of Nineteenth-Century Archaeology: Nationalism, Colonialism, and the Past.* Oxford: Oxford University Press, 2007.

Díaz-Andreu, Margarita, and Timothy Champion, eds. *Nationalism and Archaeology in Europe.* London: UCL Press, 1996.

Di-Capua, Yoav. *Gatekeepers of the Arab Past: Historians and History Writing in Twentieth-Century Egypt.* Berkeley: University of California Press, 2009.

Dodson, Alan P. *Peaceful Air Warfare: The United States, Britain, and the Politics of International Aviation.* Oxford: Clarendon Press, 1991.

Doresse, Jean. *Des hieroglyphs à la croix: ce que le passé pharaonique a légué au Christianisme.* Istanbul: Nederlands Historisch-Archeologisch Instituut in het Nabije Oosten, 1960.

Dowling, Archdeacon. *The Egyptian Church.* London: Cope & Fenwick, 1909.

Doyon, Wendy. "On Archaeological Labor in Nineteenth-Century Egypt." In *Histories of Egyptology: Interdisciplinary Measures,* edited by William Carruthers, 141–56. London: Routledge, 2015.

Dreyer, Günter, and Daniel Polz, eds. *Begegnung mit Vergangenheit: 100 Jahre in Ägypten: Deutsches Archäologisches Institut Kairo 1907–2007.* Mainz: P. von Zabern, 2007.

Drower, Margaret S. *Flinders Petrie: A Life in Archaeology.* London: Gollancz, 1985; repr., Madison: University of Wisconsin Press, 1995.

Duara, Pransenjit. *Rescuing History from the Nation: Questioning Narratives of Modern China.* Chicago: University of Chicago Press, 1995.

Dunham, Dows. *Recollections of an Egyptologist.* Boston: Museum of Fine Arts, 1972.

Dyson, Stephen L. *In Pursuit of Ancient Pasts: A History of Classical Archaeology in the Nineteenth and Twentieth Centuries.* New Haven: Yale University Press, 2006.

Edwards, I.E.S. *From the Pyramids to Tutankhamun: Memoirs of an Egyptologist.* Oxford: Oxbow, 2000.

Edwards, Jill, ed. *Historians in Cairo: Essays in Honor of George Scanlon.* Cairo: American University in Cairo Press, 2002.

Egger, Vernon. *A Fabian in Egypt: Salamah Musa and the Rise of the Professional Classes in Egypt, 1909–1939.* Lanham, MD: University Press of America, 1986.

Egypt Travel Magazine.

The Egyptian Directory: L'Annuaire égyptien (Égypte et Soudan). Cairo, 1921.

Egyptian Gazette (EG).

El-Daly, Okasha. *Egyptology: The Missing Millennium: Ancient Egypt in Medieval Arabic Writings.* London: UCL Press, 2005.

El-Daly, Okasha and Stephen Quirke. "Arabic Transliteration of Ancient Egyptian." In *Managing Egypt's Cultural Heritage: Proceedings of the First Egyptian Cultural Heritage Organisation Conference on Egyptian Cultural Heritage Management,* edited by Fekri A. Hassan, L. S. Owens, A. De Trafford. Egyptian Cultural Heritage Organisation (ECHO). Discourses on Heritage Management Series, No. 1: 15-26. London: Golden House Publications, 2009.

Eldamaty, Mamdouh Mohamed, and Mai Trad, eds. *Egyptian Museum Collections around the World.* Cairo: Supreme Council of Antiquities, 2002.

El-Gawhary, Major Mahmoud. *Ex-Royal Palaces in Egypt from Mohamed Aly to Farouk.* Cairo: Dar al-maarif, 1954.

El-Habashi, Alaa El-Din Elwi. "The Preservation of Egyptian Cultural Heritage through Egyptian Eyes: The Case of the Comité de Conservation des Monuments de l'Art Arabe." In *Urbanism: Imported or Exported,* edited by Joe Nasr and Mercedes Volait, 155–75. Chichester, UK: Wiley-Academic, 2003.

El Shakry, Omnia. *The Great Social Laboratory: Subjects of Knowledge in Colonial and Postcolonial Egypt.* Stanford, CA: Stanford University Press, 2007.

El Sharif, Sayed Desokey. *Egyptian Paper Money / al-Umlat al-misriya al-waraqiya.* Cairo: al-Faris lil-diaya wa-l-ilan, 2003.

Elston, Roy. *Traveller's handbook for Egypt and the Sudan.* Cook's Travellers' Handbooks. London: Simpkin, Marshall, 1929.

Emberling, Geoff, ed. *Pioneers to the Past: American Archaeologists in the Middle East 1919–1920.* Chicago: Oriental Institute, University of Chicago, 2010.

Empereur, Jean-Yves. *Alexandria Rediscovered.* New York: G. Braziller, 1998.

Engel, A. J. *From Clergyman to Don: The Rise of the Academic Profession in Nineteenth-Century Oxford.* Oxford: University of Oxford Press, 1983.

Erman, Adolf. *Mein Werden und Mein Werken: Erinnerungen eines Alten Berliner Gelehrten.* Leipzig: Von Quelle & Meyer, 1929.

Ernst, Carl W., and Richard C. Martin, eds. *Rethinking Islamic Studies: From Orientalism to Cosmopolitanism.* Columbia, SC: University of South Carolina Press, 2010.

Etman, Ahmed. "Translation at the Intersection of Traditions: The Arab Reception of the Classics." In *A Companion to Classical Receptions,* edited by Lorna Hardwick and Christopher Stray, 141–52. Malden, MA: Blackwell, 2008.

Evans, Trefor, ed. *The Killearn Diaries, 1934–1946.* London: Sidgwick & Jackson, 1972.

Fahmi, Zaki. *Safwat al-asr fi tarikh wa rusum mashahir rijal Misr*. Cairo: Matbaat al-itimad, 1926.

Fahmy, Khaled. *All the Pasha's Men: Mehmed Ali, His Army and the Making of Modern Egypt*. Cambridge: Cambridge University Press, 1998.

———. "For Cavafy, with love and squalor: some critical notes on the history and historiography of modern Alexandria." In *Alexandria, Real and Imagined*, edited by Anthony Hirst and Michael Silk, 263–80. Aldershot, Hampshire, UK: Ashgate, 2004.

Fahmy, Ziad. *Ordinary Egyptians: Creating the Modern Nation through Popular Culture*. Stanford: Stanford University Press, 2011.

[al-Falaki], Mahmoud Bey. *Mémoire sur l'antique Alexandrie*. Copenhagen: Imp. de B. Luno, 1872.

Fanus, Wajih. "Sulayman al-Bustani and Comparative Literary Studies in Arabic." *Journal of Arabic Literature* 17 (1986): 105–19.

Farnall, Harry. "Polémique de press au sujet des fouilles à Foustât." Comité de conservation des monuments de l'art arabe, *Bulletin* 32 (1915–19): 279–300.

Fathy, Hassan. *Architecture for the Poor: An Experiment in Rural Egypt*. Chicago: University of Chicago Press, 1973.

Fawzi, Husayn. *Sindibad Misri*. Cairo: Dar al-maarif, 1961.

Finkelstein, Israel, and Neil Ashe Silberman, eds. *The Bible Unearthed: Archaeology's New Vision of Ancient Israel and the Origin of Its Sacred Texts*. New York: Free Press, 2002.

Fiqi, Mustafa. *Copts in Egyptian Politics, 1919-1952*. Cairo: General Egyptian Book Organization, 1991.

Forster, E.M. *Alexandria: A History and a Guide*. 3rd ed. Garden City, NY: Anchor Books, 1961.

———. *Pharos and Pharillon*. 2nd ed. Surrey, UK: Leonard and Virginia Woolf: Hogarth Press, 1923.

Fouad I National Research Council. *Guide to Scientific and Technical Workers in Egypt*. Cairo: Fouad I National Research Council ,1951.

Fowler, Montague. *Christian Egypt: Past, Present and Future*. London: Church Newspaper Co., 1901.

Frend, W.H.C. *The Archaeology of Early Christianity: A History*. London: Geoffrey Chapman, 1996.

Gabra, Sami. *Chez les derniers adorateurs de Trismegiste: la nécropole d'Hermopolis Touna El Gebel (Souvenir d'un archéologue)*. Cairo: al-Haya al-misriya al-amma lil-kitab, 1971.

———. *Rapport sur les fouilles d'Hermoupolis Ouest (Touna El-Gebel)*. Université Fouad Ier. Cairo: IFAO, 1941.

Gallagher, Nancy Elizabeth. *Egypt's Other Wars: Epidemics and the Politics of Public Health*. Syracuse: Syracuse University Press, 1990.

Gange, David. *Dialogues with the Dead: Egyptology in British Culture and Religion, 1822–1922*. Oxford: Oxford University Press, 2013.

Ghazalé, Midhat. *Pyramids Road: An Egyptian Homecoming*. Cairo: American University in Cairo Press, 2004.

Geddes, Charles L., et al. *Studies in Islamic Art and Architecture in Honour of Professor K.A.C. Creswell*. Cairo: Center for Arabic Studies: American University in Cairo Press, 1965.

Gershoni, Israel. "An Intellectual Source for the Revolution: Tawfiq al-Hakim's Influence on Nasser and His Generation." In *Egypt from Monarchy to Republic: A Reassessment of Revolution and Change*, edited by Shimon Shamir, 213–49. Boulder, CO: Westview Press, 1995.

Gershoni, Israel, and James Jankowski. *Commemorating the Nation: Collective Memory, Public Commemoration, and National Identity in Twentieth-Century Egypt*. Chicago: Middle East Documentation Center, 2004.

———. *Confronting Facism in Egypt: Dictatorship vs. Democracy in the 1930s*. Stanford: Stanford University Press, 2010.

———. *Egypt, Islam, and the Arabs: The Search for Egyptian Nationhood, 1900–1930*. New York: Oxford University Press, 1986.

———. *Redefining the Egyptian Nation, 1930–1945*. Cambridge: Cambridge University Press, 1995.

Gertzen, Thomas L. "The Anglo-Saxon Branch of the Berlin School: The Interwar Correspondence of Adolf Erman and Alan Gardiner and the Loss of the German Concession at Amarna." In *Histories of Egyptology: Interdisciplinary Measures*, edited by William Carruthers, 34–49. London: Routledge, 2015.

Goldschmidt, Arthur, Jr. *Biographical Dictionary of Modern Egypt*. Boulder, CO: Lynne Rienner, 2000.

———. "The Boutros-Ghali Family." *Journal of the American Research Center in Egypt* 30 (1993): 183–88.

Goldschimdt, Arthur, Jr., Amy J. Johnson, and Barak A. Salmoni, eds. *Re-envisioning Egypt 1919–1952*. Cairo: American University in Cairo Press, 2005.

Goode, James F. *Negotiating for the Past: Archaeology, Nationalism, and Diplomacy in the Middle East, 1919–1941*. Austin: University of Texas Press, 2007.

Gordon, Joel. *Nasser's Blessed Movement: Egypt's Free Officers and the July Revolution*. New York: Oxford University Press, 1992.

Gorman, Anthony. "Anarchists in Education: The Free Popular University in Egypt (1901)." *Middle Eastern Studies* 41 (May 2005): 303–20.

———. "Foreign Workers in Egypt 1882-1914: Subaltern or Labour Elite?" In *Subalterns and Social Protest: History from Below in the Middle East and North Africa*, edited by Stephanie Cronin, 237–59. London: Routledge, 2008.

———. *Historians, State and Politics in Twentieth-Century Egypt: Contesting the Nation*. London: RoutledgeCurzon, 2003.

Goyon, Georges. *La découverte des trésors de Tanis: aventures archéologiques en Égypte*. Paris: Persea, 1987.

Grabar, Oleg, ed. *K.A.C. Creswell and His Legacy. Muqarnas 8*. Leiden: Brill, 1991.

Graffety-Smith, Lawrence. *Bright Levant*. London: J. Murray, 1970.

Gran-Aymerch, Ève, Jean Leclant, and André Laronde. *Les chercheurs de passé, 1798–1945: la naissance d' archéologie moderne: dictionnaire biographique d'archéologie*. Paris: CNRS, 2007.

Graves, Robert. *Good-bye to All That*. London: Johnathan Cape, 1929.

Greenfield, Jeanette. *Return of Cultural Treasures*. 3rd ed. Cambridge: Cambridge University Press, 2007.

Gregory, Derek. "Colonial Nostalgia and Cultures of Travel: Spaces of Constructed Visibility in Egypt." In *Consuming Tradition, Manufacturing Heritage: Global Norms and Urban Forms in the Age of Tourism*, edited by Nezar AlSayyad, 111–51. London: Routledge, 2001.

———. "Emperors of the Gaze: Photographic Practices and Productions of Space in Egypt, 1839–1914." In *Picturing Place: Photography and the Geographical Imagination*, edited by Joan M. Schwartz and James R. Ryan, 195–225. London: I.B. Tauris, 2003.

———. "Scripting Egypt: Orientalism and the Cultures of Travel." In *Writes of Passage: Reading Travel Writing*, edited by James Duncan and Derek Gregory, 114–50. London: Routledge, 1999.

Guide to Egypt and the Sûdân. Macmillan's Guides. 7th ed. London: Macmillan, 1916, reprinted 1918.

Guirguis, Magdi, and Nelly Van Doorn-Harder, *The Emergence of the Modern Coptic Papacy*. Vol. 3 of *The Popes of Egypt*. Cairo: American University in Cairo Press, 2011.

Habib, Tawfiq. "Dars al-athar fi-l-jamia al-misriya," *al-Muqtataf* 72 (1928): 438–43.

Hagerman, C.A. *Britain's Imperial Muse: The Classics, Imperialism and the Indian Empire, 1784-1914*. Houndsmill, Basingstoke, Hampshire, UK: Palgrave Macmillan, 2013.

Hahn, Peter. *The United States, Great Britain, and Egypt, 1945–1956: Strategy and Diplomacy in the Early Cold War*. Chapel Hill, NC: University of North Carolina Press, 1991.

Haikal, Fayza. "Egypt's Past Regenerated by its Own People." In *Consuming Ancient Egypt*, edited by Sally MacDonald and Michael Rice, 123–138. London: UCL Press, 2003.

al-Hakim, Tawfiq. *The Maze of Justice*. Translated by A. Eban. London: Harvill, 1947.

———.*Return of the Spirit: Tawfiq al-Hakim's Classic Novel of the 1919 Revolution*. Translated by William M. Hutchins. Washington, DC: Three Continents Press, 1990.

Halim, Hala. *Alexandrian Cosmopolitanism: An Archive*. New York: Fordham University Press, 2013.

Hamid, Ahmad. *Hassan Fathy and Continuity in Islamic Architecture: The Birth of a New Modern*. Cairo: American University in Cairo Press, 2010.

Hamilakis, Yannis. *The Nation and Its Ruins: Antiquity, Archaeology, and National Imagination in Greece*. Oxford: Oxford University Press, 2007.

Hamilton, Alastair. *The Copts and the West, 1439-1822*. Oxford: Oxford University Press, 2006.

Hamilton, R.W. "Keppel Archibald Cameron Creswell, 1879–1974," *Proceedings of the British Academy* 60 (1974): 1–20.

Hamouda, Sahar. *Omar Toussoun, Prince of Alexandria*. Alexandria: Bibliotheca Alexandrina, 2005.

Hamza, Abd al-Qadir. *Ala hamish al-tarikh al-misri al-qadim*. Cairo: Matbaat dar al-kutub al-misriya, 1940.

Hankey, Julie. *A Passion for Egypt: Arthur Weigall, Tutankhamun and the 'Curse of the Pharaohs.'* London: I.B. Tauris, 2001.

Hanna, Sami A., ed. *Medieval and Middle Eastern Studies in Honor of Aziz Suryal Atiya*. Leiden: Brill, 1972.

Hanotaux, Gabriel, ed. *Historie de la nation égyptienne*. 7 vols. Paris: Société de l'histoire nationale, 1931–1940.

Hartleben, Hermine. *Champollion: sein Leben und sein Werk*. Berlin: Weidemann, 1906.

Hartman, Michelle. "Muhammad Husayn Haykal." In *Essays in Arabic Literary Biography 1850–1950*, edited by Roger Allen, 125–137. Wiesbaden: Harrassowitz, 2010.

Hassan, Ahlam Fathy. "Cleopatra in Dramatic Work," *Classical Papers / Awraq Klasikiya*. Cairo University, Faculty of Arts, Dept. of Greek and Latin Studies 4 (1995): 79–108.

Hassan, S.S. *Christians versus Muslims in Modern Egypt: The Century-Long Struggle for Coptic Equality*. Oxford: Oxford University Press, 2003.

Hassan, Selim. *Excavations at Giza*. Vol. 1. Oxford: Oxford University Press, 1932; Vols. 2–10. Cairo: Government Press, Bulaq, 1934–60.

———. *Excavations at Saqqara 1937–8*, edited by Zaki Iskandar. 3 vols. Cairo: Department of Antiquities, 1975.

———. *Misr al-qadima*. 15 vols. Cairo: al-Haya al-misriya al-amma lil-kitab, 1992; Cairo: Matbaat dar al-kutub al-misriyya, 1940–60.

Hassan, Zaki M. *Moselm Art in the Fouad I University Museum*. Cairo: Fouad I University Press, 1950.

Hatch, Alden. *American Express: A Century of Service*. Garden City, NY: Doubleday, 1950.

Hawass, Zahi. *Discovering Tutankhamun: From Howard Carter to DNA*. Cairo: American University in Cairo Press, 2013.

Haykal, Muhammad Husayn. *Mohammed Hussein Haikal's Zainab: The First Egyptian Novel*. Translated by John Mohammed Grinsted. London: Darf, 2010.

———. *Mudhakkirati fi-l-siyasa al-misriya*. 3 vols. Cairo: Matbaat dar al-maarif, 1951–53.

———. *Tarajim misriya wa gharbiya*. Cairo: Dar al-maarif, 1980.

Hazbun, Waleed. *Beaches, Ruins, Resorts: The Politics of Tourism in the Arab World*. Minneapolis: University of Minnesota Press, 2008.

———. "The East as an Exhibit: Thomas Cook and Son and the Origins of the International Tourism Industry in Egypt." In *The Business of Tourism: Place, Faith, and History*, edited by Philip Scranton and Janet F. Davidson, 3–33. Philadelphia: University of Pennsylvania Press, 2007.

Headrick, Daniel R. *The Tentacles of Progress: Technology Transfer in the Age of Imperialism, 1850–1940*. Oxford: Oxford University Press, 1988.

Hellman, Geoffrey T. "Herbert E. Winlock, Egyptologist." *The New Yorker*, July 29, 1933: 16–19.

al-Hilal.

Hilal, Amal. "Les premiers égyptologues égyptiens et la réforme." In *Entre réforme sociale et movement national: identité et modernizations en Égypte (1882–1962)*, edited by Alain Rousillon, 337–50. Cairo: CEDEJ, 1995.

Hingley, Richard. *Roman Officers and English Gentlemen: The Imperial Origins of Roman Archaeology.* London: Routledge, 2000.

Hirst, Anthony, and Michael Silk, eds. *Alexandria, Real and Imagined.* Aldershot, Hampshire, UK: Ashgate, 2004.

Hodgson, Marshall. *The Venture of Islam.* 3 vols. Chicago: University of Chicago Press, 1974.

Holland, Matthew F. *America and Egypt: From Roosevelt to Eisenhower.* Westport, CT: Praeger, 1996.

Hopwood, Derek. *Tales of Empire: The British in the Middle East 1880–1952.* London: I.B. Tauris, 1989.

Hourani, Albert. *Arabic Thought in the Liberal Age, 1798–1939.* Oxford: Oxford University Press, 1962.

———. *Islam in European Thought.* Cambridge: Cambridge University Press, 1991.

Hoving, Thomas. *Tutankhamun: The Untold Story.* New York: Simon & Schuster, 1978.

Humbert, J. M., M. Pantazzi, and C. Ziegler, eds. *Egyptomania: Egypt in Western Art, 1730-1930.* Exhibition catalogue. Paris and Ottawa: Musée du Louvre and National Gallery of Canada, 1994.

Humphreys, Andrew. *Grand Hotels of Egypt in the Golden Age of Travel.* New York: American University in Cairo Press, 2011.

Hunter, F. Robert. "Tourism and Empire: The Thomas Cook & Son Enterprise on the Nile, 1868–1914." *Middle Eastern Studies* 40, no. 5 (September 2004): 28–54.

Husayn, Ahmad. *Mawsuat tarikh Misr.* Cairo: Dar al-shab, 1972.

Hussein, Taha. *The Future of Culture in Egypt.* Translated by Sidney Glazer. New York: American Council of Learned Societies, 1975.

———. *A Passage to France: The Third Volume of the Autobiography of Taha Husain.* Translated by Kenneth Cragg. Leiden: Brill, 1976.

———. *The Stream of Days: A Student at the Azhar.* Translated by Hilarly Wayment. London: Longmans, Green, 1948.

Hutchins, William Maynard. *Tawfiq al-Hakim, A Reader's Guide.* Boulder, CO: Lynne Rienner, 2003.

Ibrahim, Vivian. *The Copts of Egypt: Challenges of Modernisation and Identity.* London: I.B.Tauris, 2011.

Ikram, Salima. "Collecting and Repatriating Egypt's Past: Toward a New Nationalism." In *Contested Cultural Heritage: Relgion, Nationalism, Erasure, and Exclusion in a Global World*, edited by Helaine Silverman, 141–54. New York: Springer, 2011.

Ilbert, Robert. *Alexandrie 1830–1930: histoire d'une communauté citadine.* 2 vols. Cairo: IFAO, 1996.

Ilbert, Robert, Ilias Yannakakis, and Jacques Hassoun, eds. *Alexandria 1860–1960: the Brief Life of a Cosmopolitan Community.* Translated by Colin Clement. Alexandria: Harpocrates, 1997.

Iliffe, J.H. "The Palestine Archaeological Museum, Jerusalem." *Museums Journal* 38, no. 1 (April 1938): 1–22.

Illustrated London News.

Insoll, Timothy. *The Archaeology of Islam.* Oxford: Blackwell, 1999.

Institut égyptien (later Institut de l'Égypte). *Bulletin de l'institut égyptien (BIÉ).*

International Congress of Orientalists. *Proceedings.* (Language of title varies with host country).

Iriye, Akira. *Cultural Internationalism and World Order.* Baltimore: Johns Hopkins University Press, 1997.

Jacob, Wilson Chacko. *Working Out Egypt: Effendi Masculinity and Subject Formation in Colonial Modernity, 1870–1940.* Durham: Duke University Press, 2011.

Jacobs, Jessica. *Sex, Tourism and the Postcolonial Encounter: Landscapes of Longing in Egypt.* Farnham, Surrey, UK: Ashgate, 2010.

Jamiat Fuad al-Awwal. *al-Kitab al-fiddi li-kulliyat al-adab 1925–1950.* Cairo, Matbaat Jamiat Fuad al-Awwal, 1951.

Jamiat al-Qahira. *al-Athar al-ilmiya li-ada hayat al-tadris bi-Jamiat al-Qahira.* Cairo, 1958.

———. *al-Rasail al-ilmiya li-darajatay al-majistir wa-l-dukturah, 1932–1966.* Cairo, 1967.

Jamiat al-Qahira, Kulliyat al-athar. *al-Dalil al-dhahabi lil-asatidha wa khariji al-athar, Jamiat al-Qahira mundhu sanat 1925.* Cairo: al-Haya al-misriya al-amma lil-kitab, 1975.

———. *al-Kitab al-dhahabi lil-ihtifal al-khamsini bil-dirasat al-athariya bi-Jamiat al-Qahira.* Vol. 1, *Majallat kulliyat al-athar.* Cairo, 1978.

James, T.G.H. *Howard Carter: The Path to Tutankhamun.* 2nd ed. London: Kegan Paul International, 2001.

———., ed. *Excavating in Egypt: The Egypt Exploration Society 1882–1982.* Chicago: University of Chicago Press, 1982.

Jankowski, James. *Egypt's Young Rebels: "Young Egypt:" 1933–1952.* Stanford: Stanford University Press, 1975.

Janssen, Rosalind M. *The First Hundred Years: Egyptology at University College London, 1892–1992.* London: UCL Press, 1992.

Jaritz, Horst. "The Extension of the Egyptian Museum: A Project of 1937 by Otto Königsberger." In *Egyptian Museum Collections around the World,* edited by Mamdouh Mohamed Eldamaty and Mai Trad, 581–89. Cairo: Supreme Council of Antiquities, 2002.

Journal of Egyptian Archaeology.

Jumayi, Abd al-Munim Ibrahim al-Dusuqi. *al-Jamiya al-misriya lil-dirasat al-tarikhiya wa-dirasa tarikhiya lil-muassa ilimiya 1945–1985.* Cairo: Matbaat al-Jabalawi, 1985.

———. *Taha Husayn wa-l-jamia al-misriya.* Cairo, 1981.

Junker, Hermann. *Leben und Werk in Selbstdarstellung.* Österreichische Akademie der Wissenschaften. Philosophisch-historiche Klass. Sitzungsberichte 242. Band 5. Abhandlung. Vienna: H. Böhlaus, 1963.

Kaiser, Werner. *75 Jahre Deutsches Archäologisches Institut Kairo 1907–1982.* Mainz: P. von Zabern, 1982.

Kamal, Ahmad. *Mujam al-lugha al-misriya al-qadima*. Vol. 1. Cairo: Supreme Council of Antiquities, 2002.

———. "Le procédé graphique chez les anciens égyptiens, l'origine du mot Égypte," *Bulletin de l'institut égyptienne*, sér. 5, t. 10, fasc. 1, (1916): 133–76, and rejoinder: t. 11, fasc. 2 (1918): 422-23.

Kamil, Jill. *Labib Habachi: The Life and Legacy of an Egyptologist*. Cairo: The American University in Cairo Press, 2007.

Kaplan, Flora E.S., ed. *Museums and the Making of "Ourselves": The Role of Objects in National Identity*. London: Leicester University Press, 1994.

Karnouk, Liliane. *Modern Egyptian Art*, 2nd ed. Cairo: American University in Cairo Press, 2005.

Karrarah, Azza. "Egyptian Literary Images of Alexandria." In *Alexandria, Real and Imagined*, edited by Anthony Hirst and Michael Silk, 307–22. Aldershot, UK: Ashgate, 2004.

Kashishiyan, Harant, ed. *Iskandar Sarukhan: nabdha an hayatihi wa fannihi wa injazatihi*. Cairo: Jamiyat al-Qahira al-khayriya al-armaniya al-amma, 1998.

Kelley, Thomas. *For the Advancement of Learning: The University of Liverpool, 1881-1981*. Liverpool: University of Liverpool Press, 1981.

Kerboeuf, Anne-Claire. "The Cairo Fire of 26 January 1952 and Interpretations of History." In *Re-evisioning Egypt, 1919–1952*, edited by Arthur Goldschmidt Jr., Amy J. Johnson, and Barak A. Salmoni, 194–216. Cairo: American University in Cairo Press, 2005.

al-Kharrat, Edwar. *City of Saffron*. Translated by Frances Liardet. London: Quartet, 1989.

———. *Girls of Alexandria*. Translated by Frances Liardet. London: Quartet, 1993.

Khater, Antoine. *Le régime juridique des fouilles et des antiquités en Égypte*. Cairo: IFAO, 1960.

Kirk, George. *The Middle East in the War*. London: Royal Institute of International Affairs: Oxford University Press, 1952.

Kitroeff, Alexander. *The Greeks in Egypt, 1919–1937: Ethnicity and Class*. London: Ithaca, 1989.

Klein-Franke, Felix. *Die Klassische Antike in der Tradition des Islam*. Darmstadt: Wissenschaftliche Buchgesellschaft, 1980.

Kohl, Philip, and Clare Fawcett, eds. *Nationalism, Politics, and the Practice of Archaeology*. Cambridge: Cambridge University Press, 1995.

Kohl, Philip, and Pérez Gollém. "Religion, Politics, and Prehistory: Reassessing the Lingering Legacy of Oswald Menghin." *Current Anthropology* 43, no. 4 (Aug./Oct. 2002): 561–86.

Koshar, Rudy. *German Travel Cultures*. Oxford: Berg, 2000.

Krämer, Gudrun. *Hassan al-Banna*. Oxford: Oneworld, 2010.

Kramer, Thomas W. *Deutsch-ägyptische Beziehungen in Vergangenheit und Gegenwart*. Tübingen: H. Erdmann, 1974.

Krause, Martin, ed. *Essays on the Nag Hammadi Texts in Honour of Pahor Labib*. Leiden: Brill, 1975.

Krauss, Rolf. "1913–1988: 75 Jahre Büste der Nofretete/Nefret-iti in Berlin."
  Jahrbuch. Preussischer Kulturbesitz 24 (1987): 87–124, and the author's update
  "Why Nefertiti Went to Berlin," *KMT* 19 (3, Fall 2008): 44–53.
Kubiak, Wladyslaw B. *Al-Fustat: Its Foundation and Early Urban Development.*
  Cairo: American University in Cairo Press, 1987.
Kuklick, Bruce. *Puritans in Babylon: The Ancient Near East and American Intellec-
  tual Life, 1880–1930.* Princeton: Princeton University Press, 1996.
Labib, Pahor. *The Coptic Museum and the Fortress of Babylon at Old Cairo.* Cairo:
  General Organisation for Government Printing Offices, 1953.
Lackany, R. *La société archéologique d'Alexandrie à 80 ans.* Alexandria: Impr. Don
  Bosco, 1973.
Lampson, Miles. *Politics and Diplomacy in Egypt: The Diaries of Sir Miles Lampson
  1935–1937,* edited by M.E. Yapp. Oxford: British Academy: Oxford Univer-
  sity Press, 1997.
Lane, E.W. *An Account of the Manners and Customs of the Modern Egyptians: The
  Definitive 1860 Edition.* Edited by Jason Thompson. Cairo: American Uni-
  versity in Cairo Press, 2003.
Lane-Poole, Stanley. *Cairo: Sketches of Its History, Monuments, and Social Life.*
  London: J.S. Virtue, 1898.
al-Lataif al-Musawwara.
Le Tourneur d'Isson, Claudine. *Une passion égyptienne: Jean-Philippe et Marguertie
  Lauer.* Paris: Plon, 1996.
————. *Lauer et Sakkara.* Paris: Tallander: Historia, 2000.
Leeder, S.H. *Modern Sons of the Pharaohs.* New York: Arno Press, 1973. Reprint
  of London: Hodder & Stoughton, 1918. Translated to Arabic by Ahmad
  Mahmud as *Abna al-faraina al-muhdithun: dirasa li-akhlaq aqbat Misr wa
  adatihim.* Cairo: Dar al-shuruq, 2008.
Lévi, I.G. "Le tourisme et la villégiature en Égypte." *L'Égypte contemporaine* 3
  (1912): 255–281.
————. "Pour une politique du tourisme," *L'Égypte contemporaine* 24 (1933): 573-77.
Lewis, Naphthali. *Greeks in Ptolemaic Egypt: Case Studies in the Social History of the
  Hellenistic Period.* Oxford: Clarendon Press, 1986.
Lia, Brynjar. *The Society of the Muslim Brothers in Egypt: The Rise of an Islamic
  Movement, 1928–1942.* Reading, UK: Ithaca, 1998.
Lloyd, Lord. *Egypt since Cromer.* 2 vols. London: Macmillan, 1933; New York:
  AMS Press, 1970.
Lloyd, Seton. *Foundations in the Dust: The Story of Mesopotamian Exploration.* 2nd
  ed. London: Thames & Hudson, 1980.
Long, C.W.R. *British Pro-Consuls in Egypt, 1914–1929: The Challenge of National-
  ism.* London: I.B. Tauris, 2005.
Long, Richard. *Tawfiq al-Hakim, Playwright of Egypt.* London: Ithaca Press, 1973.
Louca, Anouar. "Rifa'a al-Tahtawi (1801–1873) et la science occidentale. In *D'un
  orient l'autre,* 2: 201–17. 2 vols. Paris: CEDEJ: CNRS, 1991.
———— (Luqa, Anwar). *Ali Bahgat: raid al-bahth fi-l-athar al-arabiya bi-Misr: min
  rasailihi 1887–1919 li-tilmidhihi al-sawisri wanbirkham.* Cairo: Dar al-hilal,
  2003. The cover, however, reads *Ali Bahjat: awwal athari Misri.*

Louis, William Roger. *The British Empire in the Middle East, 1945-1951: Arab Nationalism, the United States, and Postwar Imperialism*. Oxford: Clarendon Press, 1984.
————. *Ends of British Imperialism: The Scramble for Empire, Suez and Decolonization. Collected Essays*. London: I. B. Tauris, 2006.
Luckhurst, Roger. *The Mummy's Curse: The True History of a Dark Fantasy*. Oxford: Oxford University Press, 2012.
Lutfi al-Sayyid, Ahmad. *Qissat Hayati*. Cairo: Dar al-hilal, 1962. Based on conservations with Tahir al-Tanahi.
Mabro, Robert. "Alexandria 1860–1960: The Cosmopolitan Identity." In *Alexandria, Real and Imagined*, edited by Anthony Hirst and Michael Silk, 247–62. Aldershot, UK: Ashgate, 2004.
McBride, Barrie St. Claire. *Farouk of Egypt: A Biography*. London: Hale, 1967.
MacDonald, Sally, and Michael Rice, eds. *Consuming Ancient Egypt*. London: UCL Press, 2003.
Mackail, J.W. *Classical Studies*. London: J. Murray, 1925.
MacKenzie, John. *Orientalism: History, Theory, and the Arts*. Manchester: University of Manchester Press, 1995.
McLaren, Brian. *Architecture and Tourism in Italian Colonial Libya: An Ambivalent Modernism*. Seattle: University of Washington Press, 2006.
MacLean, Derryl H., and Sikeena Karmali Ahmed, eds. *Cosmopolitanism in Muslim Contexts: Perspectives from the Past*. Edinburgh: Edinburgh University Press, 2012.
McNeill, William H. *Arnold J. Toynbee: A Life*. New York: Oxford University Press, 1989.
Madrasat al-muallimin al-ulya. *al-Kitab al-dhahabi li-madrasat al-muallimin al-ulya, 1885-1935*. Cairo, 1935.
Mahfouz, Naguib. *Autumn Quail*. Translated by Roger Allen. Cairo: American University in Cairo Press, 1985.
————. *Khufu's Wisdom*. Translated by Raymond Stock. Cairo, American University in Cairo Press, 2003.
————. *Rhadopis of Nubia*. Translated by Anthony Calderbank. Cairo: American University in Cairo Press , 2003.
————. *Thebes at War*. Translated by Humphrey Davies. Cairo: American University in Cairo Press, 2003.
Mahfouz, Naguib, and Raja Naqqash, *Naguib Mahfouz: safahat min mudhakkiratihi wa adwa jadida ala adabihi wa hayatihi*. Cairo: Markaz al-Ahram lil-tarjama wa-l-nashr, 1998.
Mahmoudi, Abdelrashid. *Taha Husein's Education from the Azhar to the Sorbonne*. Surrey, UK: Curzon, 1998.
Manning, J.G. *The Last of the Pharaohs: Egypt under the Ptolemies, 305–30 B.C.* Princeton: Princeton University Press, 2010.
Marchand, Suzanne L. *Down from Olympus: Archaeology and Philhellenism in Germany, 1750–1970*. Princeton: Princeton University Press, 1997.
————. *German Orientalism in the Age of Empire: Religion, Race, and Scholarship*. Cambridge: German Historical Institute, Washington, DC/ Cambridge University Press, 2009.

Marsot, Afaf Lutfi al-Sayyid. *Egypt's Liberal Experiment: 1922–1936*. Berkeley: University of California Press, 1977.
Maspero, Gaston. "Une inscription trilingue de C. Cornelius." In *Causeries d'Égypte*, by Gaston Maspero. 2nd ed. Paris: E. Guilmoto, 1907.
Masters, Bruce. *Christians and Jews in the Ottoman Arab World: The Roots of Sectarianism*. Cambridge: Cambridge University Press, 2002.
Matthes, Olaf. *James Simon: Mäzen in Wilhelmischen Zeitalter*. Berlin: Bostelmann & Siebenhaar, 2000.
Meade, Donald C. *Growth and Structural Change in the Egyptian Economy*. Homewood, IL: R. D. Irwin, 1967.
Meijer, Roel. *The Quest for Modernity: Secular Liberal and Left-Wing Political Thought in Egypt, 1945–1958*. London: RoutledgeCurzon, 2002.
———, ed. *Cosmopolitanism, Identity and Authenticity in the Middle East*. Surrey, UK: Curzon, 1999.
Meinardus, Otto. *Two Thousand Years of Coptic Christianity*. Cairo: American University in Cairo Press, 1999.
Meskell, Lynn, ed. *Archaeology under Fire: Nationalism, Politics, and Heritage in the Eastern Mediterranean and the Middle East*. London: Routledge, 1998.
———. "Sites of Violence: Terrorism, Tourism, and Heritage in the Archaeological Present." In *Embedding Ethics*, edited by Lynn Meskell and Peter Pels, 123–46. Oxford: Berg, 2005.
Middle East Report, no. 196 (1995). Special issue on "Tourism and the Business of Pleasure."
Mikhail, Kyriakos. *Copts and Moslims under British Control*. London: Smith, Elder, 1911.
Milwright, Marcus. *An Introduction to Islamic Archaeology*. Edinburgh: Edinburgh University Press, 2010.
Mitchell, J.M. *International Cultural Relations*. London: Allen & Unwin, 1986.
Mitchell, Richard. *The Society of the Muslim Brothers*. London: Oxford University Press, 1969.
Mitchell, Timothy. *Colonising Egypt*. Cambridge: Cambridge University Press, 1988.
———. *Rule of Experts: Egypt, Techno-Politics, Modernity*. Berkeley: University of California Press, 2002.
———. *Le mondain égyptien et du moyen-orient: l'annuaire de l'élite, 1951*. Edited by E.J. Blattner. Cairo: Paul Barbey, 1951.
Monroe, Elizabeth. *Britain's Moment in the Middle East, 1914–1971*. 2nd ed. London: Chatto & Windus, 1981.
Montet, Pierre. *La nécropole royal de Tanis*. 3 vols. Paris: Uden forlag, 1947–60.
Moon, B. *More Usefully Employed: Amelia B. Edwards: Writer, Traveller, and Campaigner for Ancient Egypt*. London: Egypt Exploration Society, 2006.
Morris, Rosalind C., ed. *Can the Subaltern Speak? Reflections on the History of an Idea*. New York: Columbia University Press, 2010.
Moser, Stephanie. *Wondrous Curiosities: Ancient Egypt at the British Museum*. Chicago: University of Chicago Press, 2006.
Moosa, Matti. *The Early Novels of Naguib Mahfouz: Images of Modern Egypt*. Gainsville, FL: University Press of Florida, 1994.

Muhammad, Muhsin. *Sariqat malik Misr*. Cairo: Markaz al-Ahram lil-tarjama wa-l-nashr: Muassasat al-Ahram., 1985.

Mukhtar, Muhammad Gamal. "al-Alim al-athari al-awwal fi Misr." *al-Majalla al-tarikhiya al-misriya* 12 (1964–65): 43–57.

———. "Selim Hassan ka-munaqqib wa alim al-athar." *al-Majalla al-tarikhiya al-misriya* 19 (1972): 73–87.

al-Muqtataf.

Musa, Salama. *The Education of Salama Musa*. Translated by L.O. Schuman. Leiden: Brill, 1961.

———. *Misr asl al-hadara*. Cairo: Matbaat al-majalla al-jadida, 1935.

Myntti, C. *Paris along the Nile: Architecture in Cairo from the Belle Epoque*. Cairo: American University in Cairo Press, 1999.

Naghi, Effat, et al., eds. *Mohamed Naghi (1888–1956): un impressioniste égyptien/ al-Fannan al-thathiri al-misri*. Cairo: Les cahiers de Chabramant, 1988.

Naguib, Saphinaz-Amal. "Survivals of Pharaonic Religious Practices in Contemporary Coptic Christianity." *UCLA Encyclopedia of Egyptology*, 2008, 1–6. http://repositories.cdlib.org/nelc/uee/1008. Accessed 1/11/2015.

National Gallery of Canada, *Egyptomania: Egypt in Western Art 1730–1930*. Ottawa: National Gallery of Canada, 1994.

Nelson, Nina. *Shepheard's Hotel*. London: Macmillan, 1960.

Noblecourt, Christiane Desroches. *La grande nubiade ou le parcours d'une égyptologue*. Paris: Stock/Pernoud, 1997.

Nora, Pierre, and Lawrence D. Kritzman. *Realms of Memory: Rethinking the French Past*. 3 vols. New York: Columbia University Press, 1996–98. Selected translations from Pierre Nora, ed., *Les Lieux de Mémoire*. 7 vols. Paris: Gallimard, 1984–92.

Noshy, Ibrahim. *Arts in Ptolemaic Egypt: A Study of Greek and Egyptian Influences in Ptolemaic Architecture and Sculpture*. London: Oxford University Press, 1937.

———. *Tarikh Misr fi asr al-batalima*. 1946; repr. Cairo: Matbaat al-anjlu al-misriya, 1966.

O'Connor, David. "The American Archaeological Focus on Ancient Palaces and Temples of the New Kingdom." In *The American Discovery of Ancient Egypt: Essays*, edited by Nancy Thomas, 79–95. Los Angeles: Los Angeles County Museum of Art and the American Research Center in Egypt, 1995.

O'Donnell Jr., J. Dean. *Lavigerie in Tunisia: The Interplay of Imperialist and Missionary*. Athens, GA: University of Georgia Press, 1979.

Ormos, István. *Max Herz Pasha (1856–1919): His Life and Career*. 2 vols. Cairo: IFAO, 2009.

Ory, Solange. "Max van Berchem, orientaliste." In *D'un orient l'autre*, edited by Jean-Claude Vatin, 2: 11–24. 2 vols. Paris: CEDEJ: CNRS, 1991.

Ostle, Robin. "Ahmad Zaki Abu Shadi." In *Essays in Arabic Literary Biography 1850–1950*, edited by Roger Allen, 32–37. Wiesbaden: Harrassowitz, 2010.

———. "Alexandria: A Mediterranean Cosmopolitan Center of Cultural Production." In *Modernity and Culture from the Mediterranean to the Indian Ocean*, edited by Leila Tarazi Fawaz and C.A. Bayly, 314–20. New York: Columbia University Press, 2002.

_____. "Literature and Art in Egypt (1914–1950): Form, Structure and Ide-
ology," In *D'un orient l'autre*, edited by J.C. Vatin. Vol 1, 524–34. Paris:
CEDEJ, CNRS, 1991.
_____. "Modern Egyptian Renaissance Man." *Bulletin of the School of Oriental
and African Studies* 57, pt. 1 (1994): 184–92
Owen, Roger. *Lord Cromer: Victorian Imperialist, Edwardian Proconsul*. Oxford:
Oxford University Press, 2004.
Pemble, John. *The Mediterranean Passion: Victorians and Edwardians in the South*.
Oxford: Clarendon Press, 1987.
Petricioli, Marta. *Oltre il mito: L'Egitto degli italiani (1917–1947)*. Milan: B.
Modadori, 2007.
Petrie, Flinders. *Seventy Years in Archaeology*. London: Sampson Low, Marston,
1931.
Politis, Athanase G. *L'Hellénisme et l'Égypte modern*. Vol. 1, *Histoire de l'hellénisme
égyptien de 1798 à 1927*. Paris: Alcan, 1929.
Pollard, Lisa. *Nurturing the Nation: The Family Politics of Modernizing, Colonizing,
and Liberating Egypt, 1805–1923*. Berkeley: University of California Press,
2005.
Powell, Eve Troutt. *A Different Shade of Colonialism: Egypt, Great Britain, and the
Mastery of the Sudan*. Berkeley: University of California Press, 2003.
Practical Guide to Alexandria, Cairo, Port Saïd, and Neighbourhood. London:
Nilsson, [1908].
Pudney, John. *The Thomas Cook Story*. London: M. Joseph, 1953.
al-Qadi, Faruq Hafiz, "al-Ruwwad al-awail fi dirasat al-tarikh al-yunani al-
rumani." *al-Majalla al-tarikhiya al-misriya* 39 (1996): 271–82.
al-Qadim. (magazine, Cairo, 1920s).
Quirke, Stephen. "Exclusion of Egyptians in English-directed Archaeology
1882–1922 under British Occupation of Egypt." In *Ägyptologen und Ägyptologien zwischen Kaiserreich und Gründen der beiden deutschen Staaten: Reflexionen
zur Geschichte und Episteme eines altertumswissenschaftlichen Fachs im 150. Jahr
der Zeitschrift für Ägyptische Sprache und Alteretumskunde*, edited by Susanne
Bickel et al., 379–405. Beiheft 1. Berlin: Akademie Verlag Berlin: de Gruyter,
2013.
———. *Hidden Hands: Egyptian Workforces in Petrie Excavation Archives, 1880–
1924*. London: Duckworth, 2010.
Rabbat, Nasser. "The Formation of the Neo-Mamluk Style in Modern Egypt."
In *The Education of the Architect: Historiography, Urbanism, and the Growth of
Architectural Knowledge*, edited by Martha Pollak, 363–86. Cambridge, MA:
MIT Press, 1997.
al-Rafii, Abd al-Rahman. *Tarikh al-haraka al-qawmiya fi Misr al-qadima min fajr
al-tarikh ila al-fath al-arabi*. Cairo: Maktabat al-nahda al-misriya, 1963.
al-Ra'i, Ali. "Arabic Drama since the Thirties." In *Modern Arabic Literature*,
edited by M. M. Badawi, 358–403. The Cambridge History of Arabic Literature. Cambridge: Cambridge University Press, 1992.
Raue, Dietrich. "Der 'J'accuse'-Brief an John A. Wilson: Drei Ansichten von
Georg Steindorff." In *Ägyptologen und Ägyptologien zwischen Kaiserreich und*

Gründen der beiden deutschen Staaten: Reflexionen zur Geschichte und Episteme eines altertumswissenschaftlichen Fachs im 150. Jahr der Zeitschrift für Ägyptische Sprache und Alteretumskunde, edited by Susanne Bickel et al., 345–76. Beiheft 1. Berlin: Akademie Verlag Berlin: de Gruyter, 2013.

Recueil d'études égyptologiques dédiées à la mémoire de Jean-François Champollion à l'occasion du centenaire de la letter à M. Dacier relative à l'alphabet des hieroglyphs phonétiques lue à l'académie des inscriptions et belles-lettres le 27 septembre 1822. Bibliothèque de l'école des hautes études publiée sous les auspices du ministère de l'instruction publique. Sciences historiques et philologiques. Fasc. 234 (Paris: E. Champion, 1922).

Reeves, Nicholas. *Ancient Egypt: The Great Discoveries: A Year-by-Year Chronicle.* London: Thames & Hudson, 2000.

———. *The Complete Tutankhamun.* London: Thames & Hudson, 1990.

Reeves, Nicholas, and John H. Taylor. *Howard Carter before Tutankhamun.* New York: H.N. Abrams, 1993.

Reid, Donald Malcolm. "Archeology, Social Reform, and Modern Identity among the Copts, 1854–1952." In *Entre réform sociale et movement national: identité et modernization en Égypte (1882–1962)*, edited by Alain Rousillon, 311–35. Cairo: CEDEJ, 1995.

———. *Cairo University and the Making of Modern Egypt.* Cambridge: Cambridge University Press, 1990.

———. "Cromer and the Classics: Imperialism, Nationalism and the Greco–Roman Past in Modern Egypt." *Middle Eastern Studies* 32, no. 1 (1996): 1–29.

———. "Cultural Imperialism and Nationalism: The Struggle to Define and Control the Heritage of Arab Art in Egypt." *International Journal of Middle East Studies* 24 (1992): 57–76.

———. "French Egyptology and the Architecture of Orientalism: Deciphering the Façade of Cairo's Egyptian Museum." In *Franco–Arab Encounters: Studies in Memory of David C. Gordon*, edited by Mathew Gordon and L. Carl Brown, 35–69. Beirut: American University in Beirut Press, 1996.

———. *The Odyssey of Farah Antun: A Syrian Christian's Search for Secularism.* Minneapolis: Bibliotheca Islamica, 1975.

———. "Remembering and Forgetting Tutankhamun: Imperial and National Rhythms of Archaeology, 1922–1972." In *Histories of Egyptology: Interdisciplinary Measures*, edited by William Carruthers, 157–73. London: Routledge, 2015.

———. "Representing Ancient Egypt at Imperial High Noon (1882–1922): Egyptological Careers and Artistic Allegories of Civilization." In *From Plunder to Preservation: Britain and the Heritage of Empire, c. 1800–1940.* Proceedings of the British Academy 187, edited by Astrid Swenson and Peter Mandler, 187–214. Oxford: Oxford University Press, 2013.

———. *Whose Pharaohs? Archaeology, Museums, and Egyptian National Identity from Napoleon to World War I.* Berkeley: University of California Press, 2002.

Reimer, Michael J. *Colonial Bridgehead: Government and Society in Alexandria, Egypt 1807–1882.* Boulder, CO: Westview, 1997.

Renoliet, Jean-Jacques. *L'UNESCO oubliée: La société des nations et la cooperation intellectuelle.* Paris: Publications de la Sorbonne, 1999.

Reynolds, Nancy Y. *A City Consumed: Urban Commerce, the Cairo Fire, and the Politics of Decolonization in Egypt*. Stanford: Stanford University Press, 2012.

Rizq, Yunan Labib. *Tarikh al-wizarat al-misriya 1878-1953*. Cairo: Markaz al-dirasat al-siyasiya wa-l-istratijiya bil-Ahram. Wahdat al-wathaiq w-l-buhuth al-tarikhiya, 1974.

Robinson, James M. *The Facsimile Edition of the Nag Hammadi Codices*. 12 vols. Leiden: Brill, 1972–77.

———. "The French Role in the Early Nag Hammadi Studies. *Journal of Coptic Studies* 7 (2005): 1–12.

Rogers, J.M. *From Antiquarianism to Islamic Archaeology*. Cairo: Istituto italiano di cultura per la R.A.E, 1974.

Romer, John and Elizabeth. *The Rape of Tutankhamun*. London: Michael O'Mara, 1994.

Rosenberg, Emily. *Spreading the American Dream: American Economic and Cultural Expansion, 1890–1945*. New York: Hill & Wang, 1982.

Rosenthal, Franz. *The Classical Heritage in Islam*. Translated by E. and J. Marmorstein Berkeley: University of California Press, 1965.

Russell, Mona L. *Creating the New Egyptian Woman: Consumerism, Education, and National Identity, 1863–1922*. New York: Palgrave Macmillan, 2004.

Ryzova, Lucie. *The Age of the Efendiyya: Passages to Modernity in National-Colonial Egypt*. Oxford: Oxford University Press, 2013.

Saad, Zaki Youssef. *Royal Excavations at Saqqara and Helwan (1945–1947)*. Cairo: IFAO, 1947.

———. *Royal Excavations at Helwan (1945–47)*. Cairo: IFAO, 1951.

Said, Edward. *Culture and Imperialism*. New York: Knopf, 1993.

———. *Orientalism: Western Conceptions of the Orient*. New York: Pantheon, 1978.

Said, Luway Mahmud. "Ahmad Basha Kamal: raid al-tanwir al-athari." In *Kamal wa Yusuf: athariyan min al-zaman al-jamil*, edited by Luway Mahmud Said and Mahmud Abd al-Munim Qaysuni, 7–132. Cairo: Supreme Council of Antiquities, 2002.

Said, Rushdi. *The River Nile: Geology, Hydrology, and Utilization*. Oxford: Pergamon, 1993.

Sakr, Tarek Mohamed Refaat. *Early Twentieth-Century Islamic Architecture in Cairo*. Cairo: American University in Cairo Press, 1993.

Sallam, Hala. "Ahmed Kamal Pasha (1851–1923): A Family of Egyptologists." In *Proceedings of the Seventh International Congress of Egyptologists: Cambridge, 3–9 September 1995*, edited by C.J. Eyre, 1015–1019. Leuven: Peeters, 1998.

Sammarco, Angelo. *Gli italiani in Egitto: il contributo italiano nella formazione dell'Egitto moderno*. Alexandria: Edizioni del Fascio, 1937.

Samuel, Alan E. *The Shifting Sands of History: Interpretations of Ptolemaic Egypt*. Lanham, MD: University Press of America, 1989.

Sanders, Paula. *Creating Medieval Cairo: Empire, Religion, and Architectural Preservation in Nineteenth-Century Egypt*. Cairo: American University in Cairo Press, 2008.

Sattin, Anthony. *Lifting the Veil: British Society in Egypt, 1768–1956*. London: J.M. Dent, 1988.

Savoy, Bénédicte, ed. *Nofretete: Ein deutsch-französische Affäre, 1912–1931.* Cologne: Böhlau, 2011.

Sayce, Rev. A.H. *Reminiscences.* London: Macmillan, 1923.

Schneider, Thomas. "Ägyptologen im Dritten Reich." *Journal of Egyptian History* 4, no. 2 (Fall 2011): 105–216.

Schroeder-Gudehus, B. "Challenge to Transnational Loyalties: International Scientific Organization after the First World War." *Science Studies* 3 (1973): 193–218.

Schultz, Bernd, ed. *James Simon: Philanthrop und Kunstmäzen / Philanthropist and Patron of the Arts.* 2nd ed. Munich: Prestel, 2007.

Schipper, Bernd. U., ed. *Ägyptologie als Wissenschaft. Adolf Erman (1854–1937) in seiner Zeit.* Berlin: W. du Gruyter, 2006.

Schwanitz, Wolfgang G., ed. *Germany and the Middle East, 1871–1945.* Princeton: Marcus Wiener, 2004.

Scott III, Gerry D. "Go Down into Egypt: The Dawn of American Egyptology." In *The American Discovery of Ancient Egypt*, edited by Nancy Thomas, 37–47. Los Angeles: Los Angeles County Museum of Art and the American Research Center in Egypt, 1995.

Scott 2012 Standard Postage Stamp Catalogue. 6 vols. Sidney, OH: Scott Publishing Co., 2011. "Egypt" is in Vol. 2: *Countries of the World C–F.*

Sedra, Paul. "Class Cleavages and Ethnic Conflict: Coptic Christian Communities in Modern Egyptian Politics." *Islam and Christian-Muslim Relations* 10, no. 2 (1999): 219–35.

———. *From Mission to Modernity: Evangelicals, Reformers, and Education in Nineteenth Century Egypt.* London: I.B. Tauris, 2011.

———. "Imagining an Imperial Race: Egyptology in the Service of Empire." *Comparative Studies of South Asia, Africa and the Middle East* 24, no. 1 (2004): 249–59.

———. "Writing the History of the Modern Copts: From Victims and Symbols to Actors." *The History Compass* 7, no. 3 (2009): 1049–63.

Segrè, Claudio. *Fourth Shore: The Italian Colonization of Libya.* Chicago: University of Chicago Press, 1974.

Seikally, Samir. "Coptic Communal Reform: 1860–1914." *Middle East Studies* 6 (1970): 247–75.

Selim, Samah. *The Novel and the Rural Imaginary in Egypt, 1800–1985.* New York: RoutledgeCurzon, 2004.

Seyfried, Friedericke. "Die Büste der Nofretete: Dokumentation des Fundes und der Fundteilung, 1912/1913." *Jahrbuch Preussischer Kulturbesitz 2010*, Band 46 (2011): 133–202.

———, ed. *In the Light of Amarna: 100 Years of the Nefertiti Discovery.* Berlin: Ägyptisches Museum und Papyrussammlung, Staatliche Museen zu Berlin, 2012.

Shafiq, Ahmad. *Mudhakkirati fi nisf al-qarn.* 4 vols. Cairo: Matbaat Misr, 1934–36.

Shahid, Irfan. "Ahmad Shawqi." In *Essays in Arabic Literary Biography, 1850–1950*, edited by Roger Allen, 304–17. Wiesbaden: Harrassowitz, 2010.

Shalabi, Hilmi Ahmad. *al-Aqbat wa-l-islah al-ijtimai fi Misr (dawr jamiyat al-tawfiq) 1891–1952*. Cairo: Maktabat al-anjilu al-misriya, 1992.

Shamir, Shimon. "Radicalism in Egyptian Historiography." In *Islam, Nationalism and Radicalism in Egypt and the Sudan*, edited by Gabriel R. Warburg and Uri Kupferschmidt, 216–17. New York: Praeger, 1983.

Sharkey, Heather. *American Evangelicals in Egypt: Missionary Encounters in an Age of Empire*. Princeton: Princeton University Press, 2008.

Shaw, Wendy M.K. *Possessors and Possessed: Museums, Archaeology, and the Visualization of History in the Late Ottoman Empire*. Berkeley: University of California Press, 2003.

el-Shayyal, Gamal el-Din. *A History of Egyptian Historiography in the Nineteenth Century*. Alexandria: Alexandria University Press, 1962.

———. *Tarikh al-tarjama wa-l-haraka al-thaqafiya fi asr Muhammad Ali*. Cairo: Dar al-fikr al-arabi, 1951.

Silberman, Neil Asher. *Digging for God and Country: Exploration, Archaeology and the Secret Struggle for the Holy Land, 1799–1917*. New York: Knopf, 1982.

———, ed. *Oxford Companion to Archaeology*. 2nd ed. Oxford: Oxford University Press, 2012.

Simaika, Marcus H. *Guide sommaire du musée copte et des principales églises du Caire*. Cairo: Imp. nationale, 1937.

———. *Note historique sur le Musée Copte au Vieux Caire à l'occasion de la visite de Sa Hautesse Fouad Ier. Sultan d'Égypte, Mardi 21 Décembre, 1920*. Cairo: Musée Copte, 1920.

Simaika, Samir and Nevine Henein. *Marcus Simaika: Father of Coptic Archaeology*. Cairo: The American University in Cairo Press, 2017.

Smith, Carl D. *Islam and the Search for Social Order in Modern Egypt: A Biography of Muhammad Husayn Haykal*. Albany: State University of New York Press, 1983.

Sobhy, Georgy. *Kitab qawaid al-lugha al-misriya al-qibtiya*. Cairo: IFAO, 1925.

———. "Notes on the Ethnology." *Bulletin de l'association des amis des églises et de l'art copte* l (1935, counted as *Bulletin de la société d'archéologie copte* 1): 43–59.

———. "Survivals of Ancient Egyptian in Modern Dialect." *Ancient Egypt* (1921): 3: 70–75.

Société archéologique d'Alexandrie. *Bulletin de la société archéologique d'Alexandrie (BSAA)*.

Société d'archéologie copte. Bulletin de la société d'archéologie copte (BSAC).

Société royale de géographie d'Égypte. *Bulletin de la société royale de géographie d'Égypte*. (Previously Société khédiviale, later Société de géographie.)

Solé, Robert. *L'Égypte, passion française*. Paris: Seuil, 1997.

Somekh, S. "The Neo-Classical Poets." In *Modern Arabic Literature*, edited by M.M. Badawi, 329–57. The Cambridge History of Arabic Literature. Cambridge: Cambridge University Press 1993.

Speiser, Philip. *Die Geschichte der Erhaltung Arabischer Baudenkmäler in Ägypten. Die Restaurierung der Madrasa Tatar al-Hiğāzīya* . . . . Heidelberg: Heidelbergerverlag, 2001.

Stadien, William. *Too Rich: The High Life and Tragic Death of King Farouk*. New York: Caroll & Graf, 1991.

Standard Catalog of World Paper Money. Colin R. Bruce and Albert Pick, eds. 8th ed. Vol. 2, *General Issues to 1960,* "Egypt." Iola, WI: Krause Publications, 1996.

Starkey, Paul. *From the Ivory Tower: A Critical Study of Tawfiq al-Hakim.* London: Ithaca Press, 1978.

Starr, Deborah A. *Remembering Cosmopolitan Egypt: Literature, Culture, and Empire.* London: Routledge, 2009.

Steele, James. *An Architecture for People: The Complete Works of Hassan Fathy.* New York: St. Martin's, 1997.

———. *Hassan Fathy.* London: Academy Editions, 1988.

Storrs, Ronald. *The Memoirs of Sir Ronald Storrs.* New York: Putnam, 1937. Published in England as *Orientations.* London: Nicholson & Watson, 1937.

Stowe, William W. *Going Abroad: European Travel in Nineteenth-century American Culture.* Princeton: Princeton University Press, 1994.

Stray, Christopher. *Classics Transformed: Schools, Universities, and Society in England, 1830–1960.* Oxford: Clarendon Press, 1998.

Subhi, Muhammad Khalil. *Tarikh al-hayah al-niyabiya fi Misr min ahd rukn al-jinan Muhammad Ali Basha.* (Vols. 4-6 and supplementary vols. 5 and 6) Cairo: Dar al-kutub al-misriya, 1939-47.

Suriyal, Riyad. *al-Mujtama al-qibti fi (al-qarn 19).* Cairo: Maktabat al-mahabba, ca.1971.

Swinglehurst, Edmund. *Cook's Tours: The Story of Popular Travel.* Poole, Dorset, UK: Blandford Press,1982.

Symonds, Richard. *Oxford and Empire: The Last Lost Cause?* London: Macmillan, 1986.

Tadrus, Ramzi. *al-Aqbat fi-l-qarn al-ishrin.* 4 vols. Cairo: Matbaat jaridat Misr, 1910–11.

Taragan, Hana. "Architecture in Fact and Fiction: The Case of the New Gourna Village in Upper Egypt." *Muqarnas* 16 (1999): 169–78.

Thabit, Karim. *al-Malik Fuad: malik al-nahda.* Cairo: Matbaat al-maarif, 1944.

Thomas, Nancy, ed. *The American Discovery of Egypt* and *The American Discovery of Egypt: Essays.* Los Angeles: Los Angeles County Museum of Art and the American Research Center in Egypt, 1995.

———. "American Institutional Fieldwork in Egypt, 1899–1960." In *The American Discovery of Ancient Egypt,* edited by Nancy Thomas, 49–76. Los Angeles: Los Angeles County Museum of Art and the American Research Center in Egypt, 1995.

Thompson, Jason. *Edward William Lane, 1801–1876: The Life of the Pioneering Egyptologist and Orientalist.* London: Haus, 2010.

———. *Wonderful Things: A History of Egyptology.* 3 vols. (Cairo: American University in Cairo Press, 2015–18).

Tignor, Robert. *State, Private Enterprise and Economic Change in Egypt, 1918–1952.* Princeton: Princeton University Press, 1984.

The Times. London.

The Times Digital Archive 1785–1985.

Tompkins, Calvin. *Merchants and Masterpieces: The Story of the Metropolitan Museum of Art.* New York: E.P. Dutton, 1970.

Toth, James. *Sayyid Qutb: The Life and Legacy of a Radical Islamic Intellectual.* Oxford: Oxford University Press, 2013.

Tregenza, L.A. *Egyptian Years.* London: Oxford University Press, 1958.

Trigger, Bruce. "Egyptology, Ancient Egypt, and the American Imagination." In *The American Discovery of Ancient Egypt,* edited by Nancy Thomas, 21–35. Los Angeles: Los Angeles Country Museum of Art and the American Research Center in Egypt, 1995.

———. *A History of Archaeological Thought.* Cambridge: Cambridge University Press, 1989. 2nd ed., 2006.

Trümpler, Charlotte, ed., *Das Grosse Spiel: Archäologie und Politik zur Zeit des Kolonialismus (1860–1940).* Cologne: Ruhr Museum, 2008.

Truscot, Bruce. *Red Brick University.* London: Faber & Faber, 1943.

"Turath Misr al-qadima." Special issue of *al-Muqtataf* (September 1936).

Turner, Eric. "The Graeco–Roman Branch." In *Excavating in Egypt: The Egypt Exploration Society 1882–1982,* edited by T.G.H. James, 161–76. Chicago: University of Chicago Press, 1982.

Tzalas, Harry E. *Farewell to Alexandria.* Translated by Susan E. Mantouvalou. Cairo: American University in Cairo Press, 2007.

Urry, John. *The Tourist Gaze.* 2nd ed. London: Sage, 2002.

Van Berchem, Max. *Matériaux pour un Corpus Inscriptionum Arabicum.* Part 1: *Inscriptions de l'Égypte.* Cairo: IFAO, 1903.

Van der Spek, Kees. *The Modern Neighbors of Tutankhamun: History, Life, and Work in the Villages of the Theban West Bank.* Cairo: American University in Cairo Press, 2011.

Van der Vliet, Jacques. "The Copts: 'Modern Sons of the Pharaohs'?" *Church History and Religious Culture* 89, nos. 1–3 (2009): 279–90.

Varisco, Daniel Martin. *Reading Orientalism: Said and the Unsaid.* Seattle: University of Washington Press, 2007.

Vasunia, Phiroze. *The Classics and Colonial India.* Oxford: Oxford University Press, 2014.

———. *The Gift of the Nile: Hellenizing Egypt from Aeschylus to Alexander.* Berkeley: University of California Press, 2001.

Vatin, Jean-Claude, ed. *D'un orient l'autre.* 2 vols. (Paris: CEDEJ, CNRS, 1991).

Vaziri, Mostafa. *Iran as Imagined Nation: The Construction of National Identity.* New York: Paragon House, 1993.

Verner, Miroslav. *The Pyramids: The Mystery, Culture, and Science of Egypt's Great Monuments.* Translated by Steven Rendall. Cairo: American University in Cairo Press, 2002.

Vernoit, Stephen, ed. *Discovering Islamic Art: Scholars, Collectors and Collections, 1850–1950.* London: I.B. Tauris, 2000.

Vinson, Steve. "From Lord Elgin to James Henry Breasted: The Politics of the Past in the First Era of Globalization." In *Marketing Heritage: Archaeology and the Consumption of the Past,* edited by Yorke Rowan and Uzi Baram, 57–65. Walnut Creek, CA: Alta Mira Press, 2004.

Vitalis, Robert. *When Capitalists Collide: Business Conflict and the End of Empire in Egypt.* Berkeley: University of California Press, 1995.

Volait, Mercedes. *Architectes et architectures de l'Égypte moderne (1830–1950): genèse et essor d'une expertise locale.* Paris: Maisonneuve et Larose, 2005.

————. "Architectures de la décennie pharaonique en Égypte (1922–1932)." In *Images d'Égypte de la fresque à la bande dessinée,* edited by Jean-Claude Vatin, 163–86. Cairo: CEDEJ, IFAO, 1991.

————. *Fous du Caire: excentriques, architects et amateurs d'art en Égypte, 1863–1914.* Montpellier: L'archange minotaure, 2009.

————. "Making Cairo Modern (1870–1950): Multiple Models for a 'European-Style' Urbanism." In *Urbanism: Imported or Exported,* edited by Joe Nasr and Mercedes Volait, 17–50. Chichester, UK: Wiley-Academic, 2003.

Volkoff, Oleg V. *Comment on visitait la vallée du Nil: les guides de l'Égypte.* Cairo: IFAO, 1967.

————. *Voyageurs russes en Égypte.* Cairo: IFAO, 1972.

von Pilgrim, Cornelius. "Ludwig Borchardt und sein 'Institut für ägyptische Bauforschung und Altertumskunde' in Kairo—Ein Beitrag zur Urgeschichte des Schweizer Instituts Kairo." In *Ägyptologen und Ägyptologien zwischen Kaiserreich und Gründung der beiden Staaten: Reflexionen zur Geschichte und Episteme eines altertumswissenschaftlichen Fachs im 150. Jahr der Zeitschrift für Ägyptische Sprache und Alteretumskunde,* edited by Susanne Bickel et al., 243–66. Beiheft 1. Berlin: Akademie Verlag Berlin: de Gruyter, 2013.

Von Sabine Mangold, Wuppertal. "Die Khedivial-Bibliothekare und ihre deutschen Bibliothekare (1871–1914)." *Zeitschrift der Deutschen Morgenländischen Gesellschaft* 151, Heft 1 (2007): 49–76.

Voss, Susanne. "Der lange Arm des Nationalsozialismus: Zur Geschichte der Abteilung Kairo des DAI im Dritten Reich." In *Ägyptologen und Ägyptologien zwischen Kaiserreich und Gründen der beiden deutschen Staaten: Reflexionen zur Geschichte und Episteme eines altertumswissenschaftlichen Fachs im 150. Jahr der Zeitschrift für Ägyptische Sprache und Alteretumskunde,* edited by Susanne Bickel et al., 266–98. Beiheft 1. Berlin: Akademie Verlag Berlin: de Gruyter, 2013.

————. *Die Geschichte der Abteilung Kairo des DAI im Spannungsfeld Deutscher Politischer Interessen.* Bd. 1: *1881–1929.* Rahden, Westf.: Verlag Marie Leidorf, 2013.

————. "La representation égyptologique allemande en Égypte et sa perception par les égyptologues français du XIXe au milieu du XX siècle." *Revue germanique internationale* 16 (Nov. 2012): 171–92.

Voss, Susanne, and Cornelius von Pilgrim, "Ludwig Borchardt und die deutschen Interessen am Nil." In *Das Grosse Spiel—Archäologie und Politik zur Zeit des Kolonialismus (1860–1940),* edited by Charlotte Trümpler, 294–305. Cologne: Ruhr Museum, 2008.

Watson, John H. *Among the Copts.* Brighton, UK: Sussex Academic, 2002.

Weiner, Mina Rieur. *Edwin Howland Blashfield: Master American Muralist.* New York: Norton, 2009.

Wendell, Charles. *The Evolution of the Egyptian National Image: From Its Origin to Ahmad Lutfi al-Sayyid.* Berkeley: University of California Press, 1972.

Whidden, James. *Monarchy and Modernity in Egypt: Politics, Islam and Neo-colonialism between the Wars.* London: I.B. Tauris, 2013.

Whitcomb, Donald. "Archaeology." *Encyclopaedia of Islam*. 3rd ed. Leiden: Brill, 2009–4: 47–66.

Wickett, Elizabeth. *Seers, Saints and Sinners: The Oral Tradition of Upper Egypt*. London: I.B.Tauris, 2012.

Wilkinson, Richard H., ed. *Egyptology Today*. Cambridge: Cambridge University Press, 2008.

Williams, Caroline. *Islamic Monuments in Cairo: The Practical Guide*. 6th ed. Cairo: American University in Cairo Press, 2008.

Wilson, John A. *Signs and Wonders upon Pharaoh: A History of American Egyptology*. Chicago: University of Chicago Press, 1964.

———. *Thousands of Years: An Archaeologist's Search for Ancient Egypt*. New York: Charles Scribner's Sons, 1972.

Winstone, H. V. F. *Howard Carter and the Discovery of the Tomb of Tutankhamun*. London: Constable, 1991.

Withey, Lynn. *Grand Tours and Cook's Tours: A History of Leisure Travel, 1750–1915*. New York: W. Morrow, 1997.

Wizarat al-maarif al-umumiya. *Mathaf al-hadara al-misriya 1949*. Cairo: Matbaat wizarat al-maarif al-umumiya, 1949.

Wright, John L. "Mussolini, Libya, and the Sword of Islam." In *Italian Colonialism*, edited by Ruth Ben-Ghiat and Mia Fuller, 122–30. New York: Palgrave Macmillan, 2005.

Wynn, L.L. *Pyramids & Nightclubs: A Travel Ethnography of Arab and Western Imaginations of Egypt*. Austin: University of Texas Press, 2007.

Zaidan, Jurji. *The Autobiography of Jurjī Zaidān*. Translated by Thomas Philipp. Washington, DC: Three Continents Press, 1990.

Zakhura, Ilyas. *Mirat al-asr fi akabir al-rijal bi-Misr*. 3 vols. Cairo, 1897–1916.

Zubaida, Sami. "Cosmopolitanism and the Middle East." In *Cosmopolitanism, Identity and Authenticity in the Middle East*, edited by Roel Meijer, 15–33. Surrey, UK: Curzon, 1999.

Zvie, Alain-Pierre. "L'Égypte ancienne ou l'orient perdu et retrouvé." In *D'un orient l'autre*, edited by Jean-Claude Vatin. Vol 1, 35–44. Paris: CEDEJ: CNRS, 1991.

Online Sources

Association Internationale des Papyrologues/ International Association of Papyrologists. "Histoire – History." http://www.ulb.ac.be/assoc/aip/histor.htm. Updated Aug. 23, 2014.

Comité de conservation des monuments de l'art arabe. *Bulletin*. Issues from 1882–1961 available at Thesaurus Islamicus Foundation Islamic Art Network. http://www.islamic-art.org/comitte. Accessed August 18, 2014.

El-Aref, Nevine. "Alexandria's Graeco–Roman Museum to Reopen within 18 Months," *Ahram Online*, Oct. 30, 2013. http://english.ahram.org.eg/UI/Front/Search.aspx?Text=alexandria's%20graeco-roman%20museum%20to%20reopen. Accessed January 9, 2015.

International Committee of Mediterranean Games, History, "Les jeux

méditerranéens." http://www.cijm.org.gr/index.php?option=com_content&v
iew=article&id=19&Itemid=27&lang=en. Updated January 2015.

Maessen, Marcel and Monica. t3.wy Foundation for Historical Research in
Egyptology. "Dig House Project." http:///www.t3.wy.org/. Updated July 20,
2014.

Qurna History Project. Caroline Simpson, Secretary. http://www.qurna.org.
Last updated 2010, accessed January 9, 2015.

Schweizerisches Institut für Ägyptische Bauforschung und Altertumskunde,
"Geschichte des Instituts." http://www.swissinst.ch/html. Accessed January
9, 2015.

Steindorff, George. Letter to John A. Wilson, June 1945. Oriental Institute
Archives, University of Chicago. Included in online post by Charles
E. Jones, "Nazism and ANE Studies," October 25, 1993. http://oi.
uchicago.edu/research/library/ane/digest/v01/v01.n021. Accessed
January 9, 2015.

Archives and Privately Held Manuscripts

Egypt

American University in Cairo. Rare Books and Special Collections. Creswell
Archives.

Cairo University Archives (CUA). Université Égyptienne. Records of the private
Egyptian University, 1908–1925.

Dar al-Mahfuzat (DM). Millafat al-khidma wa-l-maash (Pension Folders).

Dar al-Wathaiq al-Qawmiya (DWQ) / Egyptian National Archives. Nizarat
al-Ashghal / Ministry of Public Works. Maslahat al-Athar / Service des
Antiquités.

Simaika Pasha, Murqus (Marcus) H. "Excerpts from the Memoirs of Marcus
H. Simaika Pasha, C.B.E., F.S.A. (1864–1944)." Typescript in the possession
of the Simaika family. These memoirs have since become the prime
source for Samir Simaika and Nevine Henein. *Marcus Simaika: Father of
Coptic Archaeology.* Cairo: The American University in Cairo Press, 2017.
"Introduction", pp. 1–6, by Donald Malcolm Reid.

France

Archives de le Ministère des affaires étrangères (MAE), Nantes.
Ambassade Le Caire. Université 1907–1940: Carton 140 (52); Enseignement
égyptien.
Service des antiquités: Cartons 174, 174bis; Carton 175, Dossier 3: Ensei-
gnement Publique, Folder: Société royale égyptienne de papyrologie.
Service des oeuvres françaises à l'étranger. Série D.—Levant/ Carton 366:
Égypte.
Facultés égyptiennes.

United Kingdom

Egypt Exploration Society Archives. London.
Unmarked folder on Amarna 1947–1949.

EES Correspondence, Box: A.H. Gardiner 1937–1949.
The Griffith Institute Archive. University of Oxford. Percy Newberry
Correspondence.
National Archives (formerly Public Record Office), Kew, Richmond, Surrey, UK
FO (Foreign Office) 141, 371, 395, 924
BW 29/34 (British Council)
MT 23
RAIL 258
School of Oriental and African Studies, University of London. Archives and
Special Collections. MS 380428/1–6, Alan J.B. Wace, Farouk lst Univer-
sity Alexandria, "Excavations at Kom Ed Dika, Alexandria" and associated
correspondence.
Thomas Cook Archives (TCA), Peterborough, UK. "Egyptian Steamers" (scrap-
book); Box: Egypt: Steamer Contracts.
University of Liverpool. Special Collections and Archives.

United States
Museum of Fine Arts, Boston (MFA). George Reisner Papers.
Box: Egyptian Department 1943–54. Folder 8/9 (folder 8 out of 9).
Oriental Institute Archives, University of Chicago, James H. Breasted Papers.
With the permission of the director of the Archives, Jeffrey Abt kindly sup-
plied me with copies of selected documents from the Breasted papers.
University of Pennsylvania. University Museum Archives. Expedition Records.
Egypt. Mitrahineh. Meydum.
National Archives. Washington DC. Records of the Dept. of State relating to
Internal Affairs of Eg, 1910–1929, 1930–39. Microfilm Publications series
numbers 571 and T 1251.
Smithsonian Institution Archives. Washington, DC. Accession No. 94–118,
records of the American Research Center in Egypt.

Unpublished Theses and Dissertations

Carruthers, William Edward. 2014. "Egyptology, Archaeology and the Making
of Revolutionary Egypt, c. 1925–1958." PhD diss., Darwin College, University of Cambridge.
Gabra, Sami. 1925. "Justice under the Old and New Kingdom in Egypt." MA
thesis, Institute of Archaeology, University of Liverpool, Special Collections
& Archives..
Gady, Éric. 2005. "Le pharaon, l'égyptologue et le diplomate. Les égyptologues
français en Égypte, du voyage de Champollion à la crise de Suez (1828–
1956)." 2 vols. PhD diss., Université de Paris IV-Sorbonne.
Hamza, M.A. 1925. "The Relations of Nubia and Egypt." MA thesis, Institute of
Archaeology, University of Liverpool, Special Collections & Archives.
El-Habashi, Alaa El-Din Elwi. 2001. "*Athar* to Monuments: The Intervention
of the Comité de Conservation des Monuments de l'Art Arabe." PhD diss.,
University of Pennsylvania.
Nobbs-Thiessen, Max. 2006. "Contested Representations and the Building of

Modern Egypt: The Architecture of Hassan Fathy." MA thesis, Simon Fraser University.

Oram, Elizabeth E. 2004. "Constructing Modern Copts: The Production of Coptic Christian Identity in Contemporary Egypt." PhD diss., Princeton University.

Stock, Raymond T. 2008, corrected 2009. "A Mummy Awakens: The Pharaonic Fiction of Naguib Mahfouz." PhD diss., University of Pennsylvania.

Interviews by the author

(In Cairo unless otherwise noted.)

Egyptologists

Abou-Ghazi, Dia. Jan. 5, 12, 13, 1999.

Bakr, Muhammad Ibrahim. Apr. 30, 1983.

Gaballa, Ali Gaballa. Several interviews, spring 2005.

Habachi, Labib. Nov. 9, 1982; Jun. 23, 1983.

Haikal, Fayza. May 23, 25, 1988; Mar. 1, Jun. 2, 1999; Jul. 17, 2005.

Labib, Pahor. Oct. 22, 1987.

al-Mallakh, Kamal. Oct. 14, 1988.

Mokhtar, Gamal. Jun. 6, 1988.

Nur El-Din, Abdel Halim. Oct. 31, Nov. 21, 1998.

Radwan, Ali. Feb. 17, Apr. 2 and 3, 1999.

Riad (Ghabur), Henry. Apr. 20, 1988.

Sadek, Abdel-Aziz. Jun. 6, 10, 12, 1988.

Salih, Ahmad. Nov. 3, 1987 (Conservation Dept., Fac. of Archaeology, Cairo University)

Trad, Mai. April 6, 1983; Mar. 2, 1988, etc.

Zayed, Abd El-Hamid. Apr. 19, 1999.

Islamic Archaeologists, Historians of Islamic Art, and Preservationists

Abd Eltawab, Abd El Rahman. Jan. 7, 10, 1999; July 12, 2005.

Asker, Farouk S. Dec. 2, 1998.

al-Basha, Hassan. Feb. 2, 1988.

Beheri, Salah El-Din. Dec. 27, 1998; June 7, 2005.

Emary, Amal El. Jan. 3, 1999.

Fathi, Sayed. Dec. 9, 1998.

Hassan, Nawal. July 17, 2005.

Nadim, Asaad. Aug. 1, 2005.

Yussef, Abdel Raouf Ali. April 18, 1988.

Greco–Roman Specialists

Awad, Mohamed. Alexandria. July 6, 2005.

El-Abbadi, Mostafa A.H. Alexandria. August 14, 2005.

Abboudi, Mohammed Ibrahim. March 3, 2005.

Ali, Abd al-Latif Ahmad. Oct. 18, 1987.

Daoud, Daoud Abdo. Alexandria. March 14, 1988.

Etman, Ahmed. Feb 15, April 22, 1999; July 17, 2005.

El-Fakharani, Fauzi. Alexandria. March 13, 1988.
Fawzi, Hanem M. May 15, 2005.
Haggag, Mona. Alexandria. July 4, 5, 2005.
Hamdi, Ibrahim. Oct. 29, 1987.
El-Khashshab, Muhammad Abd El-Muhsin. April 14, 1983.
Mattar, Amira. May 23, 1983.
El-Mosallamay, Abdallah Hassan. Oct. 29, Nov. 25, 1987.
Noshy, Ibrahim. May 22, 1983.
Omar Abdalla, Aly. May 19, 2005.
Riad (Ghabur), Henry (Henri). April 20, 1988.
Said, Doriya. Alexandria. March 14, 1988.
Salem, Muhammad Salim. Nov. 26, 1987.
Seif El-Din, Mervet. Alexandria. March 14, 1988.
Shaarawi, Abdel Moati A. May 7, 1983.

Coptic Studies Specialists
Aziz Atiya. Salt Lake City. March 29, 1986.
Gabra (Abdel Sayed), Gawdat. Feb. 13, 1988; Feb. 13, 1992; Feb. 8, March 9,
    1999; May 16, 2005.
Boutros Ghali, Mirrit. April 15, 1988.
Boutros Ghali, Wassef (or Michel). March, 2005.
Fanous, Isaac. May 12, 1988.
Guirguis, Magdi. April 25, 2005.
Guirguis, Victor. March 10, 1988.
Labib, Pahor. Oct. 22, 1987.
Shenouda, Zaki. May 12, 1988.

Other Specialists
al-Aqqad, Salah. April 17, 19, 1983. (modern Arab history).
Awad, Louis. April 20, 1982 (literature, literary criticism).
Awad, Mohamed. Alexandria. July 6, 2005 (architecture, preservation).
al-Khashshab, Yahya. March 14, 1983 (Middle Eastern languages).

Index

Fakhri, Husayn 175, 176, 204, 404
Fakhry, Ahmad 116, 119, 120, 121, 269, 271, 319, 342, 345, 357
al-Falaki, Mahmud 238
Fanon, Frantz 11
Faraj, Mansour 311–13, *313*
Farid, Muhammad 35, 176, 238, 314
Farnall, Harry 179, 180–81, 183, 187, 190
Faruq, King 54, 170, *211*, 264, 283, *283*, *284*, *287*, 329, 354; interest in archaeology and antiquities 16, 296, 330, 333, 346–51; medal 250, *252*; pharaonism 323, 350, 351; rest house 323, 346–47, *347*; stamp 349–51, *350*, *360*
Fathy, Hassan 160–62, *161*, 165; New Qurna 160, 162–63, *164*, *165*, 330; failure 163, 330; *Gournal Architecture for the Poor* 164–65; sundried mud brick 162, 163, 165
Fawzi, Husayn 256, 306, 325
Firth, Cecil 58, 82, 87, 91, 105–106, 119
Fisher, Clarence 40, 60–61, 93
folklore 12, 31, 125, 165, 237, 367
Forster, E.M. 233, 240, 241, 245
Foucart, George 41, 76, 84, 87, 89, 93, 119–20, 247; Lacau/Foucart dispute 81, 84–86
France 19, 74, 232, 352–53; the Comité 173, 194; Commission of Historic Monuments 173; Egyptology 20–21, 57, 337, 341; British/French rivalry 22, 75, 81, 82–84, 273; French 175, 234; Tutankhamun 75–76; World War I 38–39, 85; World War II 332–34; *see also* Egyptian Antiquities Service; IFAO
Franz, Julius 6, 172, 173, 174, 176, 191, 194
Free Officers 9, 16, 23, 314, 318, 330, 355–56; *see also* 1952 Revolution; Egyptian nationalism; Nasser, Gamal Abdel
Freemasonry 20, 26
Fuad I, King/Sultan 47, 54, 85, 86, 125–26, 128, 180, 184, *208*, 246–47, 380; Coptic Museum 206, 207, 210; medal *243*; Nefertiti, bust of 91; pharaonism 123, 125–27; Rockefeller-funded Cairo museum 103–104; stamps, coins, banknotes 126, *126*, 127, *127*, 170; Tutankhamun 77, *78*
Fuad I University *see* Cairo University
al-Fustat 178, 180–83

Gaballa, Gaballa A. 116
Gabra, Sami 218, *267*, *283*, 357, 365, *366*; Coptic community activities 122; education 109, 113, 114–16, 117, 357; Egyptian Antiquities Service 122, 266; Egyptology Department, Cairo University 111, 218, 266, 330, 336, 343; Tuna al-Gebel 267–68
Gabriel, Albert 181
Gady, Éric 14, 75, 292
Gallab, Muhammad 125
Gange, David 23

Gardiner, Alan 10, 39, 76, 87–88, 116, 159, 277, 279, 292, 337–38, 343, 346; ownership of the finds 82, 83
Garstang, John 115, 116, 292
Gauthier, G. 122, 279
Gauthier, Henri 91, 278, 281, 288
Generation of 1919: 110, 194, 299, 302, 320; literary leaders 295–96, 297; pharaonism 44, 47, 295–96
Germany 24, 87–93; Berlin's Egyptian Museum 23, 24, 89, 91, 178, 332; denazification 270, 272, 332; Egyptology 23–26, 57, 88, 117, 337; German House at al-Qurna 25, *25*, 38, 89, 273, 332; Imperial German Institute for Egyptian Archaeology 25, 38, 87, 88, 91; Khedival Library 6, 174; Nazism, impact on Egyptology 271–73, 293, 332; World War I 38, 57; World War II 273; *see also* DAI; Nefertiti, Queen
Gershoni, Israel 13, 302, 303, 315
Gertzen, Thomas 88
Ghaleb, Kamal Osman 193, 220
Ghali, Boutros 34, 201, 205, 206–207, 219
Ghoneim, Zakariya 157, 269, 323, 345, 353, 354, 365, *366*
Ghurbal, Shafiq 33, 220, 222, 351
Girgis, Habib: Sunday School Movement 202, 226
Girgis, Victor Antun 120, 121, 202, 223, 225, 271
Glanville, Stephen 115, 336
Golenischeff, Vladimir 110, 118, 119–20, *120*, 265, 266
Goode, James 93
Goyon, Georges 294, 341
Grand Egyptian Museum 369
Grapow, Hermann 223, 272, 332
Grébaut, Eugène 31, 32
Greco-Roman Museum 1, *3*, 5, 229, 235, 240, 246, 257, 258; architecture 6, *3*, 235; collection 369; directors 234, 332, 359; founding 5–6, 233, 234; Italian influence 6, 174, 234, 258; visits to 139; *see also* Alexandria
Greek (language) 20, 40, 152, 198, 235, 236, 237, 241
Greeks 234, 255, 359
Greg, Sir Robert 159, 190, 192, 193, 278, 293, 348
Grégoire, Henri 118, 242, 244, 254
Gregory, Derek 145
Grenfell, Bernard 237, *253*
Grenfell, Francis 39
Griffini, Eugenio 87
Griffith, Francis Llewellyn 76, 115, 116, 119, 270
Guéraud, Octave 255, 332
guidebooks to Egypt 140, 143–44, 146–48, 157; Baud, Marcelle 157; Hachette guides 155, 157; local guides 155–56; Macmillan guides 140, 150, 155, *208*; Volkoff, Oleg 118, 140; *see also* Aboudi, Mohamed; Baedeker, Karl; Murray, John; Thomas Cook & Son

Mitchell, Timothy 13, 145, 158

Mixed Courts 6, 70–71, 232, 258, 337

MMA (Metropolitan Museum of Art, New York) 28–29, *29*, 40, 56, 76, 93, 356

monastery 10, 206; Monastery of Phoebammon 219; Monastery of St. Menas 222; Saint Catherine Monastery 212; Wadi al-Natrun 212

Mond, Robert 65, 266, 293, 349

Montet, Pierre 123, 294, 333, 334, 341, 345–46, 356

Montgomery, General 330

Moret, Alexandre 116, 128, 278

Morgan, J.P. 28, 29, 86, 99

mosque 8, 169–70, 186, *350*, 351; Mosque of Amr 183, 184; Mosque of al-Hakim 176; Mosque of Ibn Tulun 174; Mosque of Sayyida Zaynab 169, 299; Mosque of Sayyidna Husayn 169; Mosque of Sultan Hassan 362; Muhammad Ali Mosque 8, 139, 177, 257, 351, 362; al-Rifai Mosque 177

Mubarak, Ali 29, 31, 173, 200, 238

Muhammad Ali 8, 20, 31, 128, 173, 230, 231, 238, 247, 359

Muharram, Uthman 310, 311, 312, 324

Mukhtar, Mahmoud 45, 46, 48, 129, 357; *Aida* 46; *The Revival of Egypt* 35, 44–45, *46*, 47, 50, 109, 123, *130*, 309, 313, 323, 357; political drama 128–29; unveiling 130; *Saad Zaghlul* 16, 295, 309, 310, *311*, 312, 357

al-Muqtataf 32, 79, 301

Murad, Mahmud 132, 314

Murray, Gilbert 85, 90, 241

Murray, John 102, 137, 138, 155

Musa, Salama 16, 297, 299, 305, 325, 357; *Misr asl al-hadara* 300, 301; pharaonism 216, 296, 299–302, 320, 357

museum 1, 3, 6; four-museum paradigm 5–6, 11; *see also* Coptic Museum; Egyptian Museum, Cairo; Greco-Roman Museum; Museum of Arab Art

Museum of Arab Art 1, *4*, 5, 194, 357; architecture *4*, 6; Austro–Hungarian influence 6, 174, 194; collection 170, 176, 369; founding 5, 169, 176, 187; Khedival Library 177, 179; Museum of Islamic Art 170, 194; visits to 139, 143, 177; *see also* Bahgat, Ali

Museum of Egyptian Antiquities *see* Egyptian Museum, Cairo

Museum of Egyptian Civilization 351–52

Museum of Islamic Art *see* Museum of Arab Art

Muslim Brotherhood 222, 226, 264, 296, 303, 318, 354, 359; *see also* al-Banna, Hassan; Qutb, Sayyid

Mustafa, Muhammad 168, 190, 191, 194

Mutran, Khalil 66, 238, 246

Nag Hammadi codices 221, 223–25, 323, 336,

341; *see also* Coptic Museum

Nagi, Muhammad 45, 46–47, 48, 124, 357; *The Revival of Egypt* 44–45, *45*, 47, 50, 109, 123, 128, 130, 309, 323; *The School of Alexandria* 229, *230*, 257

Naguib, Ahmad 110, 159, 221, 325

al-Nahhas, Mustafa 54, 55, 129, 130, 186, 193, 207, 223, 249, 253, 264, 275, 282, 286, 304, 329, 330, 352, 353, 354; pharaonism 129, 130, 309, 310, *325*

Nasser, Gamal Abdel 16, 225, 296, 298, 318, 322–23, 330, 356, *362*, *364*; pan-Arabism 364; pharaonism 361–62; tourism 137, 166; *see also* 1952 Revolution; Egyptian nationalism; Free Officers

National Library/Dar al-Kutub al-Misriya 9, 38; collection 186; Khedival Library 6, 8, 174, 177, 179, 186, 204, 357–58

nationalism 1, 5, 11–12, 14; *see also* Arab nationalism; Egyptian nationalism

Nazli, Queen 130

Nefertiti, Queen: dispute over the bust of 26, 52, 81, 88–89, 91, *92*, 154–55, 332, 356

Newberry, Percy 39, 76, 95, 115, 278, 281, 288; Egyptology Department, Egyptian University 116, 223, 264–69 *passim*

Niebuhr, Karsten 212–13

NMEC (National Museum of Egyptian Civilization) 352

Noblecourt, Mme./Desroches, Christiane 111, 290, 294, 332–33, 334

Nora, Pierre 74

Noshy, Ibrahim 253, 254, 255

Nubia 162, 365

al-Nuqrashi, Mahmud 111, 280, 290, 329

OI (Oriental Institute) 81, 99–102, *100*, 292, 293, 338–39, 356; Epigraphic Survey 86, 97–98, 293; expeditions 95, *96*, 97; Rockefeller, John D., Jr. 95, 338, 356; *see also* Breasted, James Henry

Omar Toussoun, Prince of Alexandria 247–48, 266

Omm Sety / Dorothy Eady 290–91, 342

Orientalism 171, 172, 174, 199; *see also* Said, Edward

Ormos, István 168, 174, 176, 204

Ottoman Empire 125, 170, 355; World War I 8, 37, 179

Palestine 81, 83, 95, 250, 356; Palestine Archaeological Museum 107, 292

papyrology 237, 247, 253

Passalacqua, Giuseppe 23

Patricolo, Achille 173, 180, 183–84

Pauty, Edmond 183, 184, 186

Peet, Eric 39, 115, 116, 118, 345